THE LITERARY NOTEBOOKS OF THOMAS HARDY

Volume 2

The Literary Notebooks of Thomas Hardy provide a major source of information about what Hardy considered necessary or desirable reading for his craft. Compiled during more than fifty years (1876–1927) they show traces of having been reread and annotated by Hardy. And, as they incorporate materials from other notebooks, they represent to some extent Hardy's own special selection from his voluminous notetaking.

The span of Hardy's entries in the Literary Notebooks is striking both in its chronological and broadly intellectual dimensions: the entries range from the Greek dramatists to George Bernard Shaw; from the radical French utopian Charles Fourier to Cardinal Newman; and from *The Milliner and Dressmaker and Warehouseman's Gazette* to Einstein.

The Notebooks show how Hardy intensifies his determined preparatory studies in the mid-1870s; how keenly he follows the contemporary debate over realism and other aesthetic questions; how he primes himself in philosophical studies at the turn of the century for the metaphysical challenge of *The Dynasts*; and how he gradually becomes more preoccupied with poetic matters while maintaining his lifelong interest in religion and science. Thus the material presented here confirms, modifies and extends our knowledge of Hardy's intellectual background. In so doing, it also opens up avenues into nineteenth-century thought in general where Hardy is a compelling guide.

Lennart Björk's carefully compiled edition provides identification of sources and indicates how Hardy used his Notebooks both explicitly and implicitly in his own writing. The annotations thus offer unusual and interesting glimpses into Hardy's workshop. With full critical and textual introductions this two-volume work makes available for the first time the complete verbatim text of Hardy's Literary Notes.

The editor

Lennart A. Björk is Professor of English at the University of Stockholm. A graduate of the University of Gothenburg, Princeton University and Oxford University, he has held lectureships and other appointments in Britain, Sweden and the USA. He has published articles on Chaucer, Dryden, Hardy, Faulkner and O'Neill.

THE LITERARY NOTEBOOKS OF THOMAS HARDY

Volume 2

Edited by
LENNART A. BJÖRK

First edition 1985
Reprinted 1988

Published by
THE MACMILLAN PRESS LTD
Houndmills, Basingstoke, Hampshire RG21 2XS
and London
Companies and representatives
throughout the world

Typeset in Great Britain by
Photo-Graphics, Honiton, Devon.

Printed in Great Britain by
Antony Rowe Ltd
Chippenham

British Library Cataloguing in Publication Data
Hardy, Thomas, *1840-1928*
The literary notebooks of Thomas Hardy.
1. Hardy, Thomas, *1840-1928* — Biography
2. Novelists, English — 19th century — Biography
I. Title   II. Björk, Lennart A.
823'.8   PR4753
ISBN 0-333-36777-4 (the set)
ISBN 0-333-34650-5 vol. 1
ISBN 0-333-34651-3 vol. 2

To Maj, Christina and Staffan

Contents

Preface

This edition consists of the three volumes of notebooks which Hardy labelled 'Literary Notes'. An additional notebook is included in the Appendix. The flyleaf of this notebook bears the notation '1867'. It is contemporary with the other volumes and of a generally similar character. At a loss for a more adequate name, and despite the understandable objections of some critics, I retain the classification of it as the '"1867" Notebook'.

Some readers may question the inclusion of 'Literary Notes III', since it consists largely of newspaper and magazine cuttings. I have included it not for reasons of mere completeness. My overriding criterion is the fact that the cuttings represent Hardy's considered choice: he cut them out, he wrote the references and the annotations. It is true that the more focused handwritten references are generally of greater value, but the difference is one of degree rather than of kind. It is, for instance, exciting to have easily available the whole argument of the *Daily Mail* article which Hardy annotated in red ink '(Very like the "Immanent Will" of the Dynasts.)' (entry 2526). But also less immediately interesting entries contribute to our knowledge of what DeLaura calls 'the complex contemporary matrix' of Hardy's writing. There are less interesting guides into this phenomenon than Hardy's scissors.

This consolidated edition of all Hardy's 'Literary Notes' has made possible a considerable number of improvements in entries 1–1339, published separately in 1974. Thanks to the constructive criticism, both oral and written, of many generous Hardy scholars and general readers, I have been able to eliminate textual errors, to identify several entries previously left unidentified and to employ a better method of indicating spelling-errors and other irregularities in the manuscript. Also, my detailed work on the whole body of the 'Literary Notes' has given me a better perspective on Hardy's note-taking, thus making possible, for example, many cross-references between the early and the late notes. Finally, the revised annotations have benefited from the valuable scholarship of the past decade.

Not least valuable in this respect, as well as for my 'Critical Introduction', is the publication of the first volumes of *The Collected Letters of Thomas Hardy*. They have revealed new biographical data which have removed the need in some cases for the tentativeness of my suggestions in the 1974 Introduction. There is now indisputable evidence, for instance, that Hardy took a planned sabbatical in 1876 at the same time as he started compiling his 'Literary Notes I' (see 'Critical Introduction' below, pp. xx–xxi).

In my work on this edition I have incurred many debts of gratitude, which it gives me great pleasure to acknowledge.

I wish to thank the Trustees of the Hardy Estate for courteous and helpful co-operation and for permission to edit and publish the 'Literary Notes', the '1867' Notebook, and other material previously unpublished.

I should also like to thank the following institutions and their staffs for valuable assistance: the Berg Collection and Manuscript Division, New York Public Library; the Bodleian Library; the British Library; Cambridge University Library; Colby College Library; Dorset County Library; Dorset County Museum; the Fitzwilliam Museum, Cambridge; Göteborg University Library; the Houghton Library, Harvard University; the Library of Congress; the Miriam Lutcher Stark Library, University of Texas; the Nobel Library, Stockholm; the Pierpont Morgan Library; Princeton University Library; Queen's College Library, Oxford; the Royal Library, Stockholm; Stockholm University Library; University College Library, Dublin. My thanks are also due to Professor Richard Little Purdy and Mr Edwin Thorne for kindly giving me access to manuscripts in their possession and to Professor Quentin Bell for permission to quote a letter by Sir Leslie Stephen.

For material assistance making this edition possible, I am greatly indebted to the Florey Studentship at the Queen's College, Oxford, 1969–71; to the University of Göteborg and the University of Stockholm for several research grants, and to Hvitfeldska Stipendiefonden for a travel grant.

Ever since my interest in Thomas Hardy was first significantly roused in one of Professor E. D. H. Johnson's stimulating seminars at Princeton University in the early 1960s, I have in the course of my work had the pleasure of receiving assistance and encouragement from numerous individuals, who freely and generously gave me of their knowledge and time. In Oxford, Mr R. E. Alton of St Edmund Hall took an active and helpful interest in the paleographic problems of the manuscript; Mr Dennis Burden of Trinity College gave me continual help and inspiration as he followed the slow growth of the edition; Mr J. D. Fleeman of Pembroke College expertly advised me on textual problems and editorial principles. Mr J. I. M. Stewart of Christ Church shed light on several Hardy problems in a number of inspiring conversations.

During my two years at the Queen's College, Oxford, a great number of College members and other Oxford residents, permanent or temporary, made my research intellectually profitable and socially enjoyable. I should particularly like to thank Lord and Lady Blake, Lady Florey, Mr Paul Foote, Mr Peter Miller, and Mrs E. Townson. Several of my fellow Florey students, especially Mr Rainer Tamchina and Mr Frederik van Bolhuis, were subjected to lengthy and, I fear, but mildly interesting expositions of the 'Literary Notes'. Of their patience, compassion, and good friendship I am truly appreciative. I also gratefully remember the profitable discussions with George Thottungal, SJ, of St Joseph's College, Tiruchi, India, during our simultaneous work on the 'Literary Notes', as I do the stimulating help and company of Mrs C. Airaksinen, Mrs M. Arvidsson, Miss S. Anastasov, Mr Bengt Bengtsson, Mrs M. Breadmore, Mr A. Chambati, Miss D. Elliott, Mrs S. Feather, Mr J. Feather, Miss H. Heinsen, Miss L. Herbst, Mrs C. Kallie, Mr J. Kallie, Miss J. Morton, Mrs M. Rose, and Mr R. H. G. Szyszkowitz. I also recall with the greatest pleasure the liberal help and good companionship of Mr Tor Bengtsson in Dorchester, London and Oxford.

For valuable assistance in time-consuming tracing of some sources which eluded my own research, I am indebted to my wife, Maj, and my daughter, Christina; also to Miss Susan Knight, Mrs Judy Lindhé, Mr Åke Lindgren, Mr Michael Russel, Miss Susan Taylor, and Miss Susan Ward. Special thanks are due to Mrs Margaret Clerici, Miss Hilary Cooke, Mrs Catherine Sandbach-Dahlström and Mrs Chinta Kallie for their generous and efficient help with many particularly difficult identifications. In addition, Miss Cooke read the first half of the manuscript, Mrs Sandbach-Dahlström gave me perceptive criticism of all the annotations, and Mrs Kallie helped me purge the entire text of transcription errors, as did Mrs Clerici, Mrs Stina Lässman, Dr Mark Troy and Dr Hermann Wüscher. I also very much appreciate the timely help of Mrs Vera Jesty of Max Gate, whose ancestor by marriage, by appropriate coincidence, appears in entry 596.

For much valuable criticism I am also indebted to Professor Harold F. Brooks, as I am for help with particular problems and for useful general discussions to Dr Michael E. Bath, Dr Werner Bies, Mr Kenneth Carter, Professor Peter Casagrande, Dr Robert Gittings, Mr David Lister, Dr Charles Lock, Professor Harold Orel, Professor Norman Page, Dr F. B. Pinion, Professor Dieter Riesner, Mr Gregory Stevens Cox, Dr Jeremy V. Steele, Dr Richard H. Taylor and the Revd J. M. C. Yates. Mrs Margareta Hammarkrantz kindly helped me with a manuscript drawing, and Mr J. W. Brown with the technical examination of the notebooks. Dr Evelyn Hardy very generously put at my disposal a work copy of her own projected edition of Hardy's notebooks.

I am very grateful to Mr Roger Peers, Curator of the Dorset County Museum, for his extraordinary help and patience during my many visits to Dorchester.

I should also like to express my warm appreciation of the help of Professors Michael Millgate and Richard Little Purdy. In addition to my reliance, acknowledged throughout the edition, on their outstanding published contributions to Hardy scholarship, I have also had the privilege of their personal counsel and generous hospitality.

Professor Robert C. Schweik and Dr Simon Gatrell have given me their expert advice on textual problems and editorial principles in addition to their generous help in other ways. Dr Eleanor Wikborg has followed my work from the start and has enhanced the quality of the edition through her careful and perceptive comments and queries.

I am also obliged to friends and colleagues at the University of Göteborg and the University of Stockholm: to Professor Alvar Ellegård for his friendly interest and encouragement over many years; to Professor Erik Frykman for his keen and perceptive comments on the manuscript of the 1974 edition; to Mr Michael Cooper, Dr Olof Lindström, and Mrs Elisabeth Mercer for suggestions on various parts of the early manuscript; to Dr Johannes Hedberg, Mrs Ann-Britt Höglund, Dr Göran Kjellmer, Dr Ishrat Lindblad, Professor Magnus Ljung, Dr Monica Mannheimer, Dr Britta Olinder, Dr Christina Stendahl, and Dr Mall Stålhammar for their help with particular queries and problems; to Mrs Ingegerd Folker, Mrs Susanne Francke, Mr David Jones and Professor Magnus Ljung for their help in facilitating my indulgence in Hardy studies in recent years.

In the various stages of preparing the typescript of this edition I have received valuable help from Mr Marian Czernek and Mrs Irja Sanden, but above all from Mrs Ann Westrell, who has expertly typed the entire manuscript – and more than once, owing to editorial indecision and whimsy.

The edition has also benefited greatly from the constant and courteous support of Mrs Julia Steward of the Macmillan Press, and the helpful and efficient copy-editing of Mrs Valery Rose.

I am greatly indebted to my mother, Olga Björk-Olsson, and my stepfather, the late Gunnar Olsson, as I am to Mrs Elsa Ljungqvist and the late Mr Bertil Ljungqvist. My greatest debt, however, is to my wife Maj, and to Christina and Staffan, for their support, encouragement and help in so many ways, over so many years.

Critical Introduction

I

The correlation between an author's conscious preparations for his craft and his artistic achievement is always difficult to establish satisfactorily. That some correlation exists, however, is recognized by anyone who believes that a literary work owes its birth to the nature and efforts of its mundane creator rather than to divine impulse or inspiration. So, for instance, when there are indications that in the mid 1870s Hardy's deliberate preparations for his profession increased significantly in scope and seriousness, this merits some attention, especially since the first novel to appear after this noticeable increase, *The Return of the Native*, by critical consensus marks the beginning of a new phase in Hardy's literary career, a phase both ideologically and aesthetically more ambitious than the previous one.

This is not to imply that Hardy had been unambitious earlier, or that he had neglected preparatory studies. *The Life of Thomas Hardy* testifies to the contrary in, for instance, the well-known note of March 1875: 'Read again Addison, Macaulay, Newman, Sterne, Defoe, Lamb, Gibbon, Burke, *Times* leaders, etc. in a study of style.'[1] What is meant by a marked increase in his literary aspirations – and preparations – is, therefore, a change of degree rather than kind. Nor do I mean to imply that the success of *The Return of the Native*, or that of any other novel, can be explained by an examination of the groundwork for Hardy's fiction. It seems reasonable to assume, however, that, of the many tangible and intangible elements of the complex background of Hardy's art, evidence of his own professional preparations is likely to offer some insight not only into that background but also into his works of art.

[1] Florence Emily Hardy, *The Life of Thomas Hardy 1840–1928* (London, 1962; repr. 1965) p. 105. The *Life* was first published in two volumes: *The Early Life of Thomas Hardy* (1928) and *The Later Life of Thomas Hardy* (1930). Subsequent references to this work will be made parenthetically in the text and refer to the one-volume edition. The existence of other notebooks from 1865 onwards (see Textual Introduction) is, naturally, further proof of Hardy's early 'literary' studies.

Hardy's 'Literary Notes' are very much part of his propaedeutic literary activities. The notes do not, of course, provide a comprehensive account of his general autodidactic endeavours or of his more specifically 'literary' studies. Yet, external characteristics alone indicate the importance of the 'Literary Notes' as one of the major sources of information about what Hardy considered necessary or desirable reading for his craft: they cover all but the first few years of his career as a writer; they show traces of having been reread and annotated by Hardy; and, they incorporate notes from other notebooks and thus seem to constitute a special selection, or edition, of Hardy's voluminous note-taking. The significance of the 'Literary Notes' is, of course, mainly to be inferred from their internal characteristics and from their reflection in, or direct appropriation into, Hardy's work. Before these matters are exemplified in more detail, however, a brief consideration of Hardy's situation as a novelist at the time he started compiling the 'Literary Notes' may help to explain the psychological background of the note-taking and the benefits Hardy hoped to derive from the notes.

With the publication of *Far from the Madding Crowd* (1874), Hardy firmly established himself as a novelist – but as a novelist of rustic life and manners only. From the very first, critics had praised his descriptions of the countryside and urged him to limit himself to this subject. Even the predominantly unfavourable *Spectator* review of his first published novel, *Desperate Remedies* (1871), had acknowledged his 'unusual and very happy facility in catching and fixing phases of peasant life' and suggested that the then-anonymous author's 'powers might and ought to be extended largely in this direction'.[2] Whether Hardy consciously followed this advice or not – advice which he had also received in regard to his unpublished first novel, 'The Poor Man and the Lady' (*Life*, pp. 58–9, 86) – is not of much concern here. The fact is that the largely rural tales that followed, *Under the Greenwood Tree* (1872) and *A Pair of Blue Eyes* (1873), increased his popularity to an early high level, reaching its climax with *Far from the Madding Crowd*. By 1875 then, Hardy was recognized as a major rural author not only in England but also in France: in that year Léon Boucher devoted the greater part of an article in the *Revue des deux mondes*, 'Le Roman pastoral en Angleterre', to *Far from the Madding Crowd* (*Life*, p. 106; Cox, p. xviii).

[2] R. G. Cox (ed.), *Thomas Hardy: The Critical Heritage* (London, 1970) pp. 3–4. Subsequent references to this work will be made parenthetically in the text.

Pleasing as such recognition must have been, there also seems to have been some ground for resentment on Hardy's part, especially over the limitations on ideological matters which he could find both implicitly and explicitly attached to the critical classification of him as a mere chronicler of country life. Hardy had, after all, ideological pretensions from the very beginning of his literary career, judging from what we know about 'The Poor Man and the Lady'.[3] The other early novels also show some speculative aspirations, but, and this seems pertinent here, such tendencies were usually noted rather condescendingly by the critics. For instance, not even the basically positive *Saturday Review* mention – attributed to Hardy's friend Horace Moule – of *Desperate Remedies* refrained from taking to task Hardy's delight 'in running off to sententiae, in generalizing abstractions out of the special point in hand'; Hardy inclined, the critic complained, 'to this intellectual pastime a little bit too often' (Cox, p. 7). In a similar manner the *Academy* review of *Far from the Madding Crowd* somewhat patronizingly rebuked Hardy for 'attempting too much', for contemplating 'his shepherds and rural people with the eye of a philosopher' (Cox, p. 36; see also pp. 9, 11, 23, 41).

It is interesting in this context to note Hardy's own interpretation of the critical reaction to *The Hand of Ethelberta* – his first real attempt to transcend pastoral themes and settings. For to a remarkable extent he misconstrues the general tone of the contemporary reviews. In the 1895 Preface, for instance, he states that on 'its first appearance the novel suffered ... for its quality of unexpectedness in particular – that unforgivable sin in the critic's sight – the immediate precursor of *Ethelberta* having been a purely rural tale';[4] later, in his autobiography, he refers to the 'general disappointment at the lack of sheep and shepherds' in the novel (*Life*, p. 103). In fact the reviews were more mixed, and with more pronounced praise, than Hardy's account implies; that the negative remarks should have assumed such proportions in Hardy's own impression of the criticism may partly be owing to the fact that the first notices to appear were in general slightly

---

[3] See the *Life*, pp. 58–64, and Richard L. Purdy, *Thomas Hardy: A Bibliographical Study* (London, 1954; repr. 1968) pp. 275–6. Subsequent references to Purdy's study will be made parenthetically in the text.

[4] Harold Orel (ed.), *Thomas Hardy's Personal Writings* (London, 1967; orig. publ. Lawrence, Kan., 1966) p. 11. Subsequent references to this work will be made parenthetically in the text and refer to the London printing.

less favourable than the later ones.[5] Above all, however, Hardy seems
to have resented the criticism that might be interpreted as personal, as
slighting his social and intellectual background in general and his rural
connection in particular. The *Graphic*, for example, while
acknowledging that the novel was 'unquestionably the work of a true
artist and humourist', regretted Hardy's change of setting: 'We take it
ill of Mr Hardy that he should have abandoned that rustic life which
few can portray as he can ... for London drawing-rooms and "good
society", ground on which he seems much less at home.'[6] Many years
later, when writing the *Life*, Hardy is still frustrated as he remembers
that the critics would not credit him with any knowledge of the capital:
'if he only touched on London in his pages, [the reviewers] promptly
reminded him not to write of a place he was unacquainted with, but to
get back to his sheepfolds' (*Life*, p. 62). The impact of this kind of
criticism was probably intensified by coming not long after a specific
derogatory remark of a personal nature in another context. Explaining
the circumstances under which *The Hand of Ethelberta* was written,
Hardy recalls how the request for more of his writing after the success
of *Far from the Madding Crowd* 'coincided with quizzing personal gossip,
among other paragraphs being one that novel-writing was coming to a

[5] The *Athenaeum*, 15 April 1876, relegated *The Hand of Ethelberta* to the 'branch of fiction
that ... may be called the modern romantic. ... This must be called the second order of
fiction, as it is distinctly inferior, in an artistic point of view, to that which produces its
effects solely with the materials of everyday life ...' (p. 523). Within its sphere, however,
the novel was praised. A few days later the *World*, 19 April, was more positive but found
traces of 'hurried and incurious writing' (p. 20). The *Spectator* review on 22 April was
mainly negative and complained about the artificiality of the characters, who resembled
'rather full-grown marionettes than independent characters, really seen and studied in
the world, which the novelist can ask us to accept as representing what he has actually
seen and known' (p. 531). The *Graphic*, 29 April, was somewhat more positive but
objected to Hardy's change of setting: see quotation in the text. On 13 May two mainly
favourable reviews appeared: in the *Academy* and, especially, in the *Examiner*, whose
reviewer undertook to defend the improbabilities that earlier notices had detected (p.
545). The *Guardian*, 19 July, offered some positive remarks but complained about 'stage
trickiness' (p. 953). The *Morning Post*, 5 August, found Hardy's delineations of
'uncommon characters' commendable. The most negative and insulting mention of *The
Hand of Ethelberta* appeared on 29 September 1877, when the *London* called it 'with all its
cleverness, about as bad a novel as one would care to see' and speculated that 'Mr
Hardy, it may be assumed, knows the world of boors very well, and the world of society
very ill' (p. 212). Despite some undeniably unpleasant remarks, the reviews are thus less
consistently negative than Hardy's complaints lead us to believe. Cf. also Michael
Millgate's conclusion that 'Hardy had little reason to be seriously dissatisfied with its
[*Ethelberta's*] first reception' – *Thomas Hardy: His Career as a Novelist* (London, 1971) p. 116.
[6] *Graphic*, 29 April 1876, p. 419.

pretty pass ... the author of *Far from the Madding Crowd* having been discovered to be a house-decorator (!)'; Hardy's own account of the immediate effects of such publicity is revealing: 'Criticism like this influenced him to put aside a wood-land story he had thought of (which later took shape in *The Woodlanders*) and make a plunge in a new and untried direction. He was aware of the pecuniary value of a reputation for a specialty; ... Yet he had not the slightest intention of writing for ever about sheepfarming ...' (*Life*, p. 102). Hardy states explicitly, that is, that his experimentation in *The Hand of Ethelberta* was a deliberate and self-assertive step to break out of his pastoral mode.[7]

Despite Hardy's rebellion against being labelled a rural author only, it is easy to exaggerate his disapproval of the critical insistence on the limitation of setting *per se*. Years later, for instance, referring to the example of Greek plays, Hardy refuted the notion that 'novels that evolve their action on a circumscribed scene' should not be 'so inclusive in their exhibition of human nature as novels wherein the scenes cover large extents of country, in which events figure amid towns and cities' (Orel, p. 45).[8] Allowing for a possible, or likely, element of rationalization in this late comment, it still seems probable that the idea should not have been foreign to Hardy in the mid 1870s.[9] In fact a note in the *Life* assigned to the time of his writing *Ethelberta*, while corroborating his rebellious move in an 'untried direction', also indicates that he may not have been very comfortable with the new setting and subject matters: 'He perceived ... that he was committed by circumstances to novel-writing as a regular trade ... and that hence he would, he deemed, have to look for material in manners – in ordinary social and fashionable life as other novelists did. ... So far what he had written had not been novels at all, as usually understood – that is pictures of modern customs and observances ...' (*Life*, p. 104). In the light of Hardy's well-known aversion to the novel of manners (see, for instance, Orel, p. 119), the prospect could not have seemed very attractive to him.

---

[7] For an excellent consideration of the scope of Hardy's experimentation in *The Hand of Ethelberta*, see Richard H. Taylor, *The Neglected Hardy: Thomas Hardy's Lesser Novels* (London, 1982) esp. pp. 57–68.

[8] Cf. also Hardy on the implications of the setting of *The Woodlanders* 'where, from time to time, dramas of a grandeur and unity truly Sophoclean are enacted in the real, by virtue of the concentrated passions and closely-knit interdependence of the lives therein' (Wessex Edn, pp. 4–5).

[9] See also Millgate, *Thomas Hardy: His Career as a Novelist*, pp. 95–104, on the genesis of Wessex in Hardy's fiction.

   The critical recommendations to limit himself to the Dorset setting are not likely, therefore, to have been altogether unpalatable. On the other hand – and in addition to his own explicit statements drawn attention to above – the whole body of his work suggests that from an early date Hardy resisted being classified as a rural chronicler with the critical restriction this seemed to impose on the ideological scope of his writing; Hardy had a higher vision of his art, that is, than to write merely what Leslie Stephen so readily associated him with as late as 1880: 'Now it seems to me that you might write an exceedingly pleasant series of stories upon your special topic. I mean prose idyls [*sic*] of country life – short sketches of Hodge & his ways, wh. might be made very attractive. ...'[10]

   Whether these speculations on Hardy's literary ambitions and on his reaction to the critical reception of his early works are valid or not, the fact remains that the frequent early critical exhortations to restrict his literary aspirations to pastoral idylls did not have the intended effect. This is perhaps particularly remarkable after his rising popularity suddenly fell off – at least, as we have seen, according to his own assessment of the reviews – with his exploration of new themes and settings in *The Hand of Ethelberta*; for, instead of complying with critical opinion and thereby possibly reclaiming lost admirers, Hardy's literary ambitions seem to have been boosted rather than daunted, particularly as regards the ideological scope of his art: as is well known, from *The Return of the Native* onwards, Hardy's rural settings do not noticeably restrict his ideological ambitions.

   Hardy's increased literary ambitions in his creative works from the second half of the 1870s are also reflected in some initiatives he took after the mixed reception of *Ethelberta*, initiatives indicating his interest in extending his preparatory literary studies: as we shall see below, he approached Leslie Stephen for advice; he took a rest from his novel-writing; and, he started the 'Literary Notes'.

   In the spring of 1876 Hardy wrote to Leslie Stephen for suggestions as to what literary criticism he should read in order to improve his own writing. Stephen answered on 16 May,

   ... if you mean seriously to ask me what critical books I recommend, I can only say that I recommend none. I think as a critic that the less authors read of criticism the better. You e.g., have a perfectly fresh

---

[10] Stephen to Hardy, 19 Nov. 1880 (Dorset County Museum).

& original vein, and I think that the less you bother yourself about critical canons the less chance there is of your becoming selfconscious and cramped. I should, therefore, advise the great writers – Shakespeare, Goethe, Scott, &c. &c., who give ideas & don't prescribe rules. Sainte Beuve and Mat. Arnold (in a smaller way) are the only modern critics who seem to me worth reading – perhaps, too, Lowell. We are generally a poor lot, terribly afraid of not being in the fashion.... If I were in the vein, I think I should exhort you above all to read George Sand, whose country stories seem to me perfect, and have a certain affinity to yours. The last I read was the 'Maitres-Sonneurs' which (if you don't know it) I commend to you as well nigh perfect. You could do something of the kind, though I won't flatter you by saying that I think that you could equal her in her own line, I don't think any one could.[11]

Hardy had read the 'great writers' before and possibly also some Arnold and Sand (see entries 101n and 477n). So, despite the many Arnold and Sand entries in the 'Literary Notes', Stephen's letter is here primarily interesting as an indication of Hardy's determination at the time to strengthen what he considered a sound basis for his literary career.

A more significant manifestation of Hardy's growing professional aspirations – and almost a prerequisite for any serious preparations – is the rest he took from his novel-writing at this time. He had in fact already decided to take time off for study and reflection while he was still at work on *The Hand of Ethelberta*. Declining an offer to publish his next novel in the *Examiner*, Hardy wrote to the editor on 4 November 1875, 'My intention is to suspend my writing – for domestic reasons chiefly – for a longer time than usual after finishing *Ethelberta*, which I am sorry to say is not nearly done yet.'[12] In March 1876 he confirmed his decision in a letter to another publisher stating plainly that 'I do not wish to attempt any more original writing of any length for a few months, until I can learn the best line to take for the future' (*Letters*, I, 43). Actually, Hardy took a leave of just about one whole year; for, if we

[11] Frederic William Maitland, *The Life and Letters of Leslie Stephen* (London, 1906) pp. 290–1. The letter is also partly quoted in *The Life of Thomas Hardy*, p. 109.
[12] *The Collected Letters of Thomas Hardy*, ed. Richard L. Purdy and Michael Millgate, I (Oxford, 1978) 41. Subsequent references will be made parenthetically in the text.

are to judge from a passing remark in his own contribution to Maitland's *Life of Leslie Stephen*, he does not seem to have commenced the next novel until the following year: 'in 1877, on my starting another novel, "The Return of the Native"...'.[13] As Hardy had completed five novels within about five years, mere exhaustion may well suffice as a plausible explanation for an extended rest. But he may also, as the letters suggest, have listened to the critical recommendations he had received to leave off writing for a while and gain some perspective on his art.[14] Whatever the reasons for the rest, the main point here is that it afforded Hardy time to broaden his general education – about which he seems to have felt insecure for the greater part of his life – as well as to concentrate on and collect whatever specialized material he conceived of as useful or mandatory for his profession. The 'Literary Notes' alone show that he availed himself assiduously of this time for extensive reading: approximately one third of the 'Literary Notes' appears to be from the interval between the completion of *The Hand of Ethelberta* and the start on *The Return of the Native*.[15]

As argued above then, Hardy felt that he had reasons to be concerned about his situation as a novelist in the mid 1870s. That he resented being classified as a novelist of rural life only is implicitly indicated by his creative works thereafter, and, as we have seen, explicitly testified to by his own recollections, decades later, in the *Life*. Against this background the fact that the letter to Stephen and the sabbatical coincide with the inception of the 'Literary Notes' strongly suggests that in the spring of 1876 – intent on broadening the scope and changing the direction of his literary career – Hardy embarked on a planned and determined course of study and note-taking, and that a significant part of this course is reflected in the 'Literary Notes'.

[13] Maitland, *Life and Letters of Leslie Stephen*, p. 276. F. B. Pinion has shown that Hardy submitted the first fifteen chapters of the novel to John Blackwood on 12 April 1877, and suggested, consequently, that Hardy started writing *The Return of the Native* quite early in the year: 'The Composition of "The Return of the Native"', *TLS*, 21 Aug. 1970, p. 931. See also Millgate, pp. 123–4, and Purdy, p. 27.

[14] In its review of *The Hand of Ethelberta*, the *Athenaeum* reminded Hardy of its earlier advice: 'We have ventured, if our memory serves, once before to suggest that he [Hardy] should allow himself longer intervals of silence. To novelists, if to any people, *sua mortifera est facundia*' (15 April 1876, p. 523). The previous occasion was in its review of *Far from the Madding Crowd*: 'He [Hardy] ought to hold his peace for at least two years...' (5 Dec. 1874, p. 747; repr. Cox, p. 20).

[15] Of the 1649 entries of this volume, no. 880 is the first entry with material published in 1877.

II

The most rewarding way, perhaps, of attempting to indicate the importance and relevance of the 'Literary Notes' to Hardy's art within the scope of this essay, may be to look at them primarily in relation to some of his own aesthetic theories. This procedure may also help us to approximate his own conception of the notes. Hardy's essay 'The Profitable Reading of Fiction' (1888) will serve as a convenient starting-point. In it Hardy outlines what he values in fiction and makes a rough distinction between, on the one hand, 'the accidents and appendages of narrative', among them 'trifles of useful knowledge, statistics, queer historical fact' (Orel, pp. 112–13), and, on the other hand, those essential literary elements which offer 'intellectual and moral profit to active and undulled spirits' (Orel, p. 113).

A similar classification may be applied to the 'Literary Notes'. A great number of entries have the potential function of providing 'trifles of useful knowledge'. A typical example is entry 604: 'Link between extinct animals & those present now – The Dodo, last seen in 17th cent.' When, in *The Return of the Native*, Hardy came to describe the precariousness of the reddleman's profession, the dodo was called upon to help stress the point: 'He [Diggory Venn] was one of a class rapidly becoming extinct in Wessex, filling at present in the rural world the place which, during the last century, the dodo occupied in the world of animals.'[16] Another entry of the same general kind is 611: 'Miraculous animation. It is said that Albertus Magnus & Thos Aquinas between them animated a brass statue, wh. chattered, & was their servant.' The passage came to Hardy's mind when he good-humouredly analysed the relationship between Johnny and Eustacia, as the little boy reluctantly tended her bonfire: 'The little slave went on feeding the fire as before. He seemed a mere automaton, galvanized into moving and speaking by the wayward Eustacia's will. He might have been the brass statue which Albertus Magnus is said to have animated just so far as to make it chatter, and move, and be his servant' (*Return*, pp. 66–7). In view of Eustacia's almost magic sway over males of different ages (Johnny, Charley, Clym) and her local reputation as a witch, the comparison is perhaps not as far-fetched as it might seem at first. However this may be, the entries are obvious instances of material from the 'Literary

---

[16] *The Return of the Native*, p. 9. Subsequent references to Hardy's fiction will be given parenthetically in the text. The Wessex Edn is used.

Notes' appearing in Hardy's fiction as 'accidents and appendages of narrative'.

Entries of this kind are more common in the early than in the later part of the 'Literary Notes', and *The Return of the Native*, written close to the time when the early notes were being compiled, shows much greater use of such material than any other novel.[17] Since it is usually easier to detect the appropriation of factual matters – and to prove their immediate source in the 'Literary Notes' – than to establish aesthetic or ideological influence or borrowings, Hardy's use of, and overall dependence on, 'the trifles of useful knowledge' type of notes might easily be exaggerated at the expense of the other notes. It is to be remembered, of course, that the dodo and Albertus Magnus exemplify a more superficial relationship between the notes and Hardy's creative works than do, for instance, the many entries on non-realistic aesthetics, so essential to his own art, or, above all, the numerous entries which reveal a general but profound ideological accord with Hardy's writing. As we shall see below, these entries too are clearly reflected already in *The Return of the Native*.

This latter category of notes corresponds, in terms of Hardy's own evaluations in 'The Profitable Reading of Fiction', to those primary elements of literature which give 'intellectual and moral profit' as well as aesthetic training (Orel, pp. 112, 120); the nature of these notes, therefore, is best considered in relation to Hardy's central critical beliefs, that is, the anti-realistic basis of his aesthetic principles and his corollary emphasis on the intellectual and moral essence of literature.[18]

The general battle over realism in Hardy's days, as intensive as it was undecided, is reflected in entry 1304 on 'the realistic & poetical schools of painting'. Hardy quotes here that the 'two tendencies are indestructible ... the endeavour of the artist now to forget himself in

---

[17] There are over twenty explicit uses of 'Literary Notes' material in *The Return of the Native*: see annotations for entries 22, 35, 75, 79, 122, 161, 197, 204, 274, 306, 321–2, 331, 415, 443, 528, 604, 611, 613, 880, 885 and 907. For a more general discussion, see Lennart A. Björk, 'Hardy and his "Literary Notes"', in *A Thomas Hardy Annual*, ed. Norman Page, I (1982) 115–28.

[18] For authoritative and stimulating discussions of Hardy's theoretical aesthetics, see William J. Hyde, 'Hardy's View of Realism: A Key to the Rustic Characters', *Victorian Studies*, II (1958–9) 45–9; S. F. Johnson, 'Hardy and Burke's "Sublime"', *Style in Prose Fiction* (English Institute Essays, 1958: New York, 1959) pp. 55–86; Penelope Vigar, *The Novels of Thomas Hardy: Illusion and Reality* (London, 1974) esp. pp. 1–12; Morton Dauwen Zabel, 'Hardy in Defence of his Art: The Aesthetic of Incongruity', *Hardy: A Collection of Critical Essays*, ed. Albert J. Guérard, *Twentieth Century Views* (Englewood Cliffs, NJ, 1963), pp. 24–45; originally published in the Hardy Centenial number of the *Southern Review*, IV (Summer 1940) 125–49.

what he sees, & now to transfuse all the external world with his own thought and emotion'. As is well known, Hardy's own theoretical position does not display any such conflicting tendencies. Hardy is strictly anti-realistic in the following sense: art is a 'representation', not a 'transcript'; thus 'all art is only approximative', and hence '"realism" is not art' (*Life*, pp. 163, 229).[19]

Hardy seems to have found support for his unequivocal anti-realistic bias in both ideological and moral aesthetics. At the very centre of these strands of aesthetic principles is his acceptance of Matthew Arnold's concept of 'the application of ideas to life' – quoted in entry 1102.[20] At the same time, however, he embraced the idea of the unity of a work of art; he felt disinclined to distinguish between ideological and aesthetic qualities. When Hardy discussed the 'matter' and the 'rendering' (Orel, p. 27) separately, it was usually only for the sake of clarifying – and justifying – his treatment of certain issues raised in the criticism of his work.[21] It is also, it seems to me, in this context that one may, at least partly, understand Hardy's disclaimers of any 'consistent philosophy'. For, although he approved of 'the application of ideas to life', he did not respect 'novels with a purpose', presumably because

---

[19] For some additional 'Literary Notes' material on the realism issue, see entries 1218, 1219, 1321. See also Björk in *Thomas Hardy Annual*, I, pp. 125–26. Hardy's published anti-realism statements are well known, but there is an interesting item in the '1867' Notebook. Under a heading '[Examp. of more-true-than-truth: –]' Hardy quotes a passage from Zola's *Germinal* (London, 1885) p. 116: 'A warm odour of woman arose from the trodden grass.' The entry provides a good illustration to Hardy's observation in 'The Profitable Reading of Fiction' that 'The most devoted apostle of realism, the sheerest naturalist, cannot escape, any more than the withered old gossip over her fire, the exercise of Art in his labour or pleasure of telling a tale. ... If in the exercise of his reason he select or omit, with an eye to being more truthful than truth (the just aim of Art), he transforms himself into a technicist at a move' (Orel, p. 134).

[20] An interesting reflection of the same concept is found in, among several other places, Hardy's marking of the following passage in his own copy of Frederic Harrison's *The Choice of Books and Other Literary Pieces* (London, 1886): 'All great art, from the beginning of the world, has been the child of corresponding religion, philosophy, and manners. Greek drama, Roman epic, mediaeval poetry, architecture, and painting: Aeschylus, Pheidias, Virgil, Dante, Giotto, Shakespeare, Calderon, Raffaelle, Milton, were but interpreters of a civilisation which rested ultimately on profound religious and social ideas' (p. 229).

For one of the most succinct and interesting discussions of the potentially far-reaching effects of Hardy's ideological aesthetics on the structure of his novels, see Barbara Hardy, *The Appropriate Form* (London, 1964; repr. 1971) pp. 70 ff.

[21] See especially his prefaces to *The Hand of Ethelberta*, *Two on a Tower*, *The Woodlanders*, *Tess of the d'Urbervilles*, *Jude the Obscure* and *The Dynasts*, as well as 'The General Preface to the Novels and Poems' and the 'Apology', prefaced to *Late Lyrics and Earlier*.

they put ideological consistency before art.[22] He believed that the best
way of conveying what he wanted to say was to appeal, not by the
'logical reason' of disguised didactic pamphlets, but by the 'emotional
reason' of the imaginative representation of a true work of art: 'A
representation', he contended in 'The Profitable Reading of Fiction', is
'less susceptible of error than a disquisition; the teaching, depending as
it does upon intuitive conviction, and not upon logical reasoning, is not
likely to lend itself to sophistry'; it is therefore possible for the average
reader to 'discern, in delineative art professing to be natural, any stroke
at variance with nature, which, in the form of moral essay, *pensée*, or
epigram, may be so wrapped up as to escape him' (Orel, p. 114). It is
clear from this piece of reasoning alone that Hardy did not deny the
appropriateness of ideological substance in works of art: he only asked
for a fusion of emotion and ideology in literature – in accord with his
idea that 'a poet should express the emotion of all the ages and the
thought of his own' (*Life*, p. 386).

In the light of Hardy's emphasis on the contemporary ideological
background of literature, it is not surprising to find so much
nineteenth-century thought reflected in the 'Literary Notes'. The
ideological span of the notes is well illustrated by the first two entries:
charts and notes from the revolutionary Utopian Socialist Charles
Fourier face quotations from the conservative Christian speculations of
Cardinal Newman's *Apologia Pro Vita Sua*. Although Hardy's fictional
use of entries of this kind in general is difficult to establish with
reasonable certainty – as compared with his direct appropriation of
more factual material – there are nevertheless some explicit
occurrences. *Jude the Obscure* offers a good example. During Jude's first
night in Christminster he imagines that he hears the voice of Newman
and the sentences from the *Apologia* quoted in entry 11: 'My argument
was ... that absolute certitude as to the truths of natural theology was
the result of an assemblage of concurring and converging probabilities
... that probabilities which did not reach to logical certainty might
create a mental certitude' (*Jude*, p. 95). Newman plays an important
role in Jude's early career and is a prominent stimulus in that complex
of dreams epitomized by Christminster (*Jude*, p. 120). It is appropriate,

---

[22] Cf. also entry 1217. There is, however, substantial weight to Millgate's psychological
argument that Hardy's hesitancy and ambiguity in his handling of ideas should be seen
in relation to his 'extreme vulnerability' (p. 40) and 'fundamental lack of assurance' (p.
39), characteristics possibly explained by Hardy's 'experience, as a young man, of social,
economic, and educational insecurity' (p. 40).

therefore, that when Jude finally rejects Christminster and her
theology, and thus no longer enjoys the 'mental certitude' that
Newman offered him in his less rational youth, it should be Newman's
books that he throws into the bonfire of his theological works (*Jude*, p.
262).

As these examples have shown, it is easy to detect Hardy's direct
quotations of 'Literary Notes' material in his fiction. It is, however, also
possible to recognize a more implicit integration of his 'Literary Notes'
into his works throughout his career as a novelist. Again, *The Return of
the Native* is perhaps the most striking example. In fact, it is legitimate
to propose, as Gittings does, that almost 'all the main themes which
critics have discussed in *The Return of the Native* have their origins in his
[Hardy's] note book entries'.[23]

Similarly, Hardy's central concerns in *A Laodicean* can be related to
the 'Literary Notes'. As Michael Millgate persuasively points out, the
basic concept of Matthew Arnold's essay on Heine (quoted from in
entries 1017 and 1173–5) 'responds to the whole situation of *A
Laodicean*, lays down, indeed the lines of its central battle'.[24] In
addition, direct quotations from Arnold's 'Pagan and Mediaeval
Religious Sentiment' (quoted in entries 1018, 1176–8) in the final
chapter of the novel, as well as Hardy's allusions to other essays by
Arnold, read and excerpted from at the same time, suggest that Hardy
deliberately incorporated the Arnoldian themes into the novel as a
whole (see Millgate, pp. 174 ff.).

It is perhaps a little more surprising to find such ideological
reflections of early Literary Notes also in Hardy's late novels. In *Tess*,
for instance, there are unmistakable impressions of Hardy's reading of
Comte and other positivists in the 1870s. Indeed, no less a positivist
than Frederic Harrison greeted *Tess* as a 'Positivist allegory or sermon'
(see entry 618n).

In *Jude*, finally, it might be argued that Fourier's psychological vision
– as charted in entry 1 – is very similar to Hardy's own view of human
nature. Fourier's emphasis on the primary role of the emotions in
human life and the consequent struggle between Intellect and Passions,
the subject of Hardy's diagram in the first entry, constitutes a
conspicuous background to, for instance, the main theme of *Jude the*

[23] Robert Gittings, *The Older Hardy* (London, 1978) p. 9. See also Lennart A. Björk,
'"Visible Essences" as Thematic Structure in Hardy's *The Return of the Native*', *English
Studies*, 53 (Feb. 1972) 52–63, and Frank R. Giordano, 'Eustacia Vye's Suicide', *Texas
Studies in Literature and Language*, xxx (1980) 504–21.

[24] Millgate, *Thomas Hardy: His Career as a Novelist*, p. 175. See also Taylor, *The Neglected
Hardy*, pp. 191–2.

Obscure: the 'deadly war waged between flesh and spirit' (Preface to
Jude, p. vi). Although it is hardly feasible to prove direct influence,
Hardy's preservation of the early psychological charts is certainly
suggestive.[25]

It is easier to support Matthew Arnold's claim to a significant part of
the ideological structure of *Jude the Obscure* and other Hardy novels. The
general effect of the many Arnold entries in the 'Literary Notes' is to
confirm David J. DeLaura's convincing discussion of Arnold's overall
influence on Hardy.[26] More specifically, it is possible to point to the
juxtaposition of Hebrew and Hellene in some of Hardy's novels. One
example will suffice: Arnold's observation quoted in entry 1176 – that
the 'ideal, cheerful, sensuous pagan life is not sick or sorry' is echoed in
Sue's happy outburst at the agricultural show: 'I feel that we have
returned to Greek joyousness, and have blinded ourselves to sickness
and sorrow, and have forgotten what twenty-five centuries have taught
the race since their time, as one of your Christminster luminaries
says ...' (*Jude*, p. 358).

Many entries of the above kind thus indicate that the 'Literary
Notes' may both confirm, modify, and extend the account of Hardy's
intellectual background which previous scholarship has outlined:
several entries testify to Hardy's continued interest in evolutionary
philosophy, the Classics, Carlyle, von Hartmann, Mill, Schopenhauer,
Spencer, Leslie Stephen, and other major intellectual forces previously
discussed in Hardy studies. In such cases the notes offer specific
documentation and, in a few instances, may help to date certain
influences. For example, Hardy's interest in, and imaginative use of,
the Classics has been admirably considered by William R. Rutland and
others.[27] Numerous and extensive quotations from Mahaffy's *Social Life*

[25] For a further discussion of Hardy and Fourier, see Lennart A. Björk, 'Psychological
Vision and Social Criticism in *Desperate Remedies* and *Jude the Obscure*', in *Budmouth Essays
on Thomas Hardy*, ed. F. B. Pinion (Dorchester, 1976) pp. 86–105.

[26] David J. DeLaura, '"The Ache of Modernism" in Hardy's Later Novels', *Journal of
English Literary History*, 34 (Sep. 1967) 380–99. See also Dorothy Reimers Mills, 'The
Influence of Matthew Arnold's *Culture and Anarchy* on the Novels of Thomas Hardy'
(dissertation, Oklahoma State University 1966); and Lennart A. Björk, 'Hardy's
Reading', in *Thomas Hardy: The Writer and his Background*, ed. Norman Page (London,
1980) esp. pp. 117–24.

[27] William R. Rutland, *Thomas Hardy; A Study of his Writings and their Background*
(Oxford, 1938) pp. 20–45. See also Dieter Riesner, '"Veteris Vestigia Flammae":
Thomas Hardy und die klassische Humanität', *Lebende Antike: Symposium für Rudolf Sühnel*,
ed. Meller, Horst and Hans-Joachim Zimmermann (Berlin, 1967) pp. 370–96; M. A.
Springer, *Hardy's Use of Allusion* (London, 1983); Jeremy Steele, 'Hardy's Debt to the
Classical World: A Study of his Reading and his Fiction' (dissertation, University of
Sydney, 1979.)

in Greece, Symonds's *Greek Poets,* Arnold's *Essays in Criticism,* and various other sources will verify and specify Hardy's interest in Greek culture in general and the Greek view of life in particular. It seems significant that Hardy studied these secondary sources on the classics not long before the appearance of *The Return of the Native,* the first of his novels to employ 'Hellenism' as a criterion against which modern life is assessed.[28]

Other entries extend earlier information about Hardy's reading. The *Life,* for instance, indicates that he read periodicals quite regularly during his early years in London (*Life,* p. 39).[29] The 'Literary Notes' confirm this by a wealth of entries from various periodicals suggesting several potentially important sources of influence which have hitherto received but scant critical attention. The same is also true of Hardy's familiarity with Auguste Comte. The *Life* records that 'in May [1870] he was reading Comte', and, with reference to 1873, that he 'had latterly been reading Comte's *Positive Philosophy,* and writings of that school' (*Life,* pp. 76, 98). Entries 618–20, 640–2, and 645–769 reveal that Hardy also read Comte in 1876 and then took some twelve pages of quotations from the French philosopher. Of no less interest is the evidence in entries 2086–140, subtitled 'Notes in Philosophy', that Hardy was priming himself for the metaphysical challenge of *The Dynasts* by reading and taking notes from Spencer, Fiske, Clifford, Christlieb and, above all, von Hartmann's *Philosophy of the Unconscious.*

Hardy's ability to penetrate and assimilate profound intellectual matters has long been a topic of critical dissension. Although most students of Hardy today would hesitate to subscribe to Chesterton's famous characterization of Hardy as 'the village atheist brooding and blaspheming over the village idiot', there is still widespread reluctance to give him much credit as a thinker.[30] The 'Literary Notes' will not, of course, settle this question either way. They do show, however, that through his autodidactic course of study Hardy became familiar with

[28] The 'Hellenism' of this novel is emphasized by Evelyn Hardy in *Thomas Hardy: A Critical Biography* (London, 1954) p. 162; the contrast between 'Hellenism' and modern life is further developed in Björk, '"Visible Essences"', *English Studies,* 53.

[29] See also Maitland, *Life and Letters of Leslie Stephen,* p. 272; and Robert Gittings, *Young Thomas Hardy* (London, 1975) pp. 39 ff.

[30] G. K. Chesterton, *The Victorian Age in Literature* (London, 1913; repr. 1923) p. 143. See also, however, his *Autobiography* (London, 1936) p. 278, where he argues that the remark was not meant derogatorily. One should not, however, ignore A. O. J. Cockshut's observation that 'the influence exercised by a professional philosopher, like Schopenhauer, is a literary one. Hardy is not concerned with his reasoning but with the *tone* of his thinking' – 'Hardy's Philosophy', in *The Genius of Thomas Hardy,* ed. Margaret Drabble (London, 1976), p. 144.

contemporary thought in several fields, both in the sciences and the humanities, and thus made possible 'the application of ideas to life' in his own works of art.

Closely related to – or part of – 'the application of ideas to life' principle is, in Hardy as in Arnold, the notion of literature's *moral* interpretation of life. Arnold's distinction between 'the two kinds of interpretation, the naturalistic and the moral', which Hardy quotes in entry 1171, serves in fact as a structural basis for Hardy's main 'critical' essays. In 'The Science of Fiction' (1891) Hardy disparages the naturalistic approach, asserting that a 'sight for the finer qualities of existence, an ear for the "still sad music of humanity", are not to be acquired by the outer senses alone'; these aspects of life require a 'mental tactility that comes from a sympathetic appreciativeness of life in all its manifestations' (Orel, p. 137); in 'The Profitable Reading of Fiction' he argues that literary masterpieces are 'based on faithful imagination' rather than on 'the transcript ... of material fact', and that, whatever new technical innovations literature will indulge in, its 'general theme' will remain intact; 'the higher passions must ever rank above the inferior – intellectual tendencies above animal, and moral above intellectual –' (Orel, pp. 116, 114). The same argument is, of course, implicit in the many prefaces in which Hardy defends the morality of his fiction.

It is only to be expected that Hardy should have been almost equally interested in the often concomitant question of the morality of the artist. In entry 1217 he quotes, for instance, at some length from Leslie Stephen's 'The Moral Element in Literature', in which Stephen emphasizes the intimate bond between an author's 'artistic revelations' and his 'moral qualities': 'In a man's books if they are good for anything, I expect to have the highest part of the man. ... I measure the worth of a book by the worth of the friend whom it reveals to me.' There is, naturally, no certainty that Hardy concurred completely with Stephen in this matter, but in 'The Profitable Reading of Fiction' he voices a similar notion: 'In pursuance of his quest for a true exhibition of man, the reader will naturally consider whether he feels himself under the guidance of a mind who sees further into life than he himself has seen' (Orel, p. 115). Stephen's emphasis on the artist's personality is, furthermore, in general accord with Hardy's own insistence upon the right and value of 'the author's idiosyncratic mode of regard' (*Life*, p. 255), and with the sentiment Hardy quoted from Goethe, in Arnold's rendering, on the subject: 'as man must live from within outwards, so the artist must work from within outwards, seeing that make what contortions he will, he can only bring to light his own individuality' (entry 1017).

Hardy's personality in general and his 'idiosyncratic mode of regard' in particular are also reflected in the 'Literary Notes'. It is possible, that is, to detect some of the idiosyncracies which J. I. M. Stewart has drawn attention to in the *Life*, especially Hardy's 'fondness for the macabre and bizarre' and his 'sense of the power of incongruity to "intensify the expression of things"'.[31] Yet, in addition to giving glimpses into Hardy's workshop as he weaves the 'accidents and appendages' into the texture of his narratives and thereby stimulating studies of Hardy's technique of allusion,[32] the 'Literary Notes' are perhaps even more likely to encourage scholarly interest in the contemporary ideological background of Hardy's writings. As the notes help to trace Hardy's self-educating course of study over many years, they contribute to our knowledge of what David J. DeLaura aptly terms 'the complex contemporary matrix of Hardy's fiction'.[33] In so doing, the 'Literary Notes' will also provide material and stimulus, it is hoped, for further explorations of the relevance to our reading of Hardy of one of his central critical beliefs. This belief is perhaps best summarised by his own quotation from Arnold: 'a great poet receives his distinctive character of superiority from his application ... to his subject whatever it may be, of the ideas "on man, on nature, & on human life", which he has acquired for himself' (entry 1104). Read open-mindedly together with the fiction and poetry, these notes may even lead us part of the way towards an experience of how Hardy's characters and thematic concerns 'walk[ed] out from the chambers of memory through the gates of the imagination'.[34]

[31] J. I. M. Stewart, *Thomas Hardy: A Critical Biography* (London, 1971) p. 5. For examples of Hardy's eye for the macabre and bizarre, see entries 171, 318, 379, 414, 415, 429, 497, 498, 779, 851; for his readiness to appreciate incongruity, see entries 55, 57, 86, 128, 174, 387, 593, 770, 824, 1219, 1317.

The importance of these idiosyncrasies for the understanding of Hardy's art has been persuasively pointed out also by Penelope Vigar in *The Novels of Thomas Hardy*, pp. 1–12; and by Paul Zietlow in *Moments of Vision: The Poetry of Thomas Hardy* (Cambridge, Mass., 1974) esp. pp. 1–7.

[32] See, for instance, Peter J. Casagrande, 'A New View of Bathsheba Everdene', in *Critical Approaches to the Fiction of Thomas Hardy*, ed. Dale Kramer (London, 1979) esp. pp. 57–68; William F. Hall, 'Hawthorne, Shakespeare and Tess: Hardy's Use of Allusion and Reference', *English Studies*, 52 (Dec. 1971) 533–42; Marlene Springer, *Hardy's Use of Allusion* (London, 1983); Michael Wheeler, *The Art of Allusion in Victorian Fiction* (London, 1979) pp. 137–58.

[33] DeLaura, in *Journal of English Literary History*, p. 280.

[34] R. R. Bowker's apt phrase (possibly Hardy's own) quoted in Michael Millgate, *Thomas Hardy: A Biography* (Oxford, 1982), p. 279.

Textual Introduction

Towards the end of his life, Thomas Hardy destroyed most of his personal notebooks and diaries. After his death in 1928, his second wife and his literary executor Sir Sydney Cockerell, following his instructions, further reduced their number (see Purdy, p. viii). Only a few notebooks survived. With the exception of a small notebook of 1865 entitled 'Studies, Specimens &c' and a photocopy of a 'Poetical Matter' notebook – both in the private collection of Professor Richard L. Purdy – the extant notebooks are now in the Thomas Hardy Memorial Collection in the Dorset County Museum.[1] Among these are four notebooks of a stationery account-book or ledger style, listed in the Museum files as 'Commonplace Books I–IV'. They were deposited and made publicly available in 1962, after someone, possibly Irene Cooper Willis, co-executor of the second Mrs Hardy's will, had given the books their present classification, as to both title and numbering.

Although to some extent the four notebooks are of a commonplace-book character, this categorization will not be used in the present edition, since it somewhat obscures the distinct differences between the various volumes as well as Hardy's own classification of them, for, in Hardy's lifetime, the notebooks had been labelled as follows: 'Commonplace Book I' and 'Commonplace Book II' were entitled 'Literary Notes I' and 'Literary Notes II' respectively; 'Commonplace Book III' was headed 'Facts from Newspapers, Histories, Biographies, & other chronicles (mainly Local)'. Whether 'Commonplace Book IV' had a proper title is unknown: the first leaves are now removed, and it has '1867' on the front flyleaf as the only heading.

A fifth notebook, a guarded scrap album, entitled 'Literary Notes III', was added to the Memorial Collection in 1972.

[1] The two 'Memoranda' notebooks, the 'Schools of Painting Notebook' and the 'Trumpet-Major Notebook' have been expertly edited by Richard H. Taylor as *The Personal Notebooks of Thomas Hardy* (London and New York, 1979). A brief but helpful account of the existing notebooks is given by Millgate, in *Thomas Hardy: His Career as a Novelist*, pp. 39 and 366–7; and, in his *Thomas Hardy: A Biography*, pp. 87 ff., he provides an excellent account of the 'Studies, Specimens &c' notebook, along with the first mention in print of the 'Poetical Matter' notebook

DESCRIPTION

1 'Literary Notes I'

Cover. Half-bound (maroon brown leather, turquoise paper with printed gold flowers), gilt lines on spine, gilt edges, printed endpapers (yellow paper with a gold floral pattern).

Size and condition. 18 sewn-in gatherings of eight leaves measuring 18.5 × 22.5 cm. The title 'Literary Notes I', in pencil and underlined, is written on the verso of the front free endpaper. Although a few individual letters are not characteristic of Hardy's normal hand, the title is, in the absence of any likely alternative, probably written by Hardy himself, the slight differences presumably due to the title being written in a large cursive hand. Since, furthermore, Hardy himself assigned the term 'Literary Notes' to the second volume (see below) – which directly follows volume I chronologically and incorporates the same kind of notes – it seems reasonable to accept this title also for the first volume, whether the writing on its front endpaper is Hardy's own or not. Also onto the verso is pasted a leaf (16.5 × 20.5 cm), with charts, diagrams and text. Two front flyleaves: the rectos are blank; on the verso of the first is written, in pencil, and in Irene Cooper Willis's hand 'Extracts from Newman, Macaulay, (much), Saturday Review, Daily News, Fortnightly. Many of these notes appear to be in the handwriting of Mrs Emma Hardy.' Onto the verso of the second flyleaf, otherwise blank, are tipped four small leaves with text (9.5 × 15.8 cm); about 2.2 cm are cut off from the fourth leaf; rectos are paginated 518, 520, 522, 524 in pencil and are obviously salvaged from one of the destroyed notebooks. On fl^r is a partially erased line '[To be destroyed uncopied].' There are 143 leaves of text (paginated consecutively in pencil 1–141; thereafter only rectos are paginated, with the number 163 left out by mistake so that the rest of the notebook is incorrectly paginated) plus two inserted leaves (not paginated). The pagination is Hardy's (see entry 1419). Onto the edge of fl143 is attached one leaf of ruled paper (19.5 × 22.5 cm) with text. The recto of the first back flyleaf is written on. Onto the recto of the second back flyleaf is tipped one leaf of unruled paper (11.4 × 17.7 cm) with text on both sides. The back flyleaves are otherwise blank, as is the back endpaper. The notebook is ruled.

The entries are in ink unless described otherwise.

Period of use. Mid 1870s until 1888. The dating of the early entries is difficult, see 'Dating' below.

2 *'Literary Notes II'*

Cover. Full-bound, blind stamped rules on spine, marbled edges, printed endpapers (marble pattern).

Size and condition. 12 sewn gatherings of 12 leaves measuring 18.1 × 22.9 cm. 'Literary Notes II' is written, in pencil, and in the same large cursive hand as in 'Literary Notes I', on the verso of the front free endpaper. The front flyleaf is blank. The first page of text is entitled 'Literary Notes', underlined and in Hardy's hand. A subtitle, in pencil and also in Hardy's hand, reads '[188–, onwards.].' At the top of the page is Hardy's underlined notation 'Not to be printed or promulgated'. The top 2.5 cm of fl are cut off with traces of writing in red ink visible. 128 leaves of text (rectos 1–77 only are paginated, in pencil) plus some inserted material and a few loose pieces of paper. F65^r is headed 'Notes in Philosophy', in Hardy's hand. This classification, however, seems to apply only to ten pages of 'philosophical' notes, for, although Hardy did not bother to reintroduce 'Literary Notes' as a heading, the remaining entries are of the mixed 'Literary Notes' character. The rest of the notebook is blank. The notebook is ruled.

The entries are in ink unless described otherwise.

Period of use. 1888–1927.

3 *'Literary Notes III'*

Cover. Half-bound (sheepskin, diced grain) with cloth sides (pebble finish), spine tooling (three palette lines in four-panel style), waterwave silk endpapers.

Size and condition. Guarded scrap album made up of 16 gatherings, each consisting of four leaves, measuring 21.5 × 26.5 cm, and six small stubs. 'Literary Notes III', in pencil and underlined, is written in the same large cursive hand as in the previous notebooks, on the inside of the front cover, On the recto of the front free endpaper is written, in

Hardy's hand and underlined, 'To be destroyed uncopied'. Most of the material is made up of cuttings pasted onto the leaves but with some tipped onto the stubs so that both pages of the cuttings can be read. There are also 28 typewritten pages (ff43^r–63^r) and a few loose cuttings (indicated in the notes). The album is not paginated. Several passages are marked in the margin. All handwritten references and comments are in Hardy's hand and in ink unless described otherwise.

Period of use. Uncertain; most of the material is from 1906–10, but see 'Dating' below.

4 '1867' Notebook

Cover. Half-bound; blind lines on spine; marbled edges; printed endpapers (marble pattern).

Size and condition. 15 sewn gatherings of 12 leaves measuring 11.4 × 17.6 cm. On the verso of the front flyleaf is written in pencil '1867'. A number of leaves are cut out. The first page with text is numbered 29, although I have been able to detect only 10 stubs for the removed leaves. There are 23 leaves with text, rectos only paginated, in pencil, 29–73. Bottom 7.2 cm of f16 cut out. There are also eight stubs underpasted in strip 14 leaves from the end of the volume; before f156 there is a single stub and after f156 there are three stubs. On f143^v is a reference in an unidentified hand 'p. 40.4 Swin. At Eleusis P & B 1st Series' (to entry 82). On f156^r the word 'Points' is written, upside down, and partly encircled. On f156^v is written, upside down and in Hardy's hand, 'Subjective adj^s for objective e.g. "a girl ... so gladdening to see" (for so fair'; and two lines further down: 'Utilitarian romance'. The rest of the book is blank, except for an index, in an unidentified hand, on ff148–9. The notebook is ruled and the entries are in ink unless described otherwise.

Period of use. From the '1867' heading on the front flyleaf it has generally been assumed that this book was used in the late 1860s and thus chronologically preceded the other notebooks here described. This is not the case. The first twenty entries that now remain are possibly from the 1860s. Entry A21, however, is from an 1874 translation of Victor Hugo's '*Ninety-Three*', and several other entries show that Hardy copied material into the notebook as late as the second half of the 1880s. A few entries, for instance, are from the Norwegian writer Bjørnstjerne Bjørnson's *The Bridal March and Other Stories*, trs. R. B. Anderson (London, 1884); there are also quotations from Émile Zola's *Abbé Mouret's Transgressions* (London, 1886) and *Germinal; or Master and Man* (London, 1885).

HANDWRITING

The majority of entries in the 'Literary Notes' were written by Hardy himself. He enlisted the help of his first wife, however, to do some copying, especially in the early part of the first volume: it seems, in fact, as if Hardy wrote the first entry of the notebook proper (entry 20 – the inserted leaves from earlier notebooks are also in his hand) only to show how he wanted the material copied; his wife then penned the next 228 entries. Much of this material appears to be copied from earlier notes, particularly the passages from Macaulay, which are in no chronological order (see also 'Dating' below).

The two handwritings are superficially similar but there are important differences, both in matters of detail and in general appearance: Emma Hardy's hand is regularly sloped to the right; her husband's gives a slightly more irregular impression, heightened by the fact that in his hand the arch of *h* and the minims of *m, n,* and *u* are often splayed. Individual letters are otherwise not unequivocally safe criteria. Normally, however, the following traits are recognizable: his *d* is more often than not round-backed, hers straight-backed; his *t,* when crossed at all, usually has a stroke at the head of the stem, hers is crossed below the head.[2] A few years into the notebook, the letter forms of Emma Hardy's hand seem to be influenced by those usually employed by her husband, but the general appearance of each hand remains fairly distinguishable.

In both handwritings the displayed matter is, in the case of the rubrics, normally underlined and written in a hand which is often larger than the body of the text and sometimes without joining-strokes between the letters.

---

[2] For another discussion of the two handwritings, see Dale Kramer, 'A Query Concerning the Handwriting in Hardy's Manuscripts', *Papers of the Bibliographical Society of America* (Third Quarter, 1963) pp. 357–60. See also Kramer's account in his outstanding edition of *The Woodlanders* (Oxford, 1981) pp. 60–1.

The entries which are in Emma Hardy's hand are indicated in the individual annotations.

The '1867' Notebook is in Hardy's hand.

DATING

The 'Literary Notes' entries do not follow any regular day-by-day diary pattern. On the contrary, they seem to have been made at irregular intervals, sometimes, it appears, from notes in earlier pocketbooks, notebooks, or on loose pieces of paper. This is true especially of those which Hardy's wife helped him copy. Her assistance may also account for the chronological irregularities of many of these notes. However, the dating of the late notes is also very complicated.

From the evidence of the 'Literary Notes' proper it is not possible, therefore, to establish with any exactness either the date of Hardy's reading of the cited works or of the entering of the notes and quotations into the notebooks. As regards the reading of articles in newspapers and periodicals, it seems reasonable to assume that, with a few exceptions, he read these as they appeared or not very long afterwards, particularly in the case of publications frequently copied from.

Book excerpts are more complex. If they appear among entries from periodicals, some help is obtained. On several occasions Hardy's page references indicate which edition of a specific work he used, and in rare circumstances such information together with extrinsic evidence may help to specify the date. This is the case, for instance, with the quotations from G. H. Lewes, *The Life of Goethe* (entries 105–20), an abridged version of *The Life and Works of Goethe* (London, 1857); entry 118 reads: 'Modern Art wants. – The deepest want & deficiency of all modern Art lies in the fact that the Artists have no mythology. Quoted from Schlegel – 310.' The page reference proves that Hardy did not use any of the unabridged editions of the biography (1855, 1864, 1875) but the abridged edition of 1873. But for the page reference the 1875 edition might have seemed the most likely source, especially as another notebook attributes the reading to that year: in a small notebook headed 'Memoranda of Customs, Dates, &c – (viz. Prose Matter) 1', Hardy has entered for 16 June 1875, 'Reading Life of Goethe. Schlegel says that "the deepest want & deficiency of all modern art lies in the fact that the artists have no Mythology"'. The entry is quoted in *Thomas Hardy's Notebooks*, ed. Evelyn Hardy (London, 1955), p. 51.[3]

In a few of the cases where page references are not given, textual matters may reveal the edition used: entry 1015, for instance, 'The huge Mississippi of falsehood, history', from Arnold's 'The Literary Influence of Academies', is only three entries from material dated 29 July 1876, and it might be tempting to assume that Hardy used the then latest edition (3rd, 1875) of *Essays in Criticism*. The passage quoted, however, is deleted from this edition, and Hardy must have used either the 1865 or the 1869 edition; some scant evidence from the accidentals points to the 2nd edition (see also entries 1015n and 1018n). When, in 1880, however, Hardy again entered some material from *Essays in Criticism*, he seems to have used the 1875 edition (see entries 1018n and 1176n; 1022n and 1179n).

The exact date on which Hardy started keeping the 'Literary Notes' cannot now be established. The scant evidence, extrinsic and intrinsic, at present available gives only vague clues, especially as to the latest likely date for the inception of the notebooks. The most substantial evidence here is Hardy's use of a few entries in his fiction. The incorporation, for example, of material from entries with numbers as high as 604 and 611 in the manuscript (fols 7 and 66 respectively) in the first seven chapters of *The Return of the Native*, which were completed in the early spring of 1877, suggests that these entries were made before that date at least – assuming that Hardy would not have bothered to copy material which he had already used in his creative writing.

The evidence for the earliest possible date is a little more reliable. As we have seen (p. xxxvi), what is now entry 118 in the 'Literary Notes' was read and taken down into the 'Memoranda' notebook in June 1875. Since a preceding entry in the 'Literary Notes' (entry 82) draws on an article printed in January 1876, it is clear that Hardy, with his wife's assistance, had at least the Goethe passages incorporated into the 'Literary Notes' after the date of that article. This does not account for the earlier notes – for the dating of which there is no evidence – but there are other clues strongly suggesting the first half of 1876 as the most likely starting-point.

This dating is, above all, supported by the obvious enthusiasm for the whole project reflected in the great number of entries with material published in 1876, particularly in the late spring of that year: of the

[3] For another example of helpful extrinsic evidence, see entry 2423n.

total 2641 entries about 850 are extracted from publications dated 1876, and a substantial number is based on sources printed in the three months between 18 March and 17 June. It may also be significant in this context that it was Mrs Hardy who copied entries 21 to 249: they are in no chronological order and may therefore be presumed to be old notes entered *en masse*. The first material thereafter – the publication of which is traceable to a specific day, April 1876 – is found in entry 258 and is in Hardy's hand. From then on the chronology improves considerably, although there are also later entries in chronological disorder. A tempting, and not impossible, hypothesis is that Hardy temporarily took over some of the copying himself when, in April 1876, his wife had finished transcribing a good many old notes she had been entrusted with, and some new material was to be entered.

With a few exceptions Hardy kept his 'Literary Notes I' and 'Literary Notes II' in tolerably chronological order up to around entry 2296 (from January 1905). There are, however, some insertions of old notes. Entries 2263–83, for instance, are on tipped-in leaves and constitute a mixture of notes from November 1883 to June 1904, suggesting a cleaning-up operation on Hardy's part in the summer of 1904. There are also entries of a younger date inserted here: the material in entry 2257 is from October 1907 and in 2289 from March 1905; but these entries are cuttings which Hardy pasted in later just because space was available on the leaves already used for other cuttings. So, up to 1904–5 (entry 2296), Hardy seems to have entered his notes on a continuous, but not entirely regular, basis.

After that the chronology disintegrates at the same time as more cuttings are inserted. But the fact that already some fifty entries later (entry 2310) we find material from August 1908 suggests that Hardy made another attempt at organizing his notebook stuff in 1908, for the surrounding entries (2290–340) contain several cuttings from 1904 to 1907, with material from 1908 becoming more frequent from entry 2320 onwards. Then there seems to be a lapse of some five years before, in 1913, he makes another effort at a chronological arrangement: in entries 2321–420 he collects materials from 1908–13. But, again, old notes are inserted, and the chronology is far from strict.

The best piece of evidence for dating an entry in 'Literary Notes II' is Hardy's letter of 21 December 1914 (*Life*, p. 449), asserting that he had not yet read Bergson's *Creative Evolution* (1911), from which he quotes in entries 2423–8. And, since the following entry is from a book published in 1916, Hardy's interest in his 'Literary Notes' seems to have waned for more than a decade: that is, between 1914 and 1926 he made only some thirty entries (2423–52). Then, however, some time late in 1926 or early in 1927 (see entry 2455), he regained sufficient interest to collect once more some old materials, a few going back almost twenty years. Among these are several old scraps of paper, which Hardy headed 'Old Notes' (see entry 2459) and pasted in (entries 2459–72). Not counting loose cuttings, three handwritten excerpts from an article appearing in October 1927 conclude 'Literary Notes II'.

'Literary Notes III' is the most difficult volume to date with any precision. Since it is a scrap album with leaves and stubs, the tipped-in or pasted-in materials are not necessarily inserted in the order in which they now appear. Thus, for instance, the fifth entry of the volume (entry 2487) from 1907 or 1908 is found among cuttings from 1904. It is equally difficult to interpret the fact that the first part of entry 2509 (from May 1906) is in Hardy's hand, which might suggest that he started keeping 'Literary Notes III' in 1906. But the handwritten part is on a piece of paper pasted in, and two earlier entries (2491 and 2499) are from 1907. Yet, they could have been inserted there later just as the physical arrangement of entries 2503 and 2505 shows that these notes on Ibsen (from 24 and 23 January 1908) were pasted in later simply to have the various Ibsen entries in one place.

Another piece of tantalizing evidence to consider here is the collection of pages (entries 2544–628) typed by Florence Dugdale. Since entry 2542, the penultimate entry before the typed pages, is from November 1908, and since entry 2629, immediately following the typed insertions, cannot have been pasted in before February 1909, it seems likely that Florence Dugdale typed these pages for her future husband some time in 1909.[4] If this is so, these pages may well be among the earliest typing she did for Hardy. Biographical data suggest that Florence Dugdale started working for Hardy in April 1907 (Millgate, *Thomas Hardy: A Biography*, p. 453). She possibly did some typing for him in 1908, and certainly before July 1909, since then Hardy wrote to

---

[4] A further complication here is that the pages might have been typed at different times, since two ribbons seem to have been used (unless some pages are carbon copies, a difficult thing to decide with the kind of ribbons used at the time): f43^r (entries 2544–7) is mauve; ff44^r–55^r (entries 2548–607) are black; the rest (entries 2608–28) are mauve. Florence Dugdale had been given a typewriter by Sir Thornley Stoker: see Robert Gittings and Jo Manton, *The Second Mrs Hardy* (London and Seattle, 1979) p. 42. She acknowledged this in her correspondence with Rebekah Owen in 1916 (Robert Gittings, private letter to Lennart A. Björk, 1 Feb 1983). The exact date of the gift is unknown, but it was presumably not later than 1908.

his friend Edward Clodd that 'she is not really what is called a "typist"', but that she did his 'typewriting as a fancy' (quoted by Millgate, p. 463).

Mindful of the conflicting pieces of evidence, I suggest that Hardy started keeping 'Literary Notes III' late in 1907 or early 1908, perhaps between finishing the manuscript of Part III of *The Dynasts* in October 1907 and before reading the proofs in December 1907 (Millgate, p. 451). His late insertion (discussed above) of the Ibsen material from January 1908 supports this hypothesis, though one could wish for more substantial support. If this suggestion is correct, 'Literary Notes III' span some two years, since the latest inserted material (loose cuttings not counted) dates from August 1910 (entry 2630).

THE TEXT

The principal aim is to present a *literatim* text both as to substantives and accidentals. Fortunately, the manuscripts of the 'Literary Notes' and the '1867' Notebook are clear and with the exception of a very few words easily legible. Editorial intrusion can, therefore, be kept to a minimum; its most conspicuous feature is the numbering of the entries, undertaken to facilitate general handling and reference problems. For the most part such entry division has been easy: the first line of a new entry is normally indented and the first words are often underlined; generous space usually separates various entries, and sometimes horizontal strokes further emphasize the divisions. In a few instances, however, such distinct demarcation signs are absent, and a slight indent may be the only potential indication. Such uncertain cases will be discussed in the annotations.

There are also occurrences of words and phrases inserted above the line or elsewhere in the text; they may be simple corrections, or later comments or afterthoughts. All such insertions are enclosed by angle brackets (see 'Editorial Symbols').

Occasionally, the haste of some of the note-taking shows in the punctuation marks. It is, for instance, difficult at times to determine whether an entry ends with a period or a more expressive dash or hyphen. So, whereas every care has been taken to follow the original, there may be instances where the materially minute, but psychologically or ideologically significant, difference between a full-inked period and a short dash has not been discerned.

·Hardy used both square and round brackets. Both have been retained as they were possibly intended to serve different functions, although I have not been able to detect any consistent criteria. The few editorial insertions are enclosed by obliques. Folio numbers in bold type indicate the point in the manuscript where a new page begins.

Some regularization has seemed desirable and the following silent emendations have been performed:

1 All dashes, of whatever length, have been reduced to an en dash. Rules and other marks indicating division are standardized.
2 Ellipses are indicated by three spaced periods, irrespective of the number of periods in the original.
3 Quotation marks are completed but not otherwise corrected or regularized.
4 Commas and periods are put inside quotation marks: the original varies. Where, however, the manuscript repeats quotation marks both before and after an ellipsis within a quotation the manuscript is followed.
5 A period is put after the abbreviation 'ib.' but 'ib.' is not underlined. The original varies in both matters.
6 No period is put after the page references in the text. The original varies.
7 The periods or/and dashes in abbreviations with raised letters (e.g. 3.rd and 3rd) are transcribed as a single period under the raised letter(s). Abbreviations with neither periods nor dashes are not emended.
8 Irrelevant material, wholly or only partly legible, on some cuttings has not been transcribed.
9 In newspaper cuttings, newspaper names and titles of articles – sometimes pasted onto the page in the middle of the text – are moved up front for the sake of clarity and ranged left. The layout of extracted quotations is standardized.
10 Newspaper or magazine ornamentations are not transcribed.
11 Partly cut-off words in newspaper or magazine cuttings are completed within obliques.
12 Misprints in cuttings are corrected.
13 The accents in French quotations are corrected. The list of errors would have been too cumbersome (other irregularities are indicated in the annotations).
14 Capitalized words are printed in small capitals.

15 The desire to present the material as intact as possible has been weighed against the aims of practicality and clarity. Therefore, obvious misspellings have been corrected but recorded in the annotations.

EDITORIAL SYMBOLS

pf	Preliminary folio material.
⟨word⟩	A later insertion, above or below line, by Hardy.
/? word/	An uncertain reading.
/... /	An illegible word. Each additional period indicates another word.

Other brackets, parentheses, dashes, strokes, and signs are transcribed from the manuscript. In the absence of evidence to the contrary, they are presumed to be Hardy's own.

ANNOTATIONS

Despite the expenditure of a considerable amount of time and effort, and despite the generous help of friends and colleagues, I have not been able to trace all the sources for the 'Literary Notes' or the '1867' Notebook. It is a partial consolation that – unless unconscious rationalization be here at work – the unidentified entries seem of only minor significance.

The identifications given refer to the editions Hardy used – whenever these are known. In addition, complementary references are offered, wherever possible, to more modern and, it is hoped, more authoritative and easily available editions. For references to Hardy's own works, the Wessex Edition[5] has been used; but, unless otherwise indicated in the relevant annotations, the manuscripts, magazine publications, and other editions of his novels and short stories have also been studied for possible textual variations involving 'Literary Notes' material.

Cuttings are pasted in unless described otherwise.

---

[5] Although Purdy's conclusion – that the 'Wessex Edition is in every sense the definitive edition of Hardy's work and the last authority in questions of test' (*Thomas Hardy: A Bibliographical Study*, p. 286) – has been criticized to some extent by Robert C. Schweik in 'Current Problems in Textual Scholarship on the Works of Thomas Hardy, *English Literature in Transition*, 14 (1971) 239–40, the Wessex Edn remains the best edition for the purposes of the present work. For special purposes, of course, there are better editions of individual works.

I have attempted to indicate as briefly as possible the basic relationships between the entries and their sources; to note, that is, whether the entries are quotations, summaries or comments. The necessary brevity precludes any more detailed and comprehensive account, especially since most entries are mixtures of the various categories, which, in turn – as regards summary and comment – often overlap. The standardized terminology of these compressed descriptions is detrimental, it is feared, to the aesthetics, but beneficial, it is hoped, to the clarity of the annotations. Departures from the original sources are indicated as 'variations' as regards substantive, and as 'slight variations' as regards accidental deviations. Borderline cases, such as abbreviations of words – for example, 'w^{d}' for 'would', and '&' for 'and' – are not individually accounted for but classed as 'slight variations'. It is hoped that what information is provided in these matters will be sufficient for most purposes.

In a few cases when the elusive relationships between the entries and their sources have seemed especially significant – or when the sources *per se* have seemed so – the relevant source passages have been transcribed in full in the annotations. Since, however, deciding what is significant, and what is not, is a highly subjective process, it would have been preferable to err more often on the side of generosity, particularly as regards rare publications not available outside the most outstanding libraries. However, publishing costs have made such indulgence impossible.

The principle of affluence has not guided the scope of the annotations in other respects either. There are, admittedly, a few notes of some length on, for instance, Hardy and Fourier (entry 1n), Hardy and Newman (2n), Hardy and Arnold (101n), Hardy and Comte (618n), Hardy and McTaggart (2377n) and Hardy and Bergson (2423n). It will easily be seen, however, that these notes are also subjected to the principle of economy: they are mere outlines with no pretence whatever at completeness on the subjects dealt with. Since superficiality is often the corollary of brevity in matters of this kind, it would have been preferable perhaps to refrain from making such general notes. On the other hand, taken for what they are intended to be, mere starting-points for further research into subjects that seem well worth investigating, they may nevertheless be of some usefulness. The great majority of the annotations, however, are brief. As the 'Literary Notes' are primarily relevant to Hardy's prose works, there are but few references made to his poetry, and I have attempted to limit my comments on the many-faceted relationship between the 'Literary Notes' and his creative writing, in terms of influence, parallels and appropriations, to what in my opinion seemed not only potentially important but also reasonably demonstrable cases. It is my hope that this attempt to exercise restraint has to some extent reduced the number of editorial indulgences, prejudices and idiosyncrasies – that, in other words, the annotations will not too often remind the reader of Washington Irving's celebrated remarks on commentators who 'send up mists of obscurity from their notes'.

Literary Notes II

Entries 1650–2482

Literary Notes.

[188–, onwards –]

1650   To the old Theology the Earth was the grand centre & sum of the Universe, & the other heavenly bodies were adjuncts and auxiliaries to it. With a geo-centric astronomy, as the root-idea of science, the anthropomorphic Creator, the celestial Ressurection, & the divine Atonement, were natural & homogeneous ideas. No one can conceive the scheme of salvation growing up with anything but a geo-centric system of thought. With a geo-centric science, & an anthropomorphic philosophy all this was natural enough. But with a science where this planet shrinks into an unconsidered atom, with a transcendental philosophy to which the anthropomorphic is the contemptible, the Augustinian Theology goes overboard. And then Natural Theology calmly descends upon the waters to save a few fragments of supernaturalism out of the shipwreck of a mighty religious system. ...

There are thousands of acute minds wh. have abandoned all dogmatic Christianity, whilst they cling to its spirit of Transcendentalism & mystery. The evil legacy of Theology (**fl^v**) has been to bequeath to those who surrender Revelation a craving for Absolute objects of belief, absolute tests of truth, transcendental & mystical sources of hope.

Now this temper of mind is quite artificial; nay, it is unmanly morbid, & special to certain ages & races of men. Some of the noblest races of men in the most active ages were conspicuously free from any such weakness. The problem of the Universe & the problem of Immortality never troubled the great Greeks & Romans of the best times. ... Neither the Universe nor Paradise provided the source of their morality or the inspiration of their lives. ...

The grand difference between the humanitarian & the supernatural

3

views is this, that the former is content with a <u>relative</u>, the latter insists on an <u>absolute</u> basis of life. ...

The religion of humanity is a frank return upon the healthy, instinctive, anthropomorphic view of religion. ... The God adored by Abraham, by Job, & by David, was in every sense an anthropomorphic being. ...

Religion does not mean a metaphysical doctrine about the origin of the Universe & man's condition after death: it means the combination of beliefs & emotions which train him to live the best life in the completest way.

Fred^k Harrison. (F. Rev^w 11.88.)

1651 (**fla^r**) Mr. Frederic Harrison on History Books.
[BY PRIVATE WIRE: FROM OUR OWN REPORTER.]
Yesterday evening Mr. Frederic Harrison lectured on "History Books," at the head-quarters of the English Positivists, Fetter-lane, London. He said that the history of all studies most needed methodised application. The history of the world might be divided into – (1) The ancient theocratic world. (2) The rise and fall of the Greek Republic. (3) The rise and fall of the Roman Empire. (4) The Catholic and feudal world. (5) The formation and fettlement of European monarchical systems; and (6) the political and industrial revolution of modern times. In recommending history books he should only choose those suitable for the fireside for men and women whose time was limited, and who were not going in for competitive examinations. Everyone should know something of Herodotus. He could be read very well in translations by Canon Rawlingson, or in Church histories. Thucydides was a strict scientific writer, which Herodotus was not. Thucydides' description of Pericles and his age was a masterpiece. He was not easily read, as his whole matter was so charged with epigram. The translation by Dr. Jowett, the master of Balliol, Oxford, was as good as any. The histories of Rome were too much broken up into sections, and were not so worthy their attention as the Greeks. Livy was the greatest of the Romans. It was one of the greatest sorrows of literature that out of 142 of his books all but 35 had been lost. His narrative was not so easy to translate as the simple garrulity of the benign Herodotus. The spirit of the Master was well caught in Dr. Arnold's history of Rome. Tacitus was greater than Thucydides in the power of understanding human character. Carlyle alone of historians came anywhere near him. Dean Merivale's "Rome Under the Empire," vol. 2, gave a good idea of

Tacitus. Plutarch was a moralist rather than an historian, a painter of character rather than a narrator of events. There were numerous translations, both of him and of Julius Caesar, whose commentaries Mr. Harrison eloquently praised. A rational knowledge of history was, of course, not complete without the study of geography and the ancient arts. He could hardly praise Gibbon's "Decline and Fall" sufficiently. The just estimate of competent men was that his work was perfect of its kind. Hallam's "Middle Ages," Guizot's "Lectures on the Civilisation of Europe," and Dr. Milman's "Latin Christianity" were not to be shelved because modern research threw more light on these subjects. They had never been superseded. But it was necessary to go to the fountain head – to read the great contemporary writer at first hand. Coming to more modern times, Mr. Harrison recommended Robertson's History of Charles V., and Carlyle's "Cromwell" and "French Revolution." The "French Revolution" was an interesting instance of the poetic method applied to history. Guizot's revolution was useful as a corrective. "Frederick the Great" Mr. Harrison censured as preposterous in length, full of tiresome digressions and trivialities. The best historical handbook he thought to be "Hume's Student," as re-written by Brewer. In conclusion, he commended the historical work of the Positivists, amongst them Professor Beesley's Studies of Roman History, Dr. Congreve's Roman History and Elizabeth of England, and Mr. Cotter Morrison's "St. Bernard."

1652 (**f2ʳ**) Since all progress of mind consists for the most part in differentiation, in the severance of an obscure complex into its parts or phases. ...   Pater. F. R. 12. 88.

1653 Brahms – The individual character of his ideas. ...With him beauty seems to hold a place subordinate to expression.
                                        Grove. Mus. Dic.

1654 The roman romanesque ... of Balzac & G. Sand, is it so completely worn out as they wish us to believe [Paul Bourget, R. de Bonnierès, & G. de Maupassant, also H. Rabusson & Pierre Loti]. ...
   All five seek to do otherwise than others have done before them. But in doing otherwise do they do better? Or do they even otherwise? ... This novel of real life ... has it not also, like the other, its methods,

processes, conventions, which they have not invented?

... That largness, that freedom, that fine & tranquil audacity of execution wh. characterizes M. Guy de M's talent. ... His subjects are not <u>distingue</u>.   R. D. M.

~~~~~~~~//~~~~~~~~

1655   <u>Fuller's Ch. History</u>. – Many precious books were embezzled at the dissolution of abbeys. ... Few printed books in comparison of the many MSS. These, if carefully collected, would have amounted to a library exceeding that of ~~the~~ Ptolemy's for plenty, or many Vatican's for choiceness.

~~~~~~~~//~~~~~~~~

_____

1656   (**f2ᵛ**) Blame ... a stratagem, as some theologians have argued. ...

~~~~~~~~~~~~~~~~

1657   <u>Tropical education</u>. The tropics are the norma of nature: the way things mostly are & always have been. ... The biological head-quarters ... the standard or central type by wh. we must explain all the rest of nature, both in man & beast, in plant & animal.

... Men feel themselves in closer touch than elsewhere with the ultimate facts & truths of nature. ...

In the tropics we seem to get down to the very roots of things. Thousands of questions, social, political, economical, present themselves at once in new & more engagingly simple aspects. Difficulties vanish, distinctions disappear, conventions fade, clothes are reduced to their least common measure, man stands forth in his native nakedness. Things that in the North we had come to regard as inevitable – garments, firing, income-tax, morality – evaporate or simplify themselves. ...

How can Mrs Grundy thrive where every woman may rear her own ten children on her ten-rood plot without aid or assistance from their indeterminate fathers? ...

There are things wh. can only be learnt in the crowded haunts & cities of men – in Lⁿ, Paris, N. Y., Vienna. There are things wh. can only be learnt in the centres of culture or of artistic handicraft – in Oxford, Munich, Florence, Venice, Rome. There is only one Grand

Canal, (**f3ʳ**) & only one Pitti Palace. We must have Shakesp. Homer, Catullus, Dante ... Pheidias, Fra Angelico, Rafael, Mendelssohn; ... Aristotle, Newton, Laplace, Spencer. But ... something more left to learn ... & unlearn ... coming back with broken faiths & shattered gods ... an outlook undimmed by ten thousand preconceptions wh. hem in the vision & obstruct the view. ...

All these things (of the new environment ... topsy-turvy) are highly conducive to the production of that first substratum of philosophic thinking, a Socratic attitude of supreme ignorance, a pure Cartesian frame of universal doubt.

I admit that cold has done much for human development – has been the mother of civilization in somewhat the same sense that necessity has been the mother of invention. ... Clothing, the house, fire, steam-engine. ...

⟨The Tropics are even now the rule of life; the colder regions are but an abnormal & outlying eccentricity of Nature. Yet it is from this starved & dwarfed & impoverished northern area that most of us have formed our views of life. ...⟩

Views formed exclusively in the North tend too much to imitate the reduced gentlewoman's outlook upon life.

Influence of the tropics is by no means an ascetic one ... encourage a genial & friendly tolerance. ... They are essentially democratic, not to say socialistic, revolutionary. By bringing us all down to the underlying verities of life, apart from its conventions. ...

Grant Allen. (Long 8. '89)

1658 (**f3ᵛ**)

Ritter, treue Schwesterliebe	⟨Knight! a true sister-love⟩
Widmet euch dies Herz;	~~Sir Knight, a sister's love for thee~~
Fordert keine andre Liebe,	This breast ~~shall~~ retains;
Denn es macht mir Schmertz.	Ask me no other love:
	That way lie pains!
Ruhig mag ich euch erscheinen	Calm can I view thee come
Ruhig gehen sehn	Calm see thee go
Eurer Augen stilles Weinen	⟨Thy⟩ ⟨tearfulness⟩
Kann ich nichts verstehn	~~Thine eyes~~ silent ~~weeping~~
	⟨I must not⟩
Schiller.	~~My eyes cannot~~ know! (T.H.)

1659   R. D. Mondes.
Satanism: if Baudelaire had invented vice
Le Baudelaire sadique. Le Baudelaire satanique.
Delacroix.

1660   "Derrière lui traînaient un long mugissement." Baudelaire.
Désespoir de Lamartine –
Le Don Juan de Musset.
La Barque de Dante d'Eugène.

1661   "Ce flot d'anathèmes" (Alf.ᵈ de Vigny) [on Baudelaire?]

1662   "Les sanglots ... sont une symphonie enivrante. ..."   ib.

1663   (f4ʳ) B. M. 9 Mar.
R. d. Mondes. The dream: the disarray of souls: Renovation &
Dissolution: elements of renovation mingled with elements of
dissolution & corruption: des quolibets: senility: honest people find
there (Baudelaire's Fleurs du mal) a vegetation fantastic & hideous,
with bizarre leafage, with disquieting colourations, corrupt perfumes,
... a flora of vice & putridity. 'You have taken Hell, & made yourself
the Devil,' wrote Sainte-Beuve to him ... ~~as if B. had discovered or
invented vice~~ ... [Satanism.]
   Instead of making the object of art the imitation of nature & the
expression of truth, to make it uniformly consist in artifice, & to use
artifice itself only for the expression of paradox – such in four words
might be the formula of Baudelairism: ... [berquinades: sadism:]. ...
Pessimism, sadism, & satanism are, with him, only poses.

1664   "The Age of Apologies" – (in Christian literature) – the second
century, because of the large proportion of an apologetic kind. S.
Justin's two apologies are prominent among these. (Pref. Justin
Martyr. Pusey. Library of the Fathers) π "Hideous as it was 'the grove
of Thammuz or Adonis' which overshadowed it, & the idolatrous
wailings over Adonis, marked, during the 180 years from Adrian to
Constantine, the cave where Jesus was born."   (ib. Preface.)

1665   (f4ᵛ) Orval, or the Fool of Time. Lᵈ Lytton.
"Could those events [of 1789] be cancelled from the memory of man,
this nineteenth century wᵈ be a social orphan. ..."   Preface.

1666   "Who can undo
What time hath done? Who can win back the wind?
Beckon lost music from a broken lute?
Renew the redness of a last year's rose?
Or dig the sunken sunset from the deep?"

                                        ib. Poem.

1667   The poem is in 5 Epochs.

Epoch 1. Bride & Bridegroom.
      2. Husband & wife
      3. Father & Son.
      4. Man & man
      5. Man & Fate.

The Preface gives a sketch of the idea, wh. is mostly an imitation of that of the Infernal Comedy – (polish poem). A young noble (who has been interested in a young locksmith, & has ultimately seduced a girl whom the locks.th has saved from the criminal life of her parents) is married to a virtuous lady. ⟨Friend of seduced one comes – is hustled out. ...⟩ His past comes back upon him: antagonism between his class & that of the locksmith, &c, &c. ... He loves the memory of the seduced one. Lower class revolts. (Fch. Revolution). ...

1668   (**f5ʳ**) <u>Salon</u>. "There is a fine rush & impetus of life about these big pictures. ... They show a fine scorn for the thistle-and-ass kind of painting, to deal with matters of strong human interest & emotion to be conceived by men ~~whol~~ whose pulses beat freely & in a masculine manner. ... These are <u>men's</u> work as well as artists pictures. ...

    Turn in thought ... to the B. Academy & notice how rarely our artists escape beyond the groove of prettiness & thin sentiment. The fear of unconventionality seems to beset them all; the subjects & the way of regarding them are like boy's conversation on a Sunday afternoon in their schoolmaster's drawing-room – demure trivial & uncharacteristic. You dont suppose that English painters are at heart less subject to the passions & defects of humanity than their Gallic brethren.   Harry Quilter.

1669   "Be it so; then minimize pain." Words of Jeremy Bentham when his physician told him he was about to die   F. R. E. Dowden. ~~ib~~.

1670   Thackeray could not acquiesce in the ways of the world, its shabbiness, its shams, its snobbery, its knavery; & yet it is only for born prophets to break with the world & go forth into the wilderness crying "Repent! ... Why affect to be a prophet? ... The club is a pleasant lounge ... one can (**f5ᵛ**) ~~even~~ always preserve a certain independence by that unheroic form of warfare suitable to an unheroic age – satire; one can even in a certain sense stand above one's own pettiness by virtue of irony. ... Thackeray had not the austerity & lonely strength needful for a prophet."   ib.

1671   The contributions towards an ideal reconstruction of society by Fourier, by Robert Owen, by Aug. Comte, by Lassalle & Karl Marx. ...
                                                                          E. Dowden.

1672   P. & his island. G. Moore.
[opens] Dublin.
     This is Dalkey, a suburb of Dublin. From where I stand I look down upon the sea as upon a cup of blue water ... my thoughts turn involuntarily to the Bay of Naples which I have never seen. ... The character of Dublin is the absence of any characteristic touch. ... Nobody reads, nobody thinks. To be considered a man of the world it is only necessary to have seen one or two plays in London before they are six months old & to curse the Land League. ... Dublin is divided into four parts: The Castle, The Shelbourne Hotel, The Kildare Street Club, & Mʳˢ Rusville the fashionable dressmaker.

1673   (**f6ʳ**) "Again I saw another angel."

               ...
     I saw this monstrous grave the earth
     Shake with a spasm as though of birth,
     And shudder with a sullen sound,
     As though the dead stirred in the ground.
     And that great angel girt with flame
     Cried till the heavens were rent around,
     "Come forth ye dead!" Yet no man came.

     Then there was silence overhead;
     But far below the ancient dead
     Muttered as if in mockery;

And there was darkness in the sky,
And rolling through the realm of death,
Laughter & some obscure reply,
With tongues that none interpreteth.

Margaret L. Woods.
(cf. Heine.)

1674 (**f6ᵛ**) One cannot repeat too often that what makes the work of art is the force of the sentiment that an individual fixes in it, & eternizes in it; nature is only the arsenal, always open, where he goes to look for his means of expression.

La Peinture a l'Exposition. G. Lafenestre. R. D. M. 1.11.89

—————————//—————————

1675   Plain Tales from the Hills. Rudyard Kipling. (May 10.90)
   Some of the best are –
"Lispeth," – who is brought up as a Christian servant at the Chaplains. She finds the Chaplains wife has lied to her in saying her English lover will come back – thereupon 'verts to her mother's gods. ... "She took to her own unclean people savagely ... " married a wood-cutter, who beat her after their manner ... died a very old woman. "She always had a perfect command of English, & when she was sufficiently drunk could sometimes be induced to tell the story of her first love affair."

1676   "Thrown away" – subaltern commits suicide – They destroy his letters to his friends, & write to tell his mother he has died of cholera.

1677   "Yoked with an unbeliever" – Phil Garron, who, having gone out to India, is beginning to forget his fiancée in England, rises (**f7ʳ**) to the level of a heart-broken man when she tells him she has married another. He marries a Hill-woman. His former sweetheart, widowed, comes out to look for him, still loving him.

1678   "The other man" – Mrs S. marries S. while she loves another. She gets ill – her husband leaves her at Simla – The other man is coming there, ill. She appoints to meet him – He arrives one wet night – dead.

1679   "Beyond the Pale" – Englishman makes Hindoo widow his mistress – goes to her some weeks after: her hands have been cut off.

1680   "In error." Man is saved from drunkenness by believing in Mrs Reiver, a bad woman. "He thought her something that she never was."

1681   "In the Pride of his Youth" – Man of 20 marries girl, & goes to India – sends greater part of salary home to her – she complains – has child – he is hoping to have her out when she writes that she has gone to another man. He does not care for anything afterwards, retires, refusing rise in salary.

1682   "The Madness of Private Ortheris." Longs for home.

1683   (**f7ᵛ**) "The strength of a likeness" – (an excellent story of the delicate sort) – Man, disappointed in love, sees, 4 yrs. after, a woman like the one he has lost. She is also a married woman. He seeks her society because she reminds him of the lost one. At parting he tells her the reason, & as a matter of fact, does not care for her personal life. When she is gone he gets to love her for herself.

1684   "To be filed for reference" – A scholar & an Oxford fellow, is found living as the drunken husband of a native woman. He does not regret his position. "Little incidents wh. wᵈ vex a higher life are to [me] of no consequence. Last night my soul was among the gods."

———————— // ————————

1685   Journal of Marie Bashkirtseff –   (May 13, 90)
To see through stone walls, & to hear the thoughts as they pass through a man's head.   Introd. by transʳ

1686   The drama of a woman's soul; at odds with destiny, as such a soul must needs be, when endowed with great powers & possibilities, under the present social conditions; where the wish to live, of letting whatever energies you possess have their full play in (**f8ʳ**) action, is continually thwarted by the impediments & restrictions of sex.
                                                      Introd.

1687   "The fever called living."

1688 At 12 she is desperately in love. "O God, give me the Duke of H—!" This is a nobleman whom she has only seen in the street, & who does not know of her existence. He marries – she is in despair. (1873).

In 1877 she accidentally sees him in a cab – He has developed into a rubicund Englishman – "Half an hour after I thought no more about him." "... How awfully excited I was!"

1689 Description of her life in Julian's studio.

1690 "It is amusing when you feel that you are making some one love you. ... The love one inspires is a sensation unlike anything else, wh. one feels oneself & wh. I formerly mistook for love."   I. 395

1691 "On my dress depended my temper; on my temper my manner & the expression of my face – everything, in fact."   399

1692 (**f8ᵛ**) "Departmental Ditties," &c. R. Kipling. (14.5.90) There is a cry as of a race in trouble, in such lines as: –

"What part have Indian exiles in their mirth?"

and

"Say that we be a feeble folk who greet her,
    But old in grief, & very wise in tears
Say that we, being desolate, entreat her
    That she forget us not in after years."

1693 "The Ballad of Fisher's Boarding house" is excellent –

At a boarding house for sailors of all nations there is a woman who belongs to each man for a week. She fancies Hans the Dane – he is cold to her, being true to a girl at home. He sneers at her – She says he has insulted her – the men stab him. She takes from his corpse the charm of silver his mistress had given him.

'Twas Fultah Fisher's boarding house
    Where sailor-men reside,
And there were men of all the ports
    From Mississip to Clyde,
And regally they spat & smoked
    And fearsomely they lied.

South, down the Cattegat – What's here?
    There-are- no- lights-to -guide!"
The mutter ceased, the spirit passed,
    And Anne of Austria cried
In Fultah Fisher's boarding-house
    When Hans the mighty died.

In Anne of Austria's trembling hands
  The weary head fell low: –
"I ship mineselfs to-morrow straight
  For Besser in Saro;
Und there Ultruda comes to me
  At Easter, and I go

Thus slew they Hans, the blue-eyed Dane
  Bull-throated, bare of arm,
But Anne of Austria looted first
  The maid Ultruda's charm –
The little silver crucifix
  That keeps a man from harm.

1694   (**f9ʳ**) He adroitly mixes two tones, the gay & the bitter: e.g.

"The leg-bar chafed the ankle & we gasped for cooler air,
But no galley on the water with our galley could compare!"
                                (The Galley Slave.)

1695   "Soldiers three."
  They lounged about cantonments – it was too hot for any sort of game, & almost too hot for vice – & fuddled themselves in the evening, …. Then the tempers began to wear away, & men fell a-brooding over insults real or imaginary. They had nothing else to think of. The tone of the repartees changed. … Losson had for a long time been worrying Simmons. … Simmons was afraid of Losson, & dared not challenge him to a fight. He thought over the words in the hot still nights. –

———————————————⊹———————————————

1696   "The New Spirit." Havelock Ellis. (May '90)
"Wᵐ Morris looks back wistfully towards the popular art of the middle ages, & deals out scorn to the novel."   31

1697   "'In founding morality on the relationships wh. must always exist between men, the religious law becomes perhaps superfluous; & the civil law should only be the enunciation of the law of nature, which we bear engraved on our hearts.'"   (quot. from Diderot.) 60

1698   (**f9ᵛ**) "'I am convinced' he [Diderot] wrote, 'that there can be no true happiness for the human race except in a social state in which there is neither king nor magistrate, nor priest nor laws, nor <u>meum</u>, nor <u>tuum</u>, nor property in goods or land, nor vices nor virtues.' This is the anarchism that stands at the end of all social progress, but as an attainable social state it is still certainly, as Diderot adds, 'diablement idéal.'"   62

|| 1699   "When men begin to say that everything has been done, the

‖ men come who say that there has yet nothing been done. We have congratulated ourselves that many sciences of nature & of man are in the main settled, but we are always compelled to begin again, & on a larger & perhaps simpler scale." 67

1700 "Heine never mentioned her name: it was not till after his death that the form standing behind this Maria, Zuleima, Evelina, of so many sweet, strange, or melancholy songs, was known to be that of his cousin, Amalie Heine." 75

‖ 1701 "'One must be able' Millet said, 'to make use of the trivial for the expression of the sublime.' They ⟨[Millet & Whitman]⟩ both insisted that the artist must deal with the average & typical, not with the exceptional." 107

1702 (**f10ʳ**) "What marked the Dutch artists was the ineradicable conviction that every action, social or physiological, of the average man, woman, child, around them might be, with love & absolute faithfulness, phlegmatically set forth." 124

———————— *//* ————————

1703 The Miner's Congress – in the Belgian town of Jolimont ... "almost within a stone's throw of fields rendered historic by great battles in which British, French, Belgian, & Prussian soldiers – men having no personal cause of quarrel – had shed one another's blood in deadly strife." Burt. M. P. May 1890.

————————————

1704 "The New Spirit" (contᵈ)
"'No real circumstance is unpoetic so long as the poet knows how to use it.'" (quot. from Goethe). 165

1705 A woman, married: former lover returns: she wants to fly with him. Husband at length consents to allow her to choose as she will. Then at once she feels able to decide against the lover. The moral is that without freedom of choice there can be no real emancipation or development. 171

1706 The Scythians of 23 centuries ago are the Russian <u>moojiks</u> of to-day. Features & dress have scarcely changed. 179

1707   (**f10ᵛ**) "In some parts of Russia, even to-day, it is said, a kind of
<u>Pervigilium Veneris</u> is held periodically; the young people ascend a
mountain to sing & dance, after which it is <u>de rigueur</u> to separate & to
spend the night in couples."   180

1708   Those frantic devotees, the Skoptsy, who mutilate themselves
after the manner of the Phrygian worshippers of Cybele.   182

1709   He (Tolstoi) became a yunker, at 23, doing the work of a
common soldier & associating with the officers – as usual with
noblemen entering the army   188

1710   Both mothers [the prostitute & the lady] possess the same view
of life, namely that a woman must be fed, clothed, & taken care of, to
satisfy the wantonness of a man   200

1711   Tolstoi has nothing to say in favour of the Xty of today, wh.
approves of society as it now is. … It is unreasonable to make use of the
labours of others that you & yours may be clothed in the height of
fashion & maintain that source of <u>ennui</u>, a drawing-room. … 'In my own
life,' he says, 'I can reckon up as much suffering caused by following
the doctrine of the world as many a martyr has endured for the doctrine
of Jesus. All the most (**f11ʳ**) painful moments of my life … are only so
much martyrdom exacted by fidelity to the doctrine of the world.'"
(Tolstoi)   204

1712   "'You will find, perhaps to your surprise, that nine-tenths of all
human suffering endured by men is useless.'" (Tᵒⁱ)   204

1713   "The first condition of happiness, he (T.) tells us, is that the link
between man & nature shall not be broken."   205

1714   Zola's rule for novels – one must get one's human documents …
frequent the society of people one is studying … record their
surroundings. "But have we got reality then? Does the novelist I
casually meet … takes note of my condⁿ … furniture &c. … know
anything whatever of the romance or tragedy which to me is the reality
of my life, these other things being but shreds or tatters of life. Or if my
romance or tragedy has got into a law-court or a police-court, is he
really much nearer then? The unrevealable motives, the charm, the

mystery ... were not deposed to. ... Certain disagreeable details: do they make up reality? ... A great artist, a Shakespeare or a Goethe, is not afraid of any fact, however repulsive it may seem, so long as it is significant. – Without a severe [sifting] of details the truly illuminating facts will be missed or lost in the heap."

1715 (**f11ᵛ**) ~~Tolstoi~~ ⟨Gogol⟩ "... is perpetually insisting on the importance to the artist of those 'little things which only seem little when narrated in a book, but wh. one finds very important in actual life.'" 217

1716 Pater. "<u>Appreciations</u>."
"All progress of mind consists for the most part in differentiation, in the resolution of an obscure & complex object into its component aspects."
1

1717 [Different centuries] different intellectual needs. 3

1718 "De Quincey's distinction between 'the literature of power & the literature of knowledge,' in the former of which the composer gives us not fact, but his peculiar sense of fact." 4

1719 "'The artist may be known rather by what he omits'"
(quot. fr. Schiller)

1720 "Your historian, for instance, with absolutely truthful intention, amid the multitude of facts presented to him, must needs select, & in selecting assert something of his own humour, something that comes not of the world without but of a vision within." 5

1721 "The transcript of his sense of fact rather than the fact." 6

1722 (**f12ʳ**) "All art does but consist in the removal of surplusage." e.g. gem-engraver.

1723 With Flaubert the search, the unwearied search, was not for the smooth, or winsome, or forcible word, as such, as with false Ciceronians, but quite simply & honestly, for the word's adjustment to

its meaning.   ~~28~~
The first condition of this must be, of course, to know yourself, to have
ascertained your own sense exactly. Then, if we suppose an artist he
says to the reader, – I want you to see precisely what I see.   28

1724   If Music be the ideal of all art whatever. ...   35

1725   Impassioned contemplation͵ ... is with Wordsworth the
end-in-itself.

1726   The distinction between what is desirable in itself, & what is
desirable only as machinery. ...   61

1727   To treat life in the spirit of art.

1728   The humourist to whom all the world is but a spectacle in which
nothing is really alien from himself, who has hardly a sense of the
distinction between great & little among things that are at all.
                                                                131

1729   (**f12ᵛ**) We carry with us, as Browne writes, the wonders we seek
without us.   132

1730   Nature "the art of God"   Browne.

1731   Bacon's striking doctrine of the Idola, the "shams" men fall
down & worship.

1732   "A student of perpetuity"   Sir T. Browne.
    Mortuary customs: a kind of grey & aged colour:

1733   The veneration of relics became a part of Xtian (as some may
think it a part of natural) religion. All over Rome we may count how
much devotion in fine art is owing to it.   162

1734   Browne's real interest is in what may be called the curiosities of
our common humanity.   162

1735   In handling a subject of Greek legend, anything in the way of an actual revival must always be impossible. Such vain antiquarianism is a waste of the poet's power. The composite experience of all the ages is part of each one of us: to deduct from that exp.ᶜᵉ to obliterate any part of it, to come face to face with a people of (**f13ʳ**) a past age, as if the Middle Age, Renaissance, the 18ᵗʰ cent. had not been, is as impossible as to become a little child. ... But ... it is possible to isolate such a phase, to throw it into relief, to be divided against ourselves in zeal for it; as we may hark back to some choice space of our own individual life

224

1736   Classical – romantic. – It is the addition of strangeness to beauty that constitutes the romantic character in art: & the desire ~~248~~ of beauty being a fixed element in every artistic organization, it is the addition of curiosity to this desire of beauty, that constitutes the romantic temper. ... When curiosity is in excess, when it overbalances the desire of beauty, then ... inartistic ... ⟨grotesque⟩ ... Pope too little curiosity ... Balzac too much. These two tendencies are ... really at work at all times in art. ... If the union of strangeness & beauty ... be successful ... & entire ... then ... very exquisite ... attractive. ...
   ... Stendhal argues that all good art was romantic in its day (in his work Racine & Shakespeare, pub.ᵈ 1823, full of 'dry light' & fertile ideas). ... Note how the element of curiosity, the love of strangeness, insinuates itself into classical design, & record the effects of the romantic spirit there, the traces of struggle, of the grotesque even. ... To Sainte-Beuve C.ᵐ is ... the char.ᶜ of certain epochs ... given to the working out of refinements of manner on some authorized matter

258–262

1737   (**f13ᵛ**) Obiter Dicta – (June '90)
   In considering a poet:– ... How are we the better for him? Has he quickened any passion, lightened any burden, purified any taste? Does he play any real part in our lives? Has he had anything to say, which wasn't twaddle, on those subjects which are alone of perennial interest –

"On man, on nature, & on human life"

on the pathos of our situation, looking back on to the irrevocable & forward to the unknown.

1738 Have we not all some correspondents, though probably but few from whom we never receive a letter without feeling sure that we shall find inside the envelope something written that will make us either glow with the warmth or shiver with the cold of our correspondent's life? But how many other people are to be found, good, honest people too, who no sooner take pen in hand than they stamp unreality on every word they write.

1739 Mr Bagehot – a man who carried away into the next world more originality of thought than is now to be found in the Three Estates of the Realm. – Whilst remarking upon the extraordinary reputation of the late Francis Horner, & the trifling cost he was put to in supporting it, Mr Bagehot said that (**f14r**) it proved the advantage of 'keeping an atmosphere....'

... These awkward questions are not put to the lucky people who keep their own atmospheres. The critics before they can get at them, have to step out of the everyday air, where only achievements count, & the decalogue still goes for something, into the kept atmosphere, which they have no sooner breathed than they begin to see things differently.... Cellini is an admirable example.

1740 To suppose that no person is logically entitled to fear God, & to ridicule Januarius at the same time, is doubtless extravagant, but to do ⟨so⟩ requires care. ib. 'The Via media.'

1741 ... In a period like the present, wh. is so notoriously transitional, a logician is as much out of place as a bull in a china-shop, and that unless he is quiet, & keeps his tail well wrapped round his legs, the mischief that he will do to his neighbours' china creeds & delicate porcelain opinions is shocking to contemplate. But this excuse is no longer admissible, &c – v. Carlyle's 'Characteristics.' 182

1742 Logic is the prime necessity of the hour. Decomposition & transformation is going on all around us, but far too slowly. Some opinions, bold & erect as they may still stand, are in reality but empty shells. One shout would be fatal. Why is it not given?

(**f14v**) The world is full of doleful creatures who move about demanding our sympathy. I have nothing to offer them but doses of logic, & stern commands to move on or fall back. Catholics in distress about Infallibility; Protestants devoting themselves to the dismal task of paring down the dimensions of this miracle, & reducing the credibility of that one – as if any appreciable relief from the burden of faith could be so obtained; sentimental sceptics, who, after labouring to demolish what they call the chimera of superstition, fall to weeping as they remember they have now no lies to teach their children; democrats who are frightened at the rough voice of the people, & aristocrats flirting with democracy. Logic, if it cannot cure, might at least silence these gentry.   The Via Media. 199

1743   Morley's Voltaire. (June '90)
   Nobody is more free from the ostentatious correctness of the literary precisian, & nobody preserves so much purity & so much dignity of language with so little formality of demeanour   122

1744   The strain that society has undergone since V's day has taught men to qualify their propositions. ... New notes have been struck in human feeling, & all thought has now been touched by complexities that were then unseen.   123

1745   (f15ʳ) The hyper-hellenistic collegian: negativism (in religion):

1746   That brutal truth which is always very near being the most subtle kind of lie.   133

1747   a theology, not a theosophy (present Xty the latter)

1748   V.'s instruments were purely literary & dialectical [i.e. of the letter not of the spirit]

1749   The religiosity (of prosperous people): the ferocity of authority.

1750   The 'refined insolence' of Candide. Aristotles definition of wit as ὕβρις πεπαιδευμένη marks one of Voltaire's chief talents with entire accuracy.   283

1751   Besides the prominent men of a generation there is a something at work underneath.   308

1752   The death of Lally ... parallel to execution of Byng.

1753   'Time' s^d D'Alembert, apologising for some whiff of orthodoxy wh. V. scented in one or two articles in the Encyclopædia, 'will make people distinguish what we thought from what we said.' Condorcet, as we know, deliberately defended (**f15^v**) these deceptions, wh. did not deceive, while they did protect. He contended that if you rob a man of his natural right of publishing his opinions, then you lose your own right to hear the truth from the man's lips. Undoubtedly all laws admit that duress introduces new conditions into the determination of what is right & wrong in action. ...   339

~~~~~~~~//~~~~~~~

1754   Browning. <u>Asolando</u>.   (July '90)
"<u>Prologue</u>" ...

"And now a flower is just a flower:
    Man, bird, beast are but beast, bird, man –
Simply themselves, uncinct by dower
    of dyes which, when life's day began,
Round each in glory ran."

[cf. Coleridge's "Youth & Age.' But Browning ends with a conventional piece of optimism; while Coleridge is true throughout]

1755   "Yet here in the flesh you come –
        Your same self, form and face, –
    In the eyes, mirth still at home!
        On the lips, that commonplace
    Perfection of honest grace!"

1756   "Royally lone."

1757   (**f16^r**) "Proud solitary traverser,
　　　　My soul, of silent lengths of way –"

1758   "A City, yes, – a Forest, true, –
　　　　But each devouring each. Perfidious
　　　　　　Snake-plants had strangled what I knew
　　　　　　Was a pavilion once: each oak
　　　　　　Held on his horns some spoil he broke
　　　　By surreptitiously beneath
　　　　　　Upthrusting: ... –
　　　　Oh, Nature – good! Oh, Art – no whit
　　　　　　Less worthy! Both in one – accurst!"

1759   "That strong stern man my lover came
　　　　　　– Was he my lover? Call him, pray,
　　　　My life's cold critic bent on blame
　　　　　　Of all poor I could do or say
　　　　To make me worth his love one day. –"

1760   "Artistry's haunting curse – the Incomplete."

1761   "... And it befell
　　　　That after the first incontestably
　　　　Blessedest of all blisses ...
　　　　　　... There somehow came
　　　　The coolness which as duly follows flame."

                              ("Beatrice Signorini.")

1762   (**f16^v**) (Augustus Caesar): –

　　　　"... This masterdom o'er all the world
　　　　Of one who was but born, – like you, like me,
　　　　Like all the world he owns."

1763   "Let's sink – and so take refuge, as it were,
     From life's excessive altitude – to life's
     Breathable wayside shelter at its base!

              (from "Imperante Augusto natus est –")

(N.B. A person at the baths is talking to another on Caesar's greatness.)

–––––––––––––– // ––––––––––––––

1764   "No dream's worth waking."

1765   Life in the star Rephan, –
     "No change ... nowhere deficiency nor excess. ...
     No hope, no fear: as to day, shall be
     To-morrow. ...
          ... In that uniform universe."

–––––––––––––– // ––––––––––––––

1766   Epilogue: – (containing, curiously enough, an epitome of B's views) –

"One [himself] who never turned his back but marched breast forward,
     Never doubted clouds would break,
Never dreamed, though right were worsted, wrong would triumph,
Held we fall to rise, are baffled to fight better,
     Sleep to wake."

––––––––––––––––––––––––––––

1767   (**f17ʳ**) She Stoops to Conquer. (At its 1ˢᵗ performance, 15ᵗʰ March 1773)
   Smith & Woodward, who were designed to play young Marlow & Tony Lumpkin, threw up their parts. To this unlooked for & unnecessary resignation Lee Lewes & Quick (who took their places) owed much of their early celebrity   Cunningham's Goldsmith.

––––––––––––––––––––––––––––

1768   "With Steele the unlucky notion began of setting Comedy to reform the morals instead of imitating the manners of the age. Fielding slily glances at this, when he makes Parson Adams declare 'The Conscious Lovers' to be the only play fit for a Christian to see, & as good as a sermon."   Forster's Goldsmith.

1769   "/? The well-known/ saying of G."

1770   The application of the historical meth^d to the domain of Jurisprudence: –
   Savigny & his friends pointed out that the juristic system is not a fixed phenomenon, but variable according to the circ^s of social progress. ...Applied also to political economy of course it followed ... that no one economic system c^d be regarded as applicable to every social stage.
                     Ethic's & Politics. Sir R. Blennerhassett, b^t.
                              F. R. Aug. 90.

1771   German hist. sch^l of Pol. econ^y ... has learnt from Hegel the great truth that the state is an ethical organism.   ib.

1772   (f17^v) The well-known saying of Göthe, that reading Kant was like going into a lighted room.   ib.

1773   Mr Lillys book "On Right & Wrong."   ib.

1774   Sir J. Pope Hennessy evidently thinks that there is more need for the negroes to come to civilize us than there is for our going to civilize the negroes. 'What a contrast between the smiling faces to be seen in the crowded streets of that negro town [Kambia: Africa: thriving] and the careworn faces of Cheapside.' Would that we c^d all learn the secret. ...

                     (Rev^w of Rev^ws on 19th Cent. Sept. '90.)

1775   What is the best thing with which to entertain the masses? ...
The greatest conceptions of the worlds best minds. If you take three of
your persons singly & give them Corneille & Racine they may possibly
not understand. But the people, the masses, will always understand. It
is the difference between man & mankind. The greatest effort that man
can make is to represent humanity.
                              D. N. 3.11.90. (Address of Jules Simon
                                    to Soc. for Readings & Recitations.)

1776   The question is, s^d Sainte-Beuve, not merely whether we are
pleased, but whether we ought to be pleased. ... The secret of true
success in drama seems to be in "actuality. ..." A drama should not be
(**f18ʳ**) real in the sense of exhibiting a verisimi⟨li⟩tude of insignificant
things, but it may be as real as the author knows how to make it in
regard to the essential truths of passion & feeling.
[By actuality is meant relation to real life, modernness.] To all but the
very best work, the work that is independent of time & change, this
note of modernness seems indispensable.
            Stage-Realism – True & False – D. News. leader 3.11.90.

1777   Lord Acton on Dr Dollinger the historian:
"He felt that sincere history was the royal road to religious union."
"History, he affirmed, left to itself & pursued disinterestedly, will heal
the ills it causes."
"Throughout the measureless distance which he traversed, his
movement was against his wishes, in pursuit of no purpose, in
obedience to no theory, under no attraction but historical research
alone"

                              (Quoted from the book, in Speaker.)

1778   – The Red Indian "Ghost Dance" – in wh. the dancers with
joined hands wheel monotonously round a tree all night, to a low wail –
some in white cloth, these being the ghosts.   Times 9.12.90

1779   – Sometimes (in Early Church) the still-born child was baptized in the hope that Heaven w.d antedate the ceremony.
– The theologian who said he doubted not there were infants not a span long crawling about the floor of Hell.

Lecky. [taken from Gibbon]

1780   (**f18ᵛ**) Our two brains. It w.d seem that to the left brain we must assign the chief control over speech, writing, & gesture – the methods, that is, of expressing ideas ... also ... reasoning ... & control of motions & organs of right side of body. ... Right side of brain ... emotional manifestations, including those called hysterical ... also nutrition ... also left side of bodily organs.   Proctor – Knowledge.

1781   "The Facility of Life."   Feb. 21. 1891.
   Were it ... true that man had this agony of life for a constant purview poor Nature had long since fallen in the wretched neighbourhood.
   ... Phs it is the Xtian faith that has most favoured the error ... yet Socrates had the same thought.... This profession [of life being sorrow] is, as it were, a mere habit of the outward features ... a grimace. ...
   It is not hope inspires the most of us with content; it is rather the immediate & manifest delights of living ... : While we thrust our hideous ancestry from our rarer minds, we yet derive from it our greatest blessing, for 'tis only so far as we are of common clay with the brute that we can forget & enjoy. ... For to forget & to enjoy – these are the capacities that serve us best, & these are of the brute's prerogative.
   ... The joys of living may be of no great proportions, but they are ever recurrent, small, unexpected, immediate, grateful. You w.d account them meagre & unsatisfying did you regard them as a philosopher; yet by their continuous passage they yield a sense of repletion. ... They ~~flesh~~ are incessant & multitudinous. The flesh ... will exult in them. ... (**f19ʳ**) They are in your delicate senses ... everywhere. ... Is the wind soft, it is a charm; be it chill, how brightly burns the fire; does it snow, you may admire a white world! You must snatch these delights from the hour, neither remembering evil nor forecasting. ... There ⟨is always magic in the air if you will forget.⟩
   Life is very facile to animals; it is facile also to the supreme animal.

National Observer 7.2.91.

[I have long ago ⟨(March 19.1889. see P. B.)⟩ applied some such view

as this to the <u>poor</u> ... & animal natured. But I question its truth as to
the refined]

1782   Studies in <u>pessimism</u>. Schopenhauer.   (May 13.91)
   "Unless <u>suffering</u> is the direct & immediate object of life, our
existence must entirely fail of its aim."
   Evil: not negative but positive – it makes its own existence felt. But –
if the world were a paradise of luxury & ease men w^d die of <u>ennui</u> – .
Children ... condemned not to death but to life – "He who lives to see
two or three generations is like a man who sits some time in the
conjurors booth at a fair, & witnesses the performance twice or thrice in
succession. The tricks were meant to be seen only once; & when they
are no longer a novelty & cease to deceive, their effect is gone."

   "In early ~~life~~ youth, as we contemplate our coming life, we are like
children in a theatre before the curtain is raised, sitting there in high
spirits & eagerly waiting for the play to begin."

   (**f19^v**) "Every state of welfare, every feeling of satisfaction, is
negative in its character; that is to say, it consists in freedom from pain,
which is the positive element of existence. It follows, therefore, that the
happiness of any given life is to be measured, not by its joys &
pleasures, but by the extent to which it has been free from suffering –
from positive evil. If this is the true standpoint, the lower animals
appear to enjoy a happier destiny than man."
   Thought for what is absent & future – real origin of man's cares. "In
his powers of reflection, memory & foresight, man possesses as it were a
machine for condensing & storing up his pleasures and his sorrows. But
the brute has nothing of the kind. ..."
   "It is a wonderful thing that the mere addition of thought sh^d serve
to raise such a vast structure of human happiness & misery. ..."
   "Following upon this there is one respect in which brutes show real
wisdom when compared with us – their quiet placid enjoyment of the
present moment."   20

1783   "In its explanation of the origin of the world Judaism is inferior
to any other form of religious doctrine professed by a civilized nation ...
& is the only one wh. presents no trace whatever of any belief in the
immortality of the soul."   23

1784   Man is a burlesque of what he should be.   24

1785   (**f20ʳ**) "The spirit of the New Testament is undoubtedly asceticism, however your protestants & rationalists may twist it to suit their purpose."   26

1786   "Regard this world as a penitentiary – a sort of penal colony" – for crime committed in another state of existence   27

1787   "A man finds himself, to his great astonishment, suddenly existing, after thousands & thousands of years of non-existence: he lives for a little while; & then, again, comes an equally long period when he must exist no more. The heart rebels against this, & feels that it cannot be true. The crudest intellect cannot speculate on such a subject without having a presentiment that Time is something ideal in its nature." [v. Kant]   34

1788   "Life presents itself chiefly as a task."   37

1789   Man – like <u>infusoria</u> in a drop of water under microscope –

                                                                        39

1790   <u>Tragedy</u>. "Only when intellect rises to the point where the vanity of all effort is manifest, & the will proceeds to an act of self-annulment, is the drama tragic in the true sense"   69

1791   "Everything that is really fundamental in a man, & therefore genuine, works, as such, unconsciously; in this respect like the power of Nature."   70

1792   (**f20ᵛ**) Unconscious origin ... those fundamental ideas which form the pith & marrow of all genuine work.   70

1793   An objective view – impossible without the leaven of a grain of malice. (i.e. – of a person, to criticize him)   72

1794   A man is great or small according as he leans to the one or the other of these views of life. [that it is not worth any great anxiety, or that it is momentous]   73

1795   Many a man has a degree of existence at least ten times as high as another – exists ten times as much ... the savage ... the slave ... merchant ... man of learning ... poet or philosopher. ... Between the two extremes everyone will be able to find the place at which he himself stands.   78

1796   Imagination active in prop.[n] as our senses are not excited by external objects. ... However, if the imag.[n] is to ~~receive~~ ⟨yield⟩ any real product, it must have rec.[d] a great deal of material from the external world. ... To this very food it owes its power ... at the right time.
                                                                  80

1797   Education. – The ordinary method is to imprint ideas & opinions, in the strict sense of the word prejudices on the mind of the child before (**f21**[r]) it has had any but a very few particular observations. ... Afterwards views the world through the medium of these ready made ideas.   94

1798   Afterwards children will either see things in a false light, or try in vain to remodel the world to suit their views, & so enter upon false paths.   96

1799   Our abstract ideas, wh. are merely phrases fixed in the mind: real knowledge = result of our own observ.[n] .... A man's knowledge may be said to be mature when he has corrected his abst. ideas by obs.[n] ⟨& vice versa.⟩   99

1800   On Women. Schiller's poem in honour of women Würde der Frauen, is the result of much thought. ...
   Jouy says: "Without women, the begin.[g] of our life w.[d] be helpless; the middle, devoid of pleasure; & the end, of consolation."
   Look at way in wh. she is formed – not meant to undergo great labour. She pays the debt of life not by what she does but by what she suffers [might say, not by what she thinks but by what she feels]
   Women are childish, frivolous, & short sighted – big child.[n] all their life long. ... For a few years, a wealth of beauty, charm, at the expense of all the rest of their life – man is thereby hurried to take charge of them as long as they live – a step for wh. there w.[d] not appear to be any sufficient warranty if reason only directed his thoughts.... (**f21**[v])

Woman lives more in the present than man, & if it is tolerable, enjoys it more eagerly.... Women fix their eyes upon what lies before them; we see far beyond, overlooking what is under our noses.... Do not see things in such an exaggerated form as men ... more sympathy for the unfortunate – less just.... Concrete things exercise a power over them, wh. is seldom counteracted by abstract principles of thought.

Dependent not upon strength but upon craft – tendency to say what is not true.... Dissimulation innate in woman, & almost as much a quality of the stupid as of the clever.

Natural feeling between men, indifference; between women, enmity. The reason is trade-jealousy. When they meet in the street women look at one another like Guelphs & Ghibellines.

"It is only the man whose intellect is clouded by his sexual impulses that c^d give the name of <u>the fair sex</u> to that undersized, narrow-should^d broad-hipped & short-legged race.... Neither for music, nor for poetry nor for fine art, have they really & truly any sense or susceptibility.... Incapable of taking a <u>purely objective interest</u> in anything.... It lies in woman's nature to look upon everything only as a means for conquering man.... Have never managed to produce a single achievement in the fine arts that is really great, genuine, or original.... Never got beyond a subjective point of view.

Taken as a whole, women are, & remain, thorough-going philistines, & quite incurable. Hence ... they are a constant stimulus (**f22^r**) to ignoble ambitions.... It is because of this ... that modern society, where they take the lead, is in such a bad way.

Eastern view of women ... more correct than ours. –

In our part of the world, where monogamy is the rule, to marry means to halve one's rights & double one's duties.

Monogamy bestows upon certain women an unnatural privilege by depriving others of their natural rights. Among polygamous nations every woman is provided for.

Prostitutes ... are human sacrifices offered up on the altar of monogamy.

The vanity of women ... takes an entirely material direction (?)

The influence of women in France was to blame for the gradual corruption of the Court.... Every woman placed in the unnatural position of complete independence, immediately attaches herself to some man ... because meant to obey.   105–123

———————————//———————————

1801   "Essays Speculative & Suggestive." J. A. Symonds – (May '91)
... All things are in process ... the whole universe is literally in
perpetual <u>Becoming</u>, it ... is impossible for us to believe that any one
creed or set of opinions possesses finality.   Vol I. p.7

1802   Science ... has prepared the way for the identification of Law
with God.   25

1803   (**f22ᵛ**) Finding thought to be the very essence of man considered
as a natural product, we are compelled to believe that there is thought,
implicit or explicit, in all the products which compose this universe

1804   Primitive Xty fused the Jewish conception of God as Jehovah
with the Gk. philosophical conception of God as Law; these being the
two grand monotheistic ideas then present to the world   30

1805   This highly anthropomorphic & almost polytheistic Xty ... (the
man-god Xt, his mʳ, his cortège of saints, disciples, apostles, martyrs) –
devotionally more potent than the metaphysical fabric out of wh. it had
emerged, controlled the imagination of the Middle Ages.   31

1806   The Xtian pantheon: Theolatry or God-service. Panathenaic
⟨procession, (frieze of Panthenon):⟩

1807   The mysteries of sin, pain, disease, ... are quite as well
accounted for by formulas of evolutionary strife & imperfect
development as by the old hypothesis of a devil.   34

1808   After the <u>first</u> stage in Art ... cyclopean, pregnant with
symbolism, ... & the <u>second</u> ... a combination of full thought &
spiritual intensity with technical perfection ... comes the <u>third</u> – in wh.
the shape abides, & new motives are extracted from it, impairing its
strength ... & unity   50–51

1809   (**f23ʳ**) Lastly a <u>fourth</u> stage ... formality & affectation – & the
meaning of the type comes to be forgotten.   52

1810   Impossible to revitalize a type of art which has fulfilled the
curve of its existence   75

1811   "What is a man, & what is not a man?" cried Pindar long ago
                                                                82

1812   The Principle of Evolution must be applied not only to
humanity but to everything which humanity has brought forth. ...
Abandon the old paths of caprice & predilection. ...   83

1813   Excellent rules for the critic   pp. 106,107
e.g: –
  "Since then all art expresses what the artist has perceived, thought,
& felt, concerning external nature, mankind, & himself, the critic asks:
How far in this case is perception just, accurate, penetrative, subtle, ⟨...
how far is the represent.ⁿ adequate to fact?⟩ Does the artist show himself
to be a man of normal or abnormal temperament? ... By right of what
particular quality, moral, intellectual, & sensuous, does he claim
attention? ... How is he related to the spirit of his age & nation; & what
has he contributed to the sum of culture? ...

1814   (**f23ᵛ**) Penetrating further into the spirit of the past, students
began to perceive in what respects the thinkers of the classic age
differed from themselves, & in what points humanity remained
unaltered.   111

1815   "Art", said Goethe, "is but form-giving" ... might vary this
defin.ⁿ & say "Art is a method of expression or presentation. ...." To
what does it give form – what express? ... the spiritual content. ...
Beauty is not the final end of art, but is the indispensable condition
under which the artistic manifest.ⁿ of the spiritual content must be
made. It is the business of art to create an ideal world, in which
perception, emotion, understanding, action, all elements of human life
sublimed by thought, shall reappear in concrete forms as beauty.
  ... It is not necess.ʸ that the ideas embodied in a work of art sh.ᵈ be
the artist's own. They may be common to the race & age; as, for
instance, the conception of sovereign deity expressed in the Olympian
Zeus of Pheidias ... divine maternity in Raphael's Madonna di San
Sisto. Still, the personality of the artist ... will determine his specific
type of beauty.   125–6

1816   What distinguishes art from religion or from life is, that this
subject matter ~~must~~ – though deep as religion, wide as life ...
commensurate with what man thinks & feels & does – must assume
beautiful form, & must be presented directly or indirectly to (**f24ʳ**) the
senses. Art is not the school or the cath!, but the playground, the
paradise of humanity.... Nothing abstract enters into art's domain.
Truth & goodness are transmuted into beauty there.... Whatever art
has touched acquires a concrete sensuous embodim!   127

1817   The genius of the Greeks, ... translated by their sculptors into
statues, ... expired in Rome; the cycle of their psychological
conceptions had been exhaustively presented through this medium.
During that long period of time, the most delicate gradations of human
personality, divinised, idealized, were [exhibited] in appropriate types.
Strength & swiftness, massive force & airy lightness, contemplative
repose & active energy, voluptuous softness & refined grace,
intellectual sublimity & lascivious seductiveness – the whole rhythm of
qualities wh. can be typified by bodily form – were anal^{zed} selected,
combined in various deg. to incarnate the religious concept^{ns} of Zeus,
Aphrodite, Herakles, Dionysus, Pallas, Fauns & Satyrs, Nymphs of
woods & waves, Tritons, the genius of death, heroes & hunters,
law-givers & poets, presiding deities of minor functions, man's lustful
appetites & sensual needs. All that men think, or do, or are, or wish for,
or imagine in this world, had found exact corporeal equivalents. Not
physiognomy alone, but all portions of the body ... were employed as
symbolism   134–5

1818   (**f24ᵛ**) Words – Music
    The exact value of the counter [symbol] is better understood when it
is a word than when it is a chord, because all that a word conveys has
already become a thought, while all that musical sounds convey
remains within the region of emotion which has not been
intellectualized.   140

1819   "Thought," s^d Novalis, "is only a pale, desiccated emotion."

1820   Literature. The best poetry is that which reproduces the most of
life, or its intensest moments.   145

1821   The Italian Renaissance – bred individuals of Cellini's stamp, captains like Giovanni de'Medici & the Strozzi, popes of the calibre of Julius II., scholars as world-famous as Poliziano, thinkers like Bruno & Sarpi, despots of the force of Cosimo de'Medici, saint-like souls of the purity of Carlo Borromeo & Filippo Neri, gentlemen fit to rank with Castiglione, well-tempered spirits of the kith of Contarini, freelancers of the intellect as keen as Aretino.   166

1822 Realism & Idealism. – A hackneyed antithesis, like Subject & Object, which are posed as antithetical only to be resumed as the conditions of experience. ... A work of art = on the one hand, an act of mental intuition, whereby the nature of the object is imaginatively grasped. (**f25^r**) On the other ... certain materials & processes, the technical part. ...

The result will be more ~~or less~~ idealistic or more realistic, according to the bent of the artist's sympathy with nature, acc^g to his choice of mat^{ls} & processes, & acc^g to his method of employing these. ... Prosaically accurate, ⟨like the pedlar in Peter Bell⟩* or ... pure fancy ... like the Poet in Shelley's "On a Poet's lips I slept."

1823 Art ... utilizes man's inferiority to a copying machine in graphic accuracy, while it exercises man's superiority to the machine in power of intellect! suggestion. To turn defects into forces is the privilege wh. man possesses. ... Idealism in art is the ultimate elaboration of that comparative inaccuracy /? ~~by~~ / and that imported subjective quality.
                                                                      182

1824 "Nature has the will but not the power to realize perfection" (Aristotle)   183

1825 "To disengage the elements of beauty," says Sainte-Beuve.
                                                                      185

1826 The artist may lean more to one side than the other ... may choose to concentrate his powers upon the literal imit^n of objects rather than upon the developm! of subjective qualities. Or, on the other hand,

---

* A primrose by a river's brim,
 A yellow primrose was to him,
 And it was nothing more.

he may devote his whole att.ⁿ to the refinem! of an intell! type of beauty
or to the express.ⁿ of thoughts, remaining content with slovenly
execution & feeble grasp on fact.   191

1827   (**f25ᵛ**) <u>Realism</u> – "truth to actual fact" –   189

1828   We find in the art-history of the present century a false Idealism
superseded by a false Realism. Both are false, because neither recognˢᵉˢ
the correlation of these elements. ... The idealist sought to dispense with
the necessary interrogation of nature; the realist seeks to ignore the fact
that art must aim at selection & must disengage the elements of beauty
inherent in N.   196

1829   The artist cannot avoid modifying his imitation of the chosen
object by the infusion of his own subjective quality; but he is at liberty
to reduce this subjective element to a minimum, or, on the other hand,
to regard it as his chief concern.   199

1830   The artist's mind cannot be inoperative in the processes of Art.
The imported element of subjectivity will be definite or vague,
according to the intensity of the artist's character. ... It will be genial or
repellent, tender or austere, humane or barbarous, depraving or
ennobling, chaste or licentious, sensual or spiritual, according to the
bias of his temperament.   206

1831   It follows that no two men can treat the same subject in the
same way. Each ... has his own style. ... To eliminate the mental
element from art, the element of style, the element of interpretation, is
therefore impossible.   209

1832   (**f26ʳ**) Man's mind is the most perfect of existences at present
known to us. Being the most perfect, whatsoever is presented to its
observ.ⁿ in the external world lacks something in comparison with
itself. This something it is the proper business of the mind to supply.
                                                                         215

1833   Art is bound to introduce an equivalent for what it cannot
represent.   222

1834   It is the artist's duty to perpetuate ... fugitive perfections
                                                                         223

1835   Much diff.ᶜᵉ of opinion exists as to whether artists ought to aim deliberately at expressing thoughts & emotions [to the eye]. The elder schools of criticism assumed, pps too confidently, that such ... is ... ultimate end ... of art: Younger students advance a counter theory ... to create beautiful schemes of form, col.ʳ, light, & shade, in harmony with Nature. ... [It is] the old antithesis of idealism & realism. ...

   The question is ... how far revelation or expression ... can be legitim.ˡʸ carried ... whether aim at uttering the thought of his brain ... emotion of his heart, through forms selected with deliberate intention for the purpose. ... [It is] legitimate enough in poetry or fiction.

225

1836   Incapable of rivalling reality in its own sphere, the arts assert compensatory advantages, by the adroit uses of their limitations & by the introduction of subjective elements ... the controlling (**f26ᵛ**) sense of beauty ... sympathy, reserve, delicacy, self-restraint, those preferences for refinement, those tendencies making for spiritual progress, rather than for relapse into bestial conditions.

   [In common words, he says the artist makes what he can't do be that which he doesn't want to do]   229

1837   [Sometimes] characterization borders upon caricature. In all cases it implies a willing sacrifice of superf! beauty for the sake of force & uncompromising veracity.   230

1838   Civilization only accepts art under the condition of its making for the nobler tendencies of human nature   250

1839   Poetry. If thought predominates too crudely ... product is prosaic. Must be impassioned.   255

1840   Those mighty works of art which we call languages   268

1841   'Men go abroad to gaze ... at ... mountains ... stars ... & leave themselves unheeded.' (Confessions of St Augustine.)   297

~~~~~~~~//~~~~~~~~

1842   "Virginity, mysticism, melancholy ... diseases brought in by the Christ." Th. Gautier.   (Pref. to Mlle de Maupin)

~~~~~~~~//~~~~~~~~

1843   (**f27ʳ**) J. A. Symonds – (cont.ᵈ) –
~~The more remarkable a p~~ Whatever a man utters from his heart & head
is the index of his char.ʳ. The more remarkable a person is, the more
strongly he is differentiated from the average of human beings, the
more salient will be the characteristic notes of his expression. But even
the commonest people have, each of them, a specific style. The marks of
difference become microscopical as we descend from Dante or Shakesp.
to the drudges of the clerk's desk in one of our great cities. Yet these
marks exist. ...
  Not all the actions & ⟨the⟩ utterances of an individual betray the
secret of his personality. You may live with men & women through
years, by day, by night, yet you will never know the whole about them.
No human being knows the whole about hims.ᶠ   II.3

1844   For examples of satire = Archilochus & Aristophanes. Juv.ⁱ &
Persius, Rabelais, & Regnier, Cervantes & Swift, Dryden & Pope,
Heine & V. Hugo.   28

1845   We cannot, in the present conditions of culture, affirm that any
monuments of art are absolutely authoritative. ... If the art of style c.ᵈ be
reduced to a fixed science, then certain masterpieces w.ᵈ have to be
recognized as indisputable standards, & production w.ᵈ merge in
imitation.   29

1846   (**f27ᵛ**) Democratic Art – Modern classical schools rehandled
mat.ⁱ & observed rules supplied from Greece & Rome through
scholarship. The romantic schools reverted to the lit.ᵉ & arch.ᵉ of
feudalism – Cla.ˢᵐ was aristocratic; Rom.ˢᵐ revolutionary, but it drew
its insp.ⁿ from arist.ᶜ sources. "Neither mode possessed finality, because
neither corresp.ᵈᵉᵈ to the cardinal phenomenon of the 19.ᵗʰ cent. wh. is
the advent of the people. ..."
  D. Art – an art free in its choice of style ... ch. of subject ... an art wh.
retains from the romantic reactionary movement one precious principle
– that nothing in nature or man is unpoetical, if treated by a mind wh.
feels its poetry & can interpret it.
  ... We need not accept the postulate that Dem.ᶜʸ must prove itself ... by
creating intellectual types wh. shall displace all that previously existed.
But ... will differ. ... The Gk & Roman & mediaeval ideals are
inadequate to the modern, democ.ᶜ scientific stage upon wh. humanity
has entered. ...

What sort of art does D. require?

Delivered from scholastic trad.^{ns} regarding style & ... subjects ... deliv^d from pedantry & blind reactionary fervour ... from depend^{ce} upon aristoc^c & eccles! authority – sharing the emancip^n of the intellect by mod^n science ... new political conceptions ... the whole of nature, seen for the first time with sane eyes, the whole of human^{ty} liberated from caste & class distinc^{ns} ... invite his sympathy.... (**f28^r**) He discovers that love is a ~~dignity~~ ⟨deity⟩ in the cottage no less than in king's chambers; not with the supercilious condescension of Tasso's "Aminta" or Guarini's "Pastor Fido," but with a reverent recognition of the <u>praesens deus</u> in the heart of every man & woman – In order to make Florizel & Perdita charming, it is no longer necessary that they sh^d be prince & princess in disguise....

Meanwhile we need not preach the abandonment of high time-hon^d themes.... Achilles ... lovely knights ... have lost nothing because others have gained   43

1847   Caste & high birth have no monopoly of physical loveliness.... Goethe, I think, defined good society as that wh. furnished no material for poetry.... There is a characteristic beauty in each several kind of diurnal service, wh. waits to be elucidated ... muscles of the smith ... the girl hanging linen on the line ... it is the business of D. art to unfold these beauties....

Snobbery of middle class.... The man of letters ... artist ... must emerge from earthy vapours of complacent self, & artific! circ^s, & decaying feudalism.... It is his function to find a voice ... wh. shall be on a par with nature delivered from unscientific canons of interpret^n....

                                                      47

1848   (**f28^v**) Democracy implies the absolute equality of heritage possessed by every man & woman in the good & evil of this life. It also involves the conception that there is nothing beautiful or noble which may not be discovered in the simplest human being. As regards physical structure

'Whoever you are, how superb & divine is your body....' (W. Whitman)

As regards emotion ...

'Wherever the human heart beats with terrible throes out of its ribs'
                                                                    ib.

... Here there & everywhere, the seeing eye finds majesty. ...

The same principle is applied to the whole sphere of nature. Miracles
need not be sought in special occurrences, in phenomena which startle
us. ...

'To me, every hour of the light & dark is a miracle,
Every inch of space is a miracle
Every square yard of the surface of the earth is spread with the same,
Every cubic foot of the interior swarms with the same;
Every spear of grass – the frames, limbs, organs of men & women, &
all that concerns them,
All these to me are unspeakable miracles!'   (W. Whitman)
                                                                    49

1849   He (W. W.) discrowns the heroes of myth & romance; but
greets their like again among his living comrades. What is near ... in
the men & women he consorts with, bears comparison with things far
off & rarities imagined.   50

1850   (**f29ʳ**) 'The great poems – Shakespeare included – are poisonous
to the idea of the pride & dignity of the common people. ... The models
of our literature ... have had their birth in courts, & basked & grown in
castle sunshine; All smells of princes' favours. ... As now taught,
accepted, & carried out, are not the processes of culture rapidly
creating a class of supercilious infidels, who believe in nothing.'
(W. Whitman)   62

1851   'When I mix with these interminable swarms of alert, turbulent,
good-natured, independent citizens, mechanics, clerks, young persons,
... this mass of men ... I feel, with dejection & amazement, that among
our geniuses ... few or none have yet really spoken to this people, or
created a single image-making work that could be called for them – or
absorbed the central spirit & the idiosyncrasies wh. are theirs, & wh.
thus, in highest ranges, so far remain entirely uncelebrated,
unexpressed.' (W.W.)   64

1852   In Europe as in America, the founts of earlier inspiration are failing. Classical antiquity & romance cannot supply perennial nutriment for modern art. ... A more ethereal spirituality ... begins to penetrate our conceptions of the universe, of law, of duty, of human rights & destinies. Art & literature, if they are to hold their own, must adapt themselves to these altered conditions. They must have a faith in their mission ... & their power to present the genius of the age, its religion, & its char! with the same force as the Gk sculptors presented Paganism & the Italian painters presented mediaeval Xty.   67

1853   (**f29ᵛ**) We now understand what Whitman means by "the divine average"; Why he exclaims: "Ever the most precious is the common."   68

1854   The upshot of W. Whitmans message – the people have as yet found no representative in poetry & art. The <u>sacer vates</u> of Democracy has not appeared.   70

1855   The faculty for seeing beauty in the simplest people & the commonest things has indeed been granted to all poets & all artists worthy of the name. But ... need to be exercised in a very different way, & with far other earnestness. ... Gk pastorals & Latin ... note of condescension ... avoidance of bare fact ... selection agreeable to the cultivated sense. The rustics pose, or are transfigured. Their humanity is toned down to elegance, landscape ... Arcadia. ... A suppression of the true & a suggestion of the false. ... what Democr! art demands is ... not such a distorted picture as ... <u>La Terre</u> ... neither prettify nor brutalize. ...   73

[throw light upon the beautiful–true is what he seems to mean.]

1856   <u>Landscape</u>
Contemporaneously with Dante ... there began what is known as the Revival of Learning. ... This contact with antiquity was not an unmixed blessing. It did much to emancipate ... from theological. ... But it brought back the old mythology ... when no longer believed in ... reappeared as mere ... artistic artifice. ....Fettering restrictions on (**f30ʳ**) creative fancy. ... Must imitate Virgil or Horace ... manufacture Tritons &c.   97

1857   We cannot return to the state of thought about the world, out of which the primitive myths sprang. ... But in its place the modern theory of the universe tends to establish the conviction that men & beasts & plants & inorganic subs^{ces} are parts of one mind-penetrated unity. That abrupt separation of men from their environment, wh. formed the leading principle of phil^y & religion during the last 2000 yrs, begins to disappear.   131

1858   Is poetry, &c –
   If one thing is proved with certainty by the whole history of lit^{re} down to our own time, it is that the self-preservative instinct of humanity rejects such art as does not contribute to its intellectual nutrition & moral sustenance.   153

1859   Of the two less perfect kinds of poetry, the p. of revolt & the p. of indifference, the latter has by far the slighter chance of survival. Powerful negation implies that wh. it rebels against. The energy of the rebel^s spirit is itself a kind of moral greatness. We are braced & hardened by contact with impassioned revolutionaries, with Lucretius, Voltaire, Leopardi.   154

1860   The poet ... sh^d not turn aside to comment. That is the function of the homilist. We must learn to live from him less by his precepts ~~157~~ than by his examples.   158

1861   (**f30^v**) The prime aim of all art is at bottom only presentation.
                                                                      158

1862   The poet is less a judge than a seer & reporter. If he judges, it is as light, falling upon an object, showing its inequalities, discovering its loveliness, may be said to judge.   159

1863   Mr. M. Arnold ... insisted somewhat too strenuously on the purely intellectual & moral aspects of art. There is a widely different way of regarding the same subject matter, which ... ignores the criticism of life altogether, & dwells upon sensuous presentation, emotional suggest^n & technical perfection as the central & essent! qualities of art.   181

1864   Mr. Pater says ⟨(in Fort<u>y</u> R.<u>w</u> Oct. 1887)⟩ that all the arts in common aspire 'towards the principle of music, music being the typical or ideally consummate art. ... The identification of form & matter. ...' If this means ~~183,5~~ that art, as art, aspires toward a complete absorption of the matter into the form – toward such a blending of the animative thought or emotion with the embodying vehicle that the shape produced shall be the only right & perfect manifestation of a spiritual content to the senses, so that, while we contemplate the work, we cannot conceive their separation – then in this view there is nothing either new or perilous. It was precisely this wh. constituted the consummate excellence of Gk sculpt<u>r</u>. ... But it does not seem that Mr P. means this only ... he has in (**f31ʳ**) view the more questionable notion that ... a well defined subject in poetry & painting & sculpture is a hindrance to artistic quality. Art, he says is ... 'always striving ... to get rid of its responsibilities to its subject or material. ... Lyrical poetry, just because in it you are least able to detach the [essential] matter from the form without a deduction of something from that matter itself, is artistically the highest form of poetry ... [its] perfection seems to depend *on a certain suppression or vagueness of mere subject, so that the definite meaning almost expires. ...*' Cf. my theory of naked souls, no clothes]

   This is ingenious; yet ... sh<u>d</u> have to prefer Popes "Verses by a Person of Quality" to the peroration of the "Dunciad," & a noble specimen of Japanese screenpainting to Turner's Temeraire or Raphaels School of Athens [Why?]

1865   'The range of human thoughts & emotions greatly transcends the range of such symbols as man has invented to express them; & it becomes therefore the business of Art to use these symbols in a double way. They must be used for the direct repres.<u>n</u> of thought & feeling; but they must also be combined by so subtle an imagination as to suggest much which there is no means of directly expressing. ... 'In poetry of the first order, almost every word (to use a mathem.<u>l</u> metaphor) is raised to a higher power. It continues to be an articulate sound & a logical step in the argument; but it becomes also a musical sound & a centre of emotional force.

   (**f31ᵛ**) '... The poet, therefore, must avoid two opposite dangers. If he thinks too exclusively of the music & the colouring of his verses – of the imaginative means of suggesting thought & feeling – what he writes will lack reality & sense. But if he cares only to communicate definite

thought & feeling according to the ordinary laws of eloquent speech, his verse is likely to be deficient in magical & suggestive power.'
(Quot. from Myers's 'Essays Classical.')   189

1866   Art ... communicate a mood: the Paphian (Venus):

1867   The time is not yet ripe for poetry to resume the results of science with imaginative grasp. What has been called the cosmic enthusiasm is too undefined as yet, too unmanageable, too pregnant with anxious and agitating surmise, to find free utterance in emotional literature. ...   271

1868   Yet signs are not wanting ... shorter poems of Tennyson ... in the great neglected work of Roden Noel.   "

------------------------|--------------------

1869   Mumbo Jumbo, Indra, Shiva, Jahve, Zeus, Odin, Balder, Christ, Allah – what are these but names for the Inscrutable, adapted to the modes of thought wh. gave them currency?   287

1870   The subjective element in art – appears in all reports made by credible witnesses of events – none identical – each idealized by prepossession   300

1871   (**f31a**[r]) Le roman de demain. ... Il ne sera pas naturaliste. ... Mais le naturalisme ne périra pas pour cela tout entier. Les morceaux en seront bons. ... Cette probité d'observation ... l'obligation pour le romancier de situer ses person(n)ages dans un milieu qui les explique en partie; celle de ne laisser passer de sa personne dans son oeuvre que le moins qu'il pourrai – mais encore, deux ou trois choses qu'il a ~~volue~~ voulues sans les faire, parce que les temps n'en étaient pas venus, le roman de demain les fera.
   Il étudiera de plus près dans les hommes 'ces combinaisons infinies de la puissance, de la richesse, des dignités de la force, de l'industrie, de la capacité, de la vertu, du vice, de la faiblesse, de la stupidité, de la pauvreté, de l'impuissance, de la roture et de la bassesse." (La Bruyère). ...
                                 R. deux Mondes. 1.6.91. Ferd[d] Brunetière.

1872 (**f32ʳ**) The Golden Bough. J. G. Frazer, M. A. vol. I. (July. 7.91)

This is a work on primitive superstitions & religion. As he fears, the author seems to have pushed the theory of the G. Bough too far.

In the sacred grove & sanctuary of Diana Nemorensis or Diana of the Wood near the town of Aricia (the modern La Riccia) grew a certain tree round which a strange figure prowled, drawn sword in hand. He was a priest & a murderer. A candidate for the priesthood cᵈ only succeed by slaying him, & having slain him he held office till he was himself slain.

The book treats of Priestly kings, sympathetic magic, rain making, inspiration by blood drinking (at Argos, blood of a lamb – India &c) – live human gods (in South Sea islands). also

Tree-worship. Many tribes ascribe souls to trees. Tree-spirits, May King – queen. Man – god (the Mikado):

1873 Instances of soul-absence (like the belief about Melbury Osmund &c. in Dorset) 125–8. (evidently the same superstition out of wh. I constructed the story about the "Miller's soul." in ~~Harper~~ ⟨Life's Little Ironies – ⟩).

1874 The soul in the reflection. Some of the Fijians thought that man has two souls, a light one & a dark one: dark one goes to Hades, the other is his reflection in water or in a mirror.   145

1875 Cuttings of hair & nails prevented falling into enemy's hand – (cf. Dorset, about burning a drawn tooth)   200–2

1876 (**f32ᵛ**) At the court of the King of Uganda, when the king laughs every one laughs; when he sneezes every one sneezes; when he has a cold, everyone pretends to have a cold; when he has his hair cut, so has every one.   222
also,
Human sacrifices: building=in a shadow: temporary kings (Siam):

1877 Of taboo: 169 ... The Zafimanelo in Madagascar lock their doors when they eat.... The Warua will not allow any one to see them eating & drinking   161

1878   A Book of Verses – By W.ᵐ Ernest Henley.

      "Bland as a Jesuit, sober as a hymn;
      Humorous, & yet without a touch of whim." ("House-surgⁿ")

                                     27

1879   Thin-legged, thin chested, slight unspeakably,
      Near-footed & weak fingered: in his face –
      Lean, large-boned, curved of beak, & touched with race,
      Bold-lipped, rich tinted, mutable as the sea,
      The brown eyes radiant with vivacity –
      There shines a brilliant & romantic grace,
      A spirit intense & rare, with trace on trace
      Of passion & impudence & energy –

                         41 ("Apparition")

- -

1880   (**f33ʳ**) "At the barren heart of midnight,
      When the shadow shuts & opens
      As the loud flames pulse & flutter,
      I can hear a cistern leaking"

-   ("Nocturn"–) 43

1881   What is to come we know not. But we know
      That what has been was good – was good to show,
      Better to hide, & best of all to bear.
      We are the masters of the days that were.
      We have lived, we have loved, we have suffered ... even so.

      Shall we not take the ebb who had the flow?
      Life was our friend. Now, if it be our foe –
      Dear, though it spoil & break us! – need we care
                    What is to come?

Let the great winds their worst & wildest blow,
Or the gold weather round us mellow slow;
We have fulfilled ourselves, & we can dare
And we can conquer, though we may not share
In the rich quiet of the afterglow
>What is to come.

>(175)

1882 (**f33ᵛ**) Specimen of Rudyard Kipling's style: –
"Some of the dâk-bungalows or rest houses on the Grand Trunk
Road have handy little cemeteries in their compound – witnesses to the
changes & chances of this mortal life in the days when men drove
behind horses from Calcutta to the North West. ...

Not long ago it was my business to live in dâk-bungalows. ... When I
arrived there was a fitful undecided rain on the face of the land,
accompanied by a restless wind; – every gust made a noise like the
rattling of dry bones in the stiff toddy-palms outside. The butler
completely lost his head on my arrival. He had served a Sahib once.
Did I know that Sahib? He gave me the name of a well-known man who
had been buried more than a quarter of a century, & showed me an
ancient daguerreotype of that man in his prehistoric youth. I had seen a
steel engraving of him at the head of a double volume of Memoirs a
month before, & I felt ancient beyond telling.

While he was cutting up the dead bodies of animals [i.e. cooking
dinner] I settled myself down ... second-hand palaces: a maternity case

It was just the sort of dinner & evening to make a man think of every
single one of his past sins, & of all the others that he intended to
commit if he lived. Sleep, for several hundred reasons, was not easy.
The lamp in the bathroom threw the most absurd shadows ... & the
windows beginning to talk nonsense.

>From "My own true ghost story."

1883 (**f34ʳ**) The Rediscovery of the Unique (Fortnightly R. July
1891) or the Fallacy of the Common Noun.

We only arrive at the idea of similar beings (& things) by an
unconscious or deliberate disregard of an infinity of small differences. ...
Nothing is strictly like anything else. ... When a man speaks of a
thousand years, it never crosses his mind that he is referring to a unique
series of unique gyrations on the part of the earth we inhabit.

[The proverb] embalms a misconception. ... A negligible quantity.

>– Wells.

1884   "We can only utter the message of our temperament."

A. Lang.

————————————//————————————

1885   Maurice Maeterlinck.
La Princesse Maleine (drame en 5 actes): Les Aveugles & L'Intruse
(2 other dramas). Lacomblez, Bruxelles.
A weird creepiness about all these plays – terrible murder scene in
the first-mentioned. The terror of the old King Hjalmar is well set
forth, & the timidity of the Princess. In L'Intruse, a blind grandfather,
his sons, daughters &c are sitting in antechamber to wife of one, who
has just given birth to a child. The blind man hears noises &c. It is
found the patient in next room is dead. All blind in Les Aveugles.

1886   (**f34ᵛ**) Dowden. F. Revᵂ Nov. 1891. "The Interviewer abroad."
(apropos of Enquête sur l'Evolution Littéraire. by M. Jules Huret.):
"The possibility of a 'spiritual naturalism' has been conceived by M.
Huysman" ['spiritual naturalism' nearly defines my own old idea of
the principle of novels of the future]

1887   "The themes of which future singers will treat must include all
in thought, action, & emotion wh. is susceptible of poetic handling, &
these themes will not be presented directly & four-square after the
manner of those old rhetoricians the Parnassian poets; the younger
poets will choose rather to suggest than to depict; they will not fear the
indefinite or the mysterious; if they present an object it will be in order
that the object may call up or adumbrate some spiritual, some
emotional state or mood; or they will, through some state of the soul,
shadow forth an object; they may be charged with obscurity, but all art
which demands the co-operation of the spectator's or the reader's
feelings & imagination is obscure to those who do not bring that one
thing needful. In this statement of M. Mallarmé we have a good
account of the symbolist school."

1888   (**f35ʳ**) The Pessimism of Europe. "It needs no very long stay in
Europe to detect a strange drooping of spirit. The rank corn-&-cotton
optimism of the west quickly feels the deep sadness that lurks behind
French balls, Prussian parades & Italian festivals. ...
The final blow to the old notion of the ego is given by the doctrine of

multiple individuality. Science tells of the conscious & the sub-conscious, of the higher nerve-centres & the lower, of the double cerebrum & the wayward ganglia. It hints at the many voiceless beings that live out in our body their joy & pain, & scarce give sign, dwellers in the sub-centres, with whom, it may be, often lies the initiative when the conscious centre thinks itself free. This I is, no doubt, a hierarchy or commonwealth of psychical units that at death dissolves & sinks below the threshold of consciousness. ...

"... The naïve balance of pleasure & pain is disturbed. Suffering becomes an almost supernatural fact hid in a halo of mystery, & is not to be blotted out by any quantity of joy. One single pang is enough to condemn the world as worse than nothingness. This inexplicable fact of suffering takes on a mystical meaning & becomes thereby the pivot of a new faith. And so, as the altar-lights of the old worship of sorrow grow dim, there rises the legend of a suffering unconscious."

"Turning towards Nirvana." E. A. Ross. Arena. nov. 91

Jan. 1892

1889 (**f35ᵛ**) Ideas. "The ideas which at any moment go to form our mental life are ... full of movement, & melt into each other, & are ever developing anew. A book is no sooner finished & done with than it strikes its author as inadequate. It becomes antiquated as soon as its ideas have been assimilated by the public mind, & that because the thought of the author and the public alike is alive, & ever moving onward." Principal Gore, in Lux Mundi.

1890 "The blessings of Christianity are not so obvious as they were."
Saturday Review. "The Slave Trade" 16.1.92

———————————#———————————

1891 The cry is now that we should have a firm foothold on the earth. If, in France, the cry has been for Realism, here the cry has been for Reality. In politics the increasing tendency is no longer to make leaps into the dark or the ideal, such as are involved in the extension of the franchise, but in "real" questions like those bound up with the land. "We are Socialists now" simply means that we are all interested in social questions now. The literature of essayism has shared in this reaction like everything else. Get on solid ground here, too, has been the cry. And here in this literary movement, as in others that have

distinguished the present century, we have been affected on one side by
America, and on another by France. The *mot d'ordre* of the forces that
be, or at all events have been, in what Emerson has termed "the great
sloven continent" on the other side of the Atlantic, has been Back to
Nature, Trust in Nature, Joy in Nature, above all things be not
ashamed of Nature. The true Naturalists are not the Zolas and the
Goncourts, but the Thoreaus and the Whitmans. "All the day long on the
alert," says Thoreau of modern civilisation, "at night we unwillingly
say our prayers, and commit ourselves to uncertainties." But when one
trusts to Nature and to Nature only, "I am convinced that to maintain
oneself on this earth, is not a hardship, but a pastime, if we live simply
and wisely; as the pursuits of simpler nations are still the sports of the
mere artificial." Thoreau tried to work out his life on his own theory of
Naturalism, with what success – or want of success – the world
generally now knows. Whitman has walked in the same path as
Thoreau, with more freedom, more joyousness, more swagger in his
gait; he is not, like Thoreau, one of Nature's prigs. With him open air
and free comradeship are everything. "The passionate tenacity of
hunters, woodmen, early risers, cultivators of gardens and orchards
and fields, the love of healthy women for the manly form, seafaring
persons, drivers of horses, the passion for light and the open air – all is
the old unvaried sign of the unfailing perception of beauty, and of a
residence of the poetic in outdoor people." Whitman has tried
deliberately to break down "the barriers of form between Prose and
Poetry." He has even set himself, as did Milton before him, although in
a different manner, to accomplish a still more difficult task. "No one,"
says one of his critics, "speaks of maternity with his tongue in his cheek;
and Whitman made a bold push to set the sanctity of fatherhood beside
the sanctity of motherhood, and introduce this also among the things
that can be spoken of without either a blush or a wink." A whole
Atlantic rolls between the Thoreau and the Whitman of the States and
the Zola and the Bourget and the Daudet of France – Daudet, that
Derby winner that tries to drag a manure-cart. They also claim a right
to state facts. Human baseness and depravity of the most appalling
kind surround them, and their business, they say, is to paint it. In this
matter of Naturalism or Realism, as in so many other matters, Great
Britain is the half-way house or *via media tutissima* between America and
France. There is no room here for the practice of Whitmanism; and
Zolaism is alien to the soil. Realism, as the revelation of human
wretchedness, takes the forms of philanthropy, of schemes for the

recovery of the Submerged Tenth, of Mr Frederic Harrison's passionate cry – "What do we all gain if in covering our land with factories and steam-engines we are covering it also with want and wretchedness!   From – Glasgow Herald Feb 27. 1892

1892   (**f36ʳ**) THE PAINTER–ETCHERS.
The Visions, to use the dialect of William Blake, which seems here the most appropriate, have been rather angry with Mr. Strang. He has been afflicted by strong Feminine Delusions, and before those Female Tabernacles washing themselves (No. 238) the mild Emanations of Albion cover their face. That spell-bound troupe of the artist's dreams, the man with the fixed eyes and the tall hat, the woman with the mutch, and the rest of them, are becoming more blank and puzzled at every fresh treat that is provided for them. This time they are summoned from perilous seas and Christian pews to listen to a Socialist of the Chair in Regent's Park (No. 254); and, *pejora passi*, rally with hypnotic docility. Marks of a recent starvation have not faded from their faces, nor the frost of long listening to sermons; they settle themselves as for another, and one gives himself a countenance by hastily taking a collection where no collection is. But the decent old woman with the mutch has even a harder lot. She who was trained up to abhor all carnal sounds of music save those appointed by the General Assembly to be made in churches, has to stand by while a child of this world performs on the 'cello (No. 60). It was more fitting that she should sit against that Chelsea wall (No. 270), where a famous fellow-countryman has left his hat and umbrella. Such are the accidents of the dream; without surprise you meet a Dutch family flying into Egypt (No. 219), and patriarchs selling trinkets (No. 38), skies of paper and woods of Legros. But now and then things are less mixed. The ballet of skeleton monks on stilts has no intruders to upset its fantastic logic and *macabre* sportiveness. Bones prances by Bones, and Deadhead whispers Deadhead in a natural nightmare way (No. 281).
                                        Spectator. 26.3.92

1893   From Pierre Loti's (M. Jules Viand) address on his reception into the French Academy:
"We [Feuillet & himself] were both made to be charmed by the same savage simplicities as well as by the same refinements ... a common disgust of all that is rather gross or only vulgar. ...
"I never read ... from a sort of indolence of mind, from some

inexplicable terror of written thought. But ... quite capable of passionately delighting in a book. ...

"Happy men do not write such fine books as he did. ...

"... As a child he was a little sensitive creature, vaguely suffering from everything, uneasy at the unknown of life – ... tendency to suffer from everything, even from happiness.

"This hothouse of Paris, which is capable, it is true, of bringing out in some people very acceptable half talents, or rather surprising cleverness, is rather detrimental to those who have some charming dream to translate, some mental plaint to communic!ᵉ to their brethren, or merely a sincere cry to utter.

(**f36ᵛ**) "Great ladies ... their familiar tone ... their silent heroisms ... the polished & secretly terrible passions.

"I myself have never composed a novel. I have never written but when my mind was haunted with a thing. ... There is always too much of myself in my books. ⟨He, on the contrary was personally absent from his work. He had to find the plot of a book, to place the personages ... the scene in the original void. ...⟩

"Realism & the naturalism which is the excess of it. ... The condemnation of naturalism lies in that it takes its subjects solely amongst those dregs of the people of the large towns. ... The fashionable people its authors endeavour to depict ... peasants ... artizans ... are shams. ... This is why naturalism, as now understood ... is destined to pass away when the unhealthy curiosity which backs it is worn out. The ideal, on the contrary, is everlasting. ...

"Life & charm. ... This secret can never be won; it must have been received at birth from some fairy. This secret for a writer is everything, & it is enough, moreover, to give to his works that not too long endurance which we agree to call immortality."

Quot. from Feuillet:

"Les femmes sont à l'aise dans la perfidie comme le serpent dans les broussailles. ...

"Dans cette étrange serre chaude de Paris, l'enfant est déjà une jeune fille, la jeune fille est une femme et une femme est un monstre. Elle se conduit quelquefois bien, quelquefois mal, sans grand goût pour l'un ni pour l'autre, parce qu'elle rêve quelque chose ... (**f37ʳ**) de mieux que le bien, et de pire que le mal. Cette innocente n'est souvent séparée de la débauche que par un caprice et du crime que par une occasion. ..."

"That mysterious 20ᵗʰ century will soon look at ours to see what there was of little & great in it. All our literature for which we are so much disputing will pass through that sieve of years which lets fall into the bottomless void the small things, the profusion of impersonal, commonplace, hollow, pretentious, simply clever works, & retains only those worth something."   Times   April 8. 1892

1894   <u>Carlyle</u>. – "With regard to German metaphysics & metaphy^ns he referred us to Sir Wm Hamilton ... but meanwhile there was one assurance he could give us on that subject. Kant was the prime author of the new spiritual world, & the systems of Schelling, Fichte, & Hegel were mere superficial modifications & obscurations of his. ... There was far more to be gained from Goethe Schiller & Jean Paul Richter than from all bodies of philosophy."
<u>The Carlyles, & a segment of their circle. Bookman, Oct. 91.</u>

1895   That custom wh. history attributes to some ancient peoples: when anyone was born the parents & friends of the family met to weep, & when there was a death, it was made a day of rejoicings.
Leopardi.

1896   (**f37^v**) Those deceive themselves who think that man's misfortunes are the result of his iniquities in the eyes of the Gods: on the contrary, his perversities are born of his misfortunes.   ib.

1897   Phantoms ... called Justice, Virtue, Glory, Patriotism, &c, and another named Love. ... Also Wisdom.

1898   Before there were clothes there was no love, only a spurt of desire.   ib.

1899   Having withdrawn the phantoms from the earth, save Love, the least noble of all, Jupiter sent Truth among men.   ib.

1900   Love himself, the same name as the phantom, descended from the sky ... remained in hearts for one short instant, filling them with noble passions.   ib.

~~~~~~~~//~~~~~~~~

1901   Michelet studies, as an important document, the journal of Louis XIV.'s digestion, & divides his reign into two periods – before & after the fistula. In the same way Francis I.'s reign ... before & after the abscess. – Lombroso – Insanity of Genius.   229

1902   (**f38ʳ**) <u>Domesday population of Dorset</u>.   (Sept 5.92)
<u>Censores</u>, more correctly <u>censuarii</u> = free tenants who held their
quotas of land not by military or other service, but by payment of a
fixed⌐rent⌐money⌐
<u>Coliberti</u> = half-free, free as to their persons but not as to their
tenements
<u>Villani</u> = the villeins, the highest of the classes which had no sort of
freedom: condition not servile: tilled land for his own use as well as for
that of his lord.
<u>Bordarii</u> = (boors) a sort of villeins.
<u>Cotarii</u> = (cotters) ditto.
<u>Servi</u> = serfs, mere slaves, cᵈ be sold by the landlord. <u>Ancillæ</u> = female
ditto.
From "A Key to Domesday ... a digest of the Dorset Survey."
                              By Revᵈ R. W. Eyton.

1903   <u>Man is the only</u> animal that laughs & weeps; for he is the only
animal that is struck with the difference between what things are &
what they ought to be.   Hazlitt.

1904   <u>Persepolis</u>. "The rock-platform of, which supports the
monumental structures erected by successive Achæmenid Kings. ...
This unique spot, the mutilated but still impressive remnant of 'the
most sumptuous framework of regal magnificence ever wrought by
man.'"   Times. Sept 9. 1892

1905   The <u>Bacchæ</u> of Euripides. There is nothing more fascinating for
a modern mind than to study the essential forces of Paganism. Much
that to ourselves seems merely strange & senseless may have been
august & impressive to a Gk. ... But there is something abnormal in
these riots of nakedness, those nocturnal orgies on the hill-tops. ... Some
passages appear to hint that the enthusiasm inspired by Dionysus
(**f38ᵛ**) was not entirely different from a common 'drunk &
disorderly. ...' We can recognize that the ecstacies of the cult were
inherent in a system of Nature worship; we can realize that the worship
of Dionysus & Aphrodite was but the fulfilment of the Hellenic idea of
religion, wh. must be as many-sided as Hellenic man himself; we can

see the virtue of Paganism in making a virtue of joy.,
... The Bacchæ is a play of surpassing interest. Dramatically &
artistically it is pps the poet's most finished work: instinct with a feeling
for nature, it is ever suggestive of the charm of mountain, wood, &
river, &c.

Nat. Obs.ʳ of Tyrrell's Bacchæ. (Macmillan.)
[I quite agree with the above criticism]

———————— # ————————

1906   The Meaning of Life.   F. W. H. Myers says, concerning modern
Poets, that we thrill to the old music of the word Liberty, but that
that motif can be worked afresh no more by the poet. Liberty represents
the next stage of progress after Peace & Plenty.... Before the race can
make out for itself a new practical ideal – such as Plenty & Liberty were
once to the many, & such as Science is now to the few, we must
somehow achieve a profound readjustment of our general views of the
meaning of life & of the structure of the universe.

Now ... we may say that just as Liberty represents the next stage ⟨of
human progress⟩ after Peace & Plenty, Love represents the next stage
after Liberty.   ("19ᵗʰ Cent." Jan 1893.)

1907   (**f39ʳ**) Does the law of the conservation of energy condemn
man's consciousness to extinction when the measurable energies which
build up his chemical texture pass back into the inorganic world, or
may his conscious life be a form of activity which, just because it is not
included in our cycle of mutually transformable energies, is itself in its
own proper form as imperishable as they? What does evolution mean
when we get below the.... Does it apply to the moral, or only to the
material world?   ib. id.

————————————————

1908   Revᵈ S. A. Alexander on The Decline of Pessimism –
  Byronism has almost spent itself.... Browning has become the
prophet of the rising generation.... In philosophy Schopenhauer has
given place to Hegel – the hope of cosmic suicide to the thought of a
spiritual society, the vision of that City of God to wh. the race of men is
slowly climbing nearer. Pessimism has had its day.

Contempʸ Review, Jan. '93 [comforting, but false]

1909   EMMY.
                              By Arthur Symons.

Emmy's exquisite youth and her virginal air,
   Eyes and teeth in the flash of a musical smile,
Come to me out of the past, and I see her there
   As I saw her once for a while.

Emmy's laughter rings in my ears, as bright,
   Fresh and sweet as the voice of a mountain brook,
And still I hear her telling us tales that night,
   Out of Boccaccio's book.

There in the midst of the villainous dancing-hall,
   Leaning across the table, over the beer,
While the music maddened the whirling skirts of
b/   the hall,
   As the midnight hour drew near;

There with the women, haggard, painted and old,
   One fresh bud in a garland withered and stale,
She, with her innocent voice and her clear eyes, told
   Tale after shameless tale.

And ever the witching smile, to her face beguiled,
   Paused and broadened, and broke in a ripple of fun,
And the soul of a child looked out of the eyes of a child,
   Or ever the tale was done.

O my child, who wronged you first, and began
   First the dance of death that you dance so well?
Soul for soul: and I think the soul of a man
   Shall answer for yours in hell.

              (From "Silhouettes" (Matthews and Lane.)

1910   (**f39ᵛ**) <u>Peer Gynt</u>. by Henrik Ibsen. Transl. by W. & C. Archer.
(May 1893)
<u>Peer</u>. "Dearly one pays for one's birth with one's life."   273

1911 <u>Peer</u> (to the Lean one) My demands [on life] are in no way
excessive
I shouldn't insist on a salary
but treatment as friendly as things will permit ...
                                    ... and chiefly
the power of departing in safety & peace.   267

1912 <u>Peer.</u>   One is born only once,
      and one's self, as created, one fain would stick to.   250

————————————— // —————————————

1913 "<u>The Heavenly Twins</u>"   (May. 1893)
  "'We are long past the time when there was only one incident of
interest in a woman's life, & that was its love affair. ... It is stupid to
narrow it [life] down to the indulgence of one particular set of emotions
... to swamp every faculty by ~~the~~ constant cultivation of the animal
instincts'"   I. 119.

1914   (June 30. 1893)
      (**f39a^r**) (From the <u>Spanish</u> of G. <u>Becquer</u>.)

We were together, – her eyes were wet,
But her pride was strong, & no tears would fall;
And <u>I</u> would not tell her I loved her yet,
And yearned to forgive her all!

So, now that our lives are for ever apart,
<u>She</u> thinks – "Oh! had I but wept that day!"
And <u>I</u> ask in vain of my lonely heart –
"Ah! why did I turn away?"

                                        F. H.

————————————— —————————————

1915   An Autumn Lyric
                           ⌠after Drèves.

    (**f39b^r**) High o'er the forest the storm-clouds are flying,
The little birds haste to the south & the sun,
Darling, – the red leaves are dropping & dying –
Darling – how soon is life over & done!

Hardly the hawthorn-tree blossoms & blushes,
Hardly has opened the first rose of May, –
Scarce o'er the heart Love tumultuous rushes.
E'er the rose-petals fall, & all passes away!

The love & the weeping; – the rapture & sorrow,
Are they but dreams that come never again?
What will be left when the day knows no morrow?
Darling, we sigh, but we question in vain.

Though the perfumes be shed, & the rose-leaves be blighted,
(**f39c^r**) The new year must come, & the new roses blow,
And lovers will kiss, & their vows shall be plighted
On the green of our graves, while we slumber below.

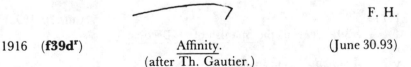

                                                      F. H.

1916   (**f39d^r**)   Affinity.   (June 30.93)
                           (after Th. Gautier.)

In an old-world temple two blocks of stone,
Where the sky of Athens burns hotly blue,
Have been standing stately, & still, & lone
Dreaming together the ages through.

There were two pearls hid in the self-same shell,
(Like sweet sea-tears that for Venus weep,)
They have whispered secrets that none may tell,
Side by side in the heart of the deep.

When Boabdil ruled in the land of Spain,
Two roses grew in a garden rare,

They drank of the fountain's silver rain,
And mingled their scents in the drowsy air.

In Venice, to rest on a golden dome,
Two doves came floating on pinions white,
(**f39d^v**) And they loved eachother, & made their home
Under the stars on a still May night.

But the changeless laws that our lives involve
Are the laws of death, & cold decay,
So the temple falls, & the pearls dissolve, –
The birds & the roses must pass away.

Yet each, by a strange metamorphosis
Is born anew in some fairer form;
And the rose may live in red lips that kiss, –
The marble in limbs that are white & warm!

And in hearts of lovers once more may greet
Those doves who dwelt on the dome of gold, –
And in mouths of velvet those pearls may meet
To gleam more white than those pearls of old.

For how otherwise grew the wondrous birth
Of the strange & sweet affinity,
(**f39e^r**) That warns two souls in this desert of earth,
They must claim eachother, where'er they be?

They recall, in a new-found exstasy,
The dreams of their mystic Long-ago,
By the marble temple, or stormy sea,
Or Moorish garden where roses blow.

And they feel the flutter of snowy wings
On the golden dome of a stately fane; –
And the faithful atoms the wild wind brings
Must find eachother, and love again!

So my heart, that within me burns & glows,
Would read <u>your</u> heart, – ask you whether

You were pearl, or marble, or dove, or rose
In that fairer world, when we were together?

                                                          F. H.

1917   (**f40ʳ**) "Oh dearest, while we lived and died   (Aug. 5.1893)
                A living death in every day,
            Some hours we still were side by side
                When where I was you too might stay
                And rest and need not go away.
            O nearest, furthest! can there be
                At length some hard-earned heart-won home
            Where – exile changed to sanctuary –
                Our lot may fill indeed its sum,
                And you may wait, and I may come?"

                                          D. G. Rossetti.

───────────//───────────

1918   Keynotes – by George Egerton.   Jan 3. 1894
   She laughs softly to herself because of the denseness of man; his
chivalrous conservative devotion to the female idea he has created
binds him, perhaps happily, to the problems of her complex nature.
                                                          21

1919   The key to woman's seeming contradictions. ... The why a
refined, physically fragile woman will mate with a brute, a mere male
animal with primitive passions – and love him ... [is] the untamed
primitive savage temperament that lurks in the mildest, best woman ...
each woman in God's wide world will deny it – for the woman (**f40ᵛ**)
who tells the truth & is not a liar about these things is untrue to her sex
& abhorrent to man, for he has fashioned a model on imaginary lines,
& he has said, 'so I would have you,' and every woman is an
unconscious liar, for so man loves her. And when a Strindberg or a
Nietzsche arises & peers into the recesses of her nature and dissects her
ruthlessly, the men shriek out louder than the women, because the
truth is at all times unpalatable, and the gods they have set up are dear
to them.   23

1920   It seems as if all the religions, all the advancement, all the culture of the past, has ⟨only⟩ been a forging of chains to cripple posterity, a laborious building up of moral & legal prisons based on false conceptions of sin & shame. ... Men manufactured an artificial morality, made sins of things that were as clean in themselves as the pairing of /?as/ birds on the wing; crushed nature, robbed it of its beauty & meaning, & established a system that means war, and always war, because it is a struggle between instinctive truths and cultivated lies.   41

1921   The untrue feminine is of man's making, whilst the strong, the natural, the true womanly is of God's making.   42

1922   There has been a·mighty storm, it has been raging for two days. (**f41ʳ**) A storm in which the demon of drink has reigned like a sinister god in the big white house, & the frightened women have cowered away, driven before the hot blast of the breath upon which curses danced, & the blaze of ire in the lurid eyes of the master.   124

1923   <u>Treachery of Women</u>. In <u>Woman,</u> Jan 3. 94 Lady Constance Lytton says women have no code of honour. Spectator, Jan 13. contests the point. She says that "a woman who breaks with a man after an intimate friendship will not hesitate to betray the confidence reposed in ~~him~~ her during that intimacy." The Spectr says, once convinced that the secret she is keeping ought to be kept, & she is silent as the grave.
                                                                      Spectr   Jan 13. '94.

1924   Truth ... never comes into the world but, like a bastard, to the ignominy of him that brought her forth; till Time, the midwife rather than the mother of Truth, have ... declared her legitimate.
                                                J. Milton, "Divorce." Introduction.

1925   Do you remember what Stevenson says of 'Style'; that conversation is an attempt – mostly ineffective – to express, to picture our inner selves? Well, what the ordinary person cannot do, that the dramatist does for him; he is falsely true in expressing his chars out of their own mouths.   Zangwill   Pall Mall M.

1926   (**f41ᵛ**) Life of Shelley.

Pieces of verse "possessing a character & distinction of their own."

1927   With admirable temper & the grace of perfect manner Sh.
replied (to a scolding letter of Godwin's)

1928   "The fire – & – faggot system of suppressing heresy."

1929   Gk. & Roman Poets, '"… Perpetuation of the noxious race of
heroes." (Godwin.) Lucretius forms pps the single exception. Through!
the whole of ancient lit., honour & fame, or pub. opinion, are set above
virtue.'   329

1930   'Facts are not what we want to know in poetry, in history, in the
lives of individual men, in satire, or panegyric. They are the mere
divisions, the arbitrary points on wh. we hang, & to wh. we refer those
delicate & evanescent hues of mind wh. language delights & instructs
us in precise proportion as it expresses.'   (Shelley.)

1931   "That record of crimes & miseries – history."   (Shelley.)

1932   (**f42ʳ**) "We are afraid to put men to live & trade each on his own
private stock of reason, because we suspect that this stock in each man
is small, & that the individuals wᵈ do better to avail themselves of the
general bank & capital of nations & of ages. Many of our men of
speculation, instead of exploding general prejudices, employ their
sagacity to discover the latent wisdom wh. prevails in them. If they find
what they seek – & they seldom fail, – they think it more wise to
continue the prejudice with the reason involved, than to cast away the
coat of prejudice, & to leave nothing but the naked reason; because
prejudice, with its reason, has a motive to give action to that reason, &
an affection which will give it permanance. … Prejudice renders a man's
virtue his habit, & not a series of unconnected acts."
                                    Burke, Reflections on the F. R.

1933   Psychology of the Emotions. Th. Ribot.

... M. Ribots theory of the order in which "decay of the affective life" takes place ... probably the reverse of its ascending order of development. "As the decay of the feelings progresses from the higher to the lower, from complex adaptation to simple adaptation, gradually narrowing the area of the affective life, we may, (**f42ᵛ**) in this decadence, distinguish four phases, marked by the successive disappearance of (1) the disinterested emotions, (2) the altruistic emotions, (3) the ego-altruistic emotions, (4) the purely egoistic emotions." To the first group belong "the æsthetic & scientific cravings"; to the second "the social & moral emotions"; to the third, Love, & "the religious sentiment in its medium forms"; to the last group, emotions such as anger & fear, & "the nutritive cravings." These last, which are most directly associated with self-conservation in its primitive form, as they are the earliest to appear, are the latest to disappear. The general order of decay, however, is interfered with in cases such as those where devotion to some science or art has become the dominant tendency. Thus, "the æsthetic sentiment, one of the most delicate & latest in formation, is of very late extinction in an artist."

1934   In the present instance, "The Tinker" affords curious and valuable evidence as to where Wordsworth drew that line. Still more interesting is a cancelled passage of prose which was to have appeared in the appendix to the edition of 1802: – [of Wordsworth]

The reader, I hope, will believe that it is with great reluctance I have presumed, in this note, to censure so freely the writings of other poets, and that I should not have done this could I otherwise have made my meaning intelligible. The passages which I have condemned, I have condemned upon principle, and I have given my reasons, else I should have been inexcusable. Without an appeal to laws and principles there can be no criticism. What passes under that name is, for the most part, little more than a string of random and extempore judgments, a mode of writing more cheap than any other, and utterly worthless. When I contrast these summary decisions with the pains and anxiety of original composition, especially in verse, I am frequently reminded of a passage of Drayton on this subject, which no doubt he wrote with deep feeling: –

Detracting what laboriously we do
Only by that which he but idly saith.

Artists of every order will read these words with a thrill of sympathy; and yet – there is something to be said from the critic's point of view, as well.

1935   (**f43^r**) Life of Tennyson.

If, wrote Venables, an artist could only now find out where these objects ... of high imagination & intense popular feeling, similar to those of the Catholic painters ... are, he w^d be <u>the</u> artist of modern times. ... They were to be sought in the convergent tendencies of many opinions, on religion, art, & nature.   I. 123.

1936   Mablethorpe.

> Here often when a child I lay reclined
>   I took delight in this fair strand and free;
> Here stood the infant Ilion of the mind,
>   And here the Grecian ships all seemed to be.
> And here again I come, & only find
>   The drain-cut level of the marshy lea,
> Gray sand-banks, & pale sunsets, dreary wind,
>   Dim shores, dense rains, & heavy-clouded sea.

     161

1937   Annihilate within yourself these two dreams of Space & Time.

     171

1938   My father's poems were generally based on some single phrase like "Someone had blundered" –   268

1939   As if we c^d destroy facts by refusing to see them.   278

1940   (**f43^v**) The constant reading of the new poems aloud was the surest way of helping him to find out any defects.   378

1941   He looked forward to 'a warless world, a single race, a single tongue.'   401

1942   "In this world there are few voices & many echoes."

     II.11.

1943   Tennyson goes to Waterloo ... stayed at the Hôtel du Musée ... impressed with the wailing of the wind at night, as if the dead were lamenting ... all around us ... the graves of so many thousand men. Stayed there a week.   24

1944   Thence to Luxembourg, & Trèves ... Mülheim ... down the Moselle ... to Coblentz ... Eisenach ... Weimar ... Leipzig ... Dresden ... Brunswick ... Aix-la-Chapelle.   27

1945   "The muse may give thee, but the gods must guide."

quot. by Locker.   80

1946   The "grand style" of poetic diction ... he considered that of Milton even finer than that of Virgil "the lord of language."   284

1947   Verse should be "<u>beau comme la prose</u>" [i.e. apart from the rhyme & the rhythm, the sentences sh^d be elegant & balanced]

1948   (**f44^r**) Browning, he said, never greatly cares about the glory of words or beauty of form. ... As for his obscurity in his great imaginative analyses, I believe it is a mistake to explain poetry too much, people have really a pleasure in discovering their own interpretations.

285

1949   Browning is ... quite incapable of correcting his literary faults, which at first sprang from carelessness & an uncritical habit. ... His thought & feeling & knowledge are generally out of all proportion to his powers of expression.   (Letter from Jowett.) 344

1950   "I can understand the Persian dualism; there is much [in life] which looks like the conflict of the powers of light & darkness."

(Tennyson.) 373

1951   "Dryden's paraphrase of Virgil is stronger than any of the translations."   (Ten.) 385

1952   'He said that his poems sprang often from "a nucleus": some one word, maybe, which had floated into the brain'

F. T. Palgrave. 496

1953   "I hate inversions, but this line is strong in its inversion:

'And over them triumphant Death his dart
Shook. ...' (Milton)"

                                                    (T.) 523

1954   (**f44ᵛ**) "The powerful union of pathos & humour in Marvell's
'Lines to his coy mistress" (F. T. Palgrave)

'Had we but world enough, & time,
This coyness, lady, were no crime. ...
                          ... I would
Love you ten years before the Flood,
And you should, if you please, refuse
Till the conversion of the Jews. ...
   But at my back I always hear
Time's winged chariot hurrying near;
And yonder all before us lie
Deserts of vast Eternity.'

                                                    501

1955   <u>Poetry</u> ... must be Emotional, concrete, artistic. ...
   Before the poet begins to write he shᵈ ask himself which of these
artistic methods is natural to him ... the weighty ⟨(1)⟩ <u>iambic</u>
movement, whose primary function is to state, or those <u>lighter</u>
movements which we still call for want of more convenient words ⟨(2)⟩
anapæstic & dactylic – whose primary function is to suggest. ...
   [Whenever Wordswᵗʰ or Keats pass from (1) to (2) they ... doggerel.
Reason: <u>conciseness</u> is the virtue of all <u>statemᵗ</u>] (**f45ʳ**) The moment the
Eng. poet tries to "pack" his anapæstic or dactylic line as he can pack
his iambic line, his versification becomes harsh & pebbly. Nor is this
all – anap. & dac. verse must in Eng. be obtrusively (?) alliterative, or
the same pebbly effect begins to be felt.
   The anapᶜ line is so full of syll. that in a langᵍᵉ where the consonants
dominate the vowels (as in Eng.) these syll. grate agˢᵗ e. o. unless their
corners are artfully bevelled by one of the only two smoothing processes
at the command of an Eng. versifier – obtrusive alliterⁿ or an obtrusive

use of liquids. Now these demands of form may be turned to good account if his appeal to the listener's soul is primarily that of suggestion by sound & symbol. But if his appeal is that of direct & logical statement the diffuseness inseparable from good anapæstic verse is a source of weakness.   T. W. in Enc. Brit.

———————————//———————————

1956 Animism "Mr Im Thurn ... speaking of the natives of Guiana: 'Every object, animate & inanimate, seems to the Indian exactly of the same nature, & is a being consisting of a body & spirit'"
(Review by "C." of Grant Allen's
'Evolution of the Idea of God.' D. C.)

1957 Origin of Religions. Two theories: 1, Ancestor worship; 2, Animism.   ib.

1958 Egyptian Religion – Sun-worship; Ancestor worship, &c
ib.

1959 (**f45ᵛ**) Les sept filles d'Orlamonde,
      Quand la fée est morte,
    Les sept filles d'Orlamonde,
      Ont cherché les portes.

    Ont allumé leurs sept lampes
      Ont ouvert les tours
    Ont ouvert quatre cent salles
      Sans trouver le jour.

(Quoted in Speaker. 27.11.97)

1960 ... Had the devotion spent on another world been given to this, we might lament less over our "vale of tears," which, with all its drawbacks, is improvable.

          Is it so small a thing
            To have enjoy'd the sun,
          To have loved light in the spring,
            To have loved, to have thought, to have done;

To have advanc'd true friends, and beat down baffling foes;
That we must feign a bliss
Of doubtful future date,
And, while in dream on this,
Lose all our present state,
And relegate to worlds yet distant our repose?

Tract by J. M. Wheeler.

1961 Literature (Dec 18. 97) reviewing Worsfold's "Principles of Criticism" says the author constantly presents Aristotle as a critic of form as opposed to the criticism wh. he thinks to be triumphant & justly triumphant at the present day – the criticism of thought. This is surely a blunder. Aristotle almost sneers at "style." He insists on the "worthiness" of the subject, on the necessity of its thorough conception (**f46ʳ**) & realization by the poet.

The reviewer goes on to ask how Mr W. faces such an all important contrast as that between the critical doctrine & the practical performance of two such men as Dante & Wordsworth. ... Wordsworth, flouting poetic diction, protesting that for his part he does not consider metre necessary for poetry at all, & dismissing "the power of producing the harmony of numbers" as "invariably attendant" upon the ethical & intellectual faculties which he thinks necessary for the poet, yet in practice always falsifies his theories in his best passages, & hardly ever writes a good passage in carrying them out.

1962 "Realism." Was Daudet a realist? M. Lemaître holds that he was more rᶜ than M. Zola, who takes the same view. La Vérité moyenne was Daudet's aim, while Zola & the others are of the lyrical kind, more or less disguised. So says the author of the Rougon-Macquart history, conscious that, despite his achievements in naturalism, he is one of the romantics.   Speaker.

1963 "Art begins where observation ends."

National Observer.

1964 (**f46ᵛ**) <u>Sculpture</u>. "The ideality of the art of Sculpture – each object presenting beauty or passion in an immortal abstraction from all that is temporary & accidental – appealed in a peculiar degree to Shelley's imagination." Dowden's Shelley. II. 283.

1965 <u>Poetical necessities</u>: –
1. A message. 2 Exaltation 3. Sincerity.
All poetry is the outcome of
1. Absolute vision. (dramatic). 2 Relative vision (lyric).
(condensed from Enc. Brit.)

1966 "Language is everywhere half sign; its hieroglyphics, the dumb modes of expression, surpass the speech. All action, indeed, is besides being action, language; if you do a thing for another, that is language; if you do not do it, that is language. ... Fragments at the very pick of expression – that reality which just comes to the surface for a moment. ... The proverb is true which says, that half is more than the whole; fragments mean most." <u>Mozley's Sermons. "Nature."</u>

1967 (**f47ʳ**) <u>Symbolism</u> – the association of material images with moral. ... A consensus & uniformity in the interpretation of physical things, i.e., the mode in which our feelings are affected by them ... thunder, the impress of awe, &c. ib.

1968 <u>The Family & Socialism</u>.
"'If I had the power," said the Italian Socialist Rossi, "to banish the greatest afflictions of this world, plagues, wars, famines, &c., I would renounce it, if instead I could suppress the family. ...'" Family life, as Mr Mallock does well to point out, presents a fatal difficulty to practical socialism.' <u>Literature</u> 2.4.98.

1969 "Gibbon, Grote, Mommsen, & in a less degree Macaulay, wrote history much as they thought, & with an eye to colour. Thirwall, Stubbs, Creighton, bishops all, are keen for facts, & chary of imagination. Gibbon & Macᵞ are the greatest artists of this goodly

company. They are of the same school. ... A greater genius still, akin to
them for colour & style, was Tacitus."   D. Chronicle.

————————————— // —————————————

1970   "That only is great in art which comes from the depths of a pure
& true soul."   Quot. by D[r] W. R. Nicoll.

1971   (**f47ᵛ**) Cnut's song on the monks of Ely. There are indications in
the late text handed down to us that the dialect in wh. these verses were
written was the Mercian dialect from wh. the English of to-day is, for
the most part, derived, & not the West-Saxon dialect – the language of
King Alfred.   8.10.98. Literature. A. L. Mayhew.

1972   Verse. "In works of imagination there is only one secret of
vitality, & that is power. ...
   We are ready to accept a great deal that we sh[d] not accept if it were
500 yrs. old (?); for the poetic interpretation of its own thoughts is a
need of every age in turn. ... There are poets who bring just the message
that their own day asks for – that & no more. There are others who
possess the secret of speaking to all nations through their own – to all
ages through the present. ...   Literature. 8.10.98.

1973   The Dissecting-room: –

   "Through the dim window of the narrow gable,
   The moonlight decks, in ivory & sable,
   The silent tenant of each leaden table.

   Not here the gold-piped organ ebbing slowly
   To chant of priests with censers swinging lowly,
   Nor waxen tapers burning tall & holy."

                                    – Nightshade & Poppies.
                              Dugald Moore (Long. 3/6)

1974   (**f48ʳ**) Where the poet is bound by history he can hardly have a
real plot with a real dramatic unity. ... The dramatist instead of one
central action is often obliged to content himself with a panorama of
shifting scenes. ... No one who has read a Greek play side by side with
one even of Shakespeare's ... will deny ... Attic tragedian ... immense

advantage. Literature 8.10.98
[an instance of the <u>non sequitur</u>; but suggestive.]

———————————#———————————

1975 <u>Verse</u> which sustains the Siege of Time: –
... Primitive force ...
... Large outlook on life. "see life steadily & see it whole"
... Swinburne, if he live ... mastery of words, rather than any
interpretation of life. ...
"... Browning was rather a spy on life than a spectator or critic"
<u>Spectator</u>. 29.10.98.

1976 <u>Art</u> – "An artist must be able to persuade himself either that he
is carrying to completion something begun by his forerunner, or that it
is his to denounce the fraud of his predecessors, & to discover afresh the
secret of art. He may find it in another country, in a past century, or in
his own head." SR. on Turner ("D. S. M.")

1977 (**f48ᵛ**) <u>A Gospel of Cowardice</u>. – "Browning's ... morbidly
healthy, all-inquiring intellect that never quite grasped the idea of
intelligence. – 'I was ever a fighter. ...' The apathy of strength, [is]
Unintelligence. To be strong to the end it is necessary to shut up many
windows, to be deaf on either side of the head at will, to fetter the
mind. ... To know, to understand, & therefore to sympathize with, & a͟l͟
love, all men even the worst, & yet to have to rule them, to have to
punish them – the greatest men die of that.

"You cannot be
Both strong & free."

"J. S. – It is a Gospel of Cowardice."
John Davidson. D. C. 14.11.98

1978 <u>Ruskin</u>. – A mind that has always refused to take anything at
second hand. The most imposing phrase & acceptable commonplace
never escaped the scrutiny of his insight. ... All the accepted rules &
reputations [in Art] went by the board. ... "All art" he said, "which
involves no reference to man, is inferior or nugatory"
D. Chron. Feb 8. 99

———————————#———————————

1979   "Accustom yourself to regard this world as a penitentiary or ἐργαστήριον ...."

1980   (**f49ʳ**) Observers of character know that the cliché of custom lies so strongly on individuals that it is only in one action out of twenty that the average man expresses his own idiosyncrasy in a recognizable form. ...
... The number of cleverish novelists who falsify or neglect real happenings, to chime with a gross optimism.   C. in Bookman.

1981   Ostrovsky's "The Storm." (trans. from Russian.)
'The keynote of Russian invention has been the Triumph of Sorrow, Man & God are banded together to fight against an overmastering ἀνάγκη. Sometimes it is the power of Winter, of famine, of government; in Ostᵧ it is the inevitable evil of human relations. "The Storm" ıs a picture of fate as embodied in the reactions of character. Katerina is a study in "original virtue" brought to nought by education & environment. It is not tragedy as we know it in the traditions of the Classical School; it is the Sadness of life itself, reduced to dramatic dimensions. ... It is the triumph of useless "social needs" over "the strength of youth."'   Lit. 21.1.99.

1982   (**f49ᵛ**) "To bring the invisible full into play
Let the visible go to the dogs – what matters?"

1983   Law in Poetry – Professor Courthope lectures to the effect that all fine poems combine the Individual, or peculiar, with the Universal, or common: "In all these [great verses] the total effect produced was simple, natural, universal: & yet the individual character was strongly marked. ... Such a reconciliation of opposing qualities was the universal condition of all fine art."

1984   The newspaper press, that huge engine for keeping discussion on a low level, and making the political test final. To take off the taxes on knowledge was to place a heavy tax on broad and independent opinion.   John Morley

1985   Pleasure saps high interests, and the weakening of high interests leaves more undisputed room for pleasure.   John Morley

1986   Pyrrho's teaching may be summed up in the three following statements: (1) We can know nothing about the nature of things. (2) Hence the right attitude towards them is to withhold judgment. (3) The necessary result of suspending judgment is imperturbability –

Zeller. 'Stoics' &c.

1987   (**f50ʳ**) WHAT – if any – are the relations of art to morality? is a question which, as the French say, has "defrayed the expenses" of innumerable discussions from the dialogues of Plato to the latest tract of Tolstoy. It is a familiar commonplace of our academic lecture-rooms, "University Extension" platforms, the studios; even Bayswater (if we may use that expression without prejudice and in a Pickwickian sense) has been known to toy with it at afternoon tea. Our Puritan forefathers, of course, settled the question very summarily. For them, all art was immoral. The opinion was a little excessive – but not more excessive, perhaps, than the contrary opinion which we have seen come into fashion in our own day – the opinion that art is outside morality, not to say above it. This is the "advanced," the "emancipated" view; not to share it is to convict oneself of Philistinism, fogeyism, the "vestry mind." Undismayed, however, by these epithets, there are a few fastidious spirits who reject this view as too "cheap." They are aware of all that has been urged by the æsthetic philosophers of the century in favor of some mysterious transformative agency of art; how it "transfigures" and "purifies" whatsoever it touches. Art is essentially "disinterested," therefore necessarily moral. Art "liberates the spirit," said Hegel; art purges us of the will-to-live said Schopenhauer, in a theory which has come direct from that old Aristotelian one of the "Katharsis" – though "diablement changé en route." Signs are not wanting, however, of a reaction against this somewhat absolute doctrine. Only the other day, in a trenchant article on Maupassant, to which we drew attention in these columns, Tolstoy "went for" the fashionable theory "baldheaded." But Tolstoy is accounted a crank – a crank of genius, if you like – but still a crank; and most of us, perhaps, will be willing to give more heed to M. Ferdinand Brunetière, if only because he "keeps his hair on." In a lecture, republished as a pamphlet (Paris: Hetzel), on "L'Art et la Morale," M. Brunetière boldly carries the war into the artists' camp. He makes it his business to show that there is a secret germ of immorality in all art. In all art, be it noted. To take the lower forms of art – an Empire ballet, a Palais Royal farce, or some specimen of "Le Nu au Salon" – would be making the game too easy. No, it is of art in general, high art, Art with a big A, that the statement is advanced.

And it is based upon three considerations. The first of these is the tendency of art to separate manner from matter. That treatment is everything and subject nothing, we hear from artists on all hands. This exaggerated importance of form – or, as a recent Italian critic, Francesco de Sanctis, has called it, *l'indifferenza del contenuto*, indifference to content – has brought us to dilettantism and the art of the Decadents. Dilettantism – despite its seductive air of "sweet reasonableness," of freedom from prejudice – is in another aspect only an incapacity for taking sides, an enfeeblement of the will. Decadentism makes the beauty (or ugliness) of things the measure of their absolute value. The essential immorality of these frames of mind needs no demonstration. If you want to see what they lead to, you have but to look at the French art of the closing eighteenth century, the novels of Duclos and the younger Crébillon, the sculpture of Clodion, the paintings of Boucher and Fragonard. We have had more recent illustrations nearer home – which it would be cruel to mention. The second danger for art on the moral side, according to M. Brunetière, consists in the too faithful imitation of nature. Whatever we may say of nature, we cannot say that it is moral. It is often hideous, often cruel, often "red in tooth and claw." Representation of the ugliness and ferocity of life was an essential part of the romantic creed; the naturalism which superseded that creed "went one better" – or worse. Nature worship lands art in a gross animalism. And even if it stops short of that, we are to remember that facts do not become moral merely because they are faithfully transcribed. Here M. Brunetière draws a suggestive parallel between two great artists who, unlike in everything else, are alike in having forsworn their art on this ground – Racine and Tolstoy. "When the great dramatist abandoned the stage, what feelings do you suppose dictated his conduct? He took fright at himself, fright at the truth of the pictures he had drawn; at the terrible fidelity with which he had rendered the nature of passion; at the justification he had found for its excess in its conformity to instinct; and that is why, from that moment, his life was one long expiation for the errors of his genius. And remember that this very example has been followed by the man who was at one moment the illustrious author of 'War and Peace' and of 'Anna Karenina.'" Mention of Tolstoy comes pat to the occasion, for he has lately been insisting upon the tendency which M.

Brunetière reckons as the third immoral factor in art. This is the tendency towards isolation, towards an aristocratic distinction between the "artist" and the "crowd." Nietzsche formulates the creed of the "Over-man," and before Nietzsche, Flaubert writes to George Sand to assert his belief that "the crowd, the herd, will always be hateful." And so Flaubert poured out his hatred for the crowd in his caricatures of Bouvard and Pécuchet. Such a creed cuts off art from its communications with life, it is anti-social, inhuman – and therefore immoral.

What is M. Brunetière's conclusion? That the artist should take to sermonising? By no means. His conclusion is that art cannot usurp the liberty to absolve itself from its obligations as a social function; its true morality lies in the conscientiousness with which it acquits itself of this function. No more than any other social force can it claim to regulate itself. The test of a well-ordered society is the equilibrium of its forces. No single one of them should be dominant; not a religious organisation – see the history of the mediæval Papacy; nor tradition – look at China to-day; nor art – remember the fate of Renaissance Italy and of Decadent Greece. If we knew the conditions of this equilibrium, we should have solved the social problem. That, unfortunately, is still a hard nut to crack. But, at any rate, we can keep our eye on art, remind it of its moral obligations, and request it, in the language of Dick Swiveller to the Marchioness, "to moderate its transports."

D. Chronicle, May 16, 1898

1988   (**f50ᵛ**) "The extent to which the domestic affairs of the great affect the policies of nations." [e.g. Louis XIV was suffering from raging toothache at the time of the revocation of the edict of Nantes] –
(advt of "The Secret Cabinet of History."
Paris. Carrington.)

1989   Nietzsche's Genealogy of Morals. "Mr Crawfurd considers that N.'s sounder doctrines were put forth during his early life, & that his later utterances were tainted with insanity."   (Newspaper)

[The latter words are true enough.]

————————————//————————————

1990   Kipling. L'Envoi to Soldiers Three:–

> Lo, I have wrought in common clay
> Rude figures of a rough-hewn race.
> . . . .
>
> . . . I wrought them for Thy sake
> And breathed in them mine agonies.
> Small mirth was in the making. Now
> 'I lift the cloth that clothes the clay,
>   And, wearied, at thy feet I lay
> My wares, ere I go forth to sell.
> The long bazaar will praise – but Thou –
> Heart of my heart, have I done well?

1991   (**f51ʳ**) <u>Letters of Browning & Mrs B</u>.

" 'O God, if there be a God, save my soul if I have a soul.' "

(King's memoirs)

1992   "It is a principle with me to begin by welcoming any strangeness [in poetry], intention of originality in men, the other way of safe copying precedents being <u>so</u> safe."   R. B.

1993   "The lane Keats loved so much [at Highgate] – called Poets Lane by the Gods [Keats met Hunt with presⁿ copy of his poems there]. Coleridge had an affection for the place, & Shelley <u>knew</u> it."

R. B.

1994   "Carlyle sees things in broad blazing lights, but he does not analyze them like a philosopher."   E. B. B.

1995   "How the fashion of this world passes; the forms its beauty & truth take!"   R B.

1996   "Those known facts which, for practical good, we treat as supremely commonplace, but wh., like those of the uncertainty of life ... if they were not commonplace, & cᵈ they be thoroughly

apprehended, (except in the chance minutes wh. make one grow old ...) the business of the world w^d cease."
R. B.

1997 (**f51^v**) "Let us use the advantage which falls to us from our misfortune."
E. B. B.

1998 "Was ever life so like death before? My face was so close against the tombstones that there seemed no room even for the tears."
E B B.

1999 Lady Mary Wortley Montagu's Septennial Act [for marriage]
E B B.

2000 "All men are made, or make themselves, different in their approaches to different men – & the secret of goodness & greatness is in choosing <u>whom</u> you will approach, & live with, in memory or imagination, through the crowding obvious people who seem to live with you."
R. B.

––––––––––– # –––––––––––

2001 Leslie Stephen's <u>Studies of a Biographer</u>.
"Gibbon's great maxim: To the philosopher all religions are equally false; & to the magistrate equally useful."

2002 "Voltaire's <u>Essai sur les moeurs</u> is delightful reading, but a caricature of history."

2003 '"Gentlemen – butchers"' (sportsmen)   Arthur Young.

2004 (**f52^r**) "The wisest philosopher, if he honestly put down his first thoughts, would be always contradicting himself. We get the appearance of consistency only because we take time to correct, & qualify, & compare, & extenuate, & very often we spoil our best thoughts in the process. What w^d not Mr Ruskin lose if he cared for consistency? The price of suppressing first thoughts may be worth paying by a man whose strength lies in logic; but with a keen, rapid, impetuous observer like Arthur Young we w^d rather do the correcting for ourselves."

–––––––––––––––––––––

2005   "Max" on Mme Tussaud's.

"It flashed upon me that, as I watched them, they were stealing my life from me, making me one of their own kind. My brain seemed to be shrinking, all the blood ceasing in my body. I w.^d not watch them. I drooped my eyelids. My hands looked smooth, waxen, without nerves. I knew ~~not~~ now that I sh.^d never speak nor hear again, never more. I took a dull pride, even, in the thought that this was the very frock-coat in which I had been assassinated."

2006   (**f52^v**) "Viewed in the light of evolution, it is only those recently acquired functions that are perfectly conscious: repetition of functions leads to their unconscious performance."   Lancet.

2007   Our real life is not the life we live, & we feel that our deepest, nay, our most intimate thoughts, are quite apart from ourselves, for we are other than our thoughts & our dreams. And it is only at special moments – it may be by merest accident – that we live our own life. ...

Facts are nothing but the laggards – the spies & camp-followers – of the great forces we cannot see.

Maeterlinck. Treasure of the Humble.

2008   A "Hellenism was the government of communities of men, ... & the source of authority was from within: orientalism was the government of territory ... & the source of authority was from without. ...

... ~~The worship~~ Local citizenship [in the greater Greece] slowly yielded to a sense for citizenship of the world, & cosmopolitanism was born. The worship of the old city gods, based on community of blood, gave place to a (**f53^r**) yearning for something that might symbolize the higher unity of human life"

B. I. Wheeler – Century Magazine, Oct. 99.

2009   'What does a philosopher firstly & lastly require of himself? To overcome his age in himself, to become "timeless." With what, then, has he to wage the hardest strife? With the characteristics in which he is just the child of his age.'   Nietzsche.

2010   ETHICS. [From the Article (33 pages) by HENRY SIDGWICK, Litt. D., Prof., Moral Philosophy, Cambridge]. ...

The
Socratic
paradox.
There is an obvious danger to moral responsibility involved in the doctrine that vice is involuntary; which yet seems a natural inference from the Socratic identification of knowledge with virtue. Hence Aristotle had already been led to attempt a refutation of this doctrine; but his attempt had only shown the profound difficulty of attacking the paradox, so long as it was admitted that no one could of deliberate purpose act contrary to what seemed to him best. Now, Aristotle's divergence from Socrates had not led him so far as to deny this; while for the Stoics who had receded to the original Socratic position, the difficulty was still more patent. In fact, a philosopher who maintains that virtue is essentially knowledge has to choose between alternative paradoxes; he must either allow vice to be involuntary, or affirm ignorance to be voluntary. The latter horn of the dilemma is at any rate the less dangerous to morality, and as such the Stoics chose it. But they were not yet at the end of their perplexities; for while they were thus driven on one line of thought to an extreme extension of the range of human volition, their view of the physical universe involved an equally thorough-going determinism. How could the vicious man be responsible if his vice were strictly pre-determined?...

2011   (**f53ᵛ**) COMTE. [From the Article (9 pages) by THE RT. HON. JOHN MORLEY, P. C., M. A., F. R. S., LL. D., D. C. L., M. P.]. ... The exaltation of Humanity into the throne occupied by the Supreme Being under monotheistic systems made all the rest of Comte's construction easy enough. Utility remains the test of every institution, impulse, act; his fabric becomes substantially an arch of utilitarian propositions, with an artificial Great Being inserted at the top to keep them in their place. The Comtist system is utilitarianism crowned by a fantastic decoration. Translated into the plainest English, the position is as follows: "Society can only be regenerated by the greater subordination of politics to morals, by the moralization of capital, by the renovation of the family, by a higher conception of marriage, and so on. These ends can only be reached by a heartier development of the sympathetic instincts. The sympathetic instincts can only be developed by the Religion of Humanity." Looking at the problem in this way, even a moralist who does not expect theology to be the instrument of social revival, might still ask whether the sympathetic instincts will not necessarily be already developed . to their highest point, before people will be persuaded to accept the religion, which is at bottom hardly more than sympathy under a more imposing name. However that may be, the whole battle – into which we shall not enter – as to the legitimateness of Comtism as a religion turns upon this erection of Humanity into a Being. The various hypotheses, dogmas, proposals, as to the family, to capital, &c., are merely propositions measurable by considerations of utility and a balance of expediencies. Many of these proposals are of the highest interest, and many of them are actually available; but there does not seem to be one of them of an available kind, which could not equally well be approached from other sides, and even incorporated in some radically antagonistic system. Adoption, for example, as a practice for improving the happiness of families and the welfare of society, is capable of being weighed, and can in truth only be weighed, by utilitarian considerations, and has been commended by men to whom the Comtist religion is naught. The singularity of Çomte's construction, and the test by which it must be tried, is the transfer of the worship and discipline of Catholicism to a system in which "the conception of God is superseded" by the abstract idea of Humanity, conceived as a kind of Personality. ...

2012   STANLEY, ARTHUR PENRHYN. [From the Article (4 pages) by THE VERY REV. GEORGE GRANVILLE BRADLEY D.D., LL.D. Dean of Westminster, Dean of the Order of the Bath.]. ... Though he resolutely stood aloof from all connection with party, it is impossible not to recognize even in his least controversial writings the position which he held as, in the eyes of the greatest portion of his countrymen, the leading liberal theologian of his time in England. Throughout his writings in prose or poetry, on almost every subject which he touched, we see the impress, not only of his distinctive genius and of his extraordinary gifts, but also of his special views, aims, and aspirations. It may be well to describe these as nearly as possible in his own words. He looked on the age in which he lived as one of mingled hope and gloom, as a period of transition, to be followed either by an "eclipse of faith" – a "winter of unbelief" – or by a "revival of Christianity in a wider aspect," a "catholic, comprehensive, all-embracing Christianity" that "might yet overcome the world." He believed, and was never tired of asserting his belief, "that the Christian church had not yet presented its final or its most perfect aspect to the world"; that "the belief of each successive age of Christendom had as a matter of fact varied enormously from the belief of its predecessor"; that "all confessions and similar documents are, if taken as final expressions of absolute truth, misleading"; that each "successive form of theology is but the approximation to the truth, not the whole truth itself"; that it was "the glory of the church to be always advancing to perfection"; and that "there still remained, behind all the controversies of the past, a higher Christianity which neither assailants nor defenders had fully exhausted. ...."

2013 (**f54ʳ**) H. W. Mabie. in N. Y. Bookman. Sept. '99.

... Criticism is vital, penetrative, luminous, only when it is the product of the creative temper. It takes an artist to catch an artist. The key to the work of art is insight, not observation; hence the discursive quality of the criticism of men like Goethe, Herder, Joubert, Coleridge, Amiel. "Almost all rich veins of original and striking speculation," says John Stuart Mill, "have been opened by systemic half-thinkers." The half-thinker like Goethe, Coleridge, Carlyle and Emerson, who sees a whole-world, is often more inclusive and creative than the whole-thinker who sees a half-world.

"Many minds have contributed to the working out of what may be called the vital, as distinguished from the abstract, idea of history and art; but we owe to Herder, Winkelmann, Lessing and Goethe a lasting obligation for their varied but harmonious exposition of this deep and luminous conception; perhaps the most fundamental and characteristic idea which modern thought has produced. Winkelmann's contribution to the knowledge of art may be taken as an illustration of the general work of these thinkers. Instead of looking at Greek sculpture as comprising a series of detached and unrelated works, he discerned the unity and harmony of these works as expressions of a single impulse or activity; more than this, he discerned the vital relation of sculpture, as the Greeks practised it, to their genius, their temper and their life. He saw that no individual impulse or skill accounted for Greek art, but that its explanation must be sought in the Greek nature. He saw that the art of sculpture in Greek hands was of a piece with all the other arts, and that what was characteristic of Phidias, the sculptor, was also characteristic of Sophocles, the poet, of Plato, the thinker, and of Pericles, the statesman. Everything the Athenians did in their best years was of a piece, and all their arts were so many expressions of their nature. Elevation, simplicity and repose were characteristics common to sculptured figures, acted dramas, philosophic speculation and practical statesmanship; sculpture, literature, philosophy and oratory were, therefore, vitally related parts of a complete and harmonious expression of Greek life, and the Greek nature was the soil in which all these beautiful growths had their root. Winkelmann discerned the natural history of art; its response to external conditions; its large dependence on soil, sky, temperament, religion, political characters; the impress of race upon it. He saw, in a word, the unity of Greek life and history. He put a vital process in place of an abstract idea, a living organism in place of unrelated products of individual skill.

"Herder, fresh from the study of the Bible, of Shakespeare and of the English ballads, approached the study of history and literature in the same spirit. He put aside all ideas of artificial production; he saw that literature is a natural growth; that its roots are in the life of man, and that it responds to the changing conditions of that life as swiftly and surely as vegetation responds to a change of soil; each soil nourishing the growth to which it is specially adapted. The significant word with Herder was growth; because growth implies natural process as opposed to mechanical process, spontaneous impulse as distinguished from conscious action, genius as contrasted with artifice, and the personality of the writer as against abstract ideas. His thought of what goes to the making of a great work of literature is well expressed in these words of Goethe's: 'Everything that a man undertakes to produce, whether by action, word or in whatsoever way, ought to spring from the union of all his faculties.' In other words, a work of art is an expression of a man's whole nature and life; something that grows out of him and not something which he puts together with mechanical dexterity. Herder discerned the natural history of literature, its vital relation to the life behind it, its close and inevitable connection with human history and development. 'Poetry in those happy days,' he declared, 'lived in the ears of the people, on the lips and in the harps of living bards; it sang of

history, of the events of the day, of mysteries, miracles and signs. It was
the flower of a nation's character, language and country; of its
occupations, its prejudices, its passions, its aspirations and its soul.'
The epic was 'the living history of the people.' This view of life and its
arts is now familiar to us, but it was strange and revolutionary to the
contemporaries of Herder.*

*Short studies in Literature – quoted in N. Y. Bookman. Sept. '99 by
H. W. Mabie.

2014 (**f54ᵛ**) "Literature" Nov 4.99

It is with a darker, more macabre sense of the soiling mystery of
death, and the end of beauty, that a poem called "Wasted Words,"
which I have translated for a specimen, sums up the attitude of the
universe towards woman and of woman towards the universe: –

> After the bath the chambermaid
>   Combs out your hair. The peignoir falls
> In pleated folds. You turn your head
>   To hear the mirror's madrigals.

> Does not the mirror's voice remind
>   Your pride: This body, fair in vain,
> Decrepit shelter of a kind
>   Of soul, must find the dust again.

> Then shall this delicate flesh forsake
>   The bones it veiled, and worms intrude
> Where all is emptiness, and make
>   A busy nest in solitude.

> There, no more white; but brown earth strewn
>   Heavily on your bony cheeks.
> No gleaming lustres, but the moon.
>   These are the words your mirror speaks.

> You listen with a soulless smile,
>   Too proud to heed the thing they say;
> For woman mocks at time, the while
>   To-morrow feeds on yesterday.

That is characteristic enough, in its touches of old sentiment and new, in its not unsuccessful aim at effect, in its fantastic modernity; Charles Cros is very French, and in his own time was very modern.

ARTHUR SYMONS.

2015   "I was not sorrowful, but only tired
        of everything that ever I admired."

        (Ernest Dowson. "Decorations in verse & prose." Smithers 5/-)

2016   A good line: –
"They have ridden the low moon out of
the sky, their hoofs drum up the dawn."

Kipling.

2017   WAR.

        Private Smith of the Royals; the veldt and a slate-black sky.
        Hillocks of mud, brick-red with blood, and a prayer – half curse
            – to die.
        A lung and a Mauser bullet; pink froth and a half-choked cry.

        Private Smith of the Royals; a torrent of freezing rain;
        A hail of frost on a life half lost; despair and a grinding pain.
        And the drip-drip-drip of the Heavens to wash out the brand of
            Cain.

        Private Smith of the Royals, self-sounding his funeral knell;
        A burning throat that each gasping note scrapes raw like a
            broken shell.
        A thirst like a red-hot iron and a tongue like a patch of Hell.

        Private Smith of the Royals; the blush of a dawning day;
        The fading mist that the sun has kissed – and over the hills away
        The blest Red Cross like an angel in the trail of the men who
            slay.

But Private Smith of the Royals gazed up at the soft blue sky –
The rose-tinged morn like a babe new born and the
    sweet-songed birds on high –
With a fleck of red on his pallid lip and a film of white on his eye.

HERBERT CADETT.

[We do not often publish poems by writers unknown to us, but these
lines, in spite of some defects, appear to us to have a character which
promises distinction for their author.]

D. Chronicle.   28 Oct 99

2018   (**f55^r**) "Paolo and Francesca." A Tragedy in four Acts. By
Stephen Phillips. (London: John Lane. 4s. 6d)

PAOLO: You are not sad?

FRANCESCA: What is it to be sad?
Nothing hath grieved me yet but ancient woes,
Sea-perils, or some long-ago farewell,
Or the last sunset cry of wounded kings.
That can fetch down on us the eternal sleep
Anticipating the slow mind of God.

GIO.   Lucrezia! this is that old bitterness.

LUC.   Bitterness – am I bitter? Strange, O strange
How else? My husband dead and childless left,
My thwarted woman-thoughts have inward turned,
And that vain milk like acid in me eats.
Have I not in my thought trained little feet
To venture, and taught little lips to move
Until they shaped the wonder of a word?
I am long practised. O those children, mine!
Mine, doubly mine: and yet I cannot touch them,
I cannot see them, hear them – Does great God
Expect I shall clasp air and kiss the wind
For ever? And the budding cometh on,
The burgeoning, the cruel flowering:
At night the quickening splash of rain, at dawn
That muffled call of babes how like to birds;

And I amid these sights and sounds must starve –
I, with so much to give, perish of thrift!
Omitted by His casual dew!

GIO.   Well, well,
You are spared much: children can wring the heart.

LUC.   Spared! to be spared what I was born to have!
I am a woman, and this very flesh
Demands its natural pangs, its rightful throes,
And I implore with vehemence these pains.
I know that children wound us, and surprise
Even to utter death, till we at last
Turn from a face to flowers: but this my heart
Was ready for these pangs, and had foreseen.
O! but I grudge the mother her last look
Upon the coffined form – that pang is rich –
Envy the shivering cry when gravel falls.
And all these maiméd wants and thwarted thoughts,
Eternal yearning, answered by the wind,
Have dried in me belief and love and fear.
I am become a danger and a menace,
A wandering fire, a disappointed force,
A peril – do you hear, Giovanni? – O!
It is such souls as mine that go to swell
The childless cavern cry of the barren sea,
Or make that human ending to night-wind.

PAO.   What can we fear, we two?
O God, Thou seest us Thy creatures bound
Together by that law which holds the stars
In palpitating cosmic passion bright;
By which the very sun enthralls the earth,
And all the waves of the world faint to the moon.
Even by such attraction we two rush
Together through the everlasting years.
Us, then, whose only pain can be to part,
How wilt Thou punish? For what ecstasy
Together to be blown about the globe!
What rapture in perpetual fire to burn

Together! – where we are is endless fire.
There centuries shall in a moment pass,
And all the cycles in one hour elapse!
Still, still together, even when faints Thy sun,
And past our souls Thy stars like ashes fall,
How wilt Thou punish us who cannot part?

FRANC.   I lie out on your arm and say your name –
"Paolo!" "Paolo!"

PAO.   "Francesca!"

2019   The French have a proverb that "stones are thrown only at the trees which bear fruit,"

2020   *The History of Modern Philosophy*, by Prof. Harald Höffding, of the University of Copenhagen, in two volumes, has been already translated from the Danish into German. The object of the work is to trace the development of philosophic thought from the close of the Middle Ages onwards, and the method adopted is to study the personality and work of those men whose names naturally stand out in their historic sequence to indicate the special contribution or advance made by each, and to criticise their standpoint. The value of the work has been widely recognised in Germany. Perhaps the most noticeable feature of the book is its full treatment of the beginnings of modern philosophy in the period before Descartes, reviewing the thought of writers so different and so interesting as Montaigne, Machiavelli, Giordano Bruno, and the inaugurators of the new science – Leonardo da Vinci, Kepler, and Galileo, who lead up to Bacon. The first volume, which is procurable separately, deals fully with Hobbes and the later English thinkers, and the last chapter is devoted to French thought in the eighteenth century, from Voltaire and the Encyclopædists to Rousseau. The second volume passes from a brief study of Lessing to Kant, with whom begins the period of strictly "modern" philosophy. Very much less space is conceded to the later Germans, Fichte, Schelling, Hegel, Schopenhauer, and the rest, who are classed as the philosophers of Romanticism. The ninth book deals exhaustively with the Philosophy of Positivism, beginning with Comte and ending with Darwin and Herbert Spencer, and the tenth expounds the later Germans, Lotze, Hartmann, and their fellows. The book may be commended to all students of philosophy, whether ethical, metaphysical, or political, as covering a field of which no other existing work has attempted to give so comprehensive a survey. The book has been translated from the German edition by Miss B. E. Meyer.

2021   By this time most people have made up their minds upon the merits of M. Maeterlinck, and the production of his *Pelléas et Mélisande* in an English version, for a series of nine *matinées*, will hardly rekindle the fiery discussion which followed its performance in French some seasons ago by the company of the Théâtre de l'Œuvre. As every one knows, the world, according to the "*Shakespeare des marionettes*," is peopled with a strangely anaemic race, morbidly sensitive to impressions of physical or mental discomfort, and given to triple repetitions of the simple sentences in which they express themselves. With all the Ollendorffian peculiarities of their diction, and, notwithstanding the simplicity, not to say *naïveté*, of most of the situations and incidents of the dramas, an impression of remote yet vivid pathos is somehow conveyed in any adequate performance of the best of the author's plays. And [i.e. Maeterlinck]

   In the French production of the work the effect of remoteness and archaic simplicity was obtained by making the whole action pass behind a gauze curtain, and by encouraging the actors in a designedly angular style of gesture, which perpetually reminded the spectator of figures in tapestry. Here the management has, perhaps wisely, preferred to accept the ordinary conditions of theatrical production, and a succession of scenes of the usual elaborate kind pass before our eyes. The place of the intervening veil is taken, and its object as separating the drama from everyday experience partly fulfilled, by the incidental music.

2022   (**f55ᵛ**) California. "The right hand of the Continent."
                    (by C. F. Lummis. Harper's Mag. Jan 1900.)
It is a case where one man & the geography are a majority.

2023   The Pacific – prophets have foretold it the coming chief theatre of the world's activities.

2024   The Civil War. ... Tall trees are risen upon its graves. ... N. & S. are grown one ... by the slow 'intention' of time & the blood.

2025   Emigrants thither in '48 & onwards. Every man lost something in California, & found something. ... Some that had been strong so long as environment crutched them, turned weak when they tried to stand alone; & some, weakling by disuse, turned giants under exercise. Some "good men" became bad, & some "bad men" became good. It was the Circe that bewitched a man to his true inner shape – of fox or wolf or hog or man. And so is the frontier always. ... Every man jack of those men was changed – grown along his line of least resistance.

2026   (**f56ʳ**) California is above all others the land of contrasts. ... It is true, but truth is a club too heavy to be used unmercifully.

2027   I would rather think of it [the climate &c] as Nature's true normal, & of the peevish climate temper of my native coast as it were her neuralgia.

2028   ... Though one may prefer the things that merit superlatives.

2029   No one does the thing which seems to need doing.

2030   "Maeterlinck." Contempʸ Review, March 1900.
                                                        Arthur R. Ropes.
   "'The thoughts of a princess an-hungered.'"
"The hungry princess – a favourite type of M.'s – is the soul pining in vain for its birthright of sympathy. That a beggar should starve is natural, & has no especial significance; a princess is born with a presumed right to live in abundance & tender care."

2031   We have had our serious mystical poets too: William Blake in the past, & the Celtic school in the present, e.g. Mr Yeats. ...

2032   (**f56ᵛ**) "But crude & boyish as is La Princesse Maleine, & Ollendorfian as is much of its dialogue, the play already gives us the one note that M. strikes more plainly than any other. There is the sense of mystery at the back of the visible action – the unknown horror behind the closed door, the tremendous presence impending over the trivialities of ordinary life. The chief personage in the M. drama is the Dweller of the Threshold, Fate, or Death, or Love, or all in one.

2033   "One theme, however, is not enough for a symphony; this new
dramatic motive [the bar, material or mental, & the mystery going on
behind it] needs development. ... M. breaks down ... singularly limited
... possessed with a certain number of images, & he can hardly go
beyond them. Corridors, moats, & towers of old castles ...
underground passages ... marshes canals, forests, lighthouses,
convents, fountains, ponds ... through wh. move weird mournful
beings. ...

2034   "A Symbolist may be defined as a man who says something else.
Unable or unwilling to put his thoughts into definite words, he uses
certain terms or metaphors to shadow it forth. Hence symbolism is only
justifiable, (**f57ʳ**) from an artistic point of view, when the real meaning
of the writer cannot be put into plain words, or cannot be so expressed
in proper artistic form. Beyond this symbolism is unnecessary, &
simply irritating. ... A symbolist who <u>always</u> talks or paints in symbols is
a man who speaks an arbitrary language of his own. His work is mere
cryptogram. We must judge the symbolist by his non symbolᶜ work. If
we find this full of significance we may feel sure that what we do not
quite understand has yet its meaning. ... If we apply this test to M., is
his silence always so eloquent ... or ... confession of inadequacy?

2035   "We never feel the thrill of the perfect thought & the perfect
word in one of his writings. In fact, he wᵈ hardly care to give us such a
thrill. ... Thought may seem to him as lowered by becoming a definite
mental conception, & degraded by embodiment in a form of words. His
eloquence ... lies in the silences between & behind the speeches of his
characters.
   "But have we not <u>all</u> this eloquence? Can we not all outvie the
greatest poets in the dim recesses of our consciousness? ... The poet is
not ⟨necessarily⟩ he who thinks what no one has thought, but the man
that finds ... words for the ... idea."

2036   (**f57ᵛ**) "<u>The terrific oracle of Oedipus</u>: 'Mayst thou ne'er know
the truth of what thou art.'"
                                        Dᵣ J. H. Hyslop. in <u>Harper's</u>.
[The line more literally is 'Mayst thou never come to know who thou
art' – ΟΙΔΙΠΟΥΣ ΤΥΡ: 1068.]

2037 <u>Secondary Personality</u>. – Subconscious mental processes – e.g. "hypnotize a man ... suggest that he make a speech, & he may do so in a way that he could not in a normal state. He seems to be another person than himself. This is what is called secondary personality."

D.ʳ J. H. ib.

––––––––––––––// ––––––––––––––

2038 <u>Letter of D.ʳ St George Mivart</u>, just before his death: –
"... I have no more leaning to atheism or agnosticism now than ever I had; but the inscrutable, incomprehensible energy pervading the universe, & (as it seems to me) disclosed by science, differs profoundly, as I read nature, from the God worshipped by Christians."

<u>Times</u>. 4.4.1900.

––––––––––––––// ––––––––––––––

2039 <u>Heretical notions of God</u>. Tertullian (De Testimonio Animae, c. ii.) speaks of some who believe in a non-active & passionless God.

––––––––––––––// ––––––––––––––

2040 He is confounding the functions of the poet and the pamphleteer. The age of the poetry of reason has long passed, and it is only in the correspondence columns of a Church paper or in tract or pamphlet that one should discuss the infallibility of the Church of Rome, the mistaken faith of the Jews, or the contentions of the atheist.

Athenaeum 4. Aug 1900

2041 (**f58ʳ**) Style and the "Edinburgh Review."
The article in the current *Edinburgh Review* on "Some Tendencies of Modern Style" deserves attention in more ways than one. Its declared aim is to criticise some recent efflorescences of the younger phrase-mongers who follow their Meredith not wisely but too well. Herein we have every sympathy with it. The application to the novel of a style perilous in the essay is an innovation to be deplored. The aim of such style is great minuteness of word selection: the sentence is to become a mosaic of *recherchés* and carefully tested words. In the hands of a master this may succeed. It may succeed by a fastidious reticence, a

delicate sense of the too much, a chastened instinct where to stop. But in most hands – as one might prophesy, and as we see in fact – the tendency of such narrowed attention to the individual word is to throw the sentence out of focus. There should be an organic relation and subordination in the vocables of a sentence, a distinction of major and minor. But in the strained minuteness of the writer's attention to language he misses sight of this with distressing result. The words lose their perspective, and start out upon the reader with an unnatural separate distinctness:

> Each particular word doth stand on end,
> Like quills upon the fretful porcupine.

It has an effect like the painful heightening of individual objects in a nightmare vision. In fact, such a sentence (unconsciously to the writer) is veritably dislocated; as in the drawing of a beginner, where noses and other features assume abnormal proportions. Each word may be accurate and defensible in itself, but the total result is false because *relation* – comparative importance – has been neglected. It is an error parallel to the pre-Raphaelite assemblage of severally-studied details in an unrelated whole. And all this becomes tenfold worse when the writer intensifies the impression by packed audacities of imagery. The effect is phantasmagoric. One's eyes ache, seeking and finding no place of rest.

But here our agreement with the reviewer ceases. It is, unhappily, only at the close of his article that he reaches these justified animadversions. The rest of the article is consumed in an elaborate attempt to provide a foundation of principle for his forthcoming strictures. For this purpose he revives the mischievous fallacy that "you should write as you speak." When it is considered that there are whole ranges of themes which are practically excluded from speech, the fallacy and inadequacy of this principle seems evident. It is true that the reviewer modifies it by saying that speech should be the model for prose. True, in the same sense that the skeleton is the model for the flesh. But the reviewer means much more; he contends that the nearer prose is to speech the better it is. Armed with this law, he surveys the range of English prose, and makes devastating work. Passing over his loose introduction, which contains fallacies of thought enough to require an article for their discussion, it is sufficient to say that one main result, if not object, of his essay is virtually to set aside and condemn a whole mode of English prose; and with it to clear away from

our literature a stately grove of noble writers. On his principle, of
course, the eighteenth century is the great period of our prose. With
ruthless logic he carries his theory to its full consequences, brushing
aside the entire seventeenth century. A principle which condemns at
one fell swoop Milton and Sir Thomas Browne and Jeremy Taylor, and
their great brethren, stands surely self-condemned. If either they or the
principle must go, it will be hard for the principle!

The truth is, that it is pedantry to limit prose within any external
order of style. The form of prose is determined by its *aim* – by its
subject-matter and the writer's design in treating that subject-matter.
As this approaches or recedes from the aims of speech, the style should,
and must, approach or recede from the usual structure of speech.
Where it is widely different from unpremeditated speech, that is
because theme and aim are widely different from anything conceivable
in speech. But here we touch one cause of the reviewer's error. He
wishes to draw a fast line between prose and poetry. Metre, he thinks,
is the proper distinction between poetry and prose; therefore, outside
metre, the more prosaic your writing (the nearer to speech, in his
phrase), the better it will be, as a matter of style. But metre is not the
proper distinction between poetry and prose (though a distinction
convenient for general observation). As a proof, take the poetical books
of the Bible. They have been rendered into prose so superbly fit that all
attempts, even by poets, to substitute metrical form have utterly failed.
Here you have grand poetry without metre. What, then, has it which
distinguishes it, outwardly, from prosaic prose? It has *rhythm*. It is the
presence of lofty and noble rhythm which invests the poetry of the Bible
with such satisfying and wholly congruous form. And it is rhythm
which really is the *necessary* medium of poetry, not metre. But rhythm
varies gradually and imperceptibly through numberless gradations,
from the highest to the lowest, till it disappears in the pedestrian
progress of average prose. It follows that there is no such fast line
between poetry and prose as the Edinburgh Reviewer supposes. Poetry
and prose can, and sometimes do, play into each other. Prose,
therefore, becomes a vast *spectrum*, fading into poetry at one end, into
journalism at the other (or, if the Reviewer prefer the phrase, into the
forms of ordinary speech). To which of these two extremities a given
style shall approximate depends wholly on the writer's aim. Prose in
the past has divided itself into two great modes, represented by the
seventeenth and eighteenth centuries. The prose of Browne and Jeremy
Taylor was well towards the upper, or poetic, end of the spectrum,

without actually passing into it, like the poetic books of the Bible. The prose of Swift and Dryden was well towards the lower, or colloquial, end, though far from passing into it – much further than certain modern prose. But both were as legitimate as they were separate modes of prose. That the eighteenth century is a fitter model for the general requirements of prose is obvious. But that does not sweep from the ranks of the great masters of style Taylor, and Browne, and Hooker, and their fellows. And God forbid it should!

The Academy. 18 November, 1899.

2042   (**f58ᵛ**) <u>Kant & Hegel</u>, "Kant had shown that all known or knowable objects are relative to a conscious subject, & that therefore we cannot legitimately treat them as <u>things in themselves</u> – i.e. as things that ⟨would?⟩ might exist by themselves even if there were no intelligent principle in existence to know them. He had shown, in other words, that existence means nothing unless it s̶ means existence for a self. Hegel carried the argument a step further, & maintained that the world of objects is not only related to an intelligence, but that it can be nothing but the revelation or manifestation of intelligence."

Professor E. Caird (Chamber's Cyclo.)

2043   "According to Hegel's system finite things are not (as in the system of subjective Idealism) simply phenomena for us, existing only in <u>our</u> consciousness, but are phenomena <u>per se</u> by their very nature, i.e., things having the ground of their being not in themselves, but in the universal divine Idea. ... This is the system of Absolute Idealism. [idea-ism]

Ueberweg.

<center>~~~~~~~~~~~~~~~</center>

2044   <u>Market Gardening</u>. "The field is overcrowded, & prosperity is only to be found in doing something that few are engaged in; or in unmistakably excelling others."

Westmʳ Gazette

2045   to this literary craftsman words have an existence like living creatures.

2046 (**f59ʳ**) A traditional ballad. "All the more because it is so dreamlike & confused I am inclined to think that this is really a traditional version."   (A. Lang, in Longman's.)

2047 Impressionism.
R. A. M. Stevenson's monograph on Velasquez. (Bell. Gt. Masters in Painting Series) Finest statement of the theory of Impressionism in the language. Herein ... he serenely enunciates the now universally accepted proposition that the art of painting can progress but in one direction – towards Impressionism so called.   The Outlook.

2048 "In whatever way the Self is taken, it will prove to be appearance. It cannot, if finite, maintain itself against external relations. For these will enter its essence, & so ruin its independency."
          F. H. Bradley. Appearance & Reality. 1 vol. 1897.

2049 Consciousness in Nature. Schelling, in the Philosophy of Nature writings, & in the World-Soul, supplements the Fichtian Ego or Absolute Ego by showing that the whole of Nature may be regarded as an embodiment of a process by which Spirit tends to rise to a consciousness of itself.   Chamb. Biog. Dic.
[cf. Clifford's "Mind-stuff"]

2050 "As the fundamental Cause of all earthly suffering we find Darwin's struggle for existence."
          Philʸ of Mysticism. C. du Prel. transl. by C. C. Massey.

2051 (**f59ᵛ**) "Newton ... could compare infinite space to the sensorium of the Deity."   Huxley. Study of Berkeley.

2052 "According to their [Sir I. Newton's &c] doctrine, God Almighty wants to wind up his watch from time to time, otherwise it would cease to move."   ib. quot. from Leibnitz.

2053   "The passion of love invariably drives men & women to an
extreme step in one direction or another. It will send some to the
Cloister, some to the Tribune, some to the stage, some to heroism, some
to crime, & all to their natural calling."

Robert Orange – by J. Oliver Hobbes.

2054   "I cannot light my own fire; but whenever I get my fire lighted
from another life I can carry the living flame as my own into other
subjects, which have been illuminated in the flame."
(Robertson of Brighton on finding his inspiration in the writings of
others)

2055   "Every kind of ~~material~~ (information) was by the piety of his
mind, converted into theology."   (Dr Johnson on Watts.)

2056   (**f60^r**) He read a certain humanity into natural things, feeling
for them as though actually living and sentient. The Jungfrau, when
the sunset glow had gone, appalled him as being dead, and he rejoiced
to note her recovery under the moonlight: mountain streams were
always to him 'little scamps' playing mischievous merry pranks among
the hills, and he was genuinely sorry for the untimely fate of a rill in
Ireland, which, rising in a tarn on the top of a headland, only lived to
tumble abruptly over a cliff into the sea; there was pathos to him in this
short career.   J. C. Tarver in *Macmillan's Magazine*.

2057   "The Thrush": No 1.
   Another is a lyric by Mr. W. E. Henley, of which the first and last
verses read:–

> It came, the news, like a fire in the night,
>   That life and its best were done;
> And there was never so dazed a wretch
>   In the heat of the living sun.
>
> So I went for the news to the house of the news,
>   But the words were left unsaid,
> For the face of the house was blank with blinds,
>   And I knew that she was dead.

2058   "While ye have light believe in the light."   John XII.36.

2059   "Be not children in understanding. ... In understanding be
men."   1 Cor. XIV.20.

2060   "Walk while ye have the light, lest darkness come upon you."
John XII.35

2061   "Ye have been called unto liberty."   Gal. V. 13

2062   "Believe not every spirit."   I John IV.1

2063   "Kant's greatest service is to have separated the phenomenal
from the thing-in-itself by proving that between us & things there
always stands the intellect. Kant's Copernican discovery is aptly hit off
by Schopenhauer in the words: 'Before Kant we were in Time; now
Time is in us,' & so on."
Schopenhauer's Criticism of Kant. Mind 1891.

2064   (**f60ᵛ**) The painter Manet. "It has been said of Manet that ...
he kept losing & half-finding himself, never saying 'this is my rest,
at this point I set up my mastership.'"

2065   "He secures with loose liquid touches the chief constituent tones
of the effect, leaving them to float side by side, with their edges
undetermined."

2066   "Ugly buildings ... Never mind: take the lovely tones that
without premeditation these misfortunes offer to the sunlight."
"D. S. M." in S. Review. 22.9. 1900

----------------//----------------

2067   Music. "England, before doing anything of her own, must
absorb German music, even as the earlier Germans absorbed Italian
music."   "J. F. R." ib.

2068 The Grave. "The one most impressive feature of the Chinese landscape is the grave."

Dr Clark. N. American Rev^w

2069 "The Riddle of the Universe at the Close of the Nineteenth Century." By Ernst Haeckel. Translated by Joseph McCabe. Issued by the Rationalist Press Association, Limited. (London: Watts and Co. 6s. net.)

Now that Huxley is dead, Ernst Haeckel of Jena is perhaps the most famous of all those who champion science in opposition to religion. In "Die Welt-räthsel," of which this book is a translation, he returns once more to the charge against all that is most hateful to the militant naturalist. There is no withdrawing or falling away. In a strikingly large number of cases men who have been decisively ranged on the same side have modified their views with advancing years. Professor Haeckel almost ruefully reviews a number of these apostates – Wundt, Virchow, Du Bois-Reymond, Karl Ernst Baer, and others. Their entire change of philosophical principle he finds "very interesting," suggesting that it (**f61^r**) may be due, perhaps, to the gradual decay of the brain which comes with advancing years. But Haeckel expounds the faith as earnestly as ever, and does not cease to belabour the false conceptions of dualism, idealism, and Christianity.

What, then, is the reasoned belief that science has to offer as a solution of the great world-riddle? It is the homogeneity of nature. There are not two distinct forms of being, matter and spirit, but only one form. There is no such thing as spirit without matter. All nature passes through endless changes and forms; no dividing line can be drawn between the organic and inorganic, between nature and man. For man is only a part of nature, and a very unimportant part. There is no such thing as design or government or plan in the world; teleology is a conception which must be ruled out without remorse. Kant's three great postulates, God, Freedom, and Immortality, are promptly disposed of. The "wise Providence" of the Church, the "all-loving Father in heaven" is an "untenable myth." The controversy about Freedom has ended in the complete victory of the determinists. And "the belief in the immortality of the human soul is a dogma which is in hopeless contradiction with the most solid empirical truths of modern science."

To Haeckel and those who think with him the most unpardonable error is "anthropism." Man is not the central point of the universe, nor, indeed, a point of any importance at all. He is no more than a zoological species. An infinite process of development through the lower animals has produced him – somehow. There was no purpose in his production: he merely happened to come about. He is placed, too, on an unimportant planet of an unimportant sun, lost in the infinities of space. The duration of his dwelling-place is limited. "Even our mother earth ... will grow cold and lifeless, ..., and, gradually narrowing its orbit, will fall eventually into the sun." Man has little behind him and little before: he is a casual, transient and trivial animal creature. In the light of modern scientific discovery –

Our earth shrinks into the slender proportions of a "mote in the sunbeam," of which unnumbered millions chase each other through the vast depths of space. Our own "human nature," which exalted itself into an image of God in its anthropistic illusion, sinks to the level of a placental mammal, which has no more value for the universe at large than the ant, the fly of a summer's day, the microscopic infusorium, or the smallest bacillus. Humanity is but a transitory phase of the evolution of an external substance, a particular phenomenal form of matter and energy, the true proportion of which we soon perceive when we set it on the background of infinite space and eternal time.

The belittling of man, his deposition from his former place in the universe, has inspired much of the warfare that has raged around modern science. Professor Haeckel urges this consequence of his teaching with a certain gloomy zest. How strongly many refined and sensitive minds have recoiled from it is known to everyone who has read "In Memoriam." The doctrine set forth in the words we have just quoted seemed to Tennyson to be the most fatal fruit of knowledge without "reverence." By Haeckel it is urged without condition or mitigation, no condemnation being too hard for "anthropism" in all its branches.

About the energy, the vigour and the conviction with which Professor Haeckel presses his views there is as little doubt as there is of his immense attainments, and the authority with which he speaks on all questions of natural science. But how far can the authority of science be stretched? Much that is said in this book is not matter of science at all, but of belief, of interpretation, of the point of view. How far is the scientist justified in asserting that he utterly rejects "teleology," when he can hardly open his mouth without speaking of organs which show "provident arrangement" and "excellent contrivance"? Whilst using freely expressions such as these, Professor Haeckel may hold to the conviction that "teleology" is an outworn dogma, and that no one ought to speak of end or purpose in nature; but he does not make himself clear. Criticisms of even more importance suggest themselves. What justification can "anthropism" plead before the bar of science itself? The doctrine of evolution may be interpreted in two very opposite ways. Since man has sprung from the brute, it may be held that he is merely an animal showing certain accidental variations from other animals. We may explain evolution by referring everything back to its beginnings. Or we may fix our attention on the final and highest stages. The oak is the outgrowth of the acorn, or the acorn is the seed of the oak. The process of evolution may be understood in the light given by its most perfect product, man – not with the eye fixed alone on its imperfect beginnings. If we study nature from man downwards, rather than from the lowest germ upwards, we, in some measure justify "anthropism"; we are interpreting nature by man. Human life and human energies thus become the most significant thing in all the animated world. The argument might be pursued a little deeper. Most people, we believe, are haunted by a conviction that that which is the highest must also be the truest. They believe the highest form of existence to be that which finds expression in the moral and spiritual life. Moral experience seems to be the highest, and, for that very reason, the most real form of experience of which we have any knowledge. It is man alone "who battles for the true, the just." In this aspect his activities have a dignity and value that we seek for everywhere else in nature in vain.

In the whole of this book we have found only one reference to religion which does not display a desire to say something unpleasant and crushing. "When I was at Bombay in 1881," says Professor Haeckel, "I watched with the greatest sympathy the elevating rites of the pious Parsees, who, standing on the sea shore, or kneeling on their prayer-rugs, offered their devotion to the sun at its rise and setting." But not a scrap of this sympathy is forthcoming for the religion that produced Francis of Assisi and Thomas à Kempis. In Christianity Haeckel sees only a lurid vision of darkness and superstition: – Torquemada, Lourdes, the Holy Coat of Trêves, Leo X., the burning of Giordano Bruno – that is all. Nor would he have written the amazing chapter on "Science and Christianity" had he devoted to it a fraction of the critical care he has bestowed on the propagation of protozoa. "Recent historical investigation," he tells us, "teaches that Paul's father was of Greek nationality, and his mother of Jewish." On what evidence does this historical investigation rest? It cannot be better than that of Paul himself, who wrote in an Epistle which Professor Haeckel admits to be genuine, "For I also am an Israelite, of the seed of Abraham, of the tribe of Benjamin." The genuine Pauline Epistles are spoken of as "three in number, according to recent criticism – to the Romans, Galatians, and Corinthians." We hesitate to suppose that Professor Haeckel is unaware of the existence of two Epistles to the Corinthians, both of which are generally accepted: but our mind misgives us.

D. Chronicle Oct 1. 1900

2070 (**f61ᵛ**) The Literary Artist. – "The one thing that is not permitted to the artist is the absense of moral interest. To sit between the shining oriels & sing your songs alone is to be a monster. After all, it is character, the sense of values, the feeling for 'the things that are more excellent' that go to the making of the great personalities. Without these you can amuse, you can interest, you can startle, but you cannot move. This is why some find Velasquez the least dynamic of the masters. He stood outside his subjects, interpreting them perfectly by sheer intellectual power, without enthusiasms, & without predilections. Therefore many admire & respect Velasquez, but do not love him, & are not moved by him." Athenaeum. Oct 20. 1900.

2071 What is Poetry? "The modern craze for individuality is a grave symptom of a graver malady.... The poet as he [the modern critic] conceives him is not a seer charged with a spiritual message to the general heart of man, but a clever craftsman whose ingenuity is the delight of a select circle of fastidious connoisseurs.... Mannerisms of style, novelties of metre, eccentricities of diction ... an agreeable change to men whose jaded palates are ever craving new sensations.... It is difficult to say whether this conception ... (**f62ʳ**) offers the deeper insult to poetry or to human nature. As well might it be said that Art exists in order to exercise the critical acumen of the bric-a-brac hunter."

"What is poetry?" By E. Holmes. ~~Lond~~. Lane. 3/6

2072 Imaginative literature. "The first & noblest aim of imagᵛᵉ literᵘʳᵉ is not either to tickle or to stab the sensibilities, but to render a coherent view of life's apparent incoherence, to give shape to the amorphous, to discover beauty wh. was hidden, to ~~ref~~ reveal essential truth. The great artist may force you to laugh or to wipe away a tear, but he accomplishes these minor feats by the way. What he mainly does is to see for you. If, in presenting a scene, he does not disclose aspects of it which you would not have observed for yourself, then he falls short of success. In a physical & a psychical sense his power is visual, the power of an eye seeing things always fresh, virginally, as though on the very morn of creation itself."   Academy. 10 Nov. 1900.

2073   "Paint man man, whatever the issue."
                              Browning. "Old Pictures" in Fl.

2074   "After that I have spoken, mock on."   Job.

2075   (**f62ᵛ**) To Nature.
                        by Emily Pfeiffer.

Dread force, in whom of old we loved to see
A nursing mother, clothing with her life
The seeds of Love divine – with what sore strife
We hold or yield our thoughts of Love & thee!

Thou art not calm, but restless as the ocean,
Filling with aimless toil the endless years,
Stumbling on thought & throwing off the spheres,
Churning the Universe with mindless motion

Dull fount of joy, unhallowed source of tears,
Cold motor of our fervid faith & song,
Dead, but engendering life, love, pangs, & fears,
Thou crownedst thy wild work with foulest wrong
When first thou lightedst on a seeming goal,
And darkly blundered on man's suffering soul.

───────────────

2076   'Art, as Aristotle has said, should always have "a continual slight novelty"; it should never astonish, for we are astonished only by some excess or default, never by a thing being what it ought to be."
                        Arthur Symons in "The Academy"

2077 (**f63ʳ**) <u>On Genius &c.</u>

"The innocent vision of ripe genius."

"By this you may know vision, that it is not what you expected, or even what you could have imagined; & that it is never repeated."

"The power of seeing things in their living relationships, which constitutes genius."

"Poetic expression is far from having reached its last development."

"The synthetic eye = poetic imagination."

"No man can move this world unless he stand upon another."

Coventry Patmore.

2078 "I have been much struck since I have been in England by the fact that there is always one great reason for doing a thing, & another great reason for not doing it. The one great reason for doing a thing is that it has always been done, & the one unanswerable reason for not doing it is that it has never been done."

<u>Speech of Mr Choate,</u> <u>American Ambassador.</u>

2079 "He could understand the tunes & voices of [beasts, plants, fishes & birds]"   Burton's Anat. of M.

2080   (**f63ᵛ**) <u>The Donkey.</u>

The tattered outlaw of the earth
    Of ancient crooked will;
Starve, scourge, deride me; I am dumb,
    I keep my secret still.

Fools! For I also had my hour:
    One far fierce hour & sweet;
There was a shout about my ears,
    And palms before my feet.
    (Gilbert Chesterton, "The Wild Knight" – Grant Richards)

2081   WHICH IS THE BEST RELIGION, WITH ALL THE WORLD TO CHOOSE
FROM?

A hopeful question this, from a young man, on the threshold of life. It bespeaks an honesty of purpose and a desire to seek out for himself a system of thought and rule of action whereby to shape his future career. It bespeaks a mind restless under the dogmas and puerilities of ecclesiastical lore. The same with the doctrines of hell-fire; the sending into interminable tortures, and with equal complacency, the dissenters in opinion, the recreant in life.

The same with heaven, its harps and its houris. Of all of this there is no record on earth, in the skies, or among the stars, for the thunder clap has not declared it, neither has the trumpet blast of an archangel.

Religions are transitory and tentative, and there is no church or place of assembly yet existing to which I would invite my fellow-creatures of all ranks and ages for life instruction. Some there are where high and honest thoughts and warm hearts are forcing themselves into freedom of action; but these are rare, and I would urge at the outset (in answer to the given question) that the Church of the future lies primarily in human breasts, and its teachings are there also. Information and guidance will come, as steel to magnet, if an enquiring mind, and exercised will are to be found. But all churches and chapels, as we have known them, are fading out of ken, notwithstanding the erection of new fabrics, not one spire of which would I lower if it only pointed to man's elevation, and not to manufactured Gods – the nebulous Gods of many attributes and scant performance.

But in thus levelling a time-honored faith in order to inculcate a new one we must be careful to do strict justice to the old one. The peace and hope, the guidance and restraining influences, which may have gilded the lives of our forefathers and irradiated their death-beds, must not be slighted. The new birth to art as seen in all its branches was given by Christianity, and we must not forget that Christianity displaced the vicious complex paganism of ancient Rome, and this by the display of more virtues and a finer morality.[1]

A philosophic survey of the past leads to the conviction that as one of the historic religions Christianity will always have a niche in the temple

---

[1] We may note that these latter opinions have been repeatedly and carefully controverted in our pages. – Ed. N. R.

of fame. *But* inasmuch as man cannot do with the aliments of the child, or a living man with the cerements of the dead, we would now enshrine it in our casket of memories, and gently entomb it, as a butterfly its chrysalis. For among us has sprung up a spirit of enquiry, the undoubted off-shoot of scientific achievement. Among us has the verifying faculty been developed, which absolutely refuses to bow down to teachings long since past and gone. This verifying faculty, moulded on the mathematical accuracy of the schools, of which it is indeed the outcome, asserts nothing for the future in realms of religious thought; it disdains to dogmatise where all is unknown, but it is replete with hope. It *hopes* that bigotry will be assigned to the ages of darkness and ignorance. It *hopes* self-seeking and mere selfishness will give place to general beneficence. It *hopes* that spiritual pride and priestly arrogance will yield to a sense of the individual dignity of every man and woman and of the personal responsibility to which all alike are heirs.

While this verifying faculty may be said to hope all things for the advancement of the human race, it *thinks* that the majestic march of enlightenment traceable in every authentic page of history will go on in exact ratio with the increase of mental culture. It *thinks* that the self-arrogated insight into heaven and its doings, so conspicuous in professing Christians (the teacher and the taught), will ere long yield to convictions that earth and its congeners are the only wholesome, natural areas for the play of man's faculties. By plainness of speech such as this, by the exercise of common-sense, the way will be surely paved for the relinquishment of old paths and for the vigorous pursuit of new ones.

Where these new ones will lead to, I will endeavor to show. The finger on the dial plate of time present, and the pregnant teachings of time past, point to man as the cynosure of all stable religious action in the future, and this I would proclaim if I could with a thousand tongues! And here let us reflect on the essentials of worship, when it is that of the unseen and unknown. All is idealism and transcendentalism. Up in the skies, far away from man. He sees not his Maker and his God; he knows not where to look for him; he gets no answer to prayer; all is emotional, sentimental, hysterical and unreal. Yes! nothing more substantial is offered by our many churches for the rearing of children, the restraining of youth, the spur of maternity, the stay of all age.

If male aspirants to matrimony were henceforth to assert that they would take no more mindless damsels to wife, lovers of dress would become lovers of reflexion, and all useful ennobling accomplishments;

lovers of display become lovers of sterling worth. Pernicious doctrines of heaven are seen at their worst in our self-seekings. "Our own dirty sin-soiled souls" have first to be saved: we must enter heaven alone. But if man will enter into the service of man, if man will study how to make man happier, nobler, purer, the world at large will at all events reap the fruition of sight and sense, and may defy the orthodox persecutors, whose heaven is in the clouds, while ours is on earth.

The question at the head of my paper has been answered. "The religion of life," the religion of humanity from the cradle to the grave, is the best to adopt. It is found at our elbows, in the council chamber, on the mart, in the hall of judgment, in the purlieus of royalty. In *man*, his happiness, his pursuits, his attainments, prosperity and culture, lie the true principles of religion. Yet the world around us is content to leave it as it is: the church militant is triumphant, and the priest goes on his way rejoicing, for while apathy lasts he is sure of his gains. Oh! if I could impress all this on woman, the autocrat of the nursery, the comforter and prompter of man in his most impressionable hours, I should have lively hopes of a speedy adoption of "life religion".

Man is himself responsible for the vacuum in woman's brains. He leaves a void in her heart in the absence of culture, and the wily priest steps in and too often makes the kingdom of home his own, making of himself our priestly mediator at the "throne of grace," though with passions and tendencies like unto our own.

Be assured, young men and young women, that "the religion of life" is the best to adopt. It alone appeals to daily practice, capabilities, and common sense, and will undoubtedly be received as such in coming ages.   E. C. B.

2082   (**f64ʳ**) "A New Philosophy necessary for Art." The summit of ... art has been attained again & again. No man will ever write a better tragedy than 'Lear,' a better comedy than 'Le Festin de Pierre' or 'Peer Gynt,' a better opera than 'Don Giovanni,' a better music drama than 'The Niblung's Ring'. ... It is the philosophy, the outlook on life, that changes, not the craft. ... Men must rewrite all the old plays in the terms of their own [new] philosophy; & that is why, as Mr Stuart Glennie has pointed out, there can be no new drama without a new philosophy. To which I may add that there can be no Shakespear or Goethe without one either, nor two Shakespears in one philosophic epoch, since, as I have said, the first great comer in that epoch, reaps the whole harvest, & reduces those who come after to the rank of mere gleaners, or, worse than that, fools who go laboriously through all the motions of the reaper & binder in an empty field. What is the use of writing plays or painting frescoes if you have nothing more to say or show than was said or shown by Shakespear, Michael Angelo, & Raphael? ... In due time, when their phil^y wore itself out, a new race of 19th cent. poets & critics, from Byron to Wm Morris, began to ... & to rediscover in the mediaeval art wh. these Renascence masters had supers^ded certain forgotten elements ... germinating again for the new harvest."

Bernard Shaw.

2083 (**f64^v**) The unconscious, automatic, or reasonless Will. "It is necessary to remember the irrationality [non-rationality] of the Will in Schopenhauer. It includes all processes, from attraction and gravitation to motivation, which last is simply 'causality seen from within'. ..." [The irrational will ⟨under⟩ lies action which does] "not proceed from a mental initiative"

Cyclo.

2084 "The Spiritual movement in the 19th Cent. Few thinkers ever made a worse shot (?) than did J. S. Mill when he expressed wonder that there had not been a revival of the Manichaean philosophy. For whatever else may be affirmed of the thought of the century just passed & gone one thing is certain, viz. – that all schools tended to the doctrine of philosophic unity, & that the principle of dualism was thoroughly discarded. Whether we take the Hegelian system, or the idea of 'a double-faced unity' or the so-called Phil^y of the Unconscious, or the idealistic Theism of some eminent thinkers, or the Spencerian philosophy of Evolution, – in all there is a strenuous attempt to reach a universal unity, a substance (in the sense of Spinoza) from which all phenomena take their origin."

Spectator.

2085 "I have invented four systems for playing *trente-et-quarante*. They represent four different temperaments – bold to rashness, bold but wary, moderately cautious, and meanly plodding. In a word, I am a syndicate of four different men. When one is not successful another takes up the game." "But what if the four should fail in turn?" "Oh, when that happens we all go away, and I become a fifth person, who plays the violin."

"The Passing Mood" By Jacques. D. Chron. 14.9.01

2086   (**f65ʳ**) Notes in Philosophy.

Beyond our consciousness of things lies their unknown Reality
                                                              Fiske.

2087   All things known to us are manifestations of the Unknowable
                                                              Spencer.

2088   Transfigured Realism ... does not, with Idealism, say that the
object exists only as perceived ... does not, with crude Realism, ascribe
to the object something wh. belongs to the Subject [i.e. the impressions
it produces.]   ib.

2089   One substance with two sets of properties, two sides, the
physical & the mental – a double-faced unity.   Bain.

2090   The reality ... wh. underlies what we call matter [i.e.
phenomena] I shall call mind-stuff. ... A molecule of inorganic matter
does not possess mind or consciousness, but it possesses a small piece of
mind-stuff. ... When the molecules are so combined ... the
corresponding elements of mind-stuff are so combined as to form ...
consciousness.   Clifford.

2091   Spinoza's God is the one universal substance [sub-stratum,
noumenon] in wh. all isolated qualifications are resolved (**f65ᵛ**) into
unity, to wh. per se, we cannot therefore ascribe understanding or will.
                                                              Christlieb.

2092   Spinoza's God neither thinks nor creates ... the world is his
visible manifestation. ... Extension is visible Thought: Thought is
invisible Extension.
     Bodies, or Modes, like the curling waves of the ocean, are simply the
ever varying shapes of the Substance. The variety we behold in things
is a mere product of our faulty conceptions.   Cyclo.

2093   ... Absence of Free-will in man ... Will & Liberty belong only to
God (Spinoza)   ib.

2094   Spinoza conceives the Universe as one, & manifesting a single
necessary Law in its various modes.   ib.

2095   Man is but a mode of the Divine existence: his mind a spark of the Divine flame, his body a mode of the Infinite Extension.

Lewes on Spinoza

2096   Those German philosophers who hold matter to the 'petrified intelligence'. Spencer.
Cf. Clifford's "mind-stuff" (previous page)

2097   (**f66ʳ**) What is the Divine Idea's relation to the ... Forces in the World? (asks Martineau.) His thought is related to them as, in man, the mental force is related to all below it. (This is disputed by Spencer who says) In man the mental force is related to the forces below it neither as a creator of them, nor as a regulator of them, save in a very limited way: the greater part of the forces present in man, both structural & functional, defy the mental force absolutely.
   [But this may be the very relation; accounting for evil, pains &c, as the rebel forces. T. H.]

2098   To have ideas, & yet not to be conscious of them.   Kant

2099   I designate the united unconscious will & unconscious idea "the Unconscious."   Hartmann.

2100   Leibnitz assumed an <u>unconscious thinking</u> ... which is incessant. He declares unconscious ideas to be the bond wh. unites every being with all the rest of the universe.   ib.

2101   "The clear ideas," says Kant, "are but an infinitely small fraction of these same ⟨[total ideas]⟩, exposed to consciousness. That only a few spots on the great chart of our minds are illuminated may well fill us with amazement."   ib.

2102   (**f66ᵛ**) Whether, & how far, the obscure ideas without any consciousness are to be explained by the penetration of the original intellectual intuition of the primordial Being into the derived human understanding are points on which Kant never expressed himself: Schelling was the first energetically to pursue that line of inquiry

ib.

2103   According to Fichte God's <u>existence</u> is merely <u>knowledge itself</u> ... <u>substantial</u> knowledge only however, to wh., as infinite, <u>consciousness</u> can <u>never</u> be ascribed. Without doubt it is <u>necessary</u> for knowledge to <u>become</u> self conscious, but with equal necessity is it thereby <u>riven</u> into the plural consciousness of manifold individuals & persons.   ib.

2104   A number of the contrarieties & antinomies of earlier creeds & systems are reconciled by the adoption of ... the principle of the Unconscious. ... There is a general tendency of thought towards this single principle. In each succeeding chapter one piece more of the world <u>crystallizes</u>, as it were, around this <u>nucleus,</u> until, expanded to <u>all-unity</u>, it embraces the Cosmos, & at last is suddenly revealed as that wh. has formed the core of all great philosophies, the Substance of Spinoza, the Absolute Ego of Fichte, Schelling's Absolute Subject–Object, the Absolute Idea of Plato & Hegel, Schopenhauer's <u>Will</u>, &c.   ib.

2105   (**f67^r**) <u>The essential identity</u> of the conscious mind with unconscious Nature.   III.303.

2106   purposive: gradual perfection by exercise: ib.
         ⟨[<u>processive</u> would surely be truer. T. H.]⟩

2107   In Aesthetics, Carrière, after Schelling, shows the interposition [interaction?] of consc^s & unconsc^s mental activity to be indispensable for every artistic achievement.   ib.

2108   Undoubtedly since the close of the last (18th) century we have been making approaches to that ideal state where the human race <u>consciously</u> accomplishes its destiny; but, save for a few superior minds, this is still a remote condition of things. ... Results become, by combination, quite other than what each individual had imagined. ...
                                                                II.2. ib.

2109   The English ... historians of civiliz^n, instead of trying to discover the unconsciously impelling ideas of history, fancy they can explain them as a product of conscious reflection.   ib. 6

2110 <u>God as super-conscious</u>. Of this unconscious clairvoyant intellig.^{ce} we have come to perceive that in its infallible purposive ⟨[?processive]⟩ ... activity, ... it infinitely transcends the halting gait of the discursive reflection of consciousness, ever limited to a single point, dependent on sense perception, memory & inspirations of the Unconsc.^{ss} We shall ... designate this intellg.^{ce}, superior to all consc.^{sc}, at once unconsc.^s & <u>super-conscious</u>. [very obscure]   ib. II.247

2111 (**f67ᵛ**) Apart from the special problems wh. arise ... within the sphere of individuation for a limited intelligence, consciousness is <u>no excellence</u>   ib. 248

2112 Neither in Fichte ... nor in Schelling, nor in Hegel ... nor in Schopenhauer, does the Absolute possess a consciousness outside of the individuals pervaded by it.   ib. 261

2113 The unconscious-superconscious reflectionless–intuitive intelligence in the All-One.   ″

2114 Only if the existence of the world was decided by the act of a <u>blind</u> will ... only then is this existence comprehensible: only then is God as such not to be made responsible for the same. ... But why did not God when he became <u>seeing</u>, i.e., his all-wise intelligence entered into being, repair the error? ... Here we are again aided by the inseparability of the idea from the will in the Unconscious ... the dependence of the idea on the will; [and] the whole world-process [i.e. throughout time] only serves the one purpose of emancipating the Idea from the will by means of consciousness.   274

2115 I employ the expression "The Unconscious"; though I sh.^d have more right to the use of the word "God" than Spinoza & many others.   275

2116 "sealed consciousness" /? Times/

2117 (**f68ʳ**) "The old soul has gone away; another soul takes up its abode in the organism [succeeding]: "The absurdity of this way of regarding the subject is immed.^{ly} evident if one remembers that the old & new soul are activities of the same essence of the All-One.   288

2118 The indifference-point between plant and animal.   291

2119   At the beginning of life on the earth. – The Uncon^s apprehended & realized the <u>first</u> possibility of organic life. ... The animation of the germ does not follow, but <u>precedes</u> the <u>origin</u> of the germ.   292

2120   The Uncons^s ... interested only in the universal, not in the single case.   293

2121   In all combin^{ns} of circ^s wh. by their nature occur but seldom, or where for other reasons a mechanism can only be constructed with diff^y, the direct activity of the Uncon^s must display itself ... e.g., the incursions of the Uncon^s in human brains wh. determine & guide the course of history ... in the direct^n intended by the Uncon^s 359

2122   We cannot avoid ascribing to the Uncon^s absolute <u>clairvoyance,</u> wh. answers to the theol^l notion of omniscience   "

2123   If the idea of a better world c^d have lain in the omniscient [clairvoyant] Unc^s, the better one w^d have come to pass.   360

2124   (**f68^v**) The Unconscious ... is the <u>common subject</u> of pleasure & pain, wh. feels them in all the different consciousnesses. ...   366

2125   If happ^{ss} be the end, there can only be such sufferings as are unavoidable to attain on another side, or in a later stage, higher happ^{ss}, or to obviate more extensive sufferings ... otherwise it [God] w^d be only driving the teeth into one's own [his own] flesh   366

2126   Sh^d non-existence be [best, because pain altogether preponderates] ... the exist^{ce} of the world owes its origin to an irrational [non-rational] act, consummated <u>without</u> reason because Reason had no part in it   367

2127   The Uncon^s has, as Aristotle says, no memory: therefore it can learn nothing from its experience in the world   III.89

2128   [The Practical <u>philosophy</u> of the whole is] the complete devotion of the personality to the world-process for the sake of its goal, the general world-redemption. Otherwise expressed: To make the ends of the Uncon^s ends of our own Consciousness.

2129 <u>The goal</u>. – The world redemption from the misery of volition [i.e. life], a condition being that the yearning after annihilation attains resistless authority as a practical motive.   137 &c

(**f69^r**) [It appears that the author does not commit himself absolutely to this conclusion; asserting that, sh^d any believe in a future happiness of the world by evolution &c (wh. he has called the 3^d stage of illusion) the principles remain just as valid for those thinkers, since the final goal of the world-development may be conceived positively or negatively. The concession strikes me as weakening /?to/ his philosophy.]

2130 <u>Resumé</u>:–
<u>Will & Idea</u> – are principles, i.e. original elements ... every attempt to resolve them into simpler elements appears hopeless.   143

2131 Feeling or sensation & consciousness ... phenomenal conseq^{ces} of these principles.   "

2132 Affinity of ourselves with other products of Nature: transfer therefore the anthropological principia to the rest of Nature ... however, at the stages more removed from man ... more & more strip off Consciousness. ... But the unconscious spirit also dwells in him wh. he long admired in silence in ... less developed consciousnesses. ... Thus ... Unconscious Will & Unconscious Idea coalesced to form the one universal spiritual world-essence.

2133 It is the Will that accords its <u>That</u> ["let <u>something</u> be"] to the world: the Idea can only determine the <u>What</u>.

2134 ... It follows ... that Volition ... cannot be eternal. ...   164

2135 (**f69^v**) <u>Empty Volition</u> ... struggles after its realization ... cannot attain it without the accession of an external circ^{ce} . ... It remains in an unceasing <u>preparedness to spring</u>. ... The blind roving Will seizes the Idea ... drags it into the Vortex ... being is engendered

167–170

2136 The world-process may often have played the same tune before.

172

2137 The notion of the Good, in the ethical sense, must not be
referred to the All-One. ... 175

2138 The "What" of the world is at every moment determined by
logical neccess!y 185

2139 <u>The Absolute Spirit</u> ... if one may call anything original it must
be this unity of Will & Perception, of Power & Wisdom, as we have
hitherto called it, the Unconscious ... this one Substance. ... Thus ... the
apex of our pyramid coincides with the One S. of Spinoza. 196

2140 If nothing at all were, no World ... ⟨no Substance ...⟩ there w^d
be nothing wonderful – it w^d be eminently natural ... but that there is
... an ultimate on wh. everything depends is so unfathomably
wonderful, so absolutely alogical & senseless ... that poor little man ...
ceases to wonder at the details of the world. ... It is, for this metaphy!
problem ... absolutely indifferent what we regard as ultimate

196

2141 (**f70^r**) FOR ENGLAND'S SAKE

> Give us war, O Lord,
>   For England's sake,
> War righteous and true,
>   Our hearts to shake.
> We are drinking to the brim
> What will poison heart and limb,
> And our eyes are growing dim.
>   For England's sake!
>
> Give us war, O Lord,
>   For England's sake,
> War righteous and true,
> Such as our fathers knew,
>   Our hearts to shake.
> Ere the tricks and arts of peace
> Make our manliness to cease,
> While our world-wide foes increase.
>   For England's sake!

Give us war, O Lord,
  For England's sake,
War righteous and true
  Our hearts to shake.
Faith and loyalty grow cold,
Faction's tongue is waxing bold;
More and more we stake on gold.
  For England's sake!

Give us war, O Lord,
  For England's sake,
War righteous and true,
Such as our fathers knew,
By which their greatness grew,
  Our hearts to shake,
That amid the stress and strain,
And the discipline of pain,
We grow Englishmen again,
  For England's sake!

                              Paul Cushing.
        Old "National Observer." edited by W. E. Henley

2142 "But I'm certain you misunderstood him. He never would have called us a lazy people." (The English)
  "Not in matters of business: in matters of thought."

                                    George Meredith

2143 When people do not respect us we are sharply offended; yet deep down in his private heart no man much respects himself.

                                    Mark Twain

2144 Often the surest way to convey misinformation is to tell the strict truth.   *Mark Twain*

2145   these fine descriptive lines of Penelope to Ulysses:–

> When the winds
> Swoop to the waves and lift them by the hair,
> And the long storm-roar gathers, on my knees
> I pray for thee.

.   .   .   .

> My very heart has grown a timid mouse,
> Peeping out, fearful, when the house is still.
> Breathless I listen thro' the breathless dark,
> And hear the cock counting the leaden hours,
> And, in the pauses of his cry, the deep
> Swings on the flat sand with a hollow clang;
> And, pale and burning-eyed, I fall asleep
> When, with wild hair, across the wrinkled wave
> Stares the sick Dawn that brings thee not to me. ‖

When we read passages like this, or breathe delightedly at meeting such an image as –

> When the cool aspen-fingers of the rain
> Feel for the eyelids of the earth in spring,

it is impossible not to regret that Mr. Buchanan did not retain this closeness of imagination and expression together with the ampler thought of his mature work. ~~But we~~
   Daily Chron: in a review of A. S. Walker's "Robert Buchanan".

2146   Nothing is so great as it seems beforehand.   *George Eliot*

2147   If you trust a man, let him be a bachelor – let him be a bachelor.
                                                                George Eliot

2148   It has been a prevalent notion in the minds of well-disposed persons, that if they acted according to their own conscience, they must, therefore, be doing right. ... "I must act according to the dictates of my own conscience." By no means, my conscientious friend, unless you are quite sure that yours is not the conscience of an ass.
                                                                John Ruskin

2149   You must never be as mad as to have doubts of yourself.

Henrik Ibsen

2150   (**f70ᵛ**) "It is, concluded this excellent poet & true artist [M. Giraud] because we do not wish Beauty to be subordinated to a propagandist idea that we have set forward Art for Art. There can be Beauty in all conceptions – all subjects are good. There can be beautiful scientific works, catholic works, pagan works. … It is the Beauty which must predominate; make what you will, but make before all a work of art."   Mercure de France

2151   Literary & Dramatic Art. "An artist aims at the spirit of things. He deals in symbols & diagrams."

"Language, no less than music, is a way of hearing, & the presentment of character [in fiction, drama &c] a way of seeing."

J. Oliver Hobbes –

2152   "The greatest thing a human soul ever does in this world is to see something, & tell what it saw in a plain way. … To see clearly is poetry, prophecy, & religion all in one."   Ruskin. M. P. III.278

2153   Assonance
         & Rhyme   }   "The primitive lyrist is almost always exact in the repetition of his vowel. Where he is careless is in the accompanying consonants. … 'In all early European poetry, from The Song of Roland to the popular ballads, the ear was satisfied (**f71ʳ**) with assonance, that is, the harmony of the vowel sounds: hat is ass! to tag'" &c.

(Quoted by Brander Matthews from a "British Critic" in the N. Y. Bookman. July. 1901)

2154   Be brief as the essential will allow. – "Anybody can see how much more entertaining an article is if the writer confines himself to the point of interest which tempted him at first to write it. … Also a short story. … There is, or shᵈ be, some particular appeal to the reader's sensibility wh. the writer has in view when he attempts a short story; or, if he is not thinking of the reader (better if he is not) there is something wh. has especially moved himself. … It is just that which, as an artist, he has to convey. … There is a good deal that he may think

essential which is not so. We make no plea for bareness, but ... a hint is
better than elaboration."

[Excellent advice. Harpers Mag. "Ed.'s study"]

2155   Austin Dobson in "The May Book":–

In Angel Court the sunless air
    Grows faint & sick; to left & right
    The cowering houses shrink from sight,
Huddling & hopeless, eyeless, bare.

Misnamed, you say. For surely rare
    Must be the angel-shapes that light
        In Angel Court!

Nay: the Eternities are there.
    Death by the doorway stands to smite;
    Life in its garrets leaps to light:
And Love has climbed that crumbling stair
        In Angel Court!

2156   (**f71ᵛ**) Poetic symbolism & modern Music
"The theory that music is the perfect art, the ideal to which all other
arts aspire, because of its complete, irreducible fusion of the form & the
idea, is one that has been made familiar to all of us through Pater's
essay on "The School of Giorgione". ...

"... When we come to words ... we are faced by the fact that, unlike
sheer colour & sheer sound, words have an intellectual as well as an
emotional significance. They are born from, & cling to, both the inner
& outer lives of men. Hence poetical work like the drama, that deals
with life in its concrete aspects, cannot possibly attain such perfection
of achievement, such intimate blending of form & idea, as the poem of
pure inward emotion."

[A quotation from Mallarmé follows, as given in Symons's
"Symbolist Movement"]

"The symbolist poet feels, with Wagner, that it is only the essence of things that really matters; that the roundabout way in wh. the old dramatic poet, for example, found a means of penetrating us with an emotion, must be given up in favour of a more direct communication. Wagner held that music was the essential spirit of drama; poetry, therefore, had to be made more in the mould of music. According to the symbolist, (**f72ʳ**) the emotionalized vision is the essence of what we call our knowledge of external things; therefore this vision itself must be translated, at first hand, into words that will, in their very impact upon the emotion, spontaneously generate the idea. ...

"Adopting the aesthetics of Wagner, we might say that Tschaikowsky's symphonic poem "Romeo & Juliet" is more perfect than Shak.'s play, inasmuch as it contains all the broad essential emotions of the drama, intensified & made more beautiful, & at the same time set free from the mass of "waste matter" inevitable in the verbal exposition. But the impᵗ point is that neither Tsch.'s work nor a hundred others can ever displace that of Sh. for the reason that the pure emotion of music cannot satisfy all the elements of our nature. This is precisely why Wagner's theory of a fusion of all the arts in one is utterly vain. ... The defect of such theories is that they fix upon one of the points in which music greatly surpasses speech, & lose sight of the various ways in which poetry gives us a satisfaction wholly impossible to music ... &c" Ernest Newman – Speaker 15.6.01

[Suggestive – though neither the writer nor those he criticizes seem to have really got to the root of the matter.]

2157 (**f72ᵛ**) "German Literature is at last beginning to partake in that universal heightening of G. natˡ life of wh. the foundⁿ of the new Empire 30 yrs. ago was the first far-shining signal. ... Once more is litʳᵉ coming to be something more than a mere pastime or recreation; once more are writers coming forward who feel that they have a mission to fulfil, whose highest desire it is to be the interpreters of the longings & aspirations of the people; once more are novels & dramas being produced wh. arouse popular passion & enthusiasm, because they represent, in palpˡᵉ & living forms, ⟨the⟩ momentous conflicts & problems of the day."

Hist. of Germⁿ Litʳᵉ by Kuno Francke. (Bell)

2158   Ibsen. "He is obviously angry with the world at large & the ways of men, & unhesitatingly insults & belabours those whose best interests he has at heart. Darwin desired to popularize a theory which the vanity of humanity made very unwelcome, but he approached the world in so agreeable a spirit that converts to his creed were abundant. Ibsen, whose task has been infinitely more difficult in that it is spiritual instead of material, has never used the slightest effort to conciliate or persuade. Many questions are discussed in his plays which the world thinks are better dealt with in camera: he does not; therefore on to the stage they go. He ruthlessly lays bare the secrets of the (**f73ʳ**) human heart, & throws in the face of mankind the fact that they are in sad need of reforming – & then awaits popularity."

Egan Mew in Literature. Aug. 17.1901.

2159   Ibsen (cont.ᵈ) The ordinary acceptance of current ideals versus the vigilant openmindness of Ibsen. Old style, complacency with things as they are. ... Substitute for such questions as 'Have you kept the commandments?' &c. – e.g. a technical examination – "one in wh. there is no more & no less respect for chastity than for incontinence, for subordination than for rebellion, for legality than for illegality, for piety than for blasphemy, in short for the standard virtues than for the stand.ᵈ vices" ... [namely,] "what Ibsen insists on – that there is no golden rule – that conduct must justify itself by its effect upon happiness, & not by its conformity to any rule or ideal – And since happiness consists in the fulfilment of the Will, which is constantly growing, & cannot be fulfilled to-day under the conditions which secured its fulfilment yesterday, he claims afresh the old Protestant right of private judgment in questions of conduct as against all institutions, the so-called Protestant churches themselves included."

(G. Bernard Shaw. quoted in same article.)

This is excellently put. But neither writer dwells sufficiently on the fact that Ibsen's defect is a lack of /?~~insufficient sense~~/ ⟨the essentiality⟩ of beauty to art.   T. H.

2160   (**f73ᵛ**) "Realism." – "The modern English realist has confused the issues of his business; he thinks that if he is objectively 'actual,' laboriously detailed in outside observation, a photographer of the slum, he has exhausted the possibilities of his method. But the truer realism is subjective. It deals with emotions, with sensations half-realized &

misinterpreted; it shows the mind of a man moving to a spiritual crisis, not the external aspects ~~of~~ only of his struggle tow^{ds} experience."

D. Chron.

2161   The Lusiads of Camoens. (Aubertin's: Kegan Paul, 2v.)
"The nation itself is the hero of Camoens' Epic. ... The Lusaids is, in fact, the one representative maritime Epic of the world; though through the lustrous waters of the tropics, through the tempests of the Cape, we float on with even a coquettish ease, as in company with a Mistress of the Sea."   New Quarterly M. (July 1878.)

———————————#———————————

2162   "Alas, of a truth we should write against no man in this world. Each one is sick enough in this great infirmary."   Heine.

———————————#———————————

2163   Dorchester "Telegram" Nov. 1901
AN INSTRUCTIVE CRITICISM OF GEORGE ELIOT. The Rev. J. McClune Uffen addressed the fortnightly students' class in connection with the local course of University Extension lectures on Friday night. The subject of the address was "George Eliot." The speaker, in the course of his address, pointed out that literature is the art of putting thought and emotion into apt, effective, and permanent speech. Writing which is permanent is literature. It is permanent because it has seized upon and given in language effective shape and colour to what is indestructible in human life and character. The personalities of literature are not the personalities of an age, local and transitory, but personalities such as ever have been and ever will be; and what is set down as experience, is not merely what has happened, but what still happens.

2164   "I love my little gowns
    I love my little shoes
All standing still below them,
    Set quietly by twos

    "All day I wear them, careless,
      But when I put them by,

They look so dear & different,
And yet I don't know why."

. . . .

(Josephine P. Peabody, <u>Harpers</u>. Dec. 1901.)

2165   (**f74ʳ**) And what is this smile of the world, to win which we are bidden to sacrifice our moral manhood; this frown of the world, whose terrors are more awful than the withering up of truth and the slow going out of the light within the souls of us? Consider the triviality of life and conversation and purpose in the bulk of those whose approval is held out for our prize and the mark of our high calling. ... In the light of these things a man should surely dare to live his small span of life with little heed of the common speech upon him, or his life, only caring that his days be full of reality, and his conversation of truth-speaking and wholeness.   *John Morley*

2166   To the mass of people nothing is so costly as thought. The fact that, taking the world over, ninety-nine people out of a hundred accept the creed to which they were born, exemplifies their mental attitude towards things at large. Nearly all of them pursue mechanically the routine to which they have been accustomed, and are not only blind to its defects, but will not recognize them as defects when they are pointed out. And the reluctance to think, which they show everywhere else, is shown in their dealings with children.   *Herbert Spencer*

2167   The Republican form of government is the highest form of government; but because of this it requires the highest type of human nature – a type nowhere at present existing.   *Herbert Spencer*

2168   If there is an angel who records the sorrows of men as well as their sins, he knows how many and deep are the sorrows that spring from false ideas for which no man is culpable.   *George Eliot*

2169   Those who no longer place their highest faith in powers above and beyond men, are for that very reason more deeply interested than others in cherishing the integrity and worthiness of man himself.
                                                                        John Morley

2170 The higher the wisdom the more incomprehensive does it become by ignorance. It is a manifest fact, that the popular man or writer is always one who is but little in advance of the mass, and consequently, understandable by them; never the man who is far in advance of them and out of their sight. Appreciation of another implies some community of thought. *Herbert Spencer*

2171 Of the ends to be kept in view by the legislator, all are unimportant compared with character-making, and yet character-making is an end wholly unrecognized. *Herbert Spencer*

2172 If you have no faith in yourself you're on the downward path indeed. *Henrik Ibsen*

2173 Religion, whatever destinies may be in store for it, is at least for the present hardly any longer an organic power. It is not that supreme, penetrating, controlling, decisive part of a man's life, which it has been, and will be again. *John Morley*

⌣ · · ⌣

2174 Though perhaps one in ten of those who think is conscious that his judgment is being warped by prejudice, yet even in him, the warp is not adequately allowed for. *Herbert Spencer*

2175 Whoever hesitates to utter that which he thinks the highest truth, lest it should be too much in advance of the time, may reassure himself by looking at his acts from an unpersonal point of view. *Herbert Spencer*

2176 Exceptional men are above precedent. *Henrik Ibsen*

2177 (**f74ᵛ**) If, that the inferior may have benefits which they have not earned, there are taken from the superior benefits which they have earned, it is manifest that when this process is carried to the extent of equalising the positions of the two, there ceases to be any motive to be superior. *Herbert Spencer*

2178 You will find, if you think deeply of it, that the chief of all the curses of this unhappy age is the universal gabble of its fools, and the

flocks that follow them, rendering the quiet voices of the wise men of all
past time inaudible.   *John Ruskin*

2179   Every one who looks back and compares his early impressions
respecting states of things in his own society with impressions he now
has, will see how erroneous were the beliefs once so decided, and how
probable it is that even his revised beliefs are but partially true.
                                                            Herbert Spencer

2180   The Present; its characteristics. – "To scepticism & ...
iconoclasm ... has succeeded indifference – indifference to everything
except material comfort. ... Indifference is compatible with excellent
'conduct' in M. Arnold's sense. ... There is a quietness & even dignity
about it. ... We are inclined to think that this cent^y will end by a great
resuscitation of Conviction – a definite belief in & definite following of
some one ideal."   S. R. (end of the year.)

———————— # ————————

2181   Poetry. – "Primarily poetry is a purely subjective thing – the
expression of ~~that~~ emotion for the sake of the relief or heightening of the
emotion which the expression gives. The fact that the expression of the
emotion becomes at the same time the means of transmitting it to the
consciousness of others is almost accidental. ...

What is essential in poetry is, firstly, that it should be charged with
emotion, &, secondly, that the moods of this emotion should have
aesthetic or ethical value. They may be exceptional & remote, or they
may be common & broadly human."   Academy. 4.1.02

2182   (**f75^r**) 'Lowell says "When a man aims at originality he
acknowledges himself unoriginal. ..." You will find it enough to let your
work reflect yourself ... have a personal & individual character.'
                        C. H. Townsend (Arch^b) Lecture to A. Ass^n

2183   Literary Drama. – "True dramatic poetry is an integral part of
the dramatic framework, which indeed, at its best, it makes. The poetic
drama ... must hold us, as a play of Ibsen's holds us, by the sheer
interest of its repres^n of life. ... The verse must speak as straight as
prose, but with a more beautiful voice. It must avoid rhetoric, as
scrupulously as Ibsen avoids rhetoric."   Academy

2184   "Man is bathed in an ocean of sensations … these form all that he can know of the world."   De Fleury. quot by <u>Academy</u>.

2185   Primitive folk have in all ages believed in the existence of a world near our own, & filled with beings exercising control over it … [who are seen only by] a few individuals … with abnormal faculties.
<u>Academy</u>.

2186   "It is not the painter's business to make us a likeness of a tree or a rock; it is his business to communicate to us an emotion – an ecstasy, if you please – & that he may do so he uses a tree or a rock as a symbol, a word in his language of colour & form."
"Hieroglyphics" – by A. Machen.

2187   (**f75ᵛ**) <u>Poets</u>. "The better kind of these poet men did not wish to please the vague inferior tribes who might read them, but to deliver themselves of the divine warmth that thronged (?) in their bosom: & if all the readers were dead, still they would have written; & for God to read they wrote."   ib.

2188   "The lyrics that survive were mostly written for a tune."
19.4.02. F. M. Hueffer in <u>Acadʸ</u>

2189   "M. Ferdinand Khnopff's mystical art. A haggard woman, not unbeautiful, gazes at a mask attached to a slender blue column. Below … is a grey house … representing presumably the dwelling … in which the Lady with the Secret sits."   Academy.

2190   <u>Maeterlinck on Nature, Luck, & Justice</u> –
He finds "luck" in the faculties of that obscure unconscious or subconscious personality, or self, whose manifestations psychology is but dimly beginning to observe. The "lucky" are those whose "unconsciousness" is on the alert for catastrophes, while the "unconsciousness" of the "unlucky" lets them go into peril. "They have the right to ask destiny why it has withheld from them the [power of] watchful guard wh. warns their brethren. But … they have no further

cause of complaint. ... Things from without wish them no evil; the
mischief (**f76ʳ**) comes from themselves. ...

"We are poor weak useless creatures, consecrated to death, &
"playthings of the vast & indifferent forces that surround us. We
"appear for an instant in limitless space, our one appreciable mission
"the propagation of a species that itself has no appreciable mission in
"the scheme of a universe whose extent & duration baffle the most
"daring, most powerful, brain. This is a truth; it is one of those
"profound but sterile truths which the poet may salute as he passes on
"his way; but it is a truth in the neighbourhood of which the man with
"the thousand duties, who lives in the poet, will do well not to abide too
"long."

For to us, the most fruitful truths are those that are within; the truths
wh. light the soul through the region, narrow pps. but sufficient, wh. is
its own; the truths wh. make for honest living & loyal feeling within the
permitted space through which we know that living & feeling endure. ...

It is the object of M. Mᶜᵏ'ˢ essay to vindicate the conception & the
claims of justice against the prevalent sophism, reduced to logical form
by Nietzsche, that we are the chⁿ of Nature, & bound therefore to
model our conduct on hers, ⟨ – [that]⟩ Nature admittedly has no care
for justice, for she is indifferent to all things save the multiplⁿ &
intensificⁿ of life. ... The counter argument is briefly this, that the real
ends & aims of Nature are a profound mystery:
(**f76ᵛ**) "Nature does not appear to be just from our point of view; but we
"have absolutely no means of judging whether she be not just from her
"own. The fact that she pays no heed to the morality of our own actions
"does not warrant the inference that she has no morality, or that ours is
"the only one there can be."

2191   Shame of being one's self.
"A man will talk brilliantly, fancifully ∴ but that same man with a
pen in his hand will, through innate fear of the printed word, & of the
self revelation that it forebodes, make his prose as colourless as a
leading article" –   Academy.

2192 <u>Poetry</u> – [ap<u>ro</u>pos of Matthew Arnold] "... whether he was primarily a poet or a prosateur. ... Whether his primary impulse of expression was to seize upon the innate suggestive power of words, or whether his primary impulse was to rely upon the logical power of the sentence. ...

... Those magical effects which poets of the rarer kind can achieve by seizing that mysterious suggestive power of words which is far beyond all mere statement. ..."   T. Watts Dunton.

2193   "I, singularly moved
          To love the lovely that are not beloved. ..."

                                                            C. Patmore.

2194 (**f77ʳ**) <u>Nietzsche</u> <u>on Tragedy</u>. – (translated by the "Mercure de France" as "L'Origine de la Tragédie, ou, Hellénisme et Pessimisme.") "... We are apt to look on the Chorus in G^k plays as almost a negligible part of the structure; as, in fact, hardly more than the comments of that 'ideal spectator' whom Schlegel called up. ... We know, however, that the chorus was the original nucleus of the play, that the action on which it seems only to comment is no more than a development of the chorus. ... ~~The chorus is the 'lyric cry' the vital ecstasy; the drama is the projection into vision, into a picture, of the exterior, temporary world of forms. "We now see that the stage & the action are conceived only as visions~~. Here is the problem to which N. endeav^{rs} to find an answer. He finds it, unlike the ~~pr~~ learned persons who study Gk. texts, among the roots of things, in the very making of the universe. Art arises, he tells us, from the conflict of the two creative spirits, symbolized by the Gks. in the two gods Apollo & Dionysus; & he names the one the Apollonian spirit, wh. we see in plastic art, & the other the Dionysiac spirit, wh. we see in music. A. is the god of dreams, D. the god of intoxic^n; the one represents for us the world of appearances, the other is, as it were, the voice of things in themselves. The Chorus, then, wh. arose out of the (**f77ᵛ**) hymns of Dionysus, is the 'lyric cry,' the vital ecstasy; the drama is the projection into vision, into a picture, of the exterior, temporary world of forms. 'We now see that the stage & the action are conceived only as vision; that the sole reality is precisely the chorus, wh. itself produces the vision, & expresses it by the aid of the

whole symbolism of dance, sound, & word.' In the admirable phrase of
Schiller, the chorus is 'a living rampart against reality,' against that
false reality of daily life wh. is a mere drapery of civilization, & has
nothing to do with the primitive reality of nature. ...

"There are many pages ... in wh. Pater has dealt with some of the
Gk. problems very much in the spirit of Nietzsche; with that problem,
for instance, of the 'blitheness & serenity' of the Gk. spirit, & of the gulf
of horror over wh. it seems to rest, suspended as on the wings of the
condor. P. has shown, as N. shows in greater detail & with a more
rigorous logic, that this 'serenity' was but an accepted illusion, & all
Olympus itself but 'intermediary,' an escape, through the aesthetics of
religion, from the trouble at the heart of things; art, with its tragic
illusions of life, being another form of escape. To N. the world &
existence justify themselves only as an aesthetic phenomenon, the work
of a god wholly the artist: '& in this sense the object of the tragic myth
is precisely to convince us that even the horrible & the monstrous are
no more than an aesthetic game, played with itself by the Will in the
eternal (**f78ʳ**) plenitude of its joy'. 'The Will' in Schopenhauer's 'Will,'
the vital principle."   A. Symons.

———————————//———————————

2195   Mr. Kidd's closing paragraph sums up the tendencies of current
development thus:
    The changes which the doctrine of evolution is thus beginning to
effect in its applications to sociological theory are to all appearance
only in their initial stages. In psychology and ethics they can hardly fail
to be as important as they already promise to be in the domain of
political philosophy. The survival in social and political philosophy of
the Ptolemaic standpoint, as represented in the tendency to conceive
the principles of the evolutionary process in society as centred in the
ascendant interests in the struggle for existence of those comprised
within the consciousness of the political State, has still its correlative in
psychology and ethics. For instance, it has been hitherto impossible to
fit into any theory of empirical psychology.certain qualities which Kant
found in the human mind. But the basis in the evolutionary process of
many of the qualities with which Kant was concerned, and which could
not be accounted for in relation to experience, just as they could not be
accounted for by Mr. Wallace in relation to current environment, is

now evident. For when the evolutionary process is considered in the wider and more organic relations that have here been discussed, it is clear that the peoples who represent the advanced sections of the race at the present day do so in virtue of qualities in the minds of those who preceded them which had no relation to current environment. The peoples amongst them who are destined to inherit the future will similarly do so in virtue of qualities which have no utilitarian relationship to existing environment. In the statement of the principles of the human mind the tendency hitherto in all empirical systems has necessarily been to endeavour to construct a theory of human society and of human progress from an introspective examination of the interests and emotions of the individual mind. But this tendency can hardly fail to be reversed with the continued application of the doctrine of evolution to society. It is the principles of the evolutionary process in society, considered in its more organic aspects, that must now be considered to be the controlling factor; and it is therefore to be expected that it will be from this wider standpoint that the study of the content of the individual mind itself will in future be approached.

2196   Mr. Swinburne's article on Victor Hugo is Swinburnian in its contagious enthusiasm, its warmth and glow, and its light and shade. To Mr. Swinburne Hugo is 'the greatest man born since the death of Shakespeare,' and 'Les Misérables' the greatest epic and dramatic work of fiction ever created or conceived. This is truly Swinburnian appreciation. The final estimate is no less exalting.

> ... The author (Victor Hugo) was one of the very greatest among poets and among men; unsurpassed in sublimity of spirit, in spontaneity of utterance, in variety of power, and in perfection of workmanship; infinite and profound beyond all reach of praise at once in thought and in sympathy, in perception and in passion; master of all the simplest as of all the subtlest melodies or symphonies of song that ever found expression in a Border ballad or a Pythian ode.

from Ency. Britannica.

2197   THE MEANING OF MIND.   { cf. Hartmann,
                                      Schopenhauer, &c

Another factor in the matter has been the difficulty of arriving at a
definite understanding as to the meaning of the word "mind" in its
relation to the functions of the body. This difficulty was made vividly
apparent in 1888, when the Aristotelian Society held a meeting to
discuss the question "Whether mind is synonymous with
consciousness," and a decision was arrived at that it was not. Ribot, in
his book on "Heredity," said, "Mind has two parallel modes of activity,
the one conscious, the other unconscious"; while Dr. Henry Maudesley
declared that "It cannot be too distinctly borne in mind that
consciousness is not co-extensive with mind, that it is not mind, but an
incident accompaniment of mind." Mind, indeed, as Dr. Schofield
points out, "may be conscious, sub-conscious, or unconscious," and it
is the sub-conscious or unconscious mind which is the great factor to be
used in the curing of disease, as it is the great factor which produces
disease.   D. Mail   Sept 17. 1902

2198   Wordsworth's poetry. "The consecration of the Commonplace."

———————————————//———————————————

2199   The imaginative faculty "seizes outward things from within".
                                                                Ruskin.

2200   (f78ᵛ) A NEO-ELIZABETHAN.
"The Princess of Hanover." By Margaret L. Woods. (London:
Duckworth and Co. 5s. net.)
    "The Princess of Hanover" is a five-act tragedy on the familiar theme
of Köningsmarck and the hapless Sophia Dorothea. It follows the
Elizabethan form in its looseness of construction, its frequent changes
of scene, and, we must add, in its rhetorical prolixity. How long will
men and women of talent go on reproducing in cold blood a form
begotten and justified by the conditions of·the Elizabethan theatre, but
meaningless for the modern world? It is not by mock-Elizabethanism,
but by its negation, that Mr. Stephen Phillips and Mr. W. B. Yeats
have, of recent years, to some extent revitalisèd poetic drama. Time
alone can show whether this flickering revival is destined to grow into a
great flame; but the experience of two centuries has proved the

hopelessness of getting any real light or heat out of the Elizabethan embers.

In her former play, "Wild Justice," Mrs. Woods was much more nearly on the right track than in this one. There, though the period was modern, she was able to plunge her whole subject in that atmosphere of poetry which is the primary essential of modern poetic drama. The remote and solitary household which she depicted seemed entirely aloof from the commonplaces of life. She was able to keep her style on one level. It seemed almost natural and probable that the intense soul-life of these secluded and hapless creatures should express itself in verse. The convention once accepted, at any rate, there was nothing to jar upon it and break it up. In "The Princess of Hanover," though the period is more remote, the environment is absolutely commonplace and prosaic. The idea of the Elector Ernest Augustus, his wife, his mistress, his son, our George I., and the whole powdered and periwigged Court at Herrenhausen expressing themselves in passionate blank verse is sufficiently inacceptable to the imagination. But when, with an effort, we have admitted the convention, we are always being shaken out of it. There is no consistency, no continuity of style. Take, for instance, the following three speeches, occurring in the course of one scene, not three pages long, between the Duchess of Zell and her daughter, the Princess Sophia:–

Duchess: You exaggerate, my dear, for what in sum
  Makes your despair? Your husband is unfaithful.
  Why, so are thousands, millions of common men,
  Princes invariably. ...

Then, eight lines further on:–

Duchess: Compelled, I brought thee to an abhorred bridal,
  Yielding thy cherished youth to a house of hate.

Then, on the next page:–

Princess: Happiness –
  Hush! What a sinister word! If any utter it
  At festivals it falls as hollowly
  As when a stone drops echoing down a well,
  Hinting of deep, deep darkness and drowned things

Far underneath, and phantoms that may rise,
When midnight holds the house, shrouded and pale
And deadly cold, to haunt with long, long sighs
And endless iteration of old grief
The hushed rooms of the heart.

The first of these three speeches might quite well come from
Sheridan Knowles, the second from Aeschylus, the third from Webster
or Ford. Thus, throughout the play, we are perpetually being jolted
from plane to plane of convention. Mrs. Woods has not succeeded in
creating a poetic atmosphere and keeping us in it. She has made some
attempt to do so, by giving Köningsmarck a musical "secretary" and
letting him wander through the play singing snatches of a symbolic
ballad. But this equivalent for the "slow music" of the melodramatic
stage is scarcely a happy expedient.

It is idle to criticise the construction of a drama which is not intended
for the stage. Dramatic construction means nothing else than the telling
of a story in such a way as to make it clear, interesting and effective in
the theatre; and when that purpose is renounced in advance, the laws
which govern construction cease to apply. There are two or three really
dramatic scenes in "The Princess of Hanover"; and there is one passage
– the murder of Königsmarck and the subsequent entrance of Sophia
Dorothea and her lady-in-waiting – which contains all the elements of
tragedy, and might, with a little remodelling, be made effective in
action. Several of the characters, too – and notably the heroine – are
well drawn. Fine passages abound in the dialogue; for Mrs. Woods is a
true poet. The third of the speeches quoted above is as admirably
poetic as it is questionably dramatic. How fine, with its Shakespearean
echo, is the third of these lines:–

Your moods are more inconstant
Than the chameleon's colour, more deceiving
Than April's sun, the sharp wind's playfellow.

It would be difficult to express a sense ·of fatal predestination more
beautifully than in the following lines:–

I think I never shall return. The needle
Is drawn to the Pole, and I am drawn as surely
To some unvisited place my star looked down on
When I was born, saying "Thou shalt have his blood."

What a pity that a lady who can write so admirably should be betrayed by a misapplied theory of prosody into strewing every page of her work with metrical briars and brambles that render the reader's progress not only slow, but often really painful! We read with some misgiving Mrs. Woods's prefatory "Remarks on English Verse"; and our forebodings were only too amply justified. No amount of argument, no array of precedent, can make beautiful or even tolerable blank verse of such lines as these:—

> Will come stealthily along the corridor ...
> Hurry those long kisses, for I, I too ...
> I, Philip of Königsmarck, here dying ...
> Our sunlit past, and in my long dreams ...

It is sad to see Mrs. Woods casting in her lot with the school of metrists who would make rules of certain very rare exceptions in the blank verse of our early masters, and think they are following Milton's example when they use three times in a page abnormalities which he, perhaps, did not admit three times in an epic.   D. Chron. Oct 11.02

2201   (**f79ʳ**) The author of "The Loom of Years" is a symbolist. In other words, Mr. Alfred Noyes belongs to that school of singers which regards natural phenomena as the outward expression of a "divine idea," and holds that the mission of all true art is to interpret to men the soul, the spirit, the intelligence which resides as a unifying and co-ordinating principle within the visible world. Let Mr. Noyes be his own witness:

> Help me to seek that unknown land,
>   Help me to see the shrine,
> Help me to feel the hidden hand
>   That ever holdeth mine.

> The Temple opens wide; none sees
>   The love, the dream, the light;
> Oh blind and finite, are not these
>   Blinding and infinite?

> Help me to seek: I would not find,
>   For when I find I know
> I shall have clasped the hollow wind
>   And built a house of snow.

While the symbolistic movement has given a fresh impulse to poetic thought, it has also been a prolific cause of abstractions and mannerisms. Divested of its technical meaning, symbolism has always been a great, though unconscious, force in literature. "What distinguishes the symbolism of our day," says one of its foremost apostles, Mr. Arthur Symons, "from the symbolism of the past is that it has become conscious of itself." There lies its danger. Poetry must ever remain a matter of temperament rather than theory. If Shakespeare and Goethe had started with the set purpose of revealing the Infinite, we should never have had either Hamlet or Faust. It would be sheer ingratitude to deny that modern symbolism has given us some fine things. Too often, however, in spite of Carlyle's warning, it serves "to furnish a languid mind with fantastic shows and indolent emotions." In its search for the unseen it has a fatal tendency to utter hazy nothings in a very portentous fashion. Instead of revealing the divine in the Universe, it gives us too many glimpses of the neurotic and the fantastic in man. Mr. Alfred Noyes has many graces of style; but he has dropped the substance for the shadow. These slight poems may afford a passing gratification, but they leave no enduring impression. We are sorry that it should be so. Some of these exotic verses, "The Song of Re-Birth," "In the Heart of the Woods," "Echo and Narcissus," and others, have a beauty which deserves a better fate than to bloom for a brief day in the marketplace or the opera-stall, but one must feel, after all, that the sentiment is factitious and the emotion foreign to the common experience of mankind. The following stanzas from "The Song of Re-Birth" will convey an adequate idea of these verses in matter and style:

> In the light of the silent stars that shine on the struggling sea,
> In the weary cry of the wind and the whisper of flower and tree,
> Under the breath of laughter, deep in the tide of tears,
> I hear the Loom of the Weaver that weaves the Web of Years.
>
> The leaves of the winter wither and sink in the forest mould
> To colour the flowers of April with purple and white and gold,
> Light and scent and music die and are born again
> In the sigh of a weary woman that wakes in a world of pain.
>
> One with the flower of a day, one with the withered moon,
> One with the granite mountains that melt into the noon,

One with the dream that triumphs beyond the light of the
  spheres,
We come from the Loom of the Weaver that weaves the Web of
  Years.

R. A. G.   Daily News. 27.11.02.

————————————//————————————

2202   The following, from Pendennis, is a good example of the sort of
criticism wh. prevents born poets from discovering themselves:–

"You have got the sacred flame," said Warrington to his young
friend, "a little of the real poetical fire, sir, I think; and all our oil lamps
are nothing compared to that, though ever so well trimmed. You are a
poet, Pen, my boy."

Pen was very much pleased with the assurance. "Thank you,
Warrington," he said, "thank you for your friendship to me, and – and
what you say about me. I have often thought I was a poet – I will be one
– I think I am one, as you say so, though the world mayn't. Is it – is it
the 'Ariadne in Naxos' which you liked – I was only eighteen when I
wrote it – or the Prize Poem?"

Warrington burst into a roar of laughter. "Why, you young goose,"
he yelled out, "of all the miserable, weak rubbish I ever tried, 'Ariadne
in Naxos' is the most mawkish and disgusting. The Prize Poem is so
pompous and feeble that I'm positively surprised, sir, it didn't get the
medal. You don't suppose that you are a serious poet, do you, and are
going to cut out Milton and Aeschylus? Are you setting up to be a
Pindar, you absurd little tom-tit, and fancy you have the strength and
pinion which the Theban eagles bear, sailing with supreme dominion
through the azure fields of air? No, my boy, I think you can write a
magazine article and turn out a pretty copy of verses; that's what I
think of you."

2203   A Call for a Poet.

What we need is a poet who shall do for science what Kipling has
done for Imperialism. In spite of all the abuse showered from pulpits on
human nature, it still values kisses more than bread and cheese, and
never forgets for long that it was created in the image of God. It will

only respond enthusiastically to appeals pitched in a high key. – "Traction and Transmission."

2204   Most of the things that have been said might as well have remained unsaid for all the benefit they are to humanity.

2205   (**f79ᵛ**) Euripides. – Imperialism. 'Half a century elapsed between "Hippolytus", & the "Bacchae." In the interval the tragedy of Athens had been played. All the high hopes had faded. Hegemony had degenerated into empire. And then came the war, with its pitiful relaxation of moral & intell! fibre. Athens, once "farther removed from primitive savagery" than any other people had learnt from Cleon not to be "misled by the three most deadly enemies of empire, Pity & Eloquent Sentiments, & the Generosity of Strength. Euripides himself had incurred the dislike of his fellow countrymen, & had had to leave Athens.'
           – Euripides. trans. by Gilbert Murray. (Review in Acad℣)

———————— // ————————

2206   R. L. Stevenson's letters – S. Colvin.
   The letter written in the emigrant train (I.144) to Colvin is one of the most sincere, manly, & interesting ones in the book.

2207   "Ugliness [in literature] is the prose of horror. It is when you are not able to write Macbeth that you write Thérèse Raquin. Fashions are external: the essence of art only varies in so far as fashion widens the field of its application; art is a mill whose thirlage, in different ages, widens & contracts; but in any case & under any fashion, the great man produces beauty, (**f80ʳ**) terror, & mirth, & the little man produces cleverness (personalities, psychology) instead of beauty, ugliness instead of terror, & jokes instead of mirth."   (to Henley) I. 275

2208   "There is but one art – to omit! O if I knew how to omit, I wᵈ ask no other knowledge. A man who knew how to omit wᵈ make an Iliad of a daily paper.
   "Your definition of seeing is quite right. It is the first part of omission to be partly blind. Artistic sight is judicious blindness. ... The selective criterion ... he learns ... in changing, not in copying fact. ..."
                                                          [to R. A. M. S] 290

2209   "I feel that all my friends have lost one thickness of reality since that one passed"   [i.e. death of W. Ferrier] 300

2210   "Hegel's antinomies: the contrary of everything is its postulate."
302

2211   "They think that the ... fine thoughts & sentiments in Shakesp. impress by their own weight, not understanding that the unpolished diamond is but a stone" [very characteristic of R. L. S.]   341

2212   "Your [W. Archer's] ⟨wonderful⟩ statement that happiness tends to die out & misery to continue"   370

2213   (**f80ᵛ**) "Not only do I believe that literature shᵈ give joy, but I see a universe, I suppose, eternally different from yours; a solemn, a terrible, but a very joyous & noble universe, where suffering is not at least wantonly inflicted, though it falls with dispassionate partiality."
[to Archer] 373

2214   ... Too great realism of some chapters & passages ... wh. disprepares the imagination for the cast of the remainder. Any story can be made <u>true</u> in its own key; any story can be made <u>false</u> by the choice of a wrong key of detail or style   II.19

2215   If there is anywhere a thing said in two sentences that could have been ~~said~~ as clearly & as engagingly & as forcibly said in one, then it's amateur work.   93

2216   Granted that life is tragic to the marrow, it seems the proper function of religion to make us accept & serve in that tragedy as officers in that other & comparable one of war. ... The pious man is he who has a military joy in duty – not he who weeps over the wounded.   100

2217   This civilizⁿ of ours is a dingy, ungentlemanly business; it drops out too much of man ... the beauty of the poor beast.   153

2218   (**f81ʳ**) A delightful letter to Colvin on the voyage in the Janet Nicoll.   184–6

2219   ... The truth of yʳ ⟨[H James's]⟩ remark on the starving of the

visual sense. ... I <u>hear</u> people talking, & I <u>feel</u> them acting, & that seems
to me to be fiction. My two aims may be described as

> 1ˢᵗ War to the adjective
> 2nd. Death to the optic nerve.

Admitted that we live in an age of the optic nerve in literᵗᵉ For how
many centuries did litᵗʳᵉ get along with! a sign of it?   316

2220   Daily I see the sunrise out of my bed, wh. I still value as a tonic,
a perpetual tuning fork, a look of God's face once in the day.   333

2221   All that you can do is to civilize ⟨the⟩ man in the line of his own
civilization, such as it is ... never believe in thaumaturgic convers=
⟨ions.⟩ They may do very well for St Paul. ... Andaman islᵗ – nothing.
                                                                          341

2222   They [the multitude] don't do anything <u>because</u>; they do things,
write able articles, stitch shoes, dig, from the purely simian impulse.
                                                                          355

2223   "The part that lives in the body is a small part of one's
personality."   <u>A spiritualist, in the D. News.</u>

2224   (**f81ᵛ**) THE DRAMA.
A FORECAST.
<u>Times</u> sup! Feb 6. 1903
   The second Mrs. Tanqueray remarked that she believed the future to
be "only the past again, entered through another gate," and her
husband answered, "That's an awful belief." It was an uncomfortable
reflection, no doubt, for Aubrey and Paula, seeing that the lady's past
was of the peculiar sort denoted by turned commas; but as a general
theory there is nothing "awful" about it. It is merely the imaginative
statement of a rigorously scientific truth.. To-morrow and to-morrow
and to-morrow this petty pace creeps in from day to day, and in
forecasting the future of an art we can have no surer guide than its past
history. That is the course wisely taken by Professor Brander
Matthews, of Columbia University, N. Y., in his paper in the *Monthly
Review* on "The Future of the Drama." He sees that the process known

as "specialization of function" has always been at work in the arts as elsewhere, and it does not cost him much expenditure of prophetic inspiration to predict the continuance of this process in the playhouse. There was a time when the drama was history, essay, novel, sermon, newspaper, and street-gossip, and *pari passu* with changes in the material conditions of the playhouse, in the intellectual demands of the audience, and in the artistic impulse of the dramatists, it has been shedding all the elements extraneous to it. Conclusion: the drama will go on minding its own business more and more exclusively, will aim at greater and greater purity of type, will become more and more dramatic. Among future improvements in the mechanical conditions of the stage which are bound, as all such improvements are, to influence its artistic form, Professor Matthews lays great stress upon the illumination. "The power," he says, "of directing at will whatever light may be desired confers an advantage upon the modern stage-manager denied to his predecessors; and it is certain to impress its mark upon the drama of the next half century." One of the results will be the closer adherence of drama to the well-known fact of life that great passions are mute. In other words, dumb-show, at critical moments will supersede talk. "In the ill-lighted theatres of old, the dramatic poet had to take care that his plot was made clear in words as well as in deeds; and he was tempted often to let his rhetoric run away with him. But in the well-lighted modern houses, he can, if he chooses, let actions speak louder than words. Being able to reach the playgoers through their visual as well as their auditory sense, he sometimes plans to let a self-betraying movement do its work without any needless verbal elucidation. He recognizes that there are moments in life when a silence may be more eloquent than the silver sentences of any soliloquy."

About this there are one or two things to be said. In the first place, have we not reached finality in this matter of localizing the illumination at will? The electric light can be thrown upon any actor, in any part of the stage, whom it is desirable for the audience to see, rather than to hear. What advantage then can the future expect to have over the present in the way of dumb-show scenes? It has also to be borne in mind that, though art changes, the laws of optics do not. When once the incidence of the light is settled for a particular scene it cannot be altered. The light cannot follow the actor about the stage, the actor will still have to move into it, Mahomed to come to the mountain. But these are purely mechanical considerations; there is one of another kind which, we think, ought to qualify the forecast that the drama of the future will tend to minimize speech. No doubt, as Professor Matthews says, "the set speech, the oratorical display, the *tirade*, will tend to disappear;" but if he means that the dialogue will be reduced to such speech as merely carries on the immediate action – and, whether he means it or not, it is a currently accepted view – we think it is a mistake. In a remarkable essay on "Le Tragique Quotidien" (one of the series called "Le Trésor des Humbles") M. Maeterlinck insists upon the necessity of the apparently superfluous dialogue:–

> Indeed, the only words that count in the play are those that at first seemed useless, for it is therein that the essence lies. Side by side with the necessary dialogue you will almost always find another dialogue that seems superfluous; but examine it carefully and it will be borne home to you that that is the only one that the soul can listen to profoundly, for here alone it is the soul that is being addressed. You will see, too, that it is the quality and the scope of this unnecessary dialogue that determine the quality and the immeasurable range of the work. Certain it is that in the ordinary drama the indispensable dialogue by no means corresponds to reality; and it is just those words that are spoken by the side of the rigid, apparent truth that constitute the mysterious beauty of the most beautiful tragedies, inasmuch as these are words that conform to the deeper truth, and one that lies incomparably nearer to the invisible soul by which the poem is upheld.

M. Maeterlinck gives illustrations from the *Master Builder*, into which it is unnecessary to follow him. All we desire to do is to enforce the point that there will always be something over and above the directly significant word or the eloquent action to which Professor Matthews would reduce drama. There will always be the "harmonics" of the fundamental notes, the minor or ostensibly "superfluous" dialogue, which is really there to make us aware of the peculiar *timbre* in the dramatist's voice, to enable him to unbosom himself to us in that intimacy of soul and soul which is the ultimate aim of drama, as it is the ultimate aim of all art.

In pointing out the continual movement in the direction of severer simplicity in form, which is involved in the tendency of drama to become more and more dramatic, Professor Matthews remarks that "Ibsen stretches back across the centuries to clasp hands with Sophocles." Many commentators, of course, have already shown how Ibsen's formula of the "amplified catastrophe" "throws back" to Greek tragedy. The "story" has happened before the play begins; in the play it leaks out and is so pieced together as to have a terrible meaning. The Professor compares *Ghosts* and the *Oedipus Tyrannus*. He might have added that, while Ibsen's preliminary story is obviously true and would have appeared true if shown on the stage, that of Sophocles is as obviously a "large order," and if shown instead of being merely alluded to would have been rejected as incredible. Oedipus has killed his own father without knowing it, has innocently married his mother, and, it would seem, during several years of matrimony has never mentioned the homicidal business. While Ibsen's "amplified catastrophe" then is Sophoclean, his unseen prologue is his own, and a great improvement on the old sort. It might also be noted that two centuries before Ibsen the formula of the amplified catastrophe was (**f82ʳ**) prescribed by the Abbé d'Aubignac in his "Pratique du Théâtre" (1657). The dramatist, says the Abbé, ought to fix the action of the piece for the day of the catastrophe, and to begin the piece as near the catastrophe as possible. D'Aubignac, like all strict dramatic unitarians of the seventeenth century, has often been reviled as a pedant. It is amusing to note how modern drama is tending to justify the much-abused "rules" – the minor unities of place and time not excepted. One begins to see a new meaning in Paula Tanqueray's reflection that "the future is only the past again, entered through another gate."

But all this is to discuss merely dramatic form. More important than the form of the drama is its content. Granted that the drama of the future will have to use certain modes of expression; the great question is, What will it be able to express? It is when we ask ourselves this question that we are less confident than Professor Matthews about its future. "There is evidence," he says, "that it is on the threshold of a new youth"; unfortunately, he does not bring the evidence into Court. "Signs of its refreshed vitality can be found by who so cares to keep his eyes open and his mind free from prejudice"; but he does not tell us what these signs are or where to find them. This is tantalizing. For our part we think the future career of the drama is likely to be hampered by its inability to tell cultivated and curious people of to-day a tithe of the things they want to know. What the drama can tell, it can tell more emphatically than any other art. The novel, for instance, is but a report; the drama makes you an eye-witness of the thing in the doing. But then there is a whole world of things which cannot be done – of thoughts and moods and sub-conscious states which cannot be expressed – on the stage, and which can be expressed in the novel. In earlier ages which could do with a narrow range of vivid sensations the drama sufficed; it will not suffice for an age which wants an illimitable range of sensations and, being "quick in the uptake," can dispense with vividness. If any one considers for a moment the extraordinarily complicated texture of subtle thoughts and minute sensations in such a book as Mr. Henry James's "Wings of the Dove," and then thinks of any, the most "advanced," modern play – *The Master Builder*, say, or *Le Repas du Lion* – the contrast between the abundance of the one and the meagreness of the other cannot but be ludicrous. We are brought back once more to the element of drama which Aristotle called διάνοια, its mind-stuff, its "philosophy," as our fathers used to say – the element for which the dialogue described in the passage we have quoted from M. Maeterlinck is the vehicle. Well, who can deny that it is thin, unsatisfying, and generally behind the times? For one explanation of this we should point to the rigid limitations of the dramatic medium. For the poor look-out of our own drama, in particular, there is perhaps the additional reason that few of our modern authors with the dramatic instinct seem able to accomplish any fresh, original, profound thinking. Even Mr. Barrie, though fresh and original, is not – or not yet – profound. There is Mr. Bernard Shaw. But some curious twist in his temperament, or singularity of vision, turns his plays into curios; they are morsels for intellectual epicures, not "human nature's daily food." Who else is there? One of our dramatists has recently been deploring the ill-success of serious drama in England, and seemed to think it had something to do with cockney frivolity. (Empire shares at £3 5s., Lyceum shares at 7½d.!) He, we admit, could hardly recognize the painful truth that if our drama languishes, it is largely because our dramatists have a habit of being "not good enough."

2225   THE CHARACTERS OF THEOPHRASTUS:
CONTENTS.

Introduction.	The Superstitious Man.	The Impudent Man.
Epistle Dedicatory.	The Thankless Man.	The Gross Man.
The Dissembler.	The Suspicious Man.	The Boor.
The Flatterer.	The Disagreeable Man.	The Penurious Man.
The Coward.	The Exquisite.	The Pompous Man.
The Over-zealous Man.	The Garrulous Man.	The Braggart.
The Tactless Man.	The Bore.	The Oligarch.
The Shameless Man.	The Rough.	The Backbiter.
The Newsmonger.	The Affable Man.	The Avaricious Man.
The Mean Man.		The Late Learner.
The Stupid Man.		The Vicious Man.
The Surly Man.		

2226 Sophocles. The Philo.

2227 "The Hindu Supreme God is separated by a whole series of demiurges from all care of the universe."

2228 "Rash & presumptuous magicians – torn in pieces by the potent spirit whom they c.^d summon but not control."   R. Noel.

2229 "The warfare of our higher & our lower selves."   ib.

2230 (**f82^v**) Schopenhauer. – No man loves the woman – only his dream.
– My only amusement, the wonder of those who do not understand.
– I have made one now unalterable mistake in my life – I have not been a fool. I wish to God I could be!
– Self realization kills laughter.
– This glass of Moselle does more to tempt me to remain in life than do all my hopes. – (from the sayings of S. secured by R. V. Risley from a man who knew him. pub.^d in N. Y. Reader Jan 1903)

2231 'Music is in no sense a universal language. Like its sister, speech, it is determined in every case to a special form by the physical and mental character of the people among whom it has arisen, and the circumstances of their environment. The particular nature of music is no more disproved by the fact that a melody by Wagner speaks to German, French, and English ears alike, than is the particular nature of speech by the fact that the Latin tongue was at one time the recognized vehicle of cultivated thought throughout the civilized world. ... The whole meaning of music depends upon this immediate appeal to our emotions through the association of feeling with sensation; and so the strangeness of the foreign music of to-day, and of the dead music of the past, is insuperable, for they are the expressions of emotions which their possessors could not analyse, and we can never experience. ... The incommunicable character of music finds a striking illustration in the effects which the remnants of ancient Greek melody produce on the modern hearer. ... But though it is impossible for us now to recover the meaning of this dead music of ancient Greece, and wellnigh impossible to accustom our ears to appreciate its form, we can at least study, as a matter of speculative interest, the laws of its accidence and syntax as they have been handed down to us by its grammarians.'

[From the Introduction to *The Harmonics of Aristoxenus*, edited with Translation, Notes, Introduction, and Index of Words, by HENRY S. MACRAN, M. A. Clarendon Press. *Published by Henry Frowde.* Price 10s. 6d. net ($3.50).]

2232   (**f83ʳ**) <u>Turner</u>. "For the conventional colour he substituted a pure straightforward rendering of fact, as far as was in his power; & that not of such fact as had ⟨been⟩ before even suggested, but of all that is <u>most</u> brilliant, beautiful, & inimitable; he went to the cataract for its iris, to the conflagration for its flames, asked of the sea its intensest azure, of the sky its clearest gold."   <u>Ruskin.</u>

2233   THE INSIDE. (<u>Daily News.</u>) (By G. K. Chesterton.)

The position of Maeterlinck in modern life is a thing too obvious to be easily determined in words. It is, perhaps, best expressed by saying that it is the great glorification of the inside of things at the expense of the outside. There is one great evil in modern life for which nobody has found even approximately a tolerable description: I can only invent a word and call it "remotism." It is the tendency to think first of things which, as a matter of fact, lie far away from the actual centre of human experience. Thus people say, "All our knowledge of life begins with the amoeba," It is false; our knowledge of life begins with ourselves. Thus they say that the British Empire is glorious, and at the very word Empire they think at once of Australia and New Zealand, and Canada and Polar bears, and parrots and kangaroos, and it never occurs to any one of them to think of the Surrey Hills. The one real struggle in modern life is the struggle between the man like Maeterlinck, who sees the inside as the truth, and the man like Zola, who sees the outside as the truth. A hundred cases might be given. We may take, for the sake of argument, the case of what is called falling in love. The sincere realist, the man who believes in a certain finality in physical science, says, "You may, if you like, describe this thing as a divine and sacred and incredible vision; that is your sentimental theory about it. But what it is is an animal and sexual instinct designed for certain natural purposes." The man on the other side, the idealist, replies, with quite equal confidence, that this is the very reverse of the truth. I put it as it has always struck me; he replies, "Not at all. You may, if you like, describe this thing as an animal and sexual instinct, designed for certain natural purposes; that is your philosophical or zoological theory about it. What it is, beyond all doubt of any kind, is a divine and sacred and incredible vision." The fact that it is an animal necessity only comes to the naturalistic philosopher after looking abroad, studying its origins and results, constructing an explanation of its existence, more or less natural and conclusive. The fact that it is a spiritual triumph comes to the first errand-boy who happens to feel it.

Maeterlinck's appearance in Europe means primarily this subjective intensity; by this the materialism is not over-thrown: materialism is undermined. He brings, not something which is more poetic than realism, not something which is more spiritual than realism, not something which is more right than realism, but something which is more real than realism. He discovers the one indestructible thing. This material world on which such vast systems have been superimposed – this may be anything. It may be a dream, it may be a joke, it may be a trap or temptation, it may be a charade, it may be the beatific vision: the only thing of which we are certain is this human soul. This human soul finds itself alone in a terrible world, afraid of the grass. It has brought forth poetry and religion in order to explain matters; it will bring them forth again. It matters not one atom how often the lulls of materialism and scepticism occur; they are always broken by the reappearance of a fanatic. They have come in our time: they have been broken by Maeterlinck.

Suggestive, yet only another way of saying "Life is but thought."

2234 (**f83ᵛ**) A STATESMAN'S PHILOSOPHY. (By C. F. G. Masterman.)
"The Pathway to Reality." R. B. Haldane, M. P. Pp. xix., 316. John Murray. 10s. 6d.

Mr. Haldane studied under Lotze at Göttingen, and gives an eloquent tribute to the "high moral worth" of his master. He is still accustomed for certain months of the year to cast off advocacy and the joys of political intrigue, and to take the intellectual waters, as a kind of moral tonic, of the land which is the home of all spiritual philosophies. Here in this first part of the exposition of his faith is set out, for those who will essay a little hard thinking, the philosophical position of this perplexing politician.

This, of course, is almost pure Hegel. The first exposition of the Absolute which was unfolded a hundred years ago by the philosopher of Jena, and which has exercised such a profound influence upon the intellectual and political life of Europe, has fallen upon evil days. It has been repudiated in the land of its birth, now divided between an aggressive scientific materialism and a pessimism descended from Schopenhauer; both accompanying a commercial development which is contemptuous of the things of the spirit. When good German philosophers die they go to Oxford; and for years a modified Hegelianism, speaking through the person of T. H. Green, proclaimed from the Balliol pulpit the supremacy of the Idea and the duty of the good citizen. But now even the faithful city has passed to the enemy, and last year a vigorous band of young tutors issued a defence of "personal idealism" which was essentially a repudiation of the orthodox Oxford tradition. Hegelianism finds but fitful followers in the outlying regions of the intellectual world: in distant Scotland, where men still think; in America, whence Professor Royce pilgrimages to Aberdeen to startle the students with his mystic and moral fervour. Faithful amongst the faithless, Mr. Haldane stands sure. The avalanche of speculation which has overwhelmed the thought of the past hundred years, the rise and fall of competing systems, all the advances and the tremendous claims of the natural sciences, leave him unmoved. With that imperturbability which is one of his most attractive features, with quotations from Goethe and Shelley and other writers of the Hegelian age, altogether heedless of the forces playing around him and the noise of their movement, Mr. Haldane smilingly doles out the orthodox Hegelian logic to the students of St. Andrews.

Though delivered extempore, lacking the minor graces of style, and containing much repetition, these lectures may well be commended to those readers who desire to gain some insight into the nature of this difficult thought which has exercised so profound an influence. They are if less stimulating less obscure than Dr. Stirling's exposition; more condensed than the fervent but lengthy pages of Dr. Caird. The search after God, the lecturer rightly asserts, is the object of all philosophy. Yet the modern world is, on the whole, unbelieving: dissatisfied with its ignorance, but finding no clear light. Systems have risen and fallen till the whole intellectual life of man seems but the construction of sand castles swept away by each incoming tide. Mr. Haldane refuses to accept this dreary despair. There is advance – a dialectical ᵢ dvance, with the taking up of the true in each new system, as thought progresses through the combination of opposing theories. In the first of these courses Mr. Haldane is endeavouring to get behind the "common-sense" position to the true philosophical outlook; in the second he is destroying the claim of the sciences based on this "common-sense" view to exclusive knowledge of reality. The latter is an acute but not very novel criticism of the ultimate theories of matter and life: the ground has been covered by former Gifford lecturers, with singular acuteness and power by Professor Ward. But the first part taxes all Mr. Haldane's earnest pleadings. How to get the plain man to the position of the philosopher and the mystic? He must abandon the idea of God as a First Cause, because Cause itself vanishes outside the world of space and time. He must cease to conceive of God as possessing an independent centre of self-consciousness apart from the Universe of Spirit. He must recognise that the "window" theory of existence, of a self looking out as it were from within the chamber of the brain through the senses upon a material world outside, is a conception essentially vicious. Nay, he must even abandon the conception of this self, himself which he knows to be real: he must remain dumb und r the lecturer's gibes as he hunts this self from body to brain, from brain to mind, abandoning even the cheerful suggestion of a former speculator that it resides in the pineal gland. He must acknowledge that what he proudly calls his body is nothing separate and apart; but without a clear cut surface, with molecules and motion continually passing to and fro between it and the region outside; that, in fact, existence is a continuum. He is to learn, however forlornly, not to take much account of "the finite self, a thing with a proper name, manifesting itself in a body one day to be carried off in a coffin," the notion of which is to be only secondary and derivative. With the abandonment of these "superstitions of common-sense" he will recognise the Objective world as the workings of a mind which is not another than his own, but a mind in which all reality, himself included, has a place. "From the goblet of our spiritual kingdom our infinity foams back to us." The human mind is but a degree of the appearance of Reality, the name of which is God. In the effort to transcend these individual divisions, the bridging of the "unplumbed, salt, estranging sea" which Matthew Arnold pictured as dividing "the mortal islets," the Absolute in its highest form is manifest; in the aspirations of the artist, the visions of the poet, the self-emptying of the mystic, the moral energy of the saint losing his life in the life of others, is the final revelation of the Glory of God.

To criticise Mr. Haldane's thought would be to record the progress of nineteenth century thought. Hegel's philosophy, like that of all great religions, is of the East; a reaction from the Kantian individualism, essentially a Western system. The neo-Kantian movement of the past thirty years is a revolt against this Eastern subordination of the Self to the All – a system which, as a vigorous voice from California has told us, is at bottom a product of the hot Eastern sunshine. Historically, Mr. Haldane's system has assisted those forces which make for the community and the interests of the whole, as against the individual demand of the individual freedom and conscience. With Hegel himself it exalted the Prussian State, with its militarism and its efficiency, as the highest revelation of the Divine. With its successors it formed, on the one hand, the backbone of the Catholic reaction which rolled in on the great liberal revolt, and whose echoes at Oxford have provided the intellectual basis of the Anglo-Catholic movement in England. On the other, it stimulated that Marxian Socialism which has changed the political history of Germany. These two together have effectually submerged the liberal party on the Continent. It seems somehow incongruous to the somewhat aggressive individualism, often a little rough and unpleasant, of the Anglo-Saxon mind.

Mr. Haldane promises a second volume dealing with the questions of religion and conduct. The further definition of his Absolute will be awaited with interest. At present no satisfactory reconciliation has been effected between the immanent god of the Hegelian, the world spirit which includes the All which is the theme of all the poets of this system, and the God of the Christian theology. It is a pantheism, as Dr. McTaggart has maintained, not a personality. Mr. Haldane discerns a universe of Spirit: against a blank and deadening materialism or the hopeless abandonment of the Agnostic he is fighting with the Christian. But it may yet be found that great future combat will be between belief in his impersonal Spirit, the continuum which includes alike good and evil, and holds evil the necessary condition for the development of the good; and belief in a God which, as Sir Oliver Lodge recently has pointed out, is the only God who will satisfy the spiritual demands of men. A God who will hear and answer prayer, Himself the highest form of personality, of which our human personalities are but imperfect images; who is ever maintaining in heàven, as in earth, a warfare against the forces of evil, and destined finally to trample them under His feet.

2235 (**f84ʳ**) AN APPRECIATION OF D'ANNUNZIO.

In his novels, there are no stories, only states of mind and pictures. On the one side it is a going back to the origins of the novel, in such 'confessions' as 'Adolphe,' for example; the novelty lies in the combination of what in 'Adolphe' is a consciousness vaguely placed in the world, a world absolutely invisible to us, with an atmosphere itself as much a 'state of mind' as Amiel's, and a universe as solid and coloured as Gautier's. His few personages are as little seen in their relation with society, as closely absorbed in their own sensations, as the single personage of Benjamin Constant, the man in whom one sees also the woman, as in a mirror. But with d'Annunzio, as he tells us in the preface to the 'Trionfo della Morte,' 'the play of action and reaction between the single sensibility and exterior things is established on a precise woof of direct observation.' Man, 'the model of the world,' is seen living in his own universe, which he creates continually about him; a world as personal to himself, and, to d'Annunzio and his people, as intimately realised, as the thought of the brain, or any passion.

D'Annunzio is an idealist, but he is an idealist to whom the real world is needful to the eyes, and feelings actually experienced are needful to the memory, before he can begin to make his art. All his work – all, at least, of his finest work – is something remembered, by a transfiguring act of the mind; not something which has come to him as vision, out of the darkness. With so personal an apprehension of the world, it is the world, always, that he needs, his soul being no world to him. In a monk's cell, or with dim eyes, he would have created nothing; he would never have been able to imagine beauty without a pattern.

But, to d'Annunzio, in that 'seemingly exclusive predominance in his interests, of beautiful physical things, a kind of tyranny of the senses over him' (that phrase of Pater seems to have been made beforehand for his definition) things seen are already things felt; the lust of the eye, in him, is a kind of intellectual energy. The soul of visible things seems to cry out to him, entreating a voice: he hears, and is the voice. At times, delicate human sympathies come to him, through his mere sympathy with soulless things: the sense of pity, which stirs in him over the fading of flowers, and so over the ageing of human beauty. He realises sorrow, because it is a soiling of the texture of life; death, because it is the end of the weaving. One fancies, sometimes, that his

very feeling for art, for the arts of music, painting, literature even, is the feeling of one to whom these things are of the nature of ripe fruit, golden sunshine, a luxury of the senses, rather than a need of the soul.
                              – ARTHUR SYMONS in the *Imperial and Colonial Magazine*.

2236   (By G. K. Chesterton.)
It is one of the marks of this strange era that people have to be eccentric in order to do the most obvious and human things. If there be anything right or wrong which you would think that everyone would incline at first sight to say or do, you may be perfectly certain that you will, in this age, find it founded in a Bohemian club or a mad sect. ...
the mystery is that the commonplace beliefs are held by the odd people, and the odd beliefs by the commonplace people.

2237   Music.
Now that Strauss and Elgar, acknowledged leaders of musical advance, are both in London, and beginning to near the height of their fame, it is only decent to remember those to whom the possibility of this latest music is to be ascribed. They were four great men, born very near one another in time – Chopin, Liszt, Wagner, and Schumann. These were the men who gave us the new music, built upon the chromatic, and not the diatonic scale; built, that is to say, on twelve notes instead of seven. Of these the first and the last were ill-fated; both were born in 1810 (Schumann on June 8); Chopin lived for thirty-nine, Schumann for forty-six years. To the great genius who first saw the light in Zwickau ninety-three years ago to-day, we owe much, not only in composition, but in the elevation of the whole art of music, for both he and Wagner (born three years later) were literary men as well as composers, and wrote to high purpose. Liszt was born in 1811; so that four years (1810–13) gave us the men who revolutionised an art which had been preparing itself for them since prehistoric times.
                                                                    D$\underline{y}$ C$\underline{^{le}}$

2238   The hunter stands even lower than the butcher, since the latter kills animals for the benefit of society, while the former murders them solely for his own amusement.   *Frederick the Great.*

2239   "The Goût de comparaison (as Bruyere styles it) is the only taste of ordinary minds. They do not know the specific excellence either of an author or a composition."   Gray. Poems. p. 60.

2240 (**f84ᵛ**) "Novelty is by no means a usual poetic advantage in England, but in this case [W. E. Henley's Hospital Poems] the novelty was of a kind universally comprehensible; it lay in assimilating poetry to prose – & that blessed day of the Lord when poetry shall be prose is a consummation for which the great heart of the British public ever yearns. In so far as it colourably resembled prose Mr Henley's hospital experiment was therefore inevitably popular; in so far as it distinctly, & none the less, remained poetry – the public did not know that – did not nose the contraband ware – & allowed it to pass unsuspectingly."

Francis Thompson. Acadʸ 18:7:03

2241 "Appreciation (briefly) resides in attempting to discover what your author has aimed to compass; & then setting forth the impression yourself retain of his success or failure to succeed in the elected aim. It is obvious that your achievement will be very much in the ratio of your sympathetic gift."

ib. id.

———————— // ————————

2242 "Robert Browning was one of those who achieve the reputation, in the literal sense, of eccentricity by their frantic efforts to reach the centre."

Chesterton –

2243 Art ... Literature ... Science. "An objective register of subjective changes."

Spencer.

2244 (**f85ʳ**) The Virgin Birth – theory of Bp of Worcester, Dean Alford, &c – "If genuine, the account of [it by] the first synoptist [St Matt.] was ultimately derived from St Joseph, & that of Luke from the Blessed Virgin. The Bp. even conjectures that St Joseph (who must have died before the public ministry of Jesus began) left some document detailing the circumstances of the birth of Jesus, to be given to Mary in order to vindicate her own virginity, & that after Pentecost it passed into the hands of the author of the 1ˢᵗ gospel."
– Walter R. Cassels, author of "Supᶥ Religⁿ" – in 19ᵗʰ Cent. 10.'03.

————————————

2245 ΑΙΣΧΥΛΟΥ ΧΟΗΦΟΡΟΙ. The 'Choephori' of Aeschylus ... by A. W. Verrall, Litt. D.,
... The story ... is essentially a legend of the Appoline religion. ... The

story of the Agamemnon is neither Apolline nor essentially religious.
The facts are moralized from a religious point of view, but ... so to
speak, from outside. ... No theological prepossession is required to
account for the existence of the story, which is constructed primarily to
satisfy the human appetite for exciting narrative. But ... the story of the
Ch! is a sacerdotal invention.   Introd. xi, xii

2246   The Choephori, like the plays of Aeschylus generally, consists of
scenes from a story taken as known. Some indispensable (**f85ᵛ**) parts of
it are represented only by allusions. Others can scarcely be said to be
repᵈ at all.   xvi

2247   ... There is a marked contrast between Aes., & his two
successors [Soph. & Eurip.] In [these] the child is rescued by faithful
friends, who also play a part in his restoration. In Aes. he is 'cast away'
beforehand by the undesigned effect of a base intrigue. As elements in a
romance or in a study of charᵗ the inventions of the two later
dramatists wᵈ be as much superior as they are more obvious. But the
story of Aes. is not such: it is a legend of Divine Providence. ... No event
has so much of the providential character as that wh. comes to pass by
human agency indeed, but without or against the will of the agents.
                                                                                        xvii

2248   "Nature might mean flowers to Wordswᵗʰ & grass to Walt
Whitman, but to Browning it ... meant such things as ... the
monstrosities & living mysteries of the sea."
                                                                    Chesterton's Browning.

2249   "Childe Roland [Browning's] ... is the hint of an entirely new &
curious type of poetry, the poetry of the shabby & hungry aspect of the
earth."   ib.

2250   "The sense of the terrible importance of detail was a sense wh.
may be (**f86ʳ**) sᵈ to have possessed Browning in the emphatic manner
of a demoniac possession. ... Any room that he was sitting in glared at
him with innumerable eyes & mouths gaping with a story.... If he
looked at a porcelain vase, or an old hat, a cabbage, or a puppy at play,
each began to be bewitched ... the vase to send up a smoke of thoughts

& shapes; the hat to produce souls as a conjuror's hat produces rabbits; the cabbage to swell & overshadow the earth like the Tr. of Know^{ge}, & the puppy to go off along the road to the end of the world –"   ib. [this is true of all poets – not especially of Browning]

2251 Browning. "His processes of thought are often scientific. ... Sudden conclusion ... transcendental & inept. This was not so much due to a defect in his own mind as to the circumstances of the world of thought about him. An interest in theological questions had been quickened ... and ... scientific historical criticism began to make its voice heard. ~~Hence~~ ⟨Religious people c^d not close their ears to it, but they were as yet unprepared. ...⟩ Hence ... in many minds ... confusion between two opposing strains of thought, similar to that which has been remarked in Br^g's poetry. ... A transition state ... from wh. men's minds have already moved away in opposite directions; but it has left deep traces on the lit. of the middle Vict^n period. B.'s phil^y does not fundamentally differ from that of other ... writers of the time. ... Besides, his phil^y does not all bear the stamp of the temporary" –
                    Margaret L. Woods. ⟨In⟩ "English Poets."

2252 V. Hugo could not be spoken of as a reader. ... He read the "Mysteries of Paris" wh. as he read he raised & Hugotised into Les Misérables, ... His supreme enjoy! was the exercise of his own brain."   Truth.

2253 (f86^v) Spencer's Unknowable closely resembles the Noumenon or Thing-in-itself conceived by Kant as underlying all phenomena, which is also closely allied to the sublime idea of an impersonal Deity.
                    Academy. 12.12.03

2254 Shakespeare's contempt for the "Lower Classes":–
  He practically never brought members of the lower classes upon the stage without making fun of them or exhibiting them as knaves, with the exception of a few loyal servants, a loyal servant being apparently in his eyes the only meritorious plebeian; that he usually gave them such names as "Bottom," "Snout," "Wart," "Potpan," "Sneak," etc.;

that they were almost invariably treated with contumely by the other characters in his plays; that he falsified history to their discredit by making a common drab of Joan of Arc and transforming into vulgar and ridiculous rioters the commonalty of the Coriolanus of Rome, and the followers of Wat Tyler; that his sole idea of English history was that of a pageant of royalties, while in "John" he ignores Magna Charta, and in "Henry VIII" shuts his eyes to the overthrow of the power of Rome; that he picked out the worst enemy of the people in Plutarch, Coriolanus, for a hero, disregarding that historian's wise criticism of the Roman general, and passing over such popular heroes as the Gracchi; that he saw nothing in private soldiers but cowardice, and nothing in crowds but bad smells; and that in all of this he ran counter to the drift of the best literature of his country and of his age, for Chaucer, More, Cervantes, and the English Bible delighted in the common people, and his contemporary playwrights more than once celebrated their deeds upon the stage. It seems to me that this forms a pretty substantial indictment, and that it goes to show rather clearly that Shakspere did not hold the mirror up to nature in so far as the lower classes are concerned, for I refuse to believe that the yeomen of England were all scamps or fools, or that all the virtue of the realm was confined to the nobility and gentry.

From "The Whim"   Newark. N. J. Dec. '03

2255   To Mr. Nicklin we come closer yet. He is not remarkably clever in his versification. He uses a somewhat hackneyed vocabulary. In many of his pieces, he reminds us of more than one of the most modern poets. Yet his book is decidedly individual, and not only because the smallness of the volume and compactness of its contents suggest that they are a careful selection, and because he often uses the first person singular, but also because his concentration has the effect of producing a masterful sense of personality, above all in "The Fall." He himself expresses his aloofness well in his first sonnet, called "Inspiration":–

> Not with the Morning's virginal caress,
>   The sleepy murmur of a Summer's day,
>   Laughter of children tumbling in the hay,
> Or hush of many a leafy, shy recess,
> Nor in Greek marble's tranquil loveliness –
> Eternal youth, victor of envious years! –

Or symphonies that drown, in floods of tears,
The pensive close to all their storm and stress:
Not thus the Muse comes, but in other plight
    To me who neither love nor list her note:
Who, straining with tense eyeballs, half surmise
A sudden, silent horror in the night,
    A heavy hand that grapples at the throat,
A masked face leering with a maniac's eyes.

SECRET NIGHTS, by J. A. Nicklin. London, David Nutt, 2s. 6d. net.

2256 (f87ʳ)   A "BALLAD EPIC" OF THE BOER WAR.

The pathos of the woman's part in time of war has been expressed again and again by poets, and has even found its own place in the great epics of the world. But the epic poets have usually confined it to a small space – have seldom, at any rate, allowed its consideration to keep them long from the arms and the men, the deeds and the glories which they sing. In the parting scene between Hector and Andromache in the sixth book of the Iliad the heart may well linger with Andromache as she looks back tearfully smiling, but the feet must needs hurry with Hector to the gate. We have little time allowed us to watch the wife bearing her burden among her women, and no poet has ever arisen to tell the tale of Troy from Andromache's point of view. We do not, of course, compare Mr. A. M. Buckton, the author of THE BURDEN OF ENGELA (Methuen, 3s. 6d. net), with Homer, nor his heroine with Andromache, but war is war and women are women since the beginning, and, *mutatis mutandis*, in putting his "ballad-epic" of a Transvaal farm into the mouth of Engela de Waal he does in fact present a kind of Andromachiad (if the word be permissible) of the late struggle in South Africa. The main incidents of the tale are given, as the descriptive title suggests, in a series of lyrical ballads; and Engela's hopes and fears and mother-love run through them all from the day on which, oppressed by the rumour of coming trouble, she lies awake, her husband still safe by her side, watching the dawn break, till the day of her return to a ruined homestead at the close of the war. An extract from the ballad called "The Start," may serve to introduce some of the actors. A few stanzas touch in the scene in the old church square – the saddled horses, the men awaiting orders, the bareheaded throng standing round the Predikant, the children leading the singing, and the younger women turning away to hide their tears. Then:–

Jaapie stood beside me,
    And held my hand in his,
When Piet bent down above me,
    And took his last long kiss.

My lips were dry; but my heart
    I gave him right away,
And the look in his eyes was the look
    On the morn of our wedding day!

Koos among his comrades
    Threw us a joyous word;
And Nonnie marched beside them
    Down to the Yellow Ford.

I heard the children shouting,
    "They mount, they ride away!"
And the little band had vanished
    Into the morning grey!

Nonnie has to return with Jaapie to the farm, and the next numbers are those of her love-song to Geert, to whom she has given her heart and who has just ridden with the rest down the hill. It is a fine lyric, half desolate, half triumphant, and gains much from the touch which contrives that we shall hear it through her mother's ears as she listens through a half-open door. The author has portrayed the character of Engela with real success. She is too experienced and sympathetic to misunderstand Nonnie's indignation or the gloom of Koos when she would withhold him from the war on the plea that he is under the fighting age; she has her dark hour to herself, makes her sacrifice, and is content. The lyrics of the time of waiting are touched with the peacefulness of the half-patriarchal life of the veld (we may instance, as a good example, Jaapie's Sundown song); and as the tide of war sweeps nearer, the best of them rise to a certain rugged passion, strong enough to lend dignity to the rough simplicity of their workmanship. But the pathos, which is one of the strongest features of the book, culminates, perhaps, in the section descriptive of "The Flight of the Children" whom Engela is forced to send for safety, under Nonnie's charge, a day's and a night's journey up to a mountain farm. The mother's thought follows them constantly, "As a ewe will track her ravished lamb, and follow in its bleat." She cries:–

> O Nonnie, wait till morn; out-span the lowing team,
> Release their tossing horns from the creaking shoulder-beam.
>
> Children, 'tis time for sleep! Nonnie shall make your bed,
> And draw the waggon-sail about your dreaming head.
>
> 'Tis Nonnie sits beside you, and soothes your weary sigh,
> And shields you from the fear of the lonely jackal-cry.
>
> And overhead the stars shall mount their solemn guard,
> And round your camp all night my love keep watch and ward!

Or again:–

> O little voices, quick
>   To comfort me!
> O little forms, that leaned
>   Against my knee!
>
> . . . .
>
> Behind your groaning wheels
>   I walked all day –
> My body sat at work,
>   But I – was away:
>
> You prattled with the boy,
>   And teased until
> Nonnie withdrew her gaze
>   From the distant hill,
>
> Her fair young eyes, so worn,
>   And her lips so pale,
> With the kiss of the newly dead,
>   And a dead love-tale!

Though these "ballads" vary considerably in point of execution, each contributes its own share to the making of a very complete and telling whole. There is no waste about the book, and its effect grows upon the reader on a second perusal.   Times. Jan 15. 1904

2257   *"Under North Star and Southern Cross," by Francis Sinclair (author of "Ballads and Poems of the Pacific," "Where the Sun Sets," &c.). London: Sampson Low & Co. 1907.

In the story of "Irene Middleton" there is a song entitled "*A Song of Loch Aber*," which has something of the ring of Burns in it. Here are the first four lines:

> It was only a song, a song of Loch Aber;
>   A song of the land far across the wide sea;
> A song of the glens, and the hills and the heather,
>   A song of the days that are over for me!

It is a touching melody of thirty-two lines with a pleasant lilt in it.

2258   The Inter-Veil.
       by Eliz.^th Foote.

I

Into the silent valley
    Knee to knee
I rode between two riders
    I could not see
Because the dark had fallen 'twixt them & me.

II

We passed a lonely outfire
    And one turned;
Across his eyes an instant
    The low light burned
And in that flash their blueness I had discerned

III

But he the other rider,
    Dimly scanned,
Was dark amid the darkness
    That held the land –
Only, upon the bridle, I saw his hand.

IV
Out of the silent valley
    Knee to knee
I rode between two riders
    I could not see –
Known for a day, forever unknown to me.

Century Magazine. March 1904.

2259   (**f87ᵛ**) "It is only this same wretched understanding which
supposes that a man must be either mortal or immortal: 'there is a
higher conception through which the sharp antithesis disappears.'" (p.
221)   – Mind. July 1904. Revᵂ of Haldane's Pathway to Reality.

2260   While we are far from anticipating a millennium such as would
satisfy the aspirations of Count Tolstoy, we hold it at once unwise &
ungrateful to ignore the influences which, amid wars & preparations
for war, are making for the exclusion of violence from international
relations.   Times leader. July 5. 1904

2261   Mr. Haldane dwells with pitying contemptuousness on the
simplicity of speculations as to personal reunions after death. We
generally say we must either see our friends or not see them after death.
That is a dilemma which the man whose religious consciousness is
practically sound, according to Mr. Haldane, thinks he is bound to,
and he releases himself by affirming that he will see his friends again.
Mr. Haldane assures him there is no such dilemma. Idealism has a
view which solves the difficulty; a method whose process in Mr.
Haldane's pages is a bewildering complexity of "Wells" and "Nows";
and the conclusion that friends neither will nor will not meet each other
again after death. We refer any reader to Mr. Haldane's discussion of
the relations of parent and child in the case he supposes of the death of
the child. There is much eloquent talk of the identity of the parties
through love; they undergo some treatment in Absolute Mind freed
from conditions of space and time; but the "spooks" of the Psychical
Research Society are nothing compared to them for vagueness. The
"picture" of the religious consciousness has disappeared with a
vengeance; and neither Mr. Haldane nor any other philosopher can
have the least idea of what takes its place. It is unthinkable and
therefore inexpressible; the pathway to reality leads to nowhere where
anybody, who is not a philosopher at least, wants to go.

The idealist may be right; we ought not, as he says, to think of realities under categories of time and space: that only by doing so do we get "pictures"; and that "Gates Ajar" and "Letters from Heaven" are absurd. But the point is that we are landed in utter nescience both as to God and what we call the future life, and our position in regard to them is totally unintelligible. Our "pictures" are forbidden and the religious imagination is paralysed by a philosophical doctrine. Or rather it would be if idealism did not also show that this painting of pictures is an inevitable consequence of our existence here; for while we are here we ignóre idealism and are inevitably bound to think of what we call the future life in terms of time and space. It may turn out, idealism allows so much, that in some inexplicable manner such time and space pictures will correspond in some degree more or less to absolute reality where time and space conditions are not. But that seems to be somewhat of a concession to our weakness on the part of idealism de rigueur.

2262   "Memorials of a Warwickshire Parish." By Robert Hudson. London: Methuen. 1904. 15s.
    "We have not in the parish," Mr. Hudson wrote, "one single landowner whose name goes back a century, while of the labouring class we have several who bear names, and those not common names, which have appeared steadily and without intermission in the parish register for well nigh the whole term of its existence."

2263   (**f87a^r**) Kant's greatest service is to have separated the phenomenal from the thing-in-itself by proving that between us & things there always stands the intellect. Kant's Copernican discovery is aptly hit off by Schopenhauer in the words: 'Before Kant we were in Time; now Time is in us,' & so on. It is obvious from this that Sch. accepts the negative conseq^s of K.'s phil^y as well as the pos^{ve}; we cannot know the th-in-its^f because as K. showed, the laws wh. govern the phen^n cannot be used to deduce & explain existence its! K.'s defect is that he c^d not discover the th-in-its! Sch. does not attempt a crit^m of the notion of the th-in-its^f; the th-in-its^f is to him the reality underlying & determining the world of experience, & as such, a real & not a hypothetical entity. He never allows hims^f to speak of it in the plural, as K. does, & so keeps consistently to a monistic point of view.
                    Mind. 1891. (Caldwell on Schop$^{r's}$ Criticism of Kant.)

2264 <u>Kantian philosophy</u>. Transcendental freedom is the pure self-activity of reason, or the application to one substance of a gen! notion wh., in the case of transc! freed^m embraces all substances. Freedom is inexplicable & inconceivable. We cannot prove its actuality nor even its possibility. For, what is meant by an act of spontaneous volition or by a substance wh., without any determining influence from beyond its sphere, produces the motives upon wh. it acts we are incapable of understanding. The idea of freedom takes us outside the phenomenal world into the region of things <u>per se</u>, or of noumena. Freedom, be it distinctly noted, is vested in the noumena. What is called psychological freed^m is a transparent piece of self deception. Self-determinism, wh. has sometimes been presented as a substitute for freedom, – namely the fact that, after our character has been formed by heredity, education, environment, in short, by the confluence of innumerable extraneous influences, we then act along the lines of this, our character, – such self-deter^{sm} K. dismisses with contempt. "The free^m of a mechan! turnspit" he calls it. No; genuine freedom he demands. ... But this freedom, he tells us, occurs behind the scenes. We have no consc^{ss} of it that we can build on. There is an actor in us who never takes off his mask, who never appears on the stage, & of whom, nless we are to assume that he exists because of certain effects that he produces from behind or from within: in short from the region of the unseen. This actor is our noumenon; our freedom is in our noumenon. ...

But if ... noumena do not exist, but are only assumed to exist, what profit is there in assuming them?...

Others have said, determinism or freedom. K. says determ^{sm} & freedom. ...

   Felix Adler. A Critique of Kants ethics. <u>Mind</u> ⟨April⟩ 1902.

2265 (**f87a^v**) "THE HIGHEST EXPRESSION."
"Poetry for Poetry's Sake." By A. C. Bradley, M. A., LL. D. (Oxford: Clarendon Press. 1s. net.)

In this little book Mr. A. C. Bradley has reprinted the striking lecture which he delivered last June year at Oxford. It was his inaugural lecture as Professor of Poetry, and we have seen few that justify so well the existence of that famous and now distinguished chair. "Poetry for Poetry's Sake" is full of sane discrimination, of literary delicacy and charm; and if, like a Platonic dialogue, it leads us to no distinct conclusion, like that, too, it takes us to many pleasant places by interesting paths; we are even disposed to think that no conclusion worth having could have been attained. The discourse, as he says, is upon words, and premises that poetry is to be considered in its essence, though without regarding metrical form merely as an accident or vehicle. "A poem," Mr. Bradley says, "is the succession of experiences – sounds, images, thoughts, emotions – through which we pass when reading as poetically as we can." The *poetic* value of the work is the intrinsic worth of this "imaginative experience." Everything else is ulterior, and does not affect this poetic value. That this is not a statement of the doctrine of form for form's sake it is the main business of the book to prove. The subject, of course, cannot determine the value of the work, when a perfect poem may be written on a sparrow, and a worthless one on the omnipresence of the Deity. "What the thing is in the poem" is what the writer must be judged by; and the Professor justly distinguishes between the subject and the substance of a poem. He says:–

> When you are reading a poem, I would ask – not analysing it, and much less criticising it, but allowing it, as it proceeds, to make its full impression on you through the exertion of your recreating imagination – do you then apprehend and enjoy as one thing a certain meaning or substance, and as another thing certain articulate sounds, and do you somehow compound these two? Surely you do not, any more than you apprehend apart, when you see someone smile, those lines in the face which express a feeling, and the feeling that the lines express. Just as there the lines and their meaning are to you one thing, not two, so in poetry the meaning and the sounds are one; there is, if I may put it so, a resonant meaning, or, a meaning resonance.

This is not new, but it was worth while repeating it so well. Mr. Bradley has not, however, taken into consideration the formal and especially the metrical imperfections of great poems, such as Wordsworth's "Ode on the Intimations of Immortality." In any imperfect poem, we can separate substance and outline, as, for example, in certain poems we can see where the execution has not fully rendered the original design. Nevertheless, he seems to us quite fair when he says that Arnold was deceiving himself when he said, of the lines –

> Our noisy years seem moments in the being
> Of the eternal silence,

that "quite independently of the meaning," there is one note added to the articulate music of the world.

> About the best poetry (says Mr. Bradley), and not only the best, there floats an atmosphere of infinite suggestion. The poet speaks to us of one thing, but in this one thing there seems to lurk the secret of all. He said what he meant, but his meaning seems to beckon away beyond itself, or rather to expand into something boundless which is only focussed in it; something also which, we feel, would satisfy not only the imagination but the whole of us.

Thus, with a fitting and delicate admission that there lies something incalculable and infinite beyond the horizon of criticism, Mr. Bradley brings to a close his admirable essay.

2266 Rodin.
the story of Rodin's conflict with life, of the tenacity with which, through an untiring search after form, he has held to an impassioned dream, of his indomitable resolve "to make his work of the same message for the senses within the domain of art as the Creator's work in the domain of nature." An impression is conveyed of a Titan endowed with genius enough and courage enough to defy our conventions – useful as they may be to the multitude – and to pay heed to the heroic Word audible within himself. In that sense Rodin is a solitary, as all great men are solitary; yet living water springs from the rock they dare to smite.

2267 "Les Romans de Pierre Loti." Rev. des deux M^{des}
"Les solitudes grises de la mer sont autour de nous. ..."
... Nous sommes rentrés ici dans la vérité de l'art, qui consiste à décrire les choses les plus particulières par les termes les plus généraux, et d'autant plus généraux qu'il s'agit de nous communiquer l'impression de choses plus particulières. ... Ce ne sont pas les mots propres ou spéciaux qui me donneront la sensation des f brumes intenses de la manche, mais une combinaison propre et spéciale des termes du commun usage.

2268 (f87b^r) "The paralyzing thought – what if, of all that is thus incomprehensible to us, [the Universe] there exists no comprehension anywhere?"   H. Spenser. Autob.

2269   As to the freedom of the Will, a few words must suffice. It is a well-worn topic. ... Science stands for determinism all along the line; determinism alike in the chain of objective experience, & in the subjective aspect of that experience; determinism alike in the physical world, & in the world of mental process. For science there is not & cannot be such a thing as free-will. The question then comes to this: – Is there any necessary antagonism between the determinism of science & the freewill of metaphysics. No doubt freedom & determ^m are often regarded as antithetical. The true antithesis of freedom, however, is not determinism but external constraint. My Will is free to give expression to my character just in so far as I am not thwarted by constraining influences as other expressions of the universal Cause. Within these limits I am free to determine; & such freedom cannot be antagonistic to determinism which refers to that which is determined. You must not fail to note, however, that the freedom thus claimed by the metaphysic^n is freedom to act in accordance with the essential nature of the underlying Cause. Of this essential nature determinism is the expression. Hence metaphysicians speak of freedom as self-determinism.

June 1904. Contemp^y Rev^w Professor C. Lloyd Morgan.

2270   (**f87c^r**) "Ferrier was greatly impressed by the fine rhetorical strokes that he encountered in Hegel ... one especially. ... Alluding to the displacement of philosophical systems by the constant arrival of fresh competitors, he gave the expression of St Peter on the death of Ananias, "The feet of them that are to carry thee out are already at the door."

Autobiog. of Dr Alex^r Bain.
⟨[lit. "are at the door and shall carry thee out"]⟩

2271   The very name of Freewill has been made repulsive by the metaphysical puzzles & attempts to solve those puzzles in wh. it has been involved. But is not Necessarianism, after all, merely a mental puzzle? ... Man is conscious of a power of choice, upon which his responsibility depends, & the existence of which he assumes to his fellows when he holds them responsible for their conduct to him. Not that his volition operates in a vacuum. It must always have its antecedents. The exact relation between the antecedents & the ultimate volition eludes our apprehension & will probably never be expressed. It is of course possible that our minutest actions & those which seem least material, such as our assent to religious doctrines, & our poetic compositions, may have been determined in the cosmogonic nebula; the hypothesis to which, in fact, Necessarianism apparently must come. But unless our nature lies to us, we have liberty of choice with responsibility attached to it; & if our nature lies to us, phil^y may as well spare its pains. Whence did the notion of moral freedom find its way into our minds, if we had no more of the thing than has a stock or a stone? Is there not something ludicrous in the idea of an auto^n autom^cally convinced of its own auto^sm after auto^cally fancying its^f a free agent?

Goldwin Smith. N. Am^n Rev^w (June 1904.)

2272 (**f87d^r**) <u>Mind</u>. 1900. James Ward's "Naturalism & Agnosticism"

The doctrine against which the main arg^t of D^r W's treatise is directed is of course the theory, of late years conveniently christened "naturalism" wh. teaches that in the concept of the world as a single mechanical system of constant mass & energy & rigorously conforming to the laws of kinematics we have a true & adequate account of 'what really goes on,' & that everything mental must in consequence be regarded as epi-phenomenal, as a mere 'collateral product' of a physical evolution, running 'parallel' indeed with the series of physical causes & effects, but never entering into causal relations with it. ... This now popular philosophy. ...

Having led up to the recog^n of monism as the only really satisfactory philosophy, he is able ... by eliminating the neutral or agnostic monism so often professed by the more subtly minded of our men of science, to conduct us to an idealist or spiritual interpretation of the world as the only one wh. does full justice to the concrete facts of experience.

247

2273 The Berkeleian conception of spiritual will, deepened by the ethical philosophy of Kant, & presented in a modern garb in relation to the competing claims of agnostic naturalism and a speculative idealism which seems at times to forget the limitations of human insight & to sacrifice vital realities of human experience to its overmastering desire for unity – so we might describe ... the <u>Weltanschauung</u> which lies behind all Prof. Fraser's work.

<u>Times</u> on A. Campbell Fraser's Biog.

2274   (**f87e^r**) After the death of Hegel, his system broke down, & with it German idealism. The period of materialism began.... A new philosophy arose out of the new Zeitgeist wh. had the deepest contempt for metaph.^{cs} but wh. was, nevertheless, as metaph! as Idealism. Feuerbach, the first leader of the anti-Hegelian movement, has expressed in a very neat way both his own conception & the conception of ~~the~~ ⟨his⟩ time: "God was the thought of my youth, then came Reason, last of all came Man. He, Man alone, is & must be our God. Outside of him, Salvation cannot be." It was in this subjective theory of religion that Materialism was first mirrored.

For Feuerbach God is only the projection of Man's wish. Or to put the matter antithetically:–

Hegel says: Man is the product of God
Feuerbach says: God is the product of Man.

Hegel maintains that Matter is the product of spirit. Feu.^{ch} like most of the post-Hegelian Materialists, turning Hegel topsy turvy maintains that Spirit is the product of Matter. The mot of Feuerb: "Der Mensch ist was er isst" (Man is what he eats) wittily expressed his position. [Then, through Darwin, Häckel; & through Schopenhauer Nietzsche]
        Dr Julius Goldstein. Keynote to the work of Nietzsche.
                                        Mind, April 1902

2275   What is Art? In the Academy is a definition of art which, if clearly stated, would amount to this: Art is the statement of anything with such beautiful craftsmanship as to carry its emotion ⟨(if intrinsic)⟩ on to us, or create emotion ⟨(if extrinsic)⟩ in us therefrom. The writer finds fault with the Gk. dogma that Art is the Beautiful, & with Whistler's definition of Art as the Science of Beauty.

2276   (**f87f^r**) Haldane's "Pathway to Reality" (Review, in Mind. 1903.) If he (H.) is disposed to minimize the importance of the distinction between Will & Thought, he has been affected by the insistence of recent Psychology upon "attention," & is prepared to admit that the ultimate Reality must be looked upon as Will no less than Thought.   528

2277   The great difficulty which they [Hegelians] experience is to grasp the relation which is supposed to exist between the universal

Mind & its individual manifestations. Dʳ MᶜTaggart, who professes herein to be a faithful interpreter of the Master's [Hegel's] thought, has, indeed, got rid of the difficulty of minds within a Mind by frankly admitting that the universal Mind is only a name for the organized society of individual minds. This is at least intelligible, whatever may be thought from a speculative or from a religious point of view, of the resulting Weltanschauung. ... Mr. H. has simply cut the problem altogether. ... Contempt with wh. he speaks of the individˡ. mind ... – it is merely by an abstraction that 'the mind can be regarded as one thing among many. ...'

But waiving the ~~idea~~ question of the possibility of applying the idea of part & whole to the relation between minds or 'centres of consciousness' it is at least incumbent upon a philosopher who takes this view to show that he can recognize enough individuality in the self for the purposes of ordinary life – to say nothing of morality & religion.

530

2278 "The panpsychism of Fechner & Clifford."

Mind. Apˡ 1904.

2279 (f87gʳ) The Sophoclean play of the 'Philoctetes' /?~~suggested it~~/ – the finest & the simplest of all dramas (/? Vaughan/ used to tell us) because it depends on the workings of a single /? conscience/. Theoptolemus (as you know) stole the charmed /? word/ ⟨arrows⟩ of Philoctetes – and restores them after a long inner conflict in wh. his conscience wins. It is wonderful that the play is readable, with only this & nothing more. (1800 lines?)

2280 "Men will always be sentimentalists; for a sentimentalist is simply a man who has feelings and does not take the trouble to invent a new way of expressing them."

2281 "This is the first point to remember about poetry; it is a splendid exclamation."   Chesterton.

2282 It has been said that we only see the far distant, never that which surrounds us on every side, and it is very true;

2283 (**f87g^v**) <u>Mind</u> <u>"The use & abuse of final causes"</u> (Ap! 1904)
<u>Underhill</u>.
"Men commonly suppose" he [Spinoza] says, "that all things in Nature
act, like themselves, for a purpose; insomuch that they make sure that
God himself orders all things for some fixed end; for they say that God
made all things for man's sake & man to worship him. The origin &
ground of this belief is that men, <u>being ignorant</u> of the <u>real causes</u> of
things & having a desire to seek their own interest, think themselves
free to act with a view to the desired end. Of this d. e. they are
conscious, but they know not the causes which arouse the desire. Thus
they come to regard the f.c. or final cause or purpose of an action as a
necessary & sufficient expl^n of that ac. ...

Finally Sp. goes on to explain that current notions of good & evil,
order & chaos, beauty & ugliness, &c, are relative to men's organs &
dispositions. Thus men call whatever conduces to their own b
well-being <u>good</u>; whatever is the opposite of this bad. ... And thus it is
that good & bad, beautiful & ugly, &c, – notions which are nothing but
human ways of imagining things – come to be considered by the
ignorant as the most important properties of <u>things themselves</u>.

In the same way Sp. w^d answer the common difficulties concerning
his doctrine of the perfection of the universe. If, it is objected,
everything is the result of God's perfection, whence come the many
imperfect^{ns} of Nature – corruption, ugliness, disorder, evil, sin? These,
S. answers, are merely human ways of imagining things ... things are
not more or less perf. because they delight or offend the senses of men. ...

Here S. leaves his arguments. ...

Thus final causes are to S. mere illusions. ... But, we may ask, are f.c.
any more of or less <u>humana figmenta</u> than the mechan! & mathem!
conceptions of science, wh. S. assumes to be real properties of things.
Again, are f.c. necess^{ly} interpreted in terms of human utility &
convenience? & finally, are time, change, & imperfection mere
illusions, merely relative to man?

2284 (**f88^r**) POEMS BY RICHARD CRASHAW. The Text edited by A. R.
WALLER. Cambridge English Classics. (The University Press, Cambridge. 4s. 6d.)
There are obstacles to the enjoyment of nearly all the finer poets of
the seventeenth century. Unlike the Elizabethans most of them were
lonely adventurers pursuing their own thoughts to lengths that carried
them far away from the common mind of men, and even from the

traditions of their art. Donne was the leader of the reaction against Elizabethan conventions of verse. He was ready to forgo all the traditional beauties of poetry if he could express some thought never expressed before. He hunted an idea remorselessly through images ridiculous or sublime. He strained the capacities of language, yet he enlarged them in the process; and his example, his rare but dazzling triumphs, in spite of the huge sacrifices at which they were won, tempted many other poets to be revolutionaries in their art. The seventeenth century was an age of great religious poets, and they had a reason of their own besides Donne's example for revolting against the Elizabethan traditions of poetry. It was common form for them to lament that poetry hitherto had been at the service of profane passions, and it was natural that, in trying to put it to better uses, they should be indifferent to the beauties it had acquired in that service. There is something Puritanic in the style of Herbert and Vaughan, though they were not Puritans. They make no sacrifices to beauty, and, when they achieve it, seem to do so by accident. They are never poets at large, and always write with a practical purpose; to fortify themselves against doubts and despairs, to justify the ways of God to man, to point a celestial moral in all that they see. Crashaw, no doubt, supposed himself to have the same intentions. He often tried to be homely, imitated the worst excesses of Donne, and would let any doggerel pass if only its aim was to edify. He also was a revolutionary; but in a very different way from Herbert and Vaughan. His failures are like theirs only less interesting because they are the failures, not of a writer trying to make poetry out of prosaic material, but of one seduced by the mere force of example into writing in a bad manner unnatural to him. The homely absurdities of Herbert seem part of the natural process of his thought. They are only the labours of his mind by which his sublimities are produced. The homely absurdities of Crashaw seem wantonly perverse, and nothing ever comes of them. When he is sublime it is by a different process altogether; for he was a poet at large, a poet of the vague emotions, the abstract music of youth. No doubt his piety was sincere; but, though he did not know it, he was the enthusiast of beauty rather than of holiness. Religion for him was only a symbol of all the dreams and undefined glories that haunt the brain of youth. It was what love had been to the Elizabethans and many other poets, a theme large enough and vague enough to serve as a pretext for the expression of whatever splendid images or thoughts came into his mind. Shakespeare's Sonnets are full of splendid poetry about everything that lyrical poetry can be made out of. So are Crashaw's odes. He was only 36 when he died. He was by nature a visionary, not likely to be much moved by real experiences. He was not inspired by particular events or even by particular adventures of his own mind. The world, no doubt, never tempted him as it tempted Herbert, so that he had no need to turn his religion into a practical protection against the world or to connect it in any way with realities that did not threaten or concern him. Religion for him was all an ecstasy, a state of mind into which he threw himself when he wished to enjoy the most celestial delights of thought. There were no agonies or despairs in it; no attempt and no need to support it with reason or to apply it to the problem of life. His poetry, in the words of the preface to "Steps to the Temple," is the "Quintessence of Phantasie and discourse center'd in Heaven"; centred, indeed, in a heaven that is all phantasy, and, like Shelley's visions of a golden age, all made up of the airy dreams of a mind that is happy among abstractions and never needs to rest upon the solid earth of the concrete or the particular.

It is strange to us to find a poet moved by religion as modern poets are moved by a sunset or a range of mountains; but religion in the seventeenth century was the chief concern of all visionary minds, the inspiration not only of their morality, but of their dreams. Listening to a solemn music Milton was naturally turned to thoughts of Heaven and of man redeemed to a glorious life such as that music seemed to express. Neither he nor any other poet had yet learnt to find in the beauty or the forces of nature an expression of the loftier joys and desires which possess man and which man expresses in his noblest art. The Elizabethans used the beauties of nature as mere poetic ornaments. They had more significance for Vaughan, because his piety made him search for spiritual analogies in all beautiful things. His mind worked like Wordsworth's, and he anticipated some of Wordsworth's more arbitrary fancies; but the analogies which he found were not so much felt by him as worked out with a desire to edify. Crashaw at his best had no desire to edify. He wrote to express his raptures, and if he had been a modern poet he might, like Shelley, have felt a kinship between them and the wilder forces of nature. He might have dreamt, not of a heaven of saints and martyrs quiring in unimaginable ecstacy, but of a glorified universe, such as our own in transfigured moments seemed to promise to Shelley's exalted spirit. In that case we should have understood him better. Religion to the modern mind does not seem a proper subject for vague raptures. We

demand that it shall be applied to the problems of life. We distrust its
sincerity when it seems to be made up of emotions mainly aesthetic.

2285 Criticism is not the examination of marks and prices; it is a
valuation of forces, and it is indifferent to their direction. It is
concerned with them only as forces, and it is concerned with force only
in its kind and degree.   A. Symons.

2286   I ha' harpit a shadow out o' the sun
         To stand before your face and cry;
       I ha' armed the earth beneath your heel,
         And over your head I ha' dusked the sky.

       I ha' harpit ye up to the throne o' God.
         I ha' harpit your midmost soul in three;
       I ha' harpit ye down to the Hinges o' Hell.
         And – ye – would – make – a Knight o' me!

                              one of Mr. Kipling's minor poems,

2287   (**f88ᵛ**) Musical Full Stops
   What would the critics and the cultivated public say of a writer who
spread a sentence over many pages? Can we conceive the effect of, say,
a chapter by Thackeray a lecture by Ruskin or a poem by Browning
that contained not a single full stop and only a few commas? Yet that is
what our music-makers of to-day and the near past have asked us to
accept. We are to listen by the hour to music that flows on in an
uninterrupted stream of motives and themes worked into an intricate
embroidery music – that sometimes seeks to express emotions and
complicated phases of life, for which music has no words. It has come
to such a pass that not infrequently when a new work is produced we
are warned that we must not expect to form any judgment of it upon a
single hearing, that we must not hope to be able to understand it until
we have listened to it again and again. When authors are obscure, if
they become great it is despite their faults, as was the case with such as
Carlyle, Meredith and Browning. He that has anything to say should
so say it that it can be understood of the people.
   In passing, it is noteworthy that music is the only art that advances
before its time; indeed, almost the only art that advances at all. Poetry,
prose to a great extent, painting, sculpture – they all stand where they

stood hundreds of years ago, their method of expression remaining practically the same from age to age. But the music of to-day would astound the musicians of yesterday: it would be to them an unknown tongue. And the music of to-morrow – how can we of this day understand it? Wagner was incomprehensible to his contemporaries, and he is still a difficulty to many; he speaks a language many of us have not been able to master. And what say our critics of Strauss? They seem afraid to venture an opinion; they point to Wagner's experiences and say "Let us wait and see; he may be great, and it would not be wise for us to venture an opinion of his work."

But, after all, art should express to its own age the life of the times and its emotions; if it do that truly and in a manner that can be understood and not mistaken, it is live art both for its own and for after days. Does the music of our most "advanced" composers fulfil this demand? As we sit and listen to it does one receive any message or do we wonder what it all means? Do we long for a full stop occasionally as the minutes pass by and the intricate and sometimes not lovely sounds flow on? We may – those of us who cannot accept all this new teaching – be foolish; our ears may be stopped to the voice of the wise charmer. Or we may be the wise ones, going back as we often do to old masters, with their splendid clarity and straightforward emotional expression. It is one of the charms of the old operas that they were so peppered with full stops; it is one of the weaknesses of the new that they strive to have none, seldom even a comma or a semicolon. To plead the emotional complexity of the age is no valid excuse; literature has not raised that empty plea; letters to-day are no more complex than they were before; a man who cannot put into plain words a plain meaning is not accepted as a great writer, unless he have a very great message to deliver. Must we then accept, without questioning, music that has to be heard again and again before we know what it is that the composer has attempted to speak forth; music that is so complex that its message has often to be unravelled by its writer in written words, it being necessary to tell us what it means lest we should misinterpret it; music with never a full stop?   Academy Oct 1. 1904

2288   POEMS, by Alfred Noyes. London, Blackwood, 7s. 6d.
    Here, beyond question, is the work of a genuine poet.
    Take this lilting ballad of "Sherwood," to begin with:–

    Hark! the dazzled laverock climbs the golden steep:
    Marian is waiting: is Robin Hood asleep?

Round the fairy grass-rings frolic elf and fay,
In Sherwood, in Sherwood, about the break of day.

Oberon, Oberon, rake away the gold,
Rake away the red leaves, roll away the mould,
Rake away the gold leaves, roll away the red,
And wake Will Scarlett from his leafy forest bed.

Friar Tuck and Little John are riding down together,
With quarter-staff and drinking-can and grey goose-feather;
The dead are coming back again; the years are rolled away,
In Sherwood, in Sherwood, about the break of day.

2289 There is a striking article by Dr. William Barry on the connection between "Agnosticism and National Decay," which will well repay perusal. We quote the concluding passage:–

Ignorance of God lies at the root of social anarchy. It is fatal to genius. It has no words of condemnation for prudent vice. It has never yet convinced the pleasure-seeker that he had any duty to others except to get enjoyment out of them. The evidence is abundant and is accumulating that the agnostic negation is not simply negative. Under its influence, precepts most positive, shaping the creed of no small number, have risen from the deeps. When we look at the ways of business, fashion, literature, and at social statistics, a new Decalogue appears in view. What are its commandments? I seem to read among them these: "Thou shalt make money, have no children, commit adultery, plead in the Divorce Court, and, such duties done, commit suicide." Not the individual only, but the nation, if it loses its old Christian prejudices, will enter on this journey towards Hades. The test and proof that a mistake has been made by our Agnostic philosophers are to be found in the national decay which follows on their teaching, as darkness follows on eclipse. And by national decay nothing else is meant than the suicide of the race, consequent on frauds in marriage, a dwindling birth-rate, unlimited divorce, degeneracy in offspring, the abuse of stimulants and of pleasure, the clouding of intellect, all which are fated to terminate in one disease – the denial of the will to live. Professor Huxley, to hinder this consummation, falls back on Christian ethics, which cannot flourish when the Gospel has been rejected. Mr. Herbert Spencer concludes a life spent in preaching agnostic science by affirming its bankruptcy in the past, its hopelessness in the future. We could not wish for a conjunction of proofs more formidable and more unexpected in support of Burke's great political axiom, that "the institutor, and author, and protector of civil society" is One Whom our modern teachers refuse to have in their knowledge.

(Record, 14 March 1905)

2290 (**f89ʳ**) Bishop Creighton – "Carlyle, Froude, Ruskin, all bore me in their prophetic capacity. ..." An Englishman is not only without ideas, but he hates an idea when he sees it. ... No people do so much harm as those who go about doing good."   Life.

2291 The Human Will – Reflex action. A reflex arc consists of a sensory nerve fibre, such as, let us say, the optic nerve; a sensory cell, such as those from wh. the fibres of the optic nerve are derived; & a motor cell & fibre, such as those wh. control the muscular tissues of the iris. When a beam of light enters the eye, the reflex arc is called into action, the iris is stimulᵈ & the pupil contracts. ... It is entirely independent of consciousness.
    Will, is the expression of imperfection [in this mechanism]. ...
    Whilst will emerges from reflex action, to reflex action will can return ... e.g. piano-playing & c. ...
                    17 Dec. 1904, C. W. Saleeby (in Academy)

2292 Emerson's Rules for Readers. Do not read a book wh. is less than a year old, read only books that are famed, & never read any book you do not like.
                    J. Morley (lecture). [The two latter are doubtful].
                    Times. 19:12:04

2293 Begin with Byron. He was not the greatest of poets, but he had daring, energy, & the historic sense, with a loathing for cant in all its forms. At the beginnᵍ of the last cent. he was the great central inspiring force of democracy on the Cont. of Europe & when democracy ... applied for inspirⁿ to poetry ... then B. wᵈ once more have his day.
                    J. Morley, ib.

2294 (**f89ᵛ**) <u>Miss Dickinson's Poems</u> (Methuen)

> Apparently with no surprise
>> To any happy flower
>
> The frost beheads it at its play
>> In accidental power
>
> The bland assassin passes on,
>> The sun proceeds unmoved
>
> To measure off another day
>> For an approving God.

———— # ————

2295 [definition in <u>further</u> terms]
  <u>Also</u>:–

> I died for beauty, but was scarce
>> Adjusted in the tomb
>
> When one who died for truth was lain [sic]
>> In an adjourning room.

> He questioned softly why I failed?
>> "For beauty," I replied.
>
> "And I for truth. – the two are one,
>> We brethren are," he said.

> And so, as kinsmen met a night
>> We talked between the rooms
>
> Until the moss had reached our lips
>> And covered up our names.

2296 Prose may be justified by the novelty of its matter and by ①
a hundred other things. Verse can only be justified by the
beauty and power of its expression, for it is a means of
expression and not a means of communicating knowledge or of

doing any other useful thing. Being a means of expression its subject-matter is the emotions, and whatever thought or reasoning it may contain is employed as a means of giving fuller expression to the emotions. Donne was a heretic because he employed thought and reasoning in verse often for their own sake and not to express his emotions. Much, therefore, of the subject-matter of his verse is prosaic; and he by the perverted daring of his genius gave a twist to English taste and set it looking for a prosaic interest in poetry, which it continued to do until it turned poetry into prose. In Donne's time that prosaic interest was novelty and audacity of thought. In the eighteenth century it was good sense and logic; but the one error was only a natural development from the other, and Donne and Pope alike often used similes for their ingenuity rather than for their emotional force.

Yet Donne was a great poet, and his method, mistaken as it proved to be when others used it, in his hands produced momentary beauties of an intensity beyond what any more legitimate method has ever produced. He made prosaic mistakes not because he was a man with a prosaic mind trying to write poetry, but because he was a poet of impracticable ambitions. He had both the passion and the imagination of a poet, but he was not content to express them like other poets. He wished to use as instruments for their expression all the science and philosophy which his restless questioning brain had stored up. Life was all made up of questions for him; and his love, which in youth was the intensest part of his life, bristled with them. He reasoned about it as the theologians of his time reasoned about the nature of God. He set out to explain it in verse as well as to express it, with the result that his verse is the strangest mixture of reason and passion, too often in a distracting conflict, but sometimes fused.

(2) He would prove that nothing could happen from which some encouragement of love might not be drawn. This fanaticism, this determination to turn his passion into a business and to feel it in all the commonplaces of life, is the motive of his celebrated realism. Just as an artist like Degas, convinced that art glorifies everything, will draw the ugliest objects to prove it, so Donne wrote to prove that every kind of idea and experience can be pressed into the service of love. Degas, a pupil of Ingres,

revolted against the classical system of selection; and so Donne, brought up among the Elizabethans, revolted against their conventional range of subjects easy to be versified. They seemed to him to aim at a "fugitive and cloistered" beauty, to escape the chief difficulties of poetry by a system of renunciation. It was his aim to train his art upon the whole experience of life. Nothing should be common or unclean to it. No process of thought should be too arduous to be pursued by his imagination. In fact he wished to break down the natural barriers between poetry and prose; but unlike the writers of the eighteenth century he attacked those barriers from the side of poetry. The attempt, of course, was impossible, but sometimes he seems to achieve the impossible, sometimes his poetry seems to have a greater force than any other because of the very obstructions through which it has fought its way before it blazes upon us.

Times. 27.1.05

2297 Music. there are always two classes of listeners; one which is attracted by intricacy of form and design, one which is drawn to emotion and colour. The first like to hear Bach and Mozart; the second prefer Wagner and Tschaikowsky. Both are in pursuit of satisfaction and beauty, but each seeks them in a different locality. It can hardly be said that one is superior to the other, any more than we can say that a man who prefers sculpture is better or worse than a man who exalts painting. It is merely a form of the everlasting rivalry between form and colour, in which friendly contest it is often alleged that form corresponds to dead beauty, while colour represents life; a statement which is contradicted by the fact that some of the loveliest colourings are found in close connexion with decay – when the form is beginning to shrivel – whilst on the other side, much importance is given to the contention that the truest beauty is that of shape, independent of any charming trappings. "Occasional Papers." Duncan Hume –

2298 Art & thought equal:–
"The West front of Wells is a masterpiece of art indeed, made of imagery [&....?] in just proportion so that we may call them 'vera et spirantia signa'" Fuller.

2299   "It [the first chapter of Genesis] teaches clearly that dualism, that refuge of many ancient Eastern thinkers, is entirely impossible, and foreign to the whole idea of true religion."

– The Record. "Hours with the Bible." By the Revd W. H. Griffith Thomas, D. D. – Friday, May 25. 1906.

~~~~~~~~~~~~~~~~~

2300   "War is a game which, were their subjects wise, Kings would not play at."   (Quoted by G. W. Russell)

2301   **(f89a^r)**   THE NEW ENGLISH ART CLUB.   Times   Oct 14:05

It was said of the New English Art Club not long ago that it had become a nursery for the Royal Academy; and the implication was that it had lowered its standard of revolt and was turning respectable. It is true that the Royal Academy, in its serene manner of turning all things to its own good, has been careful to benefit, in more ways than one, by the activity of the rebellious little body; it has taken some of its best men and opened its doors to work which, but for the movement expressed in the New English Art Club, might never have been seen in Burlington House. But the work is not finished yet, and the suggestion of respectability is unfounded. The revolt against the conventional and the pretty is as strong as ever; it is only that we are growing used to the New English Art Club, and are not so much surprised at it as we were.

Take for text the work of Mr. A. E. John in the exhibition that is to be opened on Monday at the gallery of the Alpine Club in Mill-street, Maddox-street. This year Mr. John gives the capital expression of the tradition (if we may mention such a thing in this connexion) and the aims of the club. He is determined, that in his pictures, at any rate, there shall be no concession to the commonplace and the pretty. Beauty – if beauty have anything to do with the matter – is truth; truth, beauty; and if in telling the truth we succeed also in shocking the *bourgeois*, why, so much the better! He will tell you exactly what he saw, and exactly as he saw it. And he paints (No. 3) a "Mother and Child" – a naked and very ugly baby, with staring eyes and open·mouth, sitting on the arm of a mother in whose face there is none of the traditional look of mothers. She wears a very ugly yellow bodice with dark blue bows, and holds stiffly up in her right hand a green toy beetle with a bright red head. The picture makes one ask whether the individuality of the artist is really so tyrannous, and whether it would not have been possible for

Mr. John to retain it and yet express it in a pleasanter manner. He would doubtless reply that so long as the picture was well painted (and that it certainly is) and was a faithful expression of his vision we had no right to ask more. There is an equally defiant challenge in his No. 96, which he names "Cupid and Nymphs." Had he called it "Three nude women and a boy in a landscape" we should merely have objected that certain parts of the figures, the foreshortened left leg, of the woman in the centre, for instance, seemed to us unworthy of his draughtsmanship, and asked whence came the enjoyable touch of yellow light between the legs of the woman on the right. To call the picture "Cupid and Nymphs" is to insist on the strength of the individuality which can so throw overboard associations of traditional beauty, and give us a fine piece of design, indeed, but a revolution in sentiment. Mr. John contributes also an uncompromising portrait called "Flora" (No. 28) and two vigorous little chalk sketches of figures (Nos. 42 and 60). Mr. L. A. Harrison's disregard for the ordinary sense of beauty is almost equal to Mr. John's. In one of his clever portraits (No. 90) he purposely throws the sitter's head round so that one of the tendons of her rather thin neck may stand out; and then he calls attention to it as loudly as possible. That tendon is a flag of revolt. In No. 100 he is kinder to us and to his sitter; the portrait of a young girl in red is brilliant and pleasing, while his No. 12, again, is as likely to be called ugly as anything of Mr. John's. It is in Mr. W. Orpen's work that we find the uncompromising and the beautiful united. We should call Mr. Orpen the fine flower of the New English Art Club. He has a picture (No. 14) which he names "The Saint of Poverty." It is the glorification of the commonplace, a picture of an old man, unshaven and ragged, with a bare breast showing very white against his dark coat, and his hands folded across. The hands are toil-stained, gnarled, and worn; but they are so well painted, so full of recognizable truth and meaning that they are incontestably things of beauty. There is individuality in every stroke of this masterly picture, and in all Mr. Orpen's work; but to be different from other people is a result of his regard for his meaning, not his first aim. His No. 74, "Lottie of Paradise Walk," a picture of a flower-girl, is of a rich colour very different from the "Saint of Poverty"; his "Spanish Woman" (No. 97), a half-nude figure with the face hidden by falling black hair, compels admiration by the quality of the flesh-painting; and his interior, "Waiting for their Cue" (No. 97), is altogether beautiful in its clarity and the arrangement of its light.

2302   what is the real essence of classicism in its good sense. Modern criticism assumes that the more a thing becomes human the more it will become modern. The best classicism says that the more a thing becomes human the less it will become modern; the less, that is to say, it will have any characteristic of any current civilization. The essence of realism is to say that the real man has a black coat. The essence of classicism is to say that the real man has no clothes at all. The one spirit seeks to find humanity by following out the modern tendencies: the other by tearing them away.

2303   Paganism is Agnosticism which is sufficiently agnostic to admit the probability of spirits.   Chesterton. D. News. 17.3.'06
   for "Paganism" read ⟨"Modern⟩ Christianity," or "Present-day Christianity"

2304   (**f89aᵛ**) '*Menippus*. Where are all the beauties, Hermes? Show me round; I am a new-comer.   'Death
   Hermes. I am busy, Menippus. But look over there to your   keeps
right, and you will see Hyacinth, Narcissus, Nireus,   his
Achilles, Tyro, Helen, Leda, – all the beauties of old.   court.'
   Me. I can only see bones, and bare skulls; most of them
are exactly alike.
   Her. Those bones, of which you seem to think so lightly,
have been the theme of admiring poets.
   Me. Well, but show me Helen; I shall never be able to
make her out by myself.
   Her. This skull is Helen.
   Me. And for this a thousand ships carried warriors from
every part of Greece; Greeks and barbarians were slain, and
cities made desolate.
   Her. Ah, Menippus, you never saw the living Helen; or
you would have said with Homer.

        Well might they suffer grievous years of toil
        Who strove for such a prize.

We look at withered flowers, whose dye is gone from them,
and what can we call them but unlovely things? Yet in the
hour of their bloom these unlovely things were things of
beauty.

Me. Strange, that the Greeks could not realize what it was for which they laboured; how short-lived, how soon to fade.

Her. I have no tune for moralizing. Choose your spot, where you will, and lie down. I must go to fetch new dead. ....'

Hermes. Ferryman, what do you say to settling up accounts? It will prevent any unpleasantness later on. ...

Charon. I can't just now, Hermes; we shall have a war or a plague presently, and then the passengers will come shoaling in, and I shall be able to make a little by jobbing the fares.

Her. So for the present I have nothing to do but sit down, and pray for the worst, as my only chance of getting paid?

Ch. There is nothing else for it; – very little business doing just now, as you see, owing to the peace.

Her. That is just as well, though it does keep me waiting for my money. After all, though, Charon, in old days men were men; you remember the state they used to come down in, – all blood and wounds generally. Nowadays, a man is poisoned by his slave or his wife; or gets dropsy from over-feeding; a pale, spiritless lot, nothing like the men of old. Most of them seem to meet their end in some plot that has money for its object.

Ch. Ah; money is in great request.

Her. Yes; you can't blame me if I am somewhat urgent for payment. ....'

> The Lack of Pence.

[From *The Works of Lucian of Samosata*. Translated by H. W. and F. G. FOWLER. In Four Volumes. Clarendon Press. *Published by Henry Frowde*. Price 14s. net ($4.75).]

2305 (**f90^r**) K̲e̲a̲t̲s̲.

He is the poet of beauty; of beauty in nature, in the art of words, in human life and story. It is true that his life is a progress from sensuousness to sympathy, and that he came to the strongest conviction, as strong as that which Tennyson put into the "Palace of Art," that self-absorbed abandonment to the aesthetic pleasures is a drinking of deadly poison, fatal to the highest possibilities that lie before men, not merely as human beings, but as artists. But though that doctrine is to be found in his poems, in "Sleep and Poetry" for instance, and in "Hyperion," it is not the prevailing impression they leave behind them. Other men might moralize beauty better than Keats; his business was to realize its presence to a unique degree. This poet and that in our history had gifts which he had not; greater gifts than his, and his gifts in a greater degree; but none had this gift in his peculiar measure – the gift of seeing beauty everywhere, till the reader who travels through his poems feels that the world, within and without, has become an enchanted garden, the small is seen not as insignificance but as delicacy, the large not as heaviness but as majesty, action takes a new grace, and rest a new dignity,

From the beginning he lived and watched "nature's gentle doings" as no one else ever did. Watched – that was his business; not interpreted – that was Wordsworth's.   Times

2306   Matthew Arnold. May I reproduce some lines from the first two paragraphs of his essay on "The Study of Poetry"? He says:

"The future of poetry is immense, because in poetry, where it is worthy of its high destinies, our race, as time goes on, will find an ever surer and surer stay. There is not a creed which is not shaken, not an accredited dogma which is not shown to be questionable, not a received tradition which does not threaten to dissolve. Our religion has materialized itself in the fact, in the supposed fact; it has attached its emotion to the fact, and now the fact is failing it. But for poetry the idea is everything; the rest is a world of illusion, of divine illusion. Poetry attaches its emotion to the idea; the idea *is* the fact. The strongest part of our religion to-day is its unconscious poetry."

He goes on to say: "Let me be permitted to quote these words of my own, as uttering the thought which should, in my opinion, go with us and govern us in all our study of poetry. ... We should conceive of poetry worthily, and more highly than it has been the custom to conceive of it. We should conceive of it as capable of higher uses, and called to higher destinies than those which in general men have assigned to it hitherto. More and more mankind will discover that we have to turn to poetry to interpret life for us, to console us, to sustain us. Without poetry, our science will appear incomplete; and most of what now passes with us for religion and philosophy will be replaced by poetry. ... Our religion, parading evidences such as those on which the popular mind relies now; our philosophy, pluming itself on its reasonings about causation and finite and infinite being; what are they but the shadows and dreams and false shows of knowledge? The day will come when we shall wonder at ourselves for having trusted to them, for having taken them seriously; and the more we perceive their hollowness, the more we shall prize 'the breath and finer spirit of knowledge,' offered to us by poetry."

––––––––– # –––––––––

2307 OLD CROME.

He was a man of the soil – that soil of East Anglia that produced Constable and Gainsborough. When we think of the great landscape painters who sprang from the "Folk Lands of Norfolk and Suffolk," and drew their inspiration from the large skies and distances, we are again reminded how local a thing painting is, and always has been. Art has boundaries: it is bounded by the limits of the district a painter feels, and feeling, interprets. When Crome had swung into his stride the work of other painters, living or dead, was nothing to him. The Norwich men would never have emerged from obscurity had they worked after the formula of Sir George Beaumont, who surrounded himself with Claudes, Poussins and Wilsons, and painted his own picture with a picture by one of those masters on an easel by his side. Old Crome is great because he was a stay-at-home; because he studied Nature, not Art; because, like Millet, he was strong, large and elemental, and because he had mastered his craft.

L. HIND in DY. CH.^{LE}

2308 (**f90^v**) "The Metaphysics of Nature" by Carneth Read. (Black 7/6) 1905

Matter, he says has empirical reality, but "in ultimate r^y matter has no place" It is merely a manifestation in consciousness of something wh. is not in [but beyond] consc^s

As to the Absolute the Profess^r denies the dogma that it is consc^ss & nothing but consciousness. ... "The conception of ultimate Reality" he says, "is not simple but contains a duality, namely consc^ss & the Transcendent Being ... that is conscious. ..." In the consc^ss wh. goes to constitute ultimate Reality is included our own consc^ss Herein Prof^r C. Read agrees with Mr F. H. Bradley. There is included also "the cons^ss of what we call inorganic Nature." This doctrine, which is becoming prevalent, the philosop^rs may be considered to have derived from the poets, esp. fr. Wordsth In our own consc^ss according to our philosopher, we have an immed^{te} knowledge of reality, but ⟨one?⟩

conscˢˢ does not comprise the whole of reality; the remainder is not in conscˢˢ, but is manifested in conscˢˢ by phenomena. "Manifested" he declares, is the right word for this relation. ... 'Objectivation' Schopenhᵣ̇ called it. ... It stands for a relation of wh. there is only one term in experience; it is therefore an Imperfect Category, not constitutive, but only indicative or orectic; for the other term, lying beyond experience, is inapprehensible.

Time is pronounced to be more real than Space, the reason (**f91ʳ**) ... being that Time is the form of all consˢˢ (wh. is reality), whereas Space is "only the form of phenomena." Time indeed belongs to ultimate reality. Space, we are told is a growth of animal intelligence – a growth wh. is complete before the rise of self-conscˢˢ. ... The same is true of nature, wh. "has been projected in organic history as an Object in contrast with a subject. ... It is because the object precedes self that by all animals as by unsophisticated man the object is assumed to be an object for all.

Such are some of the main ideas. ... Remarks we have to offer. ... If space & nature are growths of animal intelligᶜᵉ it follows that an. int. existed before Sp. & N. The natural World therefore came into being in Time. But instead of having been created by God it was the outcome of bestial intelligᶜᵉ – a conclusion wh. a pessimist might say threw light on some of its characteristics. Again intelligᶜᵉ is always accomp. by organization. How then did the intellᶜᵉ that projected space contrive to have an organism before there was space for that organism to exist in?. ... What Profʳ C.R. says of Space may stand good as a psychⁱ account of the origin of our idea of it."   S. R. 21 Oct. 1905

[The contentions of both author & reviewer show that the attempt to make consciousness, as we know it, precede matter & its evolutions, is futile]

2309   (**f91ᵛ**) <u>Amazing old man</u> – <u>Verdi</u>. "From the ashes of his [early] popularity, from the rubbish of "Il Trovatore" & its kind, there arose on a sudden a sort of phoenix Verdi. 'Had he died at Mozart's death-age he would now be practically unknown."
                                          [quot. from where?]

2310   Verdi. "... Mme Tetrazzini has been allowed to put back the clock & to revive the opera of 50 y.^{rs} ago in order that her powers may be heard fully. ... In the old Italian opera the soprano must perforce curvet & pirouette through many meaningless pages; but occasionally the composer lit upon a situation or an emotion wh. c^d be advanced by the singer's col⟨or⟩atura, & a great aria was the result. Because of the misuse of the florid aria composers have hastily made up their minds to banish the whole use of it. ... If Verdi had lived to be a centenarian he might have found the key to the problem. The letter scene in <u>Falstaff</u> shows him well on the way to it. With long enough life Verdi might have done almost anything; but the trouble with him was that he had only just arrived at maturity at the age of threescore & ten or thereabouts, so that to complete his life he ought to have lived a hundred & fifty years."

Times Lit. Sup! Aug 13.08

2311   "The materialistic assertion of a self-originating world which only comes to consciousness in <u>us</u>."   S. R. 11.5.07

2312   (**f92^r**) HOLIDAY AND OTHER POEMS. With a Note on Poetry. By JOHN DAVIDSON. (Grant Richards. 3s. 6d. net.)

Verse, like all art, produces pleasure by giving an air of naturalness to that which is not natural. Your picture or poem seems, and is not; the painter, bound to the unnaturalness of canvas, produces a man; the poet, bound to the unnaturalness of rhyme or metre, produces human speech. "On s'attendait à voir un auteur," as Pascal said, "et on trouve un homme." That is a great part of the charm of good verse – one knows that it is produced under rules and limitations, and yet it seems free and self-developed; the chains are worn so lightly that they are invisible or even ornamental. But this is equally the case whether accepted limitations have been those of rhyme or of blank verse.

There is no difference in kind. But the burden is no doubt not always on the same shoulders in the two cases. Poetry is art in nature, and also nature in art; and if in rhyme it is difficult not to lose nature in art, in blank verse it is only too easy to lose art in nature. The rhymer's danger is that his rhymes may give too much of artificiality to art; the danger of the blank verse poet is that, unless he is a master of the arts of rhythm and pause and balance, his verse so easily becomes mere divided prose.

Times 17.8.06

2313 I remember being rather taken with a little two-stanza lyric
which appeared in Mr. Ernest Myers' volume of "Poems" in 1877. It
ran as follows:–

> Stay me no more; the flowers have ceased to blow,
> The frost begun;
> Stay me no more; I will arise and go,
> My dream is done.
> My feet are set upon a sterner way,
> And I must on;
> Love, thou hast dwelt with me a summer day,
> Now, Love, begone.

I was a young man at the time, and this pleased me. Now, in my middle
age, I open the "Gathered Poems of Ernest Myers," just issued, only to
find my old favourite transmogrified into this:–

> Hold us not here; the flowers have ceased to blow,
> The frost begun;
> Hold us not here; we will arise and go,
> The dream is done.
> Our feet are set upon a sterner way,
> And we must on;
> Ease, thou has dwelt with us a summer day,
> But now begone.

There is also a third stanza, wholly new to me. It is, no doubt,
characteristic of the middle-aged Muse that in these later lines "ease"
should be substituted for "love."

2314   Or this – the high-water-mark of the poetry from the bush –

> I've had my share of pastime, and I've done my share of toil,
>   And life is short – the longest life a span;
> I care not now to tarry for the corn·or for the oil,
>   Or for wine that maketh glad the heart of man.
> For good undone, and gifts misspent, and resolutions vain
>   'Tis somewhat late to trouble. This I know –
> I should live the same life over, if I had to live again;
>   And the chances are I go where most men go.

It seems scarcely loyal to verse of that high and haunting calibre to print it side by side with some of the weary exercises which disfigure this rather tiresome little book.

D. Chron. Nov. '06 Review of an Australian book of verses.

2315 STUDIES IN SEVEN ARTS. By ARTHUR SYMONS. (Constable. 8s. 6d. net.)
he preserves a constant standard of criticism.

"For my part," he writes in one of these essays, "I know only one really reassuring test of the value of a work of art. Here is something on which time has not yet set its judgment; place it beside something as like it as possible, on which the judgment of time seems to have been set, and see if it can endure the comparison. Let it be as unlike as you please, and the test will still hold good. I can pass from an overture of Wagner to a mazurka of Chopin as easily as from a play of Shakespeare to a song of Herrick. The one may be greater than the other, but the one is not more genuine than the other."

This may be a little overstated (could Mr. Symons pass quite easily from Isolde's Death-song to an aria of Mozart?), but the principle is the right one, as Matthew Arnold proclaimed in a well-known page. Constant familiarity with the greatest art, that is the secret;

Nov. 1906

———————//———————

2316 His plan: (Lafcadio Hearn's)
I never read a book which does not powerfully impress the imagination; but whatever contains novel, curious, potent imagery I always read, no matter what the subject. When the soil of fancy is really well-enriched with innumerable fallen leaves, the flowers of language grow spontaneously. There are four things especially which enrich fancy – mythology, history, romance, poetry, – the last being really the crystallisation of all human desire after the impossible, the diamonds created by prodigious pressure of suffering. Now there is very little really good poetry, so it is easy to choose. In history I think one should only seek the extraordinary, the monstrous, the terrible; in mythology the most fantastic and sensuous, just as in romance. But there is one more absolutely essential study in the formation of a strong style –

science. No romance equals it. If one can store up in his brain the most extraordinary facts of astronomy, geology, ethnology, etc., they furnish him with a wonderful and startling variety of images, symbols, and illustrations.

(Review of Lafcadio Hearn's Life in D. News) 11.1.1907.

2317   (**f92ᵛ**) "Poems." By Thomas Boyd. Dublin: O Donoghue and Co. 2s. 6d. 1906.

The best poem in this strain is a lament upon a young Irish poet, of rare promise, who died prematurely a year or two ago. The poem is too long to quote in full, but we hope that the quotations we can give will show its beauty:

> He came from Ballyvourney, and we called him
>   "Ballyvourney,"
> The sweetest name in Erinn that we know;
> And they tell me he has taken now the last, the last long journey;
>   And it's young he is, it's young he is, so very far to go.
>
> Where are you, Ballyvourney? God is good, and will be giving
>   Their own heaven, as they wish it, to the Gael:
> In an island like our island there in joy you will be living,
>   Where the simple joys you loved will never fail.
>
> There you strike the golden ball, and there you will be dancing.
>   Who but you could foot it well? I have seen you many a time:
> And there you rest by shining trees, where lights of heaven are
>   glancing,
>   Listening to the holy birds that sing the hours in chime.

2318   COLERIDGE AND SHELLEY stand by themselves alone. The genius of Coleridge at its highest rose above the genius of any other poet on record in the special and distinctive qualities of the very highest poetry – creative imagination and coequal expression of the thing conceived. But in these qualities Shelley stands next to him, and not far off – either in power of conception, or in mastery of such verse as includes and combines the respective gifts of the painter, the musician, and the sculptor.   A. C. SWINBURNE.

2319 A DANISH THINKER. Times 25.8.06
THE PHILOSOPHY OF RELIGION. By DR. HARALD HÖFFDING, Professor in
the University of Copenhagen. Translated from the German edition by
B. E. Meyer. (Macmillan, 12s. net.)

The author seems, as he says in his concluding sentences, to be
settling his own spiritual account, making use, in so doing, of
everything which he has learnt in the school of life and of inquiry.
Hence he speaks as a man to men, and his book claims the respectful
attention of all who are prepared to discuss seriously and without
prejudice the ultimate questions of human thought.

"Science has worked up to the view that all changes in existence are
transformations from one form of life to another, transformations which
take place according to definite quantitative relations. Existence is
unrolled before us as a great web of interrelated and continuous
elements." Quite distinct from this ideal of explanation is what
theologians have called the judgment of value, the estimation of
existence in its different forms as possessing intrinsic worth or
significance; and though the scientific ideal were realized, this further
question would still remain. This is specifically the problem of ethics
and religion. Ethics deals with the recognition and co-ordination of the
supreme values of human life; "the core of religion consists in the
conviction that no value perishes out of the world."

But the general question remains, How far is the faith of religion in
the conservation of values reconcilable with a strictly scientific account
of the world? This is the chief question of the philosophy of religion.

If, with these general philosophical presuppositions, we proceed to
deal with the religious question of the fate of values, we must at least
admit the possibility that the causal web of interrelations may exist
simply for the sake of the valuable content which it unfolds.

> Existence must at any rate contain within itself the necessary
> conditions for the existence of those values which men have learnt to
> recognize or have been able to produce. No one can ever prove that
> the genesis of the valuable in the world is due to an accident. It may
> be that the innermost essence of existence only reveals itself at the
> points at which value appears.

It is no doubt difficult to reconcile this view with the presence in
existence of so much that is not valuable or the reverse of valuable; still
such a belief constitutes the essence of religious faith.

But the fundamental axiom of the conservation of value must not be rashly supposed, our author warns us, to guarantee the conservation of any definite empirical value.

Our highest values may be only elements in a more comprehensive order of things. The confusion of particular definite values with eternal values is therefore essentially irreligious; it is a species of self-will. The most deeply religious utterance was the prayer of Jesus, "Not my will, but Thine be done." Professor Höffding applies this criterion even to the supreme case of personal immortality.

> The horizon [he says] has not closed down upon me, but the more I have looked round on the world of thought and reality, the more clearly it has been borne in upon me that those who are ready to preach that, were there no future life, this life would lose all its value, take a great responsibility upon themselves. The values which existence produces, and by which we live, do not necessarily fail because their fate in time and in eternity does not lie open before us. The philosophy of religion can appeal here to an idea which, since Rousseau's time, has been the fundamental idea of modern pedagogics. Every period of life has, or ought to have, its own proper significance, and must not be regarded merely as a preparation for one that is coming. The eternal is in the present, in every valuable moment, in each ray of sunshine, in the striving which takes Excelsior as its motto. To live eternal life in the midst of time, that is the true immortality, whether there is any other immortality or not. The distinction between end and means falls away in such moments and in such strivings, as indeed it always disappears when there is any true personal life.

2320 'I wish our clever young poets would remember my homely definitions of prose and poetry; that is, prose – words in their best order; – poetry, the *best* words in the best order.'

Coleridge. Biog. Lit.

2321 (**f93ʳ**) "Wordsworth's erroneous critical views of the necessʸ of approxᵍ the langᵍᵉ of poetry, as much as possible, to that of prose, especially by the avoidance of grammǃ inversions, arose from his having overlooked the necessity of manifesting, as well as moving in, the bonds of verse. In the finest specimens of versificᵑ there seems to be a perpetual conflict between the laws of the verse & the freedom of the lang^ge, & each is incessantly, though insignificantly, violated for the purpose of giving effect to the other."   C. Patmore.

2322 "The metrical & musical element ... commonly assumes conspicuousness ... in speech ... in prop.^n to the amount of emotion. ... Metre, in the primary degree of a simple series of isochronous intervals marked by accents, is as natural to spoken language as an even pace is nat! to walking. ... Now as dancing is no more than an increase of the element of measure which already exists in walking, so verse is but an addit! degree of that metre wh. is inherent in prose speaking. ..."
                                                                    ib.

2323 "... The prose of a common law report differs from that of an impass.^ned piece of oratory just in the same way that the semi-prosaic dramatic verse differs from an elaborate lyric. This is no new doctrine; it is as old as criticism."   ib.

2324 English metre. – "... The function of marking, by whatever means, certain isochronous intervals. ... Two indispensable conditions of metre. 1: that the sequence of vocal utterance ... shall be divided into equal or proport!^e spaces; 2: that the fact of that division shall be made manifest by an 'ictus' or beat."   ib.

2325 (**f93**^v) "Accentual" division of time the sole source of metre. ... "Feet" not true measures. e.g.

For oné restraint, Lords of the world besidé.

Here, same time ... to elapse between 1 & 2, 2 & 3, 3 & 4; but between 1 & 2, one unaccented syl; betw. 2 & 3 none; betw. 3 & 4, two.
    The common notion of an exact proportion inherent in syl.^s them.^s seems to be quite untenable.   ib.

2326 Great general law ... wh. I believe I am now for the first time stating, that the elementary measure, or integer, of Eng. verse, is double the measure of ordinary prose, – that is to say, it is the space wh. is bounded by alternate accents. ...
    Every verse proper contains 2, 3, or 4, of these metres, or as they may be called 'dipodes'. ... All Eng. verses in common cadence are therefore

dimeters, trimeters, or tetrameters, & consist, when they are <u>full</u> – i.e., without <u>catalexis</u> – of 8, 12, or 16 syl. Verses in triple cadence obey the same law.   ib.

2327   "Unless we are to go directly against the analogy of music, & to regard every verse affected with catalexis (or a deficiency in the number of syllables requisite to make it a full dimeter, trimeter, tetrameter, &c) as constituting an entire metrical system in itself, (**f94ʳ**) which is obviously absurd, we must reckon the missing syllables as substituted by an equivalent pause."   ib.

2328   <u>Magna est veritas</u>.

When all its work is done, the lie shall rot;
The truth is great, & shall prevail
When none cares whether it prevail or not.

                                                                        <u>Patmore.</u>

2329   "The relation of music to language ought to be recognized as something more than that of similarity, if we wᵈ rightly appreciate either. 'The musical art' says G. Weber, 'consists in the expressⁿ of feelings by means of tones. ...' <u>Perfect poetry & song are, in fact, nothing more than perfect speech upon high & moving subjects.</u>"   ib.

2330   "In song we have gradually fallen into the adoption of an extent of scale, & a diversity of time, wh. is simply <u>nonsensical</u>; for such variations of tone & time correspond to no depths or transitions of feeling of which the human breast is cognisant"   ib.

2331   <u>Blank verse.</u> The great diffᵗʸ, as well as delight, of this measure is not in variety of pause, tone, & stress for its own sake. Such variety must be incessantly inspired by, & expressive of, ever varying emotion. Every ... deviation from the strict & dull iambic rhythm must be (**f94ᵛ**) either sense or nonsense. <u>Such change is as real a mode of expressing</u> <u>emotion as words themselves are of expressing thought:</u> & where ...

[such an end does not exist] … the variety obtained is more offensive … than the dulness avoided." ib.
[some of these ideas are suggestive – others doubtful]

2332   Review of John Davidson's "Holiday & other poems."
                                                S. R. 8 Sept '06
"We are conscious that real poetry, new poetry, is in the air of our day, if only somebody could capture it. Hence we have little patience with echoes of Tenny^n, hints of Rossetti, & broken lights of Swinb^{ne}. … Mr Stephen Philips came along with his delusive trick of whipping the cream … from the older masters. … Even Mr W. Watson … has nothing to say about the world as we know it. He issues no challenge to the mind. … Mr David^n, however, is ambitious. He is clearly conscious of a new age. We perceive at work in him a different set of susceptibilities, another order of dynamic ideas, from those which moved the Victorian poets. … He is a modern. He feels the stiffness & unsuitability of the old vehicles, he w^d break if he could those conventions of poetic form which petrify the utterance of this generation. His verse is full of experiment. He tempts us to fancy, now & then, that here is a voice at last, a small one, no doubt, but still a voice of our own time. And there he ends. Lack of strength perhaps? Perception without the intellectual (**f95^r**) force to drive it home…?
    [Scientific] accuracy [in botanical names &c] … is a merit of prose, but the 'inevitable' word in a poet's mouth has more than a scientific sanction. Poetry is nothing if not the language of the plain man rapt above himself. … Mr D's vocabulary, as a whole, is distinctly 'poetical' – a fatal sign in these days ['threnody,' 'madrigal' & c]. …
    [Pitfalls gape for the modern poet] naturally, for he is groping his way to the expression of a world which has not been expressed before. Thus preoccupied he forgets that mere statement of these gropings, however diversified by rhyme & metre, has no poetical value. … Herein lies the badness, for the most part, of Words$^{th's}$ bad work."

———————————— // ————————————

2333   Marriage. – "We are always confronted with a practical paradox. The marriage which makes for the highest welfare of the united man & woman may be actually inimical to the children of that union. The marriage which makes for the highest type of family & its highest & fullest development may often mean, & must always tend to

mean, the inhibition of much that makes for individual perfection."
(Quoted by Speaker July 14 '06 from article by Lady Welby in
"Sociological Papers.")

2334   "The practice of loyalty to one's own understanding" [that
children should be taught it] - Professor Ray Lankester. Times. 7.1.'07

2335   "Rough justice – that the minority must in all cases pay for what
the majority demands."   11.1.'07. H. H. Howorth in Times
[not written satirically]

2336   (**f95ᵛ**) The Poet. "Arnold ... does not write regularly as one who
feels that something has to be said, that it can be said only in poetry, &
that he alone can say it. This is the way of greatness, his own 'grand
style'; & it is because it is not Arnold's way in poetry that he remains a
minor poet, though the greatest of them."   Times Suppᵗ 26.9.'07

2337   God without the world were no God. Hegel.
Apart from thought, reality has no meaning.
                                             Revʷ in Nation. 30.11.07

2338   "Ideas, if they occur to him, he rejects like temptations to sin."
words of Lord Acton (on a certain professor.)
He (Lᵈ A.) was contemptuous, with reason, of the parochialism of
English thought.   Nation.

2339   Poems by Mary E. Coleridge (Elkin Matthews): e.g.

> "We were young, we were merry, we were very very wise,
>   And the door stood open at our feast,
> When there passed us a woman with the West in her eyes,
>   And a man with his back to the East." & c

2340 "Adventure is an affair of the Soul, not of circumstance. Thoreau by his pond at Walden or paddling up the Concord had more adventures than Stanley had on the Congo, or than Stanley could have." A. G. G. in D. News.

2341 (**f96ʳ**) "Strauss's "Leben Jesu" is not so much a "Life of Jesus" as a piece of applied Hegelian philosophy. It starts with the Hegelian presupposition that the fulness of the idea cannot be individualized; it is to be found in the race, & not in any of its members; it is humanity which is the incarnate God. Humanity is the child of the earthly mother & the invisible father, of the spirit & of nature." &c
"In these speculations there was no room left for the orthodox dogma. S. realized this, & the "L. J." is devoted to a critical examination of ... documents, & c. ... A third possibility – the mythical explanⁿ " Nation. 25.1.08

2342 "The youthful poet, while he is learning his craft, is apt to be altogether literary, to live in a world imagined by his masters, & to hear nothing but their voices ... & so he catches the emotions which other men have got from their experience. He may make good poetry out of these secondhand emotions. ... But there comes a time when he must experience life itself as well as literature, if his inspiration is to last, & his enthusiasm not to grow forced & stale. It is easy to feel the romance of life as represented in poetry; but not so easy to feel the romance of life itself; & many young poets have felt the one, but never succeeded in feeling the other." Times Suppl! 30:1:1908

2343 (**f96ᵛ**)Prose & Poetry. Carlyle ... would not trust to the true prose writer's art of logical arrangement or leave the facts, even when they were most eloquent, to speak for themselves. He was always aiming at the concentration of poetry, & in the process losing the continuity of prose ... he tries like a poet to force his narrative into lyrical moments ... he will not trust to the facts to move the emotions of his readers. He must express these emotions himself, as if he were a poet instead of an historian & a lyrical rather than an epic poet. Times Lit. Sup, 20:2:'08

2344 Wilde's <u>Salome</u>. What devil of mischief prompted some blunderer to have the English translation illustrated by Beardsley? To have read the play in the light of Beardsley's deadly irony is to be unable to give it independent judgment. The book becomes an amusing duel. "This is tremendous!" says the author; "This is humbug!" says the artist.   Times Lit. Sup. 18:6:08

2345 "<u>Concepts of Monism</u>" (review)
  "Monism in the hands of its most eminent disciple Haeckel, is not a philosophic creed of any moment. It is in a large measure based on assumptions as to the unity of mind & matter, the functional relationship of the soul to the body & the mind to the brain, that are accepted by no man of science or psychologist of the first rank"(!)
                                                          Spectator 14.3.08

2346 (**f97ʳ**) <u>Shelley</u>. By the late Francis Thompson. <u>Dublin Rev.</u>ʷ I
  We have among us at the present day no lineal descendant (in the poetical order) of Shelley; & any offspring of the aboundingly spontaneous Shelley is hardly possible, still less likely, on account of the defect by which (we think) contempʸ poetry in genᐮ, as comp. with the p. of the early 19ᵗʰ C., is mildewed. That defect is the predominance of art over inspiration, of body over soul. We do not say the <u>defect</u> of inspiration. The warrior is there, but he is hampered by his armour. Writers of high aim in all branches of literature, even when they are not – as Mr Swinburne, for instance, is – lavish in expression, are generally over deliberate in exprⁿ Mr H. James, delineating a fictitious writer clearly intended to be the ideal of an artist, makes him regret that he sometimes allows himself to take the second-best word instead of searching for the best. Theoretically, of course, one ought always to try for the best word. But practically, the habit of excessive care in word-selection freqᴵʸ results in loss of spontaneity; & still worse, the habit of always taking the best word too easily becomes the habit of always taking the most ornate word, the word most removed from ordinary speech. In conseq. of this, poetic diction has become latterly a kaleidoscope, & one's chief curiosity is as to the (**f97ᵛ**) precise combinations into which the pieces will be shifted. There is, in fact, a certain band of words, the Praetorian cohorts of poetry, whose prescriptive aid is invoked by every aspirant to the poetical purple, & without whose prescriptive aid none dares aspire to the p.p.; against

these it is time some banner should be raised. Pps. it is almost impos. for a contemp.ʸ writer quite to evade the services of the free-lances whom one encounters under so many standards (We are a little surprised at the fact, because so many Vict.ⁿ poets are, or have been prose-writers as well. Now acc.ᵍ to our theory, the practice of prose sh.ᵈ maintain fresh & comprehensive a poet's diction, sh.ᵈ save him from falling into the hands of an exclusive coterie of poetic words. It sh.ᵈ react upon his metrical vocabulary to its beneficial expansion, by taking him outside his aristocratic circle of language, & keeping him in touch with the great commonalty, the proletariat of speech. For it is with words as with men: constant intermarriage within the limits of a patrician clan begets effete refinement; & to reinvigorate the stock its veins must be replenished from hardy plebeian blood.) But it is, at any rate, curious to note that the literary revolution against the despotic diction of Pope seems issuing, like political revolutions, in a despotism of its own making.

This, then, we cannot but think, disting.ˢ (**f98ʳ**) the literary period of Shelley from our own. ... We are self-conscious to the finger-tips ... entailing on our poetry the inevitable loss of spont.ʸ

. . . .

Know you what it is to be a child? It is to be something very different from the man of to-day ... it is to believe in love ... in loveliness, ... in belief; it is to be so little that the elves can reach to whisper in your ear; it is to turn pumpkins into coaches ... mice into horses, lowness into loftiness, & nothing into everything ... to live in a nutshell, & count yourself King of inf.ᵗᵉ space.

. . . .

It is this gift of not merely embodying but apprehending everything in figure wh. co-operates towards creating one of his [S's] rarest char.ⁱᶜˢ ... namely his well-known power to condense the most hydrogenic abstraction. Science can now educe threads of such exquisite tenuity that only the feet of the tiniest infant spiders can ascend them; but up the filmiest insubstantiality Sh.ʸ runs with agile ease. To him, in truth, nothing is abstract. The dustiest abstractions

> Start, & tremble under his feet,
> And blossom in purple & red.

The coldest moon of an idea rises haloed through his vaporous imagin^n.... In a more intensified signific^n than it is probable that Shakesp. dreamed of, Shelley gives to airy nothing a local habit^n & a name.

. . . .

In the solar spectrum beyond the extreme red & extreme violet rays, are whole series of col^rs demonstr^ble but imperc^ble to gross human vision. Such writing as this renders visible the invisibilities of imaginative colour.

2347 (**f98ᵛ**) <u>Ibsen</u>. "Critics have read his last play, <u>When we dead awaken</u>, as a confession that at the end of his career he 'was convinced of the error of his earlier rigour, &, having ceased to believe in his mission, regretted the complete sacrifice of his life to his work,' – just as Herbert Spencer ... regretted that he had shut himself up for so long in a Bayswater boarding-house merely to generalize about evolution."

Times lit. sup.

2348 An artist's <u>self</u>. – "The most difficult thing in the world for any artist to achieve ... is to express himself, to strike out a style of writing which shall be as natural to him as the character of handwriting is to ordinary men. It is a truism to say that individuality is the last quality to be developed in a man." <u>Nation</u>.

2349 "The geologist, the antiquarian, & the farmer, gazing at a landscape, will each see totally different things in it, & the poet & the artist different things also. Similarly the mental outlook of people seems to fix itself & specialize on certain limited lines according to character, occupation & habit. ... The finer the shades of psychological truth presented by a piece of literature, the less does the modern Englishman seem to grasp it." <u>Nation</u>.

2350 She writes: "I confess I tremble a little at the prospect of your seeing me in the flesh. At present I have the charm of a 'Yarrow unvisited.' As to the portrait, I am not one bit like it – besides, it was taken eight years ago. Imagine a first cousin of the old Dante's, rather smoke-dried – a face with lines in it that seem a map of sorrows."*

---

*"Letters from George Eliot to Elma Stuart, 1872–1880." Edited by Roland Stuart. London: Simpkin, Marshall & Co.

2351 "We each individual have each our own bodies, but our conscience is only one conscience common to all of us. Therefore it is most selfish to kill the sacred conscience, which is common to others, for the sake to save our own life."

A Japanese artist in London.

2352 (**f99ʳ**) <u>Pragmatism</u>. "The essence of pragmatism is that a proposition is true if belief in it has some utility, is conducive to some ultimately desirable end. ...

"... For minds which are not omniscient with respect to the total consequences of contemplated beliefs, the pragmatic test is useless unless they (the minds) can rely on the trustworthy guidance of an Omniscient Mind. Thus ... Theism is one of the indispensable premisses of pragmatism."

M. Sopote. B. Sc. Oxon. (in Spectator. 23.1.09)

2353 "That white epic splendour which is the crown & climax of the noblest art. ... That compelling, overmastering power which can make the unexpected prove the inevitable."

"The poignant, vivid, audacious [musical] art of to-day."

<u>Times</u>. (on Mendelssohn) 3.2.'09

2354 <u>Ruskin on Style</u>. "What is usually called the style or manner of an artist is, in all good art, nothing but the best means of getting at the particular truth which the artist wanted: it is not a mode peculiar to himself of getting at the same truths as other men, but the <u>only</u> mode of getting the particular facts he desires, & which mode, if others had desired to express those facts, they also must have adopted. All habits of execution persisted in under no such necessity, but because the artist has invented them, or desires to show his dexterity in them, are utterly base." (Modern Painters)

2355 (**f99ᵛ**) <u>Swinburne</u>. "... We can see from his criticism that his theory of poetry was perfectly clear & consistent. Poetry for him was a means of expressing emotion in terms of beauty. It might do other things, but they were not essential. ... No doubt he carried this theory to an extreme in his practice. He was too determined to express emotion in every line & to make every line beautiful ever to write a good play or a good narrative poem. All the people in his plays make poetry about the situation: they do not live & thrive & have their being in it."

Times Supp! Ap¹ 15.1909.

2356   "The final question to be put about a poet is this – Has he increased our sense of the value of the noble things of life? To do that is the function of all art, not by argument but by expression. Therefore, in considering what we owe to the genius of Swinburne, we should not ask what ideas we have got from him, but what emotions. ... For emotion is our final test of the values of things."   ibid.

2357   The real fact is that Byron ought never to have married. Whatever his admirers may have said, he was not a man that any honourable or decent woman could have permanently lived with. "Don Juan" is, perhaps, sufficient literary evidence of that – for Byron, at any rate, was not a hypocrite, and he knew himself to be no better than he should be. He did not help his champions by his abrupt disappearance abroad. Nor did he soothe his wife by turning his domestic troubles into poetical "copy." In the famous and lovely lyric entitled "Fare Thee Well," Byron pleaded his cause before the public with his invincible pen. If his wife was really a wronged woman it is not astonishing that she was deeply hurt by this poem:

> Fare thee well! And if for ever
>   Still for ever, fare thee well:
> Even though unforgiving, never
>   'Gainst thee shall my heart rebel.

That is the sort of thing to irritate a saint.
It read very pathetically, and drew from a hundred eyes such tears as – Moore tells us – blotted Byron's own manuscript:

> Fare thee well! – Thus disunited,
>   Torn from every nearer tie,
> Sear'd in heart, and lone, and blighted,
>   More than this I scarce can die.

But we who know Byron's subsequent doings in Venice and elsewhere can hold back our tears. We can only say that, in view of previous and subsequent convictions, the presumption is in favour of Lady Byron.

Lady Byron, indeed, did not conduct her case very well. She gave an impression of sourness. But hers was a terrible position. Perhaps if she had been a greater woman, she would have saved Lord Byron and done a service of infinite value to her generation. But it is far safer to say that if she had been less pure she would have been dragged down.

2358 (**f100ʳ**) Predestination. Calvin's doctrine of predestⁿ was not originated by him: it started from Augustine, & was represented by great divines in the Middle Ages, such as Bradwardine, & his view of the absolute ... will of God was similar to that of the Scotists.

Times. [I have said this]

2359 A Pluralistic Universe – Wᵐ James
We live forward, we understand backward, said a Danish writer. The line of least resistance, then, as it seems to me, both in theology & in philosophy, is to accept, along with the superhuman consciousness, the notion that it is not all-embracing, the notion, in other words, that there is a God, but that he is finite either in power, or in knowledge, or in both at once.

———————— // ————————

2360 It is the same with beliefs as with art. Two artists may paint the same scene and may produce utterly different pictures of it; yet each picture may be as beautiful, and each may give as truthful a representation of reality, as the other. This does not mean that a painter can play with reality as he chooses, or that picture-making is an arbitrary game. Reality is one sure fact and the artist's mind is another, and between these two facts there is a certain relation which it is the artist's business to express. If he tries to give us the relation between reality and the mind of some other artist, his picture expresses nothing, and has no real beauty or significance.

———————— // ————————

2361 First & Last Things. H. G. Wells.
Motives. – "There are many ... very variously estimated. Some are called gross, some sublime, some ... wicked. I do not readily accept these classifications.... Most of such strike me as wanton & hasty.... To

suppress a passion or a curiousity for the sake of suppressing a passion is
to my mind just the burial of a talent. ..."   57

2362 <u>Socialism</u>. "... is to me no clear-cut system of theories &
dogmas. ... Its common quality from nearly every point of view is the
subordin.^{n} (**f100^{v}**) of the will of the self-seeking individual to the idea of
a racial well-being embodied in an organized state."   99

2363 "The belief I have, that contributing to the development of the
collective being of man is the individual's general meaning & duty, &
the formulae of the Socialism wh. embodies this belief ... give a general
framework & direction how a man or woman sh.^{d} live."   113

2364 "<u>The Idea of the Church</u>. To confuse a church with its creed, is
to prepare the ground for a mass of disastrous & life wasting errors."
                                                                               151

2365 "The theory of a religion may propose the attainment of
Nirvana or the propitiation of an irascible Deity or a dozen other things
as its end & aim; the practical fact is that it draws together great
multitudes of diverse individualized people in a common solemnity &
self-subordination however vague"   152

2366 It may be maintained very plausibly that the Catholic Church is
something greater than Xty, however much the Xtians may have
contributed to its making. From the historical point of view it is a
religious & social method that developed with the later develop! of the
world-empire of Rome, & as the expression of its moral & spiritual
side. Its head was, & so far as its main body is con(**f101^{r}**)cerned still is,
the <u>pontifex</u> <u>maximus</u> of the Roman world-empire, an official who was
performing sacrifices centuries before Xt. was born."   152

2367 <u>Reformation</u>. "There was an attempt at a Reform^{n} ... &
through a variety of causes it failed. It detached great masses from the
C.^{c} Ch. ... It fell into particularism & failed. ... Lacked ... one
fundamentally neces^{y} idea ... the idea of Catholicity. ..." It set up a vast
process of fragmentation among Xtian associations. It drove huge
fissures through the once common platform. ... The Reformation, the
Reconstruction of the Cath.^{c} Ch. lies still before us. It is a necessary
work.   157

———————————————//———————————————

2368   Virgin Birth. "The teaching & passion of Jesus had long been subjects of written tradition before any attempt was made to round off the picture of his life by describing its beginnings.

"There is something entirely new [in Matt.] ... that he was conceived & born of a Virgin. Here we unquestionably enter the circle of pagan ideas. Even the Church fathers were unable to shut their eyes to this. ... The efforts which have been made to disprove the unwelcome intrusion of heathen mythology into the substance of the gospels have been ineffectual."

[Encyclopaedia Biblica. Ed. by Revd T. K. Cheyne, D. Litt. D. D. article by Prof. H. Usener.]

2369   (f101^v) "It has happened not seldom in the history of the world that the work of a truly great artist has startled men into reconsidering their accepted standards of art, & dumbly asking themselves, as they contemplate that which fills them at once with intense admiration & deep disgust, whether that disgust is, after all, only the rancour of conservatism against the innovator."

Times Lit. sup. 3.2.'10 on d'Annunzio.

———————//———————

2370   Courthope on Keats:–
   by approximating poetry to the plastic arts, he necessarily eliminated that element in the former which is derived from the imitation of *action*. His brilliant fancy brought into prominent relief the qualities that delight the imagination in the pictorial allegory of *The Faery Queene* and in the descriptions and similes of *Paradise Lost*. But this was to exalt one side of poetry at the expense of the whole: the scope of Spenser's and Milton's creation was far more comprehensive. Whatever difficulties Spenser encountered in the execution of his poetical task, his aim was an active and social one, namely, to present the character of a perfect knight or gentleman in an ideal form. With still higher artistic powers, Milton brought all the picturesque resources of poetry to bear on the intellectual purpose of an epic work, the main end of which was "to justify the ways of God to man." The spirit of action, by which these two poets were animated, qualified one for the use of the large form of allegorical romance, and the other for the use of the classical epic. Keats, by isolating himself from the active society about him, was obliged to restrict the expression of his idea of "Abstract Beauty" within the limits of the sonnet, the ode, and the modernised "fabliau."

2371   Place-names have, so far, been omitted from the list of beautiful words. Yet many of them are full of a strange and haunting beauty. Vallombrosa is one. Another, beloved of poets, is Skye. It figures in the most beautiful stanza in that version of the Ballad of Chevy Chase which we are reluctantly forced to regard to be spurious:–

> But I have dreamed a dreary dream,
>   Beyond the Isle of Skye,
> I saw a dead man win a fight –
> I think that man was I.

Stevenson, too, has used it with magical effect in one of the best known of his shorter poems:–

> Sing me a song of a lad that is gone,
>   Say, could that lad be I?
> Merry of soul he sailed on a day
>   Over the sea to Skye.

D. Chron: 25.8.10

2372   The more a book represents important sentiments, the higher is its place in literature.   **Taine.**

2373   "Humanism is usually both attacked & defended as that philosophy which identifies truth with utility. ...
... It is convenient to restrict the term pragmatism to the logical method which asserts that the truth of all judgments is to be tested by the value they are found to possess, & to reserve the term humanism for the epistemological theory that truth itself is a kind of value."

Mind.

2374   "To define "truth" as "value" is to destroy the value of truth" (The article is unfavourable to pragmatism)   ib.

2375   (**f101aʳ**) "Foundations of the ·19ᵗʰ Century," by H. S. Chamberlain – (transl. from the German by John Lees.)
'Several critics have cavilled at Shakespeare's art for not being true to nature in the sense of so-called "Realism"; but, as Goethe says, "Art is called art because it is not nature." Art is creative shaping; that is the business of the artist & of the special branch of art; to demand absolute

truth to nature from a work is in the first place superfluous, as nature herself gives us that; in the second place absurd, as man can only achieve what is human; & in the third preposterous, as man desires by means of art to force nature to represent something "Supernatural." In every work of art, therefore, there will be an arbitrary fashioning; art can be naturalistic only in its aims, not in its methods. "Realism" as it is called, denotes a low ebb of artistic power.'   II. 559

2376   Like James and Bergson, Professor Ward finds that a universe in which, as the latter thinker phrases it, *tout est donné* leaves no room for the real activity which he accepts as the fundamental certainty of individual experience and as conterminous at least with the phenomena of life. Evolution therefore means for him, not what the term literally means, an unfolding of what is there all along, but what he calls "epigenesis" or "creative synthesis," which recognizes "the origination by integration of new properties in the whole which its constituents in their isolation did not possess." Such evolution "implies continual new beginnings, the result of the mutual conflict and co-operation of agents, all of whom, though in varying degrees, act spontaneously or freely."

Times Lit. Sup! 18.1.12

2377   (**f102ʳ**) Free-Will v. Determinism. MᶜTaggart. "Some Dogmas of Religion."
"The indeterminist might save his position if he were prepared to maintain that, although certain completely determined qualities are to be called moral excellencies, yet they are not to be ranked as the highest moral excellencies, a position wh. is to be reserved exclusively for excellencies of the Will. But if he maintained this he wᵈ have against him the authority of most of the Churches – certainly of the Xtian Ch. – & of most of the philosophers" –   159

2378   Responsibility. "Although the determinist does not hold that volitions are distinguished from all other events by not being completely determined, he admits, like every one else, that they are marked off from other events by being determinable by expectation of pleasure & pain. ... It is universally agreed that a man is not responsible in cases where his action cannot be affected by considerations of pleasure & pain."   160, 161

2379   <u>Nero</u> – possibly mad. But ... highest degree improbable that he
w^d have committed any of his crimes if he had known that he w^d
certainly have been executed for them within a month or two. And since
the volitions of such men can be affected by the expect.^n of punishment,
it is right to punish them.   162

2380   (**f102^v**) If there is an omnipotent God, we are not responsible to
him for our sins either on the determinist view or the indeterminist. ...
For such a God could have created us without free-will, or without any
~~occasion~~ temptation to misuse it.   165

2381   If there is a God who is not omnipotent, it w^d be quite possible
for the determinist to hold that we are responsible to him for our sins.
Such a God might be unable to create a universe without sin, or at any
rate unable to do so without producing some greater evil. And he might
find it possible, as men do, to check that sin by ... punishments. 166

2382   If God is omnipotent, it is impossible that he can be good at all.
                                                                    167

2383   By God I mean a being who is personal, supreme, & good.
                                                                    186

2384   Indeterminism is inconsistent with the validity of morality. ...
According to him the volition in each case is an undetermined choice
between two ~~actions~~ motives. ... It has no permanent cause ... nothing
connected with it remains in his moral nature, except the mere abstract
power of undetermined choice, wh. is just as likely to be exercised on
the next occasion in a different way.   179

2385   How far is Dr. Wrench right in his assertion that the noble and
great no longer lead the people; but that all – good, bad, and indifferent
– have equal power?
                 T. P.'s Weekly on Wrench's "<u>Mastery of Life</u>" 8:12:11

2386   (**f103^r**) And thus it follows that all ground for predicting the
action of any man, so far as it depends on his volition, vanishes. ... One
result of this is that the indeterminist is quite inconsistent in expecting
one line of conduct from one man & another from another.   183

2387 <u>Imaginative literature.</u> – "'All representations based on knowledge are interesting. ... What is not interesting is that which does not add to our knowledge of any kind.'"

(M. Arnold. Preface to Poems 1853 quot. in Brock's Shelley.)

2388 "The artist can make a beautiful work of art out of the representation of things not beautiful in themselves, provided those things move him to emotion, & he expresses that emotion in his art."

Brock's Shelley. 239

2389 <u>Poetry.</u> Milton's threefold canon – it must be simple, sensuous, passionate. G W E. Russell.

2390 "The bareness, the absence of over-writing, the freshness of the true song." Times Lit. Sup.

2391 "All things are bound in one system of Necessity." Hegel.
"Freedom shows itself as the truth of necessity." ib.
"The essential feature of the Infinite is free self-determination. The essential feature of the Finite is subjection to an Other." ib.

(Quot. Cont. Rev^w May '10)

2392 "Benedetto Croce, in his book on "Aesthetic" says "'Art is the expression of impressions, & not the expression of expressions.'"

Nation. 17 Dec. 1910

2393 (**f103ᵛ**) "Was there not, as the early Greek apologists maintained, a Christianity before Christ?" Contempᵞ Revʷ 6.'05

2394 <u>Lord Morley on Language & Literature.</u> Times. Jan 28.11
An English critic has had the courage to say that there is an insoluble element of prose in Dante, & Tennyson has hardly shown that the scientific ideas of an age are soluble in musical words. Browning ...

nearly universal in his range, was too essentially dramatic, too independent of the scientific influences of his day, too careless of expression, to be a case much in point [as to science & poets]. Tennyson said of him, he had power of intellect enough for all of them, 'but he has not the glory of words.' Whether he had or not, science was not responsible.

2395   Who does not feel ~~that~~ (how), George Eliot's creative & literary art was impaired, & at last worse than impaired, by her daily associations with science? Or would it be truer to say – I often thought it would – that the decline was due to her own ever deepening sense of the pain of the world & the tragedy of sentient being.

2396   Ld Acton. Mr Bryce once heard him explain in what wise a history of liberty might be made the central thread of all history.

2397   For style ... let me commend two qualities – Sanity & Justesse (equity, balance, a fair mind, measure, reserve.

2398   (f104^r) The saving counsel of Cicero – who has himself been called the greatest of all men of letters – you [men of letters] must always end by exposing yourself to contact with men & trying your strength in the struggles of life.

2399   Classic [English] prose-writers – Sir T. Browne, Raleigh, Bacon, Hooker, Burke (in the address to the King, notably).

2400   There is, we must admit, to-day no monarch in any tongue upon the literary throne, no sovereign world-name in poetry or prose, in whom – as has happened before now not so many generations ago, in royal succession to Scott, Byron, Goethe, V. Hugo, Tolstoy – all the civilized world, Teuton, Latin, Celt, Slav, Oriental, are interested, for whose new works it looks.

2401   Rembrandt. Art imperiously demanded absolute submission & fidelity to the inward vision [in his great latest pictures].

2402   A drawing or an etching can make no pretence of a complete representation of reality. Line is a convention in its very nature, & because of its limited powers of repres^n has a greater power of expression.

2403   Like all great artists he addresses himself to the eye, but shows it what it has never beheld.   Times. Lit. Sup. 7:12:11

2404   (**f104ᵛ**) <u>English Prosody</u>. – (Quarterly Review July 1911)

A ... fundamental difficulty ... in the comparison of poetry with music. In both alike, sound & rhythm are a medium of artistic expression. But in music they are the sole medium; whereas, when they enter into poetry they are already constituents of the symbolic code called language. Thus the sound & rhythm which the prosodist has to investigate are never 'pure'. Poetry is only one among many functions that belong to language. ...

... Words exist to convey a meaning. The poet forgets this at his peril. For the essence of art is economy. A work of art may carry no dead-weight of inert material.

The art of the poet consists in introducing variation upon this basis of equality [the co-ordination of the syllables into feet & lines]

2405   With Prof. Saintsbury's view let us now contrast those of ... Mr Ormond & Mr Bridges. According to Mʳ O. the basis of regularity in our verse is a time-basis merely. Its feet are bars; they fall into common or triple time, accordᵍ as the number of syll. predominating is two or three. ... The line, 'How happy cᵈ I be with either' actually varies in metre [Mʳ O. says] according as we emphasise the word 'I' or leave it unimportant.

2406   The principle which we deduce may be expressed thus: so long (**f105ʳ**) as the structure of a verse shows either in itself or in its context the number of accents which it ought to have and the places where they ought to fall, so long as the mind hears the implied accents in their places, the number and position of the accents which naturally occur is of no consequence. And we may at once add that, in regard to the number of syllables in the foot, a similar principle is to be applied: the verse structure must make it clear how many syllables are to be expected, how many, that is, are to be taken as normal; the poet may then substitute more or fewer at his discretion.

2407   "That profound saying of Seneca's, 'For it is all one not to desire
& to have.'"
"Life on the terms given us is an insult to the soul of man."
"'Illusion is God's method'." B. de Casseres.
                    From "The FRA." An American publ? July 1911.

--------------------//--------------------

2408   "To the imitation of Nature, the statement of fact, painting can
get no closer than it has got by now after several centuries of effort in
that direction; and painting, finding itself after all 〈[left behind?]〉 by
the photograph, has begun to wonder whether the imitation of nature
& the statement of fact are its business at all."
                              Times. Lit. Supp! 7:12:'11

2409   (**f105ᵛ**) "Beauty beyond all other beauty, horror beyond all
other horror, still lie hidden about us, waiting for some one to see them.
The thing that really matters, that makes a writer a true writer, & his
work permanent, is that he should really see."   <u>Times</u> lit. sup.

2410   "For the pragmatist pessimism is refuted by the fact that it leads
nowhere – its opposite, if an illusion, is one necessary for our state. ... So
with Necessity, or Fate. Our instinctive resentment at the former
notion shows that it does not cover the whole field of our action."
   [These are two characteristic fallacies of optimism]
                    "The Wessex Drama." Edinburgh Review. Jan 1912

2411   "Our current literature is marked by a feverish desire to be
original (sure to defeat itself)."
                    "Elizabethan Playwrᵗˢ " Edin. Revʷ Jan. 1912

2412   "The poet does not perceive <u>things</u>: the poet perceives the
hitherto unperceived <u>relations</u> <u>of things</u>." .
                    Maurice Browne in <u>Poetry Revʷ</u>

2413   (**f106ʳ**) <u>The Past & Present of Futurism</u>. "'Painting, like
speaking," says Mr Sickert, "is a form of expression, & the speaker who
is incomprehensible cannot be considered a speaker at all." Similarly
an artist who uses a shorthand so obscure & exclusive that a key is

necessary to the understanding of it, is no artist. ...

'"The perpendicular lines indicate their depressed condition & their infinite sadness dragging everything down towards the earth." All this means that Boccioni has created for himself a symbolical interpretation of line & colour which he announces to the world as a general truth."

(The Futurist vision is a blend of the impressionist & the fauvist. ... "In order to make the spectator live in the centre of the picture ... the picture must be the synthesis of what one remembers & what one sees." Monet was concerned with what one saw; Cézanne with what one remembered. The impr^st landscape is the presentation of a momentary glance. ... Fauvism is concerned with the essentials of a scene that remain in the memory. ... The Futurist w^d reconcile in one picture these two widely different aims. ... The deep significance of Fauvism.

Mr. T. H. Sadler in "The Blue Book" Oxford. May '12.

2414 (**f106^v**) The case for the "Post Impressionists." [Grafton Gallery Catal^ge]

"We all agree now that any form in wh. an artist can express himself is legitimate, & the more sensitive perceive that there are things worth expressing that c^d never have been expressed in tradit! forms. We have ceased to ask 'What does this picture represent?' and ask instead, 'What does it make us feel?' We expect a work of plastic art to have more in common with a piece of music /? ~~that~~/ than with a col^d photo^gh . ...

... Every one of them has something to say wh. c^d not have been s^d in any other form. New wine abounded, & the old bottles were found wanting. ... In choice of subject they recognize no authority but the truth that is in them; in choice of form, none but the need of expressing it. That is Post-Impressionism.

... Simplification, & plastic design. ... What I mean by "simp!." is obvious. A literary artist, who wishes to express what he feels for a forest, thinks himself under no oblig^n to give an acc! of its flora & fauna. The P. I. claims similar privileges: those facts that any one can observe for himself ... he leaves to the makers of Xmas cards. ... He simplifies, omits details, that is to say, to concentrate on something more import! – on the signif^ce of form.

... Forms & the relation of forms have been for all great artists, not means of suggesting emotion, but objects of em^n It is this em^n they have expressed. ...

(**f107^r**) ... The treatment of form as an object of em^n & the treat! of f. as a means of description ... difference."   Clive Bell.

2415   "It is not the object of these artists to exhibit their skill or proclaim their knowl^(ge), but only to attempt to express by pictorial & plastic form, certain spiritual experiences. ...

... Modern men trying to find a pictorial language appropriate to the sensibilities of the modern outlook. ...

... The difficulty springs from a deep-rooted conviction, due to long-established custom, that the aim of painting is the descriptive imitation of natural forms. Now these artists do not seek to give what can, after all, be but a pale reflex of actual appear^(ce) but to arouse the conviction of a new & definite reality. They do not seek to im^(te) form, but to create form; not to imit^(te) life, but to find an equivalent for life. By that I mean that they wish to make images wh. by the clearness of their logical structure, & by their closely-knit unity of texture, shall appeal to our disinterested & contemplative imagin^(n) with something of the same vividness as the things of actual life appeal to our practical activities. In fact, they aim not at illusion but at reality.

The logical extreme of such a method w^(d) undoubtedly be the attempt to give up all resemblance to natural form, & to create a purely abstract language of form – a visual music; & the (**f107^v**) later works of Picasso show this clearly enough. They may or may not be successful in their attempt. It is too early to be dogmatic on the point, which can only be decided when our sensibilities to such abstract form have been more practised than they are at present ... e.g. Picasso's 'Head of a man. ...'

... An equivalence, not a likeness, of nature is sought. ...

"... Others [of them] are content with the ideas of simplific^(n) of form as existing in the gen^(l) tradition of the P. O. movement & instead of feeling for new methods of express^(n) devote thems^(s) to expressing what is most poignant & moving in contemp^(y) life."   Roger Fry.

2416   (On new & original forms of Literature & Art). [Not "change for the sake of change" [F. Harrison] but –]. A style grows to perfection. Nothing more can be done in it. And no mere desire for change, no irreverence or impatience, but a necessity of artistic development pushes poets & artists into new channels of expression, new forms.

Times, on F. Harrison's "Among my books" 10.10.'12

2417   A new study of English Poetry. H. Newbolt (in Eng. Rev.ʷ)

Sept '12

"'The necessary outcome of his (Descartes') views is what may properly be called Idealism: namely, the doctrine that, (**f108ʳ**) whatever the universe may be, all we can know of it is the picture presented to us by consciousness. This picture may be a true likeness – though how this can be is inconceivable – or it may have no more resemblance to its cause than one of Bach's fugues has to the person who is playing it; or than a piece of poetry has to the mouth & lips of a reciter." [quot. from Huxley.]. ...

"Good poetry is not merely the express.ⁿ of our intuitions, it is the masterly exprⁿ of rare, complex, & difficult states of consciousness; & great poetry ... is the exprⁿ of our consciousness of this world, tinged with man's universal longing for a world more perfect. ... In a plain prosaic way we are all poets, all makers of our own world; but the great poets re-make it for us ... by an incantation ... so that we see it under a light that is not the light of time."

2418   LIFE OF THE RIGHT HON. SIR ALFRED COMYN LYALL, P. C., K. C. B., &c., by Sir Mortimer Durand, London, Blackwood and Sons, 16s. net. – Published to-day. By Edward Clodd.

steeped in uncertainty; the seeming coherency of a theory made him only the more challenge its soundness; hence his critical attitude towards the speculations, as he deemed them, of Professors Max Müller, Frazer, and other authorities.

What Do the Wisest Know?

To him philosophy was "mostly a futile exercise, except when professed by masters of the art, who are all in the end destructive." "Do they all stand gazing as ever, and what do the wisest know?" he asks in his thought-compelling "Meditations of a Hindu Prince." But although he looked on all dogmas as doomed, he was not prepared "to throw away the baby when emptying the bath." "Religion," he says in a letter that lies before me, "as an instinct and aspiration, and even as a social institution of high utility, is not to be easily or safely uprooted, and will long be a mighty force among mankind"; and pregnant is a remark which he once made to me, "You will never put religion into liquidation." In brief, Lyall was of the type happily defined by Lord Morley as "the unbelieving religious."

Daily Chron. Apl. '13

2419   Is Art a Failure? R. Fowler. 19th cent.

'Art is Art said Goethe, precisely because it is not Nature. If it were
so true to reality that it deceived the spectator who took it for Nature it
w^d not be real Art at all, but mere artifice, mimicry & deceit.' (quot.)

Reid says 'The visible appearances of objects are intended by Nature
only as signs or indications. The mind passes instantly to the things
signified without making the least reflection upon the sign, or even
perceiving that there is such a thing.' [Art – a method of raising a desired
mood in a reader or spectator ⁰]

2420   (**f108ᵛ**) The 'mad merry rogue spirit' of conny-catching life 'is
illustrated nowhere better than in a short, dateless, nameless sermon
reprinted by Viles and Furnivall from a Cotton MS. in the British
Museum – a sermon in praise of thieves and thieving. A certain Parson
Hyberdyne, so the document states, was robbed by a band of thieves at
Hartley Row in Hampshire. After the robbery the thieves compelled
their victim to preach them a sermon in praise of thieves and thieving.
This the merry parson did so well that they restored his money again
and in addition gave him two shillings to reward his eloquence. The
sermon recites the manly qualities demanded for the trade of thieving –
especially for highway robbery; it encourages boldness, fortitude, and
courage. Thieving is practised by all men, and has precedent in
Scripture. Jacob stole his Uncle Laban's kids and his father's blessing;
David stole the hallowed bread from the temple, and even Christ took
an ass and a colt that were none of his. With a burst of eloquence the
preacher concludes: "But moste of all I marvell that men can dispyse
yow theves, where as in all poyntes almoste yow be lyke vnto christe
hym selfe: for chryste had noo dwellynge place; noo more haue yow.
christe wente frome towne to towne; and soo doo yow. christe was
hated of all men, sauynge of his freendes; and soo are yow. christe was
laid waite vpon in many places; and soo are you. chryste at the lengthe
was cawght; and soo shall yow bee. he was browght before the iudges;
and soo shall yow bee, he was accused; and soo shall you bee. he was
condempned; and soo shall yow bee. he was hanged; and so shall yow
bee. he wente downe into hell; and soo shall yow dooe. mary! in this one
thynge you dyffer frome hym, for he rose agayne and assendid into
heauen; and soo shall yow neuer dooe, withowte godes great mercy,
which gode grawnte yow! to whome with the father, and the soone, and
hooly ghoste, bee all honore and glorye, for euer and euer. Amen!"'

[From *Elizabethan Rogues and Vagabonds*. By F. AYDELOTTE. (Vol. I of

'Oxford Historical and Literary Studies.') *Published by Humphrey Milford*. Price 7s. 6d. net ($2.50).]

2421 By BENJAMIN DeCASSERES
In all creation the subject wills and formulates the style. Style is fatal.

Fornaro is an intellectual romantic. The trite, the commonplace, the unimportant do not exist for him. He has felt this way about New York. Whether he has seen what is there or not is of no importance, for all art worthy of the name is a manner of feeling, not a manner of reproduction. Shakespeare, wrong and banal in so many things, never said anything sillier than when he counselled the artist "to hold the mirror up to nature." There is no such thing in art as nature, nor is there a mirror in the human mind. There are nothing but illusion, deformation and bias. Art is the record of a temperament, atrabilious or ethereal, phlegmatic or ecstatic. "Nature" is an illusory play of light and shadow on a perpetual changing network of nerves. And the "mirror" that we are told to hold up to "nature" is a hurrying torrent of feeling and thought. There are no truisms, no rules in art, as in anything else. What I see and feel, that is so. To paraphrase Max Stirner, "In art my illusion is THE truth." Fornaro, being a pure anarch, has put himself absolutely into these pictures. They are autobiographical, which in all art whatsoever is the touchstone of its worth.

B. de Casseres on Fornaro. (Italian Painter)

2422 (**f108aʳ**) BERGSON AND BALFOUR. (Review of Reviews)
The October number of the Hibbert Journal opens with two papers which are certain to arouse in non-technical circles a profound interest in the latest developments of philosophy. In the first, Mr. Balfour criticises M. Bergson, in the second, M. Bergson states his own position irrespective of Mr. Balfour. We shall therefore take the latter first.

I. – THE AUTHOR OF CREATIVE EVOLUTION.
M. Henri Bergson treats of "Life and Consciousness." He laments that in the enormous work done in philosophy from antiquity down to the present time, the problems which are for us the vital problems have seldom been squarely faced. He thinks philosophy will now give them their rightful place. There is no absolutely certain principle from which the answers to these questions can be adduced in a mathematical way.

But we possess lines of facts, he says, none of which goes far enough, or up to the point that interests us, but each of them, taken apart, will give nothing but a probability, but all together, by converging on the same point, may give an accumulation of probabilities which will gradually approximate scientific certainty.

CONSCIOUSNESS AND CHOICE.

The first line of fact is consciousness. All consciousness is memory, preservation and accumulation of the past in the present. At the same time all consciousness is an anticipation of the future. Consciousness is above all a hyphen, a tie between past and future. Consciousness is no more limited to creatures possessing a brain than digestion is to creatures possessing a stomach. Digestion exists long before a special stomach has been developed, and consciousness may exist long before the brain has been developed. Through the brain, however, consciousness works with the greatest precision, and we find that in selecting between the respective responses to given stimulai the brain is the organ of choice. It appears therefore as if from the top to the bottom of the animal scale there is present the faculty of choice, and more particularly the choice of action, of combined movements, in response to stimulation arising from without. Yet the function of consciousness has been seen primarily to retain the past and to anticipate the future. That function is natural to choice.

CONSCIOUSNESS PRESENT IN ALL LIVING MATTER.

Does, then, consciousness cover the whole domain of life? M. Bergson replies:–

It seems probable, therefore, and this is my last word on the point, that consciousness is in principle present in all living matter, but that it is dormant or atrophied wherever such matter renounces spontaneous activity, and on the contrary that it becomes more intense, more complex, more complete, just where living matter trends most in the direction of activity and movement. Consciousness in each of us, then, seems to express the amount of choice, or, if you will, of creation, at our disposal for movements and activity. Analogy authorises us to infer that it is the same in the whole of the organised world.

LIFE USING CONSCIOUSNESS ON MATTER

Consciousness and matter appear to be antagonistic forces, which nevertheless come to a mutual understanding, and manage somehow to get on together. Matter is theoretically the realm of fatality, while consciousness is essentially that of liberty; and life, which is nothing but consciousness using matter for its purposes, succeeds in reconciling them. The essence of life seems to be to secure that matter, by a process necessarily very slow and difficult, should store up energy ready for life afterwards to expend this energy suddenly in free movements. Sensation is the point at which consciousness touches matter. M. Bergson says:–

> That these two forms of existence, matter and consciousness, have indeed a common origin, seems to me probable. I believe that the first is a reversal of the second, that while consciousness is action that continually creates and multiplies, matter is action which continually unmakes itself and wears out; and I believe also that neither the matter constituting a world nor the consciousness which utilises this matter can be explained by themselves, and that there is a common source of both this matter and this consciousness.

"THE IMPULSE TO CLIMB HIGHER."

M. Bergson then puts the question, Why, if adaptation explains everything in evolution, has life gone on complicating itself more and more delicately and dangerously? He answers:–

> Why, if there is not behind life an impulse, an immense impulse to climb higher and higher, to run greater and greater risks in order to arrive at greater and greater efficiency?

It seems as if it were a force that contained in itself, at least potential and interfused, the two forms of consciousness that we call instinct and intelligence. The human brain possesses this remarkable feature, as distinguished from that of a highly developed animal, "that it can oppose to every contracted habit another habit, to every kind of automatism another automatism, so that in man liberty succeeds in freeing itself by setting necessity to fight against necessity."

VITAL AND SPIRITUAL.

The evolution of life makes obvious that there is a vital impulse towards a higher and higher efficiency to transcend itself, in a word, to create. But such a force is precisely what is called a spiritual force. Matter, by the unique nature of the resistance it opposes, and the unique nature of the docility to which it can be brought, plays at one and the same time the *rôle* of obstacle and stimulus, causes us to feel our force and to succeed in intensifying it. Nature sets up a signal every time we attain the fullest expansion of life. That signal is joy. True joy is always an emphatic signal of the triumph of life:–

> If, then, in every province, the triumph of life is expressed by creation, ought we not to think that the ultimate reason of human life is a creation which, in distinction from that of the artist or man of science, can be pursued at every moment and by all men alike; I mean the creation of self by self, the (**f108a^v**) continual enrichment of personality by elements which it does not draw from outside, but causes to spring forth from itself?

POINTING TO A LIFE BEYOND.

M. Bergson advances still farther, and argues that as the whole life of a conscious personality is an indivisible continuity, "are we not led to suppose that the effort continues beyond, and that in this passage of consciousness through matter consciousness is tempered like steel, and tests itself by clearly constituting personalities and preparing them, by the very effort which each of them is called upon to make, for a higher form of existence? We shall have no repugnance in admitting that in man, though perhaps in man alone, consciousness pursues its path beyond this early life."

II. – MR. BALFOUR.

Mr. Balfour begins his criticism of "Creative Evolution" by recalling the time of more than forty years ago, when in the English universities the dominating influences were John Mill and Herbert Spencer – Mill even more than Spencer. The fashionable creed of advanced thinkers was scientific agnosticism. This was a challenge that Mr. Balfour himself took up in his Defence of Philosophic Doubt. He bears glad witness to the reaction that has followed:–

> In the last twenty years or so of the nineteenth century came (in

England) the great idealist revival. For the first time since Locke the general stream of British philosophy rejoined, for good or evil, the main continental river. And I should suppose that now in 1911 the bulk of philosophers belong to the neo-Kantian or neo-Hegelian school.

FREEDOM V. DETERMINISM.

Mr. Balfour begins his statement of M. Bergson's position by outlining his own position towards freedom. Being neither idealist nor naturalist, he accepts freedom as reality. The material sequence is there, self and its states are there, and he does not pretend to have arrived at a satisfactory view of their relations. He keeps them both, conscious of their incompatibilities. M. Bergson takes a bolder line. Freedom is the very corner stone of his system. Life is free, life is spontaneous, life is incalculable. Then follows one of those similes for which Mr. Balfour has become famous:–

> As we know it upon this earth, organic life resembles some great river system, pouring in many channels across the plain. One stream dies away sluggishly in the sand, another loses itself in some inland lake, while a third, more powerful or more fortunate, drives its tortuous and arbitrary windings further and yet further from the snows that gave it birth.
>
> The metaphor, for which M. Bergson should not be made responsible, may serve to emphasise some leading portions of his theory. What the banks of a stream are to its current, that is matter generally, and the living organism in particular, to terrestrial life. They modify its course; they do not make it flow. So life presses on by its own inherent impulse; not unhampered by the inert mass through which it flows, yet constantly struggling with it, eating patiently into the most recalcitrant rock, breaking through the softer soil in channels the least foreseen, never exactly repeating its past, never running twice the same course.

The metaphor would suggest that life has some end to which its free endeavours are directed, and M. Bergson objects to teleology only less than to mechanical determinism. M. Bergson thinks, with other great masters of speculation, that consciousness, life-spirit, is the *prius* of all there is, be it physical or mental. In his view the *prius* is no all-inclusive Absolute. Matter is regarded by M. Bergson as a by-product of the evolutionary process. Time is of the essence of primordial activity, space is but the limiting term of those material elements which are no more than its backwash.

WHY? WHY? WHY?

Mr. Balfour then proceeds to criticism. He holds that M. Bergson has not given answer to the following questions, Why should free consciousness first produce, and then, as it were, shed, mechanically determined matter? Why, having done so, should it set to work to permeate the same matter with contingency? Why should it allow itself to be split up by matter into separate individualities? Why should it ever have engaged in that long and doubtful battle between freedom and necessity which we call organic evolution? This leads up to the main question, On what grounds are we asked to accept the metaphysic of M. Bergson? According to his theory of knowledge, M. Bergson's view is that not reason, but instinct, brings us into the closest touch, the directest relation, with what is most real in the universe. Reason is at home, not with life and freedom, but with matter, mechanism, and space, the waste products of the creative impulse. Man is not wholly without instinct, nor does he lack the powers of directly preserving life. But, asks Mr. Balfour, How is it that instinct is greatest where freedom is smallest and man, the freest animal of them all, should especially delight in the exercise of reason? Again Mr. Balfour asks, if it be granted that life always carries with it a trace of freedom or contingency, and that this grows greater as organisms develop, why should we suppose that life existed before its humble beginnings on this earth? Why should we call in super-consciousness?

"SURELY BETTER TO INVOKE GOD."

For the super-consciousness does not satisfy Mr. Balfour. It already possesses some quasi-aesthetic and quasi-moral qualities. Joy in creative effort, and corresponding alienation from those branches of the evolutionary stem which have remained stationary. But why should he banish teleology:–

> Creation, freedom, will – these doubtless are great things but we cannot lastingly admire them unless we know their drift. We cannot, I submit, rest satisfied with what differs so little from the haphazard; joy is no fitting consequent of efforts which are so nearly aimless. If

values are to be taken into account, it is surely better to invoke God with a purpose than supra-consciousness with none.

So again in the interests of religious faith Mr. Balfour concludes his brilliant analysis, of which the foregoing excerpts offer but a slight indication.

2423   (**f109ʳ**) Creative Evolution. Henri Bergson.
'Du Bois = Reymond [says] "We can imagine the knowledge of nature arrived at a point where the universal process of the world might be represented by a single mathematical formula, by one immense system of simultaneous differential equations, from which could be deduced, for each moment, the position, direction, & velocity of every atom of the world."

(Über die Grenzen des Naturerkennens.)

[and] Huxley: "If the fundamental proposition of evolution is true, that the entire world, living & not living, is the result of the mutual interaction, according to definite laws, of the forces possessed by the molecules of which the primitive nebulosity of the universe was composed, it is no less certain that the existing world lay, potentially, in the cosmic vapour; & that a sufficient intellect could, from a knowledge of the properties of the molecules of that vapour, have predicted, say, the state of the Fauna of Great Britain in 1869, with as much certainty as one can say what will happen to the vapour of the breath on a cold winter's day." In such a doctrine, time ... is deprived of efficacy, & if it does nothing it is nothing.'   41

2424   "Unorganized bodies ... are regulated by this simple law: the present contains nothing more than the past, & what is found in the effect was already in the cause."   p. 15. [But]

2425   (**f109ᵛ**) "Organic creation, the evolutionary phenomena which properly constitute life, we cannot in any way subject to a mathematical treatment."

2426   "We are creating ourselves continually."   7

2427   "For a conscious being to exist is to change, to change is to

mature, to mature is to go on creating oneself endlessly. Should the
same be said of existence in general?"   8

2428   "The enormous gap that separates even the lowest form of life
from the inorganic world."   38

2429   Harper's Wordsworth.
   'Coleridge declared it to be "not advisable to ground the belief in
Xty. on historical evidence.... Religious belief is an act, not of the
understanding, but of the will." If philos! ideas ever had discoverable
beginᵍˢ here, we might say was the found.ⁿ in Eng. thought of that
house of refuge to wh. so many souls have flocked who deem instinct &
practical workability safer guides than understanding. ...'
   Physical observation ... recorded as if Nature were an assemblage of
souls, masc. & fem., with feelings like those of men & women. (in
"Descriptive sketches")

2430   (**f109aʳ**) Freedom of the Will. "Half the controversies about the
f. of the W. ... rest upon the absurd presumption that the proposition 'I
can do as I like,' is contradictory to the doctrine of necessity. The
answer is: nobody doubts that, at any rate within certain limits, you
can do as you like. But what determines your likings & dislikings? Did
you make your own constitution? Is it your contrivance that one thing
is pleasant & another is painful? And even if it were, why did you prefer
to make it after the one fashion rather than the other.... What
opponents of the doctrine really have to do, if they would upset the
necessarian argument, is to prove that they are free to associate any
emotion whatever with any idea whatever; to like pain as much as
pleasure; vice as much as virtue; in short to prove that, whatever may
be the fixity of order of the universe of things, that of thought is given
over to chance."   T. H. Huxley, on Hume. (221)

2431   (**f109bʳ**) "It may perhaps be answered that our philosophical
faith is not in an actually existing rational system of things – experience
prevents us believing in that – but in an end, a 'final goal of ill' tow.ᵈˢ
wh. evolution moves; that the conception of evolution involves the
conception of the Absolute as Becoming, not as Being. The universe, it .
may be said, consists of a multiplicity of independent beings who

gradually come to settle down into stable equilibrium – atoms or monads making as it were a permanent social contract with one another. The world then would be the 'best of all possible worlds' in the sense that it is the arrangement best fitted to survive. Such a view undoubtedly agrees with much that is commonly said about evolution. | But it raises all the old puzzles that Zeno found in the 'many' or 'becoming' when treated as absolute categories. Thus it makes time an absolute & brings in the difficulties about a real beginning & end of time. Process & change cannot be thought out, unless in reference to a permanent & unchanging 'substance.' 'It is only the permanent that can change' as Kant said. ... Our popular 'Sophists' of the present day talk of 'Evolution evolving' & of the 'developmental process' as if it were an absolute. But it is only the carelessness of pop.ʳ lang.ᵍᵉ & the use of abstract nouns as subj.ˢ wh. allow such phrases to pass current. | Evol.ⁿ is the app.ᶜᵉ or manif.ⁿ to us of a timeless reality wh. includes & transcends change."   Philosoph! Studies.   D. G. Ritchie, 229

2432 (**f109bᵛ**) "An unfinished world, then, with all Creation, along with our thought, struggling into more continuous & better shape – such is our author's general view of the matter of Philosophy."
W. James's Preface to Höffding's
"Problems of Philosophy" (translᵈ by him)

2433 (**f110ʳ**) In reference to the belief that the universe has a Spiritual Designer ⟨William⟩ James wrote: "If not a blind force, but a seeing force, runs things we may reasonably expect better issues. This vague confidence in the future is the sole pragmatic meaning at present discernible in the terms design and designer." Does this, Professor Dewey asks, mean that the confidence in the future which belief in a Designer gives is evidence of the truth of this belief? Or does it mean that belief in a Designer really amounts to no more than having a confidence in the future, a belief that must itself submit to empirical verification?
he claims the authority of William James for the psychological view that even the primitive experience of a baby – that "big, blooming, buzzing confusion," as he called it in one of his celebrated phrases – involves the sense of an external world. James, however, also wrote:–

A baby's rattle drops out of his hand, but the baby looks not for it. It has "gone out," for him, as a candle flame goes out; and it comes back, when you replace it in his hand, as the flame comes back when relit. The idea of its being "a thing" whose permanent existence by itself he might interpolate between its successive apparitions has evidently not occurred to him.

2434 The Philosophy of Religion. Höffding trans. by R. E. Meyer – (Macmillan)
"Many free-thinkers take for granted that human life would assume richer and stronger forms did religion cease to exist; but this view ... rests on the presupposition that psychical equivalents are always at hand – equivalents in value as well as in energy."   9

2435 "The conservation of value is the characteristic axiom of religion."   10

2436 "Value denotes the property possessed by a thing either of conferring immediate satisfaction or serving as a means to procure it."
                                                                                                    12

2437 Pragmatism. ... It is de Lisle Adam's Sans illusion tout périt, or Horace's Praetulerim scriptor delirus, – the doctrine that on a certain level of thought truth must be interpreted as applicability to plain human needs. ... The one question is, says Prof. James what concrete difference will the truth of an idea make in anyone's actual life, what is its cash-value in experiential terms?   Spectator.

2438 (f110ᵛ) Guenther's Darwinism. transl. by Mᶜ Cabe.
"The lust for life":
"According to the Teleological view the construction of an organism is the end wh. the whole embryonic development is aiming to realize. The end, as it were, observes & controls the series of causes & is realized in the ultimate effect. The very first causes were controlled by a fact that was still in the future. The ordinary causes, wh. we have discussed, can only produce an effect when they themselves have already been brought into existence as an effect. Teleological causes or ends act before they are themselves realized.
We rejected in the previous chapter the notion that organisms aim at the realization of ends. Seeking an end would be the greatest conceivable form of purposiveness."   365

2439   In the eyes of science man is not "higher" than the other animals.   424

2440   Review of Ormond's "Concepts of Philosophy" in <u>Mind</u>.
(by J. Ellis M͡c Taggart)
   "It is a painful shock to come across a passage like this: 'Why should there be anything deeper than phenomena. ... Simply because consciousness in its organ of reason will not have it so. A world wh. ended here w͡d be a scandal to reason.' Here we are left in complete darkness as to whether Prof. O. means that he w͡d disapprove of such a world, or that he w͡d commit a logical error if he believed in it. The former is interesting, but inconclusive. The latter w͡d be better if it were not put in a form wh. suggests that a contradiction becomes impossible only when it is perceived to be a contradiction."

2441   (**f110aʳ**) "~~Behind its aspectual character lies concealed the real world~~"
   A. Worsley. "Concepts of Monism."
   "Philosophy warns us against any relative interpretation whatever; proclaims that our world is one of growing perception, & not one of fact; that behind its aspectual character lies concealed the real world. Between us & it is placed the great gulf of subjectivity, so that those who would pass thence, cannot. Yet there is a way in which we can grasp a something, however little, of that underlying reality. Conceptive thought (Idealism) will lead us so far on the path; not far enough, certainly, to enable us to conceive the <u>s</u>ource in its absolute & unconditioned character, but far enough to show us the bond uniting all things into one homogenˢ whole."   ⌊2
   An instantaneous photograph gives records differing from those of our own (momentary) vision, & between these Difference is evident & Discrimination possible, because the question of time has introduced the necessʸ minimum of apparent duality. But directly we eliminate the temporal element all possibility of discriminⁿ vanishes; for to the eye of eternity there is no change, no form, no difference whatever. ... ~~If~~/? we ~~eliminate~~/ ~~the~~
   Now the Vedântic doctrine of objective unreality, or of objective pluralism ⟨[multiplicity of vision]⟩ or nescience, is clearly true in this sense. That is to say if we elimᵗᵉ the minimᵐ of duality necessʸ for discrimination by deleting Time altogʳ that then we are reduced to a condⁿ of objective nescience, in wh. no phenomⁿ & no object possesses

any particularized attrib^te what^r. So that on this assumption not only are all our percept^ns faulty records, but they are also faulty rec^ds of chimeras, not of realities. Hence the doc^ne of objective pluralism, taught by some Vedantins, is unobjectionable if explained in this sense. Yet it does not appear that this was the sense in which such doctrinaires construed it, & in any other sense it seems to me objectionable."

"Nescience = the non-knowing, the antithesis to Science."

"The world of temporalities is that illusive world existing round the Ego. ... Should we view such as illusions ... or ... as misperceptions of something real (the Vedântic view)? Surely the latter."

2442   (f111^r) La Nouvelle Revue Française on Bernard Shaw:–

"... That romantic mania which considers the exception alone as interesting. M. Shaw is classic in that he only occupies himself with the rule."   May. 1909

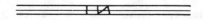

2443

And would it have been worth it, after all,
Would it have been worth while,
After the sunsets & the dooryards & the sprinkled streets,
After the novels, after the teacups, after the skirts that trail upon the
    floor.
And this, & so much more? –
It is impossible to say just what I mean!
But as if a magic lantern threw the nerves in patterns on a screen:
Would it have been worth while
If one, settling a pillow or throwing off a shawl,
And turning toward the window should say: "That is not it at all,"
That is not what I meant at all"

– – – – – – – – – – – – – – – – – –

I grow old ... I grow old. ...
I shall wear the bottom of my trousers rolled.
Shall I part my hair behind? Do I dare to eat a peach?
I shall wear white flannel trousers, & walk upon the beach.

I have heard the mermaids singing, each to each.
I do not think that they will sing to me.
I have seen them riding seaward in the waves,
Combing the white waves blown back
When the wind blows the water white & black.
We have lingered in the chambers of the sea
By sea girls wreathed with seaweed red strown
Till human voices wake us, & we drown.

> T. S. Eliot – a poet of the vers-libre school – quoted in "From Shakespeare to O. Henry" by S. P. B. Mais – Grant Richards
> 1917.

2444   (**f111ᵛ**) Odyssey I. (line 41 in transl.)

"Perverse mankind! whose wills, created free,
Charge all their woes on absolute decree;
All to the dooming gods their guilt translate,
And follies are miscalled the crimes of fate."

> Pope.

2445   "O strange, how mortals lay the blame on the gods! For they say that evil comes from us, whereas they themselves suffer for their own sins & follies, apart from what is destined."
   Od. I. 32 f. (Quoted in Times 17.3.'21, by E. A. Sonnenschein.)

2446   "La Cathédrale." J. K. Huysmans. (Paris. P. V. Stock.)
   "Avec l'aube qui commençait à poindre, elle devenait vraiment incohérente la forêt de cette église sous les arbres de laquelle il était assis. Les formes parvenues à s'ébaucher se faussaient dans cette obscurité qui fondait toutes les lignes, en s'éteignant. ...
   Autour d'elle, lentement, les autres épées encore ... ; et ces coulées de pourpre cernèrent les contours d'êtres sans doute issus des bords lointains d'un Gange; d'un côᴜté, un roi jouant d'une harpe d'or; de l'autre un monarque érigeant un sceptre. ... Puis, à gauche du (**f112ʳ**) royal musicien, se dressa un autre homme ... [etc.] ... une figure, plus déconcertante encore, se détacha ... d'un improbable lys."

> pp. 30, 31

2447   "Tchekov's art is the antithesis of realism; he never forgets that what we see is less important than what we do not see; that what happens is indefinitely less than what does not happen."

Observer. Jan 25. 1920

2448   "The inseparable propriety of Time, which is ever more & more to disclose Truth."   Bacon.

2449   (**f113ʳ**) Einstein on Time & Space –
"... The dynamic universe with time outside is replaced by a static world with time inside. Events do not happen, they are just there & we come across them in the voyage of life. ...
[But] it is quite possible to preserve the dynamic character of the universe, while still amalgamating space & time (?). ... I can see no difference between an eclipse in the year 1927, & an [a present-time] event in a remote part of the universe. ... The existence of the one is not more hypothetical than that of the other."

A. S. Eddington in Quarterly. Jan. 1920

2450   Ideas in the new theory –
"The amalgamation of space & time into one four-dimensional continuum. ..."
"The warping, or non-Euclidean charʳ, of space in a gravitational field of force. ..."
"... We recognize that the happenings of nature around us are arranged in a certain order, wh. we call an order in space. There is also an apparently independent order, an order in time. The idea that these two orders cᵈ be amalgamated into one is not new. Just as we can think of an ordinary solid as built up of a pile of plane slices, so we can think of a solid at any moment as being a slice of something four-dimensional; & the slices correspᵍ to successive moments will build up a four-dimensional figure in combined space-time. An indivˡ as he grows from childhᵈ to old age makes up such a four-dimˡ figure; what we see of him at any time is just the 3-dimˡ sectⁿ correspᵍ to that time."
"Probably at a great distance from all attracting matter this [Euclidean] geometry is correct; but Einstein made the fundamental discovery that in a gravitational field it is incorrect. ..."
"Time is not a particular direction but depends on the motion of the observer."

"... Physics is not interested in it [the distinction of past & future]. For physics, past is $-$ t, & future $+$ t, just as left is $-$ x, & right $+$ x."

ib. id.

2451 (**f113ᵛ**) "Sceptical negation ... has denied that things have any existence at all if there is no mind to perceive them, & it has occas.ˡˡʸ been haunted by the nightmare that the universe, persons & events included, was the hallucin.ⁿ of a single private mind.

Einstein's theory, as Prof. Carr sees it, leaves no absolute physical reality which can be contemplated in entire detachment from the position of the contemplator. "There is no universe common to all observers & private to none." The work of physical science is to co-ordinate the observations of perceivers for whom there is no common measure."

Times Lit. Supᵗ 9:12:20.

2452 THE MACHINE. Times Lit. Sup. 1 July 1926
OUROBOROS: OR THE MECHANICAL EXTENSION OF MANKIND. BY GARET GARRETT. (Kegan Paul. 2s. 6d. net.)

It is a commonplace that our industrial civilization is not planned. That civilization rests upon the machine; and the machine has acquired its present position, not as part of a deliberate intention but in obedience to blind impulse. To one who reflects on that rapid and tremendous growth Butler's fantasy must seem at times a mere statement of fact. The last war, for instance, was essentially a war of monstrous mechanisms with men for their attendants. And a large part of the population of the earth seems to have its *raison d'être* as machine minders. But although we are all aware that we live in a mechanical age, the extent to which the machine dominates life and controls policy is not generally realized. From Mr. Garrett's rapid survey of the whole position we gain the impression that our modern civilization can fairly be described as following in the wake of the machine.

It is convenient to treat the machine, as Mr. Garrett does, as if it obeyed laws of its own, since no rational deliberate purpose on the part of mankind can be found for its multiplication. Its law of growth is one of the most terrifying things about the machine. It is spreading over the whole world with continually increasing momentum. The reaction of this growth on human affairs can be admirably illustrated by Mr. Garrett's example of the watch. A watch was originally an extremely expensive product. A skilled craftsman might spend half his life in

making a fine one. With the rise of the machine it became possible to
make a watch at fifty dollars. Perhaps a million people want watches at
that price. The machine multiplies rapidly, and then, suddenly, it
ceases. The million people have watches. The machine can only
increase by supplying a new market. Accordingly the ten-dollar watch
is invented. The machine increases enormously, since there are twenty
million people who want watches at this price. Again there comes a lull,
to be followed by another tremendous outbreak of machinery engaged
in manufacturing the two-dollar watch. It is obvious that this process
has, in itself, no limits short of those imposed by the finite population of
the globe. And every effort is made to reach those limits. Vast credit
companies are formed to lend people money to buy watches,
gramophones, radio sets, motor-cars, and all the other products of the
machine. The "backward" nations are stimulated to desire these
products. National policies are influenced by the fact that the machine
must keep on functioning. Thrift is no longer a virtue in the modern
world. The first duty a citizen owes to his industrial civilization is to
consume. Otherwise the machines will be idle and the immense
number of people whose duty it is to mind them will find themselves
purposeless and starving. (**f114ʳ**) But more than a certain amount
cannot be consumed in spite of advertising, the instalment system, and
reduced prices. Mr. Garrett states that "the industrial equipment
already existing in the world is so great that if for one year it were
worked at ideal capacity the product could not be sold for enough to
pay the wages of labour, to say nothing of the cost of material, overhead
charges, or profit." Thus we are faced with the problem of surplus.

With the increase of the machine, so that more and more countries
(even China) are becoming industrialized, with increasing products
and diminishing markets, what are the reactions on the human minders
likely to be? One answer is that given by an Italian Minister of Finance,
defending his country's resolve to become industrial: "A man can live
on less in Italy than anywhere else," and, he says, the people will
accept the low standard of life this implies. "Because they will do
anything sooner than starve." To compete with Italy, therefore, the
standard of life in all countries would have to be lowered. Italy then
would have to go lower still, until all were sunk in misery. If this is the
logical consequence of industrialism, it seems strange that agricultural
countries should adopt it. Mr. Garrett points out that the reason is to
be found in the existence of the "trade balance." Agricultural countries
find that industrial countries pay less for what they buy than they

charge for what they sell. That is how industrial countries get rich and come to own the railroads, tramways, water works, and banks of the agricultural countries. To the commercial mind all this is quite natural – in fact, it seems to him as inevitable as a law of nature. Nevertheless it is a process which, finally, dooms man to destruction. Mr. Garrett suggests that the way out of the difficulty is to replace the principle of gain by the principle of <u>mutualism</u>. Instead of a state of parasitism let the nations live together in a state of symbiosis. The principle of gain instead of the principle of mutual service is merely a survival from those early pioneers of world-wide trade, the pirates. But Mr. Garrett does not think that commerce will ever consciously change its principles. The world has never had experience of different peoples sustaining one another on a sympathetic plan, and the general mind cannot act on a mere idea. Nevertheless, Mr. Garrett thinks that something of the kind will come to pass, although the process may be painful. The increase of the industrial population and the industrialization of agricultural countries, together with the increase in industrial commodities, all means that the price of food will rise. Twice the number of manufactures, and hence twice the labour, may be required to buy a bushel of wheat. It may even be that the "trade balance" will be in favour of the food-producing countries. In the misery of those new times mankind, taught by bitter experience, may find that he can pay too high a price for commercial gain. When he finds that profits are, after all, inconsistent with peace, security and ordinary human happiness, he may forgo them.

———————————+———————————

2453 MANKIND AT THE CROSS-ROADS Times Lit. Sup 29 July 1926
SCIENTIFIC HUMANISM. By LOTHROP STODDARD. (Scribners. 7s. 6d. net.)
Mr. Stoddard's new book is superficial and rather slipshod: but it has the saving grace of propounding a very interesting theme. It discusses the relationship between the mind of man and its material environment. On the one hand the tempo of man's conquest of nature has been immensely accelerated during the past century. On the other hand man himself is still bound by his ancient habits of thought and is staggered by the very mass of his new knowledge. It is therefore possible enough that he may not be able to support the burden of the civilization which he has made and that the road of material betterment may be leading him to a new Dark Age. Mr Stoddard is

unfamiliar with the literature of pessimism which has been produced in Europe, and particularly in Germany, since the war; nor does he, except for one incidental reference, take account of the thoroughgoing rejection of Western material civilization by a school of Indian thought. On the contrary, his outlook is optimistic, even though his cheerfulness is at times rather forced. He puts his trust in the ability of science itself to overcome the difficulties it has created, and insists again and again that science desires truth and has provided man, for the first time in his history, with precise instruments for its attainment.

What disconcerts him, however, is the character of the human mind as indicated by recent psychology. Reason no longer enjoys the easy supremacy assigned to her by the utilitarians; rather is she suspect as being the deceptive slave of the feelings. The feelings themselves are more suspect still, because they are a part of our racial inheritance from our non-moral, anti-social, primitive ancestors. Thus the pith of the problem, as Mr. Stoddard sees it, is that head and heart tend to combine against truth.

> Modern science is literally bombarding us with new conditions – and new ideas. But these novelties encounter minds mainly "set" in moulds of traditional belief and opinion handed down from pre-scientific times and usually anti-scientific in character. Ill-adjusted as we thus are to receive them, the new ideas shock and disturb us, thereby rousing emotional reactions which either close the mind to the new ideas or else admit them in muddled, distorted guise. ... In such cases the intellect becomes the slave of the emotions, the upshot being the utterance of arguments which seem to be the product of deep thought, but which are really nothing but "rationalized" feeling. Many of our radical "intellectuals" are of this type; and the same is true of certain religious spokesmen.... The amount of disguised emotion to-day masquerading as thought is literally astounding. Nowhere do we see it more plainly than in the current tendency to "think in phrases"; in other words, to avoid thinking by embracing some clever catchword or resounding "principle" which seems to settle the question and bring conviction to perplexed souls.

(**f114ᵛ**) ⟨[from back]⟩
Mr Stoddard finds his typical example of this state of mind in Fundamentalism, which he regards as a serious challenge to scientific

truth, because of the fanaticism by which it is inspired and the generosity with which it is financed. The parallel with the controversy over the "Origin of Species" sixty years ago is raised only to be rejected, since the appeal to-day is not to the educated few, but to the uneducated many. Mr. Stoddard is frankly alarmed at this mass-opposition to thought, and even suggests that as a high level of intelligence is rare, it may be bred out of the human race altogether. The fact that the movement is so far confined to the United States does not comfort him. He believes that the attitude of mind which it reveals will spread to Europe and will be thoroughly congenial to the peasants of the Central and Eastern parts of the continent. He is inclined to deplore, too, the hesitating attitude of science towards all criticism of this character. No doubt the scientific mind is right in treating its hypotheses as tentative. Still, they are based on carefully observed facts and should at least be tested by rigorous application.

In his last chapter, however, Mr. Stoddard draws encouragement from the democratic nature of modern controversy. The gay and confident humanism of the Renaissance shrivelled to nothing in an atmosphere of religious hatreds because it addressed its appeal only to the few. The new scientific humanism, on the contrary, offers its methods and its conclusions to the many: and Mr. Stoddard thinks well enough of human nature to believe that truth will prevail. It will prevail especially, he hopes, in politics; and in his closing pages he draws a picture of a State built on a proper sense of realities in which the factors making for change and the factors making for stability are equally appreciated, so that such familiar antinomies as Revolution and Reaction or Faith and Reason will <u>vanish in a wider</u> synthesis.

2454   TIMES LITERARY SUPPLEMENT, DECEMBER 23, 1926.
THE DECLINE OF THE WEST, Volume I. Form and Actuality. By OSWALD SPENGLER. Authorized Translation by C. F. ATKINSON. (Allen and Unwin. 21s. net.)

The central thesis of Dr. Spengler's system is that all the manifold achievements of a culture are but the working out of a destiny implicit in its earliest beginnings. It follows that he is keenly alive to the organic relationship between all the elements of the life of an epoch ... ⟨[next col.]⟩

The system appears not only unfamiliar but foreign – so thoroughly

German, in fact, that the doctrine of the inevitable decline of Western civilization can be dismissed as an *Oberlehrer's* patriotic reaction to his country's defeat in the war. It is no answer that the book was planned in 1911, when the author saw the war coming and thought that his country would win. On the contrary, its thoroughgoing determinism then appears as the philosophic expression of the rigidity which Prussian militarism had imposed upon German life. But this line of criticism, though in the last resort it cannot be evaded, does an injustice to the range and power of the book. Born though it may have been of the circumstances of the moment, the system is grounded upon an investigation, both wide and deep, of the innermost quality of historic cultures. The method by which this investigation is conducted is broadly Kantian. Dr. Spengler works out his ideas by the aid of a series of antinomies, causality and destiny, space and time, nature and history, thought and will, all of which he characteristically relates both to one another and to the opposed personalities of Darwin and Goethe.

To Darwin the name is used as a symbol for the nineteenth-century scientific mind – the external world appears as a multitude of facts systematized by the law of cause and effect. This Dr. Spengler calls the picture of the world-as-nature, and the reasoning which produces it is described as the logic of space. It is objected that just because it operates by dissection this method knocks life out of the universe. Accordingly Dr. Spengler sets over against it another logic, the logic of time, functioning psychologically by the will and not by thought: another picture, that of the world-as-history, and another principle, that of destiny. Appreciated in its time-setting, the external world is thus seen to be a process moving towards its predestined end by a law of internal necessity. The theory suffers from the verbal difficulty that what Dr. Spengler calls history is set up in opposition to a scientific conception which is above all things historical. This verbal confusion raises the greater doubt whether the antinomy which Dr. Spengler considers fundamental really exists at all. What is his conception of destiny except the synthesis of all the causes and effects which analysis reveals? And is it true that causality is a logic of space and not of time? On this vital point Dr. Spengler prefers assertion to argument. "Causality" he declares with the emphasis of italics, "has nothing whatever to do with time," flippantly adding that this must seem an outrageous paradox to "Kantians who do not know how Kantian they are." The reference to Kant is a red herring to enable Dr. Spengler to pass off as a paradox what is really downright nonsense. Of course, causality has nothing to do with any particular period of time. It does not matter ⟨[cont.ᵈ next page]⟩ (**f115ʳ**) whether the effect follows the cause in the length of a geological epoch or whether it is accomplished chemically in a fraction of a second. The point is that the effect does follow, that the notion of sequence is the basis of the whole doctrine of causality, that this notion implies time, and that it could not be conceived except by minds that think in time.

On this unsubstantial metaphysic Dr. Spengler founds a philosophy of history which is always stimulating, though it may not always convince. The theory is that certain specific attitudes of mind towards the external world have worked themselves out in recorded time, their initial impulse developing, maturing and fading away like the life of an individual. Our own quarter of the world has been successively dominated by five cultures – the Egyptian, the Classical, the Arabian, the Gothic or Medieval, and the Western European, to which Dr. Spengler affixes the question-begging label Faustian. The theory requires some demonstration of the specific quality of each of these cultures, and this Dr. Spengler effectively deduces from their respective conceptions of mathematics. To the Greek mind, he submits, mathematics was a study of magnitudes, never really divorced from the concrete and actual. The Arabian mind, on the other hand, held a highly abstract conception of number, and its mathematics operate by means of symbols. The modern mind, again, approaches mathematics as a study of relations, and its contribution begins with the infinitesimal calculus. Some of the best matter in the book exhibits the difference between the classical and the modern standpoints. To the Greek the essential problem of mathematics was to square the circle. If it were solved, a curved surface would be made rectangular, and therefore measurable. But for our minds this problem has lost all its urgency because our interest is not in a magnitude but in a relation stated by the symbol π. Dr. Spengler traces this contrast through all the arts, setting the precise types of beauty in Greek sculpture over against the Faustian landscape-painting, with its immense spatial perspectives; the life of Œdipus, stumbling "without warning upon a situation," against the life of Lear, maturing "inwardly towards a catastrophe" – a contrast due to the fact that Faustian man has a sense of time, and therefore of destiny, which classical man entirely lacked.

What matters, the argument continues, is the dominant idea which, in the course of its development, finds expression first in one art and then in another. Thus, in the modern culture, architecture gradually

moves to the expression of that system of relations which appears vital
to the Faustian mind. Hence it aims more and more definitely at the
expression of pure form until at last, in a baroque work, the actual
structure is felt as a hindrance and the idea passes over from
architecture into music. Under the stimulus of this notion Dr.
Spengler's thought becomes mystic, transcendent, powerfully
impressive in its insistence on the underlying unity of the most diverse
activities. The Faustian mind

> aspires towards the infinite; therefore – the discoveries of the New
> World, the circulation of the blood, and the Copernican universe
> were achieved almost simultaneously, and at bottom are completely
> equivalent: and the discovery of gunpowder (that is, the long-range
> weapon) and of printing (the long-range script) was little earlier.

All these achievements, in fact, were efforts to express the dominant
attitude of mind, and were accomplished out of an inward necessity.
But there comes a time in all cultures when this effort at expression has
reached its maximum range, when the idea has been realized in as
many forms as are possible to the type of mind which has conceived it,
and when nothing remains but to work out its implications. At this
stage, which in our own epoch Dr. Spengler believes to have been
reached about 1800, culture which is vital gives place to civilization
which is mechanical, and brain so completely replaces soul that the law
of the conservation of energy becomes a more cogent statement than
the doctrine of personal immortality.

The wealth of illustration with which these conceptions are worked
out accounts for the impression that the book has made. But again the
question arises whether the distinction between classical and
contemporary thought is really fundamental, whether Dr. Spengler has
rightly understood either of the ages which he contrasts. That the
Greeks shirked and that the moderns attack the problem of the infinite
is, of course, beyond dispute. But there is a flagrant *non sequitur* in
arguing that the Greek mind was unaware of what it refused to
investigate. The whole Platonic system is evidence to the contrary, and
the way the Greek mind handled its problem was to concentrate on the
instant so completely as to make it timeless. So, too, with the doctrine
that cultures grow, mature, and die like individuals. After all, do our
materials justify so relentless a generalization? At least Dr. Spengler
lays himself open to the charge that he has imposed his theories on the

facts. The Arabian culture, for example, whose influence and range he expounds on lines suggested by Strzygowski, is a necessity to an argument which postulates the decline and death of the classical idea. But if we are not enthralled by the postulate there is nothing to prevent us regarding Sancta Sophia as the last great constructive achievement of the Greek genius, which borrowed from Persia at the end as it had borrowed from Egypt at the beginning, and which only seemed to have lost its quality after Justinian's day because it had communicated its secrets to all mankind. Still more suspicious is Dr. Spengler's attack on modern art, which he regards with all the less favour because it is French. His argument demands that there should be no idea behind it because new ideas do not occur when a culture has died down into a civilization. And so the modern masters are bludgeone 1. "Rembrandt's mighty landscapes," we read, "lie essentially in the universe, Manet's near a railway station" – as though a station were not as effective a microcosm as a mill.

Objections such as these are not merely petty. They indicate the fundamental defect in Dr. Spengler's system – namely, that its conclusions stand in amazing contradiction to its premises. It is put forward as "the philosophy of the future ... the only philosophy which is within the possibilities of the West-European mind in its next stages." So this West European mind, whose outstanding quality is its emancipation from the world of sense, its concentration on all possible relationships, its pursuit of the infinite, is to be summed up in one philosophy, and that philosophy rigidly determinist!

2455 (f115aᵛ) G: B. Shaw on Darwinism

"As compared to the open-eyed intelligent wanting & trying of Lamarck, the Darwinian process may be described as a chapter of accidents. As such it seems simple, because you do not at first realize all that it involves. But when its whole significance dawns on you, your heart sinks into a heap of sand within you. There is a hideous fatalism about it, a ghastly & damnable reduction of beauty & intelligence, of strength & purpose, of honour & aspiration, to such casually picturesque changes as an avalanche may make in a mountain landscape, or a railway accident in a human figure. To call this Natural Selection is a blasphemy, possible to many to whom Nature is nothing but a casual aggregation of inert & dead matter, but eternally impossible to the spirits and souls of the righteous. If it be no blasphemy, but a truth of science, then the stars of heaven, the showers and dew, the winter and summer, the fire and heat, the mountains and hills, may no longer be called to exalt the Lord with us by praise: their work is to modify all things by blindly starving and murdering everything that is not lucky enough to survive in the universal struggle for hogwash."

Bernard Shaw, Preface to 'Back to Methuselah,'
Quoted in "Downland Man" by H. J. Massingham. p. 393

2456   (**f115b^r**) "Translations & Tomfooleries" by G. B. Shaw –
"When natural history (sometimes ambiguously called realism) is banished from the theatre, cruelty, horror, & death become painless there, & even luxurious, because nobody believes in them. ... The more dreadful it all is the better it is liked, because romance can never come home to reality. To preserve this delicious anaesthesia there must be no bringing down to earth of the business by the disillusioning touch of comedy. ... The fact remains that in proportion as a play succeeds in producing an illusion of real life, it must dispense with the frantic agonies & despairs & poisonings & butcheries of the romantic theatre.

&c – p. 6

[Here occurs the fallacy of Shaw, owing to his use of the word "romantic" in its depraved sense – not in its true sense. What a good play should do is "produce an illusion of real life" without being a copy of real life. This is true romance. Realism – the opposite of art – "disillusioning" does not achieve this, & makes the bad play, where the agonies & despairs ... are too much to bear, hence art no longer.]

(14 Dec. 1926)

2457   (**f116^r**) Ld Balfour on Art.
"Whether the attribution of an effect like this [emotion from paintings &c] to unthinking causes, or to an artist created & wholly controlled by unthinking causes, would not go far to impair its value," &c.   Theism & Humanism.

2458   Spinoza ... established, not (as with Descartes) an unreconciled dualism of spirit & matter, but a pure Monism of wh. the sole foundation is Substance ... which he calls God ... yet Spinoza's God neither thinks nor creates. ... Everything visible is a Mode of God's attribute of extension. God is the 'immanent idea,' the One & All, the <u>natura</u> <u>naturans</u>; World, <u>natura</u> <u>naturata</u>, is one complex whole.

His chief doctrines are: The absence of free-will in man – himself
only a Modus dependent on causes without. ... Will & Liberty belong
only to God.

(From "Spinoza" in Chambers's Cyclopaedia – an excellent article)

2459   (**f116ᵛ**) [Old notes]
"A few men & women, with the will & the power to tell in plain
words the naked truths of thought & feeling about themselves, their
relations to their fellows & the world, to vivisect their souls for the
benefit of others, can, we hold, perform the greatest practical service
demanded of literature at this time."

The Confession of Mʳ Wells. Nation. 21.11.'08 –
[Meth. /? apply/ as in "Nature Poems"]

2460   "In lyrical poetry more than in any other form of art, it is only
the distinctively individual that can outlive its period of review. It is the
personal cry, in a note that is somewhat, if not entirely, new, for which
we ask; this alone is the badge & title-deed of the true poetic lyrist; ...
~~Take the distinc~~. it is to this that every cultured nation owes its thanks
for the verbal melody which keeps its vitality from genⁿ to genⁿ Take
the distinctive personality – the mind = attitude & the ego – from
Heine, ~~Béranger~~, Burns, Moore, & the most prominent of our
Elizabethan lyrists, & what is there left?"

J. E. P. in The Academy 14.5.'10

2461   Spectator (on Swinburne)
His metrical effects were produced by a conscious, or even a
mechanical, process. This is why his verse ... in the end is apt to
weary. ... It is the difference between

"On such a night
Stood Dido with a willow in her hand"   (Mer. of Ven. V.I)

and,

"Now folded in the flowerless fields of Heaven. ..." Browning never
approached Swinburne in the matter of metrical science, yet S. could
never have written the "Toccata of Galuppi's."

—————————— // ——————————

2462 (**f117ʳ**) "The New Evolution" – 'Thought is a function of the Brain. ....'

Professor James points out that there are two kinds of function – productive & transmissive. The materialist is apt to lose sight of this fact & to think of Thought being a f. of the br. as he thinks of perfume being the function of a flower. The Old Evolutionist looked upon Thought as a productive functⁿ of the brⁿ : the New Evolutˢᵗ looks upon it as transmissive. Prof. J. points out that a prism ... has transm.ᵛᵉ function, & then reminds us that science has suggested that the whole universe of material things is but a veil over hidden & genuine realities. He asks us to think of our brains as thin & transpᵗ places in this material veil, permitting the Infinite Thought to pierce them as white light pierces glass: further, if the glass be stained or blurred the light itsᶠ will be distorted; hence the strange imperfections with wh. we are familiar in ourselves & our fellow-creatures."

Florence Gay in The Outlook 14.5.'10

2463 The noblest kind of beauty is that which does not /?ravish/ by a single stroke, does not deliver ~~stormy~~ ⟨violent⟩ ~~assaults~~ & intoxicating assaults, (/ ... / which quickly provokes distaste) but which slowly insinuates itself, ~~that~~ ⟨which⟩ one carries with him almost unconsciously, ~~that~~ ⟨which⟩ ~~one~~ ⟨on a⟩ day, in a dream, ~~he~~ ⟨one⟩ sees before him; & which finally, after having held us modestly by the heart for a long while, takes possession of us completely filling our eyes with tears, our heart with desire   Nietzsche

2464 (**f117ᵛ**) "Machiavelli said that to renew anything we must return to its origins. It is as true in literature as in life."

Fredᶜ Manning. Pref. to "Scenes & Portraits"

2465 Swinburne [His] way consisted in throwing over whatever subject the poet treated an atmosphere of poetic glamour. ... The subject does not exactly disappear, but it ceases to be more than a ~~slo~~ sort of accompaniment to the treatment. Even then, & when the accompᵗ itself is most prominent, it is universalized to an extent wh. wᵈ delight the most Aristotelian of critics. ... The heroine of "Dolores" is every woman of the enchantress kind. ... Individuality shᵈ not be looked for first in Mʳ S.   G. Saintsbury   Bookman

---

2466 "Symbiogenesis, in Nature, is 'mutual enhancement by continuous mutual effort. ...' His distinction between progressive & debased survival. ... 'Good' (i.e. symbiogenetic) survival tends more & more towards pacific & equal interchange & increase of the means of life: 'bad' survival is on the downward path of ... despoliation, & is doomed .:. to extinction. Cooperation thus begins to approximate to a moral law in Nature.

Times Rev.ʷ of "Symbiogenesis" by Hermann Reinheimer.
10:6: '15. (Knapp & Drewett. 10/6.)

2467 Italian realism & art
We [English] are not a quick-witted people, & we are not an open-minded people; serried ranks of prejudgments prevent the hostile approach of a new idea: but the Italians are the one people ... who carry with them no prevenient judments, who "cherish no idols." A man of this race has no use for an idea but to see it as it is. He has no ... cherished illusion which must be saved at all costs on the principle of tant pis pour les faits.

M. A. R. Tuker, in F. R. May '08

2468 (f118ʳ) Realities in themselves, can be there for anyone, whether Pragmatist or anti-Pragmˢᵗ only by being believed; they are believed only by their notions appearing true; & their notions appear true only because they work satisfactorily. Satisfactorily, moreover for the particular thinker's purpose. There is no idea wh. is the true idea, of anything. Whose is the true idea of the Absolute –

W. James, "The Meaning of Truth" (1909)

2469 The Claims of French Poetry. J. C. Bailey 1907.
"It is the triumph of modern art to extract interest from the common-place; to see the ordinary in such novel light that it shall be ordinary no longer. There can be no triumph more real or legitimate. But the method has perhaps been as often a trick as a triumph. Genius, just because it is genius, may for a moment make common daylight seem to rival sunset splendours; but, except for a moment, & apart from the influence of genius, the extraordinary will always be more interesting than the ordinary, the individual than the crowd."   306

2470   "Perfection of workmanship, not originality of subject ... the class of poets wh. includes Virgil, Horace, Gray, Tennyson.... The other class, in whose works wealth of matter overwhelms the ⟨effort after⟩ perfect form, as in Shakespeare sometimes, generally in Goethe, almost always in Browning. The ideal is, of course, a harmonious proportion between the two, profound thought finding perfect utterance."   ib. 307

2471   (**f118ᵛ**) Racine.... There are none of those scenes so seemingly apart from the main issue, yet so important in their bearing upon character, which Shakespeare lavished with so prodigal a hand. Instead all is ordered, precise, circumscribed; we are in the presence of the same conflict, the same fundamental situation from the first scene to the last. Another point is that in Racine, as in the Greek drama, there is little preparation, & the tragic tension is maintained from the beginning to the end. "French tragedy," says Goethe, "is a crisis." This is pre-eminently true of Racine.   Nation. May 16. 1908

2472   The Nature & function of Poetry.
   "Poetry does not mean the making of verses. He who makes beautiful verses is the artist, one for whom no praise can be too great, since he adds to the world's happiness. But the poet is beyond praise; he is something different, something, as I think, far higher, since he adds to the world's consciousness. For not only must he be artist – it may be that the understanding is more than the craft, but the craft is essential – but also he must be prophet: he must have some great new hope to offer, some great new faith to proclaim, some great new message to deliver, that men may pause awhile to listen, & wonder, & be glad."
                  Maurice Browne. Oxfᵈ & Camb. Revᵂ Mids. 1908

2473   "What we call reason is the disenchantment of life."
                                                              Mme. de Stael.

2474   THE LITERARY GUIDE   January, 1927   17
   An interesting book, by Garet Garrett, called *Ouroboros; or The Mechanical Extension of Mankind* (Kegan Paul; 93 pp.; 2s. 6d.) deals with the effect of this age of machines upon civilization. According to Mr. Garrett, the extent to which the machine rules our life and controls our policy is not sufficiently realized, and the perusal of his work leaves one with the haunting idea that present-day civilization follows the

machine and rests upon it. It is a fact that we live in a mechanical age – the Great War was strikingly unlike all those that preceded it in being less a war of nations than one of mechanisms, with men as their attendants, reminiscent of that "War of the Worlds" described by Wells, save that the combatants had more control over microbes. These mechanisms have come to their present position rather as the effect of a blind impulse than as the outcome of a rational, deliberate plan, and one wonders whether there was not an instinctive wisdom in the opposition which once arose to mechanical invention. Hence Mr. Garrett treats the machine as obeying laws of its own – a law of growth that is almost terrifying in its menace. Its reaction upon human affairs is demonstrated by the example offered of the watch. Originally a very expensive invention, taking its maker many years to perfect, it became possible to turn watches out by machinery for fifty dollars apiece, capable of satisfying possibly a million people. These supplied, fresh mechanical invention gave twenty million people a ten-dollar article. And so on to the two-dollar watch, which came within the grasp of many more. Such inventions create vast credit companies to lend people money for the purchase of watches, gramophones, radio sets, motor-cars, and a hundred other mechanical products.

But Mr. Garrett suggests yet vaster influences. National policies become influenced by the fact that the machine must keep on functioning; thrift is a virtue no longer, and the first duty of every citizen is to become a consumer lest the machines become idle and their "minders" are faced with starvation. Civilization is thus faced with the problem of surplus – in the author's words, "the industrial equipment already existing in the world is so great that if for one year it were worked at ideal capacity the product could not be sold for enough to pay the wages of labour, to say nothing of the cost of material, overhead charges, or profit." The logical outcome is that it is a process which must finally doom man to destruction; and Mr. Garrett, having followed his argument, suggests that the way out of the difficulty is to replace the principle of gain by that of mutualism: the nations must live together in a state not of parasitism, but of symbiosis. In his opinion commerce will never consciously change its principles; the world has never had experience of different peoples sustaining one another on a sympathetic plan, and the general mind cannot act upon a mere idea. Nevertheless, he thinks it is possible that some such result may be obtained, but only by a long and painful process of bitter experience. Mr. Garrett's little work deserves wide publicity. MACLEOD YEARSLEY.

2475   Literary Guide. July 1927

The most important literary event of this Spring – perhaps of this year – is surely the publication of Mr. Humbert Wolfe's *REQUIEM* (Benn; 6s). Nothing of like scope has been attempted for a very long time, and certainly nothing else at once so ambitious and so successful has been achieved. It gives its author an assured place among the major poets of our time: that is to say, among Mr. W. B. Yeats, Mr. Robert Bridges, Mr. Walter de la Mare, and – who else? Not only is it a triumph of intricate versification, but it succeeds, in a singular degree, in wedding the subtlest ideas to the most entrancing verbal music. Mr. Wolfe has fashioned for himself a highly personal idiom, the range and flexibility of which are remarkable. Sometimes his verse, like Donne's, is so heavily pregnant with meaning that it perforce staggers a little; but at its happiest it achieves that seemingly miraculous fusion of song with thought which we are in the habit of calling "pure poetry." The tracing of literary influences is the small change of criticism, the first desperate resort of a hurried reviewer; but it is worth noting that no one, so far as I am aware, has ventured to question the validity of Mr. Wolfe's inspiration, or to track down this or that of his qualities to its source in the work of other poets, whether old masters or new.

Whatever influences have played upon Mr. Wolfe (and every modern writer is influenced by his predecessors – how else could a tradition survive?), they have been so thoroughly assimilated, and are so utterly subdued to the service of his individual vision as to be now merely conjectural. More to the critic's purpose than literary influences are literary parallels; and two possible parallels occur to me. I do not and will not pretend that Mr. Wolfe's poetry is like either Browning's or Donne's: all I will say is that he is sometimes like Browning in the boldness and ingenuity of his rhyming, and that he challenges comparison with Donne (that most marvellous poet of love) by his power to cram two or three lines of verse with intellectual subtleties upon which another man might spend (and spend in vain) a page of closely-reasoned prose. But, notwithstanding all its intellectuality, this elaborately-patterned sequence of poems, with its haunting refrains and its cumulative passion, bears the mark of a genuine inspiration; of that inspiration, indeed, which the poet himself – simply, with arrogance, and without self-consciousness – claims for it in the dedicatory verses:–

This is your poem. I shall not write its fellow
Earthsides of immortality. I sing
Not here, as once, of love and his first swallow
That does not make, because it is, the spring.

   It was not mine to make, but as the pool
They called Bethesda, when the angel stirred it,
Was with some alien virtue wonderful,
So this was written, as though I overheard it

   Whispered beyond the misted curtains, screening
This world from that, so faint and yet so lit
With flame from far, that life itself was leaning
Back, like a runner storming into it.

I have refrained, with intention, from describing the subject of the book, because many thousands of words have already been devoted to it in the press; but it may be well to remind those of my readers who have short memories that what the poet offers us is no less than a requiem for the death of all the world. The book is divided into two halves; "The Losers" and "The Winners." The Losers include the Common Man and the Common Woman, the Soldier, the Harlot, the Huckster, the Nun. The Winners are lovers, saints, teachers, visionaries. Each of these pleads his cause; and for each is invoked the aid of his particular god or saint. The tale of beauty includes a dazzling variety of verse-form, and the conclusion of the whole matter is reached in "The High Song," a poem in which the note of sublimity is not merely sounded but sustained:–

   The high song is over. Silent is the lute now.
They are crowned for ever and discrowned now.
Whether they triumphed or suffered they are mute now.
Or at the most they are only a sound now.

   The high song is over. There is none to complain now.
No heart for healing, and none to break now.
They have gone, and they will not come again now.
They are sleeping at last, and they will not wake now.

   The high song is over. And we shall not mourn now.
There was a thing to say, and it is said now.

It is as though all these had been unborn now,
It is as though the world itself were dead now.

The high song is over. Even the echoes fail now;
Winners and losers – they are only a theme now,
Their victory and defeat a half-forgotten tale now;
And even the angels are only a dream now.

There is no need for blame, no cause for praise now.
Nothing to hide, to change, or to discover.
They were men and women. They have gone their ways now,
As men and women must. The high song is over.

2476   (**f119ʳ**) THE ANATOMY OF SCIENCE. By GILBERT N. LEWIS. (Yale University Press. London: Milford. 14s net.)

By illustrating the same tendency to abstraction in the case of the concepts of space and time Professor Lewis brings us right to the heart of modern physical problems. The space of Euclid is a highly refined concept, although it was for long taken not only as a description of actual physical space, but as an account of the properties of any imaginable space. We now know that it is one abstraction among many, and that it is merely a question of convenience which abstraction we use to describe the actual world. Professor Lewis describes some of the remarkable modern geometries that have been invented, particularly two that have been discussed by himself and Professor Wilson. The more important of these, the geometry of asymptotic rotation, when applied to the real world, gives us the special theory of relativity. It becomes clear that the difficulties of pre-relativity physics were due to the assumption of a less relevant geometry. On Newton's scheme velocities are added together according to the simple rules of arithmetic; the new geometry shows that velocities add together in such a way that, however many be taken, their sum can never exceed a certain limiting velocity – the velocity of light. All this, of course, has been well known since Minkowski first stated it, but Professor Lewis, beginning by giving us, as it were, several geometries to choose from, has brought the purely conventional element in scientific theories into admirable prominence. The more complicated geometry assumed by Einstein in his general theory cannot be so simply described, but Professor Lewis succeeds in giving a clear idea of the theory in its geometrical aspect. He stresses the extreme minuteness of the departures from "flat" geometry which are necessary to explain the phenomena of gravitation. And yet gravitation, although conditioned by such minute changes, is a very important fact about the world.

Having discussed relativity theory, Professor Lewis proceeds to quantum theory, and here, to the scientific reader, is the most fascinating part of his book. It is well known that the "interference" phenomena of light offer extraordinary difficulties to quantum theory. Professor Lewis suggests a solution. The technical account of this solution has already appeared. In this volume Professor Lewis tries to give, in simple language, the gist of the matter. It is nothing less than a complete revision in our notions of time and of cause and effect. We must assume, for instance, that we can affect the course of past events. If we can assume this we shall find that "certain inconsistencies between prevailing physical ideas and the geometry which so admirably interprets the kinematics of relativity are removed." This may seem a large concession to make in order to preserve a geometry. According to this geometry any two objects that exist on the path of the same light ray are in "virtual contact." But, Professor Lewis goes on: "I have spoken of virtual contact as distinguished from ordinary contact, but I do not wish to imply that it is any less a physical contact in the one case than in the other. I claim that my eye touches a star as truly as my finger touches this table." And the eye, which has been in existence only a few years, must be assumed to influence the original emission from the star, which may have occurred thousands of years ago. It is evident that this theory is one of the most startling that even modern physics has propounded. But we cannot say that it is too startling. Our ordinary notion of time comes, as Professor Lewis shows, from our experience of "one-way" time. A moving picture run backwards is ludicrous. But physics, throughout large regions, knows nothing of these irreversible phenomena. Past and future are not essentially different to it. This theory of Professor Lewis's is not so paradoxical when seen in relation to the "time" of physics. And no reader who responds to the imaginative audacity of modern physics can fail to be interested in it.   Times Lit. Sup. 3 Feb. 1927

–––––––––––––––– ┼┼ ––––––––––––––––

2477 "High poetry has got its form not by chance, but because that is the only form in which the subject-matter of high poetry can be expressed. Beauty of execution, in poetry as in all art, is not an

ornament but a means of expression; & where execution lacks beauty it
also fails in expression."

Times Lit. Sup! 25.6.'08

2478   Sometimes we are forced to say that American literature in
general lacks depth, dignity, and beauty. There are occasional and
startling exceptions; among them this beautiful and recent poem by
H. D.:–

LETHE.

Nor skin nor hide nor fleece
  Shall cover you.
Nor curtain of crimson nor fine
Shelter of cedar-wood be over you.
    Nor the fir-tree
    Nor the pine.

Nor sight of whin nor gorse
  Nor river yew,
  Nor fragrance of flowering bush,
Nor wailing of reed-bird to waken you.
    Nor of linnet
    Nor of thrush.

Nor word nor touch nor sight
  Of lover, you
Shall long through the night but for this:
The roll of the full tide to cover you
    Without question,
    Without kiss.

Times Lit. Sup. Nov. 17. 1921.

2479   (**f119ᵛ**) J. S. Mill's new propositions –
   1. What evidence we possess points to the creation of our universe by
an Intelligent Mind, benevolent but not omnipotent.
   Mill's religion displaces the idea of providential government by an
omnipotent deity, & substitutes the 'idea of the possibility, & in a low
degree even the probability,' of a universe governed by a deity with
limited powers.–   F. W. Hirst (Morley's letters).

2480   The Absolute = "The exhauster, includer, of all possibilities."
                Michael Kaye. <u>Journ!</u> of Phil. <u>Studies</u>. Oct. 1927

2481   "It is impossible that a man should be determined purely by
himself; he is always determined by others ... he is they, & they are
he.... He derives from the whole universe, & <u>is</u> in a way the whole
universe. He is an expression, a moment of the whole universe; but
since he is this he may be regard.d as being of one life with the universe,
& therefore also, its other expressions."   ib.

2482   "It may be objected to the theory of volitional determinism that
it appears incompatible with the fact of personal responsib!y Yet ... [if
so] volitional indeterminism is not less incompatible. ...

Literary Notes III

Entries 2483–2641

2483   (fl^r) his majesty's theatre.
"king henry iv." (part i.)

But what of Prince Hal? Do we care nothing for him? As King's son, nothing; the chronicle is as dull with him as it would be without him. For he does not belong to the chronicle at all, but to that other part of the play, the rich and glowing world of Falstaff, Bardolph, Poins, Peto, Gadshill, and Mistress Quickly. Shakespeare hardly brought the two worlds, the world of the Boar's Head and of the Court, into contact. They remain apart; and, to tell the truth, we suffer the scene of the chronicle for the sake of the scenes of the comedy. With a passing thought for a very fine, human, and individual performance of Hotspur by Mr. Basil Gill, we are content to forget the history; we should never be content to forget the Falstaff round which hum those merry, busy, scandalous scenes in taverns and midnight woods.

2484   mr. william morris on the printing of books.

Mr. W. Morris delivered a lecture at the New Gallery on Thursday evening "On the Printing of Books." The lecture, which was the first of a series of five to be given by different lecturers under the auspices of the Arts and Crafts Exhibition Society, was delivered in the North Gallery, which was completely filled by an appreciative audience. The chair was taken by Mr. Cobden Saunderson.

Mr. W. Morris, who was received with cheers, demonstrated by means of lantern slides the various stages which printing had passed through from the time of its invention until the third decade of the 16th century. The first slide exhibited depicted a manuscript Bible written probably about the year 1290, which was practically the form of all the subsequent books he would have to show them. The art of printing on its institution was a Teutonic art, he might even say a German art. The first books were printed actually in Germany at Mainz, on the Rhine. The German printers spread themselves all through Europe and recruited their ranks with a certain number of Frenchmen, who were educated in their school, and together they were, for the first decade at any rate, the printers of all the books printed in Europe. The next slide exhibited showed a page from the first book printed in a book form with movable type. It was a Bible printed by Gutenberg at Mainz about 1453, the year of the taking of Constantinople by the Turks. There was thus a coincidence in the dates of those two events which had so great

an influence on the new birth of letters which was shortly to be made
manifest to the world. The initials of the book were painted by hand
and not printed. The type of the book was rather stately in form, and
was afterwards called missal type because many missals were printed
in it. It was what they might call full-blown Gothic. Next came a
picture of a Psalter printed at Mainz by Gutenberg in 1457, and this
was followed by another representing a book printed by Gutenberg
with the help of Schæffer. This slide showed an initial B printed in two
colours, and the book afforded the first example of printing in two
colours. Strange to say, having succeeded in printing as well as could
be desired in two colours, printers never tried to do so again, probably
because it was a process of great difficulty. The remaining slides
illustrated the transitions from Gothic to Roman type, all the peculiar
characteristics being pointed out by the lecturer as he proceeded. Pages
were exhibited from works printed by Mentelin at Strasburg, in 1473;
by Schweinheim and Pannartz at the monastery of Sabiaco, near
Rome, in 1467; by Friburger Crantz and Gerring, at Paris, in 1471; by
G. Zeiner, at Augsburg, in 1472; by Jenson, at Venice, in 1476; by U.
Zell, at Cologne; by Schüssler, at Augsburg, in 1472; by Jean de Pres and
P. Gerard, at Abbeville, in 1486; by G. Leew, at Antwerp, in 1486; by
Caxton, at Westminster, in 1477; by Wynkin de Worde, at Westminster,
in 1495; and by Bertelette, in London, in 1532. Finally, Mr. Morris
exhibited slides representing pages from "The Golden Legend" and
"Troy" printed by himself at Chiswick last year. In summing up the
points of his lecture, he said that to produce good books as far as the
artistic point of view was concerned they must print on pretty good
paper, with good type, and the type must be put in the proper position on
the page. This last point was very important, for whenever they saw a
book that was rightly put upon the paper, even if the type was bad and
the paper not good, the book would look rather pleasant than otherwise;
whereas if the book were not properly put upon the paper it would
always seem that something was wrong. When they had paid attention
to these points they would have books which any one could read with
pleasure, and he thought it was something to feel that they were reading
a little bit through their eyes as well as through their mind. (Cheers.)

2485   "Now why is it that when I also deal in the tragi-comic irony of
the conflict between real life and the romantic imagination, no critic
ever affiliates me to my countryman and immediate forerunner,
Charles Lever, whilst they confidently derive me from a Norwegian

author of whose language I do not know three words, and of whom I knew nothing until years after the Shavian *Anschauung* was already unequivocally declared in books full of what came, ten years later, to be perfunctorily labelled Ibsenism."

G. B. Shaw. Pref. to J. Bull's other I^d *"First Aid to Critics."*

2486 But is Mr. Phillips's intensely lyrical diction – or, to widen the question, is blank verse in general – as suitable to a near and clear, as it is to a dim and distant scene and period? It is true that people did not talk blank verse in ancient Jerusalem, or in Rimini, or even in Ithaca or Calypso's Isle, any more than in Cromwell's Cambridgeshire. The medium is as unreal in Mr. Phillips's earlier plays as in this. But when the scene is laid so near us in place and time, the unreality of the medium is constantly present to our minds. We have scarcely the váguest notion as to how people talked in Judæa, but we know pretty definitely how they talked in Cambridgeshire. Consequently we can much more easily give imaginative credence to the poetic convention in the former case than in the latter.

A Singing World.

The poet asks us to join him in imagining a world steeped in an atmosphere of verbal music, where men and women spontaneously and inevitably utter their emotions in metrical language and in highly-wrought imagery. This stretch of make-believe he demands of us; and where mythical or very remote times and places are concerned, it costs us no conscious effort. The imagination works, so to speak, in a vacuum, where it encounters no resistance. But we cannot clear our minds of a more or less definite image of what England really was in 1643; and with this image the poet's metrical England is continually in conflict. Hence friction, uneasiness, and inability to yield ourselves up to the illusion. Mr. Phillips is not the first poet by many a hundred who has ignored these considerations; but no one, in our time, can ignore them with impunity.   Wm Archer.

2487 (**f2ʳ**) OSCAR WILDE (Methuen's Catalogue)

As with Wilde's life, so with his works, the tendency has been either to ignore severely, or to exaggerate. "Salome" has been called a *Weltstück*, and his other plays, poems, ballads, prose fiction, criticism of life, fairy stories, and fantasies have each and all been termed supreme in their several kinds. The great difficulty of any kind of historic estimate hitherto has been to assemble them together in any sort of uniform, authentic shape. Purged of all nauseous apocrypha, such as "The Priest and the Acolyte," it will be seen in the new edition that his work gains by the ensemble; and that it may be regarded frankly and dispassionately without fear, shame, disinfectant, or, indeed, apparatus of any kind. A chapter of Mirabeau or Willy, or a tiny duodecimo of Sterne, will contain more indelicacy than twelve volumes of Wilde, who was by no means a disbeliever in the eternal decency of things. It is true, no doubt, that his better qualities, too, have been magnified. But the historical importance of his writings is very great. He used levity as a lever to raise the incubus of humbug and dogmatic materialism with which literature was so heavily loaded, in that period of the last century between those two crises of self-complacency known as the Jubilee and the Diamond Jubilee, as no one else had done. He saw things in a newer and truer light, and he had the courage of his perceptions. He was the first of the new *Idéologues*, and his Horatian arraignment of the new "Americanismus," or haste to be rich, his new "Ars Poetica," and his rediscovery of the necessity of Individualism in Art – all these things mark the starting point of a new era in speculation. There came a change in the blood of the people which coincided with the turn of the century. Wilde did not live to see it, but he precipitated the adjustment of lagging literary opinion to the changing facts of life. A retardation of this process, as history shows, is always dangerous; and Wilde detected a chief source of this danger in the incorrigible cowardice of the press and its ineradicable terror of truth.

His early reputation as a poseur and fop – so necessary to his notoriety – recoiled upon the scholar and the gentleman (as Wilde always innately was), and even upon the artist. He could never entirely control the craft of letters of which he was in most respects a master. He could not leave the surface alone. A bright feather or bead would tempt the lurking showman within. And yet it cannot be denied that he achieved exquisite work both in prose and verse. The plays in either medium will be found here in entirety, as they have never been printed before, from "The Duchess of Padua," the draft of which was written for Mary Anderson as early as 1883, to "The Importance of being (**f2ᵛ**) Earnest, a trivial comedy for serious people," as irresistible as of old, a trifle of airy persiflage, at once insolent in its levity and exquisite in its finish. Then there are the two volumes of fairy stories, "The House of Pomegranates" and "The Happy Prince," which, concluding with that quaintly conceived irony of "The Remarkable Rocket," is, to many, the happiest of all Wilde's volumes, as "The Ballad of Reading Gaol" is the most resonant, and "De Profundis" the saddest and the most indescribable. The essays ("Intentions" and "The Soul of Man"); "Ravenna," "The Sphinx," and other poems, many "uncollected"; "Lord Arthur Savile's Crime" and the other prose stories, and a number of prose papers and one or two letters, brought together for the first time by the editor, Mr. Robert Ross, comprise the main features of this well deliberated collection.

"The Soul of Man" is full of the ideas on which we contentedly breakfast every morning in the new century on which Wilde felt that he was not destined (can we say privileged) to enter. Now quite mildly disturbing, or even tonic, these "Intentions" of his in 1888 were held to be either unhealthy or insane. Their identity in aim with the intentions of the wits of our new age, and not only in aim, but in the play of the paradoxes and similarity of the colouring (with its frequent recurrence to Christian or Biblical parallelisms) cannot be denied. And so with the turns of phrase. A good *mot* is like an aeroplane – it requires a clear run of a few rods to launch it prosperously on its volatile career. Wilde's wit and humour had not this advantage during his lifetime. But if, peradventure, you bring down a *mot* flying to-day in the upper æther, the probability is that you will find that Oscar Wilde had a hand in its flight. Much that will be accounted freshly distinctive of 1908 may be found in the original by the diligent explorer of Wilde's collected works. "Original," that is to say, in so far as it may be said of any of the best literature that it is original. For Oscar Wilde's notion of literary property (*propriété c'est le vol*) was distinctly that it belonged to the person who adorned it most. Echoes (from Vanbrugh, Foote, Sheridan, Horace Walpole, Sydney Smith, Disraeli, Whistler, Balzac, Flaubert, Baudelaire, Heredia and Anatole France), self-repetition, and irony are among the distinctive notes of most of Wilde's gayer prose. The all-pervading unsought irony that broods remorselessly over the surface of his earlier perfumed pages is one of the most terrible qualities in Wilde's writing. A type of it may be found in his reply to a question about George IV. to the effect that he was not in the habit of associating with the criminal classes (which is also an echo from Sydney Smith). Another quality of his work, as here assembled, is its variety. It contains almost everything except perhaps "open air!"

P. R. A.

2488   (**f3ʳ**) In what imaginary world do we find a virtue that is not grafted upon a defect? A virtue is but a vice that raises instead of lowering itself; and a good quality is but a defect that has turned itself to use.

"How should she have the necessary energy if she were deprived of ambition and pride? How could she thrust aside unjust obstacles if she did not possess a reserve of selfishness proportionate to the lawful exigencies of her life? How should she be ardent and fond if she were not sensual? How should she be kind if she were not a little weak? How should she be trustful if she were not often too credulous? How should she be beautiful if she knew not mirrors and did not seek to please? How should she preserve her feminine grace if she had no innocent vanities? How should she be generous if she were not a little improvident? How should she be just if she were unable to be hard, how brave if she were not rash? How should she be devoted and capable of sacrifice if she never escaped from the control of icy reason?

"What we call virtues and vices are the same forces passing along a life. They change their name according to the direction in which they go: to the left, they fall into the shallows of ugliness, selfishness and folly; to the right, they climb to the high lands of nobleness, generosity and intelligence. They are good or bad according to what they do and not according to the title which they bear.

2489 From the same ⟨(Constable)⟩ 'The Modern Pilgrimage from Theology to Religion (being some Essays in that Directon),' by Robert Locke Bremner. The day of the Atheist, if it ever really existed, is over, and we have among us instead a religion which accepts God, but rejects theology and dogma. The title of this work very fairly explains the trend of its thought. 'Spiritual culture is just as necessary to spiritual attainment as physical culture is to the acquisition of health,' says the author, which few will deny; and then, having gathered together the facts science has to teach us regarding evolution and natural laws, he proceeds to demolish the tenets of Christianity. There is a well-told parable in which three youths named Kŏkh Shûr, Agnostikos, and Discipulus apply for the post of Watchman to the City of Many Moons, over which a mist ever hangs, and one is rather inclined to connect Mr. Bremner's method with that of Kŏkh Shûr in the parable. Let us hasten to say that some of these 'Pagan essays,' as the author calls them in his dedication, contain much that is thoughtful, and even spiritual, but there is flippancy too. The paraphrase of the Apostles' Creed is in bad taste, and the statement that 'it is not now the working creed of one

Christian in a thousand' certainly lacks that reasonable proof which the author demands for all statements opposed to his views. The Divinity of Jesus, the Virgin Birth, the Ascension, and miracles generally are relegated to the region of legend; they have no place in this 'rational' belief in a God. 'Socrates was content to be known as Socrates; Jesus, as Jesus,' says the author. 'Both were assuredly in their degree sons of God.' May we humbly suggest that, when all is said and done, science as man interprets it may not be science as God knows it; and that we have still too much to learn to assert that all our fathers have taught us is mere superstition.

2490 (**f4ʳ**) EVOLUTION AND RELIGION.

The Rev. Father Coupe, s. j., m. a. (late Professor of Philosophy, Stonyhurst), on Thursday afternoon, in the Theatre Royal, Bournemouth, began a course of four lectures on "Evolution and Religion." The duties of Chairman were discharged by Colonel Colthurst.

The Lecturer said that the object of his four lectures was to show that there was no conflict between physical science and religion. As extrinsic evidence of this fact he quoted Huxley, Jevons, and the late Lord Salisbury, who had written that "few men are now influenced by the strange idea that questions of religious belief depend on the issues of physical research." The lecturer laid it down that from the beginning there had been a purposive process of evolution, and that the Cosmos, within certain limitations, had been evolved from primordial matter, just as certainly as the oak is evolved from the acorn. But he attacked extreme evolution, the materialistic theory that there existed nothing outside matter and material forces and that the universe had evolved itself by chance out of an eternal, changing, self-existent nebula. Then in detail the nebula was described. Its vast extent. The earth is distant from the sun about 93 million miles. Thus the diameter of the earth's orbit was some 186 million miles; a distance so vast than an express train going 50 miles an hour would take 400 years to cover it. Yet this was a trifle compared with the distance of the stars. The huge diameter of the earth's orbit, viewed from our nearest star, Alpha Centauri, would look less than half the thickness of one's little finger (3-16th of an inch) viewed at a distance of one-third of a mile. This nearest fixed star was 275,000 times further away from us than is the sun. Nay, this star is seen by the naked eye as one star, but is in reality a binary, i.e., two stars, each as large as our sun, and distant from one another 23 times as far as is the earth from the sun. Or measure this distance in another way. Light travels 186,000 miles a second – over seven times round the earth while your clock ticks once. The "light journey" from the sun to earth, therefore, takes about eight minutes. Yet the light journey from the nearest fixed star is 4¼ years. The second nearest star to us is 61 Cygni, distant a light journey of 7¼ years. These stars are, however, near. Canopus, the brightest star in the southern hemisphere, is distant from the earth a light journey of 400 years; so that had it been extinguished when Henry the VIII became King, in 1509, it would still be visible. It is 25 million times further off than the sun, so that it would take an express train 50 million centuries to reach it. This, however, vast a distance as it is, is but trivial compared with the extent of the whole universe, which has been calculated to be a light-journey of 36,000 years, an express train journey of 4,500 million centuries. Next the lecturer touched on the size of the Heavenly bodies. The earth is about 8,000 miles in diameter. The sun is over 100 times greater in diameter. But the sun is a comparatively small body. Arcturus, one of the brightest stars in the sky, is so much larger than the sun, that the sun, if put back to the same distance from the earth as Arcturus is, would be quite invisible to the naked eye. Yet in spite of their huge bulk these enormous bodies are moving with fearful velocity. The earth is rotating on its axis 1,000 miles an hour, and revolving round the sun 1,000 miles a minute. This, however, is comparatively, slow motion. For the mighty star Arcturus is travelling at the rate of over 720,000 miles an hour. As to the number of the stars they are computed at about 100 millions. How vast, then, must the original nebula have been! Then, putting aside the telescope and taking to the microscope, the lecturer discussed the constitution of matter. There are about 70 chemical elements, differing in weight, conductivity, melting point, chemical affinity, and the proportions in which they combine. (**f3**^{v}) These elements are so minute that in the third of a thimbleful of hydrogen there are 400 millions of millions of millions of atoms. How many then are there in the whole universe? Moreover, in each atom of hydrogen there are 1,000 electrons – particles of electricity – all moving with the velocity of light; so that each atom – a thing too utterly minute for the most powerful microscope – is a scene of such activity that it is, in itself, a piece of machinery more complicated than the whole solar system! In the primordial nebula there was also perfect arrangement. Every single atom had its exact place assigned it by the great mind that foresaw the vast universe as it is to-day, and by the great Mechanican who so ordered and disposed every single electron that the whole should evolve into the Cosmos as we now have it. The lecturer ended by pressing these questions:– First. Who made all the matter of this vast universe? The whole of matter had an efficient cause prior and exterior to itself. Who was that cause? Not matter; for it preceded and was extrinsic to matter. Then it must have been Mind. As the cause was not material, it must have been spiritual. Who was this Mind, this Spirit? Secondly, Who set the mighty mass of nebula in motion? Not the nebula itself; for by Newton's first law of motion matter cannot move itself. Matter, then, was first moved by another. Who was that Mover? Thirdly, The nebula was, according to most definite laws, to be evolved into this majestic Cosmos. A law implies a lawgiver. Who was that Legislator? Fourthly, Whose was the Mind that foresaw the ordered universe, as it is to-day? Who was the Mathematician that calculated the exact place and disposition of each separate átom, and of each electron in each atom, of the primordial nebula, so that the mighty fire-mist should develop into the present Cosmos? Who was this mighty First Cause that, by an act of will, created this stupendous nebula, set it in motion, made it subject to mechanical laws, foresaw into what it would develop, and minutely arranged each particle so that it might so develop? Who the First Cause was, the lecturer promised to discuss in his second lecture on March 8th.

2491 (**f4ʳ**) Now the first point to be grasped about poetry is that it is not prose, not even prose ornamented with rhyme and metre, but something different in its essence; and the essence of poetry is that it expresses emotion. It may express many other things; but it is poetry only because it expresses emotion, and the purpose of those formal attributes which distinguish it from prose, of metre and rhyme, is to express emotion. These things are not ornaments but means of expression. ... What poetry expresses is not an idea or an appetite or an action or any other experience of the human mind or body but the emotion aroused by such experience. It may have to make a statement of the experience which has aroused the emotion it wishes to express. The poet may have to say that he is hungry, or that he believes in God, or that his wife is dead; but these statements are not his poetry, and it is part of his art to express his emotion in the very making of them or, if possible, to leave them to be inferred from the expression of his emotion. Wordsworth, for instance, in the poem "A Slumber did my Spirit seal" does not tell us anything directly; we infer from the expression of his emotion that it has been caused by the death of some one: and it is just the same with poetry that expresses emotions aroused by moral ideas. ...

... The aim of poetry is always to express something which cannot be said in prose, which cannot be conceived by the prosaic faculties of the mind. But it is not to be assumed that the poet has not exercised the prosaic faculties of his mind because he writes pure poetry. There are some poets who are content not to write pure poetry, who do their thinking in the process of composition, and not before it; and because they exhibit the labour of their thought to the world, because their verse often contains thought and nothing else, many readers suppose them to be more thoughtful than the poets who express emotion stirred by thought but not obscured by it. Yet these are the poets who use verse for its proper purpose, which is to say what cannot be said in prose, to make words more than "sense-deep," to charge them with the music of emotion in which is implicit the logic of thought.   A. CLUTTON BROCK.

2492   The truth appears to be that in matters of literature there are two consciences, which for convenience, but for convenience only, may be called the higher and the lower. The lower conscience is that of the poet as craftsman, and Tennyson and Catullus are the crowning examples of it. It is concerned, so far as the two things can be separated, with the form rather than the matter of the work, the grammar and composition of the art, and is the power that prevents a poet from passing anything that is not expressed in the very best way that he can achieve. It may win immortality for thought of any kind, and its absence may doom the highest to extinction. Of this kind of literary conscience Mrs. Browning had little or none. She was, in spite of her bursts of lyrical beauty, careless of form. Her brain was exceedingly well equipped, but there was no file in it. She was a poet born. Thoughts and verses came to her, and she wrote them down, whether they came right or wrong. Sometimes they came entirely right:–   Times.

2493 (**f4ᵛ**) The MS. of *The Fall of Hyperion* now   *A /Keats/*
printed for the first time contains a passage cancelled   *di/scovery/*
by Woodhouse with a pencil mark, a marginal note
being added: 'Keats seems to have intended to erase
this and the next twenty-one lines.' Mr. E. de
Sélincourt denies that the evidence as it stands gives
us a right to reject the lines, particularly as they
supply a necessary climax to the argument of the

introductory allegory, which has hitherto been
presented incomplete. The passage is as follows,
beginning at line 2, and ending at line 25, and the poet
is seeking counsel of Moneta, formerly known as
Mnemosyne:—

> '"If it please,
> [Majestic shadow, tell me: sure not all
> Those melodies sung into the World's ear
> Are useless: sure a poet is a sage:
> A humanist, Physician to all Men.
> That I am none I feel, as Vultures feel
> They are no birds when Eagles are abroad.
> What am I then: thou spakest of my Tribe:
> What Tribe?" The tall shade veiled in drooping white
> Then spake, so much more earnest, that the breath
> Moved the thin linen folds that drooping hung
> About a golden censer from the hand
> Pendent – "Art thou not of the dreamer Tribe?
> The Poet and the dreamer are distinct,
> Diverse, sheer opposite, antipodes.
>
> The one pours out a balm upon the World
> The other vexes it." Then shouted I
> Spite of myself, and with a Pythia's spleen,
> "Apollo! faded! O far-flown Apollo!
> Where is thy misty pestilence to creep
> Into the dwellings, through the door crannies
> Of all mock lyrists, large self-worshippers
> And careless Hectorers in proud bad verse?
> Though I breathe death with them it will be life
> To see them sprawl before me into graves.]
> Majestic shadow, tell me where I am,
> Whose Altar this; for whom this Incense curls;
> What Image this, whose face I cannot see,
> For the broad marble knees; and who thou art,
> Of accent feminine so courteous?"'

'As poetry,' Mr. Sélincourt remarks, 'these lines may
not be very valuable, but there can be no question of
their importance to the argument of the poem. ... For

all its crudity the passage is eminently suggestive, and
supplies a valuable commentary, by no means at
variance with his other utterances, upon Keats's
conception of the poetic art. The object of the /*The a/rgu-*
(**f5ʳ**)singer, he tells us, is to pour out a balm upon the /*ment/*
world, not by luring men away from it to a fanciful
land of dreams, but by seeing things as they are, and
by concentrating his imaginative powers upon reality.
The romanticism of his own day, which, indeed,
reached its zenith in his own work, was for the most
part content with the "embroidery of dim dreams,"
and when it attempted to heal the world it presented
for contemplation "the mere fiction of what never
was." But after the return from a beautiful
dreamland, he would have us believe, the burden of
the mystery is the heavier; absence has bred
discontent with the actual, and the result is not balm
but vexation. Thus in the very height of the Romantic
movement Keats has detected the germs of its decay.

A SPECIMEN OF KEATS'S HANDWRITING REDUCED IN SIZE AND REPRODUCED
BY A PROCESS-BLOCK FROM THE COLLOTYPE FACSIMILE.

/A hit/ at
/Byron/

'But still worse than those who are admittedly dreamers are the Satirists. For under the fond delusion that they are Realists, they too are merely dreamers; though with a difference, that their dream has taken the form of nightmare – a distortion of reality. They have never felt the miseries of the world, except as a personal insult to themselves, and they have vented their spleen upon that humanity with which they should have sympathized. The shaft is here aimed at Byron, for whose work Keats had felt a growing dislike ever since, three years before, he had dedicated his own life to poetry.'

[From *Hyperion*. A Facsimile of Keats's Autograph Manuscript, with a Transliteration of the Manuscript of 'The Fall of Hyperion, A Dream.' With Introductions and Notes by ERNEST DE SÉLINCOURT. Clarendon Press. *Published by Henry Frowde*. Prices 52s. 6d. net ($35.00) and 73s. 6d. net ($45.00)]

4   *The Periodical*   *No. XXIX*

2494   (**f6ʳ**) WITHOUT COMPROMISE. BY JOHN DAVIDSON.

"Is this the thing I want to say? Is this the thing that should be said?" Only a few writers since time began have faced these questions. Many doubtless put these questions to themselves, but without in the least understanding them. They whisper, "Is this the thing I want to say?" but the meaning of these words in their suspiration is, "Will people approve of this? Will it be applauded? Will it pay?" They whisper to themselves, "Is this the thing that should be said?" only to examine still more closely the contingencies of the referendum: "Will this little book of mine be useful to the University Extensioners? Will it have the suffrage of the Socialistic mob? Will it give me kudos with this party or that? Will its publication make me feel happy and good? Will the Church be favourable? Will it be pronounced of 'the centre,' so that I shall not feel lonely, but 'in it' with the rest of them and the best of them? Will it please my friends? Will it please the public?" The true meaning of these questions, "Is this the thing I want to say? Is this the thing that should be said?" is a daily and hourly matter of life and death. Among the few who perceive the greatness and the terror of these questions, the majority look once, then turn away for ever; some stare at the flaming interrogations, fascinated, till they go mad; only two or three face them greatly without any attempt at begging them; and perhaps one in a thousand years is able to answer "Yes."

"Is this the thing I want to say?" If it is, then it will be something that nobody ever said before, something that all my contemporaries will object to, something that will turn all my friends into enemies, something that everyone will misinterpret – will set themselves to misunderstand. No other man's fingerprint has the same pressure as mine, and I shall see that it appears on everything I handle, everything I adapt, everything I own. The gloves of party, of culture, of creed, wherewith men hide their fingerprints lest they should be caught in the act of being themselves, I decline to wear. There are the whorls of my fingers and my thumbs: I, look you; not a glove, but a hand. My bones and marrow, my flesh and blood, my nerve and brain, are different from those of all other men, even as my fingerprints are; and I am conscious of that, and can make it apparent. I am not of the left, or of the right, or of the centre; but above these, and of the Universe. I say the thing I want to say, seeking out enmity as the sign of my success and the unintended warrant of my power and authority. I attack nothing; I attack no one; I say the thing I want to say with authority, and immediately all men feel themselves wounded, all ideas are in the crucible, all idols are overturned. I have authority: I write not in the name of any creed or party, revolution, or reaction, but in my own name only. Nothing but that is authority. Academic degree, the mandate of a constituency, public sanction of any kind, can place people in authority; but to have authority and to be in authority are not the same thing. Authority is inherent only in him who says, "I, of myself, announce this."

2495   (f7ʳ) LITERATURE.
MR. BRIDGES' "DEMETER."
DEMETER: A MASK. By ROBERT BRIDGES. (Oxford: Clarendon Press. Is. net.)

Mr. Bridges is the least luxurious of poets. And yet there is a kind of luxury in reading whatever he writes, the luxury of an aristocratic repose and quietness, something secret and aloof from the busy vulgarities which swallow up so much of life. It is impossible to read a single page of his work without accomplishing a delightful escape from all the "smoke and stir" and "low-thoughted care" which, for all poets, and not only for Milton, make this life seem at times a "frail and feverish" thing, from which it is the very business of poetry to lift us into other and higher regions –

Regions mild of calm and serene air.

Not that Mr. Bridges is a specially serene poet. He altogether wants the ease and smoothness that go with perfect serenity. He is always severe, often difficult, often wayward and wilful with the disdainful wilfulness of a man who has said wise things to the world to which the world has refused to listen. There is hardly a trace in his verse of the triumphant note which rings through some of Milton's greatest things, the note of one who is victoriously conscious that his words will charm or overcome the world. The tone of Mr. Bridges is quite different. He had things to say that were worth saying, and he has said them; but they are not the mighty things that Milton had it in him to say, nor has he the organ voice at the sound of which all other voices know that their part is silence; and so he seems to turn away, content to possess his own soul, think his own thoughts, and live his own life apart. And the voice that of all our living poetic voices (with one exception, little thought of as a poet's voice at all) has been the utterance of the deepest and sincerest thinking, and has uttered it in the most exact and original words, seems inclined to give itself over to metrical experiments and pedantries of orthography.

However, Mr. Bridges can still write a poem occasionally, under pressure, and, what is more, can still be persuaded to publish it; and here is one. Most people who are interested in these things heard that at the inauguration of the new buildings of Somerville College last year the members of the college performed in their garden a masque which had been written for them by Mr. Bridges to music by Mr. W. H. Hadow. This is the piece now published. It is no new departure for the poet. Those who have read *Achilles in Scyros*, or *Prometheus the Fire Giver*, will know what to expect when Mr. Bridges takes in hand the great tale of the most moving of all the figures in the Olympian hierarchy. There is the same scholarly severity of manner, the same utter refusal of all cheap triumphs of effect or emotion; and yet there is the same complete avoidance of the mere classical exercise. Some of the comedies Mr. Bridges has written do seem open to the objection that they are little more than a scholar's diversions; a graceful, dignified, even laudable

form of idleness, if you will, but still idleness, a making of things that
have no proper work to do in the world. But this is never true of the
masques or plays from Greek subjects. In them the business in hand is
not to show "how once Menander went" or to exhibit any mere
dexterity of making Greek tales run in English verse. The heart and
mind of the poet have been put into the writing of them, and the heart
and mind of the reader must go to the enjoying and understanding of
them. Every one will recall speeches and choral songs which go to the
root of the eternal things, the joys and sorrows, the problems and
ponderings, the hopes and fears which are as old as they are new and as
new as they are old, and in the presence of which man is just man,
neither primitive nor modern neither English nor Greek. And it is just
the same here. The old stories take on new meanings, and still keep the
old. At first sight so many of the Greek myths appear foolish and rather
barbarous tales. One wonders how many of the Greeks themselves
could put such meaning into them. Still the meaning was there for them
to find, and it is there for us; and, indeed, it is with these stories, as with
all the great inventions of the human mind, there is more in them than
the inventor himself knew. Some people will never forget the revelation
that Walter Pater's study of this very myth of Demeter was to them. No
doubt, only part of what Pater found in it could have been in any Greek
thought of Demeter. And so here, in a less degree, with what Mr.
Bridges does with the story. The very proof of the greatness and ideal
truth of the tale lies in its pliancy, its adaptability, its capacity to give
out new meaning under new conditions. We know what one great
English poet, happily still amongst us, has made of it; his was one way
of using it – how far from being the only way this poem is sufficient
proof. Listen to Demeter and Persephone:–

PER.   Are there not matters past the thought of men
    Or gods to know?
DEM.   Thou meanest wherefore things
    Should be at all! Or, if they be, why thus,
    As hot, cold, hard and soft; and wherefore Zeus
    Had but two brothers; why the stars of heaven
    Are so innumerable, constellated
    Just as they are; or why this Sicily
    Should be three-cornered? Yes, thou sayest well,
    Why things are as they are, nor gods nor men
    Can know. We say that Fate appointed thus,
    And are content –

PER.   Suppose, dear Mother, there wer' a temple in heaven,
Which, dedicated to the unknown Cause
And worship of the unseen, had power to draw
All that was worthy and good within its gate:
And that the spirits who entered there became
Not only purified and comforted,
But that the mysteries of the shrine were such,
That the initiated bathed in light
Of infinite intelligence, and saw
The meaning and the reason of all things,
All at a glance distinctly, and perceived
The origin of all things to be good,
And the end good, and that what appears as evil
Is as a film of dust, that faln thereon,
May, – at one stroke of the hand, –
Be brush'd away, and show the good beneath,
Solid and fair and shining: If moreover
This blessed vision were of so great power
That none could e'er forget it or relapse
To doubtful ignorance:–

It is plain that many things have passed into this which the earliest hearers of the tale of Persephone could not have had in their minds, nor the earliest of the initiated into Demeter's mysteries. Plato is there, of course, to begin with; and some suggestion of the long line of mystics and spiritual poets of whom he is the father. The questions are our questions too: the ultimate "how" and "for what reason" which never finds an ultimate "in this way" and "for this reason"; the old and new answer of silence and acquiescence, and the eternal escape from it into the answer of dream and vision, which transcends logic and defies sense.

And yet the story, as it is given here, is still just the ancient tale of Persephone, fairest flower of Sicily and lover of all fair flowers, carried off into the darkness by the King of the Darkness; and the tale of her mother, the pain she had to seek her through the world; the penalty she laid on the earth and the things that still grew where her one growth was lost, her loneliness, her sorrow, her new sympathy with man, and the ultimate reconciliation in a half-restored Persephone. How many of the most elemental human emotions are bound up in the very outline of the story! The love of the spring and the flowers is there, the dread of the darkness, the grim violence of passion, the transforming grace of

youth and innocence, the all-enduring and all-conquering power of the
first and mightiest of the loves that are not passion, the love of a mother
for her child. And what a stately, gracious, and, in the end, most
moving, figure is Demeter. No one should read the Masque without
going again to the British Museum to see the great Demeter there. It is
a pity that the poem could not have that wonderful face and figure for a
frontispiece; for the Demeter of the sculptor is exactly the Mother of
Sorrow, who learned and taught that pain could be transformed into a
sacred and fruitful thing, who, as she says here,

> bade King Keleos build for me
> A temple in Eleusis, and ordain'd
> My worship, and the mysteries of my thought:
> Where in the sorrow that I underwent
> Man's state is pattern'd: and in picture shewn
> The way of his salvation.

These last words, no doubt, have now an echo in them which could not
be in the sculptor's ear; but the figure is, in essence, the sculptor's
figure still; and the words that go beyond it are only one more proof of
the eternal significance of the tale.

But there will be people who care little about Greek myth and less
about its significance, but care a great deal about Mr. Bridges; and
they will ask whether the new poem still exhibits the familiar qualities
that have made them care more and more for his poetry every year, as
they take it up and go over the old things again. Has it his note as of a
personal confession? Has it that hesitating utterance which is soon
recognized as the hesitation of sincerity that will not speak till it has
found the only exact and truthful word? Has it his curious observation
of detail, his ranging wistfulness, his (**f7ᵛ**) grave joyfulness, his brave
and cheerful gravity? Has it the old loving watchfulness which found
pleasure for the eye, work for the mind, and food for the heart in all the
doings of nature and in all the ways of man? Such an inquirer may open
the book at the beginning of Act I., and he will be content when he
finds the first words of the chorus:—

> Gay and lovely is earth, man's decorate dwelling;
> With fresh beauty ever varying hour to hour.
> As now bathed in azure joy she awakeneth
> With bright morn to the sun's life-giving effluence,

Or sunk into solemn darkness aneath the stars
In mysterious awe slumbereth out the night,
Then from darkness again plunging again to day.

And he will be made entirely at home when he turns to the poet's very
characteristic notes on "spelling, accents, and metres," and finds that
this chorus is in the metre of

Maecenas, atavis edite regibus.

And then he may go on to the beautiful little Alcaic chorus at the
beginning of Act III.:–

Lo where the virgin veiled in airy beams,
All-holy Morn, in splendour awakening,
    Heaven's gate hath unbarred, the golden
        Aerial lattices set open.
With music endeth night's prisoning terror,
With flow'ry incense: Haste to salute the sun,
    That for the day's chase, like a huntsman,
        With flashing arms cometh o'er the mountain.

But most of all he will feel himself back among the things he knows, and
with the poet of his choice, when he comes upon the beautiful passage
in which Persephone takes the flowers for her special province, the
thing that mankind shall hold, "devote, and consecrate" to her. The
tale of beauty and death is an old one; but it is freshly handled here,
with a kind of delicacy that is perhaps the gift of gifts in Mr. Bridges:–

PERSEPHONE.   How should man, dwelling
    On earth that is so gay, himself be sad?
    Is not earth gay? Look at the sea, the sky,
    The flowers!

ATHENA.   'Tis sad to him because 'tis gay, –
    For whether he consider how the flowers,
    – Thy miracles of beauty above praise, –
    Are wither'd in the moment of their glory,
    So that of all the mounting summer's wealth
    The show is chang'd each day, and each day dies,

Of no more count in Nature's estimate
Than crowded bubbles of the fighting foam;
Or whether 'tis the sea, whose azure waves
Play'd in the same infinity of motion
Ages ere he beheld it, and will play
For ages after him; – alike 'tis sad
To read how beauty dies and he must die.

So Athena speaks; but Persephone turns from her and still chooses perishing beauty as her part, chooses the flowers,

                        but only among the flowers
Those that men love for beauty, scent, or hue,
Having no other uses:

And she knows her honour so will be no mean honour; for man's

      spirit setteth beauty before wisdom,
Pleasures above necessities, and thus
He ever adoreth flowers. Nor this I guess
Where rich men only and superfluous kings
Around their palaces reform the land
To terraces and level lawns ...

      ... That they – these lordly men –
Twixt flaunting avenues and wafted odours
May pace in indolence; this is their bliss;

      ....

But in the poorest villages, around
The meanest cottage, where no other solace
Comforts the eye, some simple gaiety
Of flowers in tended garden is seen; some pinks,
Tulips, or crocuses that edge the path;
Where oft at eve the grateful labourer
Sits in his jasmin'd porch, and takes the sun.

And where

      the children, that half naked go,
Have posies in their hands

and

> > forget
> The hour of hunger and their homely feast
> So they may cull the delicate primrose,
> Sealing their birthright with the touch of beauty;
> With unconsider'd hecatombs assuring
> Their dim sense of immortal mystery.

Any one who has ever cared for the poems of Mr. Bridges would at once recognize these lines as his; and still more perhaps the learned and yet beautiful details which follow about the various flowers from which Persephone chooses her garland. It is all in the well-known manner, and goes finely in the accustomed way from first to last. These grave, wise, primitive themes suit Mr. Bridges, and he suits them; he will never be a poet of passion; his joy and sorrow are alike touched with the quietness of wisdom, and we know from the first that each will ultimately accept calm as the end, and that, in the words with which Demeter closes the poem,

> When their bright stir is o'er, there will peace.

2496   (**f8ʳ**) Daily News, Monday, March 19, 1906.
BEGINNINGS OF LIFE. SCIENTIST ON SPONTANEOUS GENERATION. DR. BASTIAN'S EXPERIMENTS.

When Dr. Bastian, the eminent scientist, was reminded by a "Daily News" representative that his attack on the generally accepted theories of evolution and the origin of life, in his lecture at the rooms of the Medical Society the other day, had been described as "the confession of a heresy," he laughed heartily.

"Why," he said, "to talk about my renunciation of these theories is arrant nonsense. My views on evolution have been perfectly well known for many years. Between 1871 and 1876 I made a long series of investigations on the question of the origin of life, which, by the way, I often discussed with Huxley, Tyndall, and Pasteur. It was about that time that I published works on 'The Modes of Origin of Lowest Organisms,' 'The Beginnings of Life,' and 'Evolution and the Origin of Life.' It is true that, for a long period, I ceased to work at a subject which the world generally believed to have been settled in a sense adverse to my views, but that was not because I was convinced that others were right and I was wrong, but because, as a young physician, I had to devote attention to my professional career.

"During the last six years, however, I have devoted all the time I could spare from professional work to the study of one side of the subject commonly known as 'spontaneous generation.' In order to devote my time and energy to the problems which I had apparently relinquished, I resigned my professorship at University College, after thirty years' service, and also my position at the hospital. Had I not been powerfully impressed by my previous work I should not have resumed my investigations.

SOME STARTLING DISCOVERIES.

"What have been the results of those investigations? Well, one aspect of the subject of 'spontaneous generation' is known as archebiosis, which has to do with the possible synthesis of living matter from its elements in fluids. I shall soon have to announce some very startling results in that direction.

"You see this tube," continued Dr. Bastian, holding up a sealed glass tube containing clear fluid. "It contains an ammoniacal saline solution, from which, after it has been heated to 150 degrees centigrade for twenty minutes, I have obtained living bacteria as well as torulæ.

"The other aspect of the question is known as heterogenesis, by which is meant the birth of simple alien living things from the substance of higher organisms, or their germs. That was the subject of my lecture the other day, and it is one at which I have been working of late years. I have dealt with it fully in my 'Studies in Heterogenesis,' and also in the work I published last November, 'The Nature and Origin of Living Matter' – which, by the way, was well reviewed in 'The Daily News' by Mr. Bray.

"Yes, I have made some interesting experiments in heterogenesis. It is often asked whether bacteria can be made to appear where previously they were non-existent. To this query I say 'Yes.' Pasteur held strongly that the cells of healthy plants are germless, and this view is still generally regarded as true. Bacteriologists cannot obtain evidence of the existence of micro-organisms in cells taken from the centre of a healthy potato or turnip, and yet bacteria can be caused to appear in these situations, although adequate precautions are taken against infection.

THE LATENT GERM THEORY.

"Apart from heterogenesis, the only other possibility to account for the appearance of the bacteria within the closed cells would be the supposition that germs of micro-organisms have been latent within the cells. But of this no proof has ever been given, and the verdict of science has, in fact, been adverse to this supposition.

"There are, of course, many other instances of heterogenesis, one of the most interesting of which is the remarkable transformation that I have seen take place in the living matter contained in the eggs of a rotifer. No sort of kinship is known to exist between the comparatively complex rotifers and the unicellular organisms into which their eggs are transformed.

"We know that these lower living things are most mutable and sensitive to changes in their medium; yet the accredited biological doctrines of the day ask us to believe, on the one hand, that all the forms of life that have ever lived have been derived from primordial forms which were first evolved untold ages ago upon the cooling surface of our planet; and, on the other hand, we are asked to believe that bacteria, monads, amoebae, ciliated infusoria, and multitudes of other lowest forms of life which are found to teem in all kinds of situations at the present day have resisted change, and have been perpetuating their like during aeons and aeons of time. This seems to me to be absurd. Logic and the uniformity of natural phenomena would seem to negative the idea of an isolated origin of life.

"I should like to have seen more discussion after my lecture. I have raised the question at the Royal Society and at the Linnaean Society, but there has been practically no discussion. Comparatively few people seem to understand the subject, but it is coming to the front.

"Do I not think that often the heterodoxy of to-day is the orthodoxy of to-morrow?"

Dr. Bastian smiled. "Yes, I do," he said.

2497 (**f8ᵛ**) THE DAILY NEWS, THURSDAY, F/EBRUARY/
BRITAIN'S NEXT CAMPAIGN (By JULIE SUTTER, Author of "A Colony of Mercy.")
[*Author's Copyright*]

v. – Homelessness: Its Cause and Cure.

That forestry could provide for a tolerable number of workers is amply proved by the fact that whole country-sides abroad live almost solely by forest labour, and, let us add, forest ownership, individual ownership, and, what is better still, the joint ownership of a community. This altogether apart from public or Crown lands. But forestry is a science, and in Germany a professional class is trained for it, both in and out of college. It is a branch of national economy, an important factor in the "wealth of nations." Germany knows that, and therefore she watches over her forest lands, be they public or private property; no tree is struck unknown to the Ober-Förster (Ranger in Government employ), and she would laugh at the idea that forestry does not pay. It does pay. I have seen a good deal of newspaper writing lately on this question, English woodland owners as a rule declaring, "it does not pay." This is because they know only private ownership with its narrow vision. Let them go to Germany – say to Munich University – let them take a practical course with any German Ober-Förster, and they will return enlightened. British landlords, to be sure, do some planting even now, keeping the ancestral parks in repair – and fine timber some of these contain – or planting game cover; but there their forestry ceases. Park forestry is a rich man's luxury, and, in itself, a pardonable pride. But true forests, like rivers, are national things; the hand of the common-weal alone can turn them to individual gain. One could cite German towns which defray the whole of municipal expenditure out of the proceeds of their forest lands, leaving the citizens free of rates and taxes; or villages where every man gets his quota of firewood free and often a dividend in cash over and above. Surely even British landlords will admit that this is better than leaving forestry in private hands, where by their own showing it does not pay. If England could learn to husband her forest resources, she could add millions to her revenues by home growth. And how she could employ her unemployed! Abroad she appears to be more successful, training numbers of students for Indian forestry at Cooper's Hill.

But to return to our colonies. The idea should not be merely to transplant the slaves; we must set them free. And this means patiently to work for their freedom, to educate them, to raise them to that level where slum-bred slavery with its consequent degeneration, and British manhood with its crown of true freedom, needs must separate. It will be a difficult task, but it ought not to be beyond the wisdom of a great country.

Small beginnings have generally the best results; and thus it will be wisest to transplant a few dozen, a few scores, a few hundreds, to lay the foundations of future village life. There must be a patient selecting of those most fit to be saved. No one urges a random migration of the demoralised street-loafer, whose best chance is that he will rise gradually, the pressure in the strata above him lessening. He is perhaps an object for the "Labour" Colony proper.

But there should not only be Labour Colonies, not merely the thought of work for the unemployed; there should be the honest and bold confession from the outset that the hope and object is the replanting of rural England with wholesome peasant life. There should be "Own Home" Colonies, at first under guidance, but gradually growing into independent communities. Let the County Councils attempt it; let a syndicate of patriots try it; it can be done. And why should not the British Government assist a work of absolute national gain? Prussia, a few years ago, passed a law to facilitate the acquiring of small holdings. The purchase money is provided by the State. The rent is fixed at the low rate of four per cent. per annum, covering the interest, and forming a sinking fund which, at the end of sixty years, turns fixity of tenure into freehold. I am told that this provision is eagerly caught at and promises well. It is a wise law in these days of social upheavings, and a kind law, for it seeks to save the country from democracy by saving the home-life of the people.

By way of showing what is possible even in landlord Britain, one may refer to Mr. William Carter, of Parkstone (London office, Essex-street, Strand), who does business in assisting small settlers back to the land. He buys up whatever estates he can get cheap, and there seems plenty of land in the market, some of it so cheap that he retails it as low as a penny a yard, freehold – or, as he quaintly advertises, "a square yard of land at the price of a glass of beer." He builds bungalows and other homesteads on these plots, and advises his buyers about fruit growing and market gardening. He has thus settled some 500 of small freeholders in various counties. It is simple business with him, out of which he manages good profit for himself; but it is business touched by philanthropy. With such an example to hand, will anyone doubt that home colonisation would prove satisfactory? The people can be assisted back to the land, and nothing more truly patriotic could be set going. For if Britain will not apply herself to the saving of her workers, her downfall in the world market is only a question of time.

May the "Garden City" movement prosper; but it is Garden Village only – that is, the recreation of a soil-tilling people on their own freehold land – which can lead us out of our social trouble.

The cry always is that the small farmer cannot nowadays make a living by the land. But he can if he is permitted to set about it rightly. The writer remembers taking a walk one day with an English lady through a Black Forest valley, this lady expressing her astonishment "that every little strip of land, even if no larger than one's dining room table," every odd bit by the wayside, was cultivated, yielding its utmost of harvest value. "How is it," said this lady, "that these Black Foresters are so thrifty? Our people would never think of that!" She could not understand, though the answer was of the simplest: because the land is theirs, and if they cultivate even the odd strip it is for their own reward. What a gainer this country – the nation's commonwealth – would be if folk had the seeing eyes for the strongest of all economic forces – a well-directed self-interest! Set the soil-tiller free, and he will double the produce of any land.

But in seeking to replant rural England with village life, stocking her anew with true husbandmen, there is yet another economic force, doubly needed when it is a question of undoing past mischief. We have not got these thrifty people; they are the work of ages. Might one in the meantime try interdependent colonies, each upward striving man resting on the strength of his neighbour? Might co-operation not lead the way?

England could grow her own corn, at least a large portion of it; but even supposing, while present circumstances last, that wheat must be imported from other countries, what about cow-keeping? Is there any reason why English cities should not look for all dairy produce to England's own people? Cow-keeping is essentially the small owner's business. There has been some writing lately proposing dairy-farming for gentle hands, even "unemployed" ladies; but though ladies could make butter, dairy-farming cannot be divorced from the land, and England's one hope for curing her agricultural depression consists in getting a better money's worth than at present out of the land by letting in a soil-tilling people! Now some thirty million sterling a year, which might largely be kept in this country, goes to France and Denmark. Look at Denmark and her flourishing dairies, owned by a number of small farmers, combining for strength; and they apparently find it a paying thing.

And not in Denmark alone. In the Black Forest one day I came across such a co-operative dairy in a village close to where I was staying. It simply meant that all the villagers had combined for starting a machine-worked dairy. They, each and all, hand in their milk, some more, some less – for co-operation need not mean equality of ownership

– each getting back from this centre of mutual wealth his corresponding share of butter. And they find it pays, for their butter is noted all round the district. By combining they can work scientifically; they can work by strict rules of national economy, each man being the better for his neighbour's improved condition. Why should not some such arrangement be possible here also? Even a poor woman, who barely has any land, can with advantage keep a cow in such a village. One sees many humble villagers out on summer evenings in these places, women-folk mostly, cutting the grass along the hedges and ditches, and carrying home on their backs a day's fodder for the cow. Hard work this! Yes; for a village has its poor, but they are rarely paupers. What waggon loads of grass – good fodder – are wasted in Britain, both in and out side the squire's "preserves," absolutely wasted!

Yet there is more than cow-keeping. There is poultry-keeping – think of the millions of eggs imported – there is pig-fattening; there is market gardening. There are bees, rabbits – quite a number of things to which the small owner will turn his ingenuity, if only you will let him be owner, this factor of a wholesome self-interest being absolutely necessary. Those who understand these things assure me that the six-acre farm would be the most promising thing, for the simple reason that it can be worked by a man with his own family, and by the spade; hand-labour – i.e., deep-digging (intensive agriculture), yielding double or more than machine-worked fields. But I cannot forego recording here what might well move the envy of this country.

In the neighbourhood of Bielefeld, in the province of Westphalia, and within an afternoon's walk of the "Colony of Mercy," one day last autumn I came upon a peasant holding, an almost patriarchal farm, which has descended from father to son for upwards of a thousand years. That peasant's name, and family, and ownership of that particular farm can be traced in the archives of Bielefeld to the days of Wittekind.

(**f9ʳ**) And even as this old Saxon hero, the compeer of Charlemagne, was followed to the grave by his caparisoned but riderless horse, so is this peasant, many of the old Saxon customs surviving in that country-side, which, somehow, like an island in a turbulent sea, was almost the only spot in Germany not touched by the thirty years' war; and so the line of descent and ownership has never been broken.

A family property, surely; yet the owner is nothing but a peasant, and proud to be one – a peasant rising at three on a summer morning to see to his own fields, his wife rising at the same time to attend to her dairy. Naturally such people prosper. This man is lord of all he surveys, of the fields stretching away to the hill-chain, and of a couple of hills, too, well wooded and yielding their timber; yet he is but a peasant. Of course, he needs labourers, but his very labourers are small owners on his farm, holding their bits of land from which he cannot oust them, in perpetual lease, as we should call it. These lesser peasants in that part of the country are called "hirelings" (they actually have the word, being Saxons, though spelling it "heuerling," the diphthong pronounced oi), the "hireling" giving the larger peasant, instead of rent, a certain amount of labour at seed-time and harvest-time and thrashing-time, being free otherwise to work on his own little farm. And some of these "hirelings" have been in their homesteads for generations. What a manhood is grown under such conditions! Yet that man of a thousand years is nothing but a soil-tilling peasant.

The rights of inheritance are strictly guarded in that country; only one member of a family can succeed to the land, but the others are provided for. Though but peasants, and proud of it, there is no reason why a son should not enter the Church or any other profession; education can be had in Germany, and even a peasant can educate his boys. Isn't their "blood" of the soundest – country-fed, country-bred boys with a pride all their own, with qualities ingrained by a thousand years of industry, aye, of soil tilling, the contact with mother earth, even as the Grecian fable told, ever yielding the truest men?

Nor is that man an isolated specimen of his country; that Ravensberger land within the province of Westphalia is fairly stocked with them – a peasantry for a poet's dream. Not that they are angels in smock frocks; they have their own faults and shortcomings, even, maybe, an intense pride; but what they are for sterling manhood, for Christian possibilities, may be seen in the "Colony of Mercy," near Bielefeld, that unequalled creation of Christian genius having struck its roots in just such peasant soil.

I have purposely kept to the appellation "peasant" in its true sense – a freehold tiller of the soil, the wealth-producing substratum of the nation. In that particular part of Germany the larger peasant-owner is called "Meier"; but everywhere else in Germany the word "Bauer" holds, even as "paysan" does in France. I know of "peasants" in the south, in that favoured little country of Baden, for instance, who are worth their millions of marks, owning forest-land, and vineyards, and spreading fields. Yet they are just "peasants," dressing and living, and, above all, working as peasants; and the Government of that little country well knows how to appreciate them. In this country a whole class of freehold self-tilling proprietors has been absorbed by a non-tilling landlord class; and this evidently is the reason why England is complaining that she cannot feed her own people. The very name of "peasant" has in consequence received a different meaning, calling up nothing to the British mind in these days but an enslaved hind, a poverty-stricken labourer; but the loss is really a national one. Such large peasant proprietors, of course, are the minority, the real strength of the country being the thousands of lesser freehold soil-tillers, each "Bauer" on his own little farm.

Such a peasantry cannot, indeed, be manufactured; they are the patient work of a wholesome national development, forming the sure basis of a country's true wealth. It is well known that the upper classes are ever being nourished from the strata below them. Do not families decay when they have reached the top of the ladder? It is so by God's own economy, whether we like it or not. There is no individualism, but only solidarity, in the broad history of the human race. Are we, then, as a class, such a degenerate lot – we, the so-called Upper Ten – decayed physically, and aye, morally, because we have so badly husbanded the soil on which our own humanity needs must stand? Degeneration of the masses has a trick of striking the classes.

So it will indeed be for our own sakes if we endeavour to be more just to the people.

And though we cannot manufacture we can prepare the way. We can give them a health-creating environment, and health means wealth for body and soul. We can take them back to the land. As for funds, surely the money is nothing if only the idea will strike root. We do not feel the loss of a million in this country if it goes to the bottom of the sea in a foundering ironclad, and what could not be done with a million in the way of saving the people – a million which would be repaid again and again in a hundred tangible blessings? Think of the South African war cost! Nearly two millions weekly! Would to God we had spent it on home needs! But are there not nearly a hundred and fifty millions deposited in the Post Office Savings Bank, made up chiefly of the pence and shillings of the working classes? And what does this prove? That even the working classes, out of their own pockets, could provide the means, if only the public countenance were given – the honest desire of those in authority and power – to create the credit needed. For the upper strata of the British "masses" are stout-hearted people, they would glory in this sort of democracy.

At present our political economy is somewhat astray. In plain language, it connives at the people's ruin, and then some of us are busily engaged in alms-begging, in alms-giving, too, on behalf of the victims. I have heard a wonderfully true remark somewhere to the effect that Dr. Barnardo and all such philanthropic men tell us that sixteen pounds will keep one waif for a year. But the rent-value of a six-acre farm under a patriotic syndicate need not be more! And from such a farm a man could feed and clothe himself, his wife and children, and a waif to boot! Should we not, then, assist such a man? At present he and his can only inflict waifs on the nation.

2498   (**f10ʳ**) LITERATURE
The Philosophy of Religion. By Dr. Harald Höffding. Translated by B. E. Meyer. (Macmillan & Co.)

ALMOST simultaneously with his 'Problems of Philosophy' (see *The Athenaeum* for April 14th, p. 441) appeared in an English garb Prof. Höffding's more famous and almost classical work 'The Philosophy of Religion.' The recent literature of this country teems with references to its central thesis, namely, that the essence of religion consists in a belief in the

i.e. worth

"conservation of value." So long, however, as Danish, or even German, enshrouded the thought at the back of this sonorous phrase, it was calculated, like any other shibboleth, to mystify rather than to instruct. Even now that he who runs may read, it is by no means certain that he will understand. Here it is not at first sight easy to see the wood for the trees. As compared, for instance, with the highly concentrated 'Problems of Philosophy,' where we never for a moment lose sight of the main issue, this book presents a tangled skein. Perhaps the philosopher, descending from the unencumbered heights to lower levels, is less sure of his bearings. No wonder, indeed, since religion, historically considered, is a jungle. It needs a bold man to attempt a philosophy of religion. And it needs not merely a bold man, but also a wise one, to grasp, as Prof. Höffding grasps, at the sense of the whole and of the parts together – to do justice, as he seeks to do, and does, at once to religion and to the religions. But a clear-cut, immediately convincing theory it is too much to expect. We get, indeed, a pithy phrase. The phrase, however, is sufficiently hard to interpret.

"Value" is a comparatively simple and straightforward notion. It means "good" – something indefinable, perhaps, but none the less appreciable on that account. In making religion primarily concerned with value or good, Prof. Höffding is thoroughly in accord with modern tendencies. It is now customary to draw a sharp line between the judgment of fact and the judgment of value, the one being typical, say, of physical science, and the other, say, of ethics. In which direction, then, does religion incline? A strictly impartial attitude seems no longer possible. The days are gone by when theology could pose as *scientia scientiarum* and *ars artium*. A division of labour has established itself in the spiritual sphere, as Prof. Höffding insists; and for this very reason there has come to be a religious problem. Now "scientific" explanation may be said to have wholly superseded religious explanation as regards particulars. There remain certain "first" or "last" questions, which positive science is inclined to treat as insoluble riddles. Can a religious metaphysic succeed where science throws up the sponge? Of course there will be great difference of opinion on this point. Dr. McTaggart, for instance, in his recent work is all for dogma. Prof. Höffding, on the contrary, in his "epistemological" section can light on nothing absolute. Religion, as also philosophy, is with him more akin to art than science:–

"It cannot be denied that a religious community might possibly come into existence whose faith found poetic and symbolic expression, free from all dogmatic conclusions."

Or again:–

"The religious consciousness moves in a world of poetry, and is becoming increasingly aware of the fact. The more clearly it recognises the figurativeness and insufficiency of its ideas, the better it will be able to comprehend a standpoint which attaches no weight to the formation of fixed and exclusive ideas of the object of religion."

And yet, though it has become plain that religion cannot, any more than science, solve the ultimate riddles, it has not for Prof. Höffding lost its significance. There is the inner experience that the good in life is real, to the content of which it can give an emotional and imaginative expression, thus becoming, as he puts it, "a poetry of life," "a poetry of humanity." After all, has man ever worshipped God the first cause, and not rather the God who is goodness and truth? Tried even by this test of worship – a test on which Prof. Höffding, with his rather wide use of the term "religion," hardly lays stress enough – religious experience would seem mainly to be affirmative of value.

Yes; but value for whom? Before we leave the subject of what value as such means, this difficulty must be raised; and for many who would otherwise sympathize with Prof. Höffding it is likely to prove a stumbling-block. Not that our author, good psychologist that he is, underrates the principle of personality. On the one hand, he holds that "scientific work is a work of personality"; on the other, that "it is personality which in the world of our experience invests all other things with value." And yet with him the "cosmical vital feeling" which expresses itself in religion seems wholly disinterested. The validity of good which it affirms in becoming cosmical apparently ceases to be psychological. But is this strictly possible on his own principles? Has he not been misled by taking the "Not my will, but Thine, be done," of religion too literally? Is the will surrendered when it surrenders itself? And note the disastrous corollary (though Prof. Höffding would probably not accept the "argument from consequences"). Personal immortality is no concern of religion. Prof. Höffding says solemnly:–

"The more I have looked round on the world of thought and reality, the more clearly it has been borne in upon me that those who are still ready to preach that were there no future life, *this* life would lose all its value, take a great responsibility upon themselves."

Nay, he goes further than this:–

"The confusion of particular definite values with eternal values is irreligious. Nevertheless, few religions are innocent of it. The religious postulate, in such case, runs as follows: – 'If the kinds and forms of value with which I am acquainted do not persist, then the conservation of value is nothing to me, or rather I do not admit that that which persists is value or has value.' This egoistic form of religiosity is by no means rare. The belief in personal immortality is often based on this ground, – as though existence might not still have a meaning even if I were *not* immortal!"

Surely Prof. Höffding here almost deserts his chosen ground. "That which persists" and "existence" smack less of value than of fact. What sense is there in a "good" which is not for some personality, some consciousness? Is the conservation of value, then, much the same thing as the conservation of energy?

We now proceed to the even more serious question of what we are to understand by "conservation." Religion we know as the most conservative force in the world. Does this sociological fact possibly help to account for the stress laid on conservation in this context? For value or good, in its ordinary ethical sense, is rather something to be acquired than to be conserved. First you have to catch your hare; or rather life is a continual hunting. "That alone can be truly realized which is real already," it will perhaps be said. But here we immediately perceive the effect of allowing the judgment of fact to force its alien nature on the judgment of value, namely, that utter nonsense is forthwith made of the latter. What can possibly be the good, not merely for us, but also for the good itself, of realizing what is realized already? Leibnitz did well to say, "Nisi beatitudo in progressu consisteret, stuperent beati." Thus religion within its own field – unless we are ready to say with Prof. Höffding that considerations about future blessedness fall outside that field – has to face the problem why the appeal of good to us is as of something (**f10ᵛ**) yet to be *made*. If it shirk this problem, if it illicitly convert value into an Eleatic being that merely persists, then good-bye to religion. Ethics is strong in its own right, and will take its place. But it is more likely that it is Prof. Höffding's analysis of religion, and not religion itself, that is on the wrong tack.

We have left ourselves little room to consider Prof. Höffding's treatment of the actual history of religion. On the primitive forms of worship and belief he is not very illuminating. He obviously has had to depend on the researches of others, and these – as, for example, Tiele and Usener – are perhaps a little out of date. More interesting, because more his own, is the attempt to distinguish amongst the higher religions two fundamental types, namely, the Indian–Greek and the Persian–Jewish. On his view, the one favours immanence, the other evolution. According to the former, the highest value is always actually present, though hidden from men's sight by the veil of sense. According to the latter, the valuable has, and needs, a history; but only when the development of the world has run its course will the valuable be all in all to all men. The contrast is brilliantly worked out. At the same time we confess ourselves suspicious of all forms of the "philosophy of history," as this seems to be. Genuine history, based on the comparative method, does not thus set out with the explicit purpose of illustrating or confirming a doctrine established in some sense a priori. Besides, abstract similarities such as are here presented, without reference to the possibility of common derivation, are not rooted in fact, and can therefore be varied with the shifting needs of the argument. Thus, in the section on 'Buddha and Jesus,' both teachers alike are represented as laying great weight on development towards a future goal. Even so, however, let us in conclusion note, religion, as compared with ethics, would appear unsound on the subject of the *making* of good. Neither Buddha nor Christ regarded the good as able to be "reached in positive fashion by working under temporal conditions; it can only be attained through a supernatural crisis, for which men must hold themselves in readiness." The demand of many a serious mind to-day is, negatively, for absence of all naïve supernaturalism, and, positively, for a progressive, temporal, human good. Can religion satisfy this demand? If not, for such minds at least, it must either reform itself, or cease to be effective.

2499   (f11ʳ) VIEWS AND REVIEWS. Glasgow News. 31 Jan 1907.
"THE SECRET OF FORCE."

"It seems to me that the great novel will pass out of fashion: three-quarters of what is written is unnecessary – is involved simply by obedience to effete formulas and standards. As a consequence we do not read as we used to do. We read only the essential, skipping all else. The book that compels perusal of every line and word is the book of power. Create a story of which no reader can skip a single paragraph, and one has the secret of force – if not of durability. My own hope is to do something in accordance with this idea: no descriptions, no preliminaries, no explanations – nothing but the feeling itself at highest intensity. I may fail utterly; but I think I have divined a truth which may be yet recognised and pursued by stronger minds than mine. The less material the more force." In these words Lafcadio Hearn, the well-known writer on Japan, whose life and letters have recently been published, gives expression to an ideal which has probably influenced more or less every modern writer who has produced a novel. There is a naïveté almost amusing in Hearn's implication that he alone has "divined a truth" which is as old as the Sagas, and is the sole guiding principle of the talented gentlemen who write "Death Gulch" and "The Young Brigands" for those "penny bloods" whose secret of force – "no descriptions, no preliminaries, no explanations" – arrests the steps of our message boys.

PRIMITIVE STORY-TELLING.

Hearn, in the passage I quote, has seized upon some very obvious truths, and lightheartedly jumped to the conclusion that they indicate the master-truth, the formula; but they do nothing of the kind. He reminds me of the Glasgow artist who, in a fine flush of discovery, once announced to his confreres that he had at last found out the secret of producing a great picture. "What is it?" he was asked. "Distinction," he replied, fervently. "The whole thing lies in giving your picture distinction." As yet that artist remains outside the Academy, since he knew only what was wanted, but has never yet managed to produce it. Of course, distinction is absolutely essential to the great picture, and a story of which no reader can skip a single paragraph is what all storytellers aim at, but doubtless Mr. Hearn before his death discovered that knowing what is wanted is very different from knowing how to do it. The "effete formulas and standards" are really the formulas and standards of the Saga or folk-tale which is the ancient equivalent of that story without descriptions, preliminaries, or explanations, which was his ideal. The Saga and the folk-tale got their effect by the fewest possible words. They were all action and brief reported dialogue; they were designed to excite in the most direct manner the simple emotions of a primitive audience whose illusions were aroused through the ear alone. Preliminaries would have been an impertinence, long descriptions would have hampered the essential impetus of the tale, explanations were unnecessary since everything was as simple as the alphabet, and there was only one kind of story and one way of telling it.

FORMULA FOR GREAT FICTION.

The task that awaits the modern novelist is quite different from that which was undertaken by the skald and the sennachie; on him is all the burden of the intervening years, and his appeal is to a race infinitely more complex in intellect and more varied in its receptivity of emotions. There is no formula which will capture all readers; there is no recipe for a modern story "of which no reader can skip a single paragraph." Dumas, of all the moderns, seems to have come closest on the old impetuous urge, but even Dumas had many passages that might be "held as read" and in any case the Dumas convention is hopelessly out of date at present, as even Mr. Stanley Weyman must confess. The fact that the book story – unlike the old folk-tale – is to convey illusion and excite emotion in solitude through the eye and that inward ear which is the other "bliss of solitude," necessitates, too, a wholly different manner of presentation from that which was followed by the tale-tellers who swept a close-packed audience in the sheiling or the hall away upon the wings of rhetoric and personal magnetism. Even if the old folk-tale audiences had had the education and the knowledge of ourselves, their minds were kept as much intent upon the progress of the story told that they had not the opportunity and time to step aside a moment and run up the avenues of association which might diverge from the main path that led to the denouement. That is a privilege reserved for the reader alone; that is, to many readers, more delightful than the tale itself.

BLACK MAGIC.

Preliminaries, descriptions, explanations, and divagations generally form part of the written story less often by deliberate design on the part of the writer than by his own surrender to the magic power of the material in which he works. He starts with every intention of mastering the story, but soon – if it have any grace of God in it – the story more or less masters him. He needs a forest for an ambuscade, and blithely begins his chapter with what shall finish off the forest in a sentence, but no sooner has he ranked its columned trees and put the leaves upon their branches than from its heart come out the dryads and hold him prisoner for pages. He cannot tear himself away from the perfumes, the sun-glint in the glades, the song of the birds in the dim recesses, the sound of the wind, the mystery of the shades. He will delight himself though a thousand readers yawn, but it is certain that he will delight some others too. Or he takes for a supernumerary character some familiar lay figure and plants it carelessly in the midst of an early chapter looking for no more from it than that it shall be a foil for the important personages with whose society it is to be honoured, and by-and-by something happens – the figure says something utterly unexpected, or moves in some dramatic manner, and straightway, full of life, begins to dominate all the other characters, or at least to play a part far more important than was at first intended. Thus came to life and immortality innumerable characters in Shakespeare, Scott, and Dickens.

(**f11ᵛ**) MECHANICS AND MIND.

It is the primitive and uncultivated part in us that engages itself exclusively with the plot; our finer compounds find their pleasure up the avenues off the main road – in the airs peculiar to certain places (which are the only, but adequate, excuse for scenic description), in the suggestions of greater deeps in the characters than what their words and deeds reveal; in the symbolism or allegory which is in every act; in the reverie which may be found in every gesture. Unlike the old listeners to the skald, we may be profoundly interested in the storyteller's personal philosophy and in the subtle indications which, sometimes unawares, he gives to us of what his life has been, and his ideals scurvy or sublime. And again there may be in the manner of his telling an individual grace or dignity, a rhythm that, like music, charms irrelevantly since it has nothing to do with the denouement, or whether the man and the maid married at last to live happy for ever after. All those considerations that affect the various readers in various degrees no less affect the writer; he would, if he could, fascinate all – the primitive man, who loves only the bare intrigue, the plot, the mechanism; and the more supple minds that bring to their reading leisure and dreams. But, alas! he cannot please all. Let him give most of himself to the mechanism, and he may produce a novel that the public will applaud for months; yet shall win him not a single friend worth having; let him merely concede a "plot," half-heartedly, and cry across the space from heart to heart for comrades who can thrill to his imaginings, follow the trails he blazes, understand the marvels he can only feebly indicate, and he may miss the market, but he shall surely find the comrades, and he shall know content.

THE INDISCOVERABLE THING.

A story of which no reader can skip a single paragraph – no, it is indiscoverable, though we may try. It shall certainly not be attained by the methods of primitives, no matter how powerfully displayed. There is the Meredithian reader, who certainly cannot skip much or he loses all; there is the Hardy reader, who is sometimes willing to skip everything except those scenic passages in which the lonely plains at night are tenanted by old Pagan gods and the stars rain down their secret, awe-inspiring effluence; there is the Conan Doyle reader, who is hot-foot on the murderer's track, and skips in gasps to keep in pace with the bloodhounds. Lafcadio Hearn, to produce his tale that would "compel perusal of every line and word," would require to have the varied requirements of these and innumerable other classes of readers in mind continually, and the result would be a tale which would please nobody.

2500   (**f12ʳ**) And then quite suddenly I lost the desire of describing outward things, and found that I took little pleasure in a book unless it was spiritual and unemphatic. I did not then understand that the change was from beyond my own mind, but I understand now that writers are struggling all over Europe, though not often with a philosophic understanding of their struggle, against that picturesque and declamatory way of writing, against that "externality" which a time of scientific and political thought has brought into literature.

It is as the prophet of this inward spirituality that Mr. Yeats writes these essays, that in themselves are so like precious stones which beneath the surface are full of unexpected lights and flames. So in the outward world and in the world of speech he is ever on the watch for the flash of spiritual light that lurks in the heart of words as in the heart of nature. No one but a blind man or a stonecutter considers the surface of a gem; its very essence is the ray from its depths; and so it is with life and the world. Apart from the inner light, external things are of no concern to any but the blind of heart and the mechanical of soul. Mr. Yeats might have taken as motto for his book the opening lines of the last brief chorus in "Faust":–

> All that is transitory
> Is but a symbol.

All the wealth of external nature, the increase and prosperity of mankind, the inventions of the day, the dust and shouting of armies on the march, the display of riches, the authority of Parliaments and Kings – to the poet they are nothing, except in so far as they may serve to convey the inner gleam. We need no wealth or politics or novelty to afford us the symbols of the greatest truth. Those ancient things are the best which lead the soul unconsciously back through uncounted generations to the primeval thoughts and needs and interests of man. There are some words and things so full of the traditions and emotions of mankind that whenever they are finely used they seem to glow and sparkle with mysterious lights which, like the visible rays of the stars at night, started on their course unnumbered ages ago, and trail, as it were, an immemorial glory of dim associations behind them. In his essay on "Popular Poetry" Mr. Yeats says:–

> There is only one kind of good poetry, for the poetry of the coteries, which pre-supposes the written tradition, does not differ in

kind from the true poetry of the people, which pre-supposes the unwritten tradition. Both are alike strange and obscure, and unreal to all who have not understanding, and both, instead of that manifest logic, that clear rhetoric of the "popular poetry," glimmer with thoughts and images whose "ancestors were stout and wise," "anigh to Paradise" "ere yet men knew the gift of corn."

As an example of such thoughts and images, or symbols, Mr. Yeats, in a later essay, chooses the lines of Burns, which have long seemed to us almost the only words of supremely great poetry that Burns ever spoke:–

There are no lines (he writes) with more melancholy beauty than these by Burns:–

"The white moon is setting behind the white wave,
And Time is setting with me, O!"

and these lines are perfectly symbolical. Take from them the whiteness of the moon and of the wave, whose relation to the setting of Time is too subtle for the intellect, and you take from them their beauty. But, when all are together, moon and wave and whiteness and setting Time and the last melancholy cry, they evoke an emotion which cannot be evoked by any other arrangement of colours and sounds and forms.

As is natural in a book that mainly deals with such a subject as this, much of the space is taken up with the supreme creator of symbolic thought, William Blake, with whom Mr Yeats is so intimately associated by nature, as well as by his long and patient labour of interpretation in earlier years. Here, besides his use of symbolism, he dwells chiefly upon Blake's delight in what he used to call "excess" – the living passion which is for ever at war with "dead lethargies" and "tepid moderation." It is a warfare that we see continually going on in all phases of existence, though in art it is most obvious, and the triumph of passion most secure and quick. Even in political history a man like Mommsen has declared that the future always belongs to passion, and it was with the same intention that Blake said that passions, because most living, are most holy, and man shall enter eternity borne upon their wings. In Mr. Yeats's work this living and purifying passion is nearly always to be found, and by its intensity he has been able to reveal or to restore in the art of speech that inner and spiritual value which stations the poet by its infallible though secret sign apart from all followers of cautious mediocrity.

Review of Ideas of Good & Evil. W. B. Yeats. D. C. 23.5.03

2501   *An Introductory Study of Ethics.* By WARNER FITE, Ph. D. Crown 8vo. pp. xii + 383, price 6s. 6d. *June* 24. 1903. Printed in SMALL PICA type.

This volume is intended both for the general reader and for college classes. Its primary object is to give a clear statement of the chief types of ethical theory and of the point at issue between them. The endeavour to arrive at a systematic statement of their mutual relations has resulted, however, in a more or less independent reconstruction of the whole subject.

The point around which the whole treatment of the subject turns is the conflict between moral ideals and actual conditions. It is this conflict that creates the moral problem, and it is the emphasis upon one side or the other that differentiates the forms of ethical theory – hedonism, the pleasure theory, advocating a conformity to present conditions, idealism insisting upon an unqualified adherence to ideals. The moral problem thus becomes a question of the relative truth and value of the hedonistic and idealistic views.

The alternative theories are then subjected to an exhaustive analysis and criticism, each being presented not only as a specifically ethical theory, but as a theory of social relations and as the representative of a system of philosophy. In the comparison of theories hedonism appears as a relatively clear and practical view, which covers a large part of our daily life, and applies especially to the more organised commercial relations. It is, however, unable to account for the more advanced aspects of morality, as judged by the moral sense of more intelligent and cultivated men, and for the more personal of the social relations. This side of the moral life is covered more adequately by the idealistic theory. Yet idealism, while offering a more comprehensive and satisfying view of life and conduct as a whole, is relatively vague, obscure and unworkable.

Concrete morality becomes, then, a compromise between the two tendencies. The Author advances the view that, in the last analysis, the conflict of ethical theories is simply a contrast of attitude toward the existing crisis in the evolutionary process. Hedonism stands for the

wants and impulses relatively organised into a system, idealism for
those not yet organised. The life process advances through a constant
reorganisation of present conditions to realise larger ideals and a
constant broadening of ideals to call for further reorganisation. Thus
the conflict between ideals and conditions is never wholly absent; and
since neither can be disregarded, the moral problem is a question of
maintaining a condition of maximum and at the same time sustained
and regulated progress.

2502   (**f12ᵛ**) IBSEN AND HIS WORK. Daily Chronicle.
   The death of Ibsen removes from the world one of the most
stimulating forces in the literature of our time. His work has deeply
influenced both the dramatic art and the art of fiction in this country.
The very violence of those controversies, to which Mr. Archer refers in
another column, is evidence of the effect which Ibsen's work produced.
He made men think; and as with most people this is a painful process,
he was passionately abused. He challenged conventions, and set before
the world new types, new moods, new conceptions. To do this is always
to be misunderstood. Ibsen belonged to those artistic innovators of
whom Wordsworth said that they have to create the taste by which
they are to be admired. Probably he will never become popular in the
widest sense. He had neither the simplicity nor the mellowness which
lifts works of art into general acceptance. But he influenced the thinkers
and the dramatists; and to those who brought to his plays the requisite
sympathy and openness of mind, they gripped the attention as the
works of few other modern playwrights have done. Mr. Archer, in his
interesting appreciation, combats the popular fallacy that Ibsen was a
"realist." His themes were sombre, his setting of them was bourgeois,
and his work shows a certain morbid taint; but his distinction is that he
was a poet, and divined the imaginative element in the commonplace.
He was thus himself a Master-Builder. His best creations were "built to
music, therefore never built at all, and therefore built for ever."

                                                    24.5.06

2503   Mr. Gosse has written a slight, but very interesting study, of
Ibsen. It is, perhaps, a little disappointing as the work of so fine a critic
concerning a writer whom he knew so intimately. The effort to
interpret, explain, or appraise Ibsen's right place in the permanent
history of literature is hardly attempted. On the other hand, the life is
given in a form stimulating and attractive to those formerly unfamiliar

with its detail. And everywhere Mr. Gosse maintains that grave, refined, and flexible style of which he is one of the living masters.

The Changes of Fortune.

It is a study in the vicissitudes of human things. Here is one scene: Ibsen apprenticed to an apothecary in one of the meanest of Norwegian provincial towns: for six years "cooped up here among ointment boxes, pills, and plasters," later in extreme penury, "excruciatingly poor," with no hope or prospect for the future. When his financial conditions compelled him to practise the most stringent economy he tried to do without underclothing, and finally even without stockings. "In these experiments he succeeded." He separated from his family "so that when his father died in 1877 no word had passed between him and his son for nearly thirty years." In his student life at Christiania he skulked forlornly through the obscure ways of the city. "It is difficult to know how he subsisted," says Mr. Gosse, "yet he continued to exist."

For years afterwards poverty held him in its clutches and would not let him go. After an interlude as a theatrical manager at Bergen he returned again to Christiania, and married at the age of thirty, and there commenced "another six years, the most painful of Ibsen's life." He was in "disgrace with fortune and men's eyes." His genius failed to find the expression it demanded. "The struggle was an excessively distressing one. He had left Bergen crippled with debts, and his marriage weighed him down with further responsibilities." His attempts at writing everywhere failed, or were received with anger and derision. At the age of thirty-four "the second theatre became bankrupt, and Ibsen was thrown on the world, the most unpopular man of his day, and crippled with debt." He pleaded for mean sums from the Government. He received a tiny pension. Finally in despair he shook the dust of Norway from his feet and started on the pilgrimage to Rome, and Norway, if it thought at all about it, thanked God that it had got rid of a rogue.

Thirty-five years afterwards the National Norwegian Theatre is being opened by the King of Sweden and Norway at Christiania. The obscure fugitive has passed through strange places, in wanderings through the visible universe, and far beyond its borders. Now he has returned to his native land, a conqueror.

The Irony of Fortune.

And if this is a study in the vicissitudes of human life it is also a study in its ironies. Ibsen in these later days is the wealthiest man in Christiania. He honours it as an uncrowned king – with that which should accompany old age, "honour, love, obedience, troops of friends." His plays are discussed from Petersburg to San Francisco, performed in all languages. He is hailed as the voice and interpreter of the nineteenth century. But the "little pin" which spares neither royal blood nor the triumphant intellect of genius does its work; and the end – as in the case of other similar geniuses here at home – is a tragedy. The hero of "Ghosts" had proclaimed the signal for destruction in the wild cry "Give me the sun." "Now Ibsen, with glassy eyes, gazed at the dim windows, murmuring 'Keine sonne, keine sonne, keine sonne.'"

At the table where all the works of his maturity had been written, the old man sat persistently learning and forgetting the alphabet. "Look!" he said to Julius Elias, pointing to his mournful pot-hooks, "See what I am doing! I am sitting here and learning my letters – my letters! I who was once a Writer!"

It is the romantic story of the intervals between these episodes that Mr. Gosse reveals in these pages. 'It is a cosmopolitan interest developed in residence in cosmopolitan Europe – at Rome, in the Tyrol, Munich, Copenhagen, and other famous cities. There is nothing local in the outlook or criticism. His attacks are on "civilization" and its products – its ordered decencies, its conventions, its timidities and hypocrisies, its death – in life. The scene of the "Doll's House" might as easily have been laid in Tooting as in the suburbs of Christiania. The Enemy of the People is wrestling with popular demands at every British watering-place. "Less about the glaciers and the pine forests," he had cried to the poets of Norway in the earlier days; "less about the dusty legends of the past, and more about what is going on in the silent hearts of your brethren."

"Man know thyself," a modern scientist once asserted, had been converted by the increase of knowledge into the gloomy advice, "Man, may thou never know what thou art." It was the outrage of compelling man (and woman) to face the realities of his own existence which many at the first glance found it hard to forgive. Mr. Meredith in the "Egoist" has made so appalling a diagnosis of the primitive man in nineteenth century garments that to its readers life after this interpretation can never be quite the same again. And there are thousands in Europe and America who had first learnt the meaning of this complex, baffling personality of the modern man in those hurricane clashes of forces in the shabby back rooms of suburban villas which Ibsen has seen and interpreted to this and subsequent generations.

"Ibsen," says Mr. Gosse, "had not the ardour of the fighting optimist." He doubts the final success of intelligence. He questions always whether indeed the "old order changeth at all, whether, on the contrary, it has not become a Juggernaut car that crushes all originality and independence out of action." "He was at daggers drawn with all that was successful and respectable, and 'nice' from the outset of his career until near the end of it."

The poet triumphed at the end: the stifling walls of these little rooms crowded with antimacassars and horsehair cushions, and stuffed birds, fell away, revealing the stars and the peaks and the great silences. That mystic sense of presences and invisible passions behind the surface show illuminates all the later plays with a new significance and emotion, showing each moment a meeting place of great issues, and each obscure human life with all eternity for background.

2504 (**f13ʳ**) LITERARY SUPPLEMENT, FRIDAY, MAY 25, 1906.
THE ART OF HENRIK IBSEN

If we would look for the influence of a great artist, the right quarter to examine is not the band, small or great, of men who call themselves his "school"; but a far wider region, the whole body of that art which follows, and its effect upon the whole of life. We have heard it said and seen it written that the influence of Ibsen is dead, that we have outgrown it, and that his work has left no enduring mark on the drama; because the living dramatists who imitate him are none or few, because he has founded no school. The influence of artists, in whatever medium they work, who have founded schools does not end with those schools, or even fulfil its most important function through them. And so, though the French symbolists are no pupils of Ibsen, having an older tradition of their own to follow, though Mr. Pinero's little excursions into Ibsenism have ceased and Mr. Bernard Shaw is the only English playwright in whom the influence of Ibsen can be directly traced, we need not confine our attention to Mr. Shaw, or to Hauptmann and other German followers, in searching for the effects on the drama of Ibsen's work. By a strange perversity, common talk has associated his name with two kinds of plays: plays which deal with the relations of the sexes – and in these, with many which bear not the slightest resemblance to Ibsen's treatment of the theme; and with plays which lack definiteness in the drawing of character, lack clear, strongly-expounded stories and suggest a confusion between depth and vagueness.

Neither association is just. Sexual relations are not, for their own sake, of the least interest to Ibsen. Women he did not like (though their corporate homage was not unpleasant to him in his later years); they did not appeal to a nature which circumstance and will had combined to harden. They interested him only as providing the common difficulty of life, and as possessing in their own departments of action more independence and disregard of anything but their own aims – selfishness, it might perhaps be called – than men. For a story of love, licit or illicit, as a love-story, he cared nothing (though his last play, *When we Dead Awaken*, showed some such interest late born); his plays would have been more popular if he had. Of vagueness or obscurity, again, it is not too much to say that there is none in Ibsen. Difficulty there may be, but that depends on the wits of the hearer. Every play of his has a clear, strong, very definite action. (With what lies beneath that ostensible action we are not concerned for the moment). It must not be forgotten that Ibsen was in his youth a close student of Scribe, that he mastered Scribe's technique, and learned to fit a play together so that every part should be as telling as the tricks of the trade could make it. Having mastered that technique, as M. René Doumic has said, he showed that he had done so by practising, when he came to maturity, the exact opposite; very much as our Elizabethans mastered the classical technique, and then threw it away. We should rather express it thus: that, when he turned from the drama of external action to that of internal action, he adapted this technique which he had mastered to the needs of the new drama he was creating. He is still and always the playwright of consummate skill; but when it is a question of revealing what a man or woman thinks, not of putting them into "tight corners" of incident, the manner of expression naturally changes. Here Ibsen was the pioneer, and here future ages will find his influence still active. To meet the needs of the new kind of drama which he was working out for himself, he so adapted the old technique, so gave new life to the old tricks and rules of the stage, that the path has been smoothed for all who follow him. But there is no relaxation, rather a tightening of the bonds of the playwright's art. His subject being no longer the conventional situations of the stage, but the facts of life as he saw them, he found all the greater need to be exact, precise, dramatic. He keeps, until later years, very close to the unities; shears away all fustian from his dialogue, and contrives by a triumph of dramatic art to express in three words of conversation more and deeper meaning than any playwright before him had expressed in five minutes of soliloquy, and to preserve the necessary exaggeration, heightening, and clinching of action without sacrificing a jot of truth. His practice of clearing the ground by starting, so to speak, in the middle of his story, has often been observed.

Ibsen demanded to be judged as poet and playwright, not as philosopher or social reformer. He was not, in fact, a philosopher, nor a social reformer, but an artist. No amount of study of the plays nor of the commentators can lead to the discovery of any theory of life that will bind these plays together satisfactorily. Study them separately, and you think you can label their author. In *Pillars of Society* he is the democrat; in *The Doll's House* the advocate of the emancipation of women; and then *An Enemy of the People,* or *Rosmersholm,* or *The Wild Duck* comes to upset the pleasant little theory and leave you wondering what the man does mean. He means one thing, and one thing only – that you shall take from your eyes the spectacles of convention and pretence, and see things as they are. You may not see them eye to eye with Ibsen; he does not ask that you should. He asks you to be yourself and see with your own eyes, not to accept this or that theory from him nor from any one else. At the bottom of his work lies the passion to express the truth; and because the truth as he saw it was neither beautiful nor comforting, his plays are disturbing, often ugly, nearly always depressing. It is impossible to separate Ibsen the artist from Ibsen the philosopher, because his very conception of his art united the two. The duty of art in his eyes was to tell the truth, and not only to avoid the composition of theories for general use but to make it impossible for honest men to fall into the way of making them. His art is a solvent, not a cohesive; he is concerned with facts and men, not with theories and systems. How far his very closeness in depicting the men about him as he saw them – feeble, often scarcely sane, self-deceivers, cowards, and hypocrites – will prevent his plays from living, we are too close to him yet to say. It may be suggested that, so long as Euripides is read and acted and discussed, there is hope for Ibsen. And in this connexion it must not be forgotten that Ibsen has this in his favour – the burden of prophecy, as we may call it, which is found in all literature that endures. He is a symbolist, of course, in the obvious sense that he makes use of *motifs* as they are called in music; now a door, now a stream, now a tower, which, whenever they are mentioned, convey a meaning as surely as the Grail-*motif* in *Parsifal*. He was a poet before he became a dramatist, and the poetry in him is always breaking out. But he is also a symbolist in a far deeper sense. Beneath the surface dialogue of his plays, curt, bald, and commonplace as it is, there lies a deeper meaning, which the labours of modern students have done something to bring to light, but which future ages will certainly grasp more and more fully. He will have a new meaning, that is, for each generation; and, if that be so, no changes in society and belief can put these men and women and their thoughts and difficulties out of date. To us they are, for all their strangeness, modern men and women, with thoughts and difficulties which we understand; they may be just as "modern" and just as actual a thousand years hence. ⟨⟨continued at bottom of next page⟩⟩ (**f13ᵛ**) ⟨from last page⟩ If they are not, it will not matter, we might almost say: the work has been done. There is now a public, even though in England it be a small one, which has grown accustomed to the idea that the truth can be told in the theatre; and there are playwrights, though none too many, who want to tell the truth, and who see that it can be done without sacrifice of theatrical effect. Ibsen opened the windows, so to speak. The air that came in was no scented breath from Araby; it was a nipping and an eager air. But it was bracing; and the cries of "morbid," "unwholesome," and so on, that went up were only so many testimonials to its healthy influence. The atmosphere can never be quite the same again, though the man who opened the windows were as nameless as he who burned the temple of Diana.

2505 ⟨Ibsen (contᵈ)⟩ This loneliness, indeed, due in part to the circumstances of his life and in part to the quality of his genius, is one of Ibsen's differentiating characteristics. The great man whose lines lie in the pleasantest places is he who differs from the average man not in kind but only in degree – whose career and utterances can be accepted as proofs of the average man's splendid potentialities, whose message to the world the average man accepts as one which puts him up to new wrinkles, who, when we come to look at him closely, seems to be no more than the average man magnified to scale. Such men as those come into their kingdoms early, have little hostility to fight before recognition is accorded to them, conciliate sympathy (**f14ʳ**) instead of breaking themselves against the rock of prejudice, and find "roses, roses all the way" in their path as they go on from strength to strength. There have been such typical men among the leaders of art and thought in every country. Dickens in England, Victor Hugo in France, Henri Conscience in Belgium, Maurus Jokai in Hungary, Björnson in Norway, are the obvious instances that come to mind. They are not all equally great, but they all resemble one another in the fact that they became national heroes easily by marching to fame along the line of least resistance. But there is another type of great man who is so much in advance of his time that he seems to have nothing in common with it – whose whole point of view is different from that of the average man of his age, who feels that his mission is to lead, or to drive, the average man whither he has no desire to go. Ibsen was a great man belonging to that category. Isolation was at once the consequence of his idiosyncrasy and an essential condition of his growth to his full intellectual stature. He had to live alone in order that he might realize himself; because he persisted in realizing himself instead of conforming to a type he was doomed to live alone. He was the disciple of no school. He had no literary sympathies, no interest in other men's work, and, with the possible exception of Georg Brandes, no intimate personal friends. His isolation in his earlier years is sometimes ascribed to his poverty; but that can have been no more than a contributory cause. Victor Hugo, when as poor as he, was already the leading spirit of a *cénacle*, and Ibsen remained in isolation.

2506   Courthope's Poetry of the 18ᵗʰ Century
Times. Dec 1. 1905.

Pope, like most other poets of his time, was constantly at a loss for subject-matter, and restlessly casting about for it; and the subject-matter which he chose, since his choice was controlled by no principle, was often unfitted for poetry. It is, indeed, the most obvious characteristic of the eighteenth century poets that they are always versifying subjects unfit for verse. They Miltonize matter which Milton himself could not have turned into poetry. Hence the eighteenth century, always ready to laugh at its own follies, was the great period of mock heroic poems; and one of Pope's chief masterpieces was the Rape of the Lock, in which he often seems to be satirizing his own serious style. Yet the age had very strong theories about propriety in style. It held, Mr. Courthope says, that the true basis of metrical composition, was the colloquial idiom of living society refined by literary practice; and it is strange to find both Johnson and Goldsmith on the one hand and Wordsworth on the other finding fault with Gray because his diction was so far from natural speech. Wordsworth's idea of natural speech differed, however, from Johnson's and even from Goldsmith's in that he sought for a natural speech capable of expressing the deepest emotions of man, while they sought for a natural speech such as would best secure a writer from any extravagances or obscurities of expression. Theirs was the natural speech of well-bred people trained to be at ease with each other, Wordsworth's the natural speech of peasants accustomed to express their emotions without artifice or false shame. It is true, of course, that the natural speech of Wordsworth had no real existence, at least, among peasants. But it is also true that the natural speech of Johnson and Goldsmith was incapable of expressing any emotions stronger than those which in real life it was used to express. The poetry of the eighteenth century is often admirably natural and simple when it expresses the characteristic moods of the 18th century; but when it tries to express passion it almost always becomes not merely artificial but unnatural. Its merits, in fact, great as they are, are the merits of prose – even a poem so pathetic and sincere as Johnson's on the death of Robert Levett is scarcely more poetical, except for its form, than some of the tenderer passages of Lamb or Thackeray. Its defects, too, are the defects to which prose is liable when it tries to do the work of poetry.

(**f13ᵛ**) ~~reading.~~ The English of the eighteenth century, ~~however,~~ were as vigorous as ever in their history; their literary activity was as great as their political; nor, though their state of mind was prosaic, were they content only to write the admirable prose of their age. They were ambitious of producing great poetry, and threw vast energy into the task. They were not aware of their own poetic deficiencies, and they established a body of principles which made a virtue of them. Those principles admitted only a formal distinction between poetry and prose and tried to minimize even the difference of form. Poetry for us is an expression of the emotions in terms of the reason; that is to say, an attempt to express the emotions, by means of words, as exactly as the reason can be expressed by the same means. Reason, of course, plays a part in poetry as we conceive it, but chiefly as a means of expression, and as a means of showing the connexion between the different emotions expressed. But for the poets and critics of the eighteenth century reason was as much the subject-matter of poetry as of prose.

Poetry was, in fact, only a more ornamental kind of prose, the emotions serving as ornaments. And thus it came about that their poetry was so empty of objects and facts and of exact observation; for to the reason objects and facts are only interesting as they assist a logical process. The summer serves for an illustration of heat, the winter of cold, the sun of light, the night of darkness. They need therefore to be supplied only with general epithets to show why they are mentioned at all. But objects and facts are everything to the emotions, being the very means by which they are aroused. It is by the emotions, too, that objects and facts are stamped vividly upon the memory, and it is by the vivid description of those objects and facts, with which his emotions are associated, that the poet can most surely communicate those emotions to his readers. This is the reason why the romantic movement included a return to nature. Poetry became once more an instrument for the expression of the emotions; and the poets began to cast about for those means of expressing their emotions which the theories of the eighteenth century had forbidden to them.

Only a fanatic would now deny that the poetry of the eighteenth century, though mistaken, perhaps, in its aims and impoverished of much of the proper glory of poetry, is still full of power and interest and even of beauty. Take, for instance, the greatest of these poets, Pope, on whom Mr. Courthope has written an admirable chapter full both of sympathy and justice. We are heartily tired now of the old question, "Was Pope a poet?" We know that he was a poet, but one possessed by all the social sensitiveness characteristic of his age, and by that sensitiveness constantly distracted from what seem to us the proper aims of poetry. No man who was not a poet could have introduced so much beauty and passion into themes that seem to promise neither. But Pope, besides being a poet, was one of the cleverest of men; and cleverness is apt to be a worldly quality, as eager for the applause of the world as it is powerful to win it. Thus there was a constant conflict in him between his cleverness and his poetic genius. But he was too great a man of letters ever to be reduced to impotence or incoherence by that conflict.

Unlike some men of even greater genius, such as Donne, he was always effective – nearly always succeeded in what he tried to do. We may tax him with trying to do something not worth doing, but very seldom with a failure to do it. His translation of Homer is not Homer, but it is what he intended it to be, a version of Homer agreeable to the taste of his age. And yet the trouble of that conflict, though it may not affect Pope's mastery of expression, constantly betrays itself in what he expresses. He is not free, like the poets of a great age of poetry, to glorify the hopes and virtues and achievements of mankind. His time distrusted all the pretensions of man to be anything except a reasoning animal strangely inclined to forgo his reason; and Pope was a child of his time, troubled out of its characteristic contentment by his genius. So his poetry expressed the lack of that contentment and a great impatience with it, but it had nothing better to offer in its place. It is all negative and critical. It exposes the mistakes, the vices, and the illusions of men with an ardour that seems more suitable to glorification than to fault-finding. Every one must be moved by the stately close of the "Dunciad"; but who can help wondering that verses so splendid should be employed to express the triumph of dulness? What the splendour of those verses really expresses is, of course, the triumph not of dulness, but of its opposite. Yet Pope is so submissive to his age that he does not dare to show himself an enthusiast except indirectly and through his hatreds. The one great attempt he made to be a constructive poet, to reveal what is, rather than to expose what is not, produced a poem which seems to us now the most artificial and the most insincere of all his greater works. We cannot believe that any man of Pope's ability could frame arguments so contradictory as those of the "Essay on Man" without being aware of their contradictions. These contradictions are justly exposed by Mr. Courthope, yet he says that the poem must be ranked among the classical didactic poems of the world; for "the aim of the poet, as of the orator, is to persuade, not to convince." But, unfortunately, Pope tries so hard to convince that he fails to persuade. Even here he is critical rather than constructive. His object still is to reason about man rather than to express the emotions to which he is moved by the contemplation of man; and with all his miraculous skill he cannot reason so well in verse as much duller writers could reason in prose. The philosophy which Pope tried to expound in the "Essay on Man" was not a poet's philosophy at all. It was a mechanical system coldly worked out in the study, not based upon any intense experience of life nor capable of being felt with the passion which such an experience alone can produce. Hence all the poetry which Pope could supply was at variance with his philosophic purpose and distracted him from it. There is no reasoning in Shelley's "Life of Life, thy lips enkindle," but there is more philosophy in it than in all the "Essay on Man"; and it is more persuasive, to those whose experience has made them capable of understanding it, than all Pope's painful but broken logic.

2507 (**f14ʳ**) MR. STURGE MOORE'S POETRY.
POEMS by T. STURGE MOORE. Collected in one volume. (Duckworth, 6s.)

A great period of our poetry seems now to be just ended, and we are expectant of the first signs of a new age to be. There is no reason to despair because –

> The languid strings do scarcely move.
> The note is forced; the sounds are few.

There have been such intervals before, and so long as our poetry lives will be again. Meanwhile, Mr. Sturge Moore is a poet of the interval, uncertain, experimental, determined not to live in the past, yet somewhat starved by the present. The romantic movement has declined very swiftly and thoroughly in the last twenty years. In all the arts romantic ideas and emotions seem to have lost their savour, and now they only satisfy sentimentalists. Mr. Sturge Moore, if he had lived fifty years ago, would certainly have been one of the romantic poets. He cannot get away from the themes of romance, but he is not satisfied with the old treatment of them, and delights to criticize them in the light of new ideas. The characters in his little dramatic poems argue and discuss their own situations and the scheme of the universe, quite in the manner of Euripides. Pan, for instance, in *Pan's Prophecy*, seems to be a goat God tamed by introspection. He talks about the simple life he leads. He remembers his romantic past, that glorious past of Shelley's hymn, when he sang of the dancing stars and the daedal earth, and when down the vale of Maenalus he –

> Pursued a maiden and clasped a reed.
> Gods and men, we are all deluded thus!
> It breaks in our bosom and then we bleed.

That was the extent of his moralizing in those romantic days; but now love for him is not a mere blind passion, a matter of pursuing nymphs until they vanish unaccountably into reeds; now it is one of the permanent forces of life, to be analysed so that we may know the truth about it, and to be directed rightly so that we may get more good from it than harm. The analysis is laboured sometimes. Mr. Sturge Moore's Pan does not sing as wildly or sweetly as Shelley's. He is content rather to think than to sing. He is, in fact, Pan grown old and living upon memories, out of which he tries to make a new philosophy for a new generation of gods and heroes.

In the same way Mr. Sturge Moore, a poet living in the old age of a great period of poetry, is trying to make a new philosophy out of the old themes, to build a basis for the poetry of the future. He cannot therefore repeat the old romantic music, though he remembers it with delight; but, like Donne, he is studious not to fall into traditional phrases and cadences and rhythms which would carry him away from the sense which he labours to express; and, like Donne, he often grows harsh and crabbed with his labours. To him "Lilies that fester smell far worse than weeds"; any discord is better than a borrowed harmony. But his prosaic passages are, no more than Donne's, the expression of a prosaic mind. Take, for instance, one of the harshest of his poems, that meditation on the dead Don Juan, which he calls "A Spanish Picture." There is scarcely a line in it which runs easily, and scarcely any beauty of words. You might think perhaps that the terseness of the verse does not make up for its roughness and clumsiness, that it would be better in prose. But that is not so. It could not be put into prose, for it *is* poetry, and the sentences, though they may not please, could not be paraphrased. They express what the writer had to express, and if they do not move lyrically and easily, it is because his mood, when he wrote them, was not lyrical. They may be imperfect poetry, clogged with facts and checked by thought, but they are not sham poetry.

> Dull brown a cloak enwraps, Don Juan,
> Both thy lean shanks, one arm,
> That old bird-cage thy breast, where like magpie
> Thy heart hopped on alarm.

A single verse, perhaps, sounds almost absurd; but the ⟨T. O.⟩ (**f14ᵛ**) ⟨⟨continued from back⟩⟩ whole has a cumulative power. Don Juan, of course, is a romantic subject; but Mr. Sturge Moore assumes all the romance and sets to work to think over the corpse of the romantic hero. Now that he lies all tarnished and withered and shrunk to a mere bundle of bones, the question arises why was he ever a romantic hero, why did the imagination of the world glorify him in so many works of art, and was the glorification all spurious? No, says Mr. Sturge Moore. He has done his worst in his catalogue of bones and shabby finery, but, he concludes,

> Thou wast an envied man, Don Juan,
> Long shalt be envied still;
> Thou hadst thy beauty as the proud pard hath,
> And instinct trained to skill.

So Mr. Sturge Moore meditates over romanticism, and justifies its unreflecting power and glory. It had its beauty as the proud pard hath; but now its day is over, and another kind of glory is still to be born and to bewilder the world with the freshness of its unthinking youth. Meanwhile our poets must think rather than sing. And yet Mr. Sturge Moore is not always merely thinking. Sometimes the great simple themes carry him out of meditation into music, as in this passage on Alexander in his poem called "On Death."

> When to the mightiest man death did draw near,
> He shut himself within his bathing hall
> And lent to his great admiral his ear;
> Who told of voyage on the Indian main,
> The first by Grecian captains dared – that all
> The glamour of unconquered seas might reign
> Over the greatest conqueror's spirit failing.

Mr. Sturge Moore is always a poet; there is always some passion in his verse, and, though often it may struggle under a heavy burden of thought, its action can generally be felt; and in this volume of his collected poems there are many passages as well as many incidental lines and images which only a true poet could have written and which every lover of poetry must enjoy.   Times   May 18.06

2508   (**f15ʳ**) Times Lit. Sup. 29:6.06
Prosody. "There is no difference between the phrasing & accentuation of English as it is spoken & as it is written in poetry. Every effect of spoken English can be reproduced in English poetry: & even now, after so many centuries & so many varieties of poetic convention the language of our poetry is nearer than the language of our best prose to the language of our conversation. ...

The extraordinary variety and freedom of ballad rhythms was possibly due, as Professor Saintsbury points out, to a happy accident. In the fifteenth century great changes of pronunciation were occurring, and in particular the final *e* was dropping out. These changes brought anarchy and uncertainty into the written literary verse which was not subject to the continual test of recitation; but it brought variety and the discovery of new effects into oral ballad verse. Thus, to take an example given by Professor Saintsbury, in the line –

For huy ore louerd Jesu Christ: to strongue dethe broughte,

the last words were originally pronounced –

to strong*y* death*y* brought*y*.

But when the final *e* was no longer sounded they were pronounced –

to strong death brought.

And it was found that this pronunciation improved instead of spoiling the metre. So the effect, produced at first by accident, was imitated afterwards by design. You will find it all through "Love in the Valley," for instance, as in the second of these two lines –

When at dawn she sighs, and like an infant to the window
Turns grave eyes craving light, released from dreams.

And in the same way anapaestic effects came with the sounding of syllables not originally sounded. A pedantic literary poetry could not take advantage of such accidents. Its prosody was ready made and changes of pronunciation only destroyed it.

It is from examples of this kind that we can see how great is the interest of prosody if it is studied as a living thing; and also that when it ceases to be a living thing to the poets their poetry dies with it. Prosody lives only when it is obedient to speech and follows all its changes. When once it ceases to follow those changes it loses its meaning and becomes a mere set of arbitrary rules which are imperfectly observed because they are imperfectly understood; and so a blind following of the law in the end produces lawlessness. Misunderstandings of prosody may in periods of weak inspiration produce much bad verse; and for this reason it is important that we should understand our prosody and test it by our speech as closely as possible. Therefore discussions about the true nature of English versification are not so barren as they may seem provided they do not fall into mere empty theorizing. It is not, for instance, mere empty theorizing to discuss the question whether the common English decasyllabic line, the line of blank verse and the heroic couplet, is really iambic in its nature or trochaic with an anacrusis. Professor Saintsbury decides, too hastily perhaps, that it is iambic. Yet he admits that our ordinary speech takes on most readily a trochaic rhythm, and he should remember that the decasyllabic line is closer to ordinary speech than any other verse, also that many difficult and splendid lines of blank verse will scan much more easily in trochees than iambs.

Chaucer, as he points out, has a good many purely trochaic lines. Milton has some, and though they are very seldom found in modern poetry, the trochaic rhythm of much modern verse supposed to be iambic is very marked. If the natural rhythm of the decasyllabic line is trochaic, it follows that poets who are dominated by the theory that it is iambic will make bad decasyllabic verses; and it may be that the iambic theory is accountable for a good deal of the dulness of eighteenth century verse. All the laws of eighteenth century versification were based upon the iambic theory, and if that theory was wrong all the laws were wrong and eighteenth-century verse was the most incorrect, as it was certainly the most unnatural, that our poetry has produced. There are many arguments which might be advanced both for and against the trochaic theory. Professor Saintsbury does not argue the question at all; and he will say, perhaps, that it is not his business to argue such questions in his book. Yet

2509   By the Way. (On Bliss Carman)

We will also quote one or two more characteristic passages: (from his book)

"Unless the world of art be in some way more delightful than the world of our every-day experience, why should we ever visit it?"

"The one way in which art can be most immoral is by leaving us depressed and sad, and uncertain of the final issue between sorrow and gladness."

"To be a good judge of poetry, one must be a completely normal man, with a clear brain, a happy disposition, and a good appetite."

"I must believe that the world's need for great and fearless poetry is perpetual, and that without its illuminating aid we shall never come near to accomplishing our destiny."

"Life as a whole is desirable, and art as a whole is the reflection of its goodly joy."

"Poetry will return with religion."

We seldom agree with Mr. Carman, but he is a man who lives, and he is sincere, and it is our business to commend all vigorous life. With this, we leave "The Poetry of Life" to its readers. We believe that his enthusiasm and love for poetry are so genuine and sane that they will be a useful stimulus, though we must add that, whether the stimulus succeed, or fail, or pass away, little else that is memorable can come from the book.

As the Poet.

In Mr. Carman's own poetry, cheerfulness, sometimes rising to a true gusto, the beauty of Nature and men, the mystery of life, are usually in some way present. Sometimes, as in his "Dustman," he comes near to using a perfectly modern subject with dignity and magic. His descriptions of Nature are often singularly apt, and he has scores of good things about the joys of the open air like these:

Now the joys of the road are chiefly these:
A crimson touch on the hardwood trees;

A vagrant's morning, wide and blue,
In early fall, when the wind walks, too; ...

The outward eye, the quiet will,
And the striding heart from hill to hill; ...

An open hand, an easy shoe,
And a hope to make the day go through. ...

But, as it seems to us, he is diffuse, he is far too ingenious, and he is often so bent on showing us how much he has observed and how cleverly he can turn a phrase that in more than half of his pieces there is no effect at all. We believe that some of his epithets are nonsense, and that he knows it. In fact, with all his bluff sentiment and talk about vagabonds and stars, he is essentially a lover of words and phrases – a maker of verses, who writes about joy instead of expressing it. We feel little diffidence in setting him alongside men like Mr. Symons, and he ranks with them unquestionably, though, unlike them, he has that frail but genuine sympathy with wild and primitive things which is characteristic of our doubtful day. This complete edition of his work is a very handsome one.   Daily Chr. 24.5.06

2510 **(f16ʳ)** SEPTEMBER 14, 1906. SPENCER AND THE ABBEY.
"Would Offer the Devil a Christian Burial."

From a number of additional letters we have received relating to the refusal of the Dean of Westminster to allow a memorial tablet to Herbert Spencer to be placed in the Abbey we give the following extracts, as representing the point of view of those who approve of the Dean's attitude:–

"I cannot understand how any Christian can desire that Herbert Spencer should be commemorated in a Christian church. I think if the story of the last days of his life could be circulated it would be a wholesome warning to any who might be led to follow his teaching. Of course the interment of Darwin was a gross insult to the feelings of every English Churchman, but I believe that if the Devil had died Stanley or Bradley would have offered him a Christian burial as a 'distinguished person.'" – "A Radical Parson."

"If the ecclesiastical authorities in Paris had been asked to permit a memorial to Ernest Renan to be placed in Notre Dame, of course they would have refused, and no one in England would have been surprised, nor would anyone have raised the cry of intolerance. Yet it may be doubted whether Renan was such an avowed opponent of the Christian Church as Herbert Spencer. Why, then, accuse the Dean of Westminster – a truly broad and liberal-minded man – of intolerance? Westminster Abbey, is before all things, a Christian church. Would a memorial to Spencer be permitted in the new Roman cathedral at Westminster or in the City Temple?" – Rev. J. A. Richards (perpetual curate of St. Bartholomew's, Camberwell).

"It seems to have been overlooked by the many distinguished scientists who are advocating the claims of Herbert Spencer to a national memorial in Westminster Abbey that a considerable mark of respect has already been posthumously paid to him by the trustees of the National Portrait Gallery, in accepting on behalf of the nation his own bequest of two portraits of himself – one an oil painting by Burgess, representing him in the prime of life, and the other a fine marble bust executed later in life by Sir Edgar Boehm. These portraits are now exhibited in the National Portrait Gallery, where they will remain for all time. – "Limner."

2511 By his choice from so rich a vocabulary does a man reveal the secrets of his nature. And this process of selection which takes place probably quite unconsciously in the ordinary man regulated in him by his taste, natural preferences and general cultivation, becomes in the literary artist a sought-out thing deliberate and self-conscious. He is particularly alive to the magic that lies in words. He knows how terrible they can be, how clear and vivid and cruel, how they can give plastic form to formless things and have "a music of their own as sweet as that of viol or of lute". The problem of style in literary art lies in the discovery of the one word for the one thing, the one thought amid the multitude of words, terms that might just do. The joy of the musician at last able to materialise the harmony that has been haunting him is the joy also of the writer who has discovered, perhaps in a flash of insight, a happy inspiration, perhaps only after long and painful search, the one phrase or word that expresses exactly his meaning. For as Flaubert wrote "Among all the expressions in the world, all forms and terms of expression there is but one – one form, one mode – to express what I have to say." It is the possession of the sense of some mysterious harmony of expression that marks the difference between the artist and the mere stringer-together of words. Every writer is conscious how inadequately the written thing represents that deeper truer vision within and realises how hard it is to make his thoughts look anything but imbecile fools when he paints them with ink on paper.

S. R. 29 Sep'. 1906

2512 But it is not in the solitude of English field, woodland, and stream that Mr. Hueffer really finds the heart of the country. Still less is it in the "nature" of the nature poets. There is not a hint in his musings of their emotional pantheism. He admits no moral teaching in any "impulse from a vernal wood," and would perhaps agree with the late Dr. Thomas Davidson, a true Aristotelian, who baldly characterized Wordsworth's well-known lines as sheer nonsense. It is man rather than nature which most interests him. The book is much more soundly practical than "The Soul of London," and in the chapters "In the Cottages" and "Toilers of the Field" we get much keen observation and some fruitful suggestion. In the field-labourer he finds the real "heart of the country," and he has done his best to explore it –

> Its accent hit
> And partly sound its polity.

He has no Arcadian illusions as to rustic morality – "Every 'scandal' that one hears in the carrier's cart," he thinks, "is true to fact and only as to motive exaggerated." It is not a hopeful, but it is on the whole not an unpleasing, picture – this of the farm-hand, patient, good-humoured, suspicious of all wearers of clothes not weatherbeaten, often half a pagan in his superstitions, with less of class hatred than his town cousin, simply because *he* cannot rise in the social scale, and reckless of the future because he has no time to think of it, whose rests between work are so intense, says Mr. Hueffer, that he can scarcely rouse himself to think of any longer spaces of doing nothing – the man "whose days are each one a cell, shut off and unconnected, having no relation to the day which went before, and none to that which shall ensue after the black oblivion of the coming night. ... There is no time between bed and bed, and at night no lying awake." Into Mr. Hueffer's agricultural Utopia – a scheme for holdings of graduated size which should give the labourer a "prospect" – we need not here enter. But, as part of the silent, helpless exodus to the town, the business of moving comes into his picture. At certain seasons of the year

> You will see high poled waggons ponderously blocking the road, creeping onward with a great gravity as if in pensive thought. Perched on the shafts will be a child with a cat in her arms, and hanging to one of the sideboards a wicker cage ... this family has become nomadic. Its tables are woefully inverted beneath the sky; its memorial cards, these milestones of life that are the most precious decorations of all cottage walls, are packed away in some obscure corner of the creaking car.
>
> Times Supp! 8.6:06

2513   (**f17ᵛ**) /LITE/RARY SUPPLEMENT   LONDON, FRIDAY, JUNE 8, 1906.
                                      Issued Weekly with *The Times*.

LITERATURE.

PASTORAL POETRY.

PASTORAL POETRY AND PASTORAL DRAMA. A literary inquiry, with special reference to the Pre-Restoration Stage in England. By WALTER W. GREG, M. A. (Bullen, 10s. 6d. net)

When the title of a book misrepresents the contents we may generally expect to find some fault of design in the book itself, for the misrepresentation of the title is apt to be a proof that the author has not thought out the plan and the object of the book very clearly in his own mind. This is the case with Mr. Greg. As he tells us in his preface, his title does not fit his subject. His real subject, he says, "remains the pastoral drama in English literature." He began with the intention of writing about the English pastoral drama alone; but then difficulties arose – difficulties which he explains very frankly. He found that to understand that drama a general knowledge of pastoral literature generally was necessary, and, further, that no critical work existed from which such knowledge could be obtained. He therefore set to work to write a general account of pastoral literature so that he might make "the special form it assumed on the English stage appear in its true light as the reasonable and rational outcome of artistic and historical conditions." The result was that this general account "swelled to something over half of the whole work." Mr. Greg appears to think it inevitable that this should be so. Now every one will agree that the English pastoral drama could not be properly treated or explained without some kind of introductory essay upon pastoral literature in general. That drama was not a sudden, spontaneous growth. It was not a purely literary product, as Mr. Greg shows in a valuable and interesting chapter; but it owed a great deal to the general pastoral convention. Also the history of pastoral literature and its connexion with the English pastoral drama are not so well known as to justify a writer in taking them for granted. Therefore, an introduction of some kind and of considerable length was necessary. But, seeing that Mr. Greg's main subject was to be the English pastoral drama, his introduction ought to have been nothing but an introduction. What he has given us is something more. True, it is on a much smaller scale than the part which deals with the English pastoral drama, and owing to the fact that Mr. Greg wrote it with that drama always in his mind, it is not at all well proportioned. For instance, after a few pages of introduction upon the nature of pastoral poetry in general, we are plunged at once into a very summary account of the pastoral poetry of the Ancients. Considering the fact that Theocritus was both the originator of pastoral poetry and by far the greatest pastoral poet of all time, that he combines reality with beauty as no pastoral poet has done since, the few pages which Mr. Greg gives to him must seem utterly inadequate. The fact is Mr. Greg's introduction ought not to have been written in a narrative form at all. It should have been a critical and introductory essay. In that case he would have been able, without any fear of misunderstanding, to deal with different writers according to their connexion with the English pastoral drama. The difficulty in which he found himself is not a new one. It is one which besets all writers of history who do not begin with the creation of the world, and their common practice is to deal with it in an introductory chapter not in narrative form. If Mr. Greg had done this he would have displayed his considerable knowledge and his real critical power to much greater advantage.

Even in the main portion of his book, when he can write as he likes and is hampered by no introductory difficulties, Mr. Greg throws his matter too much into a narrative form. Pastoral poetry is a subject which demands a philosophical treatment. There are certain general questions which every one is prompted to ask about it, as, for instance, why it has persisted so long in so many different literatures, and why it has been put to so many incongruous uses. Mr. Greg's narrative method causes him to deal with these questions only in a casual, haphazard way. They crop up at intervals throughout the book, and provoke him to a few incidental reflexions. He never sets himself to face them squarely. In his first few pages he makes some acute remarks about pastoral poetry in general. "What does appear to be a constant element in the pastoral," he says, "is the recognition of a contrast, implicit or expressed, between pastoral life and some more complex type of civilization. At no stage in its development does literature, or, at any rate, poetry, concern itself with the obvious, with the bare scaffolding of life. Whenever we find an author interested in the circle of prime necessity, we may be sure that he himself is outside it." This is perfectly true, and, no doubt, it is the explanation why so much pastoral poetry has been produced in artificial societies. Theocritus himself, as Mr. Greg remarks, wrote about the pastures of Sicily in the streets of Alexandria, and it was the passion of his regret for them that sounded in his poetry. Pastoral poetry, in fact, is always a kind of romantic literature. Its object is not to lay bare the great forces of destiny and the human mind, but to create an atmosphere in which even the most trivial things will seem beautiful and strange. We may see what all pastoral poetry aims at perfectly accomplished in Giorgione's pastoral symphony in the Louvre. Nothing important is happening in that picture. There is simply a group of four persons in a meadow, two of them playing musical instruments. It is the atmosphere, enveloping them all in a kind of trance or dream, which makes the subject of the picture. It is not, like Michael Angelo's creation of Adam, a symbol of the highest reality, but rather a symbol of that beautiful unreality which we long for the more we know it to be unreal.

Mr. Greg obviously has this kind of idea of pastoral poetry in his mind when he begins his first chapter, but he seems to lose his grasp of it as he becomes entangled with the difficulties of his subject; and for the most part he writes without any philosophic point of view at all. He is content too often to give mere colourless accounts of the different works with which he deals, as if he did not expect his readers to read any of them, as if all they needed was secondhand acquaintance with their contents. This is a common fault not only in those who write primers of literature, but in learned authors like Mr. Greg. Thus regard themselves as travellers in unknown regions, and they produce accounts of what they have discovered for the untravelled. Mr. Greg cannot get out of this habit even when he comes to deal with quite familiar works. For instance, he gives us a kind of *précis* of *The Faithful Shepherdess* and another of *The Sad Shepherd*. He even conducts us through "Lycidas," strangely mingling quotation with paraphrase. Thus, instead of quoting "Next, Camus, reverend Sire, went footing slow," he writes, "Next footing slow, comes the tutelary deity of Alma Mater." It is pretty plain that when he wrote this he cannot have had any very clear idea in his mind of his object in writing. It is unlikely that any one who did not know "Lycidas" would ever start to read a book about pastoral poetry at all; and no one who knew "Lycidas" would want a paraphrase of it. "Lycidas" is a poem which demands a philosophic treatment above everything; for all the questions which pastoral poetry in general provokes clamour for an answer in it. Mr. Greg does raise these questions. He asks whether the allegorical pastoral, in spite of its long pedigree, is "by nature calculated to yield the highest artistic results." He seems inclined to think that it is not; but he does not attempt to argue the matter to a conclusion. Well, the first answer to that question is the fact that "Lycidas" exists. It is both an allegorical pastoral and a poem of the highest rank. It therefore is the best instance that could be found of the uses of pastoral poetry. Assuming that Milton was not moved to passionate grief by the death of Edward King, we may be quite sure that he could not have made a great poem out of a simple lamentation upon him. He had by some means to connect the death of King with other matters nearer to his heart before he could write about it. The pastoral machinery, the pastoral atmosphere, were the means which he employed. In his hands the pastoral machinery turned everything to beauty, and the pastoral atmosphere, suggesting a world neither in Heaven nor on earth, enabled him to bring together earthly and heavenly things without any incongruity. In pastoral poetry the individual is not of supreme importance. So Edward King is not of supreme importance in "Lycidas." His figure is shadowy like all the figures of pastoral poetry. He and Camus and the Pilot of the Galilean Lake all are subdued to the rich pastoral atmosphere, as the nude women and the richly-dressed youths are subdued to the atmosphere of Giorgione's picture, and as the modern poets, introduced as mountain shepherds, are subdued to the atmosphere of "Adonais." It is because pastoral poetry provides the atmosphere, in which the poet can say all that he has to say without fear of incongruity, that it has endured in literature from the time of Theocritus to the time of Matthew Arnold.

When, however, we come to Mr. Greg's main theme, the pastoral drama in Elizabethan literature, we find that the general idea of pastoral poetry does not apply altogether. That pastoral drama was not altogether an escape from reality. It was indeed half realistic. A remark of Drayton's, himself a distinguished pastoral poet, helps us to understand the Elizabethan idea of pastoral poetry. "The subject of (**f17ʳ**) pastorals," he says, "ought to be poor, silly, and of the coarsest woof in appearance. Nevertheless, the most high and noble matters of the world may be shaddowed in them, and for certaine sometimes are." Here we have Drayton insisting both on the allegorical uses of pastoral poetry and on a realistic treatment of it. Mr. Greg, in what is perhaps the most valuable part of his book, shows how this realistic treatment, for which there was but little precedent in regular pastoral literature since the time of Theocritus, came into Elizabethan pastoral poetry. Before Englishmen were aware of the literary pastoral convention, they produced a pastoral poetry, which is a purely native growth, both in their ballads and in their mystery plays. "As a result," says Mr. Greg, "the earlier native fashion affected in a noticeable degree later pastoral work, colouring and blending with, instead of being overpowered by, the regular tradition." Mr. Greg gives an interesting account of the pastoral mystery plays which were written both for rustics and about rustics. They were not, therefore, pastoral poetry at all in the literary sense of the term. They suggested no contrast between pastoral life and any more complex type of civilization. They did not offer to the mind, tired with reality, any imaginary escape from it. They are to be compared rather with the pictures of Ostade or Teniers than with the pastoral symphony of Giorgione. The Elizabethan poets, however, as soon as they became acquainted with Italian literature, began to combine the pastoral convention, with all its sense of contrast and escape from reality, with the native realism. Thus the pastoral idea is

not very clear in Elizabethan pastorals. They are half about this world
and half about a world that never was. Like Shakespeare's comedies,
they are half romantic and half realistic. Their realism gives them a
kind of savour and freshness which a great deal of pastoral poetry lacks;
but it makes them difficult to classify; and also, when it is inextricably
mixed up with a thoroughly artificial romantic convention, it produces
a certain confusion of effect.

This confusion is very evident in Fletcher's *Faithful Shepherdess*,
perhaps the chief work of the Elizabethan pastoral drama. It is the
oddest mixture of crude realism and romantic sentiment, with the
result that it has no consistent morality or lack of morality whatever.
When we are in a world altogether of nymphs and satyrs set in a
classical landscape we expect them to behave like nymphs and satyrs.
But when the landscape is purely English and there are English
shepherds and dairy-maids in it, we wince a little when nymphs and
satyrs appear and behave according to their nature. We remember that
the policeman and the Ten Commandments also belong to the English
landscape, and we are inclined to look for their interference. Mr. Greg,
therefore, has some reason when he is shocked by the moral tone of *The
Faithful Shepherdess*, but his criticism on Fletcher's conduct of his play is
not very much to the point. "Fletcher," he says, "had to fashion
characters *in vacuo* and then to weave them into such a plot as they
might be capable of sustaining. In other words, he reversed the normal
order of artistic creation and attempted to make the abstract generate
the concrete instead of making the individual example imply, while
being informed by, the fundamental idea." This is perfectly true. But it
is a criticism that will apply to nearly all pastoral poetry, and probably
to all pastoral plays. For the man who writes a pastoral play begins
with his atmosphere, not with his characters, and his characters are
generated out of his atmosphere. Fletcher's real fault was that his
atmosphere was not properly fused. Half of it was made up of the light
that never was on sea or land and half of the light of common day. Out
of this mixture he could not generate characters altogether consistent
with each other, and as soon as they begin to act their inconsistency is
obvious. It is the fault of Fletcher in all his plays. He is a romanticist in
conception, a realist often in detail; and his realistic details suddenly
make us remember reality and all its obligations, when, if we are to
enjoy his fable, we ought to forget them altogether. The beauty of *The
Faithful Shepherdess*, as Mr. Greg points out, is altogether a beauty of
detail. The pastoral atmosphere gave Fletcher the opportunity of

exercising his wonderful lyric gifts to the top of his bent. His characters can always sing beautifully even though they may act uglily; and since it is an English pastoral atmosphere, they can sing about real things such as Fletcher had seen with his own eyes, and not about mere empty classical abstractions. In fact the landscape of *The Faithful Shepherdess*, though it has not the noble lines, the balance and solemn dignity, of classical landscape, is full of dancing flowers and whispering leaves, fresh with dew, and bathed in the light of a real morning. Its beauty makes us forget how some of the figures in it behave. There is, too, the same freshness and profusion of real and detailed beauty in Ben Jonson's fragment of *The Sad Shepherd*. Even he, the most literary of Elizabethans, could not be altogether literary when he came to write of country things. Indeed his object was to produce a true English pastoral drama, carried on on English soil and by English characters. So far as he went he succeeded. Nothing could be more natural and simple and delicate than much of the dialogue, and we can enjoy it all without any of the misgivings which *The Faithful Shepherdess* provokes. That Ben Jonson should have been moved to write a pastoral of this kind is a proof how strong the old realistic tradition still was in Elizabethan pastoral poetry. That tradition made it fresher and more full of life than any pastoral poetry that had been written, perhaps, since the time of Theocritus. It was a hybrid, like many forms in Elizabethan literature, and sometimes it had some of the failings of a hybrid; but it was alive, and it is a common weakness in pure pastoral poetry to be dead.

2514 (**f18ᵛ**) FRENCH SYMBOLISTS
POÈTES D'AUJOURD'HUI, 1880–1900. MORCEAUX CHOISIS. Ad. van Bever et Paul Léautaud. (Paris; Société du Mercure de France. 3f.50c.)

An anthology is a work of art, the anthologist comparable to a jeweller; not only must the gems be of intrinsic value, but also they must be selected and combined with such cunning that while the total arrangement is harmonious the brilliance of no single gem loses anything of its potency. To produce such a work of art was not the purpose of MM. Van Bever and Léautaud, who are careful to avoid the style "anthology," rather describing their book as "un guide de la poésie récente." It consists of extracts from the works of thirty-three poets, a short biography and a complete bibliography being prefixed to each set of extracts. There is also an appendix containing various definitions by symbolists of Symbolism and of the *vers libre*. Although "anthology" and "guide" are to be distinguished, a principle of selection and arrangement is essential to both alike. The "guide" should not be a merely fortuitous aggregation. Yet in the case of this book, neither in the introduction nor in the several biographies and the appendix will it be easy to find arguments which should justify the grouping together under one classification of all its widely varying contents.

For no greater mistake is possible than to suppose that all the poets known as "Symbolists" accepted one definition of symbolism. Indeed, when we address ourselves to the actual writers we are at once lost in a whirl of conflicting theories. Thus we find Verlaine, who is generally regarded as the fountain head of this new poetic stream, strenuously denouncing symbolism:– "Ils m'embêtent, les 'cymbalistes,' eux et leurs manifestations ridicules." Again it is M. Jean Moréas who claims to have invented the name "Symbolisme." And yet M. Charles Morice protests that Moréas is no symbolist, while a third writer, M. Charles Vignier, denies that title both to Morice and to Moréas. To the question, "Il y a bien un mouvement symboliste?" M. Adrien Remacle answers, "Un mouvement, non: des mouvements sans direction, sans direction commune surtout," and adds that there are but two genuine symbolists in existence – himself and M. Mathias Morhardt. Thus it would seem as if M. Gustave Kahn were justified in asserting that one only bond unites the "symbolists" – namely, opposition to the orthodox Parnasse. And yet obviously not any kind of opposition will secure for a poet this vague appellation. This negative is a determinant. The name "Parnasse" calls to mind a very rigid technique, springing from a certain manner of regarding life – a manner essentially pessimistic. For the growth of Le Parnasse is to be traced back to Alfred de Vigny, who said:– "Je subis la prison. J'y tresse de la paille quelquefois pour oublier." And Gautier, who gathered the school about him, has written:–

> Dans l'immobilité savourer lentement
> Comme un philtre endormeur l'anéantissement,
> Voilà quel est mon voeu....

The Parnassian thinks of the world as governed by blind irrational forces, a sordid and wearisome spectacle. He retires into his inner self to find light and reason and attempts to body them forth in his poetry. This poetry then, as opposed to formless and unreasonable nature, is perfect in structure and in logical coherence. It has the clear outlines of a cameo and the hard metallic glitter of enamels. Nor were the Parnassians alone in emphasizing the sordidness of life. Whereas they had avoided life because it was banal, that very banality offered irresistible attractions to the Naturalist School. These took life at its worst and meanest, observed it and analysed it, and in imitation of the biologists proceeded to estimate the higher life by standards derived from the study of the lowest.

Before long reaction set in, declaring itself not specifically as against Naturalism, but generally as against that temper of thought of which Naturalism is a single manifestation. Naturalism was held to have failed, and its failure was attributed to exaltation of analysis and observation above simplicity and faith. But this exaltation of logic and accuracy was a defect incident also to the poetry of the Parnasse. Here was detected the fatal desire, to define, to crystallize, to set bounds, to deny the soul all way of escape into the illimitable. In short, the Parnassians were condemned guilty of description – the attempt to give the object in all its detail – every curve traced faultlessly, every surface polished to the perfection of smoothness. The new tendencies (to which the name Symbolism may now be re-attached) reacting against this were a reservation in favour of the beauty of haze. Symbolism views its object bathed in light, with contours flowing together. It will evoke rather than describe, proposing as its task to pierce to the soul of things; not to exercise critical and analytical faculties, but to contemplate, to dream, to lay the soul bare to the play of effluences from Nature. This attitude of mind is best prefigured in Rops's frontispiece to the Brussels edition of Mallarmé's poems. A figure, seated, holds a harp in front of it. The arms are uplifted, supporting the harp, and conceal the figure's countenance. Mysterious hands of spirits hover in the air and pluck at the strings. The figure is the poet, who does not himself play the harp, but holds it up for these unseen agencies to draw music from it. One may also quote Mr. W. B. Yeats, "All sounds, all colours, all forms ... call down among us certain disembodied powers whose footsteps over our hearts we call emotions." And whereas "to pierce to the soul of things" might seem a labour actually, it is but to open the heart, to be a dreamer. To be a poet, so the Symbolist might define, is to be susceptible of certain associations, such, for instance, as that which "weds" the colour of the rose, the scent of lilies, to Love and Purity, to employ the language of Mr. Yeats's "Ideas of Good and Evil." To the question, "How comes the rose to be wedded to Love?" probably there is no answer. For these associations, we are told, are too subtle to be apprehended by the unaided intellect. They do not exist for the intellect. For what, then? The French Symbolists do not extend their speculations so far, but the Neo-Celts through Mr. Kranz answer, "For the Great Memory," meaning that there is a preordained symbolic connexion between certain colours, forms, sounds, and certain emotions, the ordinant being a power or principle to which they give the name of Great Memory. To be aware of a symbolic connexion is to become, as it were, the vehicle of this Great Memory; or, varying the metaphor, to be absorbed in, taken up into this Absolute. And the result is that the poet thereby attains to a profounder Truth. Mr. Kranz in commenting upon the work of the Neo-Celtic poets in general says, "Mysticism is ... the conviction that truth is not to be come at by studious toil."

A poem, then, is for the Symbolist an arrangement of symbols, and the law which determines the sequence of these symbols is imposed from within the emotions which it is their sole function to convey. The change of symbols, in other words, is governed by the change of emotions, each new symbol as it is presented being an appropriate expression of a new stage in the emotional development, which, in turn, can be apprehended in no wise by reason. Hence symbolic poetry will often fall under the accusation of obscurity, and that obscurity must be proportionate to the rigour with which the poetic principle is carried out. Two quotations from Maeterlinck and Mallarmé respectively serve to illustrate different degrees of obscurity:–

> Toujours la pluie à l'horizon,
> Toujours la neige sur les grèves,
> Tandis qu'au senil clos de mes rêves
> De loups couchés sur le gazon,
>
> Observent en mon âme lasse,
> Les yeux ternis dans le passé,
> Tout le sang autrefois versé
> Des agneaux mourants sur la glace.

(**f19ʳ**) Here the understanding is not defeated. The comparison of our desires to wolves is a familiar and cogent metaphor. So much cannot be said of the following:–

Le vierge, le vivace et le bel aujourd'hui
Va-t-il nous déchirer avec un coup d'aile ivre
Ce lac dur oublié que hante sous la givre
Le transparent glacier des vols qui n'ont pas fui.
Un cygne d'autrefois se souvient que c'est lui
Magnifique mais qui sans espoir se délivre
Pour n'avoir pas chanté la région où vivre
Quand du stérile hiver a resplendi l'ennui.

Mallarmé's methods have been explained in some detail by Mr. Arthur Symons (in his book "The Symbolist Movement in Literature"). Briefly, they differ only from the methods of Maeterlinck in the poem quoted by the fulness with which the emotional growth is presented in all its aspects. Symbols are added to symbols as the warp is added to the woof, and the final result cannot be expressed in terms of metaphor. One is not surprised to learn that the greater part of Mallarmé's poems were incomprehensible to the author himself. In this his likeness to Browning is only superficial. Browning at the time of writing understood his own poems, but forgot the meaning afterwards. Mallarmé's poems were not, in the ordinary acceptation of the term, possessed of a "meaning" at *any* time. Their office is to convey, not definable ideas, but the sweep and play of emotions about a given centre. But more than this – according to the symbolists, when roses are presented, there should be evoked in us emotions supra-rationally associated with the particular shape, colour, and so on of the object. But the written word "rose" also represents a sound of a certain value, and this sound must itself also be associated with certain precise but indefinable emotions. And these two sets of emotions – those connected with the colour and scent of roses, and those connected with the sound of the word "rose" – may quite conceivably be incongruous, since words have been formed by pressing and material circumstances of life without regard for symbolic propriety. Hence Mallarmé's complaint – "Quelle déception, devant la perversité conférant à 'jour' comme à nuit contradictoirement des timbres obscur ici, clair là."
Insistence upon the suggestive power of words regarded as mere sounds means insistence upon the analogy between poetry and music. In order that poetry might be more perfectly assimilated to music, the old formalities of stanza, caesura, and rhyme were set aside; verse was "freed," curves of accent were complicated, need was felt for an infinitive variety of irregular harmonies, fluid wavering rhythms, and

for special application of such devices as assonance, alliteration, and refrain. Whether Verlaine is or is not the originator of the *vers libre* (that distinction is claimed also for Moréas and Laforgue), at least he alone has formulated his principles in an Art Poétique, the opening verse of which runs:–

> De la Musique avant toute chose,
> Et pour cela préfère l'Impair,
> Plus vague et plus soluble dans l'air
> Sans rien en lui qui pèse ou qui pose.

Charles Morice in his critique insists very strongly upon the significance and value of this analogy from music – "les assonances troublant délicieusement les vers d'échos mineurs, où l'éclat majeur, l'éclat de cor de la rime, perd sa brutale importance." Again, he describes the opening lines of Crimen Amoris –

> Dans un palais soie et or, dans Ecbatane.

as "Ce début où retentit tout un orchestre de cuivre." Perhaps this employment of musical terminology is an extravagance. The criticism, however, is of value as proving that, although Verlaine repudiated the title "Symboliste," he has this in common with symbolists – that by *pure* sound he attempts to evoke emotions which language in its ordinary employment (as a series of labels or indices) will hardly convey. The value of such a line as

> Qu'as-tu voulu de moi, fin refrain incertain

is *purely* musical. Even a more striking instance is the whole poem (Ariettes Oubliés, No. 3) beginning:–

> Il pleure dans mon coeur,
> Comme il pleut sur la ville. ...

Laforgue developed the musical analogy in connexion with the *vers libre* to a point far beyond the limits of Verlaine's manner. Sometimes his tone is harsh and grotesque, and he lapses into pure onomatopoetry, as in these lines:–

Les cors, les cors, les cors mélancoliques!
Mélancoliques! ...
S'en vont changeant de ton,
Changeant de ton et de musique. ...

And again –

Et tant les cors ont fait ton ton ont fait ton taine

Sometimes his music brightens where it touches, as certain
          THE TIMES LITERARY SUPPLEMENT, FRIDAY, SEPTEMBER 14, 1906.

2515   (**f20ʳ**) THE AUTHOR. Nov. 1907.   63
good X STEVENSON OF MISSOURI. (BEING STRAY LEAVES FROM A DIARY.)
   In Pago Pago, the Samoan harbour of dreams, dawn was still far off.
Under the cocoanut palms that fringed the strip of white sand on which
the little waves fell so softly, I was haggling for plantains with a
pleasant-faced aboriginal. Then, all at once, I remembered Stevenson.
The plantain-vendor appeared with difficulty to recall the name;
indeed, I suspect politeness jogged his memory. "Not here," he said,
and smiled. He waved one hand seaward. "Apia," said he. The native
guard of the governor's house came noiselessly out of the shadows, and,
drawing near, leant on his loaded carbine, regarding us and his bare
toes with equal interest and satisfaction. I had felt uplifted to speak of
the art and magic of Stevenson; I could have placed a bold finger on the
secret of his genius; but standing there in the deep velvet gloom,
breathing air odorous of spices, one was too detached, too disembodied.
Out on the water an United States cruiser and the Pacific Mail boat
rode side by side, the latter a line of brilliant port-holes. So I asked the
way to the post-office instead. The guard brought his carbine smartly
to the slope and disappeared into the darkness of tree-trunks, while,
according to directions, I followed the path along the shore.
   The building was two-storied; the ground-floor deserted; upstairs,
however, two officials were sorting the mail.
   The more melancholy came to me with a sheaf of picture post-cards
in hand, the top one showing Stevenson's grave.
   "Do you hear much of Stevenson?" I asked, pointing to the picture.
   "My name is Stevenson," he replied, peering at me.
   "I beg your pardon.. I was referring to Robert Louis Stevenson."

"I don't know the gentleman. Never did. Perhaps ... in Apia. ..." He wagged his head vaguely.

"Say, d'you know Missouri?"

I did not. Anyhow it jarred, and to avoid being drawn into a discussion of "God's own country" I withdrew.

As I strode back, bugle notes from the cruiser reverberated in the densely-wooded heights that rose so abruptly and gloriously from the beach. Daylight shimmered in the still air, expanding like the slow inevitable smile of childhood into amber dawn. ...

In San Francisco, my hotel, chosen at haphazard, stood on Kearney Street, at the corner of Portsmouth Square. In the midst of this square, known to journalists as the Old Plaza, stands a small monument – a square shaft of marble, surmounted by a green bronze barque, the *Bonaventure*, under full sail, ploughing through a curly green bronze sea. The lower part of the shaft exhibits the jet of water and appurtenances of a drinking fountain, to refresh Celestials of the adjacent China-town – should they ever fall so low as to drink with foreign devils – and the overflow of a flourishing labour agency round the corner. On the upper part are engraved the words, "To Remember Robert Louis Stevenson," and a sentence from the Christmas Sermon, beginning, "To be honest, to be kind, to earn a little and to spend a little less." The back – so I gathered from old numbers of the *Critic* – should have been adorned with a bronze pilgrim's staff and scrip, and a flageolet. However, they are not there. One especially regrets the flageolet. Here it was that he came to bask in the sun, and draw strange stories from opium-sodden wretches and derelict dock-hands.

Early one morning, about two o'clock, returning from the Press Club, I passed through the square on the way to my hotel. I have no doubt it was the effect of electric light and shadows. At any rate I thought I saw a man standing on the lawn to the south-west side of the monument. There was something about the figure that seemed strangely familiar. The great clock on the Hall of Justice struck two, and mechanically I glanced up at the illuminated dial. When I looked at the lawn again, the man had disappeared. The Plaza was quite deserted.

As I entered the hall of the hotel the night-clerk greeted me sleepily. The guest-book lay open on the office counter, and the ink was still wet upon the latest signature. It was "Stevenson."

I left the city the following afternoon. ...

In less than a week, however, I was back again. Of my quondam hotel little was to be seen except the foundations. Dynamite is very thorough. The iron skeleton of the tower of the Hall of Justice (**f20ᵛ**) leant over at right angles to its original position, China-town was a heap of smoking ruins, and the smell was indescribable. Only the gallant *Bonaventure* sailed unharmed through its curly waves, though heaped about it were trunks and sewing-machines, bird cages and gramophones, and the tents of a picket of Regulars stood upon the lawns.

Some one tapped me on the shoulder. It was the hotel clerk.

"I guess you were lucky," he said, after we had exchanged the customary congratulations on continued existence. "Your room fell in on the gentleman who was occupying it. He had only moved into it on the night."

"Indeed! Was he killed? What was his name?"

The clerk indicated a row of temporary graves to the south-west of the monument in front of us, over which a sentry stood guard, leaning on his rifle.

"He is there, the third from that end," he said. "His name was Stevenson."

"English, I suppose?"

"Why no. He came from Missouri."   Z.

2516 (**f21ᵛ**) THE WOMAN OF THE FUTURE.   X

THE trivial attention given to anthropology in this country is responsible for much misunderstanding of the "woman's movement." Romantic feminists have pieced together out of shreds of vague history and bold hypothesis a picture of a "golden age" of matriarchy, when women not only ruled the roost on the domestic hearth, but held supreme authority in public affairs, keeping the harmless necessary male for foraging and police. The future they envisage, not indeed as a complete return to this primal sway, but as a liberation from the domestic and political tyranny of man, and an equal participation in all the economic activities which men have hitherto appropriated. Not less romantic in origin are the alarms of those who, posing as defenders of the family, have dramatised the revolt of women as a strike against motherhood and home life, substituting for the ideal of chivalrous protection in life-long union, free competition in every walk of life qualified by temporary partnerships, upon agreed conditions of equal liberty. This necessarily involves a decay of all the delicate adjustments of relations between father, mother, and child, which form the strongest pillars of our social order.

Study of the natural history of man, fragmentary and uncertain though it be, serves to dispel these extravagances of hope or apprehension. Closer research into primitive society, past or present, lends little support to the notion of a general supremacy of woman. As women by physique, disposition, and maternal occupation, were more stationary, they and the "home" they made were the earliest centres in savage society. To this shelter and companionship the "motor male" would return from his roving in the chase or fight. The women and the children of a clan, living and working together with some fixity of place, would represent the beginnings of local society; they would build the huts, collect some little store of food, practise the crudest forms of agriculture, invent and make some rough utensils out of plaited twigs or earth. Thus the earliest sorts of useful property, except the weapons, nets, and other snares for fighting and hunting, were made by the women, carried about by them, and belonged to them.

Children in such an order were owned by the mother, and reckoned their descent from her alone, for, as has been said, "maternity is a matter of observation, paternity of inference," and in any case male occupations were not consistent with any regular care for the family. The superior settlement and comparative self-sufficiency of the women in some savage tribes undoubtedly gave them a strong position in dealing with their men folk; their individual inferiority of physical force was compensated by solidarity in forming habits and supporting them by public opinion, in which they were clever enough to utilise those psychic factors of taboo and other "magic" which play so conspicuous a part in savage society.

So it seems to have come about that the earliest necessary differentiation of sex activities tended to give women a *rôle* of economic, and even in some instances political supremacy. As the more arduous, adventurous, but irregular strains fell upon the men, the women figured as pioneers in the industrial arts and in peaceful group polity. The biological interpretation of these sex relations is skilfully expounded in a learned little volume just published by an American sociologist, Professor W. J. Thomas ("Sex and Society," London: T. Fisher Unwin). Though a genuine matriarchy is by no means to be inferred from the wide prevalence of the maternal system of descent in most primitive societies, Professor Thomas finds reason to believe that in not a few tribes of America, Africa, and the Pacific, the earliest condition of women, though not one of ease, was one of greater practical liberty, so far (**f21ʳ**) as male control was concerned, than that which supervened with advancing civilisation. But even in such cases, as Mr. L. T. Hobhouse has pointed out in an interesting chapter in his "Morals in Evolution," the formal equality or even authority with which women seemed to have been invested, probably did not carry in most instances an equivalent amount of real control, and in all great emergencies, the more energetic and resourceful males would assume absolute control. Moreover, there are many instances, especially in the tribes of Australia, in which women seem from the earliest times to have been a slave class, treated by their male owners with inveterate brutality.

If, however, we hold with Professor Thomas that the condition found in many tribes on the American Continent is more truly typical of the primitive sex relations, we can follow him along a fairly logical series of steps in his further analysis. The beginnings of agriculture and manufacture, due to the contrivances and industry of women round the home, developed the institution and the sense of property, and with this the dominance of man and the corresponding subjection of woman began. Now that food and other needs could be got by other ways than killing and plunder, men turned their attention to industry, and, while still leaving to the women most of the routine drudgery, applied what biology terms their "katabolic" character to industrial invention, improving the efficiency of agriculture and primitive manufactures, even taking over to themselves the arts of sewing, spinning, and weaving, because of their superior craving for adornment.

So it would appear that the three typical modern sex relations, with their correspondent "women's spheres," gradually emerged from the obscurity of early barbarism. The man asserted his supremacy in the home, wife and children became his property, for use or for ornament, as he deemed fit, an autocracy usually tempered by custom, sometimes limited by law, but commonly absolute in the general control of life. The superior male energy and initiative led to a redistribution of economic functions, by which the women were intellectually the losers, for almost all the industrial arts involving risk, skill, and interest, passed into male hands, while the drudgery of imitation and routine alone was left to women.

Modern movements have largely reference to the domestic and economic bondage thus fastened on woman partly by the superior force, partly by the cultivated aptitudes of man. But there is a third note in the demand for independence, which is most significant. It is often observed that the women who are keenest in asserting their rights have the least to complain of, as a class, so far as lack of domestic liberty and imposition of economic drudgery are concerned. A subtler injury, however, is imposed on woman than a life of toil, namely, a life of decorative idleness, supported and elaborated for the display of male power and wealth. In ancient societies profusion of domestic luxury was only possible for a few chiefs and nobles, whose type was the palace of the Oriental despot, with its harem of expensive beauties. Western mediaeval chivalry, with its romantic feint of elevating woman, was in essence a fantastic embroidery of this decorative use. Thus idleness, varied with futile frivolity, became the badge of woman's gentility. When the modern spread of wealth enabled larger numbers of new men to vie with the older aristocracy in a decorative kind of life, more women were drawn into the circle, and the merchant, the manufacturer, the professional class, imposed upon their women the same leisured round of showy ritual humorously called "social duties." It is often supposed that women prefer this life, but even if it be so, this very preference is imposed upon them in those standards and ideals of sex conduct and character which men have made and impressed through customs, laws, and literature. Those who disparage the intellectual character and achievements of the women of the educated classes should remember that the primary function, the decorative one, imposed upon them to satisfy the pride of man, has of necessity impaired the character of their intellectual life.

Professor Thomas throws interesting light upon the psychology of woman, as effected in the later stages of history by the necessity of accommodating her behaviour and her feelings to the structure of society determined by the economic and political needs and activities of man. This opens the door to a wider comprehension of some (**f22**[r]) aspects of the emancipation of woman. Just as the practical subordination of the manual workers is a source of social instability in the national economy, while the condition of the "subject races" is similarly a source of weakness and of retardation of the civilisation of the world, so it becomes manifest that the dependent character and position of women injure the growth of every social structure by disturbing the just balance of human forces in the development of social forms. Amid much extravagance and misdirection, due in large measure to an unsuccessful endeavour to "rationalise" what is essentially an instinctive movement of reform, "feminism" moves along sane lines of progress.

Biological considerations lend no support to the fear lest growing liberty and equality of opportunity should "unsex" women, and the "womanly woman" tend to disappear. Indeed, it would appear that, on the contrary, sex differences are more likely to be emphasised. For whereas under existing conditions marriage and maternity are forced upon most women as the only chance of a decent livelihood, under a régime of fuller liberty and opportunity only those women who have some vocation for matrimony will become wives and mothers. Similarly men who are less attractive than their fellows to women, will be less likely to marry and to hand down their nature to posterity, when women have an option to the career of wifehood. In other words, selection will operate more freely and with greater accuracy and stringency when women have more liberty, with the effect of securing the survival of more "womanly women" and more "manly men," thus making rather for the wider divergence of sex types than for confusion. Such at any rate would seem to be the logic of the movement.

2517   (**f22ᵛ**) THE NATION. April 13, 1907.

Neither the literary nor the respectful illiterate could believe their senses when "G. B. S." first asserted that Ibsen was a better dramatist than Shakespeare, and that to give himself his due the same must be said of Shaw. He would have been less misunderstood had he added that Mr. Arthur Jones, if not superior to the Bard, was probably his equal; though this further admission would have detracted from the piquancy of the original statement. In a sense we are all superior to Shakespeare. This simple truth so near to the eye that it escapes all except philosophers, is one of the legs, and, perhaps, the soundest, on which the polemics of "G. B. S." stand. The other leg is the fact that Shakespeare wrote from no coherent view of the world, and that the famous speeches, when paraphrased, turn into such arrant and enervating commonplaces as an energetic thinker crosses in his first stride, viz.:– "To be or not to be," or "Out, out, brief candle," &c., &c. Mr. Shaw insists that Shakespeare had nothing to say, while Ibsen and he have new and true criticisms of life to offer; his conclusion is that it is only the music of the language which makes us think such ruminations as Hamlet's profound: "in a deaf nation these plays would have died long ago." "Even the individualisation which produces that old established British speciality the Shakespearian 'delineation of character,' owes all its magic to the turn of the line, which lets you into the secret of its utterer's mood and temperament, not by its commonplace meaning, but by some subtle exaltation or stultification or slyness or delicacy or hesitancy or what not in the sound of it." Admirable criticism – completely destructive of the critic's case! Certainly it is the quality of Shakespeare's writing that his words do sweetly creep into the study of our imaginations, and are:–

> "More moving, delicate, and full of life
> Unto the eye and prospect of the soul
> Than when he lived indeed."

But it is not through sound alone that they do so. The significance is conveyed through the meanings and associations the words have for the imagination. So it would be truer to say, "In a deaf nation incapable of anything but literal interpretation" – in a nation, say, of octogenerian Duke of Wellingtons, to endow them otherwise with superior qualities – "these plays would have perished long ago."

The fallacy of taking "meaning" in a work of art to be something which can always be expressed in other terms, and of judging by that standard, crops up frequently in these criticisms. In one essay he says that the squalling of a cat on the roof means the same thing as the song of a nightingale, which is therefore really as insignificant. But they do *not* mean the same thing to the imagination, and unless a critic is prepared, in attacking romanticism, to rule out the imagination altogether, he must admit the significance of such a speech as Claudio's when the thought of death is before him, or, Macbeth's when he hears of the death of his wife, even though, when paraphrased, they may convey the merest commonplaces. So, of course, are all utterances on such themes. The facts of death, the brevity of life, the confusion of the world, are too familiar to be impressive in themselves; they only become so through the way in which they are felt. The attack on the Bard, then, in so far as it consisted in the objection that he produced his effects by a kind of hanky-panky inspiration instead of by clear statement of impressive facts or in the contention that his reflections were obvious, does not damage him much; but there is another charge to follow, the charge that Shakespeare felt these matters in no exalted spirit.

He remarks that there is not one "hero" in all Shakespeare, which is true enough in Mr. Shaw's sense of the word; for by "hero" he means a reformer. His criticisms are the criticisms of a reformer, and his own plays are the plays of a reformer. There are no villains in his plays; there are plenty of objectionable characters, but Society is the villain.

At the bottom of Mr. Shaw's philosophy there lies a Rousseauish belief that social conditions are always to blame for what is wrong in the individual. The emotions and qualities which are represented in a favourable light are those which are useful as reforming agencies; those which are not justifiable as the best means to changing society, such as love between individuals or pity or reverence, are criticised after the manner of La Rochefoucauld; that is to say, they are identified with their tainted forms. Such a spectacle is a salutary one for the public; we are apt to put too flattering interpretations on our emotions; but the picture of life thus presented is, on the whole, out of focus, because men and women are judged in his plays too exclusively from the point of view of their social usefulness. He is a puritan in art because he asks the |question "What is *the use* of beauty?" And in judging character and | emotion he asks too incessantly the same question. There is so much to be done in the world which everybody is inclined to shirk that the test is worth applying again and again. But the fact that beauties, virtues, and nameless human qualities can be good in themselves apart from their usefulness is so constantly ignored in Mr. Shaw's philosophy that his representation of life gets out of focus. Courage, efficiency, honesty, public spirit, these are the qualities he believes in. There lie the hard limits of his moral world. If you ask something from experience beyond these things, "G. B. S." will mark you as an enervating romantic. If he condescended to ask you *what* you wanted, a compendious answer would be – some of those qualities in human nature whose portraiture grew under Shakespeare's magic hand.

2518   (**f23ʳ**) A BOOK OF THE DAY. D. News. July 15. '07
THE RUSSIAN POETS.
"Poetry and Progress in Russia." By Rosa Newmarch. John Lane.
1907.

Mrs. Newmarch's interesting and agreeable volume brings home to us that we English possess no adequate translations of the great Russian poets, Poushkin and Lermontov. Poushkin's form is said by Russians, and we speak only at second-hand, to be almost perfection, and obviously he requires a translator of genius, who is also a poet, to render him. Russia appears to be remarkably rich in good translations of our great poets, and one of the reasons why Byron has preserved his reputation better abroad than at home is that many of the Continental translators have, in fact, improved on his language. Meanwhile we must be thankful for any waifs and strays in the way of verse translations from the Russian that are offered us, and "the small sheaf of acceptable English versions" that Mrs. Newmarch has gleaned, will certainly help Englishmen to "fill up some of the gaps in our scanty knowledge of Russian psychology."

Mrs. Newmarch divides her book into five sections. I. The Precursors of Poushkin. II. Poushkin and Lermontov. III. The Popular Poets. IV. Khaniakov. V. Nadson. The two last are of the least importance, though in her remarks on Khaniakov Mrs. Newmarch has given a clear and interesting account of the creed of the Slavophile Party which distrusted Russia's imitation of European institutions, and held that all social reforms should come from within, and be modelled on traditional lines. In Section II. the reader will find a very good sketch of Poushkin's life and national significance, and an adequate analysis of the Romantic movement which preceded "the great school of realistic fiction, which forms, as it were, a middle period in the national literature." At the same time we are inclined to think that in upholding the banner of the Romantics Mrs. Newmarch has identified her critical sympathies too much with the disciples of "art for art's sake," and while combating "the utilitarian tendency which for so many years hung like a blighting cloud above the horizon of Russian literature," has mistaken effects for causes. The criticism of a Pissariev, "unsound by reason of his boundless self-sufficiency and disregard of all aesthetic interests which could not be made to serve party purposes," is, no doubt, very irritating to our English writers, but admitting that his denial of Poushkin's claim to be considered a great poet is representative of "an intolerant utilitarianism have proved inimical to the development of the arts in Russia."

The National Genius.

For Dobrolioubov and Pissariev, though ultra-democratic propagandists, were children of that great national movement of self-examination and self-realisation which *is* Russian Literature from Gogol to Tchekhov. At the very time when the Russian critics, writing as party politicians on one side or the other, were most biassed in their aesthetic doctrines, we find that the chief glories of Russian literature were being produced. The Russian criticisms of that matchless artist, Turgenev, were, for the most part, extraordinarily unseeing, just as the "Edinburgh" and "Quarterly Review" attacks on Keats and Shelley were extraordinarily dense.

What Mrs. Newmarch does not seem to grasp is that when the great Russian movement in Russia from 1840–1880, of self-examination and self-realisation was at the flood the artificial romanticism, fashionable in the thirties, died a natural death. It was replaced by a much greater, deeper, and stronger movement, in which the Russian realistic genius came to its finest flower, producing the great Russian novel which beats out of the field anything that the rest of Europe could produce. Poets there were, of course, but the really significant men were those who profoundly affected their countrymen by voicing their discontent with the state of Russia, men whose song helped to swell the unrest and agitation of the time. From this point of view the remark with which Mrs. Newmarch closes her account of the great popular poet Nekrassov, seems to us very bad criticism:

> Looking back to the circumstances of his career, we understand and pardon the unquenchable fires of indignation which consumed the tenderness of his nature. But seeing the widespread influence of his poetry, it is impossible to disregard his potency as a teacher; and we cannot but confess that in that capacity it is a message of bitterness and revolt rather than of hope and self-control which his work hands on to successive generations of Young Russia.

No pardon is needed. The poet of bitterness and revolt was the spokesman of that great political movement which sent, inevitably and rightly, the flower of the Russian youth of three generations to prison, to death, and to exile. And those excellent people who, in their peaceful and comfortable English homes, preach the gospel of "hope and self-control" to the men who lived and died for the principles which mean Liberty for Russia may be compared to calm spectators on a river bank who advise men struggling in the water to keep quiet and not to lose their heads!

Mrs. Newmarch as Translator.

Putting aside, however, the polemics of criticism, let us congratulate Mrs. Newmarch on some of her translations. One of the most beautiful of Nekrassov's poems is entitled "The Soldier's Mother," which describes in the most touchingly quiet way how a soldier lad, after eight long years, comes home to his mother, the mere wreck of himself, and dies on the tenth day of his return. This is absolutely Russian in its profound and mournful resignation. Another excellent translation, perhaps the best in the book, is from Nikitin, whose unhappy life is typical of the fate of Russian poets generally who almost, without exception, died young:

THE GAFFER

Old Gaffer, with white beard and smooth, bald head,
    Sits in his chair.
His little mug of water, and his bread,
    Stand near him there.

Grey as a badger he: his brow is lined;
    His features worn.
He's left a world of cark and care behind
    Since he was born.

'Tis over now, his eyesight soon must go;
    His strength is done.
Death laid within the churchyard long ago
    Grandchild and son.

A cat the smoke-grimed hut with Gaffer shares.
    Upon the stove.
All day he sleeps. He, too, is old, nor cares
    From thence to move.

The old man still plaits shoes, with fingers slow,
    From bark of birch;
His wants are few, his greatest joy to go
    Into God's church.

He stands within the porch, against the wall,
    Mutt'ring his prayers.
A loyal child, he thanks the Lord for all
    Life's griefs and cares.

Cheery he lives – with one foot in the grave –
    In his dark hole.
Whence does he draw the strength that keeps him brave,
    Poor peasant soul?

If Mrs. Newmarch had confined herself to renderings of the poets, as happily inspired as the above, we venture to say she would have done far more for the popular Russian poets than her valuations of their teaching can do. Roughly speaking, there are two main schools of literary criticism; the first, which measures a writer by a standard of ideal perfection; the second, which holds that his value for us is inseparable from what he represents. Poets are children of their age, the spirit of its life lives in them, and the spiritual standard that our English author holds up before the Russians, "to see life steadily and see it whole," means, in fact, the annihilation of their spirit. Neither Burns, nor Shelley, nor Byron, nor Swinburne, nor Rossetti (to name but a few of our poets) saw life steadily or saw it whole. To assert that "had Nekrassov himself possessed a more robust faith in his new ideal, 'the people,' and a greater share of the uplifting spirit of hope, he might have been, indeed, the saviour of his generation and those to come," is to put the cart before the horse. Literature is the product of life, and the march of events can only be affected by literature in a minor degree. If Dostoievsky, a greater man, whose spirit and work are enshrined deep in every Russian heart, could not be the "saviour of his generation," why should it be brought against Nekrassov that he had not a faith that circumstances did not justify? The watchword of the great Russian writers – their *value* was, and is, "remorseless truth to their own sensations." Too often he relapses from this ideal view of the people, and shows them up with merciless realism," says our author. No, not too often. Merciless realism is what Russia needed from her literature and needs. The old ulcers in the national life were probed by these writers. That is why Romanticism soon lost all meaning for a Russia bleeding yesterday, as to-day, from deep intestine wounds.

2519   (**f24ʳ**) "THE INTELLECTUAL FALLACY." (London) Tribune 1907 "The Essentials of Æsthetics in Music, Poetry, Painting, Sculpture, and Architecture." By G. L. Raymond. Murray. 10s. net.

Why is it that books upon æsthetics never satisfy? Here is a book by the Professor of Æsthetics in the George Washington University, a writer who has given his life to the subject, and in this case makes a most honest and laborious attempt "to determine for the reader, if possible, the qualities causing excellence in the higher arts, and to increase his appreciation of them." The book is intended for the general reader, and it is free, or almost free, from metaphysical jargon. Dr. Raymond never theorizes at large. His method is scientific, and he constantly appeals to facts to support the principles which he lays down. And yet, when he comes to define beauty, after a great deal of hard thinking on the subject, he produces this definition: "Beauty is a characteristic of any complex form of varied elements producing apprehensible unity – that is, harmony or likeness – of effects upon the motive organs of sensation in the ear or eye, or upon the emotive sources of imagination in the mind; or upon both the one and the other." Now this definition is no worse than most others; but I do not see how it would help anyone to tell whether anything was beautiful or not; or what use it could ever be except as a theme for argument. The fact is, beauty cannot be defined, and it is worth while to ask ourselves why, as the answer will help us to understand why æsthetic theorizing is usually so futile.

BEAUTY AND REASON.

A definition of beauty is an attempt to understand beauty by means of the intellect alone. But since our experience of beautiful things is not purely intellectual, we cannot express that experience in purely intellectual terms. No amount of hard thinking will enable a man to know a good picture from a bad one, any more than it will enable a man to become a good painter. Hard thinking, of course, is necessary for both the understanding, and the consummate practise of the arts. But a work of art is produced, like an action, by the whole of a man's faculties, and not by his intellect alone. And so we can understand it only by the use of all our faculties. But it is only by an understanding of particular works of art that we can come to know and feel what art is, and when we have reached that knowledge and feeling, we can no more express it in terms of pure reason than we can express the context of one of Beethoven's Symphonies in terms of pure reason. This, I know, implies that all æsthetics expressed in terms of pure reason are futile. But surely experience shows that they are. You have only to read the first part of Tolstoy's "What is Art," in which he knocks over all the theories like ninepins, and still more the second part, in which he builds up a theory of his own just as easily destructible, to be convinced that no existing theories cover the facts.

This does not mean that æsthetic principles cannot be discovered or expressed, but only that they cannot be discovered by the intellect alone or expressed in terms of the intellect alone. When a critic is powerfully moved by the beauty of art, and when emotion and intellect work together in his expression of what art means to him, then alone can he tell the truth about it, then alone is it possible for him to attain to any understanding of the nature of beauty. Beauty eludes the pursuit of reason alone, because reason by itself cannot recognize beauty, and its power of abstraction and definition is useless where it is ignorant of the quality to be abstracted and defined.

Now the error of most writers on æsthetics, and, I fear, the error of Dr. Raymond, is that they pursue beauty through the world with the reason alone, as if it were some scientific principle that could be discovered by mere careful observation. Experiment, of course, in the production of beauty is usually denied to them; but, through a misunderstanding of the nature of the problem, they are also too apt to deny themselves the experiments of emotional experience. When they look at a work of art their intellects are so active that they suppress their emotions. They begin to theorize before they have learnt to enjoy; and the result is that they often waste their theorizing upon works so inferior that they can only mislead the mind that bases any theory upon them. In fact, to put it plainly, the writer on æsthetics usually begins to talk about art before he knows good work from bad; and he falls into this error because he thinks he can tell good work from bad by means of the reason alone. There are passages in Dr. Raymond's book which raise the suspicion that he does not know good work from bad; and I will quote one of them. He tells us that there is still a controversy between the advocates of what is called the classic, or academic, line, and the romantic, picturesque, or naturalistic line. "The former," he adds, "is a firm, clear line such as appears in the paintings of Gérôme, Bougereau, and Cabanel. The other is a misty indistinct line, such as appears in some of the works of Corot, Sargent, and Israels." Now, Bougereau's line is condemned, not because it is firm and clear, but because it expresses nothing. In fact, he, Gérôme, and Cabanel are all artists too insignificant to be brought forward as examples of any principle, since no principle can really be found in work like theirs, which, however skilful, is essentially imitative and aimless. But Professor Raymond is also in error when he says that there is any controversy about the merits of the two kinds of line. No one now says that one is absolutely better than another. Painting is an art of expression, and Michael Angelo expresses one thing with a clear outline, while Titian expresses another with an outline less clear.

ARTS OF EXPRESSION.

Dr. Raymond never seems to grasp the fact that both painting and poetry are arts of expression, and that all their peculiar characteristics are means of expression. "In mere jingle," he says, "the principles of rhythm and harmony can be fulfilled almost as perfectly as in the most inspired and sublime composition." So it might seem to anyone with a purely intellectual experience of poetry. But poetry is a means of expressing emotion as well as reason, and rhythm and harmony are not mere ornaments to it, but instruments that give it a power of expressing emotion beyond the power of prose. Therefore, the principles of rhythm and harmony cannot be fulfilled in a jingle which expresses nothing, since the only purpose of rhythm and harmony is expression. We know, by experience, that rhythm and harmony are only excellent in poetry that expresses strong emotion. In Poe's "Ulalume" there is some beauty of rhythm and harmony, because there is some vague emotion; but the rhythm is monotonous and the harmony thin, because the emotion is not closely enough connected with the sense to produce the continued delicate variations of rhythm, and the richness and complexity of sound that we find in poetry where the sense controls the harmony and rhythm. I give these particular instances of error because they seem to me to prove that Dr. Raymond's æsthetic experience is imperfect. And it is probably the imperfection of his experience that has misled him into a hopeless task. It is dull work picking holes in a book so full of labour and thought, and I can only wish that they had both been better applied. A. CLUTTON-BROCK.

2520 (**f25ʳ**) THE NEEDS OF OXFORD UNIVERSITY. Times. May 6.07
TO THE EDITOR OF THE TIMES.

Sir, – An appeal this day appears in *The Times*, signed by the new Chancellor and by the Vice-Chancellor, who say that it is their duty to issue an appeal for the assistance of which Oxford stands so much in need. They proceed to recommend a scheme, inaugurated by the Hon. T. A. Brassey, which involves the expenditure of £250,000 to be raised by subscription. They urge that this scheme was approved by the late Chancellor, Lord Goschen, and by the heads of colleges "with scarcely an exception." As I am that exception, I should like to say why I did not sign the scheme, and why I still disapprove of this appeal being made to the public *in forma pauperis*.

1. A scheme signed by these distinguished persons could hardly fail to have the appearance of the authority of the University, without the reality. It could receive that authority only by passing the Council, Congregation, and Convocation of the University, which receives benefactions only by deciding whether a proposed benefaction should be received for a proposed purpose. Nevertheless, if signed by the

Chancellor, the Vice-Chancellor, and the heads of colleges, it would be liable to be mistaken for an authoritative document. Seeing this danger, I refused to sign the scheme when delivered to me. My fears have been justified; for the scheme has lately been published by the *Daily Mail* as that of "Oxford University" and the "University authorities." Similarly, writing "as Chancellor and Vice-Chancellor of Oxford University," the authors of the appeal appear as if they were speaking with full authority; and you, Sir, give some colour to this appearance in saying that "this appeal is now made on behalf of Oxford by the Chancellor and Vice-Chancellor of the University."

2. The scheme contemplates a general fund for subscriptions, and a body of trustees, of whom two-thirds are to be non-residents; and this part of the scheme is also adopted in the appeal. I felt and feel that this proposal involves an external pressure which threatens the independence of the University. It would enable the Vice-Chancellor, or any other powerful member of the body, to come forward all at once with so large a sum for a number of objects as to tempt Convocation into accepting all the money without approving all the objects. In the present case, Mr. Brassey appears to have started with an intention of making a benefaction for scientific engineering. Why then has not that benefaction been brought before Convocation and discussed on its own merits?

3. Neither the scheme nor the appeal contemplates such an inquiry into the economy of the University as would alone justify an appeal *in forma pauperis*. There are two ways of being poor; one by having no money, and the other by wasting it. In the complex system of modern Oxford there is considerable waste. Through the attempt of Commissions to rear up a professorial by the side of a tutorial system, professors and tutors are largely doing the same work; so are readers. Piecemeal legislation in Oxford has added professor after professor, building after building, grant after grant, examination after examination, without much attempt at co-ordination and system. Learning and teaching have been cut in twain. There are some professors without pupils. Income is sometimes lost in teaching and examining people outside the University. But, even so, the University as a whole can hardly be called poor, consisting as it does of the colleges as well as of the abstract University. The accounts of the colleges of the (**f24ᵛ**) University show, after deducting external expenses, an income for 1905 of more than £350,000. The abstract University for the same year has £70,000. This total sum of £420,000 gives for each of 3,500

undergraduates (apart from his keep) £120 a year. It shows a somewhat splendid poverty. Moreover, things have been improving. The college accounts of 1902 and 1905 compared show an advance in income of £15,000. This year again the abstract University has a balance of £4,000, which at all events shows some improvement. Finally, benefactors come forward in the ordinary statutable way; such as Charles Oldham and Dr. Schorstein. In these circumstances, until real poverty pinches and spontaneous charity ceases, it would be undignified for the University to allow itself to be dragged forward as a beggar.

4. The scheme begs the question of needs, which it divides as follows:– Bodleian Library, £50,000; science, £100,000; additional buildings, £50,000; modern languages, £30,000; history, &c., £20,000 – total capital required, £250,000. No doubt, some of these so-called needs are real requirements, which may perhaps be met by internal economy and spontaneous donations. But some seem little more than demands; for example, under science, scientific engineering. In 1904 the University established a postgraduate diploma in this subject under a committee, which in its report of February 27, 1906, said that "the examination announced for June, 1905, was not held, as no candidates offered themselves"; nor since that time has there been any report of candidates or diplomas in scientific engineering. Another so-called need is more like a greed. Under the head of additional buildings, the scheme proposes to seize the building erected in 1830 for the University Printing Press out of its own profits on a convenient site of 5½ acres, and to hand it over to scientific engineering, &c. It recommends this proposal to remove the Press on the ground that the building is "unsuitable for a modern printing establishment," and it talks of "erecting a modern one-storeyed building on a new site ... at £40,000"; but without acknowledging either that a one-storeyed building can be erected on the existing site at a much less cost, or that no "new site" has been found, or is likely to be found, to compare with the old site of the Press. Curiously enough, the appeal, while mentioning other parts of the scheme, omits this audacious proposal to turn one of our most beneficial institutions out of doors. Nevertheless, the proposal remains an integral part of the scheme, for which signatures and subscriptions have been solicited. Is it to be supposed that it would have had any chance, if it had been put, as it ought to have been put, before the University?

5. The whole question, whether the University of Oxford should

condescend to appear before the world *in forma pauperis*, is a question for the University of Oxford. The scheme, therefore, inaugurated by Mr. Brassey, ought not to have been handed about marked "strictly confidential" for six months, so as gradually to ooze out, and finally to acknowledge itself in an appeal of the Chancellor and Vice-Chancellor with an appearance of authority. The Masters of Arts in Convocation, who alone could give the requisite authority, should long ago have had before them "the needs of Oxford University," and decided these questions:–

(1) How far are the so-called needs requirements?

(2) How far can the University provide for its own requirements?

(3) Is the Chancellor or his deputy to be charged with authority (1) to beg for money; (2) to assist in the formation of an external body of subscribers?

(**f25ʳ**) The appeal states that on the 16th a public meeting is to be held on "the needs of Oxford University," at which the Chancellor is to preside and the Vice-Chancellor to be present. It is significant that the meeting is to be held in London, not in Oxford, where there has been no public meeting. The meeting in London will be an informal gathering without the authority of the University of Oxford; and therefore it is to be hoped that nobody will take upon himself to say that the University is asking for money.

I am, Sir, yours faithfully,
C. C. C., Oxford, May 2.   THOMAS CASE.

2521   Jean-Jacques Rousseau. by Jules Lemaître (Times Lit Sup! 26.4.07)

Perhaps, indeed, the greatest achievement of Jean-Jacques is that he inaugurated a new state of mind. We are too apt to forget that our feelings no less than our sciences are conquests and acquirements. Some great individual enlarges the hereditary domain, and thenceforward a novel region is within the reach of all. A great man no less than a great landscape is an *état d'âme*. Rousseau invented "une nouvelle façon de sentir et comme une vibration jusque-là inconnue." He projected upon life the rays of a mind which lit up hitherto invisible summits and abysses, and impressed upon the outer world the fresh form of an original understanding. He saw things, not as they appeared to his contemporaries, nor as they had appeared to his ancestors, but in accordance with some inner image, still fragmentary, slowly formed, of which he elaborated the conception, and then imprinted it on society.

He furnished a new sentimental medium, he discovered a new ideal. And that, in our eyes, is his principal title to remembrance. He was not merely a man of letters, a novelist, a philosopher, a botanist, a musical composer, a social reformer, an apostle, and, if you will, a prophet: he brought into our ken a new sphere of our sensibility – Rousseau was an initiator.

All round the small part of our activities, which so far we have cultivated and colonized, there stretches a wide field of resources which most men never bring into any use at all. Or, to vary our metaphor, most of us are in the position of persons possessing in the bank several deposit accounts to only one of which they have obtained a cheque-book. And the excitement of some new idea, the enthusiasm created by some great individual, suddenly puts us in possession of new resources, admits us to our own, gives us access, in fact, to our hidden treasure. A new ideal is a great dynamogenic agent, unlocking innumerable energies which might have never come into play. Rousseau gave us the cheque-book to an account which we possessed already but did not utilize. For the human individual usually lives far within his limits, and fails to use a great part of the means at his disposal. With a few very simple words (such as Nature, Virtue, Equality), with a few very simple ideas, partly false (such as "Nature is good," "Be just and you will be happy," "The root of all evil is inequality"), thanks to the intense conviction with which he animated these words and ideas – making them radiant, illuminating, prophetic – Rousseau produced in the minds of his hearers a contagious optimism which brought forth great results, for good and evil. In the words of M. Lemaître, who scarcely appears to have realized the full importance of his wise remark, "il fournit à la Révolution un *état sentimental.*"

2522   (**f25ᵛ**) *Woman: her Position and Influence in Ancient Greece and Rome, and among the Early Christians.* By James Donaldson, LL. D. (Longmans & Co.)

PRINCIPAL DONALDSON has taken an engrossing subject, on which many books might be written. His present volume is, for the most part, a lucid and excellently written summary of the salient facts which may be gathered from the scattered and often conflicting testimonies available to us. He has allowed himself only 250 pages of text, but his book suggests at every step both the occasion and the best material for further study. He has a wide knowledge of the German writers who have done the "spade-work" of the subject, but he has also an advantage they generally lack – a clear and attractive style.

The ancient world did not say much about its women: Pericles in a well-known passage regarded as ideal the woman of whom least was heard for good or bad; and we do not know for certain whether Athenian women were allowed to be present at theatrical performances or not. The evidence for any single point depends, in fact, on such nice deductions from particular passages that it cannot be made interesting to readers who are not classical experts. We prefer to deal with two or three points among the many which make this book of interest. It constitutes a survey of that increasing power which, though somewhat retarded by the coming of Christianity, has, with various ups and downs, culminated in the creed of feminism.

It was not only "the passionate love of beauty which animated the Greeks" of immortal Attica in their love of women. Generally their tragedians regarded love as a disease or a madness, but a remarkable fragment of Sophocles has been preserved (Dindorf, 678, D.) which proclaims that

> "the Goddess of Love is not Love alone, but has many names: she is hell, and she is immortal life; she is unfulfilled desire and lament; in her is all of earnestness and quietness that leads to strength. ..."

A passage like this is sufficiently rare in Greek drama, but more effective as an ancient tribute to love than the unrobing of Phryne before her judges. Here is, it seems to us, an effective answer to the contention of Benecke ('Women in Greek Poetry') that Euripides and Menander were the pioneers in literature of what we now understand by the word "love." Sophocles gives us the intensity of modern passion, if not its romantic side.

Gentleness is the chief characteristic which Dr. Donaldson finds in his survey of Homeric women, and we think he is right in his contention. We wonder that he was able to resist quoting the speech of Andromache to Hector ('Iliad,' vi. 429). She finds in him father, lady mother, and brother as well as a goodly husband, and her description was to remain unparalleled in its completeness for a long period of the world. Indeed, we know of nothing in Greece or Rome equal to it until we come to Propertius, who may be regarded as the first of the decadents to analyze love in the modern style. He says of his lady:–

> Tu mihi sola domus, tu Cynthia, sola parentes,
> Omnia tu nostræ tempora lætitiæ.

He believed this perhaps for two whole days together, but Andromache, a simpler soul, strikes one as genuine and constant, at any rate while Hector lived. When the husband was dead, he was forgotten, as Homer says. Dr. Donaldson refers, of course, to the lines in the 'Odyssey' (vi. 182) about the union of a man and wife of one mind as the best thing to be had. The comment which ends the passage is

πόλλ᾽ ἄλγεα δυσμενέεσσι,
χάρματα δ᾽ εὐμενέτῃσι· μάλιστα δέ τ᾽ ἔκλυον
αὐτοί.

This epigrammatic "They hear most about it themselves" implies that connubial infelicity was a subject of gossip even in Homeric times. We are a little surprised that Dr. Donaldson regards Gladstone's views of Homer with respect, and we think he is certainly right in rejecting that statesman's ideas as to the bathing of men which are due to a false standard of modern prudishness. They would have been modified if Gladstone had known the new science of anthropology. Conventions differ, though nature remains much the same, and can be regarded by Euripides as "a great nuisance," by Coleridge as "the devil," and by Mr Snawley as a "holy thing."

Dr. Donaldson devotes some attention to the question of Sappho's good or bad repute, but it is not one which can be decided on the evidence of Germans, however ingenious. The simple fact is that we have not enough ancient evidence to deliver a verdict. Similar doubts may be felt about details in the position of the hetæræ, of whom we have here an attractive account. It is interesting to notice that Numa, if legend is to be believed, had his Aspasia as well as Pericles.

Disregarding, of course, the futile idea that Euripides was a woman-hater, Dr. Donaldson does not consider the evidence of his plays in detail. A significant line in the 'Hippolytus' (970) has been strangely omitted by some editors as pointless. Theseus, after indicating that young men are no steadier than women when love puts them off their balance, adds:–

τὸ δ᾽ ἄρσεν αὐτοὺς ὠφελεῖ προσκείμενον·

This means, we presume, that, if men give way, less disgrace attaches to them than to women similarly placed. Euripides brings out the very point of unfairness on which Mr. Hardy's 'Tess' is a bitter commentary.

Our author combats with some success the view that in the later days of Rome, when Christianity appeared, "morals were particularly low, society was in an utterly corrupt condition, and licentiousness (**f26ʳ**) universally prevailed." We have before questioned the genuineness of Juvenal as a satirist, and have little doubt that he exaggerated things. There is always to be considered the point that the virtuous have no history, whereas the bad make their mark on their time. Dr. Donaldson adds that frequent remarriage, as in the case of Caesar, Anthony, Sulla, and Pompey, is not a crime. He produces a Scotch Moderator who died in 1706, having married a seventh wife after threescore; and he notes that

> "the authentic case of the largest number of husbands is that of the woman of Samaria, who had five husbands, and was living with one who was not her husband. But her case may have been quite peculiar; and, strangely enough, it is to this notorious woman to whom the grandest revelation of universal worship ever made to mortal was vouchsafed."

He has not, however, dealt with the bad case of Catullus. There is no question of literary fiction here. Catullus was furiously in earnest. He actually likened his tainted mistress to Laodamia, and dwelt on the exceptional services rendered by the man and wife who lent him their house to prosecute his intrigue with a woman of high rank, and cover with dishonour, as Munro says, "one of the noblest and most virtuous patricians of the time."

It is especially when he comes to the position and influence of women in early Christianity that Dr. Donaldson shows admirable candour and fairness. Writing with many years' study of the Fathers behind him, he is in no way blind to the virtues of paganism. He discovers and analyzes with acuteness the "inordinate estimate of the virtue of celibacy" which became an unfortunate tradition of the early Christian Church. To St. Paul the practical ideas of the Church were chiefly due, and it is suggested that his somewhat harsh attitude towards women may have been encouraged by the fact that the women of Tarsus, his native city, were "particularly prim and modest," covering themselves, indeed, with a completeness worthy of Oriental ideals. The ascetic doctrines of the early Fathers led to the remarkable result that "there is a striking absence of home life in the history of Christians. No son succeeds the father, no wife comforts the wearied student, no daughter soothes the sorrow of the aged bishop."

Of all this we have ample contemporary evidence much more satisfactory than the notices of writers of varying periods which hint at the life of Greece and earlier Rome. Consequently this part of the book is the fullest and the most "documented," but all of it is well worth reading. A supplementary Book IV. presents some detailed evidence on special periods or points – in particular, a lively account of the women of Plautus. Finally, we have a useful Bibliography of the learning of the subject, and a good index.

2523   (**f26ᵛ**) Notice of Bowdler's *Family Shakspeare*, by LORD JEFFREY; reprinted from the EDINBURGH REVIEW, No. LXXI. October 1821.

WE have long intended to notice this very meritorious publication; and are of opinion that it requires nothing more than a notice to bring it into general circulation. We are not ourselves, we confess, particularly squeamish about incorrect expressions and allusions; and in the learned languages especially, which seldom come into the hands of the more delicate sex, and can rarely be perused by any one for the gratification of a depraved taste, we have not been very anxious about the dissemination of castrated editions; but in an author of such unbounded and deserved popularity as our great Dramatist, whose volumes are almost constantly in the hands of all who can read of both sexes, it is undoubtedly of great consequence to take care that youth runs no risk of corruption in the pursuit of innocent amusement or valuable instruction; or rather, that no offence is offered to delicacy in the midst of the purest gratification of taste.

Now it is quite undeniable that there are many passages in Shakespeare which a father could not read aloud to his children – a brother to his sister – or a gentleman to a lady:– and every one almost must have felt or witnessed the extreme awkwardness, and even distress, that arises from suddenly stumbling upon such expressions, when it is almost too late to avoid them, and when the readiest wit cannot suggest any paraphrase which shall not betray, by its harshness, the embarrassment from which it has arisen. Those who recollect such scenes must all rejoice, we should think, that Mr. BOWDLER has provided a security against their recurrence; and, as what cannot be pronounced in decent company cannot well afford much pleasure in the closet, we think it is better, every way, that what cannot be spoken, and ought not to have been written, should now cease to be printed.

We have only farther to observe, that Mr. BOWDLER has not executed his task in anything of a precise or prudish spirit; that he has left many things in the text which, to a delicate taste, must still appear coarse and reprehensible; and only effaced those gross indecencies which every one must have felt as blemishes, and by the removal of which no imaginable excellence can be affected. It is comfortable to be able to add, that this purification has been accomplished with surprisingly little loss either of weight or of value; and that the base alloy in the pure metal of Shakspeare has been found to amount to an inconceivably small proportion. It is infinitely to his credit that, with the most luxuriant fancy which ever fell to the lot of a mortal, and with no great restraints from the training or habits of his early life, he is by far the purest of the dramatists of his own or the succeeding age, – and has resisted, in a great degree, the corrupting example of his contemporaries. In them, as well as in him, it is indeed remarkable that the obscenities which occur are rather offensive than corrupting – and seem suggested rather by the misdirected wantonness of too lively a fancy, than by a vicious taste, or partiality to profligate indulgence; – while in Dryden and Congreve, the indecency belongs not to the jest, but to the character and action; and immodest speech is the cold and impudent exponent of licentious principles. In the one, it is the fantastic colouring of a coarse and grotesque buffoonery – in the other, the shameless speech of rakes, who make a boast of their profligacy. It is owing to this circumstance, perhaps, that it has in general been found easy to extirpate the offensive expressions of our great poet, without any injury to the context, or any visible scar or blank in the composition. They turn out not to be so much cankers in the flowers, as weeds that have sprung up by their side – not flaws in the metal, but impurities that have gathered on its surface – and that, so far from being missed on their removal, the work generally appears more natural and harmonious without them. We do not pretend to have gone over the whole work with attention – or even to have actually collated any considerable part of it; but we have examined three plays of a rather ticklish description – *Othello, Troilus and Cressida,* and *Measure for Measure* – and feel quite assured, from these specimens, that the work has been executed in the spirit and with the success which we have represented.

Mr. BOWDLER has in general followed the very best text – and the work is very neatly printed. We hope, however, that the publishers will soon be encouraged to give us another edition, in a larger letter; for we rather suspect, from some casual experiments of our own, that few *papas* will be able to read this, in a winter evening to their children, without the undramatic aid of spectacles.*

2524 (**f27ʳ**) THE TRIBUNE, FRIDAY, APRIL 5, 1907
ALGERNON CHARLES SWINBURNE. Born April 5th, 1837.
A BIRTHDAY APPRECIATION.

Few incidents in the course of literary history are more interesting than the constant self-renewal of the English genius in the nineteenth century. There are, of course, periods which have greater significance in the annals of culture: The Age of Pericles, the Augustan Age, the Italian and the English Renaissance. But there is something singular and unique about the way in which English literature renewed its strength in the last century, a fresh wave gathering and mounting as soon as the earlier had spent itself; Byron, Scott, Shelley, Keats, Coleridge, and Wordsworth, followed by Tennyson, Browning, Newman, Dickens, Carlyle, and they in turn by Rossetti, William Morris; Swinburne, Ruskin, Hardy, and Meredith.

Of this last group, the last which has really made its power undeniably felt, three are still with us: Meredith, only wanting a year of eighty, writing no longer, but cheery and optimist as ever; Hardy, not quite sixty-seven, saddened and grim, but turning from prose to poetry; and Swinburne, who has reached his three-score years and ten this morning, and who only the other day contributed to "Harper's Magazine" a critical essay in which his enthusiasm for the less-known Elizabethans glows with the old fervour.

FAME AND DEFAMATION.

Like Byron, Swinburne "awoke to find himself famous," and, as in Byron's case, the acclamation almost as suddenly was changed into a storm of obloquy. His first volume of poetry, "The Queen Mother and Rosamund," which appeared forty-seven years ago, was full of promise,

---

*The first edition, in 10 volumes, 12mo. printed in nonpareil type, met with great and immediate success, – the work having been often reprinted in various shapes and sizes, but never in the small type which elicited the above remark; and *Bowdler's Shakspeare* still commands a steady sale, both in one volume for the library and in six volumes for the pocket. Under these circumstances, the publishers believe that a re-issue of the thirty-six Plays, each to be had separately complete for sixpence, will bring this favourite edition of *Shakspeare* within the reach of a still wider circle of readers.

but it is only a critic here and there who has time to notice mere promise. "Atalanta in Calydon," in 1865, took the world captive – the world, that is, of poetry-loving and cultivated readers. There must have been a more appreciative audience for poets in the sixties than there is now; less jaded, sophisticated, and indifferent. Swinburne had accomplished the impossible; he had composed a real, living poem in the mould of the Attic drama. Matthew Arnold's "Merope" had been a complete failure; it suggested the great tragedians about as much as a barber's block suggests a masterpiece of Phidias. Shelley's "Prometheus Unbound" had taken a Greek myth as a kind of symbol or nucleus about which the dreams of a modern mystic could wreathe fantastic and many-hued clouds of poetry. It was the very air of Hellas that one breathed in "Atalanta in Calydon," not, however, the Hellas of Sophocles, but of the late poets of the Anthology, who saw the doings and sufferings of demigods and heroes, immortal lovers and fair, unhappy, mortal women like the frieze of a cold, marble temple, gilt by the cloudless sun and white against the deep blue sky of the Ægean. But what especially charmed and delighted Swinburne's audience was the sense of space, of elemental being with which the human spirit seemed to blend itself and be absorbed into the freedom and vastness of sky and air and sea. To this was to be added a new and marvellous music of many stops and unimagined rhythms, which carried the hearer along with the resistless stream of its melody.

(**f27^r**) ONSLAUGHT BY THE CRITICS.

It was only the next year after the appearance of "Atalanta" that the forces of Philistia, foot and horse, fell upon Mr. Swinburne's reputation with all the fury of outraged morality and all the shrillness of perplexed stupidity. There was more reason behind the outcry than that which justified the reckless onslaught upon Rossetti. Rossetti offended by his confidence in the efficacy of passion to transform what the ordinary, purblind man of the world can only look at with the oblique glance of the satyr. Rossetti thought that the poet, like the priest, may speak with a holy frankness that even the most prurient dare not receive with a disgraceful meaning. "Poems and Ballads" had quite a different inspiration from that which built up "The House of Life." Baudelaire had distilled from his "Fleurs de Mal" a strange, delirious poison that was coursing madly through the veins of French poetry. The romantic spirit demands strangeness for its essential food; at a moment when the world had grown a little weary of large hopes, and high aspirations and heroic movements, a strangely constituted genius bade Romance turn from the beauties which were beginning a little to pall, towards the fascination of abnormal ugliness; he bade her seek the strangeness that was as her very soul, not in passion, but in perverted desire; not in the rosy flush and first dawn of love, but in the dark, inscrutable hour of satiety. It was new, this idea, but only for that generation. The Renaissance, like the Romantic revival, sought to enlarge the themes of Art by sounding the dim and perilous way of the abnormal in the workings of the mind and the soul. The champions of the normal, much more numerous in Victorian than in Elizabethan England or in modern France, sounded the alarm from press and pulpit when the original sin of Baudelaire was smuggled into England in Swinburne's "Poems and Ballads."

He cared little for the horror which his book had excited among the Philistines, and replied with sonorous emphasis to their tin trumpets and cat-calls. But though all the younger generation, more intensely devoted because of the attempt to crush their idol, "went about chanting to one another the astonishing melodies" of "Dolores" and "Faustine," it was only a temporary divagation that was represented by "Poems and Ballads." Swinburne never had anything in his temperament really sympathetic to Baudelaire or Verlaine. It is much more the spirit and feelings of a healthy, clean-limbed, vigorous Englishman, with some strain of the Berserker in his blood, revelling in the more strenuous aspects of Nature, and ready to defy and battle against her – it is this that underlies the Protean changes of Mr. Swinburne's poetic themes. It is chiefly this characteristic, given, of course, his extraordinary command of verbal music, that brings us, in "Atalanta" or "Erechtheus," in direct contact with the large, elemental forces of Nature, so that these plays are "open-air books," in a more vital sense than applies to books which professedly aim at being that. In "Tristram of Lyonesse" one of the most salient distinctions between this and other romantic experiments of the same kind – Tennyson's "Idylls," for example, or William Morris's "Life and Death of Jason" – is the vivid realization of physical life, as in Tristram's exultation in battling with the waves. Again, it is the same temperament which kindles "A Song of Italy" and "Songs before Sunrise" with the white heat of passion. Those are the two passions which Mr. Swinburne is capable of – generous indignation and the joy of stimulating conflict with the forces of Nature, to breast a furious gale or a rolling sea. The cruel pleasures and voluptuous pains and frenzied raptures of "Poems and Ballads," were probably not even a passing phase, but only a curious experiment.

If anything, over-liberal in production, Mr. Swinburne soon gave the measure of himself. His trilogy, for example, on the subject of Mary Stuart – "Chastelard," "Bothwell," and "Mary Stuart" – has almost every quality that could be desired in dramatic poetry except swiftness of movement and dramatic instinct. So, too, with "Marino Faliero." It has been remarked that "he assumes the very soul of a period ... at one time he is an Elizabethan dramatist and another a French lyrist, at one moment a Hebrew prophet, at another a Greek poet." But he is always the same Swinburne. He resembles Landor – whom he warmly admired – in this: Landor, whose range of interests and subjects, as displayed in the "Imaginary Conversations," is so various and extended, but who is the sole interlocutor, whether he speaks through the masque of Pericles or Penn or Boccaccio.

WHEN JUDGMENT IS PASSED.

It is possible to become a classic even before one's claims are finally adjudicated upon. This is what has happened to Mr. Swinburne. Everyone admits his right to a place among the great English poets. But he is still a subject for controversy, in so far that there is a school of minor poets and critics who imitate him and argue about his poetical supremacy against all distinctions and discriminations. In truth, it is these unmeasured panegyrists who throw into strongest relief the limitations of Mr. Swinburne's genius. They contend for the position that metrical invention is the strongest proof of a high poetic gift, until we begin uneasily to ask ourselves whether Swinburne's fame rests on no sounder basis. They insist on the music of Swinburne's verse with such exclusiveness that it begins to look to us more colourless than it is in reality. And it must be admitted that the music, wonderful as it is, is never "the still, sad music of humanity." But whatever allowances the critic of the future will have to make, whatever other limitations he may discern, there is no doubt that to-day no living European poet, except, perhaps, Gabriele D'Annunzio, can compare for a moment with Swinburne.   J. A. N.

2525 (**f27ᵛ**) The *British Weekly* reprints from the Indian *Daily Telegraph* a leading article which affirms that "it is Theosophy which the Rev. R. J. Campbell is proclaiming from the pulpit of the City Temple to-day." There is some truth in this statement; but when we are told that Theosophy is "a belief in a wise and all-seeing Father" we are obliged to demur. The god of Theosophy is an immanent, but not a transcendent, god. It is a god which attains to consciousness only through incarnation in man and similar beings. Theosophy is pantheistic, and how a pantheistic god can be "a wise and all-seeing Father" passes the wit of man to conceive.

We believe that Christian theism is slowly tending towards pantheism, and that in this respect Mr. Campbell is leading the way to a goal which will ultimately be reached by most Christian thinkers. The old doctrine of a personal God has been utterly shaken by modern thought; but we would remind our Christian brethren that when they give up the dogma of the personality of God they must resign with it the delusive belief in "a wise and all-seeing Father."

The Literary Guide. Ap! 1. 1909

2526 (**f28ʳ**) THE 'NEW THEOLOGY' Daily Mail 12 Jan. 1907 (Very like the "Immanent Will" of the Dynasts.) 7

(**f27ᵛ**) REV. R. J. CAMPBELL'S POSITION.

"THE STORY OF THE FALL IS UNTRUE."

"LITERATURE, NOT DOGMA."

(FROM OUR SPECIAL CORRESPONDENT.)

The Churches are on the eve of a new period of controversy, one that may rival the Colenso and the Farrar ferments in the English Church, or the Robertson Smith and Marcus Dodds trials in Scotland. For some time the preaching of the Rev. R. J. Campbell at the City Temple has aroused debate among conservative theologians. Mr. Campbell proclaims himself in a way that has given him a public largely outside the usual limit of the church. A section of scientists, of whom Sir Oliver Lodge is the leading exponent, has been moving from a different standpoint in the same direction as the preacher.

A paper read by Mr. Campbell before a London ministerial body last September was the starting point of the acute stage of the controversy. Within the next few months he is going out as the apostle of a "re-stated theology," addressing gatherings of ministers in the leading provincial towns, by invitation of the ministers themselves. The orthodox are bound to take some measure to state their side against him, and thus grave developments may follow. The movement is by no means confined to Nonconformity. It is to-day agitating certain sections of the Roman Catholic Church, particularly in America, and many members of the Established Church.

What is the New Theology? How does its leading exponent define it? It was to learn the answer to these questions that I found myself in the church parlour of the City Temple in conversation with Mr. Campbell. The famous preacher, with the face of a boy, the silvery hair of an old man, and the burning, piercing eyes of a prophet, spoke with the quiet emphasis of a man who has thought out his intellectual position.

"I do not like the term 'New Theology,'" said Mr. Campbell, "but it is in common use and so must be allowed to stand. It is a term of convenience employed to describe a certain tendency towards liberalism in modern religious thought. It denotes an attitude and a spirit, rather than a creed. We object to the formal statements of belief which have distinguished the theology of the past. We object to ecclesiastical labels. Everyone knows that for the past twenty years there has been considerable uneasiness in the Churches, due largely to the development of scientific knowledge, the progress of archaeology, and the study of comparative religion. This uneasiness has affected every Church, even Rome. From the side of science the new theology is typified in the work of men like Sir Oliver Lodge.

A GREAT CLEAVAGE.

"The lines of divergence between the old and the new go down deep, and there is a great cleavage. The starting point of the New Theology is belief in the immanence of God and the essential oneness of God and man. This is where it differs from Unitarianism. Unitarianism made a great gulf and put man on one side and God on the other. We believe man to be the revelation of God, and the universe one means to the self-manifestation of God. The word 'God' stands for the infinite reality whence all things proceed. Everyone, even the most uncompromising materialist, believes in this reality. The New Theology, in common with the whole scientific world, believes that the finite universe is one aspect or expression of that reality, but it thinks of it (or Him) as Consciousness rather than a blind force, thereby differing from some scientists.

"Believing this, we believe that there is thus no real distinction between humanity and deity. Our being is the same as God's, although our consciousness of it is limited. We see the revelation of God in everything around us.

"The New Theology holds that human nature should be interpreted in terms of its own highest, and therefore it reverences Jesus Christ. It looks upon Jesus as the perfect example of what humanity ought to be, the life which perfectly expresses God in our limited human experience. So far as we are able to see, the highest kind of life that can be lived is the life which is lived, in terms of the whole, as the life of Jesus.

"Every man is a potential Christ, or rather a manifestation of the eternal Christ, that side of the nature of God from which all humanity has come forth. Humanity is fundamentally one, and all true living is the effort to realise that oneness. This is the truth that underlies all noble effort for the common good in the world to-day.

"The New Theology looks upon evil as a negative rather than a positive term. It is the shadow where the light ought to be; it is the perceived privation of good. It belongs only to finiteness. Pain is the effort of the spirit to break through the limitations which it feels to be evil. The New Theology believes that the only way in which the true nature of good can be manifested either by God or man is by the struggle against limitation, and therefore it is not appalled by the long story of cosmic suffering. Everybody knows this after a fashion. The things we most admire and reverence in one another are the things involving struggle and self-sacrifice.

"The New Theology watches with sympathy the development of modern science, for it believes itself to be in harmony therewith. It is the religious articulation of the scientific method. It therefore follows that it is in sympathy with scientific criticism of the important religious literature known as the Bible. While recognising the value of the Bible as a unique record of religious experience, it handles it as freely and critically as it would any other book. It believes that the seat of religious authority is within, not without, the human soul. The individual man is so constituted as to be able to recognise, ray by ray, the truth that helps him upward, no matter from what source it comes."

"SOCIALISTS WITH US."

Mr. Campbell laid special emphasis on one point. "We of the New Theology," he said, "look upon ourselves as representing in the sphere of religion the same movement that in the sphere of politics and sociology is making for a better social order. We believe that Mr. Keir Hardie and the social reformers who are struggling to remedy the ills of to-day are one with us, although they may not know it or

(*Continued on Page 8.*)

2527　(**f28ʳ**) THE "NEW THEOLOGY."

We print in another column to-day a statement of the new views on certain vital points of theology to which the Rev. R. J. Campbell has given able expression and utterance. They merit the most careful attention and examination, whatever the opinion entertained as to their orthodoxy. If we cannot endorse them, we can at least discuss them in the light of modern thought, and point to their significance.

Mr. Campbell feels, with many other reverent minds, that one of the great difficulties which have to be faced by the Churches is the existence of evil. By exaggerating the evil in the universe, by dwelling chiefly upon the pain and suffering of life, and not upon its redeeming features, Haeckel and his followers have produced an impression that all which exists is due to chance and necessity. They have, as they boast, left no room for a supreme moral Power, or even for morality. Their words are in thousands of mouths, and are echoed in so-called popular publications, where their wild statements are accepted as demonstrated facts. The mischief which they may do if left unanswered must be immense, for there could be no greater tragedy than a world which believed no longer in a moral God. But in his attempt to re-state the Christian position Mr. Campbell abandons much that the devout will be reluctant to lose. He discards the doctrine of the fall of man; he surrenders with it the Atonement; he appears to surrender also the freedom of the will, when he speaks of "deeds that we cannot help." And these are concessions so serious that the Churches cannot be asked to make them without stronger reasons than he has yet given.

The doctrine of the immanence of God which he emphasises is not necessarily bound up with these views, and is one for which there is ample authority in the teaching of the Church and its Founder. One of the recently discovered Logia, or sayings of Jesus, probably the oldest and most authentic record of His discourses, might well be cited in His support. "Raise the stone and there shalt thou find Me, cleave the wood and there am I." And it has been well and wisely interpreted by a modern apologist, Mr. Ballard, as pointing, not to pantheism, but to the view that the "laws of nature are really the exhibition of the mind of God," and that whatever apparent difficulties may exist owing to our present imperfect knowledge of the universe, in the interpretation of those laws from the religious standpoint, they are capable of reconciliation with a Divine purpose as we rise to a larger understanding of the meaning of life. It is, perhaps, a pity that the Logia, whose value is not disputed by any critic, are not incorporated in the

New Testament, for though few in number they should be familiar to every Christian mind.

It may be that the best answer to the assailants of Christianity is not along the lines which Mr. Campbell has followed. Yet we can learn from him, for, as Bishop Westcott pointed out many years ago, we may learn more from those with whom we disagree most fundamentally than from those with whom we find ourselves in complete agreement. Haeckel's world, in which men are mere puppets and automata, is contrary to the daily evidence of our own experience. There is no living man possessed of personality who can deny that his own fate lies in his own hands. Instinctively we feel that we have the power to choose, and to choose between good and evil. We cannot, it is true, as yet logically reconcile this freedom of the will with the uniformity of the laws of nature or with such observed facts as heredity. But it cannot be doubted that as the human mind advances the formula will be found to reconcile them. Nor can those who adopt Haeckel's position ignore the fact that modern science is shaking the very foundations of their theories as to the indestructibility and permanence of matter. Matter has been broken up into something which can scarcely be described as matter. It is no longer substance, but a "strain of the ether." The table which we see and touch, according to the working hypothesis of modern science, is ultimately composed of atoms, and these atoms again are composed of electrons, or charges of electricity, moving in space with incredible velocity, so that each atom may well be a replica in the infinitely little of the solar system. As science advances, it no longer claims to explain, but only to describe. It tells us the facts; it withholds the explanation for which humanity yearns. The function of religion and of philosophy is to give this explanation, and religion is helped, not hindered, by the growing evidence of a Purpose, of an ordered law, which is unthinkable without a dominating Intelligence, running through every phenomenon of life and existence.

2528   (**f28ᵛ**) In J. S. Mill Utilitarianism proper reached its highest term – but, if we may venture in such a connection to allude to Hegel, it was a completion which implied the absorption of its thought-process into a higher term. Almost throughout the whole of Mr. Leslie Stephen's last volume we are aware of new lights breaking through the fast-widening cracks of the Utilitarian edifice, of new vistas opening out; and it is to Mill's abiding honour that he was among the first to see clearly the inadequacy of his system. "Individualism," perhaps in a necessarily exaggerated form, had been both the lever and the stumbling-block of the Utilitarians. To Mill the external world was a series of isolated "facts" mechanically strung together by "causation"; and the consequent impossibility of asserting any universal truth about phenomena thus individualised, except what the man in the street knows, that they have been observed to follow certain laws, and will probably do so again, left him without any philosophical basis for science. In other words, the "appeal to experience" results in the discovery that we have no "experience" to appeal to. As Goethe said, the fragments lie in our hand sure enough, only "*das geistige Band*," their living unity, has vanished. And weakness of philosophic method, though it may seem a venial sin in the earnest philanthropist, has still an uncomfortable trick of reappearing, like an unlaid ghost, in the most unlooked-for places. Thus Mill's fundamental error does much to vitiate the interesting chapters in the sixth book of his logic, in which he endeavoured to lay down the outlines of social science. He failed in this attempt, as most thinkers, including Mr. Leslie Stephen, agree, through his insistence on the very Bentham-like view that to know the characters of individuals (and could we say that Shakespeare knew them?) is to know the character of the society they constitute – a view which ignores alike his own theory of chemical action and the simple experience that a crowd is something often terribly different from the people in it.

2529   MR. BERNARD SHAW ASHAMED OF HIS OPPONENTS.   D. News.
Jan 24. 08
In his concluding article on "Driving Capital out of the Country," published in the current number of the "New Age," Mr. G. Bernard Shaw says:

"The weakest point in our capitalist system is its failure to secure the application of our national capital, as fast as it is accumulated, to the provision of our national needs in the order of their urgency. Thus we want more schoolmasters and we get more jockeys, we want more recreation grounds for children and we get more racecourses and motordromes. We want more well-planned, wholesome streets, and we get more slums; we want more good houses for the people, and we get more weekend hotels for the plutocracy. We want more bakers, more tailors, more masons, more carpenters – we get more coachmen and footmen and gamekeepers. We want producers, in short, and we get parasites. Finally, wanting all these things, we often get nothing, because the capital is invested abroad instead of at home."

Mr. Shaw challenges anti-Socialists to name a single proposal made by English Socialists that would not have the effect of investing English capital in England, and says, "It is truly amazing how people lose their heads in opposing Socialism."

2530   (**f29ʳ**) THE TIMES, THURSDAY, JANUARY 23, 1908.
The Socialist Victory.

The Labour party conference, after declining on Tuesday to be delivered over to the Socialists, yesterday reversed that decision and accepted the thoroughgoing Socialist programme. MR. STEPHENSON of the Amalgamated Engineers moved that the time has come when the Labour party should have as a definite object the socialization of the means of production, distribution, and exchange, to be controlled by a democratic State in the interest of the entire community. This is the full-blown creed of theoretical Socialism in all its crudity. MR. STEPHENSON's argument was that, when they had carried their remedial measures as far as possible, they would still be confronted with iniquities in their midst which could only be removed by a commonwealth owning the means of production. MR. KELLY, who seconded, put the thing in even more direct language when he said that the workers were finding that they made little progress. Some of their trades were organized, he said, to the extent of 90 per cent. of the workers, and yet they were not able to prevent reductions in wages. It is curious that, with this fact before him, he should have implicit faith in the certainty of a better result if the odd 10 per cent. were also organized, which is really what Socialist reconstruction comes to. Nor does it seem to have occurred to MR. STEPHENSON that the iniquities he refers to are the products of degenerate human nature, which Socialism has not yet formulated any plan for eliminating from its ideal State. MR. SHACKLETON, M. P., remarked that on the previous day they refused to have a programme, and were then engaged in tying themselves up in the very thing they had rejected. He warned them that the result of voting the resolution would be very serious, and argued generally for saying nothing about ultimate Socialist ends, while working in harmony to achieve as many of them as possible. The resolution was nevertheless carried by 514,000 votes against 469,000.

It is always well to find out exactly where we stand. For some time past there has been sufficient ambiguity to confuse many excellent people. Socialism was fighting under trade union colours, and many were misled into supposing that only a few not very unreasonable reforms were in question. The Labour machine is now fairly captured by the Socialists, who openly flout all middle and moderate courses. They have proclaimed their aims in the most unequivocal way, and no one can offer any excuse for being longer deceived about the real meaning of the movement. We have yet to see what the effect will be upon the Labour party itself. There are as many shades of opinion among working men, and as many varieties of character, as there are in any other class. We shall not conclude, until we are obliged, that the vote of yesterday means the wholesale conversion of the highly individualist working classes of this country to the chimerical notions of Socialist dreamers. But, if the common sense of our workmen recoils from the wholesale robbery upon which the Socialist scheme must be founded, and from the universal poverty which must overtake alike the robbers and the robbed, it follows that we may expect shortly to see a division of the forces represented at the Labour conference. For, although the two sections may work for a time upon parallel lines, and may combine for a time to gain identical ends, the alliance cannot last. Not only are the aims of the two sections entirely different, they are also incompatible. The success of the Labour party upon its old lines raises a barrier against the advance of Socialism. For what the ordinary workman wants is more money for himself, his own children, his own home. What the Socialist wants is to break down the sense of private ownership altogether, and to make the workman dependent upon committees of wire-pullers, which, owning the capital, will be capitalists of the peculiarly harsh collectivist type, capitalists, too, with powers of inquisition and interference such as the existing capitalists cannot wield. The two ideals, though both may impel men to seek in the first instance what others possess, are absolutely incompatible. Till human nature becomes something entirely different from what we have experience of, there will always be overwhelming forces on the side of individualism. There may be nothing on hand but confiscation or robbery, but men will confiscate or rob for their own enrichment, not for the sake of an abstraction called the democratic State, though consisting in fact of all the most dexterous and unscrupulous robbers of their fellow men.

It will probably be a long time before the issues clear, and until then there will be much confusion in the minds of men, much foolish and random legislation, and many repetitions of economical experiments that have failed disastrously in the past. Already we have demands for State workshops in which high wages are to be paid for producing things that no buyers can be found for. Fixed wages, irrespective of what the business can pay, are also demanded; and both demands lead straight to aggravated unemployment. There will be other things of the same kind, together with plausible schemes for nationalizing this and the other, which mean either that one section of the community is to be robbed to satisfy another or that businesses duly paid for are to be taken out of competent hands and given over to committees of the incompetent. All this, in the face of foreign competition, does not offer a pleasing prospect for the immediate future. The disinterestedness of Socialism is illustrated by the treatment yesterday of the woman franchise question. It was discussed simply from the point of view of how it would affect the political aims of the speakers. There is nothing that would so greatly promote Socialism as the hitherto unknown spectacle of Socialists, whether "Christian" or other, themselves making some real sacrifice, or some real delegation, of their own goods without reserve to the mysterious all-wisdom to which they ask us all to bow in faith.

2531　(**f30ʳ**) Whitefriars Journal – Dinner of Club – Feb 28·1908
Literature.

FRIAR PATERSON said: In his brilliant and scholarly essay on the "Poems of Shakespeare," Mr. Wyndham makes the remark that in literature we modern people have created nothing.

But, in the essay from which I have already quoted, Mr. Wyndham reminds us that the contemporaries of Shakespeare believed that they, too, were living in a decadent age, and I find some comfort in that fact. For it means that contemporary criticism is generally only provisional. (Laughter.) Not once nor twice in the history of letters the opinion of one age has been reversed in the next, and it looks as if each generation, unable to appraise its own artistic labours, delegates to its successors the final æsthetic judgment. When I hear our poets described only as minor poets, I always remind myself of Théophile Gautier's admirable essay, in which he says: that if you wish genuine poetry, you should go to the minor poets for it. (Hear, hear.) And I notice that the minor poets of one age have a habit of becoming the major poets of the next. No doubt, during the longest part of his career, every man of letters has generally been an Athanasius *contra mundum*.

No doubt to-day we appear to be living under special disadvantages. Unlike the great writers of antiquity, unlike the mediaeval singers, we are not living on a great tradition. Disintegrating and dissolvent forces are at work around us, and they have spread the contagion of their unrest into the books that are being written to-day. It is not an age of fixed belief, and yet in its deepest form belief has always had an intimate connection with the highest kind of literature.

Mr. Wyndham's Speech.
... periods of what are called decadence are really periods of exaggerated return to a multiplicity of births no less than of deaths.
My platitude is this – Literature is the [arrested] voice of humanity. (Hear, hear.) That is wide enough to embrace all the literary world.
No doubt it can be carried to a high degree of artifice. But it ceases to be literature when it ceases to be an instinctive cry, uttering memories of all which has seemed good for man, and hopes for something unknown, but better than any good which memory records.
... all literature, pure literature, falls into two categories – the categories of song and of story, and that the highest Literature is both – the story that is sung.
I may be told that I have left out the essay. I have not left out the essay. The essay, if it be a good essay – if it be the kind of essay which Montaigne modelled upon Plutarch, and which everybody else has modelled on Montaigne – is either a narration of all the best stories, and these are the oldest stories, in the world, or else it is a song in prose. (Applause.) Not a song in lyrical form, but a lyric in prose. What is a lyric? It has been defined over and over again. And this is what all the definitions amount to. The lyric is the expression of an emotion compounded of aspiration and regret, refracted through the temperament of one human being. (Hear, hear.) Take the pure lyric:–

"O, that it were possible after long grief and pain,
To find the arms of my true love round me once again."

or you can illustrate it fantastically from Thackeray:–

"Oh, what fun!
To have a plum bun!
How I wish it never were done!"

(Laughter.) That is the archetype of the lyric, the expression of aspiration and regret refracted through the temperament of a greedy little boy of ten years old. (Laughter.) You will find that the essays which are not reflections of stories, but which are lyrics in prose, are pure lyrics, no matter what their subject may be – conviviality or the splendour of Alpine dawns, marriage, or the delight of battle with our peers –

2532 (**f30ᵛ**) Sent by the Editor THE NEW YORK TIMES. Saturday Review of Books and Art SUPPLEMENT TO THE NEW YORK TIMES. Sixteen pages.
LONDON LITERARY LETTER Written for THE NEW YORK TIMES SATURDAY REVIEW BY William L. Alden.

Of course, when a man has an established position he can write what he chooses. Mr. Hardy did not feel obliged to make his Jude happy in the last chapter, but if he had been a beginner he would have had to yield to the demand for marriage bells. It would be a great mistake for a new writer to suppose that he is permitted to do things which Hardy and Meredith can do. Even Kipling, when he wrote "The Light That Failed," had to end the book with a marriage, though he afterward put forth an edition which ended as art demanded that it should end. This fancy of the public for books which end happily is, of course, only the fashion of the moment. The day will come when the same public which now asks to be made happy will demand to be made miserable. The probability is that the day is not far off. There are signs of a revival of the Byron cult, and if we return to Byron in poetry, we will return to Byronism in novels. The one thing that a novelist should do who wishes for success is to be born at the right period. If he is born when people demand novels with happy endings, while he can write only tragedies, his fate is sealed.

2533 (**f31ʳ**) Seventeenth Century Criticism (Critical Essays. Spingarn.)

And so, while Evelyn is "disgusted" with the "old plays," Rymer, hard-headed Philistine and admirable writer that he was, tears *Othello* and *The Maid's Tragedy* and the rest to pieces. "People do not do these things." In partial opposition to this we have the "school of taste," as Mr. Spingarn well calls it, which drew its origin from the curiosity of the *virtuosi* after the peculiar nature and quality of all things in art,

science, and letters. It is here, perhaps, that the criticism of the time
becomes most interesting and most important to ourselves; for it is here
that we find rescued from oblivion that something in poetry which is
what the modern critic chiefly looks for and prizes: that

> Air and Spirit [to quote Milton's nephew, Edward Phillips (or
> possibly Milton himself?)] which perhaps the most Learned and
> judicious in other Arts do not perfectly apprehend, much less is it
> attainable by any Study or Industry; nay, though all the Laws of
> *Heroic Poem*, all the Laws of *Tragedy* were exactly observed, yet still
> this *tour entrejeant*, this Poetic *Energie*, if I may so call it, would be
> required to give life to all the rest, which shines through the
> roughest, most unpolish't, and antiquated Language, and may
> happly be wanting in the most polite and reformed; let us observe
> *Spencer*, with all his Rustie, obsolete words, with all his rough-hewn,
> clowterly Verses, yet take him throughout, and we shall find in him
> a gracefull and Poetic Majesty; in like manner *Shakespear*, in spight of
> all his unfiled expressions, his rambling and indigested Fancys, the
> laughter of the *Critical*, yet must be confess't a *Poet* above many that
> go beyond him in Literature some degrees.

Brave and enlightened words these, in an era which did not know what
to make of its great predecessors, and either damned them outright or
praised them, nine times out of ten, for the wrong things. In all this
century of transition there is no change greater than that from the
examination of a poem as an independent organism that can be
measured and appraised by rules to the search for the touch of magic,
the breath of the divine fire, the communication of the inner soul, which
this school of taste initiated by its consideration of essential "beauties"
as opposed to obedience or disobedience to the rules. And so the
ground was prepared for the criticism of later days. The process is very
incomplete. There is little as yet of the delicate analysis of the spirit and
"flavour" of an author, the subtle inquiry for his intention, at which the
modern critic aims; but the movement, of which Coleridge came to be
the outstanding figure, was at least begun.   Times 23.4.08

2534   Publishers Circʳ: 13 mar. 97
Those who are still unsatisfied on the everlasting topic of realism
should read an article on the subject which appeared in last week's
National Observer. The method of the realist is generally to go forth,

notebook in hand, and jot down details of all the sordid and unsavoury spectacles of existence that fall in his way. These, when the time comes, are faithfully transferred to story or novel, and the result, however grotesque or exceptional, is called 'life.' Then certain critics dilate on the advantages of thoroughness, counting thorough what is disagreeable, and merely romantic what is pleasant. There are, of course, realists and realists. Shakespeare and Fielding are realists: Dante is among the greatest of the race. Tolstoi and Zola are also realists, and all these are or were men of genius. When such writers go out in quest of material they may be trusted. But unhappily the latter-day realist does not invariably possess 'the ineffable something' which men are content to call genius, and he presents raw fact (the rawer the better), wondering why fastidious readers make wry faces over it.

He entirely overlooks the truth enunciated by the *National Observer*, that 'Art begins where observation ends.' He mistakes observation for imagination. Sometimes even Tolstoi and Zola appear to do this, though they generally get right at last. Art, it has been pointed out times innumerable, depends as much on what is omitted, left in the ink-pot, as Mr Lowell put it, as on what is included. The policy of the realist is to crowd in everything, especially everything that concerns the seamy side of life, though he somehow misses the potent fact that there is sunshine in the world. Men and women are not always miserable, even in slums.

2535 (**f31ᵛ**) FROM GHOSTS TO GODS.
"The Evolution of the Idea of God: An Inquiry into the Origins of Religions." By Grant Allen. (London: Grant Richards. 20s. net.)

Mr. Grant Allen's output in fiction, poetry, and scientific treatise has been large and frequent, but although working in many fields, he has reserved a wide area for cultivation of ideas to which are rightly attached a high importance. The industry of twenty years applied to the collection of material, and of ten years to its arrangement and interpretation, warrants the modest hope that a volume which is the result of such prolonged labor will have "kindly consideration from that small section of the reading public which takes a living interest in religious questions." The sympathetic spirit in which Mr. Allen treats a delicate and complex subject should have like reception from those to whom the story of man's beliefs and guesses about the unseen makes appeal. The purpose of the book, as set forth in the preface, is "to trace the genesis of the belief in a god from its earliest origin in the mind of primitive man up to its fullest development in advanced and etherealised Christian theology." In doing this, the question of "the validity or invalidity of the ideas in themselves" is not discussed, but their inevitableness is recognised, "man's relation to the external universe begetting them as of necessity."

The inquiry sets before itself the threefold problem of the origin of man's belief in many gods; of the elimination of these until belief in one supreme God was reached; and lastly, of the conception of this supreme God as Triune, "one of His Persons being identified with a particular divine and human incarnation." To this threefold question Mr. Allen gives the answer that all religions spring, directly or indirectly, from worship of the Deified Dead. By gods Mr. Allen does not mean the "vague and formless creatures which are dreaded by primitive humanity," but the deified beings standing in paternal relationship to man, and accordingly reverenced and worshipped by him. For with the products of mythological theories he will have no dealings, and perhaps one of the most interesting features of the earlier chapters is that which delimits myth and religion, defining the one as being speculations about the gods, and the other as limited to direct dealings with them. We have no liking for hard and fast definitions which assume a consistency wholly foreign to the barbaric mind, and the distinction which Mr. Allen draws would seem to wholly detach the greater gods of the world's pantheons from the affairs and actions of those who have created them, and to whom they could not have been merely passive conceptions. It is true that, as contrasted with the immediate objects of worship and ritual, these *dii majores* are remote from men's "businesses and bosoms." But, granting the greater influence on human life of what seems to touch it more closely, Mr. Allen's definition excludes that worship of maleficent spirits which is dominant among large groups of mankind, as in New Guinea, Guiana, and some parts of Africa.

Amidst many theories of the origin of religions, two may now be said to claim the attention of theorists. One is that known as ancestor-worship, the facts in support of which receive large additions and illuminative treatment, at Mr. Allen's hands. The other, known as animism, is based on the evidence of universal attribution of soul to everything, whether dead or alive, thus tersely put by Mr. Im Thurn, when speaking of the natives of Guiana: "Every object, animate and inanimate, seems to the Indian exactly of the same nature, and is a being, consisting of a body and spirit." Mr. Allen's book, which he describes as a "summary of probabilities," is offered as "to some extent a reconciliation between the conflicting schools of humanists and animists, though with a leaning rather to the former than the latter."

No student of religions will deny the overwhelming preponderance of ancestor-worship over every other cult; a preponderance largely explained by the constant supply of fresh material (the working-up of men into godlings goes on apace to-day, notably in India and other parts of the East), and by the concrete and personal character of that material, since man cannot worship an abstraction. But preponderance is no proof of primitiveness. Nothing that is cited by the humanists, from Mr. Herbert Spencer onwards, helps us to determine whether the worship of the dead is prior to attribution of intelligence to phenomena generally. Mr. Allen says that "nothing can be clearer than the fact that the early Egyptian religion bases itself entirely upon two main foundations, ancestor-worship and totemism." Against this we have the statement of Wiedemann, a high authority on the subject, that it cannot be proved historically which of the various forms of the Egyptian religion, as, *e.g.*, sun-worship or ancestor-worship, are earlier, and which are later. And, on the general question, we cannot ignore the vast body of evidence which shows how barbaric conceptions extend life and intelligence of some sort to phenomena unconnected with birth or death, as when the savage predicates an indwelling, malign-working spirit in the stone over which he stumbles – an idea which, strangely enough, survived in our statutes within the present reign, any object, say a tree or a car-wheel, causing the death of anyone being "deodand," *i.e.*, given to God, and forfeited or sold for the poor. Interpreting motion of the wind-driven cloud, the rushing water, the rolling stone, and the leaping flame, as due to life and will corresponding to his own within each of these things, why should not the "adumbration of the notion of a soul" have been cast by those phenomena on man at as early stages in his history as those when from breath, and shadows, and swoonings, he wove the diaphanous tissue of "another self"? Such a theory of interfusion of complementary ideas seems more in accord with all that is known of his behaviour before the powers of nature, and with the continuity of thought, than the theory that every god was once a ghost, and never anything else. But we fear that all our speculations will remain "summaries of probabilities." No documents are extant to enlighten us; we have only mobile, complex, and confused ideas, incarnate in eccentric, often contradictory, forms. That such character attaches to these ideas should keep us on guard against framing theories whose symmetry is sometimes their condemnation. The under-world whence we invoke these strange objects of man's worship holds a motley company, and if we venerate and deify a majority of the dead, there remain the undeified minority, who awaken compassion and pity; the pallid shades of Sheol who welcomed with mockings the arrival of the great King of Babylon, and that son of Peleus who declared he would rather be ploughboy on earth than ruler in Hades. But if it seems to us that Mr. Allen has travelled on somewhat too rigid lines in not allowing fuller play to man's animistic tendencies in the making of his gods, this may not lessen the tribute we pay to a book which is the outcome of careful, scholarly research.   c.

2536 (**f32ʳ**) A NOTE ON AMIEL. (Continued from p. 148.)
THIS dualism, this union of synthetic absorption with individual persistency, which prevented Amiel finding the Oriental refuge of monoideism, was further at work in him in another quarter. The words of Renan are something of a key to the moral nature of Amiel: "He speaks of sin, of salvation, of redemption, and conversion, as if these things were realities." Amiel himself declares, time after time, that the intellectual life is not sufficient. He blames Goethe's lofty standing aloof from the petty movements of the world; he censures theological writers and lecturers, novelists, historians, and critics for an undue disregard of elements in human nature that ask for faith before all else; and he quotes approvingly Pascal's distinction between "the order of thought and the order of charity." It was another of the strange contradictions in Amiel. In spite of all his French and German studies, his travels, his thought, he was still a Genevese at heart. He was for ever hovering between Buddha and Christ, between Schopenhauer, Hegel, and Calvin. Not that he was a Christian in the ordinary sense of the word; he seems to have rejected the historical Christianity in part, if not wholly; his Christianity was general Stoical morality, with a flavor of the prophets. "Religion," he says, "is not a method, but a life." Soar as he will in the empyrean, emancipate himself as he will from the immediate and the transitory, he is inexorably brought down to consider himself again as an individual, by a secret moving some-(**f32ᵛ**)thing within him that always disturbs and terrifies him, and makes life for him a perpetual Gethsemane. From the extreme of mind, of expansiveness, of intellectual freedom, he is brought down to pressing personal problems of life and duty and renunciation. He will have none of the *amor intellectualis*, for, lucid and all-embracing as it is, it

cannot be all, and he stands shuddering and self-doubting before the great problems of good and evil. Nay, so firm is the hold of the Christian theory upon him, that he even thinks himself sinful at times because the tendency of his intellect is to carry him away far out into the wider connexions of things, to the neglecting of his own small being and its duties. Then he attempts a fresh re-adjustment, and characteristically tries to find the solution to the problem along the line that is easiest for him to take. As formerly his supreme happiness consisted in losing himself in the general meaning of the universe, so now he will satisfy his moral craving by putting himself into complete harmony with the will of God. He comes to a solution that is a mixture of early Christian sentiment and Buddhist Nirvana. "Self-interest is but the survival of the animal in us," he says; "humanity only begins for man with self-surrender." It is the question of the ego and the universal starting up again within him in another form, and this time he tries to lay the spectre by a Christian conjuration. Baffled in his attempts to scale the heights of existence, beaten back in his desire to know the sum of things, he consoles himself with the thought that man has no right to ask so much, and that worthiness of living consists in self-surrender, in sinking unmurmuringly into the general scheme, in trying to fall into harmony with the will of God. So he posits a beneficent Creator, and goes through a curious series of spiritual contortions in his attempt to justify the idea; sees it to be unjustifiable from the point of view of mind, and falls back on faith, on intuition. All nature is in a ceaseless flux and reflux, but behind it all is the unchangeable, inscrutable will of God. "From the theistic point of view, is it the purpose of God to make souls, to augment the sum of good and wisdom by the multiplication of himself in free beings – facts which may flash back to him his own holiness and beauty? This conception is far more attractive to the heart. But is it more true?" And he replies "The moral consciousness affirms it. If man is capable of conceiving goodness, the general principle of things, which cannot be inferior to man, must be good." But he does not see that the argument is invertible; for if man is capable of conceiving *evil*, the general principle of things, which cannot be inferior to man, must be evil. The argument proves either too much or nothing at all; but we cannot expect the "moral consciousness" to be logical.

Thus Amiel hovers about between monism and dualism, the latter having generally the advantage. The soul of man is a battlefield between the two rival athletes, good and evil, with God as spectator; "the Abel in us must labor for the salvation of Cain". At times he conceives the highest duty to consist in total self-renunciation to what he calls God. "No, rebel as we may, there is but one solution – to submit to the general order, to accept, to resign ourselves, and to do still what we can. (In the next breath he will speak of the misery involved in the growing triumph of Darwinism, which is nothing more nor less than the expression of the 'general order'.) It is our self-will, our aspirations, our dreams, that must be sacrificed. We must give up the hope of happiness once for all! Immolation of the self – death to self – this is the only suicide which is either useful or permitted. Absolute disinterestedness is only reached in that perfect humility which tramples the self under foot for the glory of God." That is, he explicitly asserts the goodness of the principle of the universe, and then implicitly denies it by his efforts to escape from the real life of the universe into a state of religious absorption. What is this but Schopenhauer's "renunciation of the will to live"; and what is the legitimate conclusion from it all but pessimism; for a good principle that puts life into man and then tells him he can only find happiness in the painful renunciation of all that makes life pleasant for him, day by day, week by week, year by year, what is it but a very travesty of words?

Yet Amiel's dualism and his fundamental Christian sentiment prevent him seeing that not optimism but pessimism is what his faith comes to. He still holds to the fiction of a good God, and like most believers is careful to justify his Deity at his own expense. It is curious, as an instance of how dishonest the human mind can unconsciously be with itself, to notice how it will justify evil proceedings in the Deity on the ground that they are called for by the wickedness of man, this wickedness, even where it really exists, being necessarily a product of the God-given activity, while in nine cases out of ten no wickedness as such does exist, the individual being overwhelmed by misfortunes that have come upon him solely by the misdeeds of others. It is certainly a gratifying instance of the flexibility of the human mind when it can convert all these things into a proof of a good God, and sing paeans in praise of his justice. No amount of practical incongruities, it would seem, is ever able to make these men conscious of the incongruities of their systems; nor can they even reach consistency through contradiction. At one moment Amiel embraces the whole of the universe in thought, and finds happiness, forgetting that this is simply the *amor intellectualis* he elsewhere professes himself dissatisfied with. "On all sides stretched mysteries, marvels, and prodigies, without limit, without number, and without end. I felt the unfathomable thought of which the universe is the symbol live and burn within me; I touched, proved, tasted, embraced by nothingness and my immensity; I kissed the hem of the garment of God, and gave Him thanks for being Spirit and for being Life. Such moments are glimpses of the divine. They make one conscious of one's immortality; they bring home to one that an Eternity is not too much for the study of the thoughts and works of the Eternal; they awaken in us an adoring ecstasy and the ardent humility of love." Then, when the sense of his individuality comes over him, the previous intoxication has weakened him, left him unable to see his course clearly over a ground that is strewn with obstacles, and consequently he sinks into an agony of fear and despair. "Always and everywhere salvation is torture, deliverance means death, and peace lies in sacrifice. If we would win our pardon, we must kiss the fiery crucifix. Life is a series of agonies, Calvary, which we can only climb on bruised and aching knees. We seek distractions; we wander away; we deafen and stupefy ourselves that we may escape the test; we turn away our eyes from the *via dolorosa*; and yet there is no help for it – we must come back to it in the end. What we have to recognise is that each of us carries within himself his own executioner, his demon, his hell, in his sin; that his sin is his idol, and that this idol, which seduces the desire of his heart, is his curse."

It is the voice of Geneva speaking; and the strange thing is that it should come from the mouth of a man who is at other times partly Schopenhauer, Hegel, Stoic, Epicurean, and Oriental quietist. The dualism of Amiel's nature was his destruction; he cannot harmonise everything within him, and yet tortures himself because of his failure, ultimately seeking a fictitious harmonisation by strangling philosophy in the arms of religion. Geneva is at the bottom of him, suggesting dark problems of sin, and evil, and death, and salvation. And since he cannot attain the inward peace he strives for, and since he cannot flout God in the face and show him the cardinal blunder he has made in the clumsy creation of mankind, he takes ascetic comfort in the Christian theory of the innate perversity of man, *"das radicale Böse"* of Kant. This in turn troubles him, for how is it to be harmonised with the general beneficent scheme of things? Finally he takes refuge from the spectres that haunt him, in the Christian theory of the forgiveness of sins. This is indeed the pressing problem to Amiel. "The best measure of the profundity of any religious doctrine," he says, "is given by its conception of sin, and the cure of sin." Is then the Christian doctrine so perfect a thing in this respect? Was there ever a more grossly immoral doctrine than the forgiveness of sins, a doctrine so based on selfishness, disregard for others, callousness of the evil inflicted so that the individual soul but makes its peace with God? It is the most striking proof of the innate incapacity of the majority of men to think at all on deep moral principles, that such a doctrine should ever be regarded as the be-all and the end-all of moral obligation. Of all the specious lies that have ever blinded humanity to the sense of duty, this is surely the worst. It is an immoral doctrine because it avoids the real question of obligation; it moves the moral centre of gravity from man to the skies; and such a displacement as this is regarded, even by thinking men, as compatible with notions of justice, not merely human but divine.

ERNEST NEWMAN.

(To be continued.)

2537 (**f34ʳ**) Nearly ready.

PLANT RESPONSE AS A MEANS OF PHYSIOLOGICAL INVESTIGATION. (By JAGADIS CHUNDER BOSE, C. I. E., M. A. (Cantab.) D. SC. (Lond.), Professor, Presidency College, Calcutta. Author of 'Response in the Living and Non-Living.' With Illustrations. 8vo. 21s.

In this work Professor Bose shows through an extended series of observations that there is no physiological response given by the highly organised animal tissue, which is not seen also in the plant. He demonstrates these by means of mechanical response given by means of even ordinary plants, usually regarded insensitive. Discarding the theory of specific sensitiveness, he shows that all the various movements of plants in response to light are traceable to a single fundamental reaction. By his discovery of the multiple response in plants he endeavours to show that the autonomous movements in plants are brought about by the absorption of stimulus from external sources.

2538 In the course of his address PROFESSOR GOTCH said that the late Sir John Burdon-Sanderson, in an admirable and concise manner, thus described the aims and methods of physiology:– "The investigators who are now working with such earnestness in all parts of the world for the advance of physiology have before them a definite and well-understood purpose, that purpose being to acquire an exact knowledge of the chemical and physical processes of animal life and of the self-acting machinery by which they are regulated for the general good of the organism." This sentence set forth with scientific precision his enlarged conception of living phenomena, for whilst it asserted that the characteristics of processes formed the true aim of all physiological investigation, it defined the particular processes which should be investigated as chemical and physical, and it particularized two further aspects of these, the machinery for their co-ordination described as self-acting, that is automatic, and the *raison d'être* of their occurrence, which was said to be the welfare of the whole organism. All these various aspects were strikingly exemplified in the progress of physiology in this country and in the researches now being carried on both at home and abroad. At the outset it was desirable to refer to certain wide issues which were involved in the statement that the business of the physiologist was to "acquire an exact knowledge of the chemical and physical processes of animal life." The limitation of physiology to ascertainable characters of a chemical and physical type did not commend itself to certain physiologists, physicists, and chemists, who had revived under the term "neo-vitalism" the vitalistic conceptions of older writers. They denied that physiological phenomena could ever be adequately described in terms of physics and chemistry, even if these terms were in the future greatly enlarged in consequence of scientific progress. It was undoubted that there were many aspects of living phenomena which in the existing state of our knowledge defied exact expression in accordance with chemical and physical conceptions; but the issues raised had a deeper significance than the mere assertion of present ignorance, for those who adopted "neo-vitalism" were prepared to state not only that certain physiological phenomena were, from the chemical and physical point of view, inexplicable to-day, but that from the nature of things they must for ever remain so. This attitude implied that it was a hopeless business for the physiologist to try by the use of more appropriate methods to remove existing discrepancies between living and non-living phenomena, and this was accentuated by the use of a peculiar nomenclature which, in attributing certain phenomena to vital directive forces, left them cloaked with a barren and, from the investigator's point of view, a forbidding qualification.

NEO-VITALISM FOUND WANTING.

Neo-vitalism, like its parent vitalism, was fostered by the imperfect and prejudiced view which man was prone to take in regard to his own material existence. This existence was, for him, the most momentous of all problems, and it was therefore not surprising that he should assume that in physiology, pathology, and, to a lesser degree, in biology, events were dealt with of a peculiarly mystic character, since many of these events formed the basis of his sensory experience and occurred in a material which he regarded with a special proprietary interest. He was reluctant to believe that those phenomena which constituted the material part of his existence could be intellectually regarded as processes of a physico-chemical type, differing only in complexity from those exhibited in the non-living world, and impelled by this reluctance he fabricated for them, out of his own conceit, a special and exclusive realm. The logical pressure of physical and chemical conceptions forbade the postulation, by either the public or the neo-vitalist, of such an incongruous entity as a vital chemical element capable of blending with the familiar chemical elements recognized in the material world; yet the physiological processes of life were in popular estimation still held to be due to peculiar forces blending with those of the material world, but so essentially different that they could only be described as "vital." The neo-vitalistic school, without adopting this popular view in its entirety, retained the same term for such physiological characteristics of cell processes as, with our present limited knowledge and with our present inadequate methods of investigation, seemed to be in disagreement with present chemical and physical conceptions. This disagreement was accentuated by the assumption of directive vital forces, and since these could not be ranged alongside those of chemistry and physics, transcendental phenomena might be always expected to occur whose orderly array as part of natural science was not merely a futile but on *a priori* grounds an absolutely impossible task. What possible justification was there for branding as hopeless all further physical and chemical investigation of certain aspects of the phenomena by attributing these to vital directive forces?

AUTOMATIC BODY-MECHANISMS.

It was remarkable how many of strictly chemical automatic mechanisms had been discovered in the last few years, thus substantiating the views of Brown-Séquard. The automatic character of the mechanism which determined the secretion of the pancreatic fluid was revealed by the experiments of Bayliss and Starling, which showed that definite chemical compounds were formed in the lining cells of the small intestine, and that treatment with weak acid, such as occurs in the acid chyme, liberated a substance which, absorbed into the blood, had the special function of stimulating the pancreatic cells. A similar automatic mechanism had been found by Edkins to exist in the stomach, for although the flow of gastric juice was initiated by nervous channels, the subsequent peptic secretion was largely augmented through the presence in the blood of chemical substances elaborated and absorbed in the pyloric portion of the stomach wall. These were only a few instances of a class of mechanisms, strictly chemical in character, by which the activities of remote and dissimilar organs were automatically co-ordinated; a further class of such mechanisms, although involving a chemical substance conveyed by the blood, carried out the actual regulation by means of the central nervous system. The nervous process, which rightly seemed to us so recondite, did not, in the light of this conception, owe its physiological mystery to a new form of energy, but to the circumstance that a mode of energy displayed in the non-living world occurred in colloidal electrolytic structures of great chemical complexity. There was a natural prejudice against the adoption of this view, but such prejudice should surely be mitigated by the consideration that this full admission of physiology into the realm of natural science, by forcing a more comprehensive recognition of the harmony of Nature, was invested with intellectual grandeur. If objective phenomena formed the subject-matter of the physiologist, then "the legitimate materialism of science" must constitute his working hypothesis; and his "well-defined purpose" must be to adapt and apply the methods of physics and chemistry for the analysis of such phenomena as he could detect in all physiological tissues, including the nervous system. The trend of such a strictly physiological analysis was towards a conception in which the highest animal appeared as an automaton composed of differentiated structures exquisitely sensitive to the play of physical and chemical surroundings. The various parts of the animal body were linked by circulating fluids and by one special structure, the nervous system; in this linking of parts the physiologist detected the working of automatic chemical mechanisms of great delicacy which, once developed, were retained and perfected in proportion as they efficiently regulated the various bodily activities and co-ordinated them for the welfare of the whole organism.

(Bsh. Assoc.ⁿ 1906)

2539   (**f35ʳ**) Times Literary Supplement
Literature.
From Wordsworth to Byron.
Main currents in nineteenth century literature. Volume IV.:
Naturalism in England. By George Brandes. (Heinemann, 12s. net.)
    It is a relief to have at last Mr. Brandes's admission that, in the
history of European literature, English literature counts. The
postponement of the tribute, however, only results from some
disturbance of the chronological order of issue of the translated
volumes, and we now find it paid ungrudgingly and even with
enthusiasm. Whether our literature counts at the present moment (and
if so how and why) is another question. What is quite certain is that, in
the past, it has counted for a great deal, has exercised an influence both
wide and deep, and has anticipated and inspired several of the great
Continental movements. The Encyclopaedists are deeply in the debt of
the Baconians. Rousseau did not hesitate to acknowledge obligations to
Richardson. Balzac's earliest models were "Monk" Lewis and Mrs.
Radcliffe; while the romantic French school of the thirties owed more to
Scott than to any literary predecessor of their own race. It might be
argued, no doubt, in these cases – or at all events in most of them – that
the disciples excelled the masters; but in the period under review in the
present essay in criticism – the period, that is to say, from the French
Revolution to the beginning of the revolt against the Holy Alliance – no
such point can with any plausibility be made. The great names of that
epoch, if we exclude the metaphysicians and confine our survey to
poetry, fiction, and the "belles lettres," are English almost without
exception. Certainly no French name, whether among those that made
a noise in the world or those that were neglected, even approaches them
in significance. Chateaubriand swam gracefully and artistically with
the flowing reactionary tide which has long since turned and left him
stranded in a backwater. Sénancour's writings – other than his hack
work – are one long, helpless wringing of the hands; and his confession
of failure is faithfully rendered by his epitaph:– *Eternité, deviens mon asyle.*
Madame de Staël has left us the memory of an amazing personality,
but no work of quite commanding merit. Benjamin Constant, though
brilliantly clever, is only an interesting invalid – the typical sufferer
from the *maladie du siècle*, continually cossetting and doctoring himself in
vain. Joseph de Maître was ingeniously paradoxical; but literature
cannot live on paradox alone. The others, like Mme. de Souza and

Mme. de Krudener, are not even worth depreciating. And that is all that France has to show in an age in which the great English names are those of Wordsworth, Coleridge, Landor, Scott, Keats, Shelley, and Byron. England, it will be observed, in that golden age, produced practically all the poetry, while France produced only a portion of the prose; and poetry is, after all, the kind of literature that wears the best, and lasts the longest, and least shows the marks of age, when we know by the calendar that it is old. A work from a Continental critic of the calibre and insight of Mr. Brandes on our poetry in this era of literary renaissance is warmly to be welcomed.

There is, perhaps, only one way in which one can profitably criticize a critic – by looking for the personal equation, and discovering the bias which upsets or steadies (according to our point of view) the equilibrium of his judgements. There is no attempt in Mr. Brandes's case, to suppress the personal equation, or to conceal the bias, he has very little interest in literature as mere composition. What chiefly concerns him is always its relation to life – to the life not only of the writer, but of his times, not only of his country but of the world, not only of the present but of the future. The poet for him is not merely *poeta* but *vates sacer*. Mere beauty is not all he asks from him. He requires him also to be a prophet, and, if not a politician, at least on the right side in politics. Poetry is for him, so to say, a higher kind of politics; and he always applies the political test, though without relaxing any of the others, before delivering his verdict. And his own political opinions, to which the poet is expected to conform, are clear cut and aggressive. He is, quite frankly and even somewhat obtrusively, a Radical and an anticlerical. Kings are, for him, oppressors, and priests (including Nonconformist ministers) are the gaolers of the human spirit. Both are obstacles to human progress; both must be overthrown. Poetry is one of the weapons by which war can be waged against them. Other things being equal, he is the greatest poet who proves himself the most formidable fighter in this interminable revolutionary war. That is the fixed idea which Mr. Brandes brings to the task of criticism. It might easily have made him an unjust judge; but two things save him from ever being glaringly unfair. The first is his own feeling for beauty which enables him to enjoy Keats, even though he is painfully conscious that Keats "proves nothing." The second is the accident that the Conservatives of the period were on the whole inferior as poets to the Radicals – that Southey, for instance, cannot be preferred to Shelley by any critic of whatever political school of thought. None the less his prepossessions colour his criticisms throughout, and even, on occasions, somewhat distort his point of view. His admiration for Moore is really a reflection of his enthusiasm for Robert Emmett. It seems, as it were, to give Moore an additional good mark because he did not fear to "speak of '98"; and he also appears, for purely political reasons, to make too little of Wordsworth, and too much of Byron, though that, of course, is a tendency which he shares with the generality of continental critics of our literature.

One must not say that Mr. Brandes has failed to understand Wordsworth. He has understood him, and even, up to a point, enjoyed him. But his enjoyment has been marred by the poet's Conservatism, and especially by what he calls his Protestantism, and should, perhaps, more properly call his Pietism – his inclination, that is to say, to the use of modes of expression and manners of thought in vogue among orthodox Christians of the milder evangelical school. The habit, no doubt, involved him in inconsistencies; since the Wordsworthian Pantheism – which is the best thing in Wordsworth – is not properly expressible in Christian formulae, and is especially antagonistic to the kind of Christianity taught in pre-Victorian times. They are inconsistencies, however, which most of us can tolerate, knowing how hard it is, even for a poet, to "keep up" his Pantheism; and the irritation which they cause to Mr. Brandes appears exaggerated. He has the air of deliberately punishing – we had almost written bullying – Wordsworth for giving way to them. He reminds him that there is nothing essentially ennobling in the mere act of living in the country, suggests that he vegetated there, and even quotes with gusto Dickens's description of him as "a dreadful old ass" and another contemporary's representation that he "blew like a whale and uttered truisms in oracular tone." It is a true complaint, of course, but not really an important part of the truth. The "longueurs" of Wordsworth, rightly considered, represent the long journey which his slow-moving genius had to take in order to reach the heights to which he beckons us. The reader is not obliged to travel all the way with him, but may, so to put it, meet him by appointment at the journey's end, avoiding "Spade with which Wilkinson has tilled his lands," and resolutely declining to allow anything of that sort to impede his appreciation of "The world is too much with us," and

> Two voices are there; one is of the sea,
> One of the mountains; each a mighty voice.

And that, no doubt, is what Mr. Brandes himself would have felt if he were less of a politician, and if Conservatism and orthodox Christianity were not to him like red rags to a bull.

Very different is his treatment of Byron, to whom the whole book leads up as to a dramatic curtain and culmination, the "argument" being somewhat as follows:– The purpose of poetry is to assert and celebrate the emancipation of the human spirit from the fetters of political and ecclesiastical control – to carry out, in its own sphere, and by the means proper to it, the work begun by the French Revolution, and cynically set back by the Holy Alliance. The poet must be an artist, of course; but the great poet must also be a rebel. That he should be an enlightened patriot is much; but that he should be an enlightened cosmopolitan is more. These being our standards, let us apply our tests, and see which of the poets bear them and which break down under them. The poets of the so-called Lake School break down at once. The French Revolution, after having inspired them, frightened them. They became renegades. Having seen the better, they preferred the worse; having put their hands to the plough, they turned back. Wordsworth took to Christianity and Conservatism, Southey to Christianity and hack work, Coleridge to Christianity, muddle-headed metaphysics, and opium. Let them, therefore, be bowed, or kicked, out of the competition according to their merits. Moore, Scott, and Campbell stand for nationalism and for nothing more. The best of them only understand political freedom – the (**f35ᵛ**) sort of freedom that "shrieked when Kosciusko fell"; they do not perceive that, even under a constitutional Government, the human spirit may be enslaved. Let them too be dismissed. Keats is very beautiful, but inadequate, because purely sensuous. Landor had the right ideals in the main; but he was crotchety, and not born to command: "he had not the power of inspiring a multitude of other minds." Shelley had the root of the matter in him. He breathed the very spirit of defiance, making it also a spirit of beauty. In religion as well as in politics he was the most uncompromising Radical of the band. But he died without coming into his kingdom; and he was too vague and ethereal – too much, to quote another critic, the "beautiful, ineffectual angel" – to command attention, exert authority, and exercise direct and immediate influence. He inspired his generation by first inspiring Byron, whose voice was louder, and who could, indeed, like the west wind,

> Drive his dead thoughts over the universe
> Like withered leaves to quicken a new birth.

Mr. Brandes's essay in criticism is really, therefore, a romance, with Byron for its hero. He is not, it is true, even in this case, a shameless and unblushing hero-worshipper. He is under no illusions to the value of "Hours of Idleness" and of "English Bards and Scotch Reviewers." With Byron no less than with Wordsworth he can find fault. But the tone in which he does so is very different. Partly, perhaps, the reason for his greater leniency towards shortcoming is that he has been, as he tells us, though in more modest words, a bit of a Byron himself. He was once driven from Copenhagen, as Byron was driven from London (though on other grounds) by the Danish mania for petty persecution, and has found in his experience of the bitterness of exile a bond of sympathy with the English poet. Mainly, however, the change in his critical temper is due to his perception that Byron gradually developed the ideals which Wordsworth gradually discarded. He can be tender to his hero's faults, because his hero grew out of them; he cannot be severe upon his orgies and his addiction to rum and water, because he views these, if not as a part of his general scheme of revolt, at least as essentially instrumental in the formation of his audaciously rebellious spirit.

Here, of course, we have, in an extreme form, the Continental view of Byron. In England he has been largely accepted for what Continental critics would consider the wrong reasons – because "Don Juan" is amusing, because "Childe Harold" is full of graphic descriptions of scenery, or because of the morbid sentimentalism of "The Corsair." For Europe – and perhaps for Mr. Brandes more than for any one else in Europe – he is, above all things the poet of Revolution. He defies old-fashioned theology; he mocks at conventional morality; and he shakes his fist in the face of the Holy Alliance. There is a certain sort of English reader who regards him as great "in spite of" these excesses, as he considers them. It is precisely because of them that he is great in the eyes of Europe and of Mr. Brandes. He is for Mr. Brandes the great prison breaker – the one man who successfully burst the bars against which weaker spirits beat in vain, and behind which meaner spirits resigned themselves to dwell. "Don Juan" is great for him, not because of its rollicking humour or the idyllic charm of the Haidée episode. The jests and the idyll are only incidentally contributory to its greatness. It is fundamentally great because it is "a passionate work, instinct with political purpose, full of wrath, scorn, threats, and appeals, with from time to time a loud, long blast on the revolutionary war trumpet." Only an Englishman, Mr. Brandes is good enough to add, could have blown that trumpet quite as Byron blew it, or have been capable of such withering scorn towards Principalities and Powers. Only an Englishman could have written:–

> Shut up the bald-coot bully Alexander!
>   Ship off the Holy Three to Senegal;
>   Teach them that "sauce for goose is sauce for gander,"
>   And ask them how *they* like to be in thrall.

Granted. Even Victor Hugo denouncing Napoleon the Little from the Guernsey beach never rose quite to these heights, his style being too polished, and his hatred unsupported by humour; and, if Mr. Brandes is right in holding that this sort of thing is what poetry is principally for, then there can be no doubt whatever that he is also right in placing Byron head and shoulders above every other poet of his period.

2540 (**f37ʳ**) THE GRAND PASSION. CATCH IT YOUNG AND GET IT OVER. A PLEA FOR EARLY MARRIAGES.
INTERVIEWS WITH DR. CHALMERS MITCHELL AND MR. PLOWDEN.

In the first of a series of lectures on "The Evolution of Man," now being delivered at University College, Professor Chalmers Mitchell referred to the modern tendency to defer the age of marriage, and said that this was physiologically undesirable. People should get over their love-making early in their history. Then, when they have become sane, they should turn to the more serious problems of improving themselves and doing the work of the world.

OUT OF FASHION.

In an interview with a DAILY GRAPHIC representative yesterday Professor Mitchell explained that these remarks were only introduced incidentally in the course of his lecture, which was delivered to an audience of teachers and intelligent persons, and that they were intended to be merely suggestive, and not the statement of a theory carefully thought out and investigated. On the other hand, he had not said these words flippantly, and he would not have uttered them if he had not been strongly of opinion that this aspect of biology and sociology was worthy of considerable attention.

"There is no doubt," said Professor Mitchell, "that our statistics show that early marriages are out of fashion, except among the poor. Economic and social conditions generally prohibit most men from marrying before they reach the age of thirty. To my mind this is a bad thing for the well-being of the nation.

"WHEN PRACTICALLY CHILDREN."

"The social philosopher Metchinkoff has endeavoured to prove that the age of maturity may be considerably prolonged, and that the life of natural decay may be considerably postponed. There is no reason, he thinks, why, in the future, a man may not produce his best work up to the age of ninety or a hundred, instead of becoming senile so early as he now does. At present, however, according to our pathological knowledge, very few men are in a perfect state of health after the age of, say, thirty-five. They have traces of gout, of anaemia, of blood troubles, and the effects of smoking and drinking. It is, therefore, inadvisable that they should marry when they have reached that stage of life. It seems to me far better that they should do so when they are practically children, and get over the disturbance of love so early that they may use their full powers for the other business of life, when they are in the finest physical condition.

EXPERIMENTS WITH FROG-LIKE CREATURES.

"We have got too much into the belief that the various states of life are fixed. But experiments with frog-like creatures and other animals show that the reproductive age may be pushed either backwards or forwards. I am not at all sure whether the State should not endeavour to push the marrying age of men and women forwards, helping young people to marry early, if they are physically sound, by giving a bounty on healthy children of a high standard, while handicapping, if possible, the physically unfit. This would do much to get rid of vice, which is very expensive to the State, while increasing the intellectual output of the nation.

HEALTHY INFLUENCE OF THE NOVEL.

"There is no doubt," continued Professor Mitchell, "that love absorbs a great deal of the energies of any man and woman of a good intellectual and moral standard. Biology teaches us that love has a profound influence upon the body and brain while the passion lasts. And personally I think that the 'grand passion' is essential to the highest birth-supply. In that way the novels which do much to foster this psychological and physiological turmoil have a healthy influence. I do not approve of the man of thirty-five, who, meditating over his pipe, comes to the conclusion that it is time he should marry, and calmly looks round for a wife. That is not love in the highest sense. The 'grand passion' is a fever which, as I have said, should be got over and done with in youth.

"SOME ALTERATION OF OUR SOCIAL CODE."

"But all our social economy and our educational system is pushing the age of marriage steadily backward in life. Our polytechnics and evening classes, and University Extension lectures, and all that sort of thing, tend to keep young men and women still unmarried. Of course my theory reduces itself to the somewhat startling suggestion that boys should have married before they go to college. Then comes in the question of the children, and that raises a big economic problem; but I fancy some of our best thinkers and social scientists are of opinion that some alteration in our social code is necessary to promote healthy parentage upon broader lines than at present allowed by convention."

THE OTHER SIDE OF THE CASE.

The well-known magistrate, Mr. Plowden, was interviewed on this subject by the DAILY GRAPHIC representative, as having an extensive practical experience of the marriage problem as it affects the poor. "It is a big subject," he said, "and I do not care to enter the lists of controversy. If I once began, I should want pages to express my ideas. But certainly I know that under present conditions it is impossible to prevent early marriages of those people who are most unfitted for marriage. I assure you they, at least, need no encouragement!"

"CRIME, DESPAIR, POVERTY, AND CRUELTY."

Mr. Plowden has before him almost every day of his life cases of young people who have rushed into matrimony and repent at leisure, the husband unable to support the wife, and both of them prematurely overburdened with parental responsibilities, above their means, above their moral force, and the cause of crime, despair, and frightful poverty, to say nothing of cruelty to the children. He admits, of course, that this is due in part to our present economic conditions, but so long as they exist so also will the evils of early marriage among the physically and morally unfit. "With all my experience," said Mr. Plowden, "I am unable to lay down the law at a moment's notice upon a subject so complicated and so serious." Daily Graphic Oct. 04.

2541   (**f38ʳ**) THE PHILOSOPHY OF RELIGION.*

"In its golden ages," says Professor Höffding, "religion satisfies all the spiritual needs of man, including his thirst for knowledge." At such times the problem of religion is not raised, and its nature and rights are taken for granted, as matters of course. "A religious problem, in the strict sense of the word, can only arise when other sides of the spiritual life – science and art, moral and social life – begin to emancipate themselves and to claim free independent value. ... We may say, if we like, that it is only in unhappy periods that a religious problem can be said to exist."

Professor Höffding finds that such "an unhappy period" is ours. "We are living in an age of transition. There is a want of harmony between our faith on the one hand and our knowledge and our life on the other." The discord is so great and so vital that "the task of harmonising free knowledge and free development of life with that which is, for us, of the highest value cannot be evaded." We owe this condition of matters to the decay of "the inner forces that move within the holy places of personality"; and this decay we owe in turn, and in part, at least, to the rule of dogmatism and scepticism, to the "importunate propagandists and the profane scoffers."

All these phrases are a little indefinite; and the reader will desire a clearer indication of what is meant by the "free development of life"; and by that thing of highest value which conflicts with it? Possibly we are to identify the former with morality, which is "the process of finding and producing values," and the latter with religion, which consists essentially in faith in the conservation of values – the God of religion being also called "the principle of the conservation of values." It is the conflict between the ideal regarded as real and the same ideal regarded as in process of being realised; for religion assumes that the Best eternally *is*, and morality presupposes that it has to be brought about through struggle and striving. In that case the discord is not fundamental, or, at least, it is not final. The Best manifests itself in our "strivings to find and produce values," and is operative in them. "Life is not the tantalising pursuit of the unattainable." "The eternal is in the present, in every valuable moment, in each ray of sunshine, in the striving which takes Excelsior as its motto. ... The distinction between ends and means falls away ... and with this vanishes also the

---

*THE PHILOSOPHY OF RELIGION. By Dr. Harald Höffding. London. Macmillan and Co. 12s. net.

distinction between religion and ethics, for the ethical includes the religious."

The other contradiction with which we are tortured – namely, that between *knowledge* and religion – is more stubborn. Their domains seem to be separate, their aims and interests different; and it would seem as if we were at once obliged to choose between them and to possess both. Knowledge seeks to explain; religion to estimate and appraise; the former would deal with existence, the latter with values; and it is difficult, if not impossible, to show that the existent has value, or that the valuable exists, or in simpler language that Reality is Good, and the Best is real.

"The intellectual interest prompts us to conceive existence as a great immeasurable system of causal groups and series; the religious interest moves us to a conception of being as the home of the development and conservation of value." "Can these two points of view be harmonised?" asks Höffding. "What is the relation between value and causality, the riddle of life and the riddle of the world?" "The problem," he answers, "is perhaps insoluble, and to solve it would be to find the Philosopher's Stone."

This "perhaps," this *probable* insolubility turns into certainty so far as "speculation and construction" are concerned. Experience is inexhaustible. "New experiences are continually appearing." "There is always a possibility that the ultimate basis of these experiences does not work in a constant manner, but is itself in the grip of becoming, of evolution." This constant change of our growing experience stultifies our constructive conceptions, or at least makes them all insecure. Intellectually we are shut up within a region of mere possibilities. "We are not able to indicate the degree and nature of the metamorphosis our points of view will have to undergo before they can be assimilated into the highest and most all-embracing inter-connexion that we are able to conceive." In short, our knowledge is in the melting pot. Nay, the object of our knowledge, the universe of reality itself, may be in no better state. "The inconclusiveness of experience and of knowledge may be bound up with the fact that being itself is not complete but is continually developing."

Ordinary readers will be tempted to call such a doctrine either Agnosticism or Scepticism. But Professor Höffding calls it a Critical Monism. It is closely allied to the doctrine which in this country goes by the name of Pragmatism, or Pluralism, although it places somewhat more accent on the unity of being. The Critical Monist assumes that being is a whole or system; but he is aware that he cannot justify his assumption, and sits loose from it. He can say nothing of this system, or whole, except that it is expected somehow to comprehend the parts; nor of the parts except that by some unknowable changes they may possibly come to fit into the whole. He sees that he cannot do without unity and order; but he recoils from the Romanticism of the pronounced idealist, and would provide for accidents. The result is that he is himself safe from refutation; for you cannot convince a man of error if he only says "Perhaps," nor condemn him if, "whenever he erects a temple to God, he sets up close by a little chapel for the devil."

But, if knowledge can not evaluate at all, nor even interpret except hypothetically and in part, can any better success be achieved from the point of view of religion? Professor Höffding, as usual, answers with a "No," tempered by a "Yes." "No," if the answer has to be couched in definite conceptions. "Yes," if "poetic expressions" will serve the purpose. "No," if you desire a dogmatic creed formulated by the intelligence; "Yes," if you permit "feeling" to do the work of the intellect as well as its own and are satisfied with emotional faith. "It is not of the essence of religion to afford an understanding or explanation of existence such as the intellectual interest demands." "If the religious ideas are to have any significance at all, it can only be in serving as symbolical expressions for the feeling, the aspirations, and the wishes of men in their struggle for existence; they are secondary not primary both in significance and origin." "Such answers to these questions as transcend the latest scientific hypotheses can only have a poetical character." (**f38ᵛ**)

But this should occasion no despair. "It may be that poetry is a more perfect expression of the highest than any scientific concept could ever be." For is not poetry "the spontaneous and living form in which that which has been actually lived through in moments of violent excitement clothes itself"? "This is a poetry which is opposed neither to will nor to thought, even though it is most apt to arise when thought and will touch their limits." And might not "a religious community come into existence whose faith found poetic and symbolic expression, free from all dogmatic conclusions"? That is to say, men might unite on a common symbolism, even though no one can tell what the symbols symbolise.

Such are the dominant conceptions which rule Professor Höffding's view of religion and of its relations to the other elements of man's spiritual life. He divides his work into three main portions, and these conceptions appear in all of them. In the first part he convicts knowledge of relative impotence, finds that it "runs up against the irrational," and that religion cannot help it out of its difficulties. Its function is other than that of knowledge: it is concerned with evaluation. In the second, a psychological part, he describes the religious life of the soul, and the various kinds and degrees of value in which it exhibits itself; and in the third, or ethical part, he discusses the relation between the belief in the conservation of value, which is religion, and the actual production and maintenance of value in practical life, which is morality. By far the most original and exhaustive of these three parts is the psychological.

Taking the book as a whole, I cannot conceive its satisfying any reader, or failing to instruct him. It will instruct through its sympathetic breadth of spirit, its psychological acumen, its historical wealth of illustration and reference, and its admirable quality of estimating conflicting doctrines by their truths rather than by their errors. It will disappoint because it is inconclusive in its treatment of vital issues, and prolific rather than rigorous in its arguments. It gives no help in a crisis. It is not original in any great way. It will transform no one's attitude towards the religious problem of the age, and give definite pause neither to those who do, nor to those who do not, consider that "religious ideas have lost their value as knowledge."

The whole doctrine rests on presuppositions which it is vital either to prove or to disprove. It is assumed, in the first place, that the evolution of human experience carries with it the independence of its elements; or, in the usual phrase, that differentiation brings the rupture of the unity of life. Religion, in consequence, comes to possess "a domain of its own," and stands over against science and art." No attempt is made to refute the view that the great interests of life, the intellectual, the ethical, the religious, the artistic, are in a relation of mutual inclusiveness. Such a method of reconciliation, according to which the arts of life are free and yet serve, and by which religion inspires and informs without limiting or enslaving, by which the secular becomes sacred through attaining its highest, does not seem to have occurred to the author. In the second place, the assumption of incompatibility between value and truth, the ends and the provinces of religion on the one hand and of systematic knowledge on the other, comes far too easy. The contradiction is asserted not proven, and there is the usual absence of any critical examination of the conception of value. Lastly, there is the facile transition from the fact, which not even a Hegelian will deny, that reality surpasses knowledge, to the notion, which requires proof, that the difficulties which knowledge finds are surds – not only unreduced but irreducible.

If I understand the attitude of reflective men in this country towards religion, there is in it a high seriousness which will preclude them from resting in a theory that faces both ways, and leaves them neither truth nor error, but "a poetic expression of religious experience" capable neither of clear denial nor of clear affirmation. Höffding's distaste to a fixed dogmatism in our creeds may be more than justified; but it does not follow that all the principles of religion are insecure; nor that its graver problems should not be confronted in a frank way. We are told that *may* be that existence is itself a becoming; it *may* be that our highest principles are false; it *may* be that our religious evaluations will stand; it *may* be that existence and value are reconcilable. But what precisely is the task of the philosopher except to investigate these possibilities? No doubt he must fall back on "experience," give its own place to "feeling," attribute its full functions to "personality," admit the distinction between "value" and existence. But these terms in which the half-hearted Idealism of the day takes refuge require explanation almost beyond all others. And no explanation is offered. The votaries of Monism-*cum*-Pluralism are right in their opposition to Intellectualism if that means a theory that allows no room or no adequate room and function for the will and feeling; but they must not allow that opposition to degenerate into dislike of clear thinking, even though the will and feelings should take to thinking instead of the intellect, and in addition to their proper tasks. When they sit down to philosophising one could desire for them more of the spirit of Mrs. Battle, when she sat down to whist. Men in earnest about the truth of religion will not be put off with "poetry" from philosophers – but they will demand "the rigour of the game."   HENRY JONES.

2542   (**f39ʳ**) Times. IN DEFENCE OF RHYME. 19 Nov. '08
Though rhyme is securely established in our poetry and we are quite familiar with its beauties, yet there still persists among us an idea that it is something arbitrary and irrational, imposed upon verse to make it more difficult, like the bunkers of a golf course. This was the idea of Campion and of Milton, who were both themselves skilful masters of rhyme yet condemned it for much the same reasons – namely, because the ancients did not use it, because it was a hindrance to expression, and because it was the invention of a barbarous age. Campion also said

that it made poets indifferent to the rules of metre, and he seems to have supposed that our metres were based upon quantity, not on accent. Milton did not fall into this error; but he failed to see that poetry of accent may be the better for rhyme, although poetry of quantity does not need it. For rhyme itself is only a kind of accent, introduced to mark the end or some period of a verse by its likeness in sound to some corresponding end or period. Rhymes are landmarks, easily recognizable, on the changing surface of accentual verse; but quantities are themselves fixed and need an incessant variety of accent to preserve them from monotony. Rhyme, therefore, would only enforce the monotony to which the verse of quantity is always liable. It is strange that Milton and Campion, when they condemned rhyme for the difficulties which it sets up, should not have seen that all the forms of verse might be condemned for the same reason. If rhyme makes composition more difficult, so does metre. If the easiest kind of composition is the best, we should all write prose and free our literature from the fetters which a childish taste for ornament has imposed upon it. The business of a serious writer is to say what he has to say as plainly as he can, not to play games with words, according to some obsolete and arbitrary rules.

Now, everyone knows that the answer to this, so far as metre is concerned, is that verse is not a game, but a means of expressing what cannot be expressed so well without it; that it gives to words an emotional power which they do not possess in a merely grammatical arrangement; that verse has grown like language itself and not been invented; and that its rules are no more arbitrary than the rules of grammar, but only statements of common practice. We know that all this is true of metre, but we do not recognize the fact that it must also be true of rhyme, if rhyme is a really valuable element in our verse. That it is a valuable element seems to be proved by the practice of our poets, who would never have hampered themselves with it, if they had found it a hindrance rather than a help to expression.

But it is worth while to ask ourselves how it can help expression. There is this difficulty to begin with, that, though we may argue theoretically that rhyme is necessary to accentual verse, yet the practice of the poets, and particularly of Milton, proves that it is not. Blank verse was a noble instrument in his hands, and in the hands of many Elizabethan dramatists, and it has been nobly used by some modern poets. Also some beautiful unrhymed lyrics exist, though they are few compared with the quantity of good blank verse. But still the great mass of our poetry is rhymed, and had long been rhymed before any blank verse or rhymeless lyrics were written. We do not say this in ignorance of the fact that Anglo–Saxon poetry was rhymeless. It was not English poetry, but composed on a different principle altogether; and as Anglo–Saxon poetry changed gradually into English, rhyme crept into it together with regular metre, so that the one was as natural a growth as the other. Thus nearly all our metres were developed with the help of rhyme, and, if some of them have since been able to do without it, it does not follow that they could have done without it from the first. Accentual verse is monotonous and devoid of subtlety without considerable licence in the shifting of accent; and it was the fixed landmark of rhyme that gave our earlier poets the courage to use that licence. Without it they would have had nothing but regularity of accent to distinguish their verse from prose, in which case they would seldom have dared any irregularity. But when blank verse was first introduced the heroic line was already thoroughly familiar, and all its subtleties had been developed by Chaucer under the safeguard of rhyme. Even so, blank verse, until Shakespeare gave it freedom, was far stiffer and more monotonous than Chaucer's rhyming lines; and that freedom which Shakespeare gave it was dangerous to lesser poets. Fletcher, for all his skill, was afraid of it, and developed for himself a monotonous kind of blank verse with feminine endings instead of rhymes for landmarks; while the blank verse of other dramatists became more and more formless, until it was given up at the Restoration, after a short struggle, for rhyme or prose. We must remember, too, that dramatic verse can do better without rhyme than other kinds, because it is written to be spoken, not read; and no doubt Elizabethan actors emphasized the rhythm when they spoke it. Rhyme is of more value in poetry that is written to be read, because accent is not so plain to the eye as to the ear, whereas rhyme is equally plain to both. The mind, unassisted by the ear, is apt to think more of sense than of sound; and even a poet, if he composes only for readers, is liable to be too much absorbed in his sense. To him and to the reader rhyme is a reminder that sound is a necessary means of expression in poetry, and that poetry which does not use it is only prose. Thus Wordsworth often falls into mere prose in the Excursion and the Prelude; and those who read these works only for the sense are quite unaware that they bring only a prosaic understanding even to the more poetic parts of them.   .

Poets who write blank verse to be read are liable to two dangers, and few of them have avoided both. Either they tend, like Wordsworth, to write mere prose in their less inspired passages, or else, like Tennyson and Milton himself, they contort their language so that it may not resemble the language of prose. The language of Milton is further removed from ordinary speech than that of any great English poet, and it is furthest removed when the sense is most prosaic.

> The virgins also shall, on feastful days,
> Visit his tomb with flowers, only bewailing
> *His lot unfortunate in nuptial choice.*
> *From whence captivity and loss of eyes.*

In lines like the last two of these he set a fashion of disguising prose, which has lasted to our own time. There is always a majesty in his disguises which has been ludicrously aped by many of his followers. Even Keats could not free himself from the Miltonic convention when he wrote blank verse, and he abandoned "Hyperion" because there were too many Miltonic inversions in it. Blank verse has this great and unexpected defect, that it can seldom, for more than a few lines at a time, be written simply without falling into prose. Without rhyme we may be sure that our poetry, in the continued effort to distinguish itself from prose, would have grown more and more artificial in its grammatical structure and would long ago have lost touch with the vernacular.

But there are other kinds of verse in our poetry besides the heroic line; and many of these could certainly not have been developed without rhyme. The form of stanzas in English poetry is made by rhyme, and we could not have them without it except on some rigid and elaborate system of accentuation that would destroy much of the expressive power of accentual poetry. It is true that a few beautiful poems have been written in rhymeless stanzas, such as Campion's "Rose-cheeked Laura, Come" and Collins's "Ode to Evening." But they were written by poets, and for readers, accustomed to rhymed stanzas. They have a music that had been developed in rhymed poetry, and their form would not, perhaps, be recognized except by readers used to poems of the same kind, emphasized by rhyme. The absence of rhyme is agreeable in them just because our ears are so delicately disappointed of it. Campion disappoints us more cunningly even than Collins, (**f39ᵛ**) because, in his stanza, the metre seems to glance away from the very possibility of rhyme.

> Rose-cheeked Laura, come;
> Sing thou smoothly with thy beauty's
> Silent music, either other
>   Sweetly gracing.

Here there could not be a complete correspondence of rhymes. If the two middle lines were rhymed as in Crashaw's poem –

> To thy lover, Dear, discover –

we should expect the first line to rhyme with the last, which could not be, since the last has a feminine ending. Campion, therefore, has made a stanza only possible without rhyme; but it does not follow that he could ever have made it unless he had been used to rhyme. He himself seems to have thought his verse was quantitative. It is really, of course, accentual, with subtle irregularities of accent that had been developed in rhymed poetry and were possible in rhymeless, only because the influence and memory of rhyme were powerful in the minds both of the poet and his readers. In fact, we may say of all our rhymeless poetry, except blank verse, that it is a kind of parasite upon rhymed poetry, and that even blank verse owes much of its freedom and beauty to the practice of rhyme.

   We cannot tell why rhyme adds to the beauty and expressive power of language any more than we can tell why metre does so. The connexion between beauty and expressive power in all the arts is a mystery. We only know by observation and experience that they are closely connected, and that those rules in any art which make for beauty make also for expressive power. Indeed they are not rules at all, but only means of expression systematized by experience, which the artist is free to discard if he can do better without them. So the poet need not rhyme, unless he chooses; but he has no right to condemn rhyme, for, however well he may express himself in blank verse, he may be sure that he could never have expressed himself so well but for the practice of former rhymers. Those fetters which he has cast off have given him the freedom which he enjoys; and to most poets they are not fetters at all, but safeguards against prosaic diffuseness and even spurs to the fancy. Many a fine image has come to a poet in his search for a rhyme, just as a good speaker often makes his best points out of interruptions. Inspiration can catch at any hint and use it for its own purposes; and the difficulty of finding rhymes is only a more intense form of that difficulty of finding words which is a necessary condition of the whole art of poetry. How troublesome it must be, we think, for the poet to be checked in the full career and momentum of his inspiration by the need to find a rhyme. Yet he is incessantly checked all through the process of composition by the need to find words and to arrange them; and the finding and arrangement of them are the creative act without which his inspiration would be incomplete and vague even to himself. If he rhymes, he takes rhyme, like language itself, as a condition of that act, one that is imposed upon him by his art, not by any fashion or convention; and unconsciously he adapts his phrasing and his very grammatical structure to his rhymes. This adaptation may be carried too far, as in the correct couplets of the 18th century, where a sentence nearly always comes to an end with the second rhyme. But verse in which the sentences are quite uncontrolled by the rhymes is just as tiresome, as we may see from the heroic poems of the 17th century, and as Keats discovered when in Lamia he refused himself the liberties he had taken in Endymion and profited by the example of Dryden.

If we choose at a venture any splendid piece of rhymed verse, whether regular or irregular, we shall certainly find that its rhymes exercise a constant control both upon its grammatical structure and upon that beautiful phrasing which comes of the poet's effort to reconcile reason with emotion; grammatical with metrical demands.

> A loftier Argo cleaves the main,
> Fraught with a richer prize;
> Another Orpheus sings again,
> And loves, and weeps, and dies.
> A new Ulysses leaves once more
> Calypso for his native shore.

Here everything is controlled by the rhymes, and but for them what is said here must have been said quite differently. They give variety, not only to the metre, but also to the three sentences, all so short and so much alike in structure that in prose or rhymeless verse they would sound snappy and monotonous. But in this rhymed stanza how simple and pointed and concise is their eloquence. It may seem a paradox, but it is a certain fact that in all kinds of art, as practised by masters, elaborate form makes for simplicity of expression, and thus our simplest poetry is nearly all in rhyme. No blank verse, not even the

dramatic blank verse of Shakespeare, is ever simple for long; and
experience seems to prove that simple narrative poetry must be rhymed
if it is to escape dulness and monotony. Homer's simplicity always
becomes dull and monotonous when he is translated into blank verse;
and we may be pretty sure that, if he had been an English poet, he
would, like Chaucer, have written in rhyme. Matthew Arnold's
arguments against a rhymed translation of Homer only amount to this,
that it is impossible to find rhymes without perverting the sense. That
may or may not be so; but, as he saw, it is far more impossible to
translate Homer into blank verse without perverting the style and with
it the quality of the emotion. It is strange that he should have rejected
both rhyme and blank verse for a medium far more impossible than
either, for a rhymeless quantitative verse to which our ears and our
language are still quite unaccustomed. Both are accustomed to rhyme;
and that fact justifies it more completely than any arguments.

2543   (**f41ᵛ**) THE EVOLUTION OF ENGLISH POETRY
A History of English Poetry. By W. J. COURTHOPE. Vol. v. (Macmillan, 10s.
net.)
PROFESSOR COURTHOPE has now reached the eighteenth century in his
elaborate History of English Poetry, and as might be expected, he
shows himself thoroughly at home in dealing with the period. Perhaps
for the purposes of the general reader, who would like to enjoy this book
much in the same way as he enjoyed John Richard Green's "Short
History of the English People," he has gone too much into detail, but
Mr. Courthope's book is primarily intended, we should think, for
purposes of reference and consultation, and in that light its
thoroughness is a virtue of the highest order. It would be a very serious
task to attempt to follow his argument in all its windings, and at times
we are almost inclined to think that he presses his theory too far. No
doubt poets, like the rest of the human race, are extremely imitative in
their character, and it is possible to trace the connection between the
primitive beginnings of literature and the books written in the
eighteenth century, just as it is possible to trace the same idea in the
shape of a motor-car and the shape of an early horse-chariot. Mr.
Courthope seems to have set out with an admirable ambition to show
that the total body of literature is part and parcel of a harmonious
whole, and it is not entirely his fault that we are occasionally reminded
of those mediaeval historians who thought that every narrative should
begin with the Fall of Troy. It would, perhaps, have been sufficient to

indicate in · more general terms the connecting links between the literature of various countries, and to treat the writers (**f42ʳ**) separately from a more individual point of view. But the author may argue very justly that his mode of treatment is peculiarly suitable to the eighteenth century. It was a time when writers were to a great extent dominated by the same spirit. In prose they had taken their inspiration directly from the French writers, and the prose of the century approximates more closely in its characteristics to the French idea than that of any other period of literary activity. Individual as are such prose men as Dean Swift, Fielding, Smollett, and even Sterne, they are alike in their taste for lucidity, directness and simplicity. The dreamy, turgid mysticism that had found its highest expression in Sir Thomas Browne had passed away out of vision: so too had the poetic style of the Elizabethans. We may willingly concede much that has been claimed for Pope and his school, and it would be a narrow definition of poetry that excluded their works, but the verse of the period has none of that far-reaching glamour which we find in Homer, in Shakespeare, and even in Chaucer, though he gave less rein to this particular quality than the rest. The neatness, the antitheses, the sparkle of the school of Pope belong to poetry, but poetry of an order not quite so high. Perhaps as good a test as can be applied to poetry would lie in a comparison of the translations. It is curious that those of the Tudor period are still almost as readable to-day as they could have been at the time of their publication, while as a rule those of the eighteenth century sound to us dead and flat. Even Pope's Homer, about which so much has been said, is no exception to the general rule. It yields less of the original poetry than did Chapman's, and will not compare with some of those published in our time, though of course, as Matthew Arnold pointed out, the tendency is always to like best that which comes from our contemporaries, with whose language and thought we have more sympathy and familiarity than with those of a departed age whose niceties of expression are constantly lost.

Perhaps the most interesting section of this book is that which deals with the early romantic movement, although we cannot profess to be able to follow the argument as closely as is desired. The first important name dealt with is Allan Ramsay, and we are told that in "The Gentle Shepherd":

his inspiration seems also to be sometimes derived from classical sources, as in the following bucolic duet:–

PEGGY.

When first my dear laddie gaed to the green hill,
An' I at ewe-milking first say'd my young skill,
To bear the milk-bowie nae pain was to me
When I at the bughting foregathered wi' thee.

PATIE.

When corn-riggs waved yellow, an' blue heather-bells
Bloom'd bonny on muirland and sweet-rising fells,
Nae birns, briars, or breckens, gaed trouble to me,
Gif I found the berries right ripen'd for thee.

PEGGY.

When thou ran or wrestled or putted the stane,
An' cam' aff the victor, my heart was aye fain;
Thy ilka sport manly gae pleasure to me,
For nane can putt, wrestle, or run swift as thee.

PATIE.

Our Jenny sings saftly the *Cowden-broom-knowes*;
And Rosie lilts sweetly the *Milking the Ewes*;
There's few *Jenny Nettles* like Nancy can sing;
At *Thro' the Wood, Laddie*, Bess gars our lugs ring:

But when my dear Peggy sings wi' better skill
The Boatman, Tweedside, or *The Lass o' the Mill*,
It's mony times sweeter an' pleasing to me;
For though they sing nicely, they cannot like thee.

PEGGY.

How easy can lasses trow what they desire!
An' praises sae kindly increases love's fire:
Gie me still this pleasure; my study shall be
To mak' mysel' better and sweeter for thee.

It is difficult to understand what Mr. Courthope means, unless he is referring to the mere accident of form. He could scarcely have taken a passage from Allan Ramsay more redolent of the Scottish border, the Scottish peasant and his blunt character, than these lines. Honest Allan himself, as is very evident from the pages of his "Evergreen," has a fine taste for the minstrels of his native land, and his style, no doubt, was formed on these, while his inspiration was drawn from his native country. Whoever has written of "the loves and the ways of simple swains" has dealt with the same material, whether it be Theocritus or Robert Burns, Moschus or Allan Ramsay. The shepherd and the shepherdess have experienced the same pains and pleasures, lived under the same suns and felt the same rains, and existed in all times and all countries, in classic Greece and in shaggy Scotland. The poetical mind naturally suggests a similar treatment, except in so far as individuals are strikingly different. The scene witnessed by Theocritus and Burns, though it might conceivably be the same, would come out in very different colours. Again, the distinguishing feature of Ramsay appears to lie in a love of simplicity and naturalness more than in romance.

Curiously enough, following this study of Allan Ramsay comes a little essay on Shenstone, who may be described as the Watteau of the poets. It was scarcely romance, however, but pastoralism, to which Shenstone was returning. The next names to greet us are those of Collins and Gray: one is elaborately contrasted with the other, not altogether to the advantage of Gray as the following passage will show:

In his odes the ethic or elegiac spirit predominates, and is expressed by the union of substantives with carefully chosen single epithets, and by the antithetical turn of the sentence. This is according to the Latin genius, of which Gray's own verse compositions in that language show that he was full; who, in his 'Elegy', for example, does not feel the stately march of Latin verse?

Th' applause of listening senates to command,
The threats of pain and ruin to despise,
To scatter plenty o'er a smiling land,
And read their history in a nation's eyes,

Their lot forbade; nor circumscribed alone,
Their growing virtues, but their crimes confined,
Forbade to wade through slaughter to a throne,
And shut the gates of mercy on mankind.

The struggling pangs of conscious truth to hide,
To quench the blushes of ingenuous shame,
Or heap the shrine of Luxury and Pride,
With incense kindled at the Muse's flame.

Perhaps the fact that the English temper is more nearly allied to the
Roman than to the Greek, joined to the superiority of Gray in point
of workmanship, is sufficient to account for the greater popularity
which his poems have always enjoyed among his countrymen
compared with those of Collins. The complete assimilation of
subject and style in the *Elegy* and the masterly treatment of English
history in *The Bard* are more potent illustrations of the civic
tendencies of the Renaissance in England than is the subtle allegory
of the *Ode to Liberty*.

Mr. Courthope tells us that his reason for dwelling on these
contrasted qualities is that Collins and Gray are the "two last lyrical
poets of England whose art is consciously directed by the genius of the
Classical Renaissance." A more definite effort at romance was first
attempted by Ossian. Mr. Courthope's true aim seems to be to show
that Macpherson was essentially fraudulent. He takes very little
account of the fact that the compositions of Ossian have certainly been
proved to contain fine fragments of Gaelic poetry, and even in the
passage which he quotes for animadversion there is a quality of
picturesqueness that has suggested many a fine touch to subsequent
poets of greater refinement than Macpherson.

As the dark shades of autumn fly over hills of grass; so gloomy,
dark, successive, came the chiefs of Lochlin's echoing woods. Tall as
the stag of Morven, moved stately before them the King. His shining
shield is on his side, like a flame on the heath at night; when the
world is silent and dark, and the traveller sees some ghost sporting
in his beam! Dimly gleam the hills around, and show indistinctly
their oaks! A blast from the troubled ocean removed the settled mist.
The sons of Erin appear like a ridge of rocks on the coast; when
mariners on shores unknown are trembling at veering winds. ...
(**f42ᵛ**) As a hundred winds on Morven; as the stream of a hundred
hills; as clouds fly successive over heaven; as the dark ocean assails
the shore of the desert; so roaring, so vast, so terrible, the armies

mixed on Lena's echoing heath. The groan of the people spread over
the hills; it was like the thunder of night, when the clouds burst on
Cona; and a thousand ghosts shriek at once on the hollow wind. ...

Such were our words when Gaul's loud voice came growing on the
wind. He waved on high the sword of his father. We rushed to death
and wounds. As waves, white bubbling over the deep, come
swelling, roaring on; as rocks of ooze meet roaring waves; so foes
attacked and fought. Man met with man, and steel with steel.
Shields sound and warriors fall. As a hundred hammers on the red
son of the furnace, so rose, so rung their swords.

A closer study of Scottish verse would have supplied Mr. Courthope
with many suggestive and beautiful examples of the early work of the
romantic school. The class of poetry to which we refer may be
exemplified in these verses from William Hamilton's "Braes of
Yarrow."

B.
Busk ye then, busk, my bonny bonny bride,
 Busk ye, busk ye, my winsome marrow;
Busk ye and lo'e me on the banks o' Tweed,
 And think nae mair on the Braes o' Yarrow.

A.
How can I busk a bonny, bonny bride?
 How can I busk a winsome marrow?
How lo'e him on the banks o' Tweed,
 That slew my luve on the Braes o' Yarrow?

O Yarrow fields! may never never rain,
 Nor dew thy tender blossoms cover;
For there was basely slain my luve;
 My luve, as he had not been a lover.

The boy put on his robes, his robes of green,
 His purple veil, – 'twas my awn sewing.
Ah, wretched me! I little little kenned
 He was in these to meet his ruin!

> The boy took out his milk-white, milk-white steed,
>   Unheedful of my dole and sorrow;
> But ere the toofal of the night
> He lay a corpse on the Braes o' Yarrow.

There must have been an atmosphere suitable to this kind of verse before it was produced, and a great deal of it came into being between the middle and the end of the century

2544   (**f43ʳ**) LIFE IN POETRY: LAW IN TASTE.   W. J. Courthope.
   "The future of poetry", says Matthew Arnold, "is immense, because in poetry where it is worthy of its high destinies, our race as time goes on will find an ever surer and surer stay.... Our religion has materialized itself in the fact, in the supposed fact, and now the fact is failing it. But for poetry the idea is everything, the rest is a world of illusion, of divine illusion. Poetry attaches its emotions to the idea: the idea is the fact. The strongest part of our religion today is its unconscious poetry."

2545   Plato thought ... great poetry ... the utterance of individual genius, half inspired, half insane.

2546   Fine art does not, like photography, imitate real nature, but the idea of nature existing in the mind.

2547   One of the most striking characteristics in modern poetical conception ... the exaggeration of the individual element and the neglect of the universal ... urging the imagination to the contemplation of its own ideas without considering them in relation to the ideas of others. Poetical conception so formed will ... command attention and respect from those whose spiritual experience has been similar, and yet, as it has been framed with reference to the wants of human nature at large, will necessarily lack the main element of enduring life.

2548   (**f44ʳ**) The art of poetry has many mansions; and it does not follow that if one mode of conceiving Nature has become trite and mechanical the resources of Nature herself are exhausted.

2549   Metre can only properly be used for the expression of universal ideas.

2550 J. S. Mill ... says, "the orator ... speaks to be heard, the poet ... to be overheard."

2551 The secret of enduring poetical life lies in individualizing the universal, not in universalizing the individual.

2552 Dryden's character of Zimri, and Pope's lines on the death of Buckingham, reach the highest level of poetic diction in satire.

2553 In the decadence of art, the individual overbalances the universal.

2554 M. Mallarmé, one of the leaders of the French symbolists, says "To name an object is to destroy three-quarters of the enjoyment of the poem."

2555 He goes on to say: "The true goal of poetry is suggestion. Symbolism consists ... in evoking, little by little, an object, so as to indicate a state of soul, or, conversely, to choose an object and to disentangle from it a state of soul" ... a little obscure.

2556 (**f44ᵛ**)Two theories of poetry ... Wordsworth's ... that the poet ³ can make all things poetical by his own imagination, and hence that the selection of distinctively imaginative subjects is not essential ... the other ... Keats' ... abstract beauty of form.

2557 He (Kipling) thinks the artist sees and imitates something in actual nature which others do not see; whereas the real superiority of the painter or the poet ... ability to find expression for imaginative ideas of nature floating unexpressed.

2558 Contemporary art ... pursuit of novelty ... new matter for artistic treatment, and the deliberate rejection of those first principles of taste which the greater artists have traditionally obeyed.

2559 Every artist ... puts into his imitation of external things something that is not to be found in the particular aspect of nature. What that something is has been a matter of dispute from the earliest days of criticism. Some of the ancients called it   , others   ; some of the moderns define it as the Beautiful, others as the Characteristic.

2560   Goethe maintained that the cause of Art was the desire of the soul to imitate the idea of the Characteristic which it notes in the objects of external nature.

2561   The three main principles underlying Aristotle's criticism are:
   (1) That the function of poetry, as of all fine art, is imitation, not instruction. [4]
   (2) (**f45ʳ**) That the object of imitation in Poetry is the Universal, not the Particular; and
   (3) that the test of the justice of poetic imitation is the permanent pleasure produced in society by the work, not merely the pleasure felt by the artist in creating it.

2562   The Greeks had perceived ... that the first aim of every artist was to imitate an object. It was for this very reason that Plato objected to Art itself as immoral; since he supposed it to be the aim of the poet and painter to copy what was essentially false, as being only an imperfect resemblance of true Being.

2563   "Poetry tends to express the Universal, History the particular. By the Universal, I mean how a person of given character will on occasion speak or act, according to the law of probability or necessity."
(from Aristotle).

2564   "The higher reality"   (from same).

2565   "A probable impossibility is to be preferred (in art) to a thing improbable and yet impossible."   (from same).

2566   "It is probable that a thing may happen contrary to probability."   (from same.)

2567   (**f46ʳ**) Richard Wagner's Prose Works.

   Goethe ... won the most unfettered freedom by completely giving up the "acting-drama." In planning out his Faust he merely retained for the literary poem the advantages of a dramatic mode of statement, but left purposely out of sight the possibility of a scenic representment. In this poem Goethe was the first to sound with full consciousness the keynote of the poetic element distinctive of the present age, the thrust of Thought towards Actuality though he could not yet give it artistic redemption in the actuality of drama. Here stands the watershed between mediaeval romance ... and the real dramatic matter of the future.

2568   Wallenstein. This "dramatic poem", as Schiller himself calls it, was ... the most conscientious attempt to win from History, as such, material for the drama. ... In drama's further evolution we see Schiller dropping more and more his regard for History: on the one hand to employ it merely as itself a clothing for an intellectual motive peculiar to the poet's own general phrase of culture – on the other to present this motive more and more definitely in the form of drama. ... With this purposed subordination ... of the Stuff; Schiller fell even deeper into the inevitable fault of a sheer reflective and rhetorical presentment of his subject.

2569   No one can address himself intelligibly (in a fancy-picture) to any but those who see things in a like measure with himself: (**f47ʳ**) a man whose mode of viewing is not that of his fellow-men neither can address himself to them artistically.

2570   Were the individual man completely reconciled with the commonwealth – nay, should he find therein the fullest satisfaction of his bent towards happiness; then would all necessity of the Christian view be done away with; and Christianity itself be annulled.

2571   The State, as abstractum, is the fixed idea of well meaning but mistaken thinkers, – as concretum, the booty for the caprice of forceful and intriguing individuals who fill the pages of history with the record of their deeds.

2572   To-day the Folk cannot conceive the human being otherwise than in the uniform of his class. ... It would be placed in the greatest bewilderment if one attempted to reconstruct before it the actual human being beneath the visible semblance.

2573   In Drama, an action can only be explained when it is completely vindicated by the feeling; and it thus is the dramatic poet's task not to invent actions, but to make an action so intelligible through its emotional necessity that we may altogether dispense with the intellect's assistance in its vindication.

2574   This condensation (of phenomena) he (the poet) could only bring about ... by taking up into the motives of the moments chosen for actual representment all those motives which lay at bottom of the moments – of – action that he had discarded.

2575   (**f48ʳ**) Wherein should consist the stren⟨g⟩thening of the motives[3] which are to condition from out themselves that strengthening of the Moments of Action? ... What is the meaning ... of a Strengthening of the Motives? ... It cannot consist in a mere addition of lesser motives? ... It cannot consist in any but the complete absorption of of many motives into this one. ... An interest common to divers men once that these men are typically alike at bottom ... is to be made the interest of one man. ... This is as good as saying that from this Interest all which savours of the Particular and Accidental must be taken away.

2576   A mode of expression similar to that still proper to the beasts was in any case alike the first employed by man: and this we can recall before us at any moment, – as far as its substance goes – by removing from our Word-speech its dumb articulations and leaving nothing but the open sounds. In these vowels, if we think of them as stripped of their consonants and picture to ourselves the manifold and vivid play of inner feelings, with all their range of joy and sorrow, as given out in them alone, we shall an image of Man's first emotional language ... a joinery of ringing tones ... melody ... gestures ... took its time-measure – its Rhythm ˈ– from (them).

2577   In exact degree as poesis ceased to be a function of the feeling and became a transaction of the understanding, did the creative league of Gesture, Tone, and Word-speech, originally united in the Lyric, disband itself; Word-speech was the child that left its father and mother to help itself along in the world alone.

2578   (**f48ᵛ**) In modern prose we speak a language we do not understand with the Feeling, since its connection with the objects, whose impression on our faculties first ruled the moulding of the speech-roots, has become incognisable to us.

2579   Our Feeling – which quite of itself found unconscious expression in the primitive speech – we can only <u>describe</u> in this language.

2580   Therefore it was altogether consequent in our modern evolution that the feeling should have sought a refuge from absolute intellectual speech by fleeing to absolute tone-speech, our Music of today.

2581   In modern speech no poesis is possible – that is to say, a poetic[4] Aim cannot be realized therein, but only spoken out as such. The poet's Aim is never realized until it passes from the understanding to the feeling.

2582   A massing of consonants around a vowel, without any justification before the feeling, robs that vowel of all emotional ring, just as a massing of side-words around a main-word, when merely dictated by the meddlesome understanding, shuts off that main-word from the Feeling. In the eyes of Feeling, a doubling or trebling of the consonant is only of necessity when the vowel thereby gains a drastic colouring, (?) in harmony with a drastic property of the object which the root expresses; and in the same way an extic number of subsidiary words is only justified before the Feeling when the (**f49ʳ**)   [5]
accented main-word is specifically enhanced thereby in its expression but not when it is lamed – as in the modern phrase.

2583   Greek dramas ... unquestionably move from the lap of the Lyric to an intellectual Reflection, just as the Song of the chorus embouches into the merely spoken iambic talk of the characters. ... The lyric-element ... recurring more strongly in their Crises.

2584   The error in the art-genre of Opera consists herein: that a means of expression (Music) has been made the end, while the end of expression (the Drama) has been made a means.

2585   The Decadence of Tragedy.
   "The desire to keep up appearances has completely overcome the natural tendency to spontaneous expression. ... If, by any conceivable accident a modern Oedipus had married his mother he would not go raging through his palace. The first footman that he met would quench

his frenzy more effectually than any chorus could.

Edith Grosmann. (Contemporary.)

2586   "The danger of the romantic is the false."

(quoted in the Westminster Gazette.)

2587   (**f49ᵛ**) "An unfinished world, then, with all creation, along with our own thought, struggling into more continuous and better shape – such is our author's general view of the matter of Philosophy."

(W. James's Preface to Höffding's "Problems of Philosophy."

2588   "It is not to be doubted that thought is not the proper stuff of poetry. ... Poetry has not been fashioned in the ages in the expression of thought. What distinguishes it and always has distinguished it from prose, what has made its more organized form, is its capacity for expressing emotion. Of course, thought has more power of profundity in poetry than in prose, but then it is always thought charged with emotion and subsidiary to emotion. Emotion can be provoked by ideas as well as by the actions of men, the changes of the sky, or the seasons of the earth. Poetry has an infinite scope because emotion has an infinite scope, but emotion always remains the motive force of poetry. Great poets before Mr Meredith – Lucretius for instance – have tried to make thought its motive force, but they have always failed.

... The emotions provoked by thought are incidental and casual. Therefore the poetry in a poem of thought is incidental and casual. It is only the ornament and not the structure that is poetical.

... Both Mr Meredith and Mr Donne are reactionaries from a great convention of true poetry. Both are sick of the ease which those conventions gave to the art, of the extent to which they subordinated thought to emotion. That cry of Mr Meredith's for more brain ... was also the cry of Donne. He too, was not content to let his mind be carried away in a golden stream of music. When (**f50ʳ**) he was in love he felt his pulse assiduously and registered the results in verse. ... Against the faint poets, afraid of life, and the poisoned idealists enraged with it, Mr Meredith exalts the old wonder and delight and courage.

A. Clutton Brock – The Speaker. 19th, May '08.

2589   "It may perhaps be assumed that our philosophical faith is not in an actually existing rational system of things, – experience prevents us believing in that – but in an end, a final 'goal of ill' towards which evolution moves; that the conception of evolution involves the conception of the Absolute as Becoming, not as Being. The universe, it may be said, consists of a multiplicity of independent beings, who gradually come to settle down into stable equilibrium – atoms or monads, making, as it were, a permanent social contract with one another. The world then would be 'the best of all possible worlds' in the sense that it is the best arrangement fitted to survive. Such a view undoubtedly agrees with much that is commonly said about evolution. But it raises all the old puzzles that Zeno found in the 'many' or 'becoming' when treated as absolute categories. Thus it makes time an absolute and brings in the difficulties about a real beginning and end of time. Process and change cannot be thought of, unless in reference to a permanent and unchanging 'substance'. 'It is only the permanent that can change,' as Kant said. ... Our popular 'Sophists' of the present day talk of 'Evolution evolving' and of the 'Developmental process' as if it were an absolute. But it is only the carelessness of popular language and the use of abstract nouns as substantives which allow such phrases to pass current. Evolution is the application or (**f51ʳ**) manifestation to us of a timeless reality which includes and transcends change."

(Philosophical Studies. D. G. Ritchie.)

2590 THE PHILOSOPHY OF RELIGION. (Hoffding.)
translated by R. E. Meyer. (Macmillan.)
"Many free-thinkers take for granted that human life would assume richer and stronger forms did religion cease to exist; but this view ... rests on the pre-supposition that psychical equivalents are always at hand – equivalents in value as well as in energy."

2591 "The conservation of value is <u>the characteristic axiom of religion</u>."

2592 Value denotes the property possessed by a thing either of conferring immediate satisfaction or serving as a means to procure it.

2593 WALTER PATER. Edinburgh Review. July 1907.
"Conception – fundamental brainwork – that is what makes the difference in all art."   <u>Pater.</u>

2594 Pater's fastidiousness in the choice of language ... hence his occasional obscurity ... over-subtlety of minute thought shading ... he strove to attain to the pliancy of vocalized expression where the modulation of the human voice renders to one same word constantly varying tinges of significance.... He demanded the whole scale of meanings the intonations of speech could alone supply ... lost hold of the simpler, stronger, and broader effects with which written diction compensates for the comparative penury of its resources ... (**f52ʳ**) too rigid an elimination of ... brilliant hues and accentuations.... This human sentiment, clothed in the lovely forms of Greek art, what is it? Dismiss the fantastic circumstances of Greek art, what is it? Dismiss the fantastic circumstances of pagan story ... the fundamental conception simplifies itself.

2595 Concepts of Monism. A. Worsley.

"Philosophy warns us against any relative interpretation whatever; proclaims that our world is one of growing perception, and not one of fact; that behind its aspectual character lies concealed the real world. Between us and it is placed the great gulf of subjectivity, so that those who would pass thence cannot. Yet there is a way in which we can grasp a something, however little, of that underlying reality. Conceptive thought (Idealism) will lead us so far on the path; not far enough, certainly, to enable us to conceive the source in its absolute and unconditional character, but far enough to show us the bond uniting all things into one homogeneous whole."

"An instantaneous photograph gives records differing from those of our own (momentary) vision, and between these, Difference is evident and Discrimination possible, because the question of time has introduced the necessary minimum of apparent duality. But directly we eliminate the temporal element all possibility of discrimination vanishes; for to the eye of eternity there is no change, no form, no difference whatever....

Now the Vedântic doctrine of objective unreality, or of objective (**f53ʳ**) ~~unreality, or of~~ objective pluralism (multiplicity of vision) or ~~n~~ nescience, is clearly true in this sense. That is to say if we eliminate the minimum of duality necessary for discrimination by deleting Time altogether that then we are reduced to a condition of objective nescience, in which no phenomena and no object possesses any particularized attribute whatever. So that on this assumption not only are all our perceptions faulty records, but they are also faulty records of chimeras, not of realities. Hence the doctrine of objective pluralism, taught by some Vedantins, is unobjectionable if explained in this sense.

Yet it does not appear that this was the sense in which such doctrinaires construed it, and in any other sense it seems to me objectionable."

2596   "NESCIENCE – the non-knowing, the antithesis to Science."

2597   "The world of temporalities is that illusive world existing round the Ego. ... Should we view such as illusions ... or ... as misperceptions of something real (the Vedantic view)? Surely the latter.

2598   "Sainte-Beuve has remarked somewhere in "Nouveaux Lundis" that the greatest poet is not he who has done the best, but he who suggests the most."   The Academy.

2599   "Like Millais, Patmore felt that beauty and romance are here and now, and that the artist's business is to see them, not to imagine them."   'Times' on Patmore.

2600   (**f53ᵛ**) THE NEW MYSTICISM.   [1]
(The Divine Adventure etc, by Fiona Macleod)
   "Long ago, Eugenius Philalethes (the brother of Henry Vaughan the Silurist), and other mystics, talked of the alchemy by which a flower might be re-created from its ash and made to bloom again. In art it is possible to "quick the dead," as an old writer termed it. ... But ... like Heine, like Hugo at his best, their imaginer and new creator is, in her historical recall, only an historian of the heart. Do not be misled ... into thinking you have ... the real presence of a barbaric prime. That life, that presence, are never to be recaptured ... the umber (must) have a modern crimson added if it is to reach your current vision. ... Miss Macleod's fantasy, whose conception is ... two people, man and woman ... in the one predicament; striving and crying to deliver their love from the obstacles of Nature and Time, and seeing in their fellow mortals and the elements alike but the demons or angels that can destroy or save. In this way the people become passions, the elements become personified: the seals become men: the ninth wave becomes a demon: the trees imprison the spirits of lost creatures. Auguries and omens hang on every cloud. The sand is the piteous dust of dead beauties; the ocean is the blood of slain princes.

Morgan Lloyd says "... I found myself full of thoughts, but very quiet, having no lust, or will, or motion of my own. ..." Morgan Lloyd, a poet born out of time to a harsh birthright, set the edge of his imagination against the beauty of the visible and revealed world – It is a truer mysticism which holds with the **(f54ʳ)**   2
writer of "The Divine Adventure" that the soul has to learn to become 'one with the wind and the grass and with all that lives and moves; to take its life from the root of the body, and its green life from the mind, and its flower and fragrance from what it may of itself obtain not only from this world, but from its own dews, its own rainbows, dawn stars and evening stars' In this way the body becomes the friend, and not, as with the ascetics, the clog and foul garment of the soul.

Ernest Rhys, "Fortnightly" June 1900.

2601   "So does Love represent the next stage beyond Liberty. When men have got their communities arranged to their mind, they will find time – as a number of leisured persons find time already – to devote their main attention to such happiness as the relation between the sexes can bring. But here, almost for the first time, the question of the unknown future begins to have a practical bearing on life. If love is at once brought thus into prominence and also deprived of all beyond its earthly fruition, is not there a fear lest it should either sink into mere animal passion or lose its tranquility in yearning pain. Morris, (Wm, the poet) has treated this question in two ways."

Myers. "Meaning of Life."

2602   "The materialistic assertion of a self originating world which only comes to consciousness in us."

2603   **(f54ᵛ)** "TIMES" ON COLERIDGE.
"If a poet philosophizes at all, his philosophy should be the raw material of his poetry. It was so in the case of Wordsworth, and often it remains raw material in his verse. But it was not so in the case of Coleridge, and the reason was that his philosophy had no connection with his conduct ... Coleridge's thought was disconnected from his passion, and seldom became poetry; because poetry like action, issues

from a man's whole life, and philosophy cannot be heightened into poetry until it has grown to be part of the poet's life, and not merely a game of his intellect. It must be felt as well as thought; it must turn from a theory into a faith"

> "The harbour bar was clear as glass
>   So smoothly it was strewn,
> And on the bay the moonlight lay
> And the shadow of the moon."

   Here, and again and again in the poem (The Ancient Mariner) Coleridge achieves what all the poets are always attempting. He fills a plain statement with such beauty of sound that it has the precision of prose and the force of music."

———————————

2604   A flattering Illusion.

> "I thank you for the flowers you sent," she said,
> And then she pouted, blushed, and drooped her head.
> "Forgive me for the words I spoke last night;
> The flowers have sweetly proved that you are right."
>
> Then I forgave her, took her hand in mine,
> Sealed her forgiveness with the old, old sign;
> And as we wandered through the dim-lit bowers
> I wondered who had really sent the flowers.

[by] Geoffrey Clark. (It appeared originally in KOTABOS. the old T. D. C. magazine, and was reprinted in "Echoes from Kottabos", reviewed in the Academy of February 2nd '07.)

                                        Academy 25.5.'07.

2605 (f55ʳ) 'THE HUMANIST.'   Nation. 18th May 1907
   It is exactly Buchanan's (Scotch poet, temp. Mary Queen of Scots) kind of Humanism which has unhappily, exercised the strongest effect upon our literature and life. Other Humanists have saved themselves, like Milton, Sir Thomas Browne. ... But to Buchanan and his fellows we owe all the paralyzing falsity that invokes the Muse, the Pierian spring,

Venus, Cupid, Jove, Cynthia, Sylvan solitudes, the Penates, the
charms of Chloe. For nearly two centuries after Buchanan's death
whose tiresome fictions lay like a dead hand upon the heart of our
literature. ... Yet Buchanan's Humanism and no other, has been the
base of our highest education for nearly four centuries.

2606   "The CLARITY OF SCIENCE proves upon a close examination to be
no more than this, that its results are more easily demonstrated than
are other results. The advantages which the truths of physical science
have over the truths of metaphysic is not that the former are more true
than the latter – in truth there is not a more or less – but that they are
more demonstrable."   C. F. Keary. Albany Rv. May 1907.

2607   PRAGMATISM. – It is de Lisle Adam's 'Sans illusion tout perit,' or
Horace's Praetulerim scriptor delirus, – the doctrine that on a certain
level of thought truth must be interpreted as applicability to plain
human needs. ... The one question is, says Professor James, What
concrete difference will the truth of an idea make to anyone's actual
life? What is its cash value in experiential terms?   Spectator.

2608   (f56ʳ) A Rebel.   Albany Review. May. 1907.
   ... This enormous construction of mechanical industry, business ...
and the heaped up wealth of the world ... transforming the ancient
East, awakening China with rude blows, converting Japan into a huge
factory ... swinging steel bridges across the Zambesi ... this is the white
man's burden ... changing the world, but finding no intelligible reason
for the change; destroying what he cannot understand.
   What is the aim of it all? What is the end? Dominance of individual
or nation ... say some. ... And when dominance is obtained? ... no reply.
Happiness in wide commonalty spread, bravely assert others; to which
an examination of those who are triumphant ... would seem an even
more convincing negative than investigation of those who have failed. ...
'He gave them their hearts' desire, and sent leaness withal into their
souls,' is written over all these gorgeous palaces (of the millionaires). ...
The 'Will to Live' says the philosopher, blind and unconscious ... like
some wild beast that has captured the control of intelligent machinery,
and is directing it in ruinous courses. ... That is the unending end of
Progress. 'It is worth while,' says President Roosevelt to Mr Wells.

What 'it' is worth whose 'while', remains conjectural. "This is the Law" so chant in pitiful asseveration Mr Wells' deformed monsters. ... There are a few who escape. Their freedom is bought at a price. ... They are rebels against the accepted order of the world. ... Lafcadio Hearn was a rebel. ... He rejected with a kind of terror and a kind of disdain the whole scheme and system of modern civilisation (**f57ʳ**) ... life directed to such unimaginable ends.   G. F. G. Masterman.

2609   Freedom of the Will.
"Half the controversies about the freedom of the will ... rest upon the absurd presumption that the proposition 'I can do as I like,' is contradictory to the doctrine of necessity. The answer is: 'Nobody doubts that, at any rate within certain limits, you can do as you like. 'But what determines your likings? Did you make your own constitution? Is it your contrivance that one thing is pleasant and another is painful? And even if it were, why did you prefer to make it after the one fashion rather than the other? ...'

   What opponents of the doctrine really have to do, if they would upset the necessarian argument, is to prove that they are free to associate any emotion whatever with any idea whatever; to like pain as much as pleasure; vice as much as virtue; in short, to prove that, whatever may be the fixity of order of the universe of things, that of thought is given over to chance."   T. H. Huxley. on Hume. (221)

2610   'The 'external' novel is probably done with; nothing but the 'internal' remains' – quoted by G. Saintsbury from an American publication.

2611   (**f58ʳ**) A classic, according to a great French writer, is 'an[3] author who has enriched the human mind, who has really added to its treasures, who has got it to take a step further, who has discovered some unequivocal moral truth, or who has penetrated to some eternal passion (previously unconsidered) in that heart of man where it seemed as though all was known and explored, who has produced his thought or his observation or his emotion under some form, no matter what, so it be great, large, acute, and reasonable, sane and beautiful in itself, who has spoken to all in a style of his own, yet a style which finds itself the style of everybody, in a style which is at once new and antique and is the contemporary of all the ages.'

This is a satisfactory, full and instructive account of what is a classic.

John Morley.

2612 The decline of Philistinism.

"The true romance lives in the present, or in a future not merely of vision but of hope. Most of our chief modern poets have so far submitted to Philistinism that they have looked back to the past for romance, and so have degraded what should be the source of all pure and high energies into a luxury and a toy." 'Speaker', 10.6.05.

2613 (**f58v**) Ibsen was from first to last an artist.... He was a profound[4] thinker and like all great minds he 'felt' his thoughts. His whole endeavour was the pursuit of truth; his single aim the study of man. He had, and sought, no theory of life; he propounded no system: evolved no doctrine. Men their minds and the facts concerning them, alone interested him: and because true life as he saw it, was not always beautiful or inspiring, his plays are cheerless, ugly, painful and distressing. (?) As artist and poet – and he was both – his vision was ever concentrated on fact, not fantasy.... What he gave to the stage was the focus of thought as distinct from illusion.... For intrigue, plot, convention, he cared nothing; scenery he ignored. His puppets were human beings: to him the stage was a human document.

Observer.

2614 "Learn what common things are to uncommon minds ... an intenser day poured out upon them." 'Nation', on Literature.

2615 (**f59r**) <u>Religion</u>.

"The characteristic axiom of religion is the conservation of value – the conviction that no value perishes out of the world."
(Hoffding – Philosophy of Religion quoted by A, S. Pringle Pattison in "The Philosophic Radicals.")

2616 Value resides only in the experience of conscious beings.

Mc Taggart

2617   Mind. July '07. Review of Hoffdings "Philosophy of Religion" by H. R. Mackintosh.

"The manner in which Professor Hoffding ignores the theistic solution cuts him off from the argument, which another thinker might have employed, that an eternally existent Deity might derive some ultimate gain from the contemplation of human life, value thus surviving in HIS experience, though not in ours.

2618   Religious ideas ... he (Prof. H.) would say, are true in the sense in which the Antigone or Macbeth is true; but they are true in no other sense. ... Religious men may borrow arguments from Hoffding to prove that the truth of Theological doctrines is irrelevant. I do not myself see what is meant by saying that 'God is Love' is symbolical; though I can understand the statement that it is true or false.

2619   Religion. "faith in an ultimate harmony between our ideals and the nature of things. ... An immensely important question is whether Prof. H. has any ground in reason to offer for the truth of what, (**f59ᵛ**) in his view, is the basal ontological postulate of religion, the conviction that we and the universe are, at bottom, in harmony. ... It does not appear that he has."

––––––––––––––

2620   Matthew Arnold defined religion as 'morality touched with emotion"; Huxley as "reverence and love for the ethical ideal and the desire to realize it in life. ..." Hegel's definition, "the knowledge acquired by the finite spirit of its essence as an absolute spirit" has inspired many others ... cases of obscurum per obscurious. In so far however as these attempts hint at a psychical origin of religion they are steps in a right direction."   (Tree of Life.)

––––––––––––––

2621   You must not expect a reasoned system of ethics from any work of art, although you can, and should, demand that it has an ethical basis. Moreover it may be demanded of art that if finality be not its end, it should make a clear and suggestive appeal – A picture of life, or a picture of ideas of life, which is not presented with more concentration and charms than may be aroused by non-artistic contemplation of the facts of existence, is not art at all."

'Nation' on Wagner's 'Ring'.

2622   "ON SOME FORMS OF IRONY IN LITERATURE." Arthur Sidgwick 'Cornhill' April '07.

"Thirlwall's definition of verbal irony:–

'The most familiar species of irony may be described as (**f60ʳ**) a figure which enables the speaker to convey his meaning with a greater force by means of a contrast between his thought and his expression; or, to speak more accurately, between the thought which he evidently designs to express and that which his words properly signify."

But – irony of feeling ... (is accomplished by) understatement. ... The powerful and tragic poem (of Browning's) called 'Too Late'. ... The verse (quoted)

> "I liked that way you had with your curls
>   Wound to a ball in a net behind:
> Your cheek was chaste as a quaker-girl's,
>
>   . . . . .
>
>   like a bird's
> Your hand seemed – some would say, the pounce
> Of a scaly-footed hawk – all but!
> The world was right when it called you thin."

The penetrating effect is due to the irony of the tone.

————————

2623   Guenther's Darwinism. trans. by Mc Cabe.

"the lust for life:–

"According to the teleological view the construction of an organism is the end which the whole embryonic development is aiming to realize. The end, as it were, observes and controls the series of causes and is realized in the ultimate effect. The very first causes were controlled by a fact that was still in the future. The ordinary causes, which we have discussed, can only produce an effect when they themselves have already been brought into existence as an effect. Teleological causes or ends act before they are (**f61ʳ**) themselves realized.

We rejected in the previous chapter the notion that organisms aim at the realization of ends. Seeking an end would be the greatest conceivable form of purposiveness.

In the eyes of science man is not higher than the other animals.

2624 REVIEW OF ORMOND'S CONCEPTS OF PHILOSOPHY IN MIND. by J. Ellis McTaggart.

"It is a painful shock to come across a passage like this 'Why should there be anything deeper than phenomena?... Simply because consciousness in its organ of reason will not have it so. A world which ended here would be a scandal to reason.'

Here we are left in complete darkness as to whether Professor Ormond means that he would disapprove of such a world, or that he would commit a logical error if he believed in it. The former is interesting, but inconclusive. The latter would be better if it were not put in a form which suggests that a contradiction becomes impossible only when it is perceived to be a contradiction."

2625 CREED OF A LAYMAN. Frederick Harrison.

'L'hypocrisie Anglicane' (Comte of the English Church.)

"A religious life means conscious devotion to human welfare."

"The Essayists (of Essays and Reviews) are now all gone, full of honours and public repute: ... But the same intellectual double-dealing in things theological exists, and is far wider spread."

(Benn's History of Rationalism. 2 vols. "able" Fr, Hn.)

2626 (**f62ʳ**) "THE APOSTACY OF A WAGNERIAN." Fortnightly Review. July. '06.

"... It can easily be shown that human beings have ever sought for a means of expressing themselves with more poignancy than is possible with words, even when cast in the decorative form of poetry. It is as natural to the human being to sing as to speak. The difficulty is that music becomes an artificial mode of expression when emotions do not transcend the power of speech, and it is hardly possible so to construct a drama that it shall demand musical expression throughout. ... I doubt if (this difficulty) ever can be solved without having recourse to a mixed drama in which only that would be sung which demands song as its expression. In the old days composers unconsciously recognized this by inserting spoken dialogue. The change from speech to song is not pleasant to the musical ear. ... As a compromise the set recitative was invented but it sounds intolerably wearisome to modern ears.

Wagner's melodious declamation made the expression of opera homogen⟨e⟩ous ~~but it did~~ but it did not really ~~really~~ solve the essential difficulty of the art. As a means to this end he invented his orchestral commentary. ... By keeping the vocal writing free from a melody which was only natural when the emotion expressed demanded music he thought he had hit on a plastic musical speech which would blend easily with the orchestra. In moments of tension the vocal part could become more melodious; and when there was not this impetus the orchestra could discourse on the dramatic ideas."

E. A. Baughan.

2627   (**f63ʳ**) "Some physicists are clinging to ether as their last plank, may not perhaps atoms, they ask, be 'knots' in the ether, or perhaps vortices in it, or 'strains'? Mr Whetham's language in his rapid sketch of modern positions (The recent development of Physical Science – W, C, D. Whethan. Murray 1904) is almost poetical: 'Matter is a persistent strain-form flitting through a universal sea of ether.'
     But there is something ghost-like here' etc.

"Scientists and common sense" Armitage. Cont. Review.

May '05.

2628   "Haeckel ... sees consciousness emerge first at a late moment in the evolution of the world, so that it had no part in the world's beginnings and no control over its course.
     ... The hardy few who are content to follow Büchner to the end, and roundly to declare that consciousness is itself nothing more nor less than a movement of particles. ...
     "Haeckel writes '... I must lay down the following thesis – as indispensable for a truly monistic view of substance, and one that covers the whole field of organic and inorganic nature: the two fundamental forms of substance, ponderable matter and ether, are not dead and only moved by extrinsic force; but they are endowed with sensation and will (though naturally of the lowest grade); they experience an inclination for concentration, a dislike of strain they strive after the one and struggle against the other. ... Even the atom is not without a rudimentary form of sensation and will ... or feeling and inclination – that is, a universal soul of the simplest character'."

ib.

2629   (**f63ᵛ**) THE CARDINAL IMPORTANCE OF POE
     "The cardinal importance, then, of Poe as a poet is that he restored to poetry a primitive faculty of which civilisation seemed successfully to have deprived her. He rejected the direct expression of positive things and he insisted upon mystery and symbol. He endeavoured to clothe unfathomable thoughts and shadowy images in melody that was like

the wind wandering over the strings of an æolian harp. In other words, he was the pioneer of a school which has spread its influence to the confines of the civilised world, and is now revolutionising literature. He was the discoverer and founder of symbolism."

Gosse, in Contemp. Rev.

2630   Saintsbury's Hist. of Prosody
August 13, 1910   THE OUTLOOK

The presumption, to which Professor Saintsbury commits himself too easily, that musical analogies are necessarily anathema to the prosodist is a source of incompleteness in his work, and perhaps accounts for something unmusical and disproportionate in some of his judgments and in his manner of expressing them. A musical ear and musical experience cannot but promote the enjoyment and understanding of poetical effects, and their value consists, or should consist, in the livelier consciousness they bring of the difference between the two arts and of the lines of development proper to each. Only a very thoughtless musician could think of sound and rhythm as constituting the essence of poetry. For if sound and rhythm are the essence, why, he would ask, the enormous and fatal concession by which a clumsy instrument like language is imposed upon them and allowed to dominate its betters? To him it will be obvious that wisdom is on the side of those poor folk whom Professor Saintsbury calls "subject-people"; and that a poet is not primarily the man who can charm us with the harmony and melody of his speech, but the man whose thought and vision is such as to demand harmony and melody for its expression. Those therefore who rave, however devotedly, about the rhythmical triumphs of the poet and his mellifluous oppositions or combinations of consonant and vowel sounds, will always seem to him a little extravagant and inexperienced. For he knows that the poet, so far as sound and rhythm are concerned, is getting what best he can out of a compromise.

It is because of the large part that the element of compromise plays in poetry on its formal side that Professor Saintsbury's sensible rather than philosophic methods carry him so far. A rather more delicate appreciation of the theories of some of his opponents would perhaps have enabled him to go further. He is particularly hard in his dealings with the modern "quantitative" school of experimentalists. Yet reason is probably a better method to employ against them than invective. Language, the material of the poet, has several disadvantages; it was not devised for artistic purposes, and it is used for the most part by persons gifted with only moderate powers of discrimination in matters that appeal to the ear. The question is at least worth asking whether the poet is or is not to take the instinct of the people as authoritative where their language is concerned and to make the language as commonly spoken the vehicle of his art, or whether he is to call upon them for a more discriminating and more attentive pronunciation on the ground that a more expressive, a more responsive instrument will thereby come into his hands. When Dante decided to write his *Divine Comedy* in the vulgar tongue he answered an analogous question, and no one doubts that he answered it on the right side. The Quantitativists are for persuading us not only to break with the traditions of our own poetry, but, one may almost say, to plunge back into mediævalism. The game is not worth the candle. Rather more attention is certainly desirable on the part of most verse writers to actual quantities. But no compensation could suffice to the poet for the loss of popular sympathy and understanding. If a new system of pronunciation is wanted poetry must wait to profit by it until it is in force.   BASIL DE SELINCOURT.

2631 (**f64ʳ**) 'As to which among so many matchless and unapproachable masterpieces may be Shakespeare's masterwork in tragedy or in comedy it is impossible for any critic or any poet, and impossible it would be if even some celestial chance could possibly send us a second Coleridge, to pronounce judgement with the decision of a final authority. But as to which among his historic and patriotic plays or poems is the crowning and consummate masterpiece of the supreme poet there can be no possible question among any imaginable readers. The trilogy of *King Henry IV* and *King Henry V* would suffice to show, not that Shakespeare was the greatest poet, but assuredly that Shakespeare was the greatest dramatist and the greatest humourist of all time. The majestic and impassioned poetry of the graver scenes should not, if it is possible that it should not, be eclipsed or overshadowed in the sight of students young or old by the presence and the rivalry of the greatest comic figure that ever dawned upon the conception

Swinburne
on
Shakespeare.

Henry V
and the
Persae.

of the greatest comic poet ever born. ...
Shakespeare is himself alone: he could have taken
up Homer in his right hand and Dante in his left.
In the third play of this trilogy he has
unconsciously matched himself against a greater
than Homer or than Dante. In all poetic or
dramatic or patriotic literature there is nothing of
its kind comparable with the *Persae* of Aeschylus
but Shakespeare's *King Henry V*, there is nothing
that can be set against the tragedy which revolves
round Agincourt but the tragedy which is based on
Salamis. As Shelley so justly saw and so admirably
said, the comic humour of Shakespeare supplies
the place filled and affords the relief given by lyric
poetry in the tragedies of Aeschylus and Sophocles.
And here above all is this the case: and here above
all is the harmony of tragedy and comedy most
manifest and most perfect. ...'

'*The Merchant of Venice* is perhaps the greatest and   Shylock.
most perfect example of tragi-comedy on record.
The tragic figure of Shylock, less sinned against
than sinning, is thrilled and vivified by comic as
well as terrific touches of character and emotion.
His incontinence of lamentation and of rage is not
less grotesque than piteous: his atrocity outweighs
the balance of his injuries.'

2632   (**f65ʳ**) From Some old Review.
   That no language is too simple for poetic purposes, and that none is
too rich (the poetic art being shown entirely in the aptness of the
selection), may be seen from the two following quotations from
Chaucer and Shakespeare:–

My lord, ye wote that in my fadres place
Ye did me stripe out of my poure wede,
And richely ye clad me of your grace;
To you brought I nought elles out of drede,
But faith, and nakednesse, and maidenhede;
And here agen your clothing I restore,
And eke your wedding ring for evermore.

> Thou remember'st
> Since once I sat upon a promontory,
> And heard a mermaid on a dolphin's back
> Uttering such dulcet and harmonious breath,
> That the rude sea grew civil at her song,
> And certain stars shot madly from their spheres,
> To hear the sea-maid's music.

Now the truth is that, in order to explain why each of these widely different passages is not only poetic, but as poetic as language can possibly be, it is necessary to touch upon the deepest of all subjects in literary criticism – the subject of consciousness and unconsciousness in poetic art.

Without pretending to discuss so important a topic here, we may say in a few words that the difference between richness and simplicity in poetic style is so fundamental, that while the rich style can display consciousness of its richness (as we see notably in the above lines from Shakespeare, in such a poem as Keats's 'Lamia,' and above all in the work of a poet so self-conscious as Gray) and yet remain poetic, consciousness is absolutely destructive of the simple style. The moment, as in so many of Wordsworth's would-be simple poems, we trace the faintest suspicion of consciousness, the passage is turned into prose. Indeed, it may be said axiomatically that whether simplicity of language is poetic or prosaic is determined not so much by the inherent poetic or prosaic *timbre* of the words used as by the consciousness or unconsciousness of the writer who uses them. Hence, with all our admiration of Mr. Tennyson's genius as a master of the rich style, we cannot place those poems of his whose appeal is that of simplicity (such, for instance, as 'Dora') quite on a level with the work of less conscious writers – with the idyls of Mr. Barnes, for instance, or with some of these poems – while they must be placed far below the work of Scottish song and ballad writers such as Motherwell, Lady Anne Barnard, and others. In the rich style, however, consciousness, so far from being a weakness, is an added strength. In the gorgeous descriptions of the 'Faerie Queene,' in the sonorous movements of Virgil, in the tremendous perorations of Marlowe and Milton, and in the word-weavings of Shakespeare and Keats, the poet adds to his effects by displaying his conscious pride in his wealth; while in poets like Gray this glow of consciousness is actually needed to warm the glittering carcanet into poetic life at all. Hence it would not be difficult to show that simple and ornate poetry are two different kinds of art, though rhythmical language be the medium of both. It follows from what has been said, perhaps, that to write in the simple style is exceedingly difficult unless the poet calls in the aid of *patois*, as Mr. Tennyson does in his successful attempts at simple poetry, when another element is introduced, that of rusticity. Unless the poet has a special gift for familiar poetry it is apt to degenerate into mere colloquial prattling.

2633 TYPES OF TRAGIC DRAMA. Times. 28.5.1908
TYPES OF TRAGIC DRAMA. By C. E. VAUGHAN, Professor of English Literature in the University of Leeds. (Macmillan 5s. net.)

The tragic drama is, in one respect, rather a melancholy subject to handle to-day. The most obstinate of optimists could not persuade himself that the theatre, especially the tragic theatre, is at this moment playing the part in the intellectual and moral life of Europe which it might play and has played in the past. It is true that there are names of some real distinction, two or three Germans, one Italian, and perhaps one Englishman, who will occur to every one as having done something to redeem the poverty of the theatre in the last and present generation, and, in consequence, as having had a right to share some part of Mr. Vaughan's last lecture with Ibsen and Maeterlinck. But they are not enough, either in number or in importance, to affect the general truth, that neither the higher emotion nor the higher imagination of the present day find their way to the theatre. Dignity, greatness of mind and matter, that ancient σπουδαιότης which Matthew Arnold used to translate as "high seriousness," exist among us still, but it is not our dramatists to whom we owe them. That is the contrast. It was precisely from their dramatists that the Greeks of the great age, the French of the seventeenth century, the English Elizabethans, the Germans of a hundred years ago, did get these great things. Everywhere, even in England, and till quite lately, the theatre was in close relations to the best literature of the day. Johnson, for instance, from age, deafness, and lack of inclination, did not often go to the theatre. But it would have been impossible for Boswell to keep the drama out of his biography. It is not an accident, but the natural and inevitable result of the relations then existing between letters and the theatre, that the life of the dictator of literature is full of such names as Goldsmith and Sheridan, Garrick, or Mrs. Siddons. No such thing would be necessary to-day. We go to the play to be amused, or to be excited, not to satisfy any hunger of imagination, any thirst for poetry, in our nature. There are still tears in the theatre, as there is still laughter; but tragedy is no more to be measured by tears than comedy by laughter. Indeed, as Mr. Vaughan points out in speaking of Euripides, the greatest tragedy calls for a sterner note than that of pathos. "Nothing is here for tears"; that, as he says, is the unspoken feeling which the greatest creations of tragedy call out.

The truth is, perhaps, that the theatre is essentially a public place, and we are no longer capable of high emotions in public. In spite of much political talk about Collectivism, the world, in its higher life at any rate, grows more and more individualist. Neither religion, nor art, nor literature affords any longer a means of public expression of feelings held by the people as a whole. There is no more carrying of great religious pictures in a procession of joy, there is no more national pride in the adornment of the national citadel or sanctuary, there are no more national theatres in which the art, and the poetry, and the patriotism, and the religion of a nation find, as they found in the theatre of Dionysus, a common and public expression. The lovers of art love it with a love at least as ardent as any Greek or Roman, but, whether they keep the beloved objects in their own cabinets or give them to the public, they no longer expect the people to share their enthusiasm. The lovers of poetry read great poems alone in their studies. Of religion itself the truest part is become a secret thing of which men no longer speak easily. Our highest moments are now those of solitude, not those of society. In the company of our fellowmen we find that both they and we are shy of lifting the conversation above the level of the ordinary and obvious topics of business and pleasure. What place has the tragic drama, the great drama of the poetic imagination, in such a world as this? Its very essence is open expression of the deepest things in the human soul, even open representation of them visibly on a public stage. How is such a world, so secretive of its deepest self, to face this ordeal of publicity? It cannot; and the result is that though *l'homme moyen sensuel* is no more the whole of humanity now than he ever was, he is become the whole of that small part of humanity which is allowed to tread the boards of the modern stage.

It is difficult to avoid asking these painful questions after going through the long and splendid history of tragedy as Mr. Vaughan gives it to us. But he himself deals mainly in retrospect, and his final lecture on Ibsen and Maeterlinck is the least satisfactory in the book. It is impossible here to follow him in his minute analyses of the work and methods of the various dramatists with whom he deals. One may say, though, that the ever-increasing fame of Aeschylus, who has been so much longer coming to his own than other Greek poets, will not be diminished by anything said by Mr. Vaughan. But perhaps the world of late has been still more occupied with Euripides; and there is nothing better in the book than the chapter on that strange denier of the gods who yet more than any one else crowded his stage with gods, that humanitarian Radical who hated democracy, that romantic born out of due time who was bent on securing the picturesque at any cost, especially at that of the stately traditions of the great style which preceded him. But all this will be less new to most readers than the interesting account of Alfieri, who appears as "the last great representative of classical tragedy." Probably few readers of this book will even have opened Alfieri; one, at any rate, who had just, and only just, done so, has been sent back to him by Mr. Vaughan, and hopes he will never fail in that due measure of gratitude which Ben Jonson found so sadly wanting in a certain lawyer to whom he had rendered a still greater service. "Why, I was the man that first made him relish Horace!" People who take an interest in the drama might easily spend their time worse than in reading Alfieri. "His supreme greatness," according to Mr. Vaughan,

> lies in this: that, retaining the classical model in its most severe form, he gave to it an intensity of action and of passion, he breathed into his characters a fire and fury, he informed the whole with a dramatic subtlety and vividness, which were hardly to be supposed possible within these narrow limits. ...The result is that in his greatest plays the characters are painted with such fullness and richness of colour, such subtle mastery of light and shade as is elsewhere to be found only in the looser structure of the romantic drama – we might almost say, only in the tragedies of Shakespeare.

This is very high praise, and perhaps does something less than justice both to Aeschylus and to Shakespeare. One would have supposed that Aeschylus had not left it to Alfieri to prove that "the classical model" is capable of as much

But he has done students of the drama a real service by recalling attention to Alfieri. Whether we ultimately prefer the classical or the romantic method in tragedy, no competent critic will deny that the classical method has some very important advantages. Unity is the essential quality of all works of art, and, that being so, a method which makes unity comparatively easy has an initial advantage over one that makes it comparatively difficult. How great that advantage is may be seen without going outside the English language by comparing Dryden's *All for Love* with Shakespeare's *Antony and Cleopatra*. But the English critical tradition has, for the last hundred years at any rate been so "romantically" disposed that it is apt to be simply dazzled by Shakespeare's strokes of genius, and consequently blind to the defects of his method. But not even Shakespearian idolatry can blind any one who really faces the study of the drama as a whole and from the beginning, to the fact that the intense concentration of interest exhibited by ancient and modern classical drama is, so far as it goes, a great source of strength to that drama. Now, if we put the ancients aside for the moment, there is no one who is more likely to convince Englishmen of this than Alfieri. For good or for evil Englishmen do not generally like Racine. His formal beauties escape them, and they do not recognize humanity in a world which is never seen out of court dress. In fact, they find him somewhat insipid, and they will be slow to think *Britannicus*, for instance, so great a play as Mr. Vaughan thinks it. It is not there that they will learn to value the modern classical drama. But let them try Alfieri. There is no fear of his being found insipid. "Love plays a far less prominent part," as Mr. Vaughan says, "in his tragedies than in those of Racine." "The Courtly atmosphere is swept away. ... The language, so far from being smooth, errs, if anything, on the side of abruptness, of what Alfieri would have himself called 'ferocity.'" And yet Racine himself has not a tenser concentration of interest. Not a moment, not a word, is wasted. The action pursues its rapid course without ever being turned aside, and the *dramatis personae* never take their eyes off what Hamlet called "the necessary question of the play." This has, as we can all see, some disadvantages; we should not know Hamlet as we do know him if he had made no digressions from the business of avenging his father. But the present point is that it also has advantages, and that no one really understands the art of drama who has not perceived them. Take the two plays, *Agamemnone* and *Oreste*, which deal with the old story of the Aeschylean Trilogy; is it not difficult to deny that they absorb and possess the reader in a way that would be almost impossible to the looser structure of the romantic drama, except where reinforced by the genius of Shakespeare? Nor is this intense unity incompatible with subtlety of portraiture. On the contrary, as Mr. Vaughan says, "that subtlety is often surprisingly great." The character of Clytaemnestra, in particular, torn between passion for Aegisthus on the one hand, and honour, shame, and the love of her children on the other, is nobly conceived and finely carried out. It was, indeed, Voltaire, as Mr. Vaughan ought to have mentioned, who first attempted that reading of character, and he may have taken it, as Professor Jebb suggested, from a couple of lines put into her mouth by Sophocles. But nothing can deprive Alfieri of the glory of having given us one of the most living of tragic figures. Nor can such things as the chevalieresque absurdity of Orestes, Pylades, and Electra all clamouring for the right of being the victim of Aegisthus while Aegisthus looks on and hesitates till it is too late, nor that other absurdity of Orestes ultimately killing Clytaemnestra by accident, and without discovering it, while he kills Aegisthus, deprive the dramatist who devised the scene between Clytaemnestra and Electra in the first play, and those between Orestes and Pylades and Electra in the second, of the name of one of the great masters of his art. It is true that the classical form has its penalties as well as its gains. Its very sanity and simplicity allow it no such means of concealing incongruities as are afforded by the fine frenzies of the romantic poet hurrying us from heaven to earth and from earth to heaven. Fire enough it has room for; and fire enough Alfieri has; the flame of passion, the white heat of the tragic situation; but it only burns true when it is fed solely on the proper business of the drama. And that, to do Alfieri justice, is what, in his case, it is commonly fed on. No dramatist ever kept more closely to his text. The amazing impression of energy he makes in his best scenes is made without the assistance of fine writing, metaphors, or adornments of any kind. He truly is what he called himself in the letter prefixed to his tragedies, *forte, breve, caldo e tragico.*

What, then, is it which, in the presence of all these great qualities, we still find wanting in Alfieri, and, indeed, in all the modern classical drama? Is it not, as Mr. Vaughan argues in one of his best chapters, that lyric escape of the human spirit, that brooding and reflecting self-revelation, which the Greeks provided through their choral odes and the Romantics by their soliloquies? In these serried plots of Racine and Alfieri the pressure of the business in hand seems to have overbalanced the sense of the world as a whole and of the heights and depths of human existence in a way that makes the play seem unsatisfying and incomplete as a picture of life. What would the *Agamemnon* be without its great choruses? Not what it is, certainly.

What would *Hamlet* or *Faust* be without the great soliloquies? If there is sometimes loss, how much gain there often is in the lyrics and lyrical dialogues with which the greater Romantics have sprinkled their plays! Alfieri argues in his letter against a lyric style in drama; and what he says has one obvious side of the truth in it. But is there not another? After all it is the very claim and essence of poetry that it is the only right and natural utterance of things that lie at the very heart of humanity; and if the drama leaves these things out, is it painting all the picture of life? Mr. Vaughan thinks that the whole movement of dramatic history has been from the external to the internal, from action to character, from visibility to intimacy, and that this movement is still in progress. That may, or may not, be so. There is Maeterlinck no doubt; but can most of us feel as sure as Mr. Vaughan apparently does that we know the true soul of Ibsen's *Enemy of the People* as well as we know that of the *Antigone* or Sophocles? Or is it only that there is not so much to know? In any case, whether there be such a development as Mr. Vaughan thinks, or whether, as others might argue, this inwardness & intimacy are less an affair of date & method than of the genius of the dram⁵ poet, there can be no question of their importance. The whole of life is the province of the dramatist. Thought as well as action, the soul & the body, secrets & externals, poetry & prose, they are all his to take & use, if he can. His problem is how to use as much of them as he may within the limits of time & the law of unity that are the necessary conditions of his art. ... Great as the past is, small as the present may appear, the weal of art is always in the future.

2634   – Dante's philosophy –

'Since Dante himself has chosen to enter the philosophical arena making loud proclamations to the people, we cannot afterwards allow him to be hustled out by an emergency exit on the plea that he is only a poet. ... It was no fault of Homer's that the Greeks mistook him for a theologian and so excluded him from Plato's Republic, nor do we readily imagine Horace in cap and gown because he joined himself to the herd of Epicurus. Even Browning was not a professional psychologist, and Shakespeare's "stuff that dreams are made of" is not an orthodox variety of metaphysical substance. Yet in regard to these matters every poet must be treated as an individual, with proper reference to his tastes and training, to the style of poetry affected by him, and to the literary traditions dominant in his time. And when these simple tests are applied to Dante, we cannot but acknowledge that of all the poets who have attained to great celebrity he is (with the possible exception of Lucretius) the one most likely to have aimed at accuracy in his philosophical utterances. ... When we remember, too, that in the thirteenth century the accepted method of interpreting serious poetry favoured the view that poets were scholars, historians, philosophers, and mystical theologians; when we add to this that it was part of Dante's own vindication of his mother tongue to prove it capable of expressing the loftiest speculations; then, surely we cannot think that out of pure indifference to accuracy he would court the censure of every learned reader by introducing chaos into his moral system? ...'

'One of the best-known facts about the *Inferno* is that the name of Christ is never mentioned there. ... What Dante leaves out is not merely the name of the Saviour but the whole theological presentation of evil. Set aside for a moment the sixth circle, and you will hardly detect the slightest intimation that any sinner is damned for offending against Christianity as such. Even in Limbo the one fact insisted upon is the necessity of the baptismal rite; all the remaining deficiency in virtuous Pagans being summed up in the vague words:–

> e se furon dinanzi al Cristianesmo,
> non adorar debitamente Dio.

This is the solitary allusion (if such it can be called) in the whole *Inferno* to the Christian view of conduct; and here, too, we must remember that Virgil is speaking of those who were not and could not possibly have been Christians. ... The plain objection to distinguishing Pagan and Christian views of *morality* is that no such distinction exists. ... If, therefore, we are right in assuming that Christianity is, as far as possible, kept out of sight in the *Inferno*, the most plausible hypothesis must be that all, or nearly all, sinners can be damned on the moral level, and that the theological aspect of sin can be treated as secondary. ... The most reasonable conclusions about the sixth circle seem to be, (1) that Dante wished to make the scheme of the *Inferno* suitable to the character and knowledge of Virgil; (2) that, nevertheless, he did not propose to omit any sin that a good Catholic must condemn; (3) that, in practice, all sins could be presented in a moral form save only the sin against *fides*; (4) that even with this sin he laid as little stress as possible upon theological errors.'

[From *The Moral System of Dante's Inferno*. By W. H. V. READE, M. A. Clarendon Press. *Published by Henry Frowde*. Price 12s. 6d. net ($4.15).]

2635   Machiavelli's principle of "reason of State," even to the sacrifice of their moral and religious principles. Such were William the Silent, Henry of Navarre, glorious Queen Bess, Frederick the Great, and most stupendous example of all, Napoleon. And why not add Baby Boris and his father? Napoleon was "reason of State" incarnate. Mr. Morley describes him:

> Napoleon, a Caesar Borgia on a giant scale, deliberately called evil good and good evil; and, almost alone among the past masters of all the arts of violence and fraud, he sacrificed pity, humanity, faith, religion, and public law, less for the sake of the State than to satisfy his own ravening egotism and exorbitant passion for personal domination. Napoleon, Charles IX., the Committee of Public Safety, would all have justified themselves by reason of State, and the Bartholomew massacre, the September massacres, and the murder of the Duc d'Enghien, only show what reason of State may come to in any age, in the hands of the practical logician with a knife in his grasp.

Even Mazzini, "in some respects the loftiest moral genius of the century," could not bring himself to condemn the assassin of a Judas tyrant. In the strong, eloquent passages which conclude his address, Mr. Morley disposes of "the sophistries" of reason of State. New ideals have arisen since the Machiavellian age of intellect without morals. "Is the State means or end?" Mr. Morley asks. Is justice the true test of a civilization? "The modern conception of a State has long made it a moral person, capable of right and wrong, just as are the individuals composing it. Civilization is taken to advance, exactly in proportion as communities leave behind them the violences of external nature, and of man in a state of war." 1897

2636   D. News. 14.9. '07 (BY JOHN MASEFIELD.)
"The Dead God." By James Blackhall. Greening and Co., 2s. 6d.
"The Secret Key." By George E. Evans. Angus and Robertson. 5s.
   Mr. James Blackhall's poem of "The Dead God" is an impressive

piece of work, new in idea, sincerely felt, and strongly imagined. It tells of the finding of the dead body of Christ in a cave in Palestine, and of the results of that discovery upon erring man and woman, until then helped and chastened by belief in Him. The dead body is brought from Palestine to a "sombre roof" (probably the British Museum) in England, where it is exhibited, with terrible results to all. Among those driven to misery by the sight of the dead Christ, no longer strong to save or to uplift, is one whose agony is greater than he can bear. To this one, in the depths of his grief, comes a new revelation, all the more strong and wonderful for the agony that came before it. As he flies from the town into the darkness he sees:

> In every wayside hedge, rude crowns of thorn;
> And every tree that rose against the sky
> Threw out its limbs and stood in cruciform;
> And when a star threw lustre 'tween the leaves,
> It was to him an eye too strong for death,
> Stinging the darkness with a look, that seemed
> Breaking a pathway through a thousand tears,
> Till, as he fled, the dumb o'erhanging night
> Fell on him as a snare, and bore him down
> Prone to the earth.
>   Beneath its chilly folds
> *He lay, as one entombed before his time.*
> *Wakes from the trance and feels the holding sheet,*
> *Hears o'er his head the falling of the sod,*
> *The last long groan of her he still loves well,*
> *And seized with terror loses will to cry*
> *Or break the fetters holding him to death!*
> So lay he, while the world and time and sense
> Went from him as a sobbing wind of night:
> Until, with agony that rent his soul
> He cried aloud, "Truly, He was the Christ,
> The Son of God."

Filled with this belief, his doubt and terror pass from him, and he returns to the city, full of a fiery divine hope, to preach the ever-living Christ to all. The passage which we have quoted (those lines especially which are printed in italics) will show the reader the imaginative strength and sincerity of Mr. Blackhall's work. He has a direct way of seeing things, his vision is as strong and as single as the vision of the writers of the old moralities. In the lines:

> Dead! as the crawling beast
> Crushed when the stone was rolled!

And in the cutting lines:

> Beneath a sombre roof the relic lay.
> The dead God's bones – the world's antiquity!
> And round it silent figures of the law
> Who, when the watch began, with head erect
> Stood at attention to the dead God's bones
> And turning, faced the emptiness around.

And in the yet more cutting quotation from the catalogue:

> The dead God – showing wound from
> Roman spear,

we see the sharpness and precision with which his images are graven. In his sonnets and lyrics he shows a power of suggestion. In the sonnet, "The Voice of the Bridge," he suggests very finely the noise of waters breaking upon cliffs,

> the roar, the clash, the passing moan
> And the long midnight hush.

In some of the lyrics (in "Lazarus" and "The Matchbox Makers") he adds to the little store of poems about the London poor. These lyrics are sincerely felt, but their intensity does not save them from a certain rhetorical looseness, which keeps them out of the first class. Mr. Blackhall would have done better with them had he given to them a setting more sharply related to life. The dialogue in verse, or the dialect ballad, would have suited them better than the purely lyrical form. The poem of "The Mere" is charming, both in verse and feeling.

2637   MUSIC. Times. Jan 15. '10.
THE FOLK-SONG IN THE MUSIC-HALL.

The Englishman loves, in his entertainments, to dwell on national characteristics – provided always they are not the characteristics of his own country: a Swiss yodel, a supposed negro dialect, or a pair of sabots fill him with delight: it does not occur to him that he has any racial characteristics of his own, or that, if he had any, they also would be worth attention. It seems quite natural to him that Spain, or Norway, or Russia should each have its own characteristic songs and dances; but that England should also have its racial characteristics and should be able to display them in beautiful folk-melodies and graceful folk-dances would seem to him almost improper. And yet the researches of the last 20 years by folk-song collectors have proved that the English folk-song and dance is as vital and as artistically important as that of any Continental nation.

The management of the London Coliseum have lately won great and well-deserved success by introducing to the public first a band of Russian players on their own national instrument, the balalaika, and, following hard on that, a beautifully trained choir of Russian singers, the "Slaviansky Russian Choir." Part of the success of these two organizations was doubtless due to their marvellous *ensemble* and to the novelty of the means employed – the simultaneous plucking of so many strings or the unheard-of depth of the Russian bass voices. But all this would have counted for very little if a special atmosphere had not been created by the fact that both orchestra and choir interspersed their more ordinary *répertoire* of valses and fantasias with specimens of genuine Russian folk-songs. These beautiful melodies, with their modal qualities, their curious rhythms, their absolute detachment from their very sophisticated surroundings, created a profound impression on all classes of the audience; and it is interesting to note that one of the most strange and unconventional of these melodies, the "Volga Boatman's Song," appeared to be the most popular.

How many of the hundreds of people who heard and enjoyed these fine Russian melodies realized that we have here in England at our very doors a store of melodies equally beautiful, equally strange in tonality, equally unconventional in rhythm, and as far removed from the ordinary phraseology of fashionable music? Our English folk-song stands at the door, only waiting to be taken in and welcomed with the same care as its Russian cousin to cause the same delighted astonishment amongst a popular audience.

Experts may possibly tell us that these Russian melodies are only "edited" versions of the real peasant song – whether that is so or not only an expert can say. But here in England there need be no question of genuineness; there is now at hand a large store of folk-song accurately transcribed from the actual mouths of country singers, and its genuineness will carry the day. We have had enough of sham national characteristics; the popular entertainer, for want of something better, has had to invent out of his inner consciousness the sham country dance, the sham sailor, the sham countryman. These would all disappear before the reality – the real morris dancer will supplant the *coryphée* doing French steps round a maypole, the real sea-chanty will drive out the "Yo-heave-ho" of the theatre sailor, and the genuine artistic emotions of the countryman will replace the stale humours of the rustic grinning through a horse-collar.

That we have our genuine folk-music, as truly traditional and spontaneous as that of any other country, there can be no doubt. If it is possible for the management of the Coliseum to declare that the Slaviansky Choir "has made known to the world the exquisite and true music of Russia," why should it not be equally possible for a Smith or a Brown choir to make known to the world the true music of England? We have the voices, we have conductors quite capable of training them to a high pitch of excellence; and the material is ready to hand. Already several volumes of folk-songs arranged for solo or chorus singing are to be had. What music-hall audience could resist the lilt of "I'm Seventeen come Sunday" as arranged for chorus by Mr. Percy Grainger, or could fail to delight in the simple grace of "The Crystal Spring" in Mr. Cecil Sharp's "Folk-songs from Somerset," or the pathos of "My true love courted me" in Miss Broadwood's "Traditional Songs"? – not to speak of the sturdy blacksmith's song, "Twankidillo," or the magnificent sea ballad, "The Golden Vanity," published in English County Songs; and, if picturesque accessoires are required to vie with the gorgeous peasant dresses of the Russian singers, what could be a greater delight to the eye than the traditional dress of the morris-man, with his gay ribbons, his beaver hat, and the jingling bells on his ankles? And surely it must add greatly to the pleasure of an English hearer to know that he is witnessing, not the songs of Italy or Hungary, but the actual fruit of his own English soil. Unless our patriots are too much occupied with hating other countries to be able to give any attention to loving their own, this surely must be an extra source of pleasure.

The experiment of giving the English folk-song a stage setting has already been tried in a tentative fashion. The most delightful item in the programme of the party of entertainers known as "The Grotesques" is a choral setting of the well-known London lavender cry. Another very successful experiment was made at a students' performance lately organized by Mme. Joachim-Gibson, when two Somerset folk-songs, "A Farmer's Son" and "The Keys of Canterbury," were acted and sung, partly by solo voices and partly by an unseen chorus; this would probably make a most successful music-hall "turn."

Our managers need not be afraid that they would be offering to their patrons something archaic or of merely antiquarian interest, or that they would be shocking the ears of their audience with what they call "scientific music." The folk-song is, of course, of supreme scientific interest; but it is something else as well; it is not a dead body, but a living organism. When a country singer sings a folk-song he is giving a version of something which doubtless dates back to a remote past; but he sings his own version of it, and is probably to a certain extent the actual inventor of that version. Thus the folk-song is both old and new. It comes to us from long-forgotten times, and in that sense it belongs to the past; but it has been constantly remodelled by the minds of generation after generation, passing from father to son by oral tradition, never stereotyped by the stiffening process of print, but always in a state of flux, adapting itself to the needs of each successive generation of singers – in that sense it certainly belongs to the present; and surely it belongs to the future also, if, as we must believe, it has the vitality to survive transplantation from the cottage to the school, the concert platform, or the stage.

This belief in the future of the folk-song is not merely the pious hope of the enthusiast. It is borne out by the facts. School children who remain cold in the presence of all other forms of music take to the true folk-song like ducks to water – and this awakening is not confined to children; to quote Mr. Cecil Sharp in his "English Folk-song" – "There are those who have always been attracted to music and who ... have had the good sense to perform and listen to nothing but the best music, but who, nevertheless, have never been really moved by it. ... To such people the advent of the folk-song has been a revelation." Nor is the less discriminating public out of the movement; a well-known concert singer once told the present writer that whereas in former days he was obliged for his living to sing "shop" ballads, he had now almost entirely discarded these in favour of folk-songs, which he found infinitely more popular. May not the English folk-song have a future in the music-hall? If those who cater for public entertainment will learn from past successes, they will discover that the folk-song has unconsciously played a great part in them. Sousa's marches owe their well-deserved popularity to the fact that his trios are usually founded on folk-songs; the most popular of Mr. Chevalier's "coster" songs are saturated in the folk-song idiom; and the most vehemently applauded number in Sullivan's *Yeomen of the Guard* was a deliberate adaptation of the "Dilly Song."

The folk-song may be introduced into a music-hall programme in many ways. Our popular singers, who are probably finding that the stock humours of the mother-in-law and the stock pathos of the starving child are wearing a little thin, might well turn to the folk-song for pretty tunes and humour, romance, vigour in the words. Then when our managers have exhausted all the possibilities of "national" dancers, Parthia, Media, Mesopotamia, Pontus, Asia, Phrygia, and Pamphylia, they might turn nearer home and bring up to London a genuine "side" of morris dancers (there are still a few left) and see if they did not prove an equal attraction. Then what possibilities lie in the orchestral number during the interval. Here is a chance for the young English composer. When the inspiration for his great symphonic poem "Watchman, what of the night?" temporarily flags he might do worse than write a brilliant march founded on some of the many suitable folk-tunes to be found in the "Folk-song Journal"; or a few English dance tunes might occasionally be introduced into our ballets in the place of the cosmopolitan hotchpotch which too often does duty at those entertainments.

Till quite recently the folk-song has been in the hands of a few collectors – refined musicians and expert folk-lorists. They got no public recognition for their work, and they wanted none; their work was purely scientific. They collected and compared and theorized, and occasionally some of their treasures were brought out and exhibited to a favoured few over a cup of tea. But now times have changed – the work of collection must be nearly done; already a few of the bolder spirits have taken their treasures out into the public places and shown them to the people to whom they rightly belong, and the people are already beginning to clamour for more. Those who hold these treasures in their possession must no longer keep them hidden in their note-books and their scientific journals, but must give them to their rightful owners, the public, in the form in which they will most appreciate them.

"But will not this vulgarize the folk-song?" some timid spirit may ask. Well, let the folk-song be vulgarized; if it has real beauty and vitality, it will stand the ordeal.

2638   AMORES: POEMS. By D. H. LAWRENCE. (Duckworth. 5s. net.)
T. Lit. Sup. Aug 10.'16

In view of recent events, it may be prudent to begin by saying that
Mr. Lawrence's poems deal with more than one kind of love. Several of
the poems are poems of passion, and Mr. Lawrence's poems of passion
are almost as outspoken as Whitman's, and with the same robust
sincerity. The strangeness of the love-fever, its urgency, its revulsions,
hesitancies, betrayals – all the nervous to-and-fro of it that makes men
"frantic-mad with evermore unrest" – of these, too, Mr. Lawrence
writes with understanding and force. But those who are afraid of him
will be relieved to learn that a large number of the poems in this volume are
struck out by the loss of the poet's mother. There is no sentimentality
about them. Mr. Lawrence is not a glib writer; we should imagine that
every line of poetry that he writes was beaten out by feeling and effort
from a stubborn nature. In these mother poems he gives nothing to
convention. There is a dash of defiance in their love and grief; an air of
reluctant yielding to an emotion that is suspiciously popular. The effect
of them is all the stronger. The mother is also the bride, the beloved. In
"Sorrow," an intimate detail of her illness is used with poignant effect.
In "The Bride" we see her lying still:

> Nay, but she sleeps like a bride, and dreams her dreams
>   Of perfect things.
> She lies at last, the darling, in the shape of her dream,
>   And her dead mouth sings
> By its shape, like the thrushes in clear evenings.

"The Virgin Mother" develops the idea of a double birth.

> My little love, my dearest,
> Twice have you issued me,
> Once from your womb, sweet mother,
> Once from myself, to be
> Free of all hearts, my darling,
> Of each heart's home-life free. ...
>
> I kiss you good-bye, my darling,
> Our ways are different now;
> You are a seed in the night-time,
> I am a man, to plough

The difficult glebe of the future
For God to endow.

In the beautiful little "Elegy," in "Brother and Sister," and in other poems may be found the longing to join the lost, "to be lost out of sight with you, like a melting foam," "to fall like a breath within the breathing wind," and the determination to go forward alone, since life has a use for men.

That use, for Mr. Lawrence, is the realization of "the coming dream." At times in this volume he shows himself exultant with the sense of life, and especially of physical life. But the struggle is severe. The flower of man breaks from roots that are "fixed in the darkness, grappling for the deep soil's little control"; in the darkness where "we are not brothers, my darling, we fight and we do not spare." And the gift of life, with the duties to life that it entails, is a terrible glory. One of his freest poems ends thus:–

Oh, the great mystery and fascination of the unseen Shaper,
The power of the melting, fusing Force – heat, light, all in one,
Everything great and mysterious in one, swelling and shaping
    the dream in the flesh,
As it swells and shapes a bud into blossom.

Oh the terrible ecstasy of the consciousness that I am life!
Oh the miracle of the whole, the widespread, labouring
    concentration
Swelling mankind like one bud to bring forth the fruit of a
    dream,
Oh the terror of lifting the innermost I out of the sweep of the
    impulse of life,
And watching the great Thing labouring through the whole
    round flesh of the world;
And striving to catch a glimpse of the shape of the coming
    dream,
As it quickens within the labouring, white-hot metal,
Catch the scent and the colour of the coming dream,
Then to fall back exhausted into the unconscious, molten life!

The tremendous force of life and the unreadiness of men to welcome the new idea and make it fruitful for the new dream are the burdens which make much of Mr. Lawrence's poetry gloomy. And it may be distinctive of his mind that he regards his interior castle as a reserve not of light, but of darkness. It is on darkness and silence that he draws for refreshment; and the theme of darkness and silence inspires him to his most poetical verse.

His attitude to life is that of a man of great vitality but bitter experience; one whose great desires, left unsatisfied, lead to a half-concealed savagery. The breaks in the gloom and intervals between the storms, such as the purely tender poems of the mother and one or two of children, come as a surprise amid much that is turbulent and rebellious. So do the pure songs amid much that is strange and wilful in form. Mr. Lawrence has been more careful to get his thoughts and feelings exactly expressed, so that their very vagueness may find being in words, than he has been to make poems that should be beautiful in sound and shape. He rhymes, or rhymes not, or rhymes loosely. His rhythms are sometimes tangled, and often rugged. He produces, in fact, what is as often as not, so far as sound and movement are concerned, ugly. The beauty of his poems must not be sought in their music, still less in such lavish warmth as we find in "Drink" or "Blue," or in occasional phrases of trenchant imagery. It lies in the sincere and deliberate fitness of matter to manner. If the thought or the feeling flows sweetly, then Mr. Lawrence will write as clear a lyric as "Listening," or "Silence." If the stream is turgid, broken, difficult, then the verse will tell us so by its mere sound and movement. In any case, we must be interested, sometimes charmed, sometimes repelled, but always forced to share the experience.

2639   THE DAILY NEWS AND LEADER, FRIDAY, AUGUST 11, 1916
LITERATURE.
THE MUSIC-MAKERS. (By J. C. SQUIRE.)
"Catholic Anthology, 1914–15." Elkin Mathews. 3s. 6d. net.
"Songs for the New Age." By James Oppenheim. Grant Richards. 2s. 6d. net.
"The Man with the Hammer." By Anna Wickham. Grant Richards. 2s. 6d. net.

In the fat white Government publications which record monthly a growth of imports as compared with exports which would have made the hair of the late Mr. Chamberlain stand on end and stay there certain columns may commonly be observed which relate to imports of partly manufactured goods. The American vers libre which is now pouring into the country in such quantities comes, perhaps, into this category. It contains a good deal of the raw material of poetry, and a certain amount of work has been done on it; but the last and most delicate processes involved in the conversion of crude thought and emotion into works of art have normally been omitted. Not quite all of the contributors to the "Catholic Anthology" (the word Catholic has here no religious implications) are not American; there are one or two interesting contributions by Mr. Harold Monro (whose "Hearthstone" is one of the most satisfying things he has done), and Mr John Rodker is represented by a series of Pierrot and Columbine sketches which are written not in free verse but in impressionist prose. But most of the names are those of Americans, Mr. Ezra Pound, and the author of Spoon River, at their head. The value of the raw material employed varies. Some of these poets are nothing but feeble descriptive journalists. Some – Mr. Pound is too often amongst these – ram down any odd notion that comes into their head and trust to the eccentricity of their arrangements, or the disjointed obscurity of their expression, to disguise their lack of anything to say. Mr. Pound in "Heather" produces what he presumably thinks a decoration, or a symbolic representation of a state of mind, or something else. But is it even "something else"?

> The black panther treads at my side,
> And above my fingers
> There float the petal-like flames.

> The milk-white girls
> Unbend from the holly-trees,
> And their snow-white leopard
> Watches to follow our trace.

Feeling Like Supermen.
   Numbers of people are now writing like this; numbers also are like Mr. Orrick Johns, and find that directly they start breaking the traditional bonds of verse they feel as if they were supermen, and start outdoing Whitman and Nietzsche. Mr. Johns' laughter is "like a sword," his muscles are "piston-rods"; he shakes the hand of nations:

I swam in the sea, and lo!
The continents assembled like islands off my coast.
My talk is with Homer and Bonaparte,
    with David and Garibaldi, with China
    and Pharaoh and Texas;
When I laugh it is with Lucifer and Rabelais.
A pathfinder is my mistress, one hard to keep, and unbridled,
I have no respect for tame women.

The most promising things in the book are the poems of Mr. T. S. Eliot. Mr. Eliot has what H. James called "the visiting mind." The detachment, close observation, swift seizure of mental atmospheres of "The Love Song of J. A. Prufrock" are remarkable. One could not read it often for the simple reason that with all its merits it is shapeless, and the artist is not really putting up a defence if he says that when he goes out to tea his afternoon is exceedingly shapeless. "The Boston Evening Transcript," which is short, is very pretty, and "Miss Helen Slingsby," if inferior to the rest, is a great deal more convincing than Mr. Master's hectic attempts at the same sort of thing:

Miss Helen Slingsby was my maiden aunt,
And lived in a small house near a fashionable square,
Cared for by servants to the number of four.
Now when she died there was silence heaven
And silence at her end of the street.
The shutters were drawn and the undertaker wiped his feet:
He was aware that his sort of thing had occurred before.
The dogs were handsomely provided for
But shortly afterwards the parrot died too.
The Dresden clock continued ticking on the mantel-piece.
And the footman sat upon the dining-table
Holding the second housemaid on his knees
Who had always been so careful while his mistress lived.

But surely the footman, in the circumstances, might have chosen a more comfortable seat?

Mr. Oppenheim, like Mr. Johns, rather affects the superman, and his resolves to seek the company of the Earth His Mother and the Planets His Brothers are rather irritating. But there is a good deal of sincerity mixed up with his affectations, and he does sometimes catch a moment's mental experience with accuracy and express it with force. "The Paradox" is characteristic:

> The wheeling heavens, at this moment wheeling:
> The self-absorbed crowds in the street ...
> Gigantic paradox!
> If they saw the sublimity of which they are part
> They would hurry and hide, like children afraid of the dark.

"Washington Square" and "A Handful of Dust" are better, but too long to quote. "Civilization" shows Mr. Oppenheim at his most formless, but illustrates the delightfully frank way in which he states his reactions to the modern world:

> Civilization!
> Everybody kind and gentle, and men giving up their seats in the
>   car for the women. ...
> What an ideal!
> How bracing!

Mr. Oppenheim, if immature, is one of the most promising of the younger Americans, and nobody who gets his book will regret it.

An Enemy of Tameness.

   The most candid remarks of Mr. Oppenheim are roundabout compared with Miss Wickham's; and Mr. Johns's objection to "tame women" seems feeble against her disgust at tameness of any sort. The sort of surprises that she springs may be illustrated by the end of her declaration against rhyme:

> Rhymed verse is a wide net
> Through which many subtleties escape.
> Nor would I take it to capture a strong thing
> Such as a whale.

But the most noticeable thing about her is that one doesn't much care how she says things (in the technical sense) or whether she writes good poems or not; what matters is what she says – which is, an unusual thing, precisely what she thinks. She is reacting hard against tameness, dullness, slackness, conventionality, ugliness, all the time. No one's moods are all of a piece and, as all her moods go down, she may not be entirely consistent in what – though she would probably shudder at the word – one must call her doctrine. But an effect of unity is produced all the same by her reiterated scorn of weakness, weak self-suppression and weak self-indulgence, her contempt of hypocrisy and cowardice, her insistence on something more than lopsided relations between the sexes, and her glorification of intelligent motherhood. Quotation, except at an impracticable length, would only illustrate the robust oddities of her speech; definition must make her seem much less spontaneous and vital than she is. But without more quotation or definition one may recommend her as anything but dull and as being, in spite of her Maenad gestures, in possession of several healthy truths.

2640 I am glad to welcome a new edition of Mr. John M. Robertson's admirable "Montaigne and Shakespeare" (Black. 7s. 6d. net). This illuminating essay, first published some twelve years ago, has been amplified, and, so far as such work can be, brought up to date. It has, of course, been generally admitted that Shakespeare owed something to Florio's translation of Montaigne – any close and intelligent reader of both authors must have noticed verbal resemblances and turns of thought – but Mr. Robertson dives more deeply into the question, and attempts to show (as I think, with conspicuous success) that Shakespeare's intellectual development was largely informed and inspired by the most enduring, and still almost the most modern, of French writers. The spirit in which Mr. Robertson conducts his task is beyond praise; it is sane, tolerant, and persuasive.

Parallelisms.

It is possible, even probable, that Shakespeare knew Florio, who was certainly a friend of Jonson, and one of the Mermaid circle. Florio's wonderful translation of Montaigne appeared in 1603, though it had no doubt been passed from hand to hand earlier in MS. Mr. Robertson bases his argument largely upon the difference between the First Quarto "Hamlet" of 1601 and the Second Quarto of 1604. But before coming to that let me interpolate here an almost direct transcription of Montaigne in "The Tempest," the last and most radiant of the plays. In Florio's translation we read:

They (Lycurgus and Plato) could not imagine a genuity so pure and simple, as we see it by experience, nor ever believe our society might be maintained with so little art and human combination. It is a nation (would I answer Plato) that hath *no kind of traffic, no knowledge of letters,* no intelligence of numbers, *no name of magistrate, nor of politic superiority; no use of service, of riches, or of poverty; no contracts, no successions, no dividences, no occupation, but idle*; no respect of kindred, but common; no apparel, but natural; no manuring of lands, *no use of wine, corn, or metal.*

In "The Tempest" Gonzalo says to the shipwrecked King:

> I' the commonwealth I would by contraries
> Execute all things; for no kind of traffic
> Would I admit; no name of magistrate;
> Letters should not be known; no use of service,
> Of riches, or of poverty; no contracts,
> Succession; bound of land, tilth, vineyard, none;
> No use of metal, corn, or wine, or oil:
> No occupation, all men idle, all;
> And women too: but innocent and pure:
> No sovereignty. ...

No case of inspired lifting could be more clear.

2641   RELIGION AND ETHICS
WAS NIETZSCHE A MADMAN OR A GENIUS?

IN HIS book on the philosophy of Nietzsche, noticed in these pages two months ago, Mr. Henry L. Mencken, of Baltimore, albeit an interpreter and admirer of Nietzsche, refers to certain parts of his teaching as "sheer lunacy." If even a disciple can make so fatal an admission, it is hardly a matter for wonder that others are taking up the same cry. "Why," asks Sidney G. P. Coryn, of the San Francisco *Argonaut,* "does Mr. Mencken discriminate against *one* portion of Nietzsche, when there is such an overwhelming majority of the same brand?" The conviction, indeed, is widespread that Nietzsche was irresponsible and unbalanced. "He was a victim of fever," says a writer in the New York *Evening Post*; "his philosophy shows the same relation to reality as a nightmare bears to the objects it distorts and magnifies." In view of the indisputable fact that Nietzsche showed "pathological" symptoms (see CURRENT LITERATURE, May), and that he actually did go mad before he died, there is a valid interest in the question: How far was his thought sane, and how far was it poisoned by incipient insanity?

It is too late in the day to question the *vitality* of Nietzsche's thought and influence; and no one responsive to the intellectual currents of our time can deny that his influence is steadily growing. His shadow has fallen over half of Europe. Germany, France, and Italy are all discussing his doctrines. And now a series of works are appearing in English, interpreting and elaborating his points of view. The latest of these is a new edition* of Alexander Harvey's translation of "Human, All Too Human."

One of the striking features of the Nietzschean influence is its penetrative power. It permeates every school of thought, and arouses as much interest in conservative as in radical circles. Emma Goldman's Anarchist monthly, *Mother Earth*, has recently printed an excellent summary of Nietzsche's doctrines. Evidently the Anarchists claim him as their own. On the other hand, Mr. Mencken boldly affirms that the leading exponent of the Nietzschean philosophy in America to-day is – President Roosevelt! "The President," he remarks, "has made embryo Nietzscheans of us all, for in all things fundamental the Rooseveltian philosophy and the Nietzschean philosophy are identical." Mr. Mencken sustains his argument by quoting parallel passages from the President's book, "The Strenuous Life," and from Nietzsche's rhapsodic poem, "Thus Spake Zarathustra."

"I wish to preach," writes the President, "not the doctrine of ignoble ease, but the doctrine of the strenuous life, the life of toil and effort, of labor and strife; to preach the highest form of success which comes not to the man who desires mere easy peace, but to the man who does not shrink from danger, from hardship, or from bitter toil, and who, out of these, wins the splendid ultimate triumph."

"I do not advise you to conclude peace," cries Zarathustra, "but to conquer! What is good? ye ask. To be brave is good. Thus live your life of obedience and war! Man is something to be surpassed."

President Roosevelt says: "When men fear righteous war, when women fear motherhood, well it is then that they should vanish from the earth." And Zarathustra says: "Thus would I have men and women: fit for warfare the one, fit for giving birth the other."

---

*HUMAN, ALL TOO HUMAN. A book for Free Spirits. By Friedrich Nietzsche. Translated by Alexander Harvey. Chicago: Charles H. Kerr & Company.

While the Anarchists are claiming Nietzsche, and Mr. Mencken is trying to convince us of the essential identity of the Rooseveltian and Nietzschean philosophies, thinkers of other schools are busy debating the worth and the implications of Nietzsche's teaching. Horace Traubel, the Camden poet and visionary, offers this suggestive criticism in *The Conservator*:

"I make out Nietzsche's superman. The superior brute living on the backs of the crowd: the herd, as Nietzsche calls the crowd. The superman, acknowledging no obligations to the people. Magnificent, imperious, taking without squeamish doubts his utmost fill of life. Shaw, too, has a superman. And other dreamers and thinkers have had supermen. Shaw looks for a race of supermen. Nietzsche scorns the idea that the race at the full can ever acquire the ascent. The supermen will always be exclusive. Always the freeman on the top. Always the slave below. But I don't see how that tub will hold water. The man on top can never be free until the man below is free. Nietzsche says somewhere that the superman owes nothing to the past or to the present. Yet he also says somewhere that the superman must be prepared to sacrifice himself for the sake of the unborn generations. Nietzsche talks magnificently about the individual. And in so far as he contemplates the individual in the crowd he is final. But when he portrays the individual set off from the crowd, disavowing the crowd, he has put him on a quicksand."

Socialism bears the strong impress of Nietzsche's thought. Bernard Shaw's play, "Man and Superman," and Jack London's novel, "The Sea Wolf," are both Nietzschean documents. John Spargo, one of the clearest thinkers in the American Socialist movement, stands bewildered before this new portent. "I have read a good deal of Nietzsche's writings," he says, in *The International Socialist Review*, "and it has always been a puzzle for me what professed radical thinkers could find in his endless negations." On the other hand, Robert Rives La Monte, the author of "Socialism, Positive and Negative," discovers a real and vital unity in the thought of Karl Marx and of Nietzsche. "The self-assertion of Nietzsche," he declares, "is not so far from the class-consciousness of Marx. What Nietzsche urges on the individual Marx urges on the proletarian class, namely, to *dare to be themselves*, go straight after their heart's desire, enjoy sweet life unhampered by convention and traditional ethics." The Free-Thought organ, *The*

Truth-Seeker, says: "Nietzsche belongs to that class of thinkers who are on their way, but do not know where they are going." At the other extreme in journalism, *Town Topics*, the society paper, devotes a page of appreciative exposition to the "sham-smashing Teuton" whose "terrific philosophy, flung like a comet into dark, interstellar spaces, shines on eternally."

The most lucid and sympathetic interpretation of Nietzsche's fundamental position that has lately appeared is published in *The International Journal of Ethics*. The author, Mr. A. C. Pigou, of Cambridge University, points out that Nietzsche's poetic imagination, while it gives his work high literary value, tends to obscure his meaning, with the result that "his exposition is disjointed, sometimes almost incoherent." But if one takes the trouble to decipher Nietzsche's meanings, the results are always worth the labor.

Much of the popular misconception in regard to Nietzsche, according to this English commentator, arises from the fact that his critics have represented him as praising *in themselves* things which he accepts only as *means*, and of condemning in themselves things which he really denounces because of their perversion. To illustrate:

"Of things admittedly bad in themselves, suffering or pain is one. Nietzsche, in my opinion, knew this perfectly well; and, *pace* certain paraders of paradox, I can find no ground for attributing to him the opposite opinion. But, while he knew this, he knew also that suffering often produces other states of mind that are good in themselves. Therefore, shaking himself angrily free from that sentimental sympathy which looks to the moment only, he welcomes suffering and will not have it done away. 'The discipline of suffering,' he writes, 'of *great* suffering – know ye not that it is only *this* discipline that has produced all the elevation of humanity hitherto? The tension of soul in misfortune which communicates to it its energy, its shuddering in view of rack and ruin, its inventiveness and bravery in undergoing, enduring, interpreting, and exploiting misfortune, and whatever depth, misery, disguise, spirit, artifice, or greatness has been bestowed upon the soul – has it not been bestowed through suffering, through the discipline of great suffering?' And, as things have been in the past, so in this respect they must always be. Even when beyond-man is perfected, this discipline must continue. The beyond-man must have a beyond-dragon that is worthy of him.

448 *Literary Notebooks of Thomas Hardy*

"Nor is suffering the only thing bad in itself that is in Nietzsche's view desirable by reason of its effects. He speaks in the same tone of that bondage of the spirit which, according to him, Christianity produced in Europe during the Middle Ages. 'This tyranny, this arbitrariness, this severe and magnificent stupidity, has *educated* the spirit; slavery, both in the coarser and finer sense, is apparently an indispensable means even of spiritual education and discipline'; and again, 'Many there are who threw away everything they were worth when they threw away their servitude.'

"In these two instances it will be noticed that the evil which Nietzsche would retain produces its good effects in the persons upon whom it itself impinges, so that each person is better on the whole than he would have been if it had not been there. This condition is, however, by no means essential to his view. If an evil will produce more than equivalent good effects, he is indifferent to where these goods are located. He is prepared to sacrifice one man for the good of other men in just the same way as he is prepared to sacrifice one aspect of a man for the good of his other aspects. Hence his thesis that there are gradations of rank among persons, that 'moral systems must be compelled first of all to bow before gradations of rank,' and that 'it is immoral to say that what is right for one is proper for another.'"

Nietzsche not only believed that there are certain things admittedly bad in themselves which nevertheless lead to good effects; he also held that there are other things, generally recognized as good, which must be destroyed *in order to obviate bad effects*. It is here that his fierce denunciations enter, and here that he has been most widely misunderstood. As Mr. Pigou explains:

"The point may be put broadly in this way. Among the qualities usually considered virtues, sympathy and love for other men occupy a high place. Nietzsche finds, however, that the *actions* to which these qualities prompt are frequently of a kind to produce bad effects. They lead to the preservation of many persons who, when the good of future generations is taken into account, had, on the whole, better be allowed to perish. Hence, he calls in the first instance for a change of *action* on the part of sympathetic and altruistic persons. 'Do I command you to love your neighbor? I rather command you to flee from your neighbor and to love the most remote. Love unto the most remote future-man is higher than love unto your neighbor. And I consider love unto things and ghosts to be higher than love unto men. This ghost which marcheth before thee, my brother, is more beautiful than thou art. Why dost thou not give him thy flesh and thy bones?' 'What is great in man is that he is a bridge and not a goal.' 'Thus my great love unto the most remote commandeth: "Spare not thy neighbor! Man is something that must be surpassed."' 'Myself I sacrifice unto my love, and my neighbor as myself, thus runneth the speech of all creators.' That this is not an easy or a light thing, Nietzsche, himself tender and pitiful, feels most keenly. 'This is hardest,' exclaims Zarathustra, 'to shut one's open hand because of love.' 'This, this is *my* declivity and my danger, that my glance hurleth upward and my hand would fain clutch and lean upon – depth!

"'My will clingeth round man; with chains I bind myself unto man because I am torn upwards unto beyond-man. For thither mine other will is longing.'

"It is thus a misunderstanding of Nietzsche to assert that he condemns sympathy and love even as a means. What he condemns is the direction which it at present takes, and it is only when he finds it impossible to alter its direction that he is driven to his sternest cry that the good men who will not change in this must perish for the sake of the greater good of the whole.

"'Be sure to love your neighbor as yourselves,' he cries in one place, 'but first be such as love themselves.' And again: 'A man who is *master* by nature; when such a man has sympathy, well! *that* sympathy has value.'"

Nietzsche's affirmations and negations were alike intended to clear the way for a humanity that should fulfil his dream and his ideal – the Superman. He used the word as the early Christians used the phrase "Kingdom of God." It was a high and holy symbol prefiguring all that the universe had been in travail to produce. And what were to be the ruling qualities of his Beyond-Man? Mr. Pigou replies:

"On this point the evidence in the two books that are reputed to contain the gist of his ethical teaching, 'Thus spake Zarathustra' and 'Beyond Good and Evil,' is scanty but fairly explicit. We learn that beyond-man is a person of 'lofty spirituality.' His morality is the noble morality as distinguished from the slave-morality; and 'faith in oneself, pride in oneself, a radical enmity and irony towards all "selflessness," belong to the noble morality.' Again: 'Brave, unconcerned, scornful, violent – thus wisdom would have us to be; she is a woman and ever loveth the warrior only.' Again: 'What is good, ye ask? To be brave is good.' And yet again: 'Free from the happiness of slaves; saved from gods and adorations; fearless and fear-inspiring; great and lonely; this is the will of the trustful ones.'

"The same view is implied indirectly in Nietzsche's manifold denunciations of men as they are. 'Verily, I laughed many a time over the weaklings that thought themselves good because they had lame paws.' 'Not your sin, your moderation crieth unto heaven; your miserliness in sin even crieth unto heaven!' 'Oh, that ye would renounce that half-willing and resolve upon idleness as one resolveth upon action! Oh, that ye would understand my *word*: "Be sure to do whatever ye like – but first of all be such as *can will*."' 'Verily, like preachers of penitence and fools, I proclaimed wrath and slaughter against their great and small things. "Oh, that their best things are so very small" Oh that their evilest things are so very small!"' 'Not unto *that* stake of torture was I fixed that I know man is wicked. But I cried, as no one hath ever cried: "Alas, that his wickedness is so very small! Alas that his best is so very small!"'

"Strength and energy, then; I take it, is for Nietzsche the primary quality of beyond-man."

Thus presented, the philosophy of Nietzsche is not mad, but may be regarded as sane and inspiring. "No man," as a writer in the London *Athenaeum* justly affirms, "would have produced the effect he has whose system was entirely false." The same writer continues:

"We must never forget that Nietzsche's system is primarily, and before all else, a reaction against Schopenhauer – that it has its antagonisms in Tolstoy and Comte and in the Eastern doctrine of Nirvana. Nietzsche stands for the affirmation of life, and Schopenhauer for the opposite. It is only because the mode of the individual's development, social service, and his notion of what makes life 'more abundant' are so different that Nietzsche's antagonism to Christianity is so marked – for, after all, it is Christians who have the saying that 'it is better to lose the world than the soul'; and no force ever known has made so strongly for the strengthening of life historically here and now among men as has Christianity. It is true, of course, that with regard to the method of developing the personality, and the nature of the elements in life that give it value, Christianity and Nietzsche are divided by a gulf as wide apart as the poles; and his rules for practice differ *in toto* from those of any Christian teacher, while those of Schopenhauer may not infrequently coincide with those (say) of St. Francis. None the less it remains true that the system of Schopenhauer, being a pessimism with the gospel of 'death' inscribed on its banner, is fundamentally and theoretically far more deeply opposed to Christianity than is that of Nietzsche, with all its blasphemy and 'immoralism.' Nietzsche, in fact, fell into the mistake of identifying Christian with purely altruistic ethics, and ignoring the immense value set by Christ and his followers on the personal worth of the individual. We are no disciples of Nietzsche, and much that he says seems not only unwarrantable, but even ridiculous; but ... we believe that the real driving force of his system came from the fact that, in protest alike against a false philosophy and a one-sided view of religion, it reaffirmed with emphasis and faith the worth of life and the splendor of human destiny. To us the foundation on which Nietzsche reared this is of the veriest sand; and the entire limitation of his view to earthly existence, together with his absurd belief in the 'repetition' of historical facts, would alone prevent the system lasting as a whole. But, at the risk of being misunderstood, we say that Nietzsche performed a real service, both to religion and morality, when he told men to believe in the glory of things, and bade them shout for the joy of living."

Appendix

The '1867' Notebook

INTRODUCTORY NOTE

The 'Critical Introduction' (pp. xiv–xxx) is, in general, applicable also to the '1867' Notebook, which is in several aspects similar to the 'Literary Notes', with which it also largely coincides chronologically. The '1867' Notebook, that is, supplements the larger volumes in offering further insight into Hardy's literary background. Like the 'Literary Notes', it both confirms and extends our knowledge of Hardy's reading: there is additional confirmation of his familiarity with, especially, Carlyle, Ossian, Spencer, Swinburne, and the romantic poets. Of particular interest is the rare documentation of Hardy's reading in modern foreign literature, from France, Germany, Italy, and Norway: there are excerpts from Baudelaire, Victor Hugo, Alfred de Musset, Emile Zola, Jean Paul Richter, Giacomo Leopardi, and Bjørnstjerne Bjørnson. Some of the passages from the French sources are Hardy's own translations. Also like the 'Literary Notes', these excerpts reflect Hardy's ideological and aesthetic predilections, his 'idiosyncratic mode of regard', his quick perception of the ironic, the bizarre, the macabre, the 'Gothic'.

There is also, however, a marked difference in the general orientations of the '1867' Notebook and the 'Literary Notes'. In contrast to the latter, the '1867' Notebook consists almost exclusively of entries from literary sources. And, despite the perilous distinction between form and content, it may be argued that the intent and purpose of the '1867' Notebook are primarily aesthetic. That is, most quotations are stylistic, singling out felicitous words and phrases. This seems to be true not only of the brief quotations from poetry, but also of the prose excerpts in which individual words and phrases are often underlined. Naturally, this does not preclude cases where Hardy has been attracted by the ideological import as well as by the form of specific passages.

To define exactly Hardy's own distinction between the two collections of notes is difficult, if at all possible. That he made a distinction is, of course, obvious from his physical separation of them alone – a separation only partially preserved in the present edition. Still, to publish them in the same volume does not imply any intent to disregard or discard Hardy's own distinction. It is simply a practical

455

solution based on the idea that both collections of notes deserve to be made more easily available, and that the juxtaposition of them in the same edition will not be detrimental to our appreciation of their individual characteristics.

Editorial Note

All ticks [√] in the left-hand margin of the text are in pencil in the manuscript.

TEXT

1 √ (**fl^r**) Time ...
   perishable & plaintive, clothed with care and mutable as sand.

2 √   The gods, ...
     many things they have given & taken
       And wrought & ruined many things. ...
They have wearied time with heavy burdens ...
And circled pain about with pleasure,
   And girdled pleasure about with pain.

3 Joy is not, but love of joy shall be.

4 √ Because Thou art cruel, & men are piteous.

———————————//———————————

5 (Sha:)

     Even as men wrecked upon a sand
     That look to be washed off the next tide.

———————————//———————————

6 Have graven his exploits upon his forehead.   Corneille.

7 (**fl^v**) To action! to evil! the good remains unknown.

                               A. de Musset

8 √ "The Universal Death" [i.e. death of the whole Universe.]
                                   H. Spencer.

9 √ The ultimate state.   ib.

10 √ The Unknowable.   ib.

———————————//———————————

11 √ The soul's frail dwelling-house (the brain)   Sha.

12 √ Care keeps his watch in every old man's eye.   "

13 Populations of stern faces, stern as any Hebrew, but capable
withal of bursting into inextinguishable laughter. ...   Carl.

14 A background of wrath.   ib.

15 (**f2ʳ**) "Markham lies low. ... Visible to us there, in the glades of
ancient Sherwood, in the depths of long vanished years! – "
                    Carlyle. (A Duel) "Two hundred & fifty years ago."

16 "Sorrow lives in us as an indestructible force ... passing from pain
into sympathy."   G. Eliot. Adam B.

17 "Mental as well as bodily pain ... becomes a habit of our lives, &
we cease to imagine a condition of perfect ease."   ib.

——————————— // ———————————

18 "All these [diamonds] on a neck of snow, slight-tinted with
rose-bloom; & within it royal Life."   "Dia. Neckᶜᵉ" Carlyle.

19 "But Mr Moulder did not get drunk. His brandy-and-water went
into his blood, & into his eyes, & into his feet, & into his hands, – but
not into his brain."   "Orley Fᵐ" Trollope.

20 (**f2ᵛ**) "Miscalculating Boehmer! The Sultana of the Earth shall
never wear that necklace of thine: no neck, either royal or vassal, shall
ever be the lovelier for it. In the present distressed state of our finances,
with the American war raging round us, where thinkest thou are eighty
thousand pounds to be raised for such a thing? In this hungry world,
thou fool, these five hundred & odd diamonds, good only for looking at,
are intrinsically worth less to us than a string of as many dry Irish
potatoes. ...
    Or why not our own loveliest Marie-Antoinette, once Dauphiness
only; now every inch a queen: what neck in the whole earth would it
beseem better? It is fit only for her, – Alas, Boehmer! ... "
                                            Diamᵈ N. Carlyle.
      [Apostᵖʰᵉ from 1ˢᵗ Dʳ]

21 (**f3ʳ**) These children were ... the great future [of the Republic.]
V. Hugo

22 Traceries [of trees] in which there is ...⎷ the mute persuasion of
unkindled melodies   Shelley.

23 [Also a passage about the song in the egg of the nightingale, by
some poet.]

24 [The above passages show the future in the present.]

25 The salt wind.

26 Revolution ... was already growling audibly   Carl.

27 Show the century as a Hypocrisy.   ib.

28 A curiosity as to what ... we can discover on the other side of that
troubled atmosphere [the Fch Revolution]   ib.

29 Cagliostrie.   ib.

30 (**f3ᵛ**) faded bowers: pale eyes: painted skies.   Hood.

31 The Gomorrhaeans who sleep under the lake.   V. H.

32 The sweat of the caverns of the night   ib.

33 The sobs of the air among the clouds.   ib.

34 There, nothing has { shape contour } nor age, And the cloud is the
phantom, & the phantom the cloud.   ib.

35 And the immobility of all the cemeteries, and the sleep of all the
tombs, & the peace of all the dead lying in the grave. ...   ib.

36 The silence held suspended ⟨[an]⟩ the anathema.   ib.

37 Man ... falling from the corpse to the skeleton.   ib.

38   (**f4ʳ**) All the joy ⟨that goes⟩ wandering in ⟨the⟩ whirls of fêtes.

ib.

39   The living ... would continue to have for their end ... rottenness, – the offering of an orgie to convivial worms.   ib.

40   The spectres, making a noise of great waters, ... take in haste their bones.   ib.

41   Making the universe turn pale –   ib.

~~~~~~~~~~~~~~~~~~~~~

42   Kissing the hand of Majesty –   Carl.

43   Gilt-edged, frilled individuals –   ib.

44   Upholstery aided by the Fine Arts –   ib.

45   Judge if Paris sat idle all this while.   ib.

46   Where ⟨select⟩ Patriotism can deliver harangues with comfort.

ib.

47   (**f4ᵛ**) The shepherd of the people has been carried home from Little Trianon heavy of heart, & has been put to bed in his own Château of Versailles: the flock knows it, & heeds it not. At most, in the immeasurable tide of French Speech (which ceases not day after day, & only ebbs towards the short hours of night) may this of the royal Sickness emerge from time to time as an article of news. Bets are doubtless depending; nay some people 'express themselves loudly in the streets.' But for the rest, on green field & steepled city, the May sun shines out, the May evening fades; & men ply their useful or useless business as if no Louis lay in danger.   Carl.

48   All Dubarrydom rushes off with tumult into infinite space.   ib.

49   (**f5ʳ**) France smitten, by black art, & lying ... with a Harlot's foot on its neck
                                                                                              ib.

50   The dull millions that ... grind at the wheel of Labour.   ib.

51   Borne over the Atlantic, to the closing ear of Louis, what sounds
are these? muffled, ominous, new in our centuries? ... Democracy
announcing that she is born.   ib.

52 √ Upland, prodigal in oil.   Tennyson.

53 √ The scornful crags.   ib.

——————————————— // ———————————————

54 √ ... Survey mankind from China to Peru,
        Remark each anxious toil, each eager strife. ...   Johnson.

55   See motley life in modern trappings dressed.   ib.

56   Where want enchained caprice ... toil crushed conceit   ib.

57   (**f5ᵛ**) pacific sceptres: joyless wines.   ib.

58   And nations on his eye suspended wait.   ib.

59   Stern famine guards the solitary coast.   ib.

60   The naked heavens.   Wordsw.

61   The surging darkness – modern –

62 √ Sceptred Care: rosy Pleasure –   Gray.

63 √ The cheek of Sorrow   "

64 √ The toiling hand of Care   "

65 √ Contemplation's sober eye.   "

66 √ Pallid Fear: Envy wan: faded Care   "

67 √ Moody Madness laughing wild.   "

68 √ Lo, in the Vale of Years beneath
    A griesly troop are seen,
  The painful family of Death,
    More hideous than their Queen.   "

69 √ Folly's idle brood: √ grinning Infamy.   "

70 √ (**f6ʳ**) Grandeur ... with a disdainful smile
    The dull cold ear of Death   "

71 √ To scatter plenty o'er a smiling land,
And read their history in a nation's eyes.   "

72 √ Pestilence-stricken multitudes (dead leaves)   Shelley.

73 √ Tasting of Flora: sun-burnt Mirth   Keats.

74 √ Leaden-eyed despairs.   "

——————————— // ———————————

75   T. played from morning until evening, & practised new tunes; at night he dreamed about them; they bore him far over the hills away to foreign lands, as though he were afloat on sailing clouds. ...

76   He threw his newest tune into the fiddle. ...

77   He played till his father told him he was fading away before his eyes. ...

78   Everywhere there penetrated a long heavy (**f6ᵛ**) tone, that shook him from head to foot, & everything he saw seemed to vibrate with that tone.   Bj.

——————————— // ———————————

79 √ Many a winged woe ...
With hearts rent, & knees made tremulous.
... ephemeral lips, & casual breath. ...
They have ... vexed the lips of life with death. ...   Swin.

80 √ What shall be done with all <u>these tears of ours?</u>   "

81 √ A great <u>well-head of lamentation.</u>   "

82 √ All fields are <u>helpless</u> in the sun, all trees
<u>Stand as a man stripped</u> out of all but skin.   "

~~~~~~~~~//~~~~~~~~~

83 √ Gentlemen of the shade, minions of the moon.   Sha.

84 Fashion crowded round him, with her meteor lights and Bacchic
dances. ... Our mad Babylon wore him and wasted him with all (**f7ʳ**)
her engines; & it took her twelve years.   Carl. (on Irving.)

85 Our phantasmagory of a world.   "

86 √ They hear a voice in every wind
       and snatch a fearful joy.   Gray.

87 √ I saw pale kings and princes too,
       Pale warriors, death-pale were they all;
       They cried – ...'
       I saw their starved lips in the gloom
       With horrid warning gaped wide. ...   Keats.

~~~~~~~~~//~~~~~~~~~

88a Angry ghost: <u>labouring</u> souls.   (Dry. Virg.)
   b <u>Touched at human fate.</u>   "
   c Those whose bones are not <u>composed in</u> graves.   "
   d Palinurus ... <u>fresh from life.</u>   "
   e The <u>dooming</u> gods: the <u>inhuman</u> coast: "
   f Droves of minds: clothed in bodies.   "
   g The soul may suffer mortal flesh again.   "
   h Spots of sin in every face.   "

89 √ (**f7ᵛ**) The talk they had with the Shining Ones was about the
glory of the place; who told them that the beauty and glory of it was
inexpressible. There, said they, is the Mount Zion, the heavenly
Jerusalem, the innumerable company of angels, and the spirits of just

men made perfect. You are going now, said they, to the paradise of God, wherein you shall see the tree of life, & eat of the never-fading fruits thereof; and when you come there you shall have white robes given you, and your walk and talk shall be every day with the King even all the days of eternity. There you shall not see again such things as you saw when you were in the lower region upon the earth, to wit, sorrow, sickness, affliction, & death, for the former things are passed away. ... You must there receive the comforts of all your toil, & have joy for all your sorrow; you must reap what you have sown even the fruit of all your prayers, & tears, & sufferings for the (**f8ʳ**) King by the way. In that place you must wear crowns of gold. ... There you shall enjoy your friends again, that are gone thither before you, & there you shall with joy receive everyone that follows into the holy place after you.

Bunyan.

90   Thy ... ⟨deep⟩ throat, fallen lax & thin,
     Worked, as the blood's beat worked therein.   Swin.

91   There [in the Shades] mighty Caesar waits his
     vital hour, [i.e. the time to be born]
     Impatient for the world. ...   Dry. Virg. Ae VI

92   A dyspeptic populace.   Carl.

93   Two hostile worlds, the upper Court-world, the nether Sans-culottic one.   ib.

94   Acrid, corrosive, as the spirit of sloes and copperas, is Marat. ... Poor is this man; squalid, & dwells in garrets; a man unlovely (**f8ᵛ**) to the sense, outward & inward; a man forbid; – & is becoming fanatical, possessed with fixed-idea. Cruel <u>lusus</u> of Nature! Did Nature, O poor Marat, as in cruel sport, knead thee out of her <u>leavings</u> & miscellaneous waste clay; & fling thee forth ... a Distraction into this distracted Eighteenth century?   F. R. Carl.

95   Wagon-loads of this Pamphleteering & Newspaper matter lie rotting slowly in the Public Libraries of our Europe –   "   "

96   Such tugging & lugging, & throttling of one another, to divide ...
the joint Felicity of man in this Earth.   "   "

97   Yonder an august Assembly sits regenerating France.

                                                           "   ib.

98   (**f9ʳ**) Which of these six-hundred individuals, in plain white
cravat, that have come up to regenerate France, might one guess would
become their King? ... In fiery rough figure, with black Samson-locks
under the slouch-hat, he steps along there. A fiery fuliginous mass. ...
But now, if Mirabeau is the greatest, which ... may be the meanest?
Shall we say that anxious, slight, ineffectual-looking man, under 30, in
spectacles; his eyes (were the glasses off) troubled, careful; with
upturned face, snuffing dimly the uncertain future time; complexion of
a multiplex atrabiliar colour, the final shade of which may be the pale
sea-green.   ib.

99   √ Whose hearts ... ache with the pulse of ... remembered song.
                                                           Swin.

100 √ Memory grey with many a flowerless year.   ib.

101 √ Thou sawest the tides of things close over heads of kings   "

102a (**f9ᵛ**) A mist of the marshy Lano, when it moves on the plains of
      autumn, bearing the death of thousands along.   O-n
   b Call back his soul to the bard.   "
   c Deaths wander, like shadows, over his fiery ⟨soul.⟩
   d Children of heroes, in a land unknown [say, the human race on
      earth].

103   [Those who] waste with me in earth.

104a No words come forth ... each soul is rolled into itself.
   b Their gleaming tribes:
   c Thou sometimes hidest the moon with thy shield. Thou kindlest
      thy hair into meteors, & sailest along the night.

d   Dark waved his shaggy brow above his gathered $\begin{cases} \text{rage.} \\ \text{smile} \end{cases}$

e   ... Looked forward a ghost half formed of the shadowy smoke. He
     poured his voice amid the roaring. ...

105   The house of the spirits of men. ... The roof (**f10ʳ**) of his dreadful
hall is marked with nightly fires.

106a   A ridge of formless shades.
   b   "Where hast thou failed?"
   c   [In his soul a] dark deed wandered in secret –
   d   He fell pale, in a land unknown; his soul came forth to his fathers,
       to their stormy isle: there they pursued boars of mist along the
       skirts of winds.
   e   Why is thy head so gloomy?
   f   There, silent, dwells a feeble race: they mark no years with their
       deeds as slow they pass along. Rear the forms of old on their own
       dark-brown years.
   g   Hill of storms, I behold my race on thy side.
   h   They mixed their gloomy strife.
   i   His [the dead one's] ghost is on our hills.
   j   Like a meteor that incloses a spirit of night.
   k   The sun will now rise, & the $\begin{cases} \text{(ghosts)} \\ \text{shadows descend.} \end{cases}$

----

107   malignant light: shivering spirits: unintombed.

108   (**f10ᵛ**) The fiery soul of the world had flown up, & the cold
crumbling giant [Rome] lay around; torn asunder were the gigantic
spokes of the fly-wheel which once the very stream of ages drove.

                                                              J. Paul.

----

109   The motions I find in my heart in favour of him.

                                                              Old Spec.

110   A Beau's head. The ogling muscles [of the eye] were very much
worn & decayed with use; whereas, on the contrary, the elevator, or the

muscle which turns the eye towards heaven, did not appear to have
been used at all.   Addison. ib.

111   What we looked upon as brains were not such in reality, but a
heap of strange materials ... smelt very strong of essence. ... One cavity
filled with ribbands, lace, & embroidery ... another with invisible
billets-doux & other trumpery. ... Cavity filled with fictions, flatteries ...
another, oaths & imprecations: a duct from earth ran to the root of the
tongue.   ib.

-------------------//-------------------

112   (**f11ʳ**) √ When the dead were now fallen down by heaps one
upon another. ...   Wisd.

113   √ For whereas they would not believe anything by reason of the
enchantments. ...   "

114   √ While all things were in quiet silence, & night was in the midst
of her swift course.   "

~~~~~~~~~~~~~~~~~~~~~~~~~

115   His arms hang disordered on his side.   O-n.

116   When ...'s dark children come forth to frighten hapless men.
                                                                     "

117a   I ... passed before his soul.   "
   b   Thy departure was like a fading light.   "
   c   The crowded sighs of his bosom rose.   "
   d   Their blood is mixing. ...   "
   e   The watery forms of. ...   "
   f   The joy of his face was dark.   "
   g   Age is on our trembling hands.   "

~~~~~~~~~~~~~~~~~~~~~~~~~

118   (**f11ᵛ**) A painted people, looking tired & overcome.

                                                                Dante.
(Hypocrites, wearing leaden cloaks.)
(gilded on the outside −)
O weary mantle for eternity!   "

119   People tired by their burden.   "
I am with the body that I have always had. ...   "
You, from whom distils such sorrow. ...   "
Two shapes appeared to us mixed in one face.   "

~~~~~~~~~~~~~~~~~~~~~~

120   ... A workshop of the last day, full of fragments of worlds ... an
enormous potsherd of time.   J. Paul.

121   Youth ... the far, low-lying time, when the spindle of (his) life ran
round as yet almost without threads.   "

122   A rainy corner of his life.   "
      The Unknown Hand (i.e. Fate, God.)   "

123   I am then no longer alone with my spirit.   "

124   (**f12ʳ**) Our library ... the concert-hall of the finest voices from all
times & places.   "

125   The earth is great, but the [universal] heart which rests upon it is
greater than the earth, & greater than the sun.   "

126   Age & sufferings had already marked out ⟨in her⟩ the first
incisions for Death, so that he required but little effort to cut her down.
                                                                                 "

127   ... A woman, whose thread of life a secret, all-wondrous hand is
spinning to a second thread, & who veils within her the transition from
nothingness to existence. ...   "

128   This Golgotha of a heavenly time.   "

129   The little human being ... borne upon a flying earth.   "

130   The quick passage [of the mind] from the inward to the outward,
& conversely.   "

131 (**f12ᵛ**) √ ... Whatever power
      Or spirit of the nethermost abyss
      Might in that noise reside.   Mil.

132 vegetable gold: life-spindle   (J. P-1):

133 The birds threw themselves into pairs.   Old Spec

134 I saw a new bloom arise in your face.   "

———————————— | ————————————

135 He is a refractory corpse. ... It has to be done again. (remark of
assassin who did not kill victim)

～～～～～～～～～～～

136 Here & there the unbodied spirit flies –
    By time, or force, or sickness dispossessed,
    And lodges where it lights ...
    From tenement to tenement is tossed
    The soul is still the same, the figure only lost
    And, as the softened wax new seals receives,
    This face ⟨[the soul]⟩ assumes, & |[forsakes that shape]
                              |that impression leaves.

                          Ovid. (free transl.)

137 (**f13ʳ**) A drop of dew, of which the sun was making a carbuncle.
                                      V. H.

138 In the subterranean passages of this life ... meets no longer men,
but mummies on crutches. ...   J. P.

139 √ Day, nor night, nor change of seasons made
    [the notes of time] but thoughts & unavailing tears.
                              Shelley.

～～～～～～～～～～～

140 Barberton contains 6000 regular inhabitants. On Saturday nights
the population of Barberton is about 8000   Times.

141 √ [God, setting about Creation] in paternal glory rode
Far into Chaos, and the world unborn.
[And] Chaos heard his voice: him all his train
Followed in bright procession, to behold
Creation ...   Mil.
... the vast profundity

142   He [portrait painter] made coxcombs of his sitters.   Paper.

143   (**f13ᵛ**) Which [times] are nothing more nor less than the arrival
of a nation at a halting-place. .... They made the first relay with
Mirabeau, the second with Robespierre, the third with Buonapᵗᵉ : they
are thoroughly exhausted.   V. H.

144   Devotions wearied out, heroisms grown old, ambitions full-fed.
fortunes made, all seek, demand, implore, solicit, what? A place to lie
down.   "

145   They [the Bourbons] were surly with the 19ᵗʰ centʸ .... They
believed that they were strong because the Empire had been swept
away before them like a scene at a theatre. They did not perceive that
they themselves had been brought in in the same way. They did not see
that they also were in that hand which had taken off Napoleon.   "

146   They [the Bourbons] believed ... they were the past. They were
mistaken: they were a portion of the (**f14ʳ**) past, but the whole past was
France.   "

147   France had done without them for twenty two years; there had
been a solution of continuity; they did not suspect it. And how should
they suspect it, they who imagined that Louis XVII reigned on the 9ᵗʰ
Thermidor, & that Louis XVIII reigned on the day of Marengo?
                                                                                        "

148   The Revolution had had its say under Robespierre, the cannon
had had its say under Buonaparte   "

149   The Bourbons were an instrument of civilization which broke in
God's hands. ... Their descent into the night was not one of those solemn
disappearances which leave a dark emotion to history. .... They faded
away in the horizon.   "

150 The nation ... touched the royal personages sadly and with precaution –   "

151 (**f14ᵛ**) ... Escape from the question between rich & poor.

Thac.

152 The right prostrating the fact ... The fact, if it contain too little of the right, or none at all, is destined infallibly to become in the lapse of time, deformed, unclean, perhaps even monstrous. If you would ascertain at once what degree of ugliness the fact may reach, seen in the distance of the centuries, look at Machiavel. Machiavel is not an evil genius, nor a demon; ... he is nothing but the fact. ~~And~~ ... the fact of the 16ᵗʰ century. He seems hideous, & he is so, in the presence of the moral idea of the Nineteenth.

This conflict of the right & the fact endures from the origin of society. To bring the duel to an end, to amalgamate the fine ideal with the human reality, to make the right peacefully interpenetrate the fact, & the fact the right, this is the work of the wise.

But the work of the wise is one thing, the work of the able another.

V. H.

153 (**f15ʳ**) The able ... have decreed to themselves the title of Statesmen. ... Wherever there is ability only there is necessarily pettiness –   "

154 It is not always easy [after a revolution] to procure a dynasty. ... There must be a certain amount of antiquity ... and the wrinkles of centuries are not to be extemporized.   "

155 Louis Philippe aimed ... that he might be obeyed rather as an intelligence than as a king.   "

156 In the multitude: – the hidden & obscure uprisings of souls – all that might be called the invisible currents of conscience.   "

157 The complaints of history against L. Philippe.   "

158 He had seen behind Louis XVI – that hapless passer-by – rising up in the darkness the fear-inspiring monarchy.   "

159   (**f15ᵛ**) The blind <u>clairvoyance</u> of the Revolution, crushing royalty in the king, & the king with the royalty, almost <u>without noticing the man in the savage overthrow of the idea.</u>
"

160   The <u>public wrath questioning Capet</u>
"

~~~~~~~~~~~~~~~~~

161   [The Royal Carriage] rushing at the rate of double drink-money.

Carl.

162   This little thread of water, working <u>at all moments</u> for thousands of years, has hollowed. ...
"

163   With a surprising vividness of eye & mind he [Friedrich] watches the signs of the times, of the hours, & the days, & the places; & prophesies from them; reads men & their procedures as if they were mere handwriting, not too cramp for him. ... 'If the Austrian cooking-tents are a-smoke before 8' notes he, 'you may calculate the Austrians will march that day'
"

164   (**f16ʳ**) London statues. ... There they stand, <u>in all weathers.</u> ...

Carl.

165   What a singular shape of a man, <u>shape of a time,</u> have we in this Abbot Samson and his history
"

166   The smoky twilight ... <u>disordered dusk of Things.</u>
"

167   To-day becomes Yesterday so fast, <u>all To-morrows become Yesterdays.</u> ... Thy very pains, once <u>gone over into yesterday</u> become joys to thee.
"

168   (**f16ᵛ**) ... You reached the second story [of the stairs] whither the yellow wallpaper & the chocolate plinth followed you with a peaceful persistency
"

169 The little green flowers on the nankeen paper came calmly & in
order to these iron bars [of the grille in the wall]   "

~~~~~~~~~~~~~~~~~~~~~~

                                                        skin]
170 The soul ... expressing itself [through the face] more fully at
some moments than at others.   Soc. Psy. Research

171 Multiplex personality   "

172 (**f17ʳ**) a philosophic journey across humanity:
                                              Pref. to Leopardi.

173 √ said Nature to a soul. ...   "

174 √ those sweet & adorable chimeras.   "

175 √ the world is only a cerebral phenomenon.   "

176 √ in the evening of human things: "

177 √ the irremediable & universal grief –   "

178 √ the emancipated: "

179 √ doctor & corrector of souls: "

~~~~~~~~~~~~~~~~~~~~~~

180 The landscape ... was ⟨dying of its thirst, &⟩ flying away in clouds
of dust at the least breath of wind.   Zola.

181 For years he had never seen the sun ... gazing inwards on his
soul.   "

182 (**f17ᵛ**) If you live all alone you get to see things queerly. The trees
are no longer trees, the earth puts on the ways of a living being, the
stones seem to tell you tales.   "

183   That fearful land, utterly consumed with ardent passions. ...
                                                                        "

184   The Artauds, even when asleep, resting with aching backs,
shrouded in shadow, disturbed him with their slumber; he could
recognize their breath in the air he breathed. ... The hamlet was not
dead enough; the thatched roofs bulged like bosoms; through the
gaping cracks in the doors came sighs, faint creaks, & hums of living
silence.
                                                                        "

185   Her laughter ... resounded from every atom of his flesh.   "

186   All the hues, all the emotions of the sky.   "

187   (**f18ʳ**) The very by-paths entreated their presence from afar. ... A
tide of impassioned emotion stirred the garden to its depths ... the old
flower-garden escorted them.
                                                                        "

188   The whole parterre was a riotous mob ... where intoxicated
Nature had hiccups of verbenas & pinks.
                                                                        "

189   He beheld the rude plants of the plain – the dreadful-looking
growths that had become iron-hard amid the arid rocks, of
close-grained fibre & knotted like snakes & bossed over with muscle –
set themselves to work.
                                                                        "

190   The rust-hued lichens gnawed away at the rough plaster like a
fiery leprosy. The thyme followed on, & thrust their roots between the
bricks like so many iron wedges.
                                                                        "

191   (**f18ᵛ**)~~On The edge of the horizon, the hills, (still hot with the s)~~
~~seemed all tremulous~~
                                                                        "

192   Far off, on the edge of the horizon, the hills, still hot with the
setting luminary's farewell kiss, seemed all tremulous & quivering, as
though shaken by the steps of some invisible army. Nearer ... all the
pebbles in the valley seemed animated with a throbbing life.
                                                                        "

193   The human beings that one felt to be lying there [in dark
chamber]
                                                                        "

194   The shaft swallowed the men by mouthfuls of twenty & thirty at one time   "

195   She walked among them, grotesquely perturbing, with her lumps of flesh exaggerated almost to infirmity.   "

196   (**f19ʳ**) [Examp. ... of more-true-than-truth: –]
   A warm odour of woman arose from the trodden grass: "
the loud sound of the men's voices was deadened as it were by the draperies of the room & the hot-house atmosphere.   "

197   Etienne was alone with La Maheude in the room downstairs. ...
Crouching over the miserable fire she was suckling Estelle. ... 'Is it good news?' she asked. 'Are they going to send us money?' Etⁿᵉ shook his head. ... She became absorbed by her recollections, droned out in a mournful voice, her eyes fixed on vacancy, her breast uncovered, while her daughter Estelle fell asleep on her lap. And Etienne, absorbed also, [in their trouble] sat staring at that enormous breast, the soft whiteness of wh. contrasted with the yellow & weatherbeaten hue of her face.
                                                                              "

198   (**f19ᵛ**) The dust rose from the floor – the dust accumulated by the various dancing-bouts [some time earlier], & poisoned the atmosphere with a strong odour of tram-girls & boys [i.e. the dancers].   "

199   The Voreux pit ... panting louder & louder with its thick & heavy breath, as if obstructed in its painful digestion of human flesh & blood.   "

200   The cage ... The monster was still there, gobbling its ration of human flesh ... without a pause, without an effort, with the facile voracity of an ogre.   "

201   Some giant belly, capable of digesting a whole people. ... Voracious silence.   "

~~~~~~~~~~~~~~~~~~~~~~~~~~~

202   The massive weight of their Harmonies, the persistent crossing of the melodies by wh. those Harmonies are produced, the bright swing of their Rhythm: Grove – Dic. Music

203   (**f20ʳ**) a cadence of gigantic proportions: "
nauseous mixtures (of sounds)   "

~~~~~~~~~~~~~~~~~~~~~~~~~~~~~~~~~~~~~

204   the personal enemy of the 18ᵗʰ centʸ – Chateaubriand. –
                                                    Brunetière.

205   the humble commencement of the planets: Vogüé
                                                    – R. D. M.

206   to catch the murmur of forgotten tombs … the ⟨meaning⟩ of our
passage across the generations.   "

207   History receives the deposition of peoples [now], & relegates to
the second place the sole witnesses that she formerly ⟨would hear⟩
~~receives~~, kings, ministers. …   "

208   Le séjour des ombres   "
Voltairean persiflage   "

~~~~~~~~~~~~~~~~~~~~~~~~~~~~~~~~~~~~~

209   On the meadow before the door lay three harrows through wh.
were blooming, as best they could, all the flowers of May.   V. H.

210   (**f20ᵛ**) He left his business in order to retire to & die upon his
paternal estate.   Sterne.
[what was not foreseen in the act is foreseen in the description of the
act]

211   my iron (my armour).   Ant. & Cleo.

212   the great vertigo of happiness –   V. H.

213   the making of climate (by glass houses &c)   Times

~~~~~~~~~~~~~~~~~~~~~~~~~~~~~~~~~~~~~

214   Letter to a friend.   (Sir T. Browne)
… He is dead & buried, & by this time no puny among the mighty
nations of the dead; for though he left his world not very many days
past, yet every hour you know largely addeth unto that dark society.

215 ... dreams, thoughtful whisperings, mercurisms airy nuncios or sympathetical insinuations.   Carl. on Novalis P. B. 31. 33

216 (**f21ʳ**) ... In my sad opinion he was not like to behold a grasshopper, much less to pluck another fig; and in no long time after seemed to discover that odd mortal symptom in him not mentioned by Hippocrates, that is, to lose his own face, & look like some of his near relations; for he maintained not his proper countenance, but looked like his uncle, the lines of whose face lay deep & invisible in his healthful visage before: for as from our beginning we run through variety of looks, before we come to consistent & settled faces; so before our end, by sick & languishing alterations, we put on new visages: and in our retreat to earth may fall upon such looks which from community of seminal originals were before latent in us.

217 ... where death had set his broad arrow.
... his soft departure
... the civil ceremony of closing his eyes.

218 (**f21ᵛ**) √ – a mortal [deathly] visage & last face;
– A weak physiognomist might say that ... this was a face of earth, and ⟨that⟩ Morta had set her hard seal upon his temples, easily perceiving what caricatura draughts death makes upon pined faces, & unto what an unknown degree a man may live backward.

219 √ easy nativities ... hard deaths:
his departure was so easy:

220 infants, ... to behold the wordly hours and but the fractions thereof; & even to perish before their nativity in the hidden world of the womb, & before their good angel is conceived to undertake them

221 In this consumptive condition & remarkable extenuation, he came to be almost half himself, & left a great part behind him wh. he carried not to the grave.

222 (**f22ʳ**) his heart ... not so big as a nut.

223 ... if the bones of a good skeleton weigh little more than twenty pounds, his inwards & flesh remaining could make no bouffage, but a light bit for the grave.

224   I never more lively beheld the starved characters of Dante in any living face; an aruspex might have read a lecture upon him without exenteration.

225   his flesh being so consumed that he might in a manner have discerned his bowels with! opening of him: so that to be carried, sexta cervice, ⟨(by six shoulders)⟩ to the grave, was but a civil unnecessity. ....

226   ... and if Asia, Africa, & America should bring in their list [of diseases] Pandora's box would swell, & there must be a strange pathology.

227   √ at good distance from the grave.

228   ... a consumed kell [caul] empty & bladder-like guts, livid & marbled lungs, & a withered pericardium. ...

229   ... his disease should die with himself, nor revive in a posterity to puzzle physic, & make sad mementos of their hereditary parent.

230   this deliberate & creeping progress unto the grave.

231   ⟨customary⟩ felicities: the crowd in their beatitudes:

232   his dying ditty. .... He conceived his thread long.

233   since every age makes a step unto the end of all things.

234   Though age had set no seal upon his face, yet a dim eye might clearly discover fifty in his actions.

235   (**f23ʳ**) the streams of the sea: Aeschy. Pers.

236   in this night God called up Winter out of his season: ib.

237   The Bibles of the World.   W. Morris.

238   Rubini (singer) the man with the "tears in his voice" (Balzac's phrase).   P. M. G.

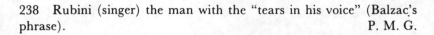

239   the enormous smile of the sea.   Baudelaire.

240   Angel full of health, do you know the Fevers which, along the pale walls of the hospital. ...

241   Ireland looks at herself on the map, in the population returns, &, finding a big blot there, rashly supposes. ...   Carlyle.

242   √ The pale nations heard it.   Shelley –

243   (**f23ᵛ**) "... Here,
           Where day bears down on day as wave on wave,
           And not man's smile fades faster than his tear."
                                                            Swinb.

244   ... In those days moustaches meant civilians, and spurs meant pedestrians.   V. H.

245   It is said that slavery has disappeared from European civilization. This is a mistake. ... It weighs now only upon woman, & is called prostitution.   "

Annotations

SOURCE ABBREVIATIONS

Anderson
J. Ford, *The Broken Heart*, ed. Donald K. Anderson, Jr, Regents Renaissance Drama Series (London, 1868).

Apologia
John Henry Newman, *Apologia Pro Vita Sua: Being a Reply to a Pamphlet Entitled 'What, Then, Does Dr. Newman Mean?'* (London, 1864).

Archer
William Archer, *Real Conversations* (London, 1904).

Archiv
Archiv für das Studium der Neueren Sprachen und Litteraturen.

Ashley Library
The Ashley Library: A Catalogue of Printed Books, Manuscripts and Autograph Letters, collected by Thomas J. Wise, 11 vols (London, 1922–36; repr. 1971).

AUMLA
Journal of the Australasian Universities Language and Literature Association.

Bailey
J. O. Bailey, *The Poetry of Thomas Hardy: A Handbook and Commentary* (Chapel Hill, NC, 1970).

Bies
Werner Bies, 'Beobachtungen zu Thomas Hardys Tagebüchern', *Archiv*, 215 (1978) 103–10.

Björk
Lennart A. Björk, 'Thomas Hardy and his "Literary Notes"', in *A Thomas Hardy Annual*, ed. Norman Page, ı (1982) 115–28.

Björk, 'Hardy's Reading'
Lennart A. Björk, 'Hardy's Reading', in *Thomas Hardy: The Writer and his Background*, ed. Norman Page (London, 1980) pp. 102–27.

Björk, 'Psychological Vision'
Lennart A. Björk, 'Psychological Vision and Social Criticism in *Desperate Remedies* and *Jude the Obscure*', in *Budmouth Essays on Thomas Hardy*, ed. F. B. Pinion (Dorchester, 1976).

Björk, 'Visible Essences'
Lennart A. Björk, '"Visible Essences" as Thematic Framework in Hardy's *The Return of the Native*', *ES*, 53 (Feb 1972) 52–63.

Blackwood's	*Blackwood's Edinburgh Magazine.*
Blunden	Edmund Blunden, *Thomas Hardy* (London, 1942; repr. 1967).
BM	British Museum
Brooks	Jean Brooks, *Thomas Hardy: The Poetic Structure* (London, 1971).
Budmouth Essays	*Budmouth Essays on Thomas Hardy*, ed. F. B. Pinion (Dorchester, 1976).
'Burleigh'	T. B. Macaulay, 'Burleigh', *Critical and Historical Essays* (London, 1854) I, 220–35.
Carlyle, *Works*	Thomas Carlyle, *Collected Works*, Library Edn, 33 vols (London, 1869–71).
Casagrande	Peter J. Casagrande, *Unity in Hardy's Novels: 'Repetitive Symmetries'* (London, 1982).
Clarendon	Edward Hyde, Earl of Clarendon, *The History of the Rebellion and Civil Wars in England in the Year 1641*, 3 vols (Oxford, 1702–4).
Clements and Grindle	*The Poetry of Thomas Hardy*, ed. Patricia Clements and Juliet Grindle (London, 1982).
'Clive'	T. B. Macaulay, 'Clive', *Critical and Historical Essays* (London, 1854) II, 83–127.
CLQ	*Colby Library Quarterly.*
Collins	Philip Collins, 'Hardy and Education', in *Thomas Hardy: The Writer and his Background*, ed. Norman Page (London, 1980). pp. 41–75.
Cont. Rev.	*Contemporary Review.*
Cornhill	*Cornhill Magazine.*
Courtney	W. L. Courtney, 'Mr. T. H. and Aeschylus', *Old Saws and Modern Instances* (New York, 1918) pp. 1–30.
Critical Approaches	*Critical Approaches to the Fiction of Thomas Hardy*, ed. Dale Kramer (London, 1979).

DCM	Dorset County Museum.
DeLaura	David J. DeLaura, '"The Ache of Modernism" in Hardy's Later Novels', *ELH*, 34 (Sep 1967) 380–99.
'Democracy'	Matthew Arnold, 'Democracy', *Mixed Essays* (London, 1879).
De Quincy	Quatremère De Quincy, 'History of the Life and Works of Raffaello', in R. Duppa and Q. De Quincy, *The Lives and Works of Michael Angelo and Raphael*, trs. W. Hazlitt (London, 1846; repr. Bohn's Illustrated Library, 1856 – same pagination).
D. News	*Daily News.*
Drabble	Margaret Drabble (ed), *The Genius of Thomas Hardy* (London, 1976).
EA	*Études Anglaises.*
EB	*Encyclopaedia Britannica.*
Duppa	R. Duppa, 'Life of Michael Angelo Buonarotti', in R. Duppa and Q. De Quincy, *The Lives and Works of Michael Angelo and Raphael*, trs. W. Hazlitt (London, 1846; repr. Bohn's Illustrated Library, 1856 – same pagination).
Edin. Rev.	*Edinburgh Review.*
E. Hardy	Emma Lavinia Hardy.
ELH	*Journal of English Literary History.*
ELT	*English Literature in Transition.*
'Equality'	Matthew Arnold, 'Equality', *Mixed Essays* (London, 1879).
ES	*English Studies.*
Evelyn Hardy	Evelyn Hardy, *Thomas Hardy: A Critical Biography* (London, 1954; reissued New York, 1970).
Fort. Rev.	*Fortnightly Review.*

'Frederic the Great'   T. B. Macaulay, 'Frederic the Great', *Critical and Historical Essays* (London, 1879) II, 244–86.

'A French Critic on Milton'   Matthew Arnold, 'A French Critic on Milton', *Mixed Essays* (London, 1879).

Friends   *Friends of a Lifetime: Letters to Sydney Carlyle Cockerell*, ed. Viola Meynell (London, 1940).

'The Function of Criticism at the Present Time'   Matthew Arnold, 'The Function of Criticism at the Present Time', *Essays in Criticism*, 1st ser. (London, 1865); from entry 1159 onwards the 3rd edn (1875) is used: see entries 1015n and 1159n.

'George Sand'   Matthew Arnold, 'George Sand', *Mixed Essays* (London, 1879).

Gittings   Robert Gittings, *The Older Hardy* (London, 1978).

Greville, *Memoirs*   Charles C. F. Greville, *The Greville Memoirs, A Journal of the Reigns of King George IV and King William IV*, ed. Henry Reeve, 4th edn (London, 1875).

Grieve   T. B. Macaulay, *Critical and Historical Essays*, Everyman's Library edn, ed. A. J. Grieve, 2 vols (London, 1907; repr. 1966).

Grolier Club *Catalogue*   *A Descriptive Catalogue of the Grolier Club Centenary Exhibition 1940 of the Works of Thomas Hardy O.M. 1840–1928*, compiled by Carroll A. Wilson (Waterville, Maine, 1940).

'Hallam's History'   T. B. Macaulay, 'Hallam's History', *Critical and Historical Essays* (London, 1854) I, 51–98.

'Hampden'   T. B. Macaulay, 'John Hampden', *Critical and Historical Essays* (London, 1854) I, 190–220.

Hasan   Noorul Hasan, *Thomas Hardy: The Sociological Imagination* (London, 1982).

'Hastings'   T. B. Macaulay, 'Warren Hastings', *Critical and Historical Essays* (London, 1854) II, 181–244.

'Heine'   Matthew Arnold, 'Heine', *Essays in Criticism*, 1st ser. (London, 1865); from entry 1159 onwards the 3rd edn (1875) is used: see entries 1015n and 1159n.

Hodgson	Sale Catalogue of Messrs Hodgson and Co., Chancery Lane, London, WC2 (26 May 1938).
Hoffman	Russell Hoffman, 'The Idea of the Unconscious in the Novels of Thomas Hardy' (dissertation, University of California, Berkeley, Calif., 1963).
Howe	Irving Howe, *Thomas Hardy* (New York, 1966; London, 1968).
Hutchins	John Hutchins, *The History and Antiquities of the County of Dorset*, 3rd edn (London, 1861).
Hyman	Virginia R. Hyman, *Ethical Perspective in the Novels of Thomas Hardy* (Port Washington, NY and London, 1975).
Jacobus	Mary Jacobus, 'Tree and Machine: *The Woodlanders*', in *Critical Approaches to The Fiction of Thomas Hardy*, ed. Dale Kramer (London, 1979) pp. 116–34.
JEGP	*Journal of English and Germanic Philology*.
'Joubert'	Matthew Arnold, 'Joubert', *Essays in Criticism*, 1st ser. (London, 1865); from entry 1159 onwards the 3rd edn (1875) is used: see entries 1015n and 1159n.
Kintner	*The Letters of Robert Browning and Elizabeth Barrett*, ed. Elvan Kintner, 2 vols (Cambridge, Mass., 1969).
Kipling, *Works*	Rudyard Kipling, *The Bombay Edition of the Works of Rudyard Kipling*, 31 vols (London, 1913–38).
Letters	*The Collected Letters of Thomas Hardy*, ed. Richard Little Purdy and Michael Millgate (1978–).
Life	Florence Emily Hardy, *The Life of Thomas Hardy 1840–1928* (London, 1962; repr. 1965). Originally published in 2 vols: *The Early Life of Thomas Hardy* (1928); *The Later Life of Thomas Hardy* (1930).
'The Literary Influence of Academies'	Matthew Arnold, 'The Literary Influence of Academies', *Essays in Criticism*, 1st ser. (London, 1865); from entry 1159 onwards the 3rd edn (1875) is used: see entries 1015n and 1159n.
Macray	E. Hyde, Earl of Clarendon, *The History of the Rebellion...*, ed. W. D. Macray, 6 vols (Oxford, 1888).

'Maurice de Guérin' Matthew Arnold, 'Maurice de Guérin', *Essays in Criticism*, 1st ser. (London, 1865); from entry 1159 onwards the 3rd edn (1875) is used: see entries 1015n and 1159n.

MFS *Modern Fiction Studies.*

Miller J. Hillis Miller, *Thomas Hardy: Distance and Desire* (Cambridge, Mass., and London, 1970).

Miller, *Fiction and Repetition* J. Hillis Miller, *Fiction and Repetition* (Oxford, 1982).

Millgate Michael Millgate, *Thomas Hardy: His Career as a Novelist* (London, 1971).

Millgate, *A Biography* Michael Millgate, *Thomas Hardy: A Biography* (Oxford and New York, 1982).

MLN *Modern Language Notes.*

MLQ *Modern Language Quarterly.*

Morley, *Works* John Morley, *The Works of Lord Morley*, Edn de Luxe, 15 vols (London, 1921).

MP *Modern Philology.*

N&Q *Notes and Queries.*

NCF *Nineteenth-Century Fiction.*

OCD *The Oxford Classical Dictionary.*

One Rare Fair Woman *One Rare Fair Woman: Thomas Hardy's Letters to Florence Henniker 1893–1922*, ed. Evelyn Hardy and F. B. Pinion (London, 1972).

Orel *Thomas Hardy's Personal Writings*, ed. Harold Orel (Lawrence, Kans., 1966; London, 1967).

'Pagan and Mediaeval Religious Sentiment' Matthew Arnold, 'Pagan and Mediaeval Religious Sentiment', *Essays in Criticism*, 1st ser. (London, 1865); from entry 1159 onwards the 3rd edn (1875) is used: see entries 1015n and 1159n.

Parton James Parton, *Life of Voltaire*, 2 vols (London, 1881).

Paulin	Tom Paulin, *Thomas Hardy: The Poetry of Perception* (London, 1975).
Personal Notebooks	*The Personal Notebooks of Thomas Hardy*, ed. Richard H. Taylor (London, 1979).
Pinion	F. B. Pinion, *A Hardy Companion* (London, 1968).
Pinion, *Art and Thought*	F. B. Pinion, *Thomas Hardy: Art and Thought* (London, 1977).
PQ	*Philological Quarterly.*
Purdy	Richard Little Purdy, *Thomas Hardy: A Bibliographical Study* (London, 1954; repr. 1968).
RDM	*Revue des deux mondes.*
REL	*Review of English Literature* (Leeds).
RES	*Review of English Studies.*
Ruskin, *Works*	John Ruskin, *The Works of John Ruskin*, Library Edn, ed. Sir Edward T. Cook and Alexander D. O. Wedderburn, 39 vols (1903–12).
Rutland	W. R. Rutland, *Thomas Hardy: A Study of his Writings and their Background* (Oxford, 1938).
Sat. Rev.	*Saturday Review.*
Smith	*The Novels of Thomas Hardy*, ed. Anne Smith (London, 1979).
Southerington	Frank R. Southerington, *Hardy's Vision of Man* (London, 1971).
SP	*Studies in Philology.*
Spencer, *Works*	*The Works of Herbert Spencer*, 21 vols (repr. of the 1891 edn, Osnabrück, 1966).
Springer	Marlene Ann Springer, *Hardy's Use of Allusion* (London, 1983).
Stewart	J. I. M. Stewart, *Thomas Hardy: A Critical Biography* (London, 1971).

Strachey and Fulford		*The Greville Memoirs 1814–1860*, ed. Lytton Strachey and Roger Fulford, 8 vols (London, 1938).

Super		*The Complete Prose Works of Matthew Arnold*, ed. R. H. Super (Ann Arbor, Mich., 1960–).

Svaglic		John Henry Newman, *Apologia Pro Vita Sua*, ed. Martin J. Svaglic (Oxford, 1967).

Tanner		H. James, *Hawthorne*, with Introduction and Notes by Tony Tanner (London, 1967).

Taylor		Richard H. Taylor, *The Neglected Hardy: Thomas Hardy's Lesser Novels* (London, 1982).

THA		*A Thomas Hardy Annual*, ed. Norman Page (London, 1982–).

THSR		*Thomas Hardy Society Review.*

TLS		*The Times Literary Supplement.*

VN		*Victorian Newsletter.*

VS		*Victorian Studies.*

Weber		Carl J. Weber, *Hardy of Wessex: His Life and Literary Career* (1940; rev. edn New York, 1965).

Weber, 'Books'		Carl Weber, 'Books from Hardy's Max Gate Library', II (Aug 1950) 246–54.

Webster		Harvey Curtis Webster, *On A Darkling Plain* (Chicago, 1947).

Webster's		*Webster's New Twentieth Century Dictionary.*

West. Rev.		*Westminster Review.*

Williamson		Eugene Williamson, 'Thomas Hardy and Friedrich Nietzsche: The Reasons', *Comparative Literature Studies*, XV (Dec 1978) 403–13.

Wreden		Sale Catalogue of William P. Wreden, Burlingame, Calif., 1938.

Wright		Walter F. Wright, *The Shaping of the Dynasts: A Study in Thomas Hardy* (Lincoln, Nebr., 1967).

ANNOTATIONS TO 'LITERARY NOTES II'

Hardy's works are cited from the Wessex Edn; entry numbers prefixed 'A' refer to the '1867' Notebook in the Appendix.

1650　Frederic Harrison, 'Apologia Pro Fide Nostra', *Fort. Rev.* L (Nov 1888) 672–7. Mixture of summary and abridged quotation. *of belief:* Hardy wrote "to belief." Third line of the heading, the dating, in pencil. First entry of 'Literary Notes II'. For Hardy and Harrison, see entry 1213n.

1651　Unidentified newspaper cutting tipped in.

1652　Walter Paper, 'Style', *Fort. Rev.*, L (Dec 1888) 728; *Works*, V, 5. Quotation with Hardy's underlining. The idea also noted in entry 1716.

1653　*A Dictionary of Music and Musicians*, ed. George Grove (London, 1879) I, 270. Abridged quotation.

1654　F. Brunetière, 'Trois Romans', *RDM*, 80 (1 Mar 1887) 202. Abridged translation and annotation.

1655　Thomas Fuller, *The Church History of Britain* (London, 1868) II, 279. Abridged quotation with variations. Hardy's edn unidentified.

1656　Unidentified.

1657　Grant Allen, 'Tropical Education', *Longman's Magazine*, XIV(Sept 1889) 479–88. Abridged quotation with annotations and variations. The educational experience here advocated is similar to the one Hardy devised – probably in the autumn of 1889 – for Angel Clare in Brazil, see *Tess*, ch. 49 (pp. 433–6).

1658　Friedrich Schiller, 'Ritter Toggenburg', *Sämtliche Werke* (München, 1965) I, 373. Quotation and Hardy's trs. of the first stanza. Hardy's edn unidentified. Final interpolated corrections in pencil. This is Hardy's draft for his poem 'After Schiller'; see Purdy, p. 117.

1659　F. Brunetière, 'Charles Baudelaire', *RDM*, 81 (1 June 1887) 697–701. Trs. and quotation of key words. Entries not in chronological order.

1660　Ibid., pp. 699–700. Quotation of key words.

1661　Ibid., p. 699. Quotation and annotations.

1662　Ibid., p. 699. Abridged quotation.

1663　Ibid., pp. 697–8. Abridged trs. with annotations. On stationery pasted in. Note Hardy's rare dating of his reading the article in the British Museum.

1664   Edward Bouverie Pusey, Preface to *The Works of S. Justin the Martyr, Library of the Fathers* (Oxford, 1861) XL, i–ix. E. Hardy's hand. Summary and quotation (final sentence) with slight variations.

1665   Robert Lytton, *Orval or the Fool of Time* (London, 1869) p. xi. Quotation with a slight variation and annotation. On stationery pasted in. Hardy's edn unidentified.

1666   Ibid., p. 39. Quotation from the opening scene of the 'Second Epoch: Husband and Wife'. Entries 1666 and 1667 on stationery pasted in.

1667   Ibid., pp. xxi ff. Summary. "The Internal Comedy," by Count Sigismund Krasinki, was published in 1835.

1668   Unidentified. E. Hardy's hand. Harry Quilter (1851–1907), art critic; editor of the *Universal Review* when it published Hardy's 'A Tragedy of Two Ambitions' in Dec 1888.

1669   Edward Dowden, 'Victorian Literature', *Fort. Rev.*, XLVII (June 1887) 836. E. Hardy's hand. Quotation and summary. Edward Dowden (1843–1913), critic and professor of English literature, Trinity College, Dublin.

1670   Ibid., p. 845. E. Hardy's hand. Abridged quotation with slight variations.

1671   Ibid., p. 838. E. Hardy's hand. Quotation with slight variations. Robert Owen (1771–1858), socialist; Antoine de Lasalle (1754–1829), French philosopher and moralist. For Comte, see entry 618n.

1672   George Moore, *Parnell and his Island* (London, 1887) pp. 1–20. E. Hardy's hand. Abridged quotation with slight variations. For Hardy and Moore, see *Personal Notebooks*, p. 79 and n. 360.

1673   Margaret L. Woods, 'Again I Saw Another Angel', in *Lyrics and Ballads* (London, 1889) p. 21; in *Collected Poems* (London, 1914) p. 136. Possibly E. Hardy's hand. Quotation with a slight variation and pencilled comment. In 1907, Hardy 'looked into' her *Poems Old and New* (London, 1907) and thought that the form of her poetry seemed 'to insist upon a poet's privilege of originality in presentation' (*Letters*, III, 279), and thus no doubt saw her as a comrade-in-arms.

   The reference to Heine is possibly to Heine's poem 'The Twilight of the Gods' ('Götterdämmerung'), esp. 11. 45 ff.; in Hardy's edn of Heine's *Book of Songs*, pp. 166–9. See entry 1017n.

1674   George Lafenestre, 'La Peinture Étrangère à l'Exposition Universelle', *RDM*, 96 (1 Nov 1889) 159. Trs.

1675   Rudyard Kipling, 'Lisbeth', *Plain Tales from the Hills*, in *Works*, I, 1–6. Annotation and mixture of summary and quotation. Hardy's edn unidentified. Hardy owned a copy of *Barrack-Room Ballads and Other Verses*, 2nd edn (London, 1892). Now in DCM, the volume has several markings and magazine and newspaper cuttings on Kipling are pasted in; Hardy's signature on the half-title. Hardy first met Kipling in May, 1890 (*Life*, p. 226), but for his possibly first reaction to Kipling's writings see Millgate, *A Biography*, p. 303; see also entry 1692n. For Hardy's reaction to Kipling's Nobel Prize, see *Letters*, III, 288. See also Harold Orel, 'Hardy, Kipling, Haggard', *ELT*, 24, no. 4 (1982) 232–248.

1676   Kipling, 'Thrown Away', *Works*, I, 12–21. Summary with key words quoted.

1677   Kipling, 'Yoked with an Unbeliever', ibid., pp. 29–33. Summary.

1678   Kipling, 'The Other Man', ibid., pp. 75–9. Summary.

1679   Kipling, 'Beyond the Pale', ibid., pp. 139–45. Summary.

1680   Kipling, 'In Error', ibid., pp. 146–50. Summary and quotation with a variation.

1681   Kipling, 'In the Pride of his Youth', ibid., pp. 173–9. Summary.

1682   Kipling, 'The Madness of Private Ortheris', ibid., pp. 230–8. Summary.

1683   Kipling, 'On the Strength of a Likeness', ibid., pp. 243–9. Comment and summary.

1684   Kipling, 'To be Filed for Reference', ibid., pp. 262–71. Summary and quotation with slight variations.

1685   *The Journal of Marie Bashkirtseff*, trs. and introduced by Mathilde Blind (London, 1890) I, vii. Quotation with variations. Maria (Bashkirtseva) Konstantinovna Bashkirtseff (1860–84), Russian memoirist. See Norman Page, 'Marie Bashkirtseff: A Model for Sue Brideshead', *THSR*, I, no. 6 (1980) 175.

1686   *Journal of Marie Bashkirtseff*, I, vii–viii. Quotation with slight variations.

1687   Ibid., pp. xxxii–xxxiii. Quotation.

1688   Ibid., pp. 1–354. Annotation and summary with key words quoted (the first paragraph mainly from p. 1, the second from pp. 353–54).

1689   Ibid., pp. 351 ff. Summary.

1690   Ibid., pp. 394–5. Abridged quotation with slight variations.

1691   Ibid., p. 399. Quotation with a slight variation.

1692   Rudyard Kipling, *Departmental Ditties and Other Verses*, 4th edn (Calcutta, 1890) pp. 58, 62; *Works*, xxi, 81, 69. Hardy's edn unidentified. Comment and quotations from the final line of the first stanza of 'Christmas in India', and the third stanza of 'The Song of the Women'. Hardy's own copy of *Departmental Ditties*, Sixpenny Series edn (London, 1890), in DCM, is signed by Hardy on the outside front cover but has no other markings.

1693   Kipling, 'The Ballad of Fisher's Boarding-House', *Departmental Ditties*, pp. 68–71; *Works*, xxi, 61. Comment, summary and quotations with variations of stanzas 1, 15, 16, 17.

1694   Kipling, 'The Galley-Slave', *Departmental Ditties*, p. 118; *Works*, xxi, 108. Comment and quotation, with a slight variation, from the first stanza.

1695   Kipling, 'In the Matter of a Private', *Soldiers Three*, 6th edn (London, 1890) p. 67; *Works*, ii, 64–5. Hardy's edn unidentified. Abridged quotation with slight variations.

1696   Havelock Ellis, 'Morris', in *The New Spirit* (London, 1890) p. 31. Quotation with slight variations. In his Preface Ellis states that a 'large part of one's investigations into the spirit of one's time must be made through the medium of literary personalities'. He then discusses Diderot, Heine, Whitman, Ibsen and Tolstoy. Henry Havelock Ellis (1859–1939), psychologist and critic. For Hardy's positive attitude to Ellis, see *Letters*, i, 117–18.

1697   Ellis, 'Diderot', *New Spirit*, pp. 59–60. Quotation with slight variations. Hardy quoted Diderot on the civil law and the law of nature in the 1912 'Postscript' to *Jude* but added, in parenthesis, 'a statement that requires some qualification, by the way' (*Jude*, p. viii). For Hardy and Diderot, see entry 709n.

1698   Ellis, *New Spirit*, p. 62. Quotation with slight variations and annotation.

1699   Ibid., pp. 66–7. Quotation with slight variations. Marginal lines in pencil.

1700   Ellis, 'Heine', ibid., p. 75. Quotation with variations.

1701   Ellis, 'Whitman', ibid., p. 107. Quotation with slight variations and annotation. Marginal lines in pencil. In connection with *vers libre* Hardy wrote to Mrs Henniker in 1916 that 'the original sinner ... [was] Walt Whitman, who, I always think, wrote as he did, formlessly, because he could do no better' (*One Rare Fair Woman*, p. 174).

1702   Ellis, *New Spirit*, p. 124. Quotation with variations.

1703   Unidentified. Thomas Burt (1837–1922), trade unionist and liberal politician.

1704   Ellis, 'Ibsen', *New Spirit*, p. 165. Quotation with slight variations and annotations. For Hardy and Ibsen, see entry 1910n.

1705   Ibid., p. 171. Summary with key words and phrases quoted. A situation similar to the one in *Jude*.

1706   Ellis, 'Tolstoi', *New Spirit*, p. 176. Summary with key words and phrases quoted. Hardy read Tolstoy's *What is Art?* (trs. Aylmer Maude, London, 1899), in July 1899 and his own copy (Purdy) has 'extensive pencil markings and a few notes' *Letters*, II, 225.

1707   Ellis, *New Spirit*, p. 180. Quotation with variations.

1708   Ibid., p. 182. Quotation with a slight variation. Hardy noted the phenomenon also in 1879; see entry 1101.

1709   Ibid., p. 188. Summary with key words and phrases quoted.

1710   Ibid., p. 200. Quotation with slight variations and annotation.

1711   Ibid., pp. 203–4. Abridged quotation with variations and annotation.

1712   Ibid., p. 204. Quotation with annotation.

1713   Ibid., p. 205. Quotation with a slight variation and annotation.

1714   Ibid., pp. 212–13. Annotation and abridged quotation with variations. Cf. Hardy's own research in law-courts, *Life*, p. 227.

1715   Ibid., p. 217. Quotation with a slight variation and annotation.

1716   Walter Pater, 'Style', *Appreciations* (London, 1889) p. 1; *Works*, v, 5. Quotation with slight variations. See also entry 1652. Most of the entries from Pater – not in chronological order – support Hardy's own anti-realistic tendencies. For Hardy's heightened interest in 'the deeper reality' at this time, see Gittings, *Older Hardy*, pp. 58–9. For Hardy and Pater, see entry 305n.

1717   Pater, *Appreciations*, p. 3; *Works*, v, 7. Annotation and quotation.

1718   Pater, *Appreciations*, p. 4; *Works*, v, 7–8. Quotation with slight variations.

1719   Pater, *Appreciations*, p. 15; *Works*, v, 18. Quotation with a variation and annotation.

1720 Pater, *Appreciations*, p. 5; *Works*, v, 9. Quotation with a slight variation. Cf. Hardy's 'idiosyncratic mode of regard' (*Life*, p. 255).

1721 Pater, *Appreciations*, p. 6; *Works*, v, 10. Quotation. Cf. Hardy's 'less the transcript than the similitude of material fact' (Orel, p. 116).

1722 Pater, *Appreciations*, p. 16; *Works*, v, 19. Quotation and annotation.

1723 Pater, *Appreciations*, p. 28; *Works*, v, 31. Quotation with variations.

1724 Pater, *Appreciations*, p. 35; *Works*, v, 37. Quotation.

1725 Pater, 'Wordsworth', *Appreciations*, p. 59; *Works*, v, 60. Abridged quotation with Hardy's underlining.

1726 Pater, *Appreciations*, p. 61; *Works*, v, 62. Quotation with slight variations.

1727 Pater, *Appreciations*, pp. 61–2; *Works*, v, 62. Quotation.

1728 Pater, "Sir Thomas Browne," *Appreciations*, p. 131; *Works*, v, 128. Quotation with slight variations and Hardy's underlining.

1729 Pater, *Appreciations*, p. 132; *Works*, v, 129. Quotation with slight variations.

1730 Pater, *Appreciations*, p. 150; *Works*, v, 146. Quotation and annotation.

1731 Pater, *Appreciations*, p. 153; *Works*, v, 148. Quotation with a slight variation.

1732 Pater, *Appreciations*, pp. 160–1; *Works*, v, 155–6. Mixture of quoted phrases with an annotation.

1733 Pater, *Appreciations*, p. 162; *Works*, v, 157. Quotation with a slight variation.

1734 Pater, *Appreciations*, pp. 162–3; *Works*, v, 157. Quotation with a variation.

1735 Pater, 'Aesthetic Poetry', *Appreciations*, pp. 223–4; not repr. in *Works*. Abridged quotation with variations.

1736 Pater, 'Postscript', *Appreciations*, pp. 248–62; *Works*, v, 246–60. Mixture of quotation and summary. The raised 'm' only is in pencil.

1737 Augustine Birrell, *Obiter Dicta* (London, 1884) pp. 58–9. E. Hardy's hand from 'How' (l. 1). Abridged quotation with variations. Augustine Birrell (1850–1933), author and statesman.

1738 Ibid., pp. 162–3. E. Hardy's hand. Quotation with slight variations.

1739 Ibid., pp. 166–8. E. Hardy's hand up to reference. Abridged quotation with variations.

1740 Ibid., p. 189. Quotation with a slight variation.

1741 Ibid., pp. 182–3. Abridged quotation with variations.

1742 Ibid., pp. 199–200. Quotation with slight variations.

1743 John Morley, *Voltaire* (London, 1886) p. 122; *Works*, VII, 98. Quotation with slight variations and Hardy's underlinings. See also entries 1589–1626.

1744 Morley, *Voltaire*, p. 123; *Works*, VII, 99. Abridged quotation with slight variations.

1745 Morley, *Voltaire*, p. 125; *Works*, VII, 101. Quotation before and annotation after the colon.

1746 Morley, *Voltaire*, p. 133; *Works*, VII, 107. Quotation with slight variations.

1747 Morley, *Voltaire*, p. 222; *Works*, VII, 180. Quotation with annotation.

1748 Morley, *Voltaire*, pp. 248–9; *Works*, VII, 201. Quotation with slight variations and annotation.

1749 Morley, *Voltaire*, pp. 277, 339; *Works*, VII, 224, 275. Summary with key words quoted.

1750 Morley, *Voltaire*, p. 283; *Works*, VII, 229. Quotation with variations. Second sentence is a footnote.

1751 Morley, *Voltaire*, pp. 307–8; *Works*, VII, 249. Quotation with a slight variation.

1752 Morley, *Voltaire*, p. 359; *Works*, VII, 291. Abridged quotation with a variation. John Byng (1704–57), admiral.

1753 Morley, *Voltaire*, p. 339; *Works*, VII, 275. Quotation with slight variations. Text partly quoted in entry 1626.

1754 Robert Browning, 'Prologue', *Asolando: Fancies and Facts* (London, 1890) p. 1; *Works*, II, 743. Quotation, from stanza 2, with comment. For Hardy and Browning, see entry 1217n.

1755 Browning, 'Bad Dreams II', stanza 14, *Asolando*, p. 24; *Works*, II, 747. Quotation.

1756 Browning, 'Bad Dreams III', l. 11, *Asolando*, p. 27; *Works*, II, 747. Quotation.

1757 Browning, 'Bad Dreams III', ll. 21–2, *Asolando*, p. 28; *Works*, II, 748. Quotation.

1758 Browning, 'Bad Dreams III', ll. 26–37, *Asolando*, pp. 28–9; *Works*, II, 748. Abridged quotation.

1759 Browning, 'Bad Dreams IV', stanza 2, *Asolando*, p. 30; *Works*, II, 748. Quotation.

1760 Browning, 'Beatrice Signorini', l. 38, *Asolando*, p. 78; *Works*, II, 757. Quotation.

1761 Browning, 'Beatrice Signorini', ll. 257–63, *Asolando*, pp. 91–2; *Works*, II, 760. Abridged quotation with a slight variation.

1762 Browning, 'Imperante Augusto natus est –', ll. 79–81, *Asolando*, p. 117; *Works*, II, 765. Annotation and quotation.

1763 Browning, 'Imperante Augusto natus est –', ll. 85–7, *Asolando*, p. 117; *Works*, II, 765. Quotation and annotation.

1764 Browning, 'Development', part of l. 87, *Asolando*, p. 128; *Works*, II, 767. Quotation.

1765 Browning, 'Rephan', excerpts from stanzas 10, 8, 14, 12, *Asolando*, pp. 133–4; *Works*, II, 768–9. Annotation and quotations with variations.

1766 Browning, 'Epilogue', stanza 3, *Asolando*, p. 157; *Works*, II, 773. Comment and quotation with annotation.

1767 *The Works of Oliver Goldsmith*, ed. Peter Cunningham (London, 1854) I, 212. Annotation and quotation with slight variations.

1768 Ibid., p. 211. Quotation, with slight variations, from an excerpt from John Forster's *The Life and Times of Oliver Goldsmith*, 7th edn (London, 1876) II, 70.

1769 The entry is partly erased. It seems to be a false start at entry 1772.

1770 Rowland Blennerhasset, 'Ethics and Politics', *Fort. Rev.*, LIV (Aug 1890) 224–34. Mixture of quotation and summary. Sir Rowland Blennerhasset, 4th baronet (1839–1909), political writer.

1771   Ibid., p. 227. Abridged quotation with slight variations.

1772   Ibid., p. 229. Quotation.

1773   Ibid., p. 228. Summary.

1774   'The Nineteenth Century: The Value of Africa', *Review of Reviews,* II (Sept 1890) 256. Abridged quotation with slight variations and annotation.

1775   'M. Jules Simon on Popular Literature', *D. News*, 3 Nov 1890, p. 6. Abridged quotation with variations and Hardy's underlining.

1776   'Stage Realism – True and False', *D. News*, 3 Nov 1890, p. 5. Mixture of summary of and quotation from an account of a lecture by Henry Arthur Jones (1851–1929), dramatist.

1777   'Döllinger's Historical Work', *Speaker*, 2 (8 Nov 1890) 512. Annotation and three separate quotations with slight variations. The quotes are not from a 'book' but from Acton's 'Doellinger's Historical Work', *English Historical Review*, 5 (Oct 1890) 711, 734 and 744. John Emerich Edward Dalberg, Lord Acton (1834–1902), historian.

1778   'The Red Indians' "Ghost Dance"', *The Times*, 9 Dec 1890, p. 15. Summary.

1779   W. E. H. Lecky, *History of the Rise and Influence of the Spirit of Rationalism in Europe* (London, 1866) I, 398, 395. Hardy's edn unidentified. Two separate quotations with slight variations and annotations. The reference to Gibbon is not in Lecky's text.

1780   Unidentified. Not found in *Knowledge*, the scientific weekly, 1886–91.

1781   'The Facility of Life', *National Observer*, 5 (7 Feb 1891) 302. Abridged quotation with variations, annotations, and comment. The text is not in chronological order. This issue also had a brief, but very positive, article on Hardy under the title 'Modern Men', pp. 301–2.

1782   Arthur Schopenhauer, *Studies in Pessimism*, selected and trs. T. Bailey Saunders (London, 1891) pp. 11–20. Mixture of summary and quotation. For Hardy and Schopenhauer, see entry 1232n, and, for a Hardy observation on pessimism, see *Personal Notebooks*, pp. 27–8. Cf. also entry 1529. There are numerous opinions on Hardy's pessimism, but for a brief and balanced discussion, see Millgate, *A Biography*, pp. 409–27.

1783   Schopenhauer, *Studies in Pessimism*, p. 23. Abridged quotation with slight variations.

1784   Ibid., p. 24. Quotation with slight variations.

1785   Ibid., p. 26. Quotation with a slight variation.

1786   Ibid., p. 27. Abridged quotation with variations. Hardy copied the view of the world as a 'penitentiary' also in 1899, see entry 1979.

1787   Ibid., pp. 33–4. Quotation with slight variations. The parenthesis is a summary of Schopenhauer's reference to Kant.

1788   Ibid., p. 37. Quotation.

1789   Ibid., p. 39. Summary with key words quoted.

1790   Ibid., p. 69. Annotation and quotation with a slight variation. As Millgate (*A Biography*, p. 315) suggests, the theme of this entry is dramatized in *Jude*.

1791   Schopenhauer, *Studies in Pessimism*, p. 70. Quotation with a slight variation.

1792–3   Ibid., pp. 70, 72. Summaries with key words quoted.

1794   Ibid., p. 73. Quotation and annotation.

1795   Ibid., pp. 75–8. Mixture of quotation and summary.

1796   Ibid., pp. 79–80. Abridged quotation with variations.

1797   Ibid., p. 95. Annotation and abridged quotation with variations.

1798   Ibid., p. 96. Quotation with variations.

1799   Ibid., p. 99. Mixture of quotation and summary.

1800   Ibid., pp. 105–23. Abridged, separate, quotations with variations and an annotation.

1801   John Addington Symonds, *Essays Speculative and Suggestive* (London, 1890) I, 7. Abridged quotation with variations. For Hardy and Symonds, see entry 167n. For illuminating letters from Symonds, indicating the close intellectual bonds between the two writers in the early 1890's, see 'Three Unpublished Letters by John Addington Symonds', *THA* I, 129–33.

1802   Symonds, *Essays Speculative and Suggestive*, I, 25. Abridged quotation. Cf. Symonds's intention of showing why the philosophy of evolution can be expected to 'reanimate religion and to restore spirituality to the universe' (p. 3).

1803   Ibid., p. 25. Quotation.

1804   Ibid., p. 30. Quotation with slight variations.

1805   Ibid., p. 31. Abridged quotation with variations.

1806   Ibid., p. 29. Summary with key words quoted.

1807   Ibid., p. 34. Abridged quotation with a slight variation.

1808–9   Ibid., pp. 50–1, 52. Mixtures of summaries and quotations with Hardy's underlinings.

1810   Ibid., p. 75. Abridged quotation with variations.

1811   Ibid., p. 82. Quotation with slight variations.

1812   Ibid., pp. 82–3. Mixture of summary and quotation.

1813   Ibid., pp. 106–7. Annotation and abridged quotation with slight variations.

1814   Ibid., p. 111. Quotation with a slight variation and Hardy's underlining.

1815   Ibid., pp. 124–6. Abridged quotation with variations.

1816   Ibid., pp. 126–7. Abridged quotation with variations and Hardy's underlinings.

1817   Ibid., pp. 134–5. Mixture of summary and abridged quotation with variations.

1818   Ibid., p. 140. Annotations and quotation.

1819   Ibid. Quotation, with variations, of a footnote to the text of the previous entry.

1820   Ibid., p. 145. Annotation and quotation.

1821   Ibid., p. 166. Annotation and quotation with variations.

1822   Ibid., pp. 172–8. Annotation and mixture of summary and quotation.

1823   Ibid., p. 182. Abridged quotation with variations.

1824   Ibid., p. 183. Quotation with variations and annotation.

1825   Ibid., p. 185. Quotation.

1826   Ibid., p. 191. Abridged quotation with slight variations.

1827   Ibid., p. 189. Quotation with variations.

1828   Ibid., p. 196. Abridged quotation with slight variations.

1829   Ibid., p. 199. Quotation with a slight variation.

1830–1   Ibid., pp. 205–6, 209. Abridged quotations with slight variations.

1832   Ibid., p. 215. Quotation with slight variations.

1833   Ibid., p. 222. Quotation with variations.

1834   Ibid., p. 223. Abridged quotation.

1835   Ibid., pp. 224–5. Abridged quotation with variations and annotations.

1836   Ibid., pp. 228–9. Abridged quotation with variations and comment.

1837   Ibid., p. 230. Annotation and quotation with slight variations.

1838   Ibid., p. 250. Quotation with a slight variation.

1839   Ibid., pp. 254–5. Mixture of summary and quotation.

1840   Ibid., p. 268. Quotation.

1841   Ibid., p. 297. Abridged quotation with variations and annotation.

1842   Théophile Gautier, *Mademoiselle de Maupin* (Paris, 1845) p. 212 (ch. 9). Parenthetical reference, in pencil, to Gautier's Preface is incorrect. The entry is probably in Hardy's own trs. of "Virginité, mysticisme, mélancolie – trois mots inconnus, – trois maladies nouvelles apportées par le Christ."

1843   Symonds, *Essays Speculative and Suggestive*, ii, 2–3. Abridged quotation with slight variations; see also entries 1801–41.

1844   Ibid., p. 28. Summary.

1845   Ibid., pp. 28–9. Abridged quotation with variations. Marginal lines in pencil.

1846   Ibid., pp. 32–43. Annotation and mixture of summary and abridged quotation with variations.

1847   Ibid., pp. 44–7. Mixture of summary and quotation with variations.

1848   Ibid., pp. 48–9. Quotation with variations. Despite the 'ib.' within the text, the present entry is written as a unit in the manuscript.

1849   Ibid., p. 50. Abridged quotation with annotation and slight variations.

1850–1   Ibid., pp. 62, 64. Abridged quotations with slight variations and Hardy's underlining in entry 1851.

1852–3   Ibid., pp. 66–7. Abridged quotations with variations; *penetrate*: Hardy wrote 'penetate' (entry 1852).

1854   Ibid., p. 70. Mixture of summary and quotation with variations.

1855   Ibid., pp. 71–3. Abridged quotation with variations and comment.

1856   Ibid., pp. 96–7. Annotation and abridged quotation with variations.

1857   Ibid., p. 131. Abridged quotation with slight variations.

1858   Ibid., p. 153. Annotation and quotation with slight variations.

1859   Ibid., pp. 153–4. Quotation with slight variations; partly quoted also in entry 1146.

1860   Ibid., p. 157. Abridged quotation with slight variations.

1861   Ibid., p. 158. Quotation with a slight variation.

1862   Ibid., p. 159. Quotation with a slight variation.

1863   Ibid., p. 181. Abridged quotation with variations.

1864   Ibid., pp. 183–7. Abridged quotation with variations, annotations and comments.

1865   Ibid., pp. 188–9. Abridged quotation with slight variations and annotation.

1866   Ibid., pp. 194–203. First four words from a line on painting (p. 194), the rest (p. 203) from a quotation of a poem by the Roman poet Ausonius (310–93).

1867   Ibid., p. 271. Quotation.

1868   Ibid., p. 272. Abridged quotation.

1869   Ibid., p. 287. Quotation with a slight variation.

1870   Ibid., pp. 299–300. Mixture of summary and quotation.

1871 F. Brunetière, 'Le Roman de l'Avenir', *RDM*, 105 (July 1891). Abridged quotation with slight variations. *celle* and *pourrai*: Hardy wrote 'cela' and 'pourra'. On Savile Club stationery tipped in. The pagination '62a' is by Hardy.

1872 J. G. Frazer, *The Golden Bough: A Study in Comparative Religion* (London, 1890) I, 2–112. Comment and summary of key words and phrases quoted.

1873 Ibid., pp. 125–8. Summary and comment.

1874 Ibid., p. 145. Annotation and quotation with variations.

1875 Ibid., p. 200. Summary and annotation.

1876 Ibid., pp. 222–29. Mixture of quotation with variations and summary with annotation.

1877 Ibid., pp. 169, 160. Reference and abridged quotation with variations.

1878 William Ernest Henley, 'House-Surgeon', ll. 6–7, *A Book of Verses* (London, 1888) p. 27. Annotation and quotation, with a slight variation. W. E. Henley (1849–1903), poet, critic and essayist.

1879 Henley, 'Apparition', ll. 1–8, ibid., p. 41. Quotation, with variations.

1880 Henley, 'Nocturn', stanza 1, ibid., p. 43. Quotation, with slight variations.

1881 Henley, 'Rondeaus', no. vii, ibid., pp. 166–7. Quotation with slight variations.

1882 Rudyard Kipling, 'My Own True Ghost Story', *Works*, III, 130–3. Annotations and abridged quotation with variations. Hardy's edn unidentified.

1883 H. G. Wells, 'The Rediscovery of the Unique', *Fort. Rev.*, LVI (July 1891), 106–9. Mixture of summary and quotation.

1884 Unidentified.

1885 Source uncertain. A volume with plays was published in Brussels in 1891, and the comment may be Hardy's own.

1886 Edward Dowden, 'The "Interviewer" Abroad', *Fort. Rev.*, LVI (Nov 1891) 731. Quotation and comment. *Spiritual naturalism*: cf. Hardy's well-known note from 4 Mar 1886: 'Novel-writing as an art cannot go backward. Having reached the analytic stage it must transcend it by going still further in the same direction. Why not by rendering as visible essences, spectres, etc., the abstract thoughts of the analytic school?' (*Life*, p. 177).

1887   *Fort. Rev.*, LVI, 725. Quotation with variations.

1888   E. A. Ross, 'Turning Towards Nirvana', *Arena*, 4 (Nov 1891) 736–43. Annotation and abridged quotation with slight variations; Hardy's underlining of 'ego'.

1889   J. R. Illingworth, 'The Incarnation in Relation to Development', in *Lux Mundi*, ed. Principal Gore (London, 1889) p. 196. Abridged quotation with variations from a very popular book; 12th edn in 1891.

1890   'The Slave-Trade – Another Point of View', *Sat. Rev.*, LXXIII (16 Jan 1892) 66. Quotation. In pencil.

1891   'Evolution of the Essayist', *Glasgow Herald*, 27 Feb 1892, p. 4. Pasted-in cutting, the reference in Hardy's hand. Several letters which were cut out have been restored in the transcription.

1892   D. S. M., 'The Painter-Etchers', *Spectator*, LXVIII (26 Mar 1892) 431. Pasted in cutting with reference in Hardy's hand.

1893   Pierre Loti at the French Academy', *The Times*, 8 Apr 1892, p. 5. Abridged quotation with variations; *une caprice*: Hardy wrote 'un caprice'; no ellipsis in source before 'de mieux que'.

1894   'The Carlyles and a Segment of their Circle: Recollections and Reflections', *Bookman*, I (Oct 1891) 21. Annotation and abridged quotation with slight variations.

1895   Giacomo Leopardi, *Poésies et Oeuvres Morales de Leopardi*, trs. F. A. Aulard (Paris, 1880) II, 96–7. Hardy's trs. He used the same text for his '1867' Notebook entries; see A172–9.

1896   Ibid., p. 97. Hardy's trs.

1897   Ibid., pp. 100–2. Hardy's abridged trs.

1898–9   Ibid., pp. 100, 109. Hardy's trs.

1900   Ibid., pp. 110–11. Hardy's abridged trs.

1901   Cesare Lombroso, *The Man of Genius* (London, 1891) p. 229n. Quotation with variations.

1902   R. W. Eyton, *A Key to Domesday* (London, 1878) pp. 46–50. Summary with key words and phrases quoted from the account of the seven classes of agricultural population mentioned in the Dorset Domesday. Hardy's dating of the entry.

1903   William Hazlitt, 'On Wit and Humour', in *The Complete Works of William Hazlitt* (London, 1931) VI, 5. Quotation with slight variations and Hardy's underlining; Hardy's edn unidentified.

1904   'Casts from Sculptures at Persepolis', *The Times*, 9 Sep 1892, p. 5. Abridged quotation.

1905   'Pedantic and Humane', *National Observer*, 7 Jan 1893, pp. 191–2. Abridged quotation, with variations and comment, from a review of R. Y. Tyrrell's rev. edn of *The Bacchae of Euripides* (London, 1893); *making a virtue of joy*: Hardy's underlining; cf. Hardy's thematic use of Paganism in *Jude* through Sue's statements: 'I feel we have returned to Greek joyousness' (v, ch. 4; p. 358); and 'We said ... we would make a virtue of joy' (vi, ch. 2; p. 408; MS leaf missing).

1906   Frederic W. H. Myers, 'Modern Poets and the Meaning of Life', *Nineteenth Century*, XXXIII (Jan 1893) 96–101. Mixture of summary and quotation. The article is also quoted in entry 2601. F. W. H. Myers (1843–1901), poet and essayist.

1907   Ibid., p. 94. Abridged quotation.

1908   Sidney A. Alexander, 'Pessimism and Progress', *Cont. Rev.*, LXVIII (Jan 1893) 83. Abridged quotation, with slight variations, and comment.

1909   Arthur Symons, 'Emmy', *Silhouettes* (London, 1892) pp. 31–2. Cutting, pasted in. Correction, in third stanza, in pencil. See John M. Munro, 'Thomas Hardy and Arthur Symons: A Biographical Footnote', *ELT*, 12, no. 2 (1969) 93–5.

1910   Henrik Ibsen, *Peer Gynt*, trs. William and Charles Archer (London, 1892) p. 273 (v.x). Annotation and quotation. Hardy was an early admirer of Ibsen and saw several of his plays in the 1890s. See *One Rare Fair Woman*, p. 1; and *Life*, pp. 234, 256, 292.

1911   Ibsen, *Peer Gynt*, p. 267 (v.x). Annotations and abridged quotation with slight variations.

1912   Ibid., p. 250 (v.vii). Quotation.

1913   Sarah Grand (pseudonym of Frances Elizabeth McFall), *The Heavenly Twins* (London, 1893) I, 118–19. Hardy's dating, abridged quotation with slight variations and annotation. The novel was a best-seller, rivalling the success of *Robert Elsmere*; see *Letters*, II, 18, 33

1914   Florence Henniker, adaptation from Gustavo A. Becquer, 'Rimas: xxx', in *Obras Completas* (Madrid, 1969) p. 425. In F. Henniker's hand. The date is in pencil and in Hardy's hand. Entries 1914–16 on ruled stationery tipped in. On 2 July 1893 Hardy wrote to Mrs Henniker: 'What beautiful translations those are! I like the two verses from the Spanish best' – *Letters*, II, 20. For illuminating discussions of these entries, see Millgate, *A Biography*, pp. 338–9 and K.G. Wilson, 'Thomas Hardy and Florence Henniker: A Probable Source for Hardy's "Had You Wept"', *Thomas Hardy Year Book*, no. 6 (1976) 62–6. For Hardy and Mrs Henniker, see, *One Rare Fair Woman*, pp. xiii–xl; Gittings, *The Older Hardy*, pp. 71–3; Millgate, *A Biography, passim*.

1915 Florence Henniker, after Lebrecht Drêves, 'Lieder der Liebe, no. 23', in *Gedichte von Lebrecht Drêves*, ed. J. von Eichendorff (Berlin, 1849) p. 154. In F. Henniker's hand. Date in pencil and in Hardy's hand.

1916 Florence Henniker, after Théophile Gautier, 'Affinités Secrètes: Madrigal Panthéiste', *Émaux et Camées* (Paris, 1852) pp. 3–7. In F. Henniker's hand. Date in pencil and in Hardy's hand.

1917 D. G. Rossetti, 'Spheral Change', *Works of D. G. Rossetti*, ed. W. M. Rossetti (London, 1911) p. 236. Quotation with a variation. Mrs Henniker gave Hardy a copy of Rossetti's *Poetical Works* in Aug 1903, see Millgate, *A Biography*, p. 339.

1918 George Egerton (pseudonym of Mary Chavelita Bright), *Keynotes* (London, 1893) p. 21. Quotation with variations, and Hardy's dating. Hardy read Mrs Henniker's copy of the novel (Purdy) and made marginal marks and comments: see Millgate, *A Biography*, pp. 356–7; and *Letters*, II, 102. For a succinct account of Egerton's status in the 1890s see Elaine Showalter, *A Literature of their Own* (Princeton, NJ, 1977) pp. 210–15. See Penny Boumelha, *Thomas Hardy and Woman: Sexual Ideology and Narrative Form* (Brighton and Totowa, NJ, 1982); and Rosemarie A. L. Morgan, 'Women and Sexuality', (dissertation, University of St Andrews, 1982), for fine and original studies of Hardy's fiction in relation to what Boumelha calls 'contemporary ideologies of sexual difference and of the nature of woman' (p. 4).

1919 Egerton, *Keynotes*, pp. 22–3. Abridged quotation with variations, annotation and Hardy's underlining; *the eternal wildness ... mildest, best woman*: in Mrs Henniker's copy (see previous note) Hardy wrote, 'This if fairly stated, is decidedly the *ugly* side of woman's nature', and added on the word 'woman' in the same passage, 'Hence her inferiority to man??' *a model on imaginary lines*: Hardy commented, '*ergo: real* woman is abhorrent to man? hence the failure of matrimony??'; *every woman is an unconscious liar, for so man loves her*: Hardy's marginal comment reads, 'This bears only on sensualism. It is untrue of man in his altruistic regard of woman as a fellow-creature; untrue of his *highest* affection for her' (quoted in Millgate, *A Biography*, pp. 356–7). For a comparison of an Egerton heroine and Sue in *Jude*, see Gail Cunningham, *The New Woman and the Victorian Novel* (London, 1978) p. 106.

1920 Egerton, *Keynotes*, pp. 40–1. Abridged quotation with slight variations.

1921–2 Ibid., pp. 42, 124. Quotations with slight variations.

1923   'The Code of Honour Among Women', *Spectator*, LXXII (13 Jan 1894) 45. Annotation and mixture of summary and quotation.

1924   John Milton, 'The Doctrine and Discipline of Divorce', *The Works of John Milton* (New York, 1931) III, 370. Abridged quotation. Hardy's edn unidentified. He used Milton's 'wormwood words' in 'Lausanne, in Gibbon's Old Garden: 11–12 p.m.', ll. 15–16; see Björk, p. 122.

1925   I. Zangwill, 'Without Prejudice', *Pall Mall Magazine,* Dec 1895, p. 649. Quotation with a slight variation.

1926   Edward Dowden, *The Life of Percy Bysshe Shelley* (London, 1886) I, 274. Abridged quotation, with slight variations, from an observation about the poetry of Thomas Love Peacock. Hardy was reading the biography in June 1896; see entry 1928n and *Letters*, II, 125.

1927   Dowden, *Life of Shelley*, I, 281. Quotation, with a slight variation, and annotation.

1928   Ibid., p. 289. Quotation with a slight variation. In a letter of 29 June 1886, Hardy associated this with the burning of *Jude* by the Bishop of Wakefield: 'But theology & burning (spiritual & temporal) have been associated for so many centuries … ' (*Letters*, II, 125).

1929   Dowden, *Life of Shelley*, I, 329. Abridged quotation, with slight variations, and annotation.

1930   Ibid., p. 335. Quotation with variations.

1931   Ibid., p. 336. Quotation with a slight variation.

1932   Edmund Burke, *Reflections on the French Revolution*, 5th edn (London, 1790) pp. 129–30; in Penguin edn (1969), p. 183. Abridged quotation with slight variations. Hardy's edn unidentified.

1933   Th. Ribot, *The Psychology of the Emotions* (London, 1897) pp. 423–32. The entry appears to be a mixture of quotation and summary from the chapter on 'The Decay of the Affective Life'. However, the many and irregular quotation marks may indicate that the entry is based on a review of the book.

1934   Unidentified newspaper cutting; bracketed annotation in Hardy's hand.

1935   Hallam Lord Tennyson, *Alfred Lord Tennyson: A Memoir* (London, 1897) I, 123. Mixture of quotation and summary. Hardy was reading the biography in Dec 1897; see *Letters*, II, 183.

1936–7   Hallam Tennyson, *Tennyson: A Memoir*, i, 161, 171. Quotations with slight variations. The poem's sense of loss of a childlike or youthful vision is of course a common theme in Hardy's poetry.

1938   Ibid., p. 268. Quotation.

1939   Ibid:, p. 278. Quotation with a slight variation.

1940   Ibid., p. 378. Quotation.

1941   Ibid., p. 401. Quotation with a variation.

1942   Ibid., ii, 10–11. Quotation with a slight variation.

1943   Ibid., p. 24. Mixture of summary and quotation.

1944   Ibid., pp. 24–7. Summary.

1945   Ibid., p. 80. Quotation.

1946   Ibid., p. 284. Abridged quotation.

1947   Ibid., p. 284. Quotation and bracketed, pencilled annotation.

1948   Ibid., p. 285. Abridged quotation.

1949   Ibid., p. 344. Quotation with variations and annotation.

1950   Ibid., p. 373. Quotation, with a slight variation, and annotation.

1951   Ibid., p. 385. Quotation, with a variation, and annotation. Hardy's mother gave him a copy of Dryden's *Virgil* before he was ten (*Life*, p. 16).

1952   Ibid., p. 496. Quotation, with variations, and annotation.

1953   Ibid., p. 503. Quotation, with a variation, and annotation.

1954   Ibid., p. 501. Abridged quotation, with variations, and annotation.

1955   Theodore Watts, 'Poetry', *EB*, 9th edn (Edinburgh, 1885) xix, 257–8. Mixture of summary and quotation with Hardy's underlinings; second and third underlinings in blue pencil; *consonants*: Hardy wrote 'consonsonants'. Cf. entry 1965. For Hardy's high opinion of the essay, see *Letters*, ii, 216.

1956   'C.', 'From Ghosts to Gods', *D. Chron.*, 10 Dec 1897, p. 3. Abridged quotation, with slight variations, and annotation. From a review of Grant Allen, *The Evolution of the Idea of God*. Hardy cut out the whole article, saved it and pasted it into his 'Literary Notes III' some ten years later: see entry 2535.

1957–8 Ibid. Summaries.

1959   A. T. Q. C., 'A Literary Causerie: Aglavaine and Selysette', *Speaker*, 16 (27 Nov 1897) 590. Quotation with slight variations from a review of Maurice Maeterlinck's *Aglavaine et Selysette*, trs. Alfred Sutro (London, 1897).

1960   Unidentified newspaper cutting; reference in Hardy's hand.

1961   Review of W. B. Worsfold's *The Principles of Criticism*, *Literature*, I (18 Dec 1897) 262–3. Summary with key phrases quoted. William Basil Worsfold (1858–1939), lawyer, historian and literary scholar.

1962   'Alphonse Daudet', *Speaker*, 16 (24 Dec 1897) 709. Annotation and quotation with variations.

1963   Unidentified.

1964   Dowden, *Life of Shelley*, II, 283. Annotation and quotation with slight variations; see also entries 1925–31.

1965   Theodore Watts, 'Poetry', *EB*, 9th edn, XIX, 259–63. Summary. Cf. entry 1955 and n.

1966   J. B. Mozley, 'Nature', *University and other Sermons* (London, Oxford, and Cambridge, 1876) pp. 152–3. Abridged quotation with variations. James Bowling Mozley (1813–78), Regius Professor of Divinity at Oxford.

1967   Ibid., p. 153. Annotation and abridged quotation with variations.

1968   'Aristocracy and Anarchism', *Literature*, II (2 Apr 1898) 371. Annotation and abridged quotation with variations from a review of W. H. Mallock's *Aristocracy and Evolution* (London, 1898).

1969   'Macaulay', *D. Chron.*, 16 Aug 1898, p. 3. Abridged quotation with slight variations. For Hardy and Macaulay, see entry 21n.

1970   Unidentified. Sir William Robertson Nicoll (1851–1923), journalist and man of letters.

1971   A. L. Mayhew, letter to Editor, *Literature*, III (8 Oct 1898) 331. Annotation and abridged quotation with variations.

1972   'Some Recent Verse', ibid., p. 318. Annotation and abridged quotation with slight variations.

1973   Ibid. Quotation from the section on Dugald Moore's *Nightshade and Poppies* (London, 1898).

1974   Ibid. Abridged quotation with variations from the section on Louisa Shore's *Hannibal* (London, 1898).

1975   'Robert Browning', *Spectator*, LXXXI (29 Oct 1898) 605. Summary with key phrases quoted.

1976   D. S. M., 'Two Turnerians', *Sat. Rev.*, LXXXVI (12 Nov 1898) 634. Annotation and quotation with slight variations.

1977   John Davidson, 'Tête-à-Tête', *D. Chron.*, 14 Nov 1898, p. 3. Annotation and abridged quotation with variations.

1978   Leader, *D. Chron.*, 8 Feb 1899, p. 6. Annotations and abridged quotation with variations.

1979   Unidentified. Hardy was struck by the expression also in 1891; see entry 1786.

1980   Unidentified.

1981   'Russian Tragic Drama', *Literature*, IV (21 Jan 1899) 59. Abridged quotation, with slight variations and Hardy's underlining in pencil, from a review of Aleksandr Nikolaevich Ostrovsky's *The Storm*, trs. Constance Garnett, (London, 1899 [1898]). A. N. Ostrovsky (1823–86), playwright.

1982   Unidentified.

1983   'Professor Courthope on Law in English Poetry', *The Times*, 7 Mar 1899, p. 13. Abridged quotation with variations and annotation. For references to Hardy and prosody, see entries 2404–5n.

1984–5   Unidentified magazine cuttings on light green paper (same paper as in entries 2165–79).

1986   E. Zeller, *The Stoics, Epicureans and Sceptics*, trs. O. J. Reichel (London, 1870) p. 492. Quotation with slight variations. Textual evidence suggests that Hardy used the 1st edn rather than those of 1880 and 1892.

1987   Leader, *D. Chron.*, 16 May 1898, p. 6. Cutting with reference in Hardy's hand in pencil. The article reflects several notions contained in Hardy's own essays.

1988   Unidentified.

1989   Unidentified newspaper extract with Hardy's comment. In 'Nietzsche: An Appreciation', *Nineteenth Century*, XLVIII (Oct 1900) 592–606, Oswald

Crawfurd distinguishes between 'the works of his [Nietzsche's] unclouded youth ... with the truer aspects of this seer's insight into contemporary life and thought' (p. 598) and 'the later utterances, when his mind was unbalanced, his reason wholly unhinged ...' (p. 605). Cf. also entry 2641. Hardy's public statements on Nietzsche are equally critical: he closes his well-known letter of 17 May 1902 on Maeterlinck's *Apology for Nature* with the observation that 'to model our conduct on Nature's apparent conduct, as Nietzsche would have taught, can only bring disaster to humanity' (*Life*, p. 315; see also p. 364). In a less often quoted letter to the *Manchester Guardian*, 7 Oct 1914, Hardy wrote (after having questioned whether the bombardment of Rheims Cathedral was accidental):

> Should it turn out to be a predetermined destruction – as an object-lesson of the German ruling caste's will to power – it will strongly suggest that a disastrous blight upon the glory and nobility of that great nation has been wrought by the writings of Nietzsche, with his followers Treitschke, Bernhardi, &c. I should think there is no instance since history began of a country being so demoralised by a single writer, the irony being that he was a megalomaniac and not truly a philosopher at all. What puzzles one is to understand how the profounder thinkers of Germany, and to some extent, elsewhere, can have been so dazzled by this writer's bombastic poetry – for it is a sort of prose-poetry – as to be blinded to the fallacy of his arguments - if they can be called arguments which are off-hand assumptions. His postulates as to what life is on this earth has no resemblance to reality. Yet he and his school seem to have eclipsed for the time in Germany the close-reasoned philosophers, such men as Kant and Schopenhauer.

A scrap album contains cuttings from the *Manchester Guardian* of extracts from Hardy's letter as well as of the other letters to the Editor which it provoked (DCM). See also Hardy's strictures on Nietzsche in a letter of 26 Feb 1914, printed in *Friends of a Lifetime*, ed. Viola Meynell (London, 1940) pp. 279–80. Here he also tries to save Kant and Schopenhauer from damnation by association by asserting that '[t]he truth is that in ethics Kant, Schopenhauer &c. are nearer to Christianity than they are to Nietzsche' (p. 280). For an interesting discussion of Hardy and Nietzsche, see also Eugene Williamson, 'Thomas Hardy and Friedrich Nietzsche: The Reasons', *Comparative Literature Studies*, xv (Dec 1978) 403–13.

1990 Rudyard Kipling, *Soldiers Three*, 3rd edn (Allahabad, 1889) p. 99. Abridged quotation from stanzas 2–3 of 'L'Envoi'. Hardy's edn unidentified. Not repr. in *Works*.

1991 *Letters of Robert Browning and Elizabeth Barrett Browning* (London, 1899) i, 406. Quotation and annotation. Kintner, i, 392. Hardy thought the letters 'made such an excellent novel, & a true one' (*Letters*, ii, 277), and late in life Hardy is said to have compared his and Emma's early correspondence with that of the Brownings (Millgate, *A Biography*, p. 131). He also chose the letters, together with Yeats's *The Wind among the Reeds*, as his contribution to the symposium 'Favourite Books of 1899' in the *Academy*, see Werner Bies, 'A Note on Hardy, W. B. Yeats, and The Brownings', *THSR*, I, no. 6 (1980) 193. For Hardy and Browning, see entry 1217n.

1992   *Browning Letters*, I, 386; Kintner, I, 365. Quotation, with slight variations, and annotation.

1993   *Browning Letters*, I, 366; Kintner, I, 352. Mixture of summary and quotation with annotations.

1994   *Browning Letters*, I, 451; Kintner, I, 443. Quotation with a variation.

1995   *Browning Letters*, I, 446; Kintner, I, 429. Quotation with variations; *its*: Hardy wrote 'it'.

1996   *Browning Letters*, I, 429; Kintner, I, 413. Abridged quotation with variations.

1997   *Browning Letters*, II, 63; Kintner, II, 616. Quotation with a slight variation.

1998   *Browning Letters*, II, 206; Kintner, II, 755. Quotation.

1999   *Browning Letters*, II, 138; Kintner, II, 688. Quotation and annotation.

2000   *Browning Letters*, II, 318; Kintner, II, 860–1. Quotation with slight variations.

2001   Leslie Stephen, *Studies of a Biographer* (London, 1899) I, 176. Quotation with variations. For Stephen and Hardy, see entry 980n.

2002   Ibid., I, 183. Quotation.

2003   Ibid., I, 89. Excerpt and annotation from a poem by John Byrom, quoted in chapter on John Byrom (1692–1763), teacher of shorthand. Hardy's reference to Young is possibly due to Stephen's account of Young's irritation in France 'at the sight of estates left waste for game-preserving' (I, 199).

2004   Ibid., I, 198–9. Quotation with slight variations.

2005   Max Beerbohm, 'Madame Tussaud's', *Sat. Rev.*, LXXXIII (13 Feb 1897) 165–6. Quotation with slight variations.

2006   Unidentified.

2007   Maurice Maeterlinck, 'The Predestined' and 'Mystic Morality', *The Treasure of the Humble*, trs. Alfred Sutro (London, 1897) pp. 55–62. Abridged quotation, with slight variations, from two separate essays. See also entry 2190n.

2008   Benjamin Ide Wheeler, 'Alexander's Death', *Century Magazine,* xxxvi (Oct 1899) 910–11. Abridged quotation, with slight variations, and annotation.

2009   Friedrich Nietzsche, *The Case of Wagner, Nietzsche Contra Wagner, The Twilight of the Idols, The Antichrist,* trs. Thomas Common (London, 1896) p. 1. Abridged quotation with variations from the Preface to *The Case of Wagner.* Entry traced by Williamson, pp. 405, 412. For Hardy and Nietzsche, see entry 1989n.

2010–12   Unidentified magazine cuttings. The bracketed texts are in red print as are the marginal texts.

2013   Hamilton W. Mabie, 'The Essay and Some Essayists', *Bookman,* x (Sep 1899) 52–3. Cuttings of part of the article; heading and final reference in Hardy's hand.

2014   Arthur Symons, 'Among my Books: A Book of French Verses', *Literature,* v (4 Nov 1899) 443. Pasted-in cutting from a brief article on the French poet Charles Gros (1842–88), whose poem Symons translated; heading in Hardy's hand and the underlining of the name in blue pencil.

2015   Ernest Dowson, 'Spleen', *Verses* (London, 1896) p. 22. Quotation of the fourth stanza. The parenthetical reference is possibly to an advertisement of *Decorations in Verse and Prose* (London, 1900).

2016   Rudyard Kipling, 'The Ballad of East and West', ll. 73–4, in *Barrack-Room Ballads and Other Verses,* 2nd edn (London, 1892) p. 78; *Works,* xxi, 187. Quotation. In Hardy's copy of the 1892 edn (DCM), the poem is marked with an X in the margin, p. 75.

2017   'War,' *D. Chron.,* 28 Oct 1899, p. 6. Cutting, with the identification in Hardy's hand.

2018   'Mr. Stephen Phillips's New Play', *D. Chron.,* 1 Dec 1899, p. 3; and 'Paolo and Francesca', *The Times,* 1 Dec 1899, p. 10. Cuttings. The first ten lines are from *D. Chron.,* the rest from *The Times.* For Hardy's opinion on Phillips's poetry, see *Letters,* ii, 188.

2019   Unidentified.

2020   Unidentified magazine cutting; Hardy's underlining in pencil.

2021 Unidentified newspaper cutting. Hardy's underlining and marginal note in pencil. The play was revived in June 1900; brief mention in the *Athenaeum*, 30 June 1900, p. 828.

2022 Charles F. Lummis, 'The Right Hand of the Continent', *Harper's*, 39 (Jan 1900) 171. Annotation and quotation with variations.

2023 Ibid., p. 172. Annotation and quotation.

2024 ibid, p. 176. Annotation and abridged quotation with variations.

2025 Ibid., p. 183. Annotation and abridged quotation with variations.

2026 Ibid., p. 184. Quotation with a variation: there is no ellipsis in the source.

2027 Ibid., p. 184. Quotation, with a slight variation, and annotation.

2028–9 Ibid., p. 185. Quotations with slight variations.

2030 Arthur R. Ropes, 'Maeterlinck', *Cont. Rev.*, LXX (Mar 1900), 422–3. Abridged quotation with variations. See also entry 2190n.

2031 Ibid., p. 425. Mixture of quotation and summary.

2032 Ibid., p. 429. Quotation with a variation.

2033 Ibid., p. 430. Abridged quotation, with slight variations, and annotation.

2034–5 Ibid., pp. 435, 436. Abridged quotations with slight variations.

2036 James Hervey Hyslop, 'Results of Psychical Research', *Harper's*, 39 (Apr 1900) 786. Quotation, with Hardy's underlining, and comment. J. H. Hyslop (1854–1920), philosopher and psychologist.

2037 Ibid., p. 792. Annotation and abridged quotation with variations.

2038 'The Late Professor Mivart', *The Times*, 4 Apr 1900, p. 9. Annotation and abridged quotation with variations.

2039 Tertullianus, *De Testimonio Animae*, II.iii, in edn by G. Quispel (Leiden, 1952), p. 7; Hardy's edn unidentified. Probably Hardy's summary. Entry division stroke in pencil.

2040 'Recent Verse', *Athenaeum*, 4 Aug 1900, p. 148. Cutting, with reference in Hardy's hand, from a negative, brief mention of C. W. Wynne's *Ad Astra* (London, 1900).

2041 'Style and the "Edinburgh Review"', *Academy*, LVII (18 Nov 1899) 576–7. Cutting.

2042 Edward Caird, 'Hegel', *Chambers's Encyclopaedia* (London and Edinburgh, 1890) v, 620. Annotation and quotation with slight variations; 'would' inserted in pencil.

2043 Friedrich Ueberweg, *History of Philosophy*, trs. Geo. S. Morris (London, 1874) II, 231. Quotation with variations and annotation.

2044 Unidentified.

2045 Unidentified cuttings of two small pieces pasted together.

2046 Andrew Lang, 'At the Sign of the Ship', *Longman's Magazine*, XXXVI (May 1900) 91. Annotation and quotation with slight variations and Hardy's underlining. For Hardy on Lang, see 'The "Life" Typescript: The Omitted Passages', in *Personal Notebooks*, pp. 237–8.

2047 'Notes', *Outlook*, 5 (21 Apr 1900) 358. Annotation and abridged quotation.

2048 F. H. Bradley, *Appearance and Reality*, 2nd edn (London, 1897) p. 119. Quotation with a slight variation.

2049 'Schelling', *Chambers's Encyclopaedia* (London and Edinburgh, 1892) IX, 205. Mixture of summary and quotation; Hardy's bracketed comment in pencil. For Hardy on Clifford's 'mind-stuff', see entry 1215n.

2050 Carl du Prel, *The Philosophy of Mysticism*, trs. C. C. Massey (London, 1889) II, 260. Quotation from a section considering various speculations on 'the question of man's place in the universe' (p. 258) and on the 'optimistic and pessimistic systems' (p. 259). Du Prel, Carl, Baron (1839–99), German occultist and philosopher.

2051 Thomas H. Huxley, *Hume with Helps to the Study of Berkeley*, in *Collected Essays* (London, 1894) VI, 247. Abridged quotation. Hardy's edn unidentified. For Hardy and Huxley, see entry 1269n. For Hardy and Hume, see Paulin, *passim*. Hardy mentioned Hume (together with Darwin, Huxley, Spencer, Comte and Mill) in his short list of mentors in his well-known letter to Helen Garwood; see entry 882n.

2052 Huxley, *Collected Essays*, VI, 248. Quotation with slight variations and annotation.

2053 John Oliver Hobbes (pseudonym of Pearl Mary Teresa Craigie), *Robert Orange*, new edn (London, 1902) p. 124. Quotation with slight variations and Hardy's underlining. The passage does not occur in the 1st edn (1900). Hardy met the author in June 1893; see *Letters*, II, 10.

2054   Stopford A. Brooke, *Life and Letters of Frederick W. Robertson* (London, 1865) II, 213. Quotation, with a variation, and annotation.

2055   Samuel Johnson, 'Isaac Watts', *Lives of the English Poets*, ed. G. Birkbeck Hill (Oxford, 1945) II, 309. Mixture of summary and quotation. Hardy's edn unidentified.

2056   J. C. Tarver, 'Thomas Edward Brown', *Macmillan's Magazine*, LXXXII (Oct 1900) 410. Cutting from a review of *The Letters of Thomas Edward Brown, Author of Fo'c'sle Yarns*, ed. S. T. Irwin (London, 1900).

2057   Unidentified newspaper cutting, with reference in Hardy's hand. The two stanzas are from W. E. Henley, 'The Way of It', in the *Thrush*, I (1 Jan 1901) 2.

2058   John 12:36. For Hardy and the Bible, see entry 102n.

2059   1 Corinthians 14:20. Abridged quotation.

2060   John 12:35. Quotation. For Hardy and the Bible, see entry 102n.

2061   Galatians 5:13. Quotation with a slight variation.

2062   John 4:1. Quotation.

2063   William Caldwell, 'Schopenhauer's Criticism of Kant', *Mind*, XVI (July 1891) 357. Quotation with slight variations. Entry on separate piece of paper pasted in. Hardy took a longer excerpt from the article in entry 2263. For an illuminating consideration of Hardy's 'inquiry into the relation of the mind to the world it inhabits', see Patricia Clements, '"Unlawful Beauty": Order and Things in Hardy's Poems', in Clements and Grindle, pp. 137–54.

2064   D. S. M., 'Art at the Paris Exhibition. – II. Manet', *Sat. Rev.*, XC (22 Sep 1900) 359. Quotation with variations and annotation.

2065   Ibid., p. 359. Quotation.

2066   Ibid. Abridged quotation with variations.

2067   J. F. R., 'Tschaikowsky', *Sat. Rev.*, XC (22 Sep 1900) 361. Annotation and quotation with variations.

2068   Francis E. Clark, 'The Empire of the Dead', *North American Review*, CLXXI (15 Sep 1900) 375. Annotation and quotation.

2069   'Science versus Man', *D. Chron.*, 1 Oct 1900, p. 3. Cutting of all but the last two sentences of a review of Haeckel's book; identification in Hardy's hand and in pencil. For a positive mention of Haeckel, see *Life*, p. 315.

2070   Review of Charles Whibley, *The Pageantry of Life in the Athenaeum*, 20 Oct 1900, pp. 504–5. Annotation and quotation with variations.

2071   Edmond Holmes, *What is Poetry?* (London and New York, 1900) pp. 68–9. Abridged quotation with variations.

2072   'Mr. J. M. Barrie. An Inquiry', *Academy*, LIX (10 Nov 1900) 445. Annotation and quotation with slight variations. J. M. Barrie (1860–1937), playwright and novelist.

2073   Robert Browning, 'Old Pictures in Florence', *Poems by Robert Browning* (London, 1897) p. 314. Quotation with a slight variation, from stanza 19, l. 5.

2074   Job 21:3. Quotation. For Hardy and the Bible, see entry 102n.

2075   Emily Pfeiffer, 'To Nature II', *Sonnets and Songs* (London, 1880) p. 8. Quotation with slight variations. Hardy's edn unidentified. On separate piece of paper pasted in.

2076   Arthur Symons, 'Technique and the Artist', *Academy*, LIX (1 Dec 1900), 521. Quotation with a variation.

2077   'Patmore's Philosophy', *Academy*, LIX (24 Nov 1900) 493–4. The exact source is uncertain but all the excerpts can be found in this article on 'the speculative opinions and unpublished fragments' of Patmore. Hardy read Patmore's *Principle in Art* (London, 1889), in 1890 (*Letters*, I, 208).

2078   'Mr Choate at Cambridge', *The Times*, 15 June 1900, p. 10. Quotation with variations. Joseph Hedges Choate (1832–1917), lawyer.

2079   Robert Burton, *Anatomy of Melancholy*, Everyman edn (London, 1961) p. 16. Mixture of quotation and summary from ch. 1, 'Democritus Junior: to the Reader'. Hardy's edn unidentified.

2080   Gilbert Chesterton, 'The Donkey', *The Wild Knight and Other Poems* (London, 1900) pp. 16–17. Quotation, with slight variations, of the last two stanzas.

2081   Unidentified cutting.

2082   George Bernard Shaw, 'Preface to the First Volume of Plays: Pleasant and Unpleasant', *Complete Plays and Prefaces*, III (New York, 1963) lvi–lvii. Hardy's edn unidentified. Annotations and abridged quotation with variations.

2083   W. Caldwell, 'Schopenhauer', *Chambers's Encyclopaedia* (1892) IX, 221–2. Abridged quotation with variations and annotations.

2084 'The Spiritual Movement in the Nineteenth Century', *Spectator*, LXXXVI (5 Jan 1901) 9. Quotation, with variations, of the opening lines of the article. Cf. Hardy on the 'wide acceptance of the Monistic theory' in his preface to *The Dynasts* (Orel, p. 40).

2085 Jacques, 'The Passing Mood', *D. Chron.*, 14 Sep 1901, p. 8. Cutting, with the identification in Hardy's hand.

2086 John Fiske, *Outlines of Cosmic Philosophy* (London, 1874) I, 81. Probably summarized from the following: 'What we refuse to admit is the legitimacy of the idealist's inference that the Unknown Reality beyond consciousness does not exist'. The heading 'Notes in Philosophy' seems to cover entries 2086–140 only. After that the entries are mixed again.

2087 Herbert Spencer, *First Principles,* 4th edn (London, 1880) p. 143; *Works,* I, 112. Quotation with a slight variation. Hardy's edn unidentified. For Hardy and Spencer, see entry 882n; cf. also A8n.

2088 Herbert Spencer, *Principles of Psychology,* 3rd edn (London, 1890) II, 505xx; *Works,* v, 570. Abridged quotation with slight variations and annotation. Hardy's edn unidentified.

2089 Alexander Bain, *Mind and Body. The Theories of their Relation* (London, 1873) p. 196. Quotation, with slight variations, from Bain's concluding paragraph of his survey of the 'History of the Theories of the Soul'.

2090 William Kingdon Clifford, 'On the Nature of Things-in-Themselves', *Lectures and Essays,* ed. Leslie Stephen and Frederick Pollock (London, 1879) II, 85. Abridged quotation, with variations, and annotation. Cf. entry 1215 and n.

2091 Theodore Christlieb, 'Modern Non-Biblical Conceptions of God: III. Pantheism', *Modern Doubt and Christian Belief: A Series of Apologetic Lectures addressed to Earnest Seekers after Truth,* trs. H. U. Weitbrecht and ed. T. L. Kingsbury (Edinburgh, 1879) p. 163. Quotation, with variations, and annotation.

2092–3 Emanuel Deutsch, 'Spinoza', *Chambers's Encyclopaedia* (1892) IX, 642–3. Abridged quotation with variations. Calling it an 'excellent article', Hardy quotes from it also in entry 2458. For Hardy and Spinoza, see entry 112n.

2094 Ibid., p. 643. Quotation with a slight variation.

2095 George Henry Lewes, *The History of Philosophy from Thales to Comte,* 5th edn (London, 1880) II, 198. Quotation with slight variations. Hardy's edn unidentified.

2096   Herbert Spencer, 'The Genesis of Science', *Works*, xiv, 28. Mixture of summary and quotation with comment in pencil. Hardy's edn unidentified. For Hardy and Spencer, see entry 882n.

2097   Herbert Spencer, 'Mr. Martineau on Evolution', *Works*, xiii, 381–2. Mixture of summary and quotation with annotations and comment. Hardy's edn unidentified.

2098   Eduard von Hartmann, *Philosophy of the Unconscious*, trs. W. C. Coupland (London, 1884) i, 1. Quotation, with a slight variation, from an excerpt from Kant. The entries from Hartmann are not in chronological order, which may suggest that Hardy made these excerpts from von Hartmann earlier than the surrounding entries (2053 from 1902 and 2145 from 1901) seem to indicate (see also entry 1443). The quotations here from the *Philosophy of the Unconscious* clearly belong to 'Notes in Philosophy' (see entry 2086n) and date back to Hardy's more specifically philosophical preparatory studies for *The Dynasts* in the late 1890s. For Hardy and Hartmann, see entry 1443n.

2099   Hartmann, *Philosophy of the Unconscious*, i, 4. Quotation with a slight variation.

2100   Ibid., pp. 17–18. Mixture of summary and quotation with Hardy's underlining.

2101   Ibid., p. 20. Abridged quotation, with slight variations, and annotations.

2102   Ibid., p. 23. Quotation with slight variations.

2103   Ibid. Abridged quotation with variations.

2104   Ibid., pp. 3–4. Abridged quotation with slight variations.

2105   Ibid., iii, 303. Quotation with a slight variation and Hardy's underlining, from 'Addenda' to i, 71, last line.

2106   Ibid., i, 90ff. Probably a summary from Hartmann's discussion in ch. 3, 'The Unconscious in Instinct', the first sentence of which is 'Instinct is purposive action with consciousness of the purpose' (p. 79). Hardy's bracketed comment in pencil.

2107   Ibid., p. 42. Annotation and abridged quotation, with variations, from 'Introductory'.

2108   Ibid., ii, 2. Abridged quotation, with variations and annotation.

2109   Ibid., p. 6. Abridged quotation, with slight variations.

2110   Ibid., p. 247. Annotation and abridged quotation, with variations and bracketed comments in pencil.

2111   Ibid., p. 248. Abridged quotation with slight variations

2112   Ibid., pp. 260–1. Abridged quotation with variations.

2113   Ibid., p. 261. Quotation with a slight variation.

2114   Ibid., pp. 273–4. Abridged quotation, with variations, and annotations.

2115   Ibid., p. 275. Abridged quotation with variations.

2116   Unidentified unless this pencilled entry is Hardy's comment on Hartmann's discussion of how 'lifeless' organisms can be brought back to life as long as 'during the lifeless condition (induced by dying or freezing, or by hermetically sealing) ... a chemical or histological change detrimental to future vital activity be prevented' (ibid., i, 286).

2117   Ibid., ii, 288. Mixture of summary and quotation.

2118   Ibid., p. 291. Quotation with a slight variation.

2119   Ibid., pp. 291–2. Annotation and abridged quotation with variations. Marginal line in pencil.

2120   Ibid., p. 293n. Abridged quotation, with a slight variation, from a footnote, testifying to the carefulness of Hardy's reading.

2121   Ibid., p. 359. Abridged quotation with variations.

2122   Ibid., p. 359. Quotation, with variations, and Hardy's underlining.

2123   Ibid., p. 360. Abridged quotation with variations and annotation.

2124   Ibid., p. 365. Quotation with variations; Hardy's ellipsis indication misleading.

2125–7   Ibid., ii, 366, 367–8; iii, 89. Mixtures of summaries and quotations.

2128   Ibid., iii, 133. Annotation and abridged quotation with variations.

2129   Ibid., p. 137. Mixture of summary and quotation with comment.

2130   Ibid., p. 143. Annotation and abridged quotation with variations.

2131   Ibid., p. 143. Abridged quotation with variations.

2132 Ibid., pp. 144–5. Mixture of summary and quotation.

2133 Ibid., p. 156. Abridged quotation with variations and annotation.

2134 Ibid., p. 164. Abridged quotation.

2135 Ibid., pp. 167–70. Mixture of summary and quotation with Hardy's underlining of the first two words.

2136 Ibid., p. 172. Quotation with a slight variation.

2137 Ibid., p. 175. Quotation with variations.

2138 Ibid., pp. 184–5. Abridged quotation with slight variations. Cf. Hardy on 'Necessity', (*Life*, p. 337).

2139 Ibid., pp. 194–6. Mixture of summary and quotation. Cf. Hardy on Spinoza, *Life*, p. 337.

2140 Ibid., p. 196. Abridged quotation with variations.

2141 Paul Cushing, 'For England's Sake', the *National Observer*, 16 Apr 1892, p. 561. Cutting of the complete poem. Identification in Hardy's hand.

2142–4 Unidentified cuttings. Parenthesis in Hardy's hand in pencil; underlining in pencil.

2145 'A Prophet of Revolt', *D. Chron.*, 13 Apr 1901, p. 3. Cutting from a review of Archibald Stodart-Walker, *Robert Buchanan: The Poet of Modern Revolt* (London, 1901). Marginal lines in blue pencil; identification in Hardy's hand.

2146–50 Unidentified cuttings.

2151 Unidentified.

2152 John Ruskin, *Modern Painters*, 3rd edn (London, 1846–60) iii, 268; *Works*, v, 333. Hardy's page reference does not tally with any edn. Abridged quotation with slight variations and Hardy's underlining of the first three words. For Hardy and Ruskin, see entry 1218n.

2153 Brander Matthews, 'A Postscript as to Rhyme', *Bookman*, xiii (July 1901) 417. Annotation and abridged quotaton, with variations.

2154 'Editor's Study', *Harper's*, 42 (July 1901) 317–18. Annotation, abridged quotation, with variations, and comment.

2155   Austin Dobson, 'Angel Court', in *The May Book*, ed. E. Aria (London, 1901) p. 12. Quotation with a slight variation. Hardy contributed 'The Superseded' to the book. Dobson's contribution was also quoted in the *Bookman*, xiii (July 1901) 404 – from which Hardy quoted in entry 2153.

2156   Ernest Newman, 'Poetic Symbolism and Modern Music', *Speaker*, 4 (15 June 1901) 298–9. Abridged quotation with variations, annotation and comment. Except for the comment, all is on Athenaeum stationery pasted in. For another excerpt from Newman on Wagner, see *Personal Notebooks*, p. 51. Ernest Newman (1868–1959), music critic and biographer.

2157   Kuno Francke, *A History of German Literature As Determined by Special Forces* (London and New York, 1901) p. 557. Abridged quotation with variations and Hardy's underlining.

2158   Egan Mew, 'Henrik Ibsen', *Literature*, ix–x (17 Aug 1901) 148. Quotation with slight variations.

2159   Ibid. Mixture of summary and quotation with annotations and comment.

2160   Unidentified.

2161   'Current Literature and Current Criticism', *New Quarterly Magazine*, 10 (July 1878) 444–5. Annotation and abridged quotation with variations. For a brief comparison of *The Lusiads* and *The Dynasts*, see Gittings, p. 113.

2162   Unidentified. For Hardy and Heine, see entry 1017n.

2163   'Dorchester News', *Dorchester Telegram*, 26 Nov 1901, p. 5. Cutting with Hardy's underlining in green pencil and the heading in his hand.

2164   Josephine Preston Peabody, 'Vanity, saith the Preacher', *Harper's*, 43 (Dec 1901) 174. Quotation, with slight variations, of the first two stanzas.

2165–79   Unidentified cuttings; the quality of the paper suggests the same source for all the entries, though entries 2165 and 2170 are on yellowish paper and the rest on light green paper.

2180   'After the Witching Year', *Sat. Rev.*, xcviii (28 Dec 1901) 799. Annotation and mixture of summary and quotation.

2181   'Reviews: Mrs. Meynell's Later Poems', *Academy*, lxii (4 Jan 1902) 647–8. Annotations and abridged quotation with slight variations from a review of Alice Meynell, *Later Poems* (London, 1902).

2182   Unidentified.

2183 Arthur Symons, 'Literary Drama', *Academy*, LXII (8 Feb 1902) 152. Annotation and abridged quotation with variations.

2184 'Correspondence', *Academy*, LXII (15 Mar 1902) 284. Abridged quotation from Maurice de Fleury's *Introduction à la Médécine de l'Esprit* (Paris, 1897).

2185 Ibid. Abridged quotation, with slight variations, and annotation.

2186 'A Critic's Eureka', *Academy*, LXII 62 (19 Apr 1902) 406. Quotation with slight variations from a review of A. Machen, *Hieroglyphics* (London, 1902).

2187 *Academy*, LXII, 406. Annotation and quotation with slight variations and Hardy's question-mark.

2188 Ford Maddox Hueffer, 'The Making of Modern Verse I', *Academy*, LXII (19 Apr 1902) 413. Quotation with slight variations.

2189 C. L. H., 'Art', *Academy*, LXII (3 May 1902) 463. Abridged quotation with variations.

2190 'Reviews: The Limits of Mystery', ibid., p. 451. Mixture of summary and quotation from a review of M. Maeterlinck's *The Buried Temple*, trs. A. Sutro (London, 1902). Hardy's highly critical reply to this article was published 17 May 1902, (*Academy*, LXII, 514–15; repr. in *Life*, pp. 314–15).

2191 'A Many-Sided Book', *Academy*, LXII (3 May 1902) 452. Annotation and quotation, with slight variations, from a review of H. Belloc's *The Path to Rome* (London, 1902).

2192 'Many Inventions', *Academy*, LXIII (19 July 1902) 79. Annotation and abridged quotation, with slight variations from a review of vols XXV–XXVII of the *E B* (1902).

2193 Coventry Patmore, 'Winter', *Poems* (London, 1906) p. 276. Quotation of the first two lines of the poem, first published in *The Unknown Eros* (London, 1890). Hardy's edn unidentified. Cf. entry 2329.

2194 Arthur Symons, 'Nietzsche, on Tragedy', *Academy*, LXIII (30 Aug 1902) 220; or in *Plays, Acting and Music* (London, 1903) pp. 9–11. Annotation and abridged quotation with variations.

2195 Unidentified cutting, probably from a report of a lecture by Benjamin Kidd (1858–1916), sociologist. The quotation is not from Kidd's *Social Evolution* (1894), *Principles of Western Civilization* (1902) or *The Science of Power* (1918).

2196 'The Encyclopaedia Again', *D. Chron.*, 11 July 1902, p. 11. Cutting of part of the review. Reference in Hardy's hand. The quotation is from A. C. Swinburne's 'Hugo' in *E B*, 11th edn (1902) XIII, 864.

2197 'Mind and Medicine', *Daily Mail*, 17 Sep 1902, p. 4. Cutting, with reference to Hartmann and Schopenhauer, 'Daily Mail' and the date in Hardy's hand; cutting from a review of Alfred T. Schofield, *The Force of Mind, or the Mental Factor in Medicine* (London, 1902).

2198 Unidentified.

2199 Ruskin, *Modern Painters*, 3rd edn (London, 1846–60) II, 159; *Works*, IV, 250–1. Summary with key words quoted.

2200 'A Neo-Elizabethan', *D. Chron.*, 11 Oct 1902, p. 3. Cutting of a review of Woods's book, with reference in Hardy's hand in pencil.

2201 R. A. G., 'Poetry', *D. News*, 27 Nov 1902, p. 8. Cutting of the final third of the article; reference in Hardy's hand and in pencil.

2202 Unidentified newspaper cutting. Introductory comment in Hardy's hand.

2203 Unidentified newspaper cutting.

2204 Unidentified newspaper cutting.

2205 'The Unrest of Euripides', *Academy*, LXIV (17 Jan 1903) 47. Annotation and quotation with slight variations.

2206 *The Letters of Robert Louis Stevenson*, ed. Sidney Colvin (London, 1899) I, 144–6. Hardy's comment on Stevenson's letter to Colvin in Aug 1879. Hardy described Stevenson's correspondence as 'very attractive' in a letter to Mrs Henniker in 1903 (*Letters*, III, 1). For Hardy's lukewarm appreciation of Stevenson, see his contribution to *I Can Remember Robert Louis Stevenson*, ed. Rosalind Masson (Edinburgh and London, 1922), repr. Orel, pp. 149–51; for more critical comments still, see *Life*, pp. 184, 246, and *Personal Notebooks*, p. 236.

2207 *Stevenson Letters*, I, 275. Quotation, with variations, and annotations.

2208 Ibid., pp. 289–90. Abridged quotation, with slight variations, and annotation. R. A. M. Stevenson (1847–1900), painter.

2209 Ibid., pp. 299–300. Quotation with variations and annotation.

2210 Ibid., p. 302. Mixture of summary and quotation.

2211 Ibid., p. 341. Abridged quotation, with a slight variation, and comment.

2212 Ibid., p. 370. Quotation, with a slight variation, and annotation.

2213   Ibid., pp. 372–3. Quotation, with slight variations, and annotation.

2214   Ibid., II, 19. Abridged quotation with slight variations.

2215   Ibid., p. 93. Quotation with slight variations.

2216   Ibid., p. 100. Abridged quotation with slight variations.

2217   Ibid., p. 153. Abridged quotation with variations.

2218   Ibid., pp. 184–6. Hardy's comment on a letter to Colvin.

2219   Ibid., pp. 315–16. Abridged quotation, with variations, and annotation.

2220   Ibid., p. 333. Quotation with a slight variation.

2221   Ibid., p. 341. Abridged quotation with slight variations.

2222   Ibid., p. 355. Quotation with annotation.

2223   'Experts on the Planchette', *D. News*, 5 Mar 1903, p. 8. Quotation with a slight variation and annotation. See also entry 2340n.

2224   'The Drama. A Forecast', *TLS*, 6 Feb 1903, p. 41. Cutting; 'Times sup!' and date in Hardy's hand and in pencil.

2225   Unidentified newspaper cutting. An 'entirely unknown' edn of Theophrastus, *Theophrasti Notationes Morum* (Oxford, 1604), was announced as having been found in the *Periodical*, XXX (June 1905) 16.

2226–7   Unidentified. Entry 2226 may be a false start for entry 2279.

2228–9   Unidentified. Roden Berkeley Wriothesley Noel (1834–94), poet. Several interesting letters from Hardy to Noel remain; see *Letters*, I, II.

2230   R. V. Risley, 'Schopenhauer', *Reader* 1 (Jan 1903) 273–5. Quotations, with slight variations, of separate sayings, and annotation.

2231   Untitled notice, *Periodical*, XXI (Mar 1903) 9. Cutting of the whole notice.

2232   Ruskin, *Modern Painters*, 3rd edn, I, 132; *Works*, III, 246. Annotation and quotation with slight variations.

2233   G. K. Chesterton, 'The Inside', *D. News*, 11 Apr 1903, p. 6. Cutting (omitting the first paragraph and with an ellipsis of 11 lines between the paragraphs) with Hardy's comment; from a review of *Thoughts from Maeterlinck* ed. E. S. S. (London, 1903). 'Daily News' and the comment in Hardy's hand.

2234   C. F. G. Masterman, 'A Statesman's Philosophy', *D. News*, 4 Mar 1903, p. 8. Cutting. Hardy also read other reviews of Haldane's work (see entries 2259, 2261, 2276–7), and it seems that Haldane's *Possible Worlds* was the last book he ever read (Millgate, *A Biography*, p. 571).

2235   Unidentified newspaper cutting with an extract from 'Gabriele D'Annunzio', *Imperial and Colonial Magazine*, I (Dec 1900) 245–6.

2236   G. K. Chesterton, 'Mr Yeats and Popularity', *D. News*, 16 May 1903, p. 8. Cutting with the ellipsis indication in pencil.

2237   Leader, *D. Chron.*, 8 June 1903, p. 5. Cutting, with the heading and reference in Hardy's hand.

2238   C. 'Whimsies', *Whim*, 6 (Dec 1903) 177. Cutting from the American publication.

2239   *The Poetical Works of Thomas Gray*, Aldine Edn of the British Poets (London, 1885) p. 60. Quotation from a footnote to 'The Bard'. In Hardy's own copy of the edn (DCM) the lines quoted are marked by pencil in the margin (as are all of the final 11 lines of the page).

2240   'W. E. Henley', *Academy*, LXV (18 July 1903) 63. Quotation, with slight variations, annotation and Hardy's underlining of the opening words, from a review of Henley's *Hospital Poems* (London, 1903).

2241   *Academy*, LXV, 62. Quotation with a slight variation.

2242   G. K. Chesterton, *Robert Browning* (London, 1903) p. 53. Quotation with variations. See also entry 2248.

2243   Herbert Spencer, 'The Genesis of Science', *Works*, XIV, 27. Mixture of summary and quotation. Hardy's edn unidentified.

2244   Walter R. Cassels, 'The Present Position of Religious Apologetics', *Nineteenth Century*, LIV (Oct 1903) 608. Quotation with variations and annotations.

2245   A. W. Verrall, Introduction to Aeschylus, *The Choephori* (London and New York, 1893) pp. xi–xii. Abridged quotation with variations. Hardy refers to Verrall's introduction in this 1903 Preface to *The Dynasts* (Orel, p. 42), and quotes a few words from entry 2246, as he recalls in a letter in 1912: 'I like what he [Verrall] says about the Greeks: indeed I have quoted him I think' (*Friends*, p. 276).

2246   Verrall, Introduction to *The Choephori*, p. xvi. Quotation with slight variations; *scenes from a story*: as part of his general explanation and defense of various aspects of *The Dynasts*, Hardy invokes 'Aeschylus, whose plays are, as Dr. Verrall reminds us, scenes from stories taken as known' (Orel, p. 42).

2247   Verrall, Introduction to *The Choephori*, p. xvii. Abridged quotation, with variations and annotations.

2248   G. K. Chesterton, *Robert Browning* (London, 1903) p. 150. Abridged quotation with slight variations. See also entry 2242.

2249   Ibid., pp. 158–9. Abridged quotation, with slight variations, and annotation.

2250   Ibid., pp. 165–6. Abridged quotation, with variations; bracketed comment in pencil.

2251   Margaret L. Woods, 'Robert Browning', in *The English Poets*, ed. T. H. Ward (London and New York, 1894) v, 667. Abridged quotation with variations. Hardy marked these lines, as well as others, in his own copy of the book (DCM).

2252   'Notes from Paris', *Truth*, LIX (2 July 1903) 29. Abridged quotation with variations.

2253   C. W. Saleeby, 'The Apostle of Evolution', *Academy*, LXV (12 Dec 1903) 674. Quotation with variations and Hardy's underlining.

2254   C., 'Whimsies', *Whim*, 6 (Dec 1903) 176–7. Quotation with slight variations; the heading and reference in Hardy's hand. Entry division strokes in pencil.

2255   Unidentified newspaper cutting; poem quoted from J. A. Nicklin, *Secret Nights* (London, 1904) p. 9.

2256   'A "Ballad Epic" of the Boer War', *TLS*, 15 Jan 1904, p. 13. Cutting with reference in Hardy's hand.

2257   Unidentified newspaper cutting; '1907' in Hardy's hand. The book was pub. in Oct. 1907; the quotation is from p. 309.

2258   Elizabeth Foote, 'The Interveil', *Century Magazine*, 45 (Mar 1904) 756. Quotation with slight variations on a loose piece of paper measuring 10.1 × 20.4 cm. The paper was originally (1968) found in this place of the volume but is now (1980) no longer in the notebook.

2259   H. Rashdall, review of R. B. Haldane, *The Pathway to Reality: Stage the Second* (London, 1904), *Mind*, XIII (July 1904) 413. Quotation. See also entry 2234n.

2260 Leader, *The Times*, 5 July 1904, p. 9. Quotation with slight variations.

2261 'Unreality and Mr. Haldane', *Sat. Rev.*, xcvii (23 Apr 1904) 524. Cutting from the middle of a critical review of R. B. Haldane, *The Pathway to Reality: Stage the Second* (London, 1904). See also entry 2234n.

2262 Newspaper or periodical cutting unidentified; quotation is from p. 7 in Hudson's book. Hardy's underlining in red.

2263 William Caldwell, 'Schopenhauer's Criticism of Kant', *Mind*, xvi (July 1891) 357–8. Quotation with slight variations. The first two sentences quoted also in entry 2063. Entries 2263–83 are on seven inserted leaves; the first, second, and fourth leaves are made of two different kinds of paper pasted together. The final 2.5 cm of the fourth leaf are cut off. The versos of leaves 2–6 are blank.

2264 Felix Adler, 'A Critique of Kant's Ethics', *Mind*, xi (Apr 1902) 168–71. Annotation and abridged quotation with variations. In pencil.

2265 'The Highest Expression', *D. Chron.*, 12 July 1901, p. 3. Cutting pasted onto inserted leaf.

2266 Unidentified newspaper cutting; heading in Hardy's hand.

2267 'Les Romans de Pierre Loti', *RDM*, 16 (1 Nov 1883) 215. Abridged quotation with variations; *propres*: Hardy wrote 'propre'; *combinaison*: Hardy wrote 'combination'. A note which seems to have been saved for almost two decades by Hardy.

2268 Herbert Spencer, *An Autobiography* (London, 1904) ii, 470; *Works*, xxi, 470. Quotation with annotation, from the final page of the autobiography. See also entry 882n. Hardy drew on this sentence for the General Preface of 1912 when emphasizing the unlikeliness that 'imaginative writings extending over more than forty years would exhibit a coherent scientific theory of the universe even if it had been attempted – of that universe concerning which Spencer owns to the "paralyzing thought" that possibly there exists no comprehensions of it anywhere' (Orel, pp. 48–9).

2269 C. Lloyd Morgan, '"The Riddle of the Universe." Five Open Letters', *Cont. Rev.*, lxxxv (June 1904) 797–8. Abridged quotation, with slight variations, from an essay, in letter form, on Ernst Haeckel's *The Riddle of the Universe*; see also entry 2069 and n.

2270 Alexander Bain, *Autobiography* (London and New York, 1904) p. 193. Abridged quotation, with variations and annotation. In pencil.

2271 Goldwin Smith, 'The Immortality of the Soul', *North American Review*, 178 (Apr 1904) 725. Abridged quotation with slight variations. In pencil.

2272   A. E. Taylor, review of James Ward, *Naturalism and Agnosticism*, in *Mind*, IX (Apr 1900) 246–7. Abridged quotation with variations from a very positive review. Entries 2272–3 on the recto of an interleaved sheet made up of two pieces pasted together; the verso is blank.

2273   'Professor Campbell Fraser's Autobiography', *TLS*, 8 June 1904, p. 171. Abridged quotation with slight variations from a review of *Biographia Philosophica* (Edinburgh, 1904). In pencil; see previous note.

2274   Julius Goldstein, 'The Keynote to the Work of Nietzsche', *Mind*, II (Apr 1902) 217–18. Quotation with variations and annotation. In pencil.

2275   Probably Hardy's response to one or two 'Art Notes' in the *Academy*, LXVI (2 Jan 1904) 21–2 and (23 Jan 1904) 106. The first is a brief mention of Walter Crane and Lewis F. Day, *Moot Points* (London, 1903). A central passage reads, 'Then he [Crane] has a little fondness for the old Greek idea that art is beauty – which it certainly is not – indeed this idea is the widespread source of confusion between art and craft. I cannot repeat too often that art is that by which the human genius transfers emotion' (p. 21). There is no explicit reference to Whistler in the review. The critic repeats his argument on 16 Jan 1904 (pp. 79–80) and also on 23 Jan 1904 (p. 106), where Whistler is mentioned.

2276   H. Rashdall, review of R. B. Haldane, *The Pathway to Reality. Being the Gifford Lectures delivered in the University of St. Andrews in the Session 1902-3* (London, 1903), *Mind*, XII (Oct 1903) 528. Quotation with slight variations and annotation. In pencil. See also entry 2234n.

2277   Ibid., pp. 528–30. Abridged quotation with variations and annotation. In pencil.

2278   Norman Smith, review of C. A. Strang, *Why Mind has a Body* (New York, 1903), *Mind*, XVIII (Apr 1904) 277. Quotation with slight variations. In pencil.

2279   Part of letter from Alfred Pretor on two pieces of blue stationery pasted in. The letter (DCM) is dated 1903 by Hardy. Alfred Pretor (1840–1908) of St Catherine's College, Cambridge.

2280–1   Unidentified magazine cuttings.

2282   Unidentified.

2283   G. E. Underhill, 'The Use and Abuse of Final Causes', *Mind*, XIII (Apr 1904) 223–6. Abridged quotation with slight variations and annotation. In pencil.

2284 'Richard Crashaw', *TLS*, 5 Aug 1904, p. 241. The cutting omits the first paragraph of the review of *Poems by Richard Crashaw*, ed. A. R. Waller (Cambridge, 1904). Hardy's underlinings in pencil.

2285 Unidentified newspaper cutting. Reference in Hardy's hand.

2286 Unidentified newspaper cutting of the two final stanzas of R. Kipling's 'The Last Rhyme of True Thomas', *Works*, xxii, 236.

2287 'Musical Full Stops', *Academy*, lxvii (1 Oct 1904) 262–3. Cutting, with reference in Hardy's hand.

2288 Unidentified newspaper cutting of stanzas 6–8 from A. Noyes's 'Sherwood', *Poems* (London, 1904) p. 8.

2289 'Magazines and Reviews for March', *Record*, 10 Mar 1905, p. 226. Cutting and annotation (Hardy's dating of his reading the note?); reference and date in Hardy's hand and in pencil.

2290 Luoise Creighton, *Life and Letters of Mandell Creighton* (London, 1904) i, 325; ii, 504, 503. Quotations of three separate sentences with slight variations and Hardy's underlining.

2291 C. W. Saleeby, 'The Human Will', *Academy*, lxvii (17 Dec 1904) 621. Abridged quotation with variations and annotations. For Hardy and Saleeby, see entries 2423n and 2428n.

2292 'Mr. Morley on Libraries', *The Times*, 19 Dec 1904, p. 11. Abridged quotation with variations and Hardy's underlining and comment.

2293 Ibid. Abridged quotation with variations and Hardy's underlining. For other excerpts from Morley on Byron, see *Personal Notebooks*, pp. 78–9.

2294 Emily Dickinson, 'Death and Life', *Poems*, ed. M. Loomis Todd and T. W. Higginson (London, 1904) p. 98. Quotation with slight variations. Hardy's edn for entries 2294–5 unidentified.

2295 Dickinson, 'I died for beauty, but was scarce', *Poems*, p. 119. Annotation and quotation with slight variations.

2296 'The Love Poems of Donne', *TLS*, 27 Jan 1905, p. 25. The cutting, starting in the middle of the second paragraph of the article, is tipped in. Marginal lines in pencil; reference in Hardy's hand. Hardy's numbering of the pages of the cutting is due to the fact that the text begins on the verso of the cutting.

2297 Unidentified cutting. Heading and reference in Hardy's hand.

2298   Unidentified.

2299   W. H. Griffiths, 'Hours with the Bible', *Record,* 25 May 1906, p. 467. Quotation with annotation.

2300   Unidentified. George William Erskine Russell (1853–1919), politician and essayist.

2301   'The New English Art Club', *The Times,* 14 Oct 1905, p. 7. Cutting with 'Times' and the date in Hardy's hand and in pencil. Entries 2301–3 pasted onto the recto of interleaved sheet from the *Periodical* (entry 2304).

2302–3   G. K. Chesterton, 'A Glimpse of Paganism', *D. News,* 17 Mar 1906, p. 6. Cuttings from a theatre review of *The Electra* by Euripides and Hardy's annotation. Reference and annotation in Hardy's hand.

2304   'Death Keeps his Court', *Periodical,* xxxi (Oct 1905) 7, 9. Cutting tipped in. Reference cut from p. 9 and pasted in.

2305   'Keats', *TLS,* 14 Apr 1905, p. 117. Cutting from first half of a review of three edns of Keats. Heading and reference in Hardy's hand.

2306   Unidentified newspaper cutting with Hardy's underlining; quotation from Arnold in Super, ix, 161–2. First passage quoted also in entry 1437. For Hardy and Arnold, see entry 101n.

2307   C. Lewis Hind, 'The Norwich School: Old Crome and East Anglian Painters', *D. Chron.,* 13 Mar 1906, p. 3. Cutting from a review of W. F. Dickes, *The Norwich School of Painting* (London, 1906). Heading and reference in Hardy's hand.

2308   'Self and Space', *Sat. Rev.,* c (21 Oct 1905) 527. Abridged quotation with variations and comment from a review of Read's book.

2309   Unidentified. When writing his autobiography Hardy used the entry to add a dimension to the account of his abandoning prose for poetry in the late 1890s (*Life,* p. 300). See also entry 2310n.

2310   'Reflections from the Opera', *TLS,* 13 Aug 1908, p. 261. Abridged quotation with slight variations. Part of this entry is also used in the *Life,* p. 300; see entry 2309n, and Björk, p. 123.

2311   'Wanted – A Satisfactory Monism: review of W. L. Walker, *Christian Theism and Spiritual Monism*', *Sat. Rev.,* ciii (11 May 1907) 592. Quotation with a slight variation and Hardy's underlining. In pencil, on stationery pasted in.

2312   'Blank Verse and Rhyme: Holiday and Other Poems. With a Note on Poetry, by John Davidson (Grant-Richards, 3s 6d net)', *The Times,*

17 Aug 1906, p. 281. Cutting, with reference in Hardy's hand. Hardy owned a copy (DCM) of Davidson's *Ballads and Songs*, 2nd edn (London, 1894).

2313   Unidentified newspaper cutting; first version of the poem quoted is called 'Song' in *Poems* (London, 1877) p. 89; second version called 'Arousal' in *Gathered Poems* (London, 1904) p. 97.

2314   'Books of the Day', *D. Chron.*, 12 Nov 1906, p. 3. Cutting from review of *An Anthology of Australian Verse*, ed. Bertram Stevens (London, 1906). Reference in Hardy's hand.

2315   Unidentified newspaper cutting. The quotation is from Arthur Symons, 'The Problem of Richard Strauss', *Studies in Seven Arts* (London, 1906) p. 327. Date in Hardy's hand and in pencil.

2316   R. A. Scott James, review of Elisabeth Bisland, *The Life and Letters of Lafcadio Hearn*, in *D. News*, 11 Jan 1907, p. 4. Cutting with reference and annotation in Hardy's hand.

2317   Unidentified newspaper cutting. Quotation of stanzas 1, 3 and 4 of the five stanza poem 'Ballyvourney', in *Poems* (Dublin, 1906) pp. 91–2. '1906' in pencil in Hardy's hand.

2318   Unidentified newspaper cutting.

2319   'A Danish Thinker', *The Times*, 24 Aug 1906, p. 286. Cutting; Hardy's dating, in pencil, refers to his reading, or cutting, of the review.

2320   'S. T. C. on Poetry', *Periodical*, xlv (Apr 1908) 228. Cutting from a series of quotations from *Coleridge's Literary Criticism*, ed. J. W. Mackail. Reference in Hardy's hand. Hardy owned a copy (DCM) of *Biographia Literaria and Two Lay Sermons*, Bohn's Standard Library (London, 1898). At the beginning of ch. 1, he copied 'The last 9 chapters are probably the greatest attempt "in English to unfold the mystery of the essence of poetry" *Times*.' In ch. 14 – of relevance to *The Dynasts* – he marked with marginal lines as well as with an X the passage arguing 'that a poem of any length neither can be, nor ought to be, all poetry' (pp. 149–50). See also Wright, pp. 85–6, 95–6.

2321   Coventry Patmore, *Amelia, Tamerton Church-Tower, etc.* (London, 1872) pp. 12–13. Quotation with slight variations. Entries from Patmore not in chronological order.

2322   Ibid., pp. 14–15. Abridged quotation with variations.

2323   Ibid., p. 15. Quotation with slight variations.

2324   Ibid., pp. 24–5. Annotation and abridged quotation with variations.

2325   Ibid., pp. 34–6. Abridged quotation with variations.

2326   Ibid., pp. 44–5. Abridged quotation with variations and Hardy's underlining of the first three words.

2327   Ibid., pp. 39–40. Quotation with slight variations.

2328   Coventry Patmore, 'Magna est veritas', *Poems* (London, 1906) p. 291. Quotation, with a slight variation, of final three lines. Hardy's edn unidentified. See also entry 2193.

2329   Coventry Patmore, *Amelia, Tamerton Church-Tower etc.*, pp. 28–9.

2330   Ibid., pp. 30–1. Quotation with slight variations.

2331   Ibid., pp. 83–4. Annotation and abridged quotation, with variations, annotation and comment.

2332   'A Minor Prophet', *Sat. Rev.*, CII (8 Sep 1906) 304. Abridged quotation, with variations and annotations, from a review of Davidson's book.

2333   J. A. Hobson, 'Eugenics and Civics', *Speaker*, 14 (14 July 1906) 332. Annotation and quotation with slight variations.

2334   E. Ray Lankester, letter to the Editor, headed 'Discipline', *The Times*, 7 Jan 1907, p. 9. Quotation and annotation.

2335   H. H. Moworth, letter to the Editor, *The Times*, 11 Jan 1907, p. 10. Quotation and comment.

2336   'Matthew Arnold', *TLS*, 27 Sep 1907, p. 289. Annotation and abridged quotation with slight variations.

2337   'George Meredith', *Nation*, II (30 Nov 1907) 311. Quotation, with variations, from a review of M. Sturge Henderson's *George Meredith, Novelist, Poet, Reformer* (London, 1907).

2338   'The Creed of a Catholic Liberal', *Nation*, III (4 Jan 1908) 505–6. Two separate quotations, the first with annotation, the second with variations and annotation – from a review of Lord Acton, *The History of Freedom and Other Essays* (London, 1908).

2339   Mary E. Coleridge, 'Unwelcome', *Poems* (London, 1908) p. 64. Quotation with slight variations. Hardy owned a copy (DCM) of the 6th edn (1910); signed 'Thomas Hardy' on the title page. The poem 'Unwelcome' is marked with an 'X' (p. 64).

2340 A. G. G[ardiner], 'G. K. C. A Character Study', *D. News*, 18 July 1908, p. 5. Quotation with variations from an article on Gilbert Keith Chesterton. On 14 Mar 1908 Hardy had read an article on himself in the same series and corresponded with Gardiner about it: see *Letters*, III, 306–7, 308. Gardiner had also written on Hardy's thought in 'A Novelist's Philosophy', *D. News,* 5 Mar 1903, p. 8, complaining about Hardy's pessimism esp. in *Jude*: 'For the deeps of pessimism can reveal no depth below the misery of this book.' For Hardy on Chesterton, see Millgate, *A Biography,* p. 571.

2341 'Daniel Friedrich Strauss', *Nation,* III (25 Jan 1908) 598. Abridged quotation with variations. For Hardy's reading of *Leben Jesu* see entry 1297n.

2342 'Mr. Noyes's New Poems', *TLS* 30 Jan 1908, p. 36. Abridged quotation, with slight variations, and Hardy's underlining in pencil. A critical review of Alfred Noyes, *Forty Singing Seamen, and Other Poems* (London, 1908).

2343 'English Prose', *TLS,* 20 Feb 1908, p. 57. Annotation and abridged quotation, with variations, from a review of *An English Prose Miscellany*, ed. John Masefield, and *Nineteenth Century Prose*, ed. Mrs. Laurence Binyon (London, 1908).

2344 'The Works of Oscar Wilde', *TLS,* 18 June 1908, p. 193. Annotation and quotation. See also entry 2487.

2345 'Concepts of Monism', *Spectator,* C (14 Mar 1908) 424. Annotations and quotation, with slight variations, from a review of A. Worsley's *Concepts of Monism* (London, 1907). For excerpts from the book, see entry 2441.

2346 Francis Thompson, 'Shelley', *Dublin Review,* 143 (July 1908) 28–44. Abridged quotation with variations; on stationery pasted in.

2347 'Ibsen', *TLS,* 23 Jan 1908, pp. 29–30. Quotation with slight variations from a review of *The Collected Works of Henrik Ibsen*, with an Introduction by William Archer, and Edmund Gosse's *Ibsen* (London, 1908). Hardy also preserved a cutting from the review, see entry 2505.

2348–9 Unidentified quotations from the *Nation*.

2350 Unidentified newspaper cutting with Hardy's capitalization of the first letter. The excerpt is from p. 11 of the edn.

2351 Unidentified newspaper quotation on a loose piece of paper, measuring 9.7 × 7.8 cm; paper originally (1968) found in this place.

2352 M. Sopote, letter to the Editor, headed 'Pragmatism and Religion', *The Spectator,* CII (23 Jan 1909) 129. Annotation and abridged quotation with slight variations.

2353   'Felix Mendelssohn', *The Times*, 3 Feb 1909, p. 8. Abridged quotation with variations and annotation.

2354   Ruskin, *Modern Painters*, 3rd edn, I, 94–5; *Works*, III, 193–94. Annotation and quotation with slight variations. Hardy's edn unidentified.

2355   'Algernon Charles Swinburne', *TLS*, 15 Apr 1909, p. 141. Abridged quotation with slight variations. For Hardy's opinion on the British attitude towards Swinburne (who died on April 10), see *Life*, p. 344; see also entry 1288n.

2356   Ibid. Abridged quotation.

2357   Unidentified newspaper cutting.

2358   'John Calvin', *The Times*, 8 July 1909, p. 10. Annotations and abridged quotation with variations. *I have said this*: Hardy's annotation refers to his letter to *The Times* (19 Feb 1904) on *The Dynasts*: 'The philosophy of *The Dynasts*, under various titles and phrases, is almost as old as civilization. Its fundamental principle, under the name of Predestination, was preached by St. Paul. ... It has run through the history of the Christian Church ever since. St. Augustine held it vaguely, Calvin held it fiercely ...' (Orel, p. 145).

2359   William James, *A Pluralistic Universe* (London, 1909) pp. 244, 311. Quotations, with slight variations. The first sentence is from lecture VI, the rest from lecture VIII. In pencil on stationery pasted in.

2360   Unidentified newspaper cutting with Hardy's underlining in pencil.

2361   H. G. Wells, *First and Last Things: A Confession of Faith and Rule of Life* (London, 1908) pp. 56–7. Annotation and abridged quotation with variations.

2362   Ibid., pp. 98–9. Annotation and abridged quotation with slight variations.

2363   Ibid., p. 113. Abridged quotation with slight variations.

2364   Ibid., p. 151. Quotation with slight variations. The underlined title is Wells's marginal title.

2365–6   Ibid., pp. 152–3. Quotations with slight variations.

2367   Ibid., pp. 156–7. Annotation and abridged quotation with slight variations.

2368   H. Usener, 'Nativity', *Encyclopaedia Biblica*, ed. T. K. Cheyne (London, 1902) cols. 3340–51. Abridged quotation with variations and annotation.

2369 'A Wasted Genius', *TLS*, 3 Feb 1910, p. 37. Quotation, with slight variations, from a review of G. D'Annunzio's *Forse che si forse che no* (Milan, 1910).

2370 Unidentified newspaper cutting. Heading in Hardy's hand.

2371 'An Office Window', *D. Chron.*, 25 Aug 1910, p. 4. Cutting with reference in Hardy's hand and in pencil.

2372 Unidentified.

2373 Oliver C. Quick, 'The Humanist Theory of Value: A Criticism', *Mind*, XIX (Apr 1910) 219–20. Abridged quotation with slight variations. In pencil on a loose piece of paper (10.2 × 15.8 cm). Originally (1968) found at this point of the volume.

2374 Ibid., p. 222. Mixture of summary and quotation with annotation. In pencil.

2375 Houston Stewart Chamberlain, *Foundations of the Nineteenth Century*, trs. John Lees (London and New York, 1911) II, 559. Quotation with variations. On Athenaeum stationery tipped in; verso is blank. Same line from Goethe quoted in entry 2419.

2376 'Pluralism and Theism', *TLS*, 18 Jan 1912, p. 21. Cutting (pasted onto the stationery [of entry 2374]) with reference in Hardy's hand and in pencil.

2377 John McTaggart Ellis McTaggart, *Some Dogmas of Religion* (London, 1906) p. 159. Annotation and quotation with slight variations. Hardy expressed his immediate and positive reaction in a letter to the author on 23 May 1906:

> Quite by chance I took up from the table here a day or two ago your recent work *Some Dogmas of Religion* (to which I was attracted by seeing on its back a name I have been familiar with in the pages of *Mind*, etc.) and I think I ought to write and tell you what a very great pleasure the reading of the book has given me, though this is a thing I very seldom do. The clearness, acuteness and vigour of the thinking throughout, its entire freedom from sophisms and the indubitable moral good to be derived from a perusal of it are cheering to others whose minds have run more or less in the same groove but have rather despaired of seeing harmful conventions shaken – in this country at least – by lucid argument and, what is more, human emotions. (*Letters*, III, 207).

In 1908 Hardy also read McTaggart's *The Relation of Time and Eternity* (Berkeley, Calif., 1908): see *Letters*, III, 329. Cf. also Hardy's seldom quoted letter of 31 Mar 1916:

I am not a philosopher any more than you are, though from your letter I think I can hardly let you off the charge of at least having associated with Philosophy. The question you open up – of Free Will *versus* Determinism – is perennially absorbing, though less so when we find how much depends, in arguments on the subject, on the definition of the terms. Your own ingenious view of Free Will as a man's privileged ignorance of how he is going to act until he has acted would hardly suit the veterans who constitute the Old Guard of Free Will, but it suits me well enough.

If we could get outside the Universe and look back at it, Free Will as commonly understood would appear impossible; while by going inside one's individual self and looking at it, its difficulties appear less formidable, though I do not fancy they quite vanish.   In H. V. Marrot, *The Life and Letters of John Galsworthy* (London, 1935) p. 751.

See also *Life*, p. 297 and *Personal Notebooks*, p. 291.

2378 McTaggart, *Some Dogmas of Religion*, pp. 160–1. Annotation and abridged quotation with slight variations.

2379 Ibid., p. 162. Annotation and abridged quotation with variations.

2380–1 Ibid., pp. 164–5, 166. Abridged quotations with slight variations.

2382 Ibid., p. 166. Quotation with a slight variation. Cf. *Life*, p. 297.

2383 McTaggart, *Some Dogmas of Religion*, p. 186. Quotation with a slight variation.

2384 Ibid., pp. 177–9. Abridged quotation with variations.

2385 'The Power of the Pyramids', *T. P.'s Weekly*, 18 (8 Dec 1911) 719. Cutting of the final paragraph of a review of G. T. Wrench's *The Mastery of Life* (London, 1911), the central thesis of which is that 'despite slavery, ancient Egypt was more free than democratic Europe' (p. 719). Reference in Hardy's hand, with date in pencil.

2386 McTaggart, *Some Dogmas of Religion*, p. 183. Abridged quotation with a slight variation. See also entries 2377–84.

2387 A. Clutton Brock, *Shelley: The Man and the Poet* (London, 1910) pp. 183–4. Annotation and abridged quotation with slight variations.

2388 Ibid., p. 239. Quotation with a slight variation. Marginal line in pencil. Cf. '*August* 5, 1888. To find beauty in ugliness is the province of the poet' (*Life*, p. 213).

2389 Unidentified.

2390 'Walter Hedlam', *TLS*, 14 July 1910, p. 251. Quotation, with variations, and Hardy's underlining.

2391 'Dr. McTaggart on Hegel', *Cont. Rev.*, xcvii (May 1910) 8. Three separate quotations, with slight variations, from a review of John McTaggart Ellis McTaggart's *A Commentary on Hegel's Logic* (Cambridge, 1910). Although the quotations are separated by 'ib' Hardy copied them as one entry enclosed by horizontal lines. See also entry 2377n.

2392 H. Watson Smith, letter to the Editor, headed 'The Poetic Basis of Music', *Nation*, viii (17 Dec 1910) 504. Quotation with slight variations and Hardy's underlining.

2393 Samuel McComb, 'What is Christianity?', *Cont. Rev.*, lxxxvii (6 June 1905) 831. Quotation with slight variations.

2394 'Lord Morley on Language and Literature', *The Times*, 28 Jan 1911, p. 9. Abridged quotation with slight variations and annotation.

2395 Ibid. Quotation with slight variations.

2396 Ibid. Annotation and mixture of summary and quotation.

2397 Ibid. Mixture of summary and quotation with Hardy's underlinings.

2398 Ibid. Quotation with variations and annotation.

2399 Ibid. Summary.

2400 Ibid. Quotation with a slight variation.

2401 'The Growth of Rembrandt', *TLS*, 7 Dec 1911, p. 497. Annotations and quotation, with a slight variation, from a review of J. C. Holmes, *Notes on the Art of Rembrandt* (London, 1911).

2402-3 Ibid., pp. 497, 498. Quotations with slight variations.

2404-5 'English Prosody', *Quarterly Review*, 215 (July 1911) 69–79, 90. Abridged quotations with variations and annotations. For good recent discussions of Hardy's prosody see Paulin, *passim*; Ronald Marken, '"As Rhyme Meets Rhyme" in the Poetry of Thomas Hardy', and S. C. Neuman, '"Emotion Put into Measure": Meaning in Hardy's Poetry', in Clements and Grindle, pp. 18–32 and pp. 33–51; Tom Paulin, '"Words, in all their intimate accents"', *THA*, i (1982) 84–94.

2406 *Quarterly Review*, 215, p. 93. Quotation; first eleven words in Hardy's hand, the rest in an unidentified hand.

2407 'Emerson the Skeptic', *FRA*, 7 (July 1911) 99–100. Three separate quotations with slight variations. The reference to Benjamin de Casseres (d. 1945) is Hardy's own and may refer to the following circumstance: in the same issue is an unsigned article on 'Thomas Hardy's Women' (pp. 108–11), which is, in fact, a reprint, with slight changes of an old article by de Casseres, originally published in the *Bookman*, 16 (Oct 1902) 131–3. For de Casseres on 'nature' and 'illusion', see also entry 2421.

2408 'On the Art of the Theatre', *TLS*, 7 Dec 1911, p. 504. Quotation, with slight variations, from a review of Edward Gordon Craig, *On the Art of the Theatre* (London, 1911). Insertion in pencil.

2409 'The Novels of George Gissing', *TLS*, 11 Jan 1912, pp. 9–10. Quotation with slight variations.

2410 'The Wessex Drama', *Edin. Rev.*, ccxv (Jan 1912) 108. Abridged quotation and comment.

2411 'The Elizabethan Playwright', ibid., p. 31. Quotation with variations.

2412 Maurice Browne, 'The Poetry of W. W. Gibson', *Poetry Review*, i (Jan 1912) 18. Quotation with slight variations; the underlined words are capitalized in the source, where the whole quoted text is in italics.

2413 M. T. H. Sadler, 'The Past and Present of Futurism', *Blue Book*, i (May 1912) 55–60. Abridged quotation with variations.

2414 Clive Bell, 'The English Group', in Grafton Galleries, *Second Post-Impressionist Exhibition, 5 Oct – 31 Dec 1912* (London, 1912) pp. 21–3. Annotation and abridged quotation with variations.

2415 Roger Fry, 'The French Group', ibid., pp. 25–8. Abridged quotation with variations.

2416 'From the Last Century', review of Frederic Harrison, *Among My Books* (London, 1912), in *The Times*, 10 Oct 1912, p. 419. Annotation and quotation with slight variations.

2417 Henry Newbolt, 'A New Study of English Poetry, iv. Poetry and Politics', *English Review*, 12 (Sep 1912) 182–5. Abridged quotation, with slight variations, and annotation.

2418 Edward Clodd, 'Sir Alfred Lyall', *D. Chron.*, 24 Apr 1913, p. 4. Cutting from the end of the review. Reference in Hardy's hand and in pencil. Clodd (1840–1930), banker and author; one of Hardy's best male friends – see Millgate, *A Biography, passim*, and *Letters*.

2419   Robert Fowler, 'Is Art a Failure?', *Nineteenth Century and After*, LXXII (July 1912) 126, 131. Quotation with slight variations and annotation. In pencil on small piece of paper pasted in. Same line from Goethe quoted in entry 2375.

2420   'A Sermon to Thieves', *Periodical*, LXXIV (Dec 1913) 224–5. Cutting.

2421   Unidentified magazine cutting. Reference in Hardy's hand and his underlinings in pencil.

2422   'Bergson and Balfour', *Review of Reviews*, 44 (Nov 1911) 473–4. Loose cutting, originally tipped onto f. 108ᵛ. Magazine reference in Hardy's hand and in pencil.

2423   Henri Bergson, *Creative Evolution*, trs. Arthur Mitchell (London, 1911) pp. 40–1. Abridged quotation with variations and annotations. Entries from Bergson not in chronological order. Letters to Dr C. W. Saleeby printed in Hardy's autobiography, show that Hardy did not read *Creative Evolution* until late Dec 1914 or early 1915, although he had come across Bergson's ideas earlier (see cutting from 1911 in previous entry and letter below). On the assumption that Saleeby is a 'fellow-philosopher' of Bergson, Hardy tactfully, and perhaps sincerely, confesses that he feels emotionally attracted by the book, but that he cannot intellectually subscribe to the ideas:

> His [Bergson's] theories are certainly much more delightful than those they contest, and I for one would gladly believe them, but I cannot help feeling all the time that he is rather an imaginative and poetical writer than a reasoner, and that for his attractive assertions he does not adduce any proofs whatever. His use of the word 'creation' seems loose to me. Then, as to 'conduct'. I fail to see how, if it is not mechanism, it can be other than Caprice, though he denies it (p. 50). And he says that Mechanism and Finalism (I agree with him as to Finalism) are only external views of our conduct....
>
> ....
>
> You will see how much I want to be a Bergsonian (indeed I have for many years). But I fear that his philosophy is, in the bulk, only our old friend Dualism in a new suit of clothes – an ingenious fancy without real foundation, and more complicated, and therefore less likely than the determinist fancy and others that he endeavours to overthrow   (*Life*, p. 450).

Hardy refuted Bergson's dualism still more forcefully several years later in a letter to Ernest Brennecke, author of *Thomas Hardy's Universe* (New York, 1924): 'You are quite right in asserting in the footnote at page 71 that I have never been influenced by Bergson ... his views seeming to me to be only a re-hashing of the old creed of Dualism' (quoted in Bailey, p. 606). And, in another letter to Saleeby (16 Apr 1915), Hardy dismisses a key Bergsonian concept:

An *élan vital* – by which I understand him [Bergson] to mean a sort of additional and spiritual force, beyond the merely unconscious push of life – the 'will' of other philosophers that propels growth and development – seems much less probable than single and simple determinism, or what he calls mechanism, because it is more complex: and where proof is impossible probability must be our guide. His partly mechanistic and partly creative theory seems to me clumsy and confused. (*Life*, p. 451).

2424 Bergson, *Creative Evolution*, p. 15. Abridged quotation with slight variations and Hardy's underlining.

2425 Ibid., p. 21. Abridged quotation with variations.

2426–8 Ibid., pp. 7, 8, 38. Quotations with slight variations. Having criticized Bergson's *élan vital* in the letter of 16 Apr 1915 to Saleeby (quoted in entry 2423n), Hardy continues,

He speaks of 'the enormous gap that separates even the lowest form of life from the inorganic world'. Here again it is more probable that organic and inorganic modulate into each other, one nature and law operating throughout. But the most fatal objection to his view of creation *plus* propulsion seems to me to lie in the existence of pain. If nature were creative she would have created painlessness, or be in process of creating it – pain being the first thing we instinctively fly from. If on the other hand we cannot introduce into life what is not already there, and are bound to mere recombination of old materials, the persistance of pain is intelligible (*Life*, pp. 451–2).

2429 George McLean Harper, *William Wordsworth* (London, 1916) ii, 195; i, 195. First paragraph abridged quotation with variations; second abridged quotation with slight variations and annotation.

2430 Thomas H. Huxley, *Hume: With Helps to the Study of Berkeley*, in *Collected Essays*, vi (London, 1894) 220–1. Abridged quotation with variations; on recto of two small pieces of stationery pasted together, folded and tipped in; the verso is blank. Also in typescript, entry 2609.

2431 David G. Ritchie, *Philosophical Studies* (London and New York, 1905) 228–9. Abridged quotation with slight variations. In pencil on two pieces of stationery pasted together and tipped in. Marginal lines in ink.

2432 William James, Preface to Harald Höffding, *The Problems of Philosophy*, trs. Galen M. Fischer (New York and London, 1905) p. xiii. Quotation with a slight variation and annotation, on small piece of stationery pasted onto the verso of the paper for entry 2431. Also in typescript, entry 2587. Entry division strokes in mauve pencil.

2433 Unidentified newspaper cutting. Interpolation in pencil.

2434   Harald Höffding, *The Philosophy of Religion,* trs. B. E. Meyer (London, 1906) p. 9. Abridged quotation. Entries 2434–7 on two pieces of paper pasted in. Also in typescript, entry 2590.

2435   Ibid., p. 10. Quotation with a slight variation. Also in typescript, entry 2591. Cf. also entry 2615.

2436   Ibid., p. 12. Quotation. Also in typescript, entry 2592.

2437   'Pragmatism', *Spectator,* xcix (6 July 1907) 10. Abridged quotation with variations. Also in typescript, entry 2607. See also entry 2468n.

2438   Conrad Guenther, *Darwinism and the Problems of Life,* trs. J. McCabe (London, 1906) p. 365. Annotation and quotation with slight variations. In pencil on paper pasted in.

2439   Ibid., p. 424. Quotation. In pencil on paper pasted in.

2440   J. Ellis McTaggart, review of A. T. Ormond, *Concepts of Philosophy* (New York, 1906), in *Mind,* xvi (July 1907) 433. Abridged quotation, with variations, from a generally critical review. In pencil on paper pasted in. Also in typescript, entry 2624. For Hardy and McTaggart, see entry 2377n.

2441   A. Worsley, *Concepts of Monism* (London, 1907) pp. 316–30. Abridged quotation with variations and annotation. In pencil on recto. of four small pieces of paper pasted together, folded and tipped in; versos blank. Also in typescript, entries 2595–7. For excerpt from review of the book, see entry 2345.

2442   'Sur Bernard Shaw', *Nouvelle Revue Française,* May 1909, pp. 386–7. Hardy's trs., in pencil.

2443   T. S. Eliot, 'The Love Song of J. Alfred Prufrock', in S. P. B. Mais, *From Shakespeare to O. Henry* (London, 1917) pp. 104–5. Quotation with slight variations and annotation. In pencil.

2444   Alexander Pope, *The Odyssey of Homer,* i. 41–4, in *Poems of Alexander Pope,* ed. Maynard Mack (London and New Haven, Conn., 1967) ix, 31. Hardy's edn unidentified.

2445   'The German Mind: When Does History Begin?: Dr. Simon's Question', E. A. Sonnenschein, Letter to the Editor, *The Times,* 17 Mar 1921, p. 8. Quotation with slight variations.

2446   Jorris Karl Huysmans, *La Cathédrale,* 30th edn (Paris, 1888) pp. 30–1. Abridged quotation with variations. The final three words are from the end of the first paragraph.

2447   'Techekhov', *Observer,* 25 Jan 1920, p. 5. Quotation, with variations, from a review of *The Chorus Girl.* In pencil on a ruled piece of paper pasted in.

2448   Unidentified. In pencil on a small piece of ruled paper pasted in.

2449   A. S. Eddington, 'Einstein on Time and Space', *Quarterly Review*, 234 (Jan 1920) 231. Abridged quotation with variations and annotations. In pencil on ruled piece of paper pasted in. For Hardy's poetic use of some of Einstein's ideas, see 'The Absolute Explains', 'So Time' and 'Drinking Song'. In 1919 he wrote to J. Ellis McTaggart that 'after what (Einstein) says the universe seems to be getting too comic for words' (quoted in Pinion, *Art and Thought*, p. 174). See also *Life*, p. 419. Hardy owned Einstein's *Relativity: The Special and the General Theory: A Popular Exposition*, 3rd edn (London, 1920); now in the DCM, it is signed 'Thomas Hardy' on the title page and there are some markings in chs 9 and 31. He also bought C. Nordmann's *Einstein and the Universe* (New York, 1922); see Orel, *The Final Years*, p. 74. In June 1921, Florence Hardy wrote that he 'ponders over Einstein's Theory of Relativity in the night' (quoted in Gittings, p. 193).

2450   *Quarterly Review*, 234, pp. 228–33. Abridged quotation with variations and annotations. In pencil on ruled piece of paper pasted in. Material not in chronological order.

2451   'From Absolute to Relative', *TLS*, 9 Dec 1920, p. 814. Abridged quotation, with slight variations and Hardy's underlining, from a review of Wildon Carr's *The General Principle of Relativity in its Philosophical and Historical Aspect* (London, 1920). In pencil on two pieces of ruled paper pasted in.

2452   'The Machine', *TLS*, 1 July 1926, p. 439. Cutting, with newspaper reference and dating in Hardy's hand and in pencil; Hardy's underlining in pencil. For another review of *Ouroboros*, see entry 2474.

2453   'Mankind at the Cross-Roads', *TLS*, 29 July 1926, p. 502. Cutting, with newspaper reference, dating and interpolation in Hardy's hand and in pencil; Hardy's underlining in pencil.

2454   'The Philosophy of History', *TLS*, 23 Dec 1926, p. 942. Cutting, with marginal lines and annotations in pencil.

2455   H. J. Massingham, *Downland Man* (London, 1926), p. 393. Annotation and quotation with variations, written on the back of a letter to Hardy (20 Dec 1926) from the National Union of Journalists; letter tipped onto f. 248, which is blank. In pencil.

2456   G. B. Shaw, *Translations and Tomfooleries* (London, 1926) p. 6. Abridged quotation, with slight variations, and comment; from Shaw's prefatory 'Note' to his translation of Siegfried Trebitsch's *Jitta's Atonement*. In pencil on back of tipped-in, undated letter offering to sell Hardy a copy of *Who's Who in Literature*, 1927 edn.

2457 Arthur James Balfour, *Theism and Humanism* (London and New York, 1915) p. 68. Annotations and quotations with slight variations. In pencil.

2458 Emanuel Deutsch, 'Spinoza', *Chambers's Encyclopaedia* (1892) IX, 642–3. Abridged quotation with variations and annotation. In pencil on paper pasted in. Quoted from also in entries 2092–4.

2459 'The Confessions of the Mr Wells', *Nation*, IV (21 Nov 1908) 299. Quotation with slight variations, annotations and comment. In pencil on paper pasted in.

2460 J. E. P., 'Wanted: A Lyrist', *Academy*, LXXVIII (14 May 1910) 466. Quotation with slight variations. In pencil on paper pasted in.

2461 'Mr. Swinburne as a Master of Metre', *Spectator*, CII (17 Apr 1909) 605. Abridged quotation with variations. In pencil.

2462 Florence Gay, 'The New Evolution', *Outlook*, 25 (14 May 1910) 715. Abridged quotation with variations. In pencil on old Athenaeum stationery pasted in.

2463 Friedrich Nietzsche, *Menschliches, Allzumenschliches*, I, in *Nietzsche: Werke, Kritische Gesamtausgabe* (Berlin, 1967) IV:2, 145–6. In pencil on stationery pasted in. Williamson (p. 406) seems unaware of a trs. of Nietzsche's book in 1908 (a review of which Hardy cut out, see entry 2641) but he is still probably right in suggesting that we here have Hardy's own attempt at translating the following passage from section 149:

> Die edelste Art der Schönheit ist die, welche nicht auf einmal hinreisst, welche nicht stürmische und berauschende Angriffe macht (eine solche erweckt leicht Ekel), sondern jene langsam einsickernde, welche man fast unbemerkt mit sich fortträgt und die Einem im Traum einmal wiederbegegnet, endlich aber, nachdem sie lange mit Bescheidenheit an unserm Herzen gelegen, von uns ganz Besitz nimmt, unser Auge mit Thränen, unser Herz mit Sehnsucht füllt.

2464 Frederic Manning, *Scenes and Portraits* (London, 1909) p. xi. Quotation, in pencil on stationery pasted in.

2465 George Saintsbury, 'Algernon Charles Swinburne', *Bookman*, 36 (June 1909) 114. Abridged quotation with variations and annotation. In pencil on stationery pasted in. Hardy also copied this passage into his 'Memoranda, I' notebook (see *Personal Notebooks*, p. 31) and is thus likely to have approved of this particular passage, but he is recorded as having believed that generally – 'Saintsbury had read too much, and he did not possess sufficient insight', quoted in Harold Orel, *The Final Years of Thomas Hardy 1912–28* (London, 1976) p. 70. See also Millgate, *A Biography*, p. 321.

2466   'Cooperation in Nature', *TLS*, 10 June 1915, p. 191. Abridged quotation with slight variations from a review of Hermann Reinheimer's *Symbiogenesis. The Universal Law of Progressive Evolution* (London, 1915). In pencil on two pieces of ruled paper pasted in.

2467   M. A. R. Tuker, 'Italian Realism and Art', *Fort. Rev.*, LXXXIII (May 1908) 874. Annotation and abridged quotation with slight variations. In pencil on two pieces of stationery pasted in.

2468   William James, *The Meaning of Truth* (London and New York, 1909) p. 240. Quotation with slight variations. In pencil on stationery pasted in. In 1925 Hardy read James's statement in *Harper's* that 'Truth is what will work', and commented, 'A worse corruption of language was never perpetrated' (*Life*, p. 428).

2469   John C. Bailey, *The Claims of French Poetry: Nine Studies in the Greater French Poets* (London, 1907) p. 306. Quotation with slight variations. In pencil on two pieces of stationery pasted in.

2470   Ibid., p. 307. Abridged quotation with variations. In pencil on stationery pasted in.

2471   'Lemaître on Racine', *Nation*, III (16 May 1908) 232. Annotation and quotation, with slight variations, from a review of Jules Lemaître's *Jean Racine* (Paris, 1908). In pencil on stationery pasted in.

2472   Maurice Brown, 'The Nature and Function of Poetry', *Oxford and Cambridge Review*, 4 (1908) 128. Quotation with slight variations. In pencil on two pieces of stationery pasted in.

2473   Unidentified, in pencil. Madame de Staël (1766–1817), French lit. critic and novelist.

2474   MacLeod Yearsley, 'Book Chat', *The Literary Guide and Rationalist Review*, no. 328 (Jan 1927) 17. Loose cutting of paragraphs 4 and 5 of the article; the date is also cut out and pasted onto this side of the cutting. Cutting originally (1968) found in this place in the notebook. For another review of *Ouroboros*, see entry 2452.

2475   Gerald Bullett, 'The Booktaster', *The Literary Guide and Rationalist Review*, no. 373 (July 1927) 119. Loose cutting of the opening three paragraphs. Cutting originally (1968) found in this place of the notebook. Heading in Hardy's hand, and in pencil.

2476   'The Anatomy of Science', *TLS*, 3 Feb 1927, p. 70. Cutting. Reference in Hardy's hand. Marginal lines in red pencil.

2477 'T. E. Brown', *TLS,* 25 June 1908, p. 201. Quotation, with slight variations, from a review of *Poems of T. E. Brown* (The Golden Treasury Series).

2478 'Young American Poets', *TLS,* 17 Nov 1921, p. 746. Cutting from a review of *Modern American Poetry,* ed. Louis Untermeyer (London, 1921). Reference in Hardy's hand.

2479 F. W. Hirst, *Early Life and Letters of John Morley* (London, 1927) I, 310–12. Annotation and abridged quotation with variations from Hirst's account of J. S. Mill's *Nature: The Utility of Religion: Theism.* In pencil.

2480 Michael Kaye, 'The Possibility of Man's Freedom', *Journal of Philosophical Studies,* II (Oct 1927) 521. Mixture of summary and quotation. Entries from this article not in chronological order. In pencil.

2481–82 Ibid., pp. 517, 519–20. Abridged quotations with variations. In pencil. This is the final entry in 'Literary Notes II'. The rest of the notebook is blank.

ANNOTATIONS TO 'LITERARY NOTES III'

Hardy's works cited from the Wessex Edn; entry numbers prefixed 'A' refer to the '1867' Notebook in the Appendix.

2483 'His Majesty's Theatre', *The Times,* 25 Apr 1906, p. 12. Cutting from the middle of the review. Marginal lines in red pencil. This is the first entry in 'Literary Notes III'.

2484 'Mr. William Morris on the Printing of Books', *The Times,* 6 Nov 1893, p. 4. Cutting.

2485 Unidentified newspaper cutting; first part of reference in Hardy's hand and in pencil. The quotation is not, as Hardy's reference suggests, from the Preface to *John Bull's Other Island* but from the fourth paragraph of the Preface to *Major Barbara.* The two plays were published in 1 vol. in June 1907.

2486 William Archer, 'Bible and Drama', *D. Chron.,* 16 Nov 1904, p. 3. Cutting of part of the review of Stephen Phillips, *The Sin of David.* Reference in Hardy's hand. William Archer (1856–1924), critic and journalist. In 1892 Hardy wrote to Archer 'I have been so drawn to yr writings by their accord with my views that I have often thought of testifying to that agreement by sending a book' (*Letters,* I, 287).

2487 Unidentified cutting tipped onto a stub. Publication reference in Hardy's hand and in pencil. Methuen published Wilde's *Collected Works,* 14 vols, in Feb 1908.

Michael Ryan suggests that Hardy mocks Wilde's *The Picture of Dorian Gray* in *The Well-Beloved*, see 'One Name of Many Shapes', in *Critical Approaches*, pp. 173ff.

2488   Unidentified newspaper cutting.

2489   Unidentified newspaper cutting; book published Nov 1904; interpolation in pencil.

2490   Unidentified newspaper cutting.

2491   A. Clutton Brock, 'Poetry and Moral Ideas', *Academy*, LXXIII (27 July 1907) 727–8. Cuttings from paragraph 6, 7, and the end of the article. Ellipsis symbol in pencil.

2492   'Elizabeth Barrett Browning', *TLS*, 5 Feb 1904, p. 33. Cutting from first half of the article. Reference in Hardy's hand.

2493   'A Keats Discovery', *Periodical*, XXIX (Mar 1905) 3–4. In the left margin only a few letters remain of the marginal texts: 'A Keats discovery', 'The Argument' and 'A hit at Byron'.

2494   Unidentified newspaper cutting.

2495   'Mr. Bridges' Demeter', *TLS*, 16 June 1905, pp. 189–90. Cutting, tipped onto stub.

2496   'Beginnings of Life', *D. News*, 19 Mar 1906, p. 8. Cutting.

2497   'Britain's Next Campaign', *D. News*, 12 Feb 1903, p. 4. Cutting.

2498   'Literature', *Athenaeum*, 12 May 1906, pp. 569–70. Cutting. Hardy's underlining, marginal annotation and line in pencil.

2499   'Views and Reviews', *Glasgow News*, 31 Jan 1907, p. 2. Cutting; newspaper reference and date in Hardy's hand.

2500   ' Poet's Criticism', *D. Chron.*, 23 May 1903, p. 3. Cutting from a review of W. B. Yeats, *Ideas of Good and Evil* (London, 1903). Reference in Hardy's hand and in pencil.

2501   Unidentified newspaper cutting.

2502   'Ibsen and his Works', *D. Chron.*, 24 May 1906, p. 6. Cutting with newspaper reference and date in Hardy's hand and in pencil.

2503   'Book of the Day', *D. News*, 24 Jan 1908, p. 4. Cutting of a review of Edmund Gosse, *Ibsen* (London, 1908).

2504 'The Art of Henrik Ibsen', *TLS*, 25 May 1906, p. 191. Cutting with inserted directions in Hardy's hand. Marginal line in pencil.

2505 Review of *The Collected Works of Henrik Ibsen*, with Introductions by William Archer (London, 1908), and Edmund Gosse's *Ibsen* (London, 1908), in *TLS*, 23 Jan 1908, p. 29. Annotation (in Hardy's hand) and cutting of the final paragrah. Hardy made a short extract from the review also in entry 2347.

2506 'The Poetry of the Eighteenth Century', *TLS*, 1 Dec 1905, p. 414. Cutting from a review of W. J. Courthope, *History of English Poetry*, vol. v (London, 1905). Reference in Hardy's hand.

2507 'Mr. Sturge Moore's Poetry', *TLS*, 18 May 1906, p. 177. Cutting with newspaper reference and date in Hardy's hand and in blue pencil; inserted directions in pencil.

2508 'English Prosody', *TLS*, 29 June 1906, p. 230. Cutting, but with the opening paragraph in Hardy's hand (on a piece of paper pasted in), from a review of George Saintsbury, *A History of English Prosody*, vol. i (London, 1906). For Hardy and prosody see entries 2404–5n.

2509 Review of Bliss Carman, *The Poetry of Life* and *Poems* (London, 1906), in *D. Chron.*, 24 May 1906, p. 3. Cutting with parentheses and final reference in Hardy's hand and in blue pencil.

2510 'Spencer and the Abbey', *D. Chron.*, 14 Sep 1906, p. 3. Cutting. Cf. *Letters*, iv, 26.

2511 'Words', *Sat. Rev.*, cii (29 Sep 1906) 390. Cutting of the penultimate paragraph of the article. Reference in Hardy's hand.

2512 'The Heart of the Country', *TLS*, 8 June 1906, p. 207. Cutting from a review of Ford Madox Hueffer, *The Heart of the Country* (London, 1906). Reference in Hardy's hand and in pencil.

2513 'Pastoral Poetry', *TLS*, 8 June 1906, pp. 205–6. Cutting tipped onto stub so that the text is not in chronological order. First half of 'Literary' in the heading cut off.

2514 'French Symbolists', *TLS*, 14 Sep 1906, p. 313. Cutting, leaving out conclusion of article.

2515 Z., 'Stevenson of Missouri', *Author*, xviii (Nov 1907) 63–4; cutting tipped onto stub. Date and marginal comment in Hardy's hand and in pencil.

2516 'The Woman of the Future', *Nation*, i (13 Apr 1907) 255–6. Cutting tipped onto stub, with the exception of p. 43, which is pasted in. Marginal cross in pencil.

2517   'Mr. Shaw on Shakespeare', ibid., p. 270. Cutting of last half of a review of B. Shaw's *One Hundred and Ninety Dramatic Opinions and Essays* (London, 1907). Marginal lines in red pencil.

2518   'The Russian Poets', *D. News*, 15 July 1907, p. 4. Cutting with newspaper reference and date in Hardy's hand and in pencil. Hardy crossed out one line in pencil.

2519   'The Intellectual Fallacy', *Tribune*, 1 Mar 1907, p. 2. Cutting with newspaper reference and '1907' in Hardy's hand and in pencil.

2520   'The Needs of Oxford University', *The Times*, 6 May 1907, p. 4. Cutting with 'Times' and date in Hardy's hand and in pencil.

2521   'Lemaître versus Rousseau', *TLS*, 26 Apr 1907, p. 132. Cutting of middle section of article with heading in Hardy's hand and in pencil.

2522   Review, *Athenaeum*, Mar 1907, pp. 248–9. Cutting.

2523   Unidentified newspaper cutting.

2524   'Algernon Charles Swinburne', *Tribune*, 5 Apr 1907, p. 2. Cutting. For Hardy and Swinburne, see entry 1288n.

2525   'Along the Way Side', *Literary Guide*, 1 Apr 1907, p. 55. Cutting with reference in Hardy's hand.

2526   'The "New Theology"', *D. Mail*, 12 Jan 1907, p. 7. Cutting with reference in Hardy's hand and with the parenthetical comment in red ink. Hardy's comment is, as the foliation indicates, pasted onto f28^r, but the piece of newspaper cutting (with page number '7') belongs to the text in entry 2526.

2527   'The Outlook: The "New Theology"', *D. Mail*, 12 Jan 1907, p. 6. Cutting.

2528   Unidentified newspaper cutting from a review, it would seem, of Leslie Stephen's *The English Utilitarians*, 3 vols (London, 1900). Vol. III is devoted to Mill.

2529   'Ousting Capital', *D. News*, 24 Jan 1908, p. 5. Cutting of first half of article, with 'D. News' and date in Hardy's hand and in pencil.

2530   'The Socialist Victory', *The Times*, 23 Jan 1908, p. 7. Cutting.

2531   'Literature', *Whitefriars Journal*, III (28 Feb 1908) 121–9. Cutting of part of the account with heading and interpolation (in pencil) in Hardy's hand.

2532   William L. Alden, 'London Literary Letter', *New York Times Saturday Review of Books*, 17 Apr 1900, p. 230. Annotation in unidentified hand.

2533 'Seventeenth Century Criticism', *TLS*, 23 Apr 1908, p. 129. Cutting of the last part of the review. Heading, final reference and date in Hardy's hand. *Springarn:* Hardy and the *TLS* have 'Spingarn'.

2534 'Notes and Announcements', *Publishers' Circular*, 66 (13 Mar 1897) 316. Cutting with heading in Hardy's hand and in pencil. The article referred to is 'What is a Realist?', *National Observer*, 6 May 1897, p. 441.

2535 C., 'From Ghosts to Gods', *D. Chron.*, 10 Dec 1897, p. 3. Cutting. Same article quoted from in entries 1956–8. Charles Grant Blairfindie Allen (1848–99), novelist.

2536 Ernest Newman, 'A Note on Amiel', *National Reformer*, 12 Mar 1893, pp. 163–4. Cutting, tipped onto a stub, of part of article.

2537 Unidentified newspaper cutting; book published in Mar 1906.

2538 'British Association: Sectional Addresses Section I Physiology', *The Times*, 7 Aug 1906, p. 11. Cutting of larger part of article. Final parenthesis in Hardy's hand.

2539 'From Wordsworth to Byron', *TLS*, 19 May 1905, pp. 157–8. Cutting tipped onto a stub.

2540 'The Grand Passion', *Daily Graphic*, 13 Oct 1904, pp. 1, 3. Cutting with reference and date in Hardy's hand and in pencil.

2541 Henry Jones, 'The Philosophy of Religion', *Speaker*, 14 (25 Aug 1906) 477–8. Cutting, tipped onto a stub, with marginal lines in red pencil.

2542 'In Defence of Rhyme', *TLS*, 19 Nov 1908, pp. 409–10. Cutting tipped onto a stub with 'Times' and date in Hardy's hand. Marginal lines in pencil.

2543 'The Evolution of English Poetry', *Academy*, LXIX (2 Dec 1905) 1254–6. Cutting of the whole review. Part of the cutting (pp. 83–4) tipped onto a stub.

2544 W. J. Courthope, *Life in Poetry: Law in Taste* (London, 1901) pp. 9–10. Abridged quotation with slight variations. Entries 2544–628 are typewritten, probably by Florence Dugdale, who became Hardy's second wife in 1914. Some folios (pp. 85, 111, 113, 115–19, 121, 123, 125) are typed with a mauve ribbon or are carbon copies. See 'Textual Introduction', p. xxxix ('Dating'). Some of the typed pages are paginated as indicated in the transcription, dividing the material into separate units. Some typed leaves are tipped onto stubs, others pasted in.

2545 Ibid., pp. 25–6. Abridged quotation with variations. Typescript.

2546 Ibid., p. 43. Quotation with a slight variation. Typescript.

2547   Ibid., p. 58. Abridged quotation with variations. Typescript.

2548   Ibid., p. 62. Quotation with variations. Typescript.

2549   Ibid., p. 83. Quotation. Typescript.

2550   Ibid., p. 85. Abridged quotation with variations and Hardy's underlining in pencil. Typescript.

2551–3   Ibid., pp. 86, 87. 91. Quotations. Typescript.

2554   Ibid., p. 115. Quotation with variations. Typescript.

2555–7   Ibid., pp. 116, 132–3, 143. Abridged quotations. Typescript.

2558–9   Ibid., pp. 145, 165. Abridged quotations with slight variations. Typescript. Florence Dugdale left out the Greek words in entry 2559: τὸ καλόν, and τὸ βέλτιον.

2560   Ibid., p. 174. Quotation. Typescript.

2561   Ibid., p. 193. Quotation with slight variations. Typescript.

2562   Ibid. Abridged quotation. Typescript.

2563–4   Ibid., p. 198. Quotations with slight variations. Typescript.

2565–6   Ibid., pp. 198, 199. Quotations. Typescript.

2567   Richard Wagner, 'The Play and the Nature of Dramatic Poetry ı', in *Richard Wagner's Prose Works*, trs. William Ashton Ellis (London, 1892) ıı, 140. Abridged quotation with variations. Typescript.

2568   Ibid., ıı, 145–6. Annotation and abridged quotation with variations. Typescript.

2569   Wagner, 'The Play and Dramatic Poetry ıı', *Prose Works*, ıı, 153. Typescript.

2570–1   Ibid., pp. 166, 192. Quotations with slight variations. Typescript.

2572   Ibid., p. 199. Abridged quotation with slight variations. Typescript.

2573   Ibid., p. 209. Quotation with variations. Typescript.

2574   Ibid., p. 220. Abridged quotation, with slight variations, and annotations. Typescript.

2575–6   Ibid., pp. 221–2, 224–5. Abridged quotations with variations. Typescript with interpolation in ink.

2577 Ibid., p. 229. Quotation with variations. Typescript.

2578–9 Ibid., p. 231. Quotations with slight variations. Typescript.

2580 Ibid. Mixture of summary and quotation. Typescript.

2581 Ibid., p. 232. Quotation with variations. Typescript.

2582 Wagner, 'The Arts of Poetry and Tone in the Drama of the Future', ibid., pp. 257–8. Quotation with variations. Typescript.

2583 Ibid., p. 283. Quotation with variations. Typescript.

2584 Wagner, Introduction to 'Opera and the Nature of Music', ibid., p. 17. Quotation with slight variations. Typescript.

2585 Unidentified. Typescript.

2586 Unidentified. Typescript.

2587 Typescript, with variations, of entry 2432.

2588 Unidentified. The final issue of the *Speaker* came out on 23 Feb 1907.

2589 Typescript, with variations, of entry 2431; *categories*: Hardy wrote 'catagories'.

2590–2 Typescripts, with variations, of entries 2434–6. For 'Conservation of value' (2591), see also entry 2615.

2593 'The Aesthetic Outlook: Walter Pater', *Edin. Rev.*, ccvi (July 1907) 29. Quotation from a review article on several works by Pater. Typescript.

2594 Ibid., pp. 29–30. Abridged quotation with slight variations. Typescript.

2595–7 Typescripts, with variations, of entry 2441. Crossing out (entry 2595) in pencil.

2598 A. Clutton Brock, 'George Meredith's Poetry', *Speaker*, 19 May 1906, p. 165. Abridged quotation with variations. Typescript with incorrect dating from review of S. M. Trevelyan, *The Poetry and Philosophy of George Meredith* (London, 1906).

2599 'Coventry Patmore', *TLS*, 17 Mar 1905, p. 85. Quotation with slight variations from a review of Edmund Gosse's *Coventry Patmore* (London, 1905). Typescript with reference in unidentified hand. Hardy copied from *TLS* on Patmore also into his 'Memoranda II' notebook in 1921; see *Personal Notebooks*, pp. 47–8.

2600   Ernest Rhys, 'The New Mysticism', *Fort. Rev.*, LXVII (June 1900) 1048–55. Abridged quotation with variations from an article which mainly deals with Fiona Macleod, *The Divine Adventure; Jona, By Sundown Shores. Studies in Spiritual History* (London, 1900). Typescript.

2601   Frederic W. H. Myers, 'Modern Poets and the Meaning of Life', *Nineteenth Century*, XXXIII (Jan 1893) 101. Quotation with variations and annotation. Hardy also quoted from the article in entries 1906–7. Typescript.

2602   Unidentified typescript.

2603   'Coleridge', *TLS*, 10 May 1907, pp. 142–3. Abridged quotation with variations. Typescript.

2604   'The Literary Week', *Academy*, LXXII (25 May 1907) 500. Quotation and annotation. Typescript.

2605   'The Humanist', *Nation*, I (18 May 1907) 446. Abridged quotation with variations. Typescript with '[by]' inserted in pencil.

2606   C. F. Keary, 'Positivism', *Albany Review*, I (May 1907) 207. Abridged quotation with variations and Hardy's underlining. Typescript.

2607   Typescript, with variations, of entry 2437; *tout*: Florence Dugdale typed 'tour'.

2608   G. F. G. Masterman, 'A Rebel', *Albany Review*, I (May 1907) 151–3. Abridged quotation with variations and annotation. Typescript.

2609   Typescript, with variations, of entry 2430.

2610   Unidentified typescript.

2611   Typescript, with variations, of entry 1401; *seemed*: Florence Dugdale typed 'seeme'.

2612   'The Decline of Philistinism', *Speaker*, 10 June 1905, p. 254. Quotation with slight variations. Typescript.

2613   'Ibsen', *Observer*, 27 May 1906, p. 4. Abridged quotation. Typescript.

2614   Unidentified typescript.

2615   A. Seth Pringle-Pattison, *The Philosophic Radicals and Other Essays* (Edinburgh and London, 1907) p. 196. Quotation and annotation. Typescript.

2616   Ibid., p. 204. Quotation. Typescript; *Philosophy*: Florence Dugdale typed 'Philosiphy'.

2617   H. R. Mackintosh, review of Harald Höffding, *The Philosophy of Religion* (London, 1906), in *Mind*, xvi (July 1907) 423. Quotation with variations. Typescript.

2618–19   Ibid., pp. 418–20. Abridged quotations with variations. Typescript.

2620   Unidentified typescript with pencilled corrections.

2621   'The Ethics of Wagner's "Ring"', *Nation*, i (11 May 1907) 415. Quotation with slight variations. Typescript.

2622   Arthur Sidgwick, 'On Some Forms of Irony in Literature', *Cornhill*, new series xxii (Apr 1907) 497–505. Abridged quotation with variations and annotations. Typescript.

2623   Typescript, with variations, of entries 2438–9; *organism:* Florence Dugdale typed 'orgasm'.

2624   Typescript, with variations, of entry 2440.

2625   Frederic Harrison, *The Creed of a Layman* (London, 1907) pp. 32–5. Mixture of summary and quotation. For Hardy and Harrison, see entry 1213n. Typescript with pencilled correction and final quotation marks.

2626   E. A. Baughan, 'The Apostasy of a Wagnerian', *Fort Rev.*, lxxxvi (July 1906) 145. Abridged quotation with variations and annotations. Typescript with interpolation in ink and corrections in pencil.

2627   E. Armitage, 'The Scientists and Common Sense', *Cont. Rev.*, lxxxvii (May 1905) 730. Quotations with variations and annotation. Typescript.

2628   Ibid., p. 734. Abridged quotation with variations. This is the last typescript entry.

2629   Edmund Gosse, 'The Cardinal Importance of Poe', *Cont. Rev.*, xcv (Feb 1909) 8. Cutting with reference in Hardy's hand and in pencil. In 1901 Hardy wrote that Poe's 'too small sheaf of verse has genius in every line, as well as music' (*Letters*, ii, 303).

2630   Basil de Selincourt, 'Saintsbury's History of Prosody', *Outlook*, 13 Aug 1910, p. 220. Cutting with heading in Hardy's hand and in pencil.

2631   'Swinburne on Shakespeare', 'Henry V and the Persae'; 'Shylock', *Periodical*, liii (Oct 1909) 43–4. Cutting.

2632   Unidentified cutting with heading in Hardy's hand and in pencil. This is the final cutting to be pasted in. Remaining entries are loose cuttings.

2633   'Types of Tragic Drama', *TLS*, 28 May 1908, pp. 169–70. Loose cutting with 'Times', date and final lines (from 'Vaughan thinks') in Hardy's hand. Marginal line in blue pencil.

2634   'Dante as Philosopher', *Periodical*, XLIX (Feb 1909) 296–7. Loose cutting with heading in Hardy's hand and in pencil.

2635   Loose unidentified newspaper cutting. The quotation is from John Morley *Machiavelli*, Romanes Lecture delivered in the Sheldonian Theatre, 2 June 1897 (London, 1897) p. 41. '1897' in pencil on a piece of paper pasted on.

2636   'Two Poets', *D. News*, 14 Sep 1907, p. 3. Loose cutting with 'D. News' and date in Hardy's hand and in pencil.

2637   'Music. The Folk-Song in the Music Hall', *The Times*, 15 Jan 1910, p. 11. Loose cutting with 'Times' and date in Hardy's hand and in pencil.

2638   'Amores: Poems. by D. H. Lawrence', *TLS*, 10 Aug 1916, p. 379. Loose cutting with 'T. Lit. Sup.' and date in Hardy's hand; cutting now (1981) no longer in the notebook.

2639   'The Music-Makers', *D. News*, 11 Aug 1916, p. 2. Loose cutting.

2640   Loose unidentified newspaper cutting from 1909. 1st edn of Robertson's study published in 1897, 2nd in 1909.

2641   'Was Nietzsche a Madman or a Genius?', *Current Literature*, 44 (June 1908) 641–4. Loose cutting. Hardy translates a passage from *Menschliches, Allzumenschliches* in entry 2463. For a general note on Hardy and Nietzsche, see entry 1989n.

ANNOTATIONS TO '1867' NOTEBOOK

Hardy's works are cited from the Wessex Edn; entry numbers prefixed 'A' refer to this notebook.

1   A. C. Swinburne, *Atalanta in Calydon,* new edn (London, 1885) p. 43. Abridged quotation with a slight variation. Hardy's own copy of this edn in the DCM is signed 'Thomas Hardy' on the title page and has several markings, but not of the passage here quoted. Hardy's edn unidentified. For a general note on Swinburne, see entry 1288n.

2   Ibid., p. 44. Abridged quotation with slight variations. Lines marked with a marginal stroke in Hardy's copy.

3 Ibid., p. 47. Quotation; underlined in Hardy's copy.

4 Ibid. Quotation with a slight variation.

5 William Shakespeare, *Henry V*, iv.i.100. Quotation. For a brief note on Shakespeare, see entry 367n.

6 Pierre Corneille, *Le Cid*, i.i.36. Hardy's edn unidentified. The entry may be Hardy's own trs. of 'Ses rides sur son front ont gravé ses exploits'.

7 A. De Musset, 'Les Vœux Stériles', *Premières Poésies 1829 à 1835* (Paris, 1881) p. 185. Probably Hardy's own trs. of the passage, which is unmarked in his copy of the edn (DCM). The original French quoted in entry 1442. See also entry 1028n.

8 Herbert Spencer, *First Principles*, vol. i of *A System of Synthetic Philosophy* (London, 1880) p. 529. Hardy's edn unidentified. Quotation, with annotation, from Part ii ('The Knowable'), ch. 23 ('Dissolution'). For a general note on Spencer, see entry 882n.

9 Ibid., p. 507. Quoted from Part ii, ch. 22 ('Equilibration'). The excerpt is from the final lines of section 174, in which Spencer argues that the equilibrations of the 'mental life' can be classified in the same way as those distinguished as 'bodily life'.

10 The term 'the Unknowable' appears in many places in *First Principles*. It is, first of all, the title of Part i. See also, however, pp. 113, 120, 122, 143, 154, 156, 157, 161, 165, 167, 397, 551.

11 William Shakespeare, *King John*, v.vii.3. Quotation.

12 William Shakespeare, *Romeo and Juliet*, ii.iii.35. Quotation and annotation.

13 Thomas Carlyle, 'The Opera', *Works*, xi, 257. Quotation. For a general note on Carlyle, see entry 94n.

14 Thomas Carlyle, 'Two Hundred and Fifty Years ago', *Works*, xi, 213.

15 Ibid., p. 217. Abridged quotation.

16 George Eliot, *Adam Bede*, Everyman's edn (London, 1906; repr. 1977) p. 468. Hardy's edn unidentified. Abridged quotation. For a brief general note on George Eliot, see entry 1297n.

17 Ibid. Abridged quotation.

18 Thomas Carlyle, 'Diamond Necklace', *Works*, x, 16. Quotation with variations and annotation.

19   Anthony Trollope, *Orley Farm* (London, 1862) ı, 40. Hardy's edn
unidentified. Quotation.

20   Carlyle, 'Diamond Necklace', *Works*, x, 17–18. Abridged quotation with
slight variations. The parenthetical annotation (in pencil, as is the marginal
marking) seems to suggest that Hardy saw a similarity between Carlyle's
apostrophe to Boehmer and the apostrophe of Moses to the Israelites in
Deuteronomy 1.

21   Victor Hugo, '*Ninety-Three*', trs. F. L. Benedict and J. H. Friswell, 3 vols.
(London, 1874) ı, 240. Quotation. This trs. was published in a new edn in 1886,
and Hardy could have used either for this entry. In the next English trs. of the
novel, however, by G. Campbell in 1887, the sentence reads, 'These little
children had a great future before them' (p. 97). The brace for entries A21–4
points to their relationship, which Hardy explains in entry A24. Hardy owned
a copy of '*Ninety-Three*', n.d. (188–); see Wreden, item 338. For a brief general
note on Hugo, see entry 1133n.

22   Percy Bysshe Shelley, 'The Woodman and the Nightingale', ll. 58–60.
Hardy's edn unidentified. Abridged quotation and annotation.

23   The source of Hardy's reminiscence is unidentified.

24   Hardy's comment, in pencil, on the three preceding entries.

25   Probably A. C. Swinburne, 'A Song in Time of Order', l. 2, *Poems and
Ballads*, 1st ser. 5th edn (London, 1873) p. 155. Quotation. See Bies, p. 106.

26   Thomas Carlyle, *History of Frederick the Great*, *Works*, xxı, 8. Abridged
quotation with a slight variation. In pencil.

27   Ibid., p. 11. Abridged quotation with variations. In pencil.

28   Ibid., p. 20. Abridged quotation with variations. In pencil.

29   Probably a mere misspelling of the name Cagliostro. Carlyle wrote an
essay on Alessandro Cagliostro (1743–95), the Sicilian adventurer, who was
involved in the 'Diamond Necklace' affair, also the subject of a Carlyle essay
(see entries A18, A20). In pencil.

30   The first part, 'faded bowers', is quoted from Thomas Hood, 'The
Departure of Summer', 1.4. The exact source of the rest of the entry (both parts of
which are in pencil) is not identified, unless Hardy rearranged the adjectives in
the following passages from 'The Haunted House':

> Their souls were looking thro' their painted eyes
> With awful speculation. ....   (ııı.x)

> The sky was pale; the cloud a thing of doubt. ....   (ııı.xvii)

31–3   Victor Hugo, 'Dieu invisible au philosophie', l. 9 in 'D'Eve à Jesus', *La Légende des siècles*, 1st ser. (Paris, 1859) i, 4. Hardy's edn unidentified, but the tentative and alternative translations of words (see entries A34, A36) suggest that the entries are Hardy's own renderings of the original French. See also entry A212.

34   Victor Hugo, 'La Trompette du jugement', ll. 16–17 in 'Hors du temps', *La Légende des siècles*, ii, 252. Hardy's trs.

35   Ibid., p. 254 (ll. 30–2). Hardy's trs.

36–41   Ibid., ii, 254–5 (ll. 37, 42, 45, 48–9, 55–6 and 58 respectively). Hardy's trs.

42   Carlyle, *The French Revolution, Works*, ii, 165. The phrase also occurs on pp. 200, 208. Quotations with a slight variation.

43   Ibid. Extracted from a description of a gala at Versailles: the Hall of *Menus* 'has loftly galleries; wherefrom dames of honour, splendant in *gaze d'or*; foreign Diplomacies, and other gilt-edged white-frilled individuals … may sit and look'.

44   Ibid. Abridged quotation with slight variations.

45   Ibid., p. 195. Abridged quotation.

46   Ibid., p. 196. Abridged quotation with slight variations.

47   Ibid., p. 2. Quotation with variations and Hardy's pencilled underlinings.

48   Ibid., p. 5. Quotation with slight variations.

49   Ibid. Abridged quotation with slight variations.

50   Ibid. Abridged quotation.

51   Ibid., p. 8. Abridged quotation with variations.

52   Alfred Tennyson, 'Palace of Art', l. 79. Quotation. For a brief general note on Tennyson, see entry 350n.

53   Ibid. l. 83. Quotation.

54   Samuel Johnson, 'The Vanity of Human Wishes', ll. 2–3. Hardy's edn unidentified. Quotation.

55   Ibid. l. 51. Quotation.

56   Ibid. ll. 53–4. Abridged quotation.

57   Ibid. ll. 197, 265. Quotations.

58–9   Ibid. ll. 206, 207. Quotations.
60   William Wordsworth, 'Milton! thou shouldst be living ... '; l. 11. Hardy's edn unidentified. Quotation. In pencil.

61   Unidentified. It is not from Wordsworth. In pencil.

62   Thomas Gray: 'Sceptred Care' is from 'The Bard', l. 141; 'Rosy Pleasure' from 'Vicissitude', l. 37. Hardy's edn unidentified. Quotations. In pencil. For a brief general note on Gray, see entry 1284n.

63   Gray, 'Vicissitudes', l. 31. Quotation. In pencil.

64   Thomas Gray, 'Ode on the Spring', l. 21. Quotation.

65   Ibid. l. 31. Quotation.

66   Thomas Gray, 'Ode on a Distant Prospect of Eton College', ll. 63, 68.Quotations. In her fine 'Hardy's Views in *Tess of the d'Urbervilles*', *ELH*, 37 (Mar 1970) 77–94, Lucille Herbert discusses the theme of 'local attachment' versus 'cosmopolitan enlightenment' in *Tess*, and, while emphasizing Hardy's debt to 'the descriptive–meditative poetry of the eighteenth century' in general, she refers specifically to this ode.

67–8   Gray, 'Ode on a Distant Prospect...' ll. 79, 81–4. Quotations.

69   Thomas Gray: 'Folly's idle brood' from 'Hymn to Adversity', l. 18; 'grinning Infamy' from "Ode on a Distant Prospect...', l. 74. Quotations.

70   Thomas Gray, 'Elegy Written in a Country Churchyard', ll. 31, 44. Abridged quotation.

71   Ibid. ll. 64–5. Quotation with Hardy's pencilled underlinings.

72   Percy Bysshe Shelley, 'Ode to the West Wind', l. 5. Hardy's edn unidentified. Quotation and annotation.

73   John Keats, 'Ode to a Nightingale', ll. 13–14. Hardy's edn unidentified. Abridged quotation. For a brief general note on Keats, see entry 416n.

74   Ibid. l. 38. Quotation.

75   Bjørnstjerne Bjørnson, 'Thrond', *The Bridal March and Other Stories*, trs. Rasmus B. Anderson (London, 1884) p. 122. Quotation with slight variations and Hardy's pencilled underlining. None of the passages quoted here is marked

in Hardy's own copy (DMC), which is signed 'Thomas Hardy' on the front flyleaf. There is no recorded statement of Hardy's impression of Bjørnson. It is likely, however, that he was attracted by the Norwegian's rural themes and settings, and in the DCM there is also a copy, signed by Hardy, of *Synnøve Solbakken*, trs. R. B. Anderson (London, 1884). In addition, Hardy once owned *A Happy Boy* (London, 1884) and *The Heritage of the Kurts* (1892): Wreden, items 9–10.

76 Bjørnson, *The Bridal March*, p. 124. Quotation with Hardy's pencilled underlining.

77 Ibid., p. 120. Quotation with variations and Hardy's pencilled underlining.

78 Ibid., p. 124. Quotation with slight variations and Hardy's pencilled underlining.

79 A. C. Swinburne, *Atalanta in Calydon* (London, 1885) pp. 48 (first three lnes) and 44 (final line). Abridged quotations with Hardy's underlinings. The first and last lines are marked in Hardy's copy (DCM). See also entries A1–4.

80 Ibid., p. 44. Quotation with Hardy's pencilled underlining. Marked with two strokes in the margin in Hardy's copy.

81 Ibid. Quotation with Hardy's pencilled underlining.

82 A. C. Swinburne, 'At Eleusis', ll. 43–4, *Poems and Ballads*, 1st ser., 5th edn (London, 1873) p. 240. Quotation with Hardy's pencilled underlinings. Hardy's copy of this edn (DCM) has his signature on the half-title. In the DCM are also his copies of *Poems and Ballads*, 2nd ser. (London, 1887), and *Songs Before Sunrise* (London, 1888); the title pages of both books are signed by Hardy. There are several markings in all the volumes.

83 William Shakespeare, *Henry IV*, I.ii.26. Quotation.

84 Thomas Carlyle, 'Death of Edward Irving', *Works*, IX, 394–5. Quotation with variations and reversed sentence order. See also entry 406n.

85 Ibid., p. 394. Abridged quotation.

86 Gray, 'Ode on a Distant Prospect of Eton College', l. 39. Quotation. The expression 'fearful joy' occurs in *Far from the Madding Crowd*, ch. 24 (p. 181), and *The Return of the Native*, II, ch. 6 (p. 166).

87 John Keats, 'La Belle Dame sans Merci', stanzas 10–11. Abridged quotation with variations.

88a 'Angry ghost' is extracted from either 'Anchises' angry ghost in dreams appears' or 'Her angry ghost, arising from the deep', ll. 506 and 558 respectively of *Aeneis*, IV, in *The Works of Virgil*, trs. John Dryden (London, n.d.) pp. 225, 226; 'labouring souls' seems to derive from either 'My lab'ring soul? what visions of the night' (IV, 12) or 'Of inborn worth, his lab'ring soul oppress'd' (x, 1249). Hardy's own copy of this edn (DCM) bears the follow inscription on the flyleaf: 'Thomas Hardy the gift of his Mother'. The copy has several markings. All underlinings in this entry are in pencil.

b Ibid., IV, 547. Quotation with a variation from

> as if the peaceful state
> Of heav'nly powers were touched with human fate,

The lines are marked by a marginal stroke in Hardy's copy.

c Ibid., VI, 450. Quotation with a variation from

> Nor dares his transport vessel cross the waves
> With such whose bones are not compos'd in graves.

The same words are underlined in Hardy's copy and in the entry.

d Ibid., VI, 461–2. Abridged quotation from

> Amidst the spirits, Palinurus press'd
> Yet fresh from life, a new admitted guest.

The same words are underlined in Hardy's copy and in the entry.

e Ibid., VI, 512–15. Abridged quotation from

> Fate, and the dooming gods, are deaf to tears.
> This comfort of thy dire misfortune take –
> The wrath of Heaven, inflicted for thy sake,
> With vengeance shall pursue th'inhuman coast,
> Till they propitiate thy offended ghost.

The first line only is marked in Hardy's copy.

f Ibid., VI, 1015, 1137. Abridged quotation from

> But, when a thousand rolling years are past
> (So long their punishments and penance last),
> Whole droves of minds are, by the driving god,
> Compell'd to drink the deep Lethaean flood   (VI, 1013–16)

and

> But when they leave the shady realms of night,
> And, cloth'd in bodies, breathe your upper light,   (vi, 1136–37)

g Ibid., vi, 1020. Quotation.

h Ibid., vi, 1001. Abridged quotation.

89 John Bunyan, *Pilgrim's Progress*, ed. J. B. Wharey (Oxford, 1928; rev. R. Sharrock, Oxford, 1960) p. 159. Hardy's edn unidentified. Quotation.

90 A. C. Swinburne, 'Aholibah', stanza 20, *Poems and Ballads*, 1st ser., p. 307. Interpolation in pencil.

91 *Aeneis*, vi, 1075–6, *The Works of Virgil* (see entry A88n). Quoted, with annotations, from

> There mighty Caesar *waits his vital hour,*
> *Impatient for the world,* and grasps his promis'd pow'r

The italics indicate Hardy's own underlinings in his copy.

92 Carlyle, *The French Revolution, Works*, ii, 289. Quotation with a slight variation.

93 Ibid., p. 290. Quotation with slight variations.

94 Ibid., pp. 291–2. Abridged quotation with slight variations.

95 Ibid., p. 293. Quotation with slight variations.

96 Ibid., p. 294. Quotation with slight variations.

97 Ibid., p. 324. Quotation.

98 Ibid., pp. 171–6. Abridged quotation with slight variations.

99 A. C. Swinburne, 'To Victor Hugo', stanza 7. Abridged quotation with a slight variation and Hardy's pencilled underlining. Not marked in Hardy's copy of *Poems and Ballads*, 1st ser., in which, however, ll. 3–8 of the third stanza have a marginal stroke and l.3 ('The splendour of a spirit without blame') of the penultimate stanza is underlined.

100 Ibid., stanza 9. Quotation with a slight variation.

101 Ibid., stanza 4. Quotation.

102a 'Fingal', *The Poems of Ossian*, trs. James Macpherson (London, 1803) I, 58. Quotation with a slight variation. Hardy's copy of this 2 vol. edn is in the DCM and has his signature on the title page of the first volume. Some of the markings in Hardy's copy are discussed by Evelyn Hardy, p. 39, and the possibility of stylistic influences from Ossian is suggested by James F. Scott in 'Thomas Hardy's Use of the Gothic: An Examination of Five Representative Works', *NCF*, 17 (Mar 1963) 363–84.

   b 'Cath-Loda', *The Poems of Ossian*, I, 209. Quoted from 'Come, thou huntress of Lutha, Malvina, call back his soul to the bard'. Hardy has underlined 'call back' in his copy.

   c Ibid., p. 210. Quotation. Underlined in Hardy's copy.

   d Ibid., p. 211. Quotation with a slight variation and annotation.

103 Ibid., p. 211. Excerpted from 'Thou shalt roll this stream away, or *waste with me in earth*'. The italics indicate Hardy's underlining in his copy.

104a Ibid., p. 211. Abridged quotation.

   b Ibid. Quotation with a slight variation.

   c–d Ibid., p. 214. Quotations with slight variations.

   e Ibid., pp. 215, 217. Quotation from 'Dark waved his shaggy brow, above his gathered smile' (p. 215) and 'His shaggy brows wave dark, above his gathered rage' (p. 217).

   f Ibid., p. 216. Abridged quotation with slight variations. In Hardy's copy 'poured his voice' is underlined.

105 Ibid., p. 218. Abridged quotation with a variation (Hardy writes 'nightly' for the original's 'mighty').

106a Ibid. Quoted from 'The race of Cruthloda advance, *a ridge of formless shades*'. The italics indicate Hardy's underlining in his copy.

   b Ibid., p. 219. Quotation.

   c Ibid. Excerpted from 'Nor feeble was the soul of the king. There, no dark deed wandered in secret.'

   d Ibid., pp. 223–4. Quotation with slight variations.

   e Ibid., p. 224. Quotation.

   f Ibid., p. 227. Abridged quotation with slight variations.

g Ibid., p. 228. Quotation with a slight variation.

h Ibid., p. 232. Quotation.

i 'Comola: A Dramatic Poem', ibid., p. 235. Quotation.

j Ibid., p. 238. Quotation with a slight variation.

k Ibid., p. 239. Abridged quotation with a slight variation and Hardy's interpolation–explanation.

107 *Aeneis*, vi, 381, 431, 508, in *The Works of Virgil*, trs. Dryden (see entry A88n). Excerpts, with a variation, from the following lines:

By the moon's doubtful and malignant light (381)

Such, and so thick, the shiv'ring army stands (431)

Think'st thou, thus unintom'd to cross the flood (508)

108 Johann Paul (Jean Paul) Friedrich Richter, *Titan*, trs. Charles T. Brooks (Boston, Mass., and Cambridge, 1868) ii, 191–2. Quotation with slight variations and annotation. The excerpt is from a description of an earthquake in Rome.
  Hardy once listed Carlyle's 'Jean Paul Richter' as one of his 'Cures for despair' (*Life*, p. 58), but I have seen no evidence of his first-hand reaction to the German writer. That his knowledge of Richter was quite extensive is suggested by the '1867' Notebook entries (see also A121–30). For a brief but fine discussion of Hardy and Richter, see Bies, pp. 108–10. Bies has identified the sources, in German, for entries A122, A124–30.

109 Richard Steele, *Spectator*, no. 278, in *The Spectator*, ed. Donald F. Bond (Oxford, 1965) ii, 584. Hardy's edn unidentified, but he owned an 1847 1 vol. edn of the *Spectator*; see Wreden, item 4: 'Very early signature of Thomas Hardy on fly-leaf.' Quotation with Hardy's pencilled underlining.

110 Joseph Addison, *Spectator*, no. 275, in *The Spectator*, ed. Bond, ii, 572. Annotations and quotation with slight variations. For Hardy's note on his reading Addison 'in a study of style' in 1875, see 'Critical Introduction', p. xiv.

111 Ibid., pp. 570–1. Abridged quotation with slight variations.

112 The wisdom of Solomon 18:23, *The Apocrypha and Pseudepigraphia of the Old Testament in English*, ed. R. H. Charles (Oxford, 1913) i, 566. Quotation with variations. Hardy's edn unidentified.

113–14 Wisdom 18:13–14, *Apocrypha*, i, 565.

115 'The War of Caros', *The Poems of Ossian* (see entry A102n), II, 4. Quotation.

116 'Fingal', ibid., p. 100. Abridged quotation.

117a 'Darthula', ibid., p. 162. Abridged quotation.

  b Ibid., p. 164. Quotation.

  c Ibid., p. 172. Quotation.

  d Ibid., p. 174. Quotation.

  e 'Death of Cuthullin', ibid., p. 181. Abridged quotation.

  f Ibid., p. 185. Quotation.

  g 'The Battle of Lora', ibid., p. 193. Quotation.

118 *Dante's Divine Comedy: The Inferno*, a literal prose trs. by John A. Carlyle, 2nd edn (London, 1867; repr. 1882) pp. 276, 271. Hardy's copy of this edn is in the DCM; it has his signature on the title page and has many markings. The entry seems to be a mixture from two sources: (1) the prose trs. of canto xxiii, 58–67: 'There beneath we found a painted people, who were going round with steps exceeding slow, weeping, and in their look tired and overcome. They had cloaks on, with deep hoods before their eyes, made in the shape that they make for the monks in Cologne. Outward they are gilded, so that it dazzles; but within all lead, and so heavy. ... *O weary mantle for eternity!*' (p. 276; italics indicate Hardy's underlining in his copy); (2) the trs. of the 'Argument' preceding canto xxxiii: 'Here they find the Hypocrites walking along the narrow bottom in slow procession, heavy-laden with cloaks of lead, which are guilded and of dazzling brightness on the outside' (p. 271). For a brief note on Dante, see entry 367n.

119 Ibid., pp. 276–7, 278, 301. Extracted, with Hardy's pencilled underlinings, from the following prose trs: (1) 'We turned again to the left hand, along with them, intent upon their dreary weeping. But that people, tired by their burden, came so slowly' (trs. of canto xxiii, ll. 68–70); (2) '"O Tuscan, that art come to the college of the sad hypocrites!" ... And I to them: "On Arno's beauteous river, in the great city I was born and grew; and I am with the body that I have always had. But you, who are ye from whom distils such sorrow as I see, down your cheeks?"' (trs. of canto xxiii, ll. 91–7); (3) 'The other two looked on, and each cried: "O me! Agnello, how thou changest! Lo, thou art already neither two nor one!" The two heads had now become one, when two shapes appeared to us mixed in one face, where both were lost' (trs. of canto xxv, ll. 67–72).

120 Richter, *Titan* (see entry A108n), II, 285. Quotation, with variations.

121 Ibid., p. 315. Abridged quotation.

122 The first line is a quotation from *Titan*, ii, 365; the second is possibly extracted from 'Amid such scenes, an unknown Hand stretches itself out in man ...' – *Life of Quintus Fixlein*, p. 352 (see entry A126n).

123 Unidentified.

124 Johann Paul Friedrich Richter, *Hesperus or Forty-Five Dog-Post-Days*, trs. Charles T. Brooks (Boston, Mass., 1865) i, 130 ('8. Dog-Post-day'). Mixture of summary and quotation. Hardy's edn unidentified.

125 Ibid., ii, 17 ('25. Dog-Post-Day'). Quotation with annotation and slight variations.

126 Johann Paul Friedrich Richter, *Life of Quintus Fixlein*, trs. Thomas Carlyle in *Tales by Musæus, Tieck, Richter, Works*, xxxiv, 342. ('Fifth Letter-Box'). Quotation with slight variations and annotation.

127 Ibid., p. 392. ('Eleventh Letter-Box'). Quotation with slight variations.

128 Ibid., p. 411. ('Chapter Last'). Quotation with a variation.

129 Jean Paul Friedrich Richter, *Levana; or, The Doctrine of Education*, Bohn's Standard Library (London, 1876; repr. 1884) p. 90 (Frag. i, ch. 1, section 7). Abridged quotation with a slight variation.

130 Ibid., p. 213 (Frag. iv, ch. 3, section 81). Quotation with pencilled underlining and slight variations and annotation from Richter's observation, 'the resemblance between women and children. The same unbroken unity of nature – the same clear perception and understanding of the present – the same sharpness of wit – the keen spirit of observation – ardour and quietness – excitability and easily raised emotions – the ready, quick passage, from the inward to the outward, and conversely, from gods to ribbons' (p. 213).

131 John Milton, *Paradise Lost*, ii, 955–7. Hardy's edn unidentified. Quotation.

132 Unidentified: see entry A108n.

133 Eustace Budgell, *Spectator*, no. 301, in *The Spectator*, ed. Bond (see entry A109), iii, 77. Quotation with Hardy's pencilled underlining. Eustace Budgell (1686–1737), essayist.

134 Ibid. Pencilled underlining.

135 Unidentified. Pencilled underlining.

136   Ovid, *Metamorphoses,* xv, 165–74. The 'free transl.' is not Hardy's own but taken from the verse trs. of the lines from Ovid in *Thoughts from Latin Authors* (see entry 175n) ii, 251. Underlinings in pencil, as are the insertions above the last line. In Hardy's copy the whole passage is marked with a stroke in the margin. For a list of allusions to Ovid in Hardy's writing, see Pinion, p. 203. For Hardy's use of Ovid in *Tess* see J. T. Laird's excellent *The Shaping of Tess of the d'Urbervilles* (Oxford, 1975) pp. 57–8. The quotation in *The Mayor of Casterbridge,* 'Video meliora proboque, deteriora sequor' (p. 247), is also found in *Thoughts from Latin Authors* and translated as 'I see the right, and I approve it too; / Condemn the wrong, and the wrong pursue' (ii, 244). Both the Latin and the English are marked with a stroke in the margin in Hardy's copy.

137   Victor Hugo, 'Marius', *Les Misérables,* trs. Charles E. Wilbour (London, 1887) i, 214. All the entries from *Les Misérables* in the '1867' Notebook are from this translation (A137, A143–50, A152–60, A244–45). Quotation with Hardy's pencilled underlining.

138   Richter, *Titan* (see entry A108n), i, 14. Quotation with variations and Hardy's pencilled underlining.

139   Percy Bysshe Shelley, *The Revolt of Islam,* vii.xxvi.2–3. Hardy's edn unidentified. Abridged quotation with slight variations. For a general note on Shelley, see entry 1175n.

140   Unidentified.

141   Milton, *Paradise Lost,* vii, 219–29. Hardy's edn unidentified. Abridged quotation and annotations.

142   Unidentified.

143   Hugo, 'Saint-Denis', *Les Misérables* ii, 286. Abridged quotation with slight variations and annotation.

144   Ibid. Quotation with a variation.

145   Ibid. Abridged quotation with an annotation and pencilled underlinings.

146   Ibid. Abridged quotation and annotation.

147–8   Ibid., p. 287. Quotations with slight variations.

149   Ibid. Abridged quotation with variations.

150   Ibid. Abridged quotation.

151   Unidentified.

152 Hugo, 'Saint-Denis', *Les Misérables*, ii, 287–8. Abridged quotation with variations and Hardy's pencilled underlinings.

153 Ibid., p. 288. Abridged quotation.

154 Ibid. Part summary, part quotation with Hardy's pencilled underlinings.

155 Ibid., p. 289. Part summary, part quotation with Hardy's pencilled underlining.

156 Ibid. Part summary, part abridged quotation with Hardy's pencilled underlinings.

157 Ibid., p. 290. Quotation with Hardy's pencilled underlining.

158 Ibid. Abridged quotation with variations.

159 Ibid. Quotation with Hardy's pencilled underlinings.

160 Ibid. Part summary, part quotation with Hardy's pencilled underlining.

161 Carlyle, *The French Revolution, Works*, iii, 218. Quotation and annotation.

162 Thomas Carlyle, *The History of Friedrich II of Prussia, called Frederick the Great, Works*, xxvii, 217. Quotation with a slight variation and Hardy's underlining.

163 Ibid., pp. 156–7. Abridged quotation with slight variations and reversed sentence order.

164 Thomas Carlyle, 'Hudson's Statue', *Latter-Day Pamphlets*, no. vii, *Works*, xix, 319. Abridged quotation.

165 Thomas Carlyle, *Past and Present, Works*, xiii, 157. Quotation with Hardy's underlining.

166 Ibid., p. 191. Abridged quotation with slight variations and Hardy's underlining.

167 Ibid., pp. 193–4. Abridged quotation with Hardy's underlinings.

168 Hugo, 'Cosette', *Les Misérables*, i, 459. Quotation with variations.

169 Ibid., p. 460. Quotation with a slight variation and annotation.

170 If this is a direct quotation the exact source is unidentified. It could, however, be a summary from Frederic W. H. Myers, 'Multiplex Personality',

or 'Automatic Writing', *Proceedings of the Society for Psychical Research*, xi (May 1887) 496–514, 209–61. Hardy quotes from this article in entry 1474.

171 Possibly the title of the article referred to in the previous annotation.

172 F. A. Aulard, 'Essai sur les idées philosophiques et l'inspiration poétique de Leopardi', *Poésies et œuvres morales de Leopardi*, trs. F. A. Aulard (Paris, 1880). Hardy's trs. of a passage in ch. 2 ('Philosophie de Leopardi'), a section called 'Theorie de l'*infelicità*', in which Aulard maintains that human unhappiness is the main theme of Leopardi's work and his explanation of human existence. See also entries 1892–8. For a comparative study of the two poets, see G. Singh, 'Thomas Hardy and Leopardi: A Study in Affinity and Contrast', *Rivista di Letteratura Moderne e Comparate*, 17–18 (1964–5) 120–35. Singh notes Hardy's possession of Aulard's trs. as well as of Leopardi's *Essays, Dialogues and Thoughts*, trs. P. Maxwell (London, 1893).

173–4 Aulard, *Leopardi*, p. 39. Hardy's trs. from Aulard's continued exposition of Leopardi's philosophy of unhappiness.

175 Ibid., p. 48. Hardy's trs. from a section entitled 'Leopardi et Schopenhauer'.

176 Ibid., pp. 123–4. Hardy's trs. from the chapter 'Les Poésies Patriotiques' of Aulard's rendering in French of a poem by Leopardi to his sister Paolina: 'Hélas! c'est trop tard, c'est dans le soir des choses humaines que celui qui naît acquiert le mouvement et le sentiment:

> ... Abi troppo tardi
> E nella sera delle umane cose,
> Acquista oggi chi nasce il moto e il senso.'

(pp. 123–4)

177–8 Ibid., p. 166. Hardy's trs. from the chapter on 'Poésies Philosophiques'; Leopardi, Aulard argues, attributed to the ancients his own 'idées sur la douleur et le néant' and he wished to find in them 'un assentiment' to his own doctrines. For a brief note on Hardy's different notion of the ancient, esp. 'Hellenic', view of life, see 'Critical Introduction', p. xxviii.

179 Ibid., p. 192. Hardy's trs. from what Aulard considers one of the most lively passages in Leopardi's *La Palinodie*, addressed to Gino Capponi (1792–1876), the Italian historian and statesman.

180 Émile Zola, *Abbé Mouret's Transgressions*, trs. without abridgement from the 34th French edn (London, 1886) p. 26. Abridged quotation. For a brief general note on Zola, see entry 1321n; for similarities between *Abbé Mouret's Transgressions* and *Tess*, see entry A187n.

181   Ibid., p. 27. Abridged quotation.

182   Ibid., p. 49. Quotation with variations.

183   Ibid., p. 71. Quotation with a slight variation.

184   Ibid., p. 107. Quotation with slight variations.

185   Ibid., p. 108. Quotation with variations.

186   Ibid., p. 120. Quotation with slight variations.

187   Ibid., p. 143. Abridged quotation with a slight variation. Zola's strongly symbolic description of the garden Le Paradou – here only briefly exemplified – is part of a potentially significant overall similarity between *Abbé Mouret's Transgressions* and *Tess of the d'Urbervilles*. Like Talbothays Dairy, Le Paradou is a place of pastoral innocence and natural emotions shielded from Christian morality. In addition to the affinity of the concepts of settings, the main characters of the novels are remarkably alike. Two girls of Nature, Albine and Tess, fall deeply and unreservedly in love with men who are emotionally frigid and under profound religious influences. In Serge, Albine discovers too late that 'a flame was lacking in the depth of his grey eyes' (p. 134), just as Tess is 'appalled by the determination revealed in the depths of this gentle being she has married – the will to subdue the grosser to the subtler emotion, the substance to the conception, the flesh to the spirit' (*Tess*, ch. 36; p. 313). Although Serge and Angel develop differently, their desertion and consequent ruin of their girls are similar and similarly motivated: Angel leaves Tess because of his Christian notions of morality and Serge Albine in order to serve the Church. Their actions dramatize the perhaps major theme of the two novels: (in Hardy's words) the 'unnatural sacrifice of humanity to mysticism' (*Tess*, ch. 40; p. 339).

     The similarities may not be far-reaching enough to indicate influence, but the possibility cannot be disregarded. Hardy read *Abbé Mouret's Transgressions* in 1886 or 1887; he started writing *Tess* in the autumn of 1888 (see Purdy, p. 71). See also Salter, pp. 129–30.

188   Zola, *Abbé Mouret's Transgressions*, p. 144. Abridged quotation with variations.

189   Ibid., p. 306. Quotation with variations.

190   Ibid. Quotation with variations.

191   A false start for the following entry.

192   Zola, *Abbé Mouret's Transgressions*, p. 304. Abridged quotation with slight variations.

193 Émile Zola, *Germinal, or, Master and Man* (London, 1885) p. 19. Quotation, annotation, and Hardy's underlining.

194 Ibid., p. 30. Quotation with variations.

195 Ibid., p. 32. Abridged quotation.

196 Ibid., pp. 116, 195. Annotation on, and quotations from (a) 'Around them, lads were tumbling their lasses, sounds of kissing and laughing were wafted to where they sat, whilst a warm odour of woman rose from the damp and trodden grass' (p. 116); (b) 'The loud sound of the voices of the miners in Monsieur Hennebeau's drawing-room was deadened, as it were, by the draperies of the room, and the hot-house-like atmosphere' (p. 195).
For a brief note on this entry see also 'Critical Introduction', p. xxiv, n. 19.

197 Ibid., pp. 203–5. Abridged quotation with variations.

198 Ibid., p. 223. Quotation with variations.

199 Ibid., p. 18. Abridged quotation with slight variations.

200 Ibid., p. 456. Abridged quotation with slight variations.

201 Ibid., p. 30. Abridged quotation with slight variations.

202–3 Exact context unidentified, but from Sir George Grove, *A Dictionary of Music and Musicians, A.D. 1450–1880*, 3 vols (London, 1879–83).

204 M. F. Brunetière, 'À propos d'une étude litteraire sur le XIXe siècle', *RDM*, 75 (1 Dec 1886) 696. Hardy's trs. of 'Chateaubriand s'est comme déclaré, dès son premier ouvrage, l'*Essai sur les révolutions*, l'ennemi personnel du XVIIIe siècle'. See also entry 1439.

205–7 Eugène-Melchior de Vogüé, 'De la littérature réaliste à propos du roman russe', *RDM*, 75 (1 May 1886) 290. Hardy translates from de Vogüé's introductory general observations on tendencies in modern literature. Hardy found this article of great interest and translated a large part of it into entries 1632–3.

208 Ibid., p. 298. Hardy's translated excerpt from de Vogüé's survey of modern French literary realism.

209 Hugo, 'Cosette', *Les Misérables* (see entry A137n), I, 109. Quotation with a slight variation.

210 Laurence Sterne, *Tristram Shandy*, Modern Library (New York, 1950) p. 7. Quotation with variations, Hardy's underlinings, and parenthetical annotation.

211 William Shakespeare, *Antony and Cleopatra*, iv.iv.1–5. Hardy's edn unidentified. Abridged quotation.

212 Victor Hugo, 'Les Chevaliers errants', iii ('Eviradnus'), xvi ('ce qu'ils font devient plus difficile à faire'), l. 70, *La Légende des siècles*, 1st ser., i, 218. Hardy's edn unidentified, but this is probably Hardy's own trs. from the line 'Vout êtes les jumeaux du grand vertige heureux'. See also entries A31–3 and Bies, p. 106.

213 Unidentified.

214 Sir Thomas Browne, 'Letter to a Friend', *Religio Medici* (London, 1886) p. 181. There is a slight piece of evidence suggesting that Hardy used the 1886 edn: in entry A224 he copied the printing error 'extenteration'. The other possible modern edn (with the modernized spelling Hardy has in all the entries) is from 1869, but it has the correct word 'exenteration' (p. 171). Quotation with slight variations and Hardy's underlinings.

215 Ibid. Quotation with Hardy's underlining. The reference, in pencil, to Carlyle on Novalis seems to be to a lost pocket-book.

216 Ibid., p. 182. Quotation with slight variations and Hardy's underlinings.

217 Ibid., p. 183. Abridged quotations.

218 Ibid., p. 187. Quotations with slight variations, annotation, Hardy's underlinings, and reversed order of the passages.

219 Ibid., p. 183. Abridged quotation.

220 Ibid., p. 186. Abridged quotation with slight variations.

221 Ibid. Quotation with slight variations.

222 Ibid. Abridged quotation.

223 Ibid. Quotation with slight variations.

224 Ibid. Quotation with a slight variation; *exenteration*: Hardy wrote 'extenteration'. For a brief textual note, see entry A214n. The entry is a direct continuation of the passage quoted in the previous entry, but a clear spatial separation in the manuscript suggests that Hardy saw them as separate entries.

225 Ibid. Quotation with slight variations and Hardy's underlinings; 'by six shoulders' is inserted in pencil.

226 Ibid., p. 189. Quotation with slight variations and annotation.

227 Ibid., p. 226. Quotation.

228 Ibid., p. 227. Quotation with slight variations.

229 Ibid., p. 192. Quotation with variations and Hardy's underlining.

230 Ibid., p. 193. Quotation with slight variations.

231 Ibid., p. 194. Abridged quotation.

232 Ibid. Abridged quotation with Hardy's underlining.

233 Ibid., p. 196. Quotation with a slight variation.

234 Ibid. Quotation.

235 Aeschylus, *The Persians, The Tragedies of Aeschylus*, trs. T. A. Buckley (London, 1849) p. 79. Quotation with Hardy's underlining from the messenger's account of the fate of the remnants of the Persian army after the Greek victory at Salamis.

236 Ibid., p. 80. Quotation with Hardy's underlining.

237 Unidentified.

238 Unidentified. 'P. M. G.' = Pall Mall Gazette?

239 Unidentified.

240 Charles Baudelaire, 'Reversibilité', *Les Fleurs du mal* in *Œuvres complètes* (Paris, 1961) p. 42. Hardy's edn unidentified, but the entry is probably his own trs. of the original:

> Ange plein de santé, connaissez-vouz les Fièvres,
> Qui, le long des grands murs de l'hospice blafard,
> Comme des exilés, s'en vont d'un pied traînard,
> Cherchant le soleil rare et remuant les lèvres?   (ll.11–14)

241 Unidentified.

242 Percy Bysshe Shelley, *Prometheus*, i, 11. Quotation.

243 A. C. Swinburne, 'In Memory of John William Inchbold', xxix, *Poems and Ballads*, 3rd ser. (London, 1889) p. 129.

244 Hugo, 'Fantine', *Les Misérables* (see entry A137n), i, 69. Quotation.

245 Ibid. Abridged quotation with slight variations.

Index: Names of Persons, Groups and Selected Titles

Editorial Note

References are to entry numbers. A number preceded by 'A' refers to an entry from the '1867' Notebook in the Appendix. A number followed by 'n' refers to the relevant editorial note in the Annotations.

The italicizing of a number and the accompanying 'n' indicates that the editorial note contains a general annotation on the indexed material.

575

Athenians, the,   2013
Atkinson, C. F.,   2454
Augustus, Caesar,   1762, 1762n, 1763,
  1763n
Augustus, Ernest,   2200
Aulard, F. A.,   [A172–79], A172 [–79]n,
  1895n
Ausonius,   1866n
Austrians, the,   A163
Aydelotte, F.,   2420

Bach, Johann Sebastian,   2297, 2417
Bacon, Sir Francis,   1731, 2020, 2399,
  2448
Baer, Karl Ernst von,   2069
Bagehot, Walter,   1739
Bailey, John C.,   2469 [–70], 2469 [–70]n
Bailey, J. O.,   2423n
Bailey Saunders, T.,   1782n
Bain, Alexander,   2089, 2089n, 2270,
  2270n
Balfour, Arthur James,   2422, 2422n,
  2457, 2457n
Ballard, Frank,   2527
Balzac, Honoré de,   1654, 1736, 2487,
  2539, A238
Barnard, Lady Anne,   2632
Barnes, William,   2632
Barrie, J. M.,   2072n, 2224
Barry, William,   2289
Bashkirtseff, Maria (Bashkirtseva)
  Konstantinova,   1685 [–91], 1685
  [–87]n, 1688 [–91]n
Bastian, Dr Henry Charlton,   2496
Baudelaire, Charles,   1659–61, [1662],
  1663, 1659 [–63]n, 2487, 2524, A239
  [–40], A240n
Baughan, E. A.,   2626, 2626n
Bayliss, Sir William Maddock,   2538
Beardsley, Aubrey Vincent,   2344
Beaumont, Sir George,   2307
Becquer, Gustavo A.,   1914, 1914n
Beerbohm, Max,   2005, 2005n
Beesly, Edward Spencer,   1651
Beethoven, Ludwig van,   2519
Bell, Clive,   2414, 2414n
Belloc, H.,   [2191], 2191n
Benecke, Edward Felix
  Mendelssohn,   2522
Benedict, F. L.,   A21n
Benn, Alfred William,   2625
Bentham, Jeremy,   1669, 2528
Béranger, Pierre Jean de,   2460

Bergson, Henri,   xxxviii, 2376, 2422,
  2422n, 2423 [–28], *2423 [–28]n*
Berkeley, George,   2051, 2051n, 2430n
Bernhardi, Friedrich von,   1989n
Bertelette (English printer),   2484
'Bess', Queen,   2635
Beuve, Sainte,   xx
Bever, van,   2514
Bible, The,   1785, 2013, 2058–62,
  2058–62n, 2074, 2074n, 2299, 2299n
Bies, Werner,   1991n, A25n, A108n,
  A212n
Birell, Augustine,   [1737–42], 1737
  [–42]n
Bisland, Elisabeth,   [2316], 2316n
Bjørnson, Bjørnstjerne,   xxxv, 2505,
  A[75–], 78, *A75 [–78]n*
Blackhall, James,   2636
Blake, William,   1892, 2031, 2500
Blennerhasset, Rowland,   1770 [–73],
  1770 [–73]n
Blind, Mathilde,   1685 [–87], 1685
  [–87]n, [1688–91], 1688 [–91]n
Boccaccio,   1909, 2524
Boccioni, Umberto,   2413
Boehm, Sir Edgar,   2510
Bonaparte, *see* Napoleon
Bond, Donald F.,   A109 [–11]n, A133n
Bonnierès, R. de,   1654
Borromeo, Carlo,   1821
Bose, Jagadis Chunder,   2537
Boswell, James,   2633
Boucher, François,   1987
Boucher, Léon,   xv
Bougereau, Adolphe William,   2519
Boumelha, Penny,   1918n
Bourbons, the,   A145–46, A149
Bourget, Paul,   1654, 1891
Bowdler, Thomas,   2523
Bowker, R. R.   xxx
Boyd, Thomas,   2317
Bradley, A. C.,   2265
Bradley, F. H.,   2048, 2048n, 2308
Bradley, George Granville (Dean of
  Westminster),   2012, 2510
Bradwardine, Thomas,   2358
Brahms, Johannes,   1653
Brandes, Georg,   2505, 2539
Brassey, T. A.,   2520
Bremner, Robert Locke,   2489
Brennecke, Ernest, Jr,   2423n
Brewer, John Sherren,   1651
'Brideshead, Sue' (*Jude the*

590 *Index*

Strzygowski, Josef, 2454
Stuart, Elma, 2350
Stuart, Mary, 2524
Stuart, Roland, 2350
Stubbs, William, 1969
Studies in Pessimism (Schopenhauer), 1782
 [–1800], 1782 [–1800]n
Studies of a Biographer (L. Stephen), 2001
 [–4], 2001 [–4]n
Sulla, 2522
Sullivan, Sir Arthur Seymour, 2637
Super, R. H., 2306n
Sutter, Julie, 2497
Sutro, Alfred, 1959n, 2007n, 2190n
Swift, Jonathan, 1844, 2041, 2543
Swinburne, Algernon Charles, 1975,
 2196, 2196n, 2318, 2332, 2346, 2355–56,
 2355 [–56]n, 2461, 2461n, 2465, 2465n,
 2518, 2524, 2524n, 2631, 2631n, A1 [–4],
 A1 [–4]n, A25n, A79 [–82], A79 [–82]n,
 A90, A90n, A99 [–101], A99 [–101]n,
 A243, A243n
Symbolists, the, 2034, 2156, 2201
Symbolists, the French, 2504, 2514,
 2514n, 2554
Symonds, John Addington, xxviii, 1801
 [–41], 1801 [–41]n, 1843 [–70], 1843
 [–70]n
Symons, Arthur, 1909, 1909n, 2014,
 2014n, 2076, 2076n, 2156, [2183], 2183n,
 2194, 2194n, 2201, 2235, 2285, 2315,
 2315n, 2509, 2514

Tacitus, 1651, 1969
Taine, Hippolyte, 2372
Tarver, J. C., 2056, 2056n
Taylor, A. E., [2272], 2272n
Taylor, Jeremy, 2041
Taylor, Richard H., xviii, xxxi
Tchekov, *see* Chekhov
Teniers, David, 2513
Tennyson, Alfred Lord, 1868, 1935
 [–54], 1935 [–54]n, 2069, 2305, 2332,
 2394, 2470, 2492, 2524, 2542, 2632, A52
 [–53], A52 [–53]n
Tennyson, Hallam Lord, 1935 [–54],
 1935 [–54]n
Tertullianus, 2039, 2039n
Tetrazzini, Mme, 2310
Thackeray, W. M., 1670, 2287, 2506,
 2531, A151
Thales, 2095n
Theism and Humanism (A. J. Balfour),

2457, 2457n
Theocritus, 2513, 2543
Theophrastus, 2225, 2225n
Theoptolemus, 2279
Thirwall, Connop, 1969, 2622
Thomas à Kempis, 2069
Thomas, W. J., 2516
Thompson, Francis, 2240, 2346, 2346n
Thoreau, Henry David, 1891, 2340
Thucydides, 1651
Thurn, Im, 1956, 2535
Tieck, Ludwig, A126n
Tiele, Cornelis Petrus, 2498
Titan (J. P. Richter), A108n, A120 [–22]n
Titian (Tiziano Vecellio), 2519
Todd, M. Loomis, 2294n
Tolstoy, Leo, 1696n, [1706–15], 1706
 [–15]n, 1987, 2260, 2400, 2519, 2534,
 2641
Torquemada, Tomás de, 2069
Townsend, Archbishop C. H., 2182
Traubel, Horace, 2641
Trebitsch, Siegfried, 2456n
Treitschke, Heinrich von, 1989n
Trevelyan, S. M., 2598n
Trollope, Anthony, A19, A19n
Tschaikowsky, Piotr Ilich, 2067n, 2156,
 2297
Tuker, M. A. R., 2467, 2467n
Turgueneff or Turgenev, Ivan
 Sergeyevich, 2518
Turner, J. M. W., 1864, 1976, 2232
Tussaud, Mme, 2005, 2005n
Twain, Mark, 2143, 2144
Tyler, Wat, 2254
Tyndall, John, 2496
Tyrrell, R. Y., 1905, 1905n

Ueberweg, Friedrich, 2043, 2043n
Underhill, G. E., 2283, 2283n
Untermeyer, Louis, 2478n
Usener, H., 2368, 2368n, 2498

Vanbrugh, Sir John, 2487
Vaughan, C. E. 2633, 2633n
Vaughan, Henry, 2284, 2600
Velasques, Diego Rodrigues de Silva y,
 2047, 2070
Venables, George Stovin, 1935
Venus, 1916, 2605
Verdi, Guiseppi, 2309, 2310
Verlaine, Paul, 2514, 2524
Verrall, A. W., 2245 [–47], 2245 [–47]n